The Psychoanalytic Study of the Child

VOLUME XX

The Psychoanalytic Study

of the Child

VOLUME XX

HOGARTH PRESS
London

The Editors announce the establishment of

THE MONOGRAPH SERIES OF
THE PSYCHOANALYTIC STUDY OF THE CHILD

to make possible the publication of papers on psychoanalytic research which, due to their length, cannot be included in the annual volumes of *The Psychoanalytic Study of the Child.*

All contributions for publication in the Monograph Series will be by invitation only. The Editors regret that they do not have facilities to read unsolicited manuscripts.

The first monographs will deal with various phases of the research work done at the Hampstead Child-Therapy Course and Clinic in London by Anna Freud and her collaborators.

CONTENTS

Diagnostic Assessments (Profiles)

Aspects of Normal and Pathological Development

Contributions to Psychoanalytic Theory

Clinical Contributions

DIAGNOSTIC ASSESSMENTS (PROFILES)

METAPSYCHOLOGICAL ASSESSMENT OF THE ADULT PERSONALITY

The Adult Profile

ANNA FREUD, LL.D., D.Sc., HUMBERTO NAGERA, M.D.,
and W. ERNEST FREUD, B.A. (London)

The need for a Profile of adult patients has made itself felt in our clinical work for some time, especially for those cases where a child and one or the other parent are in treatment simultaneously.

Our original Profile schema was devised for neurotic child patients in order to facilitate the organization of the material available about them under psychoanalytically meaningful headings (before, during, or after therapy). When the Profile was subsequently applied beyond the scope of the neurosis, a number of sections had to be amplified to embrace all the details relevant to the individual's specific pathology. In the case of the blind, this involved above all the headings concerned with phase development, fixation and regression. In the case of the borderline children, so far the sections containing information about cathexis of self and cathexis of objects have been provided with subdivisions to trace in more minute detail the location of pathology. When the Profile schema was applied to the characterization of the adolescent, it had to be widened to accommodate the variations of superego development, ideal formation, and the identity problems, which form an essential part of the adolescent's upheaval.[1]

While the Profile schema as such profited from these expansions and gained so far as its scope of application was concerned, the basic

This paper forms part of a study entitled "Assessment of Pathology in Childhood" which is conducted at the Hampstead Child-Therapy Clinic, London. It has been financed by the National Institute of Mental Health, Bethesda, Maryland.

[1] See M. Laufer in this Volume.

rationale underlying it remained untouched. For all the categories of disturbance enumerated above, assessment by Profile is made on the basis of developmental considerations, i.e., the individual is examined for his position on the progressive sequences relevant to drive development, ego and superego development, and the age-adequate developments of internal structuralization and adaptation to the environment. Pathology is evaluated in all instances according to its interference with orderly and steady progress in these respects.

This basic rationale changes with the application of the Profile schema to the adult personality. In this instance assessment is concerned not with an ongoing process but with a finished product in which, by implication, the ultimate developmental stages should have been reached. The developmental point of view may be upheld only in so far as success or failure to reach this level or to maintain it determines the so-called maturity or immaturity of the adult personality. For the rest, normality is judged by the quality of functioning (in sex, work, and sublimations), the pleasure in life derived from it, and by the quality of the individual's object and community relations. Pathology reveals itself through permanent symptomatology which interferes with any of the above aims, by suffering for internal causes, by the individual's incapacity to relate realistically to his environment, or by both.

Since childhood and adult Profiles are not identical in orientation, the comparison between such assessments of parent and child will have to be restricted to the sections which are most similar. Nevertheless, the schemas may prove invaluable for the correlation of items such as the importance within the individual structure of particular drives, the quality of the defense organization, the content of ideal self and superego, the developmental phase governing the quality of object relationships, etc.

As regards the application of what follows to individual case material, the analytic clinician has to be advised as well as warned. It would be a grave misunderstanding of what the authors have in mind if the Profile were treated as a questionnaire, if it were allowed to dominate the interviewer's attitude during diagnostic examination, if it were shared with the patient, or if its headings were merely filled in with information given by him. What the Metapsychological Profile sets out to be is of a completely different order—namely, a framework for the analyst's thinking, and a method to organize findings after they have been elicited, assimilated, and digested by him. Where a Profile is set up after diagnostic investigation, it is only natural that there will be many blanks and unanswered questions in the analyst's mind; these will be filled gradually as an analysis proceeds, to be most completely answered when analytic treatment has been terminated. Profiles set up at these different junctures will reflect the analyst's growing familiarity with the material and, by their increase in completeness, give evidence of his advances in awareness of existing problems, complications, and solutions.

Metapsychological Assessment of the Adult Personality
Adult Profile

(State the material on which the Profile is based.)

I. REASON FOR REFERRAL

Symptoms, anxieties, inhibitions, difficulties, abnormalities, breakdowns in functioning, acting out in the environment, inability to fulfill inherent potentialities, arrests in development leading to faulty ego and superego structuralization, etc.

An attempt is to be made, where possible, to distinguish between the manifest and the latent reasons for which the patient seeks help.

II. DESCRIPTION OF THE PATIENT AS DIRECTLY OR INDIRECTLY CONVEYED IN THE INTERVIEW

Personal appearance, moods, manner, affects, attitudes, etc.

III. FAMILY BACKGROUND (PAST AND PRESENT) AND PERSONAL HISTORY

(As provided by patient or derived from other sources.)

IV. POSSIBLY SIGNIFICANT ENVIRONMENTAL CIRCUMSTANCES

(Interviewer's as well as patient's evaluation where available:)

(a) in relation to the timing of referral;

(b) in relation to the over-all causation of the disturbances as evaluated by the patient himself as well as by the interviewer;

(c) in relation to the links between individual and family pathology and their interaction.

V. Assessment of Drive and Ego-Superego Positions

A. *The Drives*

1. *Libido.*—Examine and state

    (a) *Libidinal Position*

Describe the present libidinal position of the patient against the ideal normal position that he should have reached. Ideally, for women, a passive feminine position; for men, an active masculine one, with no more than the normal admixture in terms of bisexuality. At the time of assessment it is important to determine if the highest level has ever been reached, if it is being maintained, or if it has been abandoned regressively for an earlier one. Where the adult position has not been reached, it is important to assess the quality and quantity of interference contributed by previous phases.

    (b) *Libido Distribution*

        (i) *Cathexis of the Self*

whether the self is cathected, and whether there is sufficient narcissism (primary and secondary), invested in the body, the ego, or the superego, to ensure regard for the self, self-esteem, a sense of well-being, without leading to overestimation of the self. If possible, consider the regulation of narcissism; note whether this is brought about through identification, object dependence, magical means, work, etc. In the adult some information in relation to the cathexis of the self can be obtained in areas such as the patient's personal appearance, clothes, etc. (while the child's appearance in this respect reflects the adult's attitude toward him).

(ii) *Cathexis of Objects* (past and present; animate and inanimate)

The disturbances observed here should be described from the point of view of their predominant origin in one of the following phases: narcissistic, need-fulfilling, object constancy, preoedipal, oedipal, postoedipal, adolescence. As in previous sections evaluation should start at the highest level, i.e., at the level where the objects are considered and treated as partners in their own right. State:

—whether the individual in question has been able to choose his or her *sexual partner* and how far his object needs are met by the partner;

—whether the attitude necessary for *motherhood* and *fatherhood* has been achieved and on what level;

—whether and how far the infantile oedipal relationships have been outgrown or still dominate the picture;

—what part is played by *other human relationships* such as friendships, alliance to groups, or their avoidance, working relationships, etc.;

—above all, what part is played on the one hand by heterosexual object cathexes and on the other hand by homosexual object cathexes;

—whether too much libido is withdrawn from the real object world and sexual satisfaction sought in masturbation (accompanied by object-directed fantasies);

—whether and how deeply the individual is attached to objects which serve as substitutes for or extensions of ties with other human beings such as *animals, property, money,* etc.

2. *Aggression*

Note to what degree aggression is under control while being at the service of the personality in sexual life, work, and sublimatory activities.

Examine the defenses against aggression for relevant information. Aggression thus has to be assessed:

(a) according to quantity, i.e., presence or absence in the manifest picture;

(b) according to quality, i.e., correspondence with a given libidinal position;

(c) according to the direction or distribution, i.e., toward the object world (within or outside the family) or the self or both. In the latter case, state whether directed to the body or through the superego to the ego;

(d) according to the methods and defense activity used in dealing with it.

B. *Ego and Superego*

(a) Examine and state the intactness or defects of ego apparatus serving perception, memory, motility, etc.

(b) Examine and state in detail the intactness, or otherwise, of ego functions, as they are at present (memory, reality testing, synthesis, control of motility, speech, secondary-thought processes, etc.). If possible compare the present state of ego functions with functioning before the onset of the disturbance.

(c) Examine and state whether danger is experienced by the ego as coming from the external world, the id, or the superego, and whether consequently anxiety is felt predominantly in terms of fear of annihilation, separation anxiety, fear of loss of love, castration fear, guilt, etc.

(d) Examine in detail the status of the defense organization and consider:

—whether defense is employed specifically against individual drives, affects, and anxieties (to be identified here) or more generally against drive activity and instinctual pleasure as such;

—whether the patient's defense organization is mature, i.e., dependent on his own superego structure;

—whether it has remained immature, or regressed to presuperego stages, i.e., whether id control is dependent on the object world;

—whether the defense mechanisms predominantly used are

archaic or of a higher order (for example, denial, projection versus reaction formation, sublimation);

—whether defense is balanced, i.e., whether the ego has at its disposal the use of many of the important mechanisms or is restricted to the excessive use of specific and primitive ones.

—whether defense is effective, especially in its dealing with anxiety, whether it results in equilibrium or disequilibrium, lability, mobility, rigidity, or symptom formation within the structure.

(e) Note all secondary interferences of defense activity with ego functioning, i.e., the price paid by the individual for the upkeep of the defense organization.

(f) Examine the status of the superego with regard to:

—its degree of structuralization (arrested, faulty, mature, etc.);

—its sources (where obvious);

—its functions (critical, aim- and direction-giving, satisfying);

—its effectiveness (in relation to ego and id);

—its stability (under the impact of internal and external pressure);

—the degree of its secondary sexual or aggressive involvement (in masochism, in melancholia, etc.).

C (A + B). *Reaction of the Total Personality to Specific Life Situations, Demands, Tasks, Opportunities, etc.*

Drive and ego development that were viewed separately for purposes of investigation in the earlier sections of the Profile are here seen in interaction with each other, as well as in reaction to specific situations, such as: the totality of the patient's attitude to his sex life; his success or failure in work; attitude to social and community responsibilities; his disturbed or undisturbed capacity for enjoying companionship, social relationships, and the ordinary pleasures of life; his vulnerability and ability or failure to withstand disappointments, losses, misfortunes, fateful events, environmental changes of all kinds, etc.

VI. ASSESSMENT OF FIXATION POINTS AND REGRESSIONS

As character disturbances, neuroses, and some psychotic disturbances—in contradistinction to the atypical personalities—are assumed to be based on fixations at various early levels and on drive regressions to them, the location of these points is one of the vital concerns of the diagnostician. At the time of initial diagnosis such areas are betrayed:

(a) by the type of the individual's object relationships, the type of drive activity, and the influence of these on type of ego performance in cases where these are manifestly below adult level;

(b) by certain forms of manifest behavior which are characteristic of the given patient and allow conclusions to be drawn about the underlying id processes which have undergone repression and modification but have left an unmistakable imprint. The best example is the overt obsessional character where cleanliness, orderliness, punctuality, withholding and hoarding, doubt, indecision, slowing up, etc., betray the special difficulty experienced by the patient when coping with the impulses of the anal-sadistic phase, i.e., a fixation at that phase. Similarly, other character formations or attitudes betray fixation points at other levels or in other areas. Unrealistic concerns for health, safety of the marital partner, children, parents or siblings show a special difficulty of coping with death wishes; fear of medicines, food fads, etc., point to defense against oral fantasies; shyness to defense against exhibitionism, etc.;

(c) by the patient's fantasy activity. Some adult patients may occasionally be more willing than children to communicate some of their fantasy life at the diagnostic stage. Personality tests may reveal more of it (during analysis the patient's conscious and unconscious fantasy provides, of course, the fullest information about the pathogenically important parts of his developmental history);

(d) by those items in the symptomatology where the relations between surface and depth are firmly established, not open to variation, and well known to the diagnostician (such as the symptoms of the obsessional neurosis with their known fixation points); in contrast, symptoms with multiple causation such as anxiety attacks, insomnia, vomiting, some forms of headaches, etc., convey no clear genetic information at the diagnostic stage.

VII. ASSESSMENT OF CONFLICTS

By examining the conflicts which are predominant in an individual's personality, assessments can be made of

—the level of maturity, i.e., the relative independence of the patient's personality structure;

—the severity of disturbance, if any;

—the intensity of therapy needed for alleviation or removal of the disturbance.

According to quality, conflicts, which should be described in detail, may be graded as follows:

(a) *External Conflicts*

In the adult direct clashes between id and external demands occur only where ego and superego development are defective. Conflicts between the total personality and the environment (refusal to adapt to, creative attempts to modify the environment) can occur at any stage after adolescence and are not pathogenic.

(b) *Internalized Conflicts*

In the fully structured mature adult, disharmonies between instinctual wishes and external demands are mediated via ego and superego and appear as internalized conflicts. Occasionally such conflicts are externalized and appear in the guise of conflicts with the environment.

(c) *Internal Conflicts* between insufficiently fused or incompatible drive representatives (such as unsolved ambivalence, activity versus passivity, masculinity versus femininity, etc.).

VIII. ASSESSMENT OF SOME GENERAL CHARACTERISTICS WITH A BEARING ON THE NEED FOR ANALYTIC THERAPY AND THE ABILITY TO PROFIT FROM IT

An all-round metapsychological view of the patient will assist the analyst in assessing on the one hand the patient's need for internal change, and on the other hand his chances to effect this in psychoanalytic treatment.

As regards the need for internal change the following points may be considered relevant:

—whether the patient's id and ego agencies have been separated off from each other too completely by excessive use of repression, and whether better communication needs to be established between them;

—whether the ego's sphere of influence has been restricted unduly by the defenses and needs to be enlarged;

—whether ego mastery over the impulses is weakened for other than defensive reasons (ego defects, psychotic core, etc.) and whether improvement will depend in the first instance on the strengthening effect that therapy has on the ego resources;

—whether the superego structure is archaic and, through analysis of its sources, needs to be replaced by a more mature one;

—whether the libidinal and aggressive energies or only libido or aggression are bound up in countercathexes, conflicts, and symptom formation, and need to be released for constructive use.

The following characteristics, attitudes, and circumstances seem of relevance to either a positive or negative reaction to analytic therapy:

On the positive side:

—whether there is insight into the detrimental nature of the pathology, including the desire to be cured;

—whether there is ability for self-observation, self-criticism, and capacity to think and verbalize;

—whether the patient has a sufficiently high level of object relationship and a sufficient quantity of free object libido to establish a meaningful transference relationship to the analyst, and whether this relationship will serve also as a treatment alliance and withstand all the ups and downs of the resistances;

—whether there is enough frustration tolerance to cope with the necessary restrictions on wish fulfillment in the transference setting;

—whether there is enough tension tolerance to cope with the additional anxiety likely to be released by exposing conflicts and weakening defenses during the analytic process;

—whether the patient has on previous occasions shown ability to persevere in the face of difficulties;

—whether there are (past or present) areas of established sublimations which attest to the patient's capacity to displace and neutralize energies and to accept substitute satisfactions;

—whether in the absence of established sublimations there is evidence of a sublimation potential which has been interfered with by pathology;

—whether there is flexibility of libido (as contrasted with adhesiveness);

—whether there is a positive, optimistic general outlook on life (as contrasted with a crippling pessimism).

On the negative side:

—whether there is dangerously low tolerance for frustration and anxiety, coupled with the unwillingness to renounce secondary gains of the pathology;

—whether the patient's pathology is part of a pathological family or professional setting and cannot be altered without causing major upheavals and breakups in the external life situation;

—whether there are extreme self-punishing, self-destructive, and masochistic attitudes that are satisfied through the pathology and oppose improvements, i.e., which cause negative therapeutic reactions.

Example of an Adult Profile[2]

Mr. C. H.

Age: 34 years old,

Married, 3 children.

Based on:

1. Interview with a psychiatrist (Dr. A.). 1.31.1963.

2. Forty-one weekly reports to the Freud Centenary Fund Scheme for Adult Analysis, covering the period from March, 1962 to December 27, 1962.

[2] The Profile has been prepared by Dr. H. Nagera.

I. Reason for Referral

Analysis for this patient was suggested by the therapist of his daughter Alice; Mr. C. H. had been seen for some time at regular weekly or fortnightly intervals. Alice, who is four years old, had been in psychoanalytic treatment for almost two years. *Her* main complaint is a sleeping disturbance consisting of waking up and crying.

During the interview with Mrs. X (the child's therapist) Mr. H. came to realize that he tends to avoid arguments. He similarly avoids decisions leaving them to somebody else. If he has to make a decision in business, he later worries about the consequences but does not want to know what the consequences are.

He finds it difficult to deal with figures in authority and does not take well to instructions. "I always fight against them as I did at school. I would not wear the school tie and cap; I am against authority and in my political thinking I am rather left but not a communist; my father has always been rather the same."

When Dr. A. asked if there was any relation between his seeking treatment and the fact that his daughter was in treatment, the patient answered: "If something is suggested by the therapist who sees me and my wife regularly, I always make suggestions why it ought to be done, or why it will depend on my wife whether or not it will be done." The patient added that he would not have thought of having psychoanalysis if his daughter had not been in treatment. Nevertheless, he always thought he should have some help.

Dr. A.'s opinion of the patient was that "there is a very positive indication for full psychoanalytic treatment." He further expressed the opinion that this patient's basic conflicts were around his repressed oedipal rivalry and his inhibition of aggression. Once Mr. H. could free himself from the latter, Dr. A. felt, there would be an improvement in his masculinity that might bring the wife as the next patient.

II. Description of the Patient as Directly or Indirectly Conveyed in the Interview

The patient is medium height, neither thin nor fat, and has rather dark skin and dark hair. He is very punctual and usually rather anxious, restless, and a bit jerky at times, though quite capable of settling down quietly. He is rather careless of his personal appearance, as shown by his dirty hands and nails. His clothes tend to be somewhat dirty as well.

He is polite and well mannered in his behavior, especially during the initial interview. He expresses himself well and uses some technical psychoanalytic words. He works as an insurance agent for a company which does a great deal of business in this and in other countries. The patient works in the department that deals especially with foreign countries.

He describes himself as having few friends. At work he feels he has made no progress whatsoever. He attributes this to the difficulties he has in dealing with people in authority, etc. He has been employed in the present capacity for the past eight years. His net earnings are £1,200.

The patient is not particularly religious but likes to keep the forms up to a point; he observes a number of Jewish holidays mainly because of the children.

III. FAMILY BACKGROUND (PAST AND PRESENT) AND
      PERSONAL HISTORY

Past

Mr. H. comes from a very poor Jewish background. His father, now sixty-nine, works as a tailor. His mother is sixty-eight. She is very ill, having recently had an operation for cancer. Her sight has been very poor for many years.

There is a brother three years younger than the patient (thirty-one at present), married, active, outgoing, successful.

The mother is described by the patient as the strong character of the family, in contrast to the weak father. She is experienced as an overpowering character who completely controlled and dominated the father and the family.

She is further described by the patient as having had a tendency to cheat and lie, playing him and his brother against each other in order to make them behave as she wanted. For example, she is said to have moved the clock ahead several hours to try to get the children to sleep early. Mr. H. and his brother were aware of the mother's trick because of the light and activity outside.

Mr. H. feels she was always nagging and trying to make them

feel guilty. His childhood is seen as full of rules and prohibitions coming from the mother.

He thinks the mother was always hoarding, always taking home whatever other people were going to throw away, even if she had no use for it, and the objects were not even in a good condition.

The father is seen mainly as a weak and passive man by the patient. Both parents had great hopes and expectations (scholastically) for Mr. H. He feels that in this respect he has been a complete disappointment to them.

Present

Mr. H. was married about eleven years ago. His wife is thirty years old, described as very efficient, the organizing and executive power in the family. She comes from a much wealthier Jewish home. Mr. H. feels his father-in-law has no time for him because he is poor and unsuccessful. He feels his wife is now subjected to economic restrictions and anxieties that were unknown to her before.

Mrs. H. is usually affectionate and in general the relationship is not bad. The patient thinks his wife is a somewhat anxious woman, and from his description she appears somewhat obsessional. She apparently is not able to go to bed in the evening (no matter how late it may be) until she has completely cleaned up the house and finished all other household work in the most meticulous and obsessional manner. The patient frequently tries (because of the late hour) to get her to leave the unessential things for the next day, but she is quite unable to do so.

The patient is on reasonably good terms with his brother-in-law, the only sibling of his wife; he is very much preferred and favored economically by Mrs. H.'s father.

Mr. and Mrs. H. have three children, a boy, Joseph, who is nearly seven years old and had a diagnostic interview not long ago because of learning difficulties. No treatment was advised at the time but special educational help. Alice, a little girl of four, is in treatment because of her sleep disturbances, and there is a third child only one year old.

Personal History

Nothing is known of his early developmental history.

The patient is known to have grown up in tight economic and

rather crowded conditions. He has many memories of listening to primal-scene noises up to the time when he was an adolescent. He remembers being annoyed by it and thinking of his father: "Why doesn't he leave her alone?" On the other hand, apart from this exposure to primal scene, Mr. H.'s mother seems to have looked after Mr. H.'s body care until rather late in the patient's life. He believes he remembers being bathed by his mother until he was about twelve years old. At that time he was bathed occasionally by the father as well.

Mr. H. studied for two years at a university but was in effect dismissed because of his examination failures. Even at that time he had great difficulty concentrating because of his excessive fantasy life. He did his National Service in the Medical Corps for two to three years.

IV. Possibly Significant Environmental Circumstances

1. The mother's personality and the severe restrictive atmosphere at home.
2. Excessive exposure to primal scene and body stimulation through being bathed until a late age.

V. Assessment of Drive and Ego-Superego Positions

A. the drives

1. *Libido*
   (a) *Libidinal Position*

This patient is able to perform sexually in an active masculine position under favorable circumstances. He described his sexual life during his interview with Dr. A. as regular and satisfactory.

Further material elicited during treatment seems to point to the fact that this ideal state of affairs is frequently interfered with for a number of different reasons and on one occasion, so far as is known, led to temporary impotence. Thus, Mr. H. has mentioned how worried he was about not being potent at the time of his marriage, and he was in fact temporarily impotent at that time. Mr. H.'s complaints about his not being able to give his wife more money for the home and entertainment, etc., are, on another level, a reference to his dissatisfaction with his potency.

At the beginning of his married life he remained for some time very concerned about his ability to satisfy his wife sexually. He felt that his wife did not enjoy sexual intercourse. He had to ask her frequently about this. She reassured him that everything was fine. He does not worry consciously about it any more, though his wife's reactions during intercourse lead him to believe that she does not really enjoy her sexual life.

The main sources of interference in this area can be enumerated as follows:

(i) *The homosexual components of the patient's bisexual conflict.*—Mr. H.'s passive, feminine fantasies are perhaps best shown in the following examples. He had been reading a French book describing several intercourse positions. He was very excited by the one where intercourse was performed with the woman on top. He proposed it to his wife, who rejected the idea. He said his wife would have been the male in this relationship. At this point Mr. H. felt that he had my weight on him, commenting with great embarrassment that he thought in this fantasy he wanted the analyst on top of him. Mr. H. remembered how much pleasure he got when being bathed by his father at quite a late age. He always felt rejected and disappointed because his father sent him out of the room when he took his own bath. He wanted to remain to help bathe the father and look at him. Mr. H. thinks he was between ten and twelve at that time.

Some of this is now transferred to the relationship to his son Joseph (who is about seven). When treatment started Mr. H. used to get into bed with his son every morning. He explained it as being Joseph's wish resulting from his jealousy of the excessive amount of attention that Alice is said to be receiving. He still bathes Joseph frequently.

The patient described how on his way to the Underground after a session he was suddenly seized by the idea that he wanted to be loved by the analyst. He found the thought very disturbing and went on to explain that he did not really wish me to love him in a homosexual way but that he wanted me to admire him.

He described how he always finds himself in conflict with people in authority (males) while at the same time wishing to be admired and loved by them. Analysis thus is felt by the patient as a submissive experience in which he is forced to play a passive-feminine role lying on the couch while the analyst is behind him.

Mr. H. remembers having once made an overt homosexual advance by stroking a man's hair. The man was very annoyed and he was most embarrassed. This seems to have taken place during late adolescence.

(ii) *Fantasies of being damaged and castrated.*—A fantasy of having a damaged penis seems to play an important role in Mr. H.'s feeling of "insufficiency and inferiority" and in what he calls his "not being able to do well in life." Mr. H. remembers this preoccupation as going back many years. He says he remembers the following incident from his childhood. He was being bathed by his mother while another woman (a friend of his mother?) was also present. His mother then expressed some concern about his penis. He is not sure, but he thought that she meant that there was something wrong with it or perhaps that it was too short.

(iii) *Interference due to important fixations at the oedipal level with incomplete solution of the oedipal conflicts.*—For description and examples see under Section VI, Fixations and Regressions.

(iv) *Interferences due to fixation at the anal-sadistic level of libidinal development; these make sexuality into somewhat of a dirty, objectionable activity.*—Sexuality has strong anal connotations for Mr. H. These types of conflict frequently find expression through the symbolism of coal, getting dirty, cleaning the bunker, etc., either in his dreams or fantasies.

(v) *Interference coming from his conflicts with the aggressive drive in general and with anal sadism and phallic aggression in particular.*—See under Section V, 2. Aggression.

(b) *Libido Distribution*
   (i) *Cathexis of the Self*

Mr. H. has on the whole a rather poor opinion of himself. He feels ashamed because he failed at the university and has not done well for himself in life, economically or otherwise.

He attempts to compensate for his feelings of inferiority, inadequacy, and failure by a very rich fantasy life and frequent withdrawal into it. He describes himself as the "Walter Mitty" type. The fantasies occur in great numbers, the content covering a wide range, but the central theme is always connected with being successful. He is, for example, a most famous surgeon or psychoanalyst, etc., and sees himself performing difficult operations with great success. They bring fame, wealth, admiration, and great respect. (It is not without interest to note that his father wanted the patient to be a doctor. He is aware that the fantasy serves both to gratify the father's wish and to attract his admiration.)

(ii) *Cathexis of Objects* (past and present; animate and inanimate)

Mr. H. has been able to choose an appropriate sexual partner in life and there is no doubt that he can consider and treat his wife as a partner in her own right. This level of functioning with his wife and others is interfered with by his strong ambivalence and anal sadism as well as other conflicts. Although there is a basically positive attitude toward the children and fatherhood, a number of conflicts interfere in this area. Thus, the children, especially Joseph, are seen as oedipal rivals in a battle for his wife's affection and sexual favors. On the other hand, he sees them partly as extensions of the self and hopes that they will restore his damaged self-esteem through their achievements and successes. For the same reason any shortcomings and failures of the children are felt as his own failures.

Finally, the infantile oedipal relationships have not been out-grown to a sufficient degree and consequently tend to interfere at times with a more mature and adequate relationship to his wife, children, friends, colleagues, boss, etc. Examples illustrating this point can be found under Section VI, Assessment of Fixation Points and Regressions. This patient's very significant attitude to money will also be described there.

2. *Aggression*

Conflicts in this area constitute one of the essential problems of this patient's psychopathology. They are extremely important in their own right also because they make a contribution to other con-flictive areas.

Aggression is expressed mainly verbally and in fantasy, with frequent death wishes at the slightest provocation. Some of the aggression finds its way into provocative, teasing, stubborn behavior (anal-sadistic) with certain objects. Some of it seems to find an outlet in somewhat careless driving and speeding (phallic aggression). A great deal is directed toward the object world in the forms described above, but a certain amount is turned against the self, especially on certain specific occasions, as some of the examples will show. Projection, repression, and turning against the self are three favored mechanisms to deal with it.

(i) *Aggression Finding Outlet in Fantasy*

This can be seen in his fantasy of being called by the Foreign Office to work for them. He was expected to deal with a "foreign agent" (the analyst). He killed this man in the fantasy.

(ii) *Expressed Verbally*

His aggression breaks through in meetings with colleagues at work where he presents his points of view with so much provocation and hostility that they become unacceptable. Most of the time he tends to remain silent out of the fear of saying something improper and being criticized for it.

He tends to express some aggression verbally, for example, in the relationship to his brother. The brother was going on holidays. Mr. H. said that the brother was so lucky that even the weather was good for him. He did hope that something would spoil it.

(iii) *Aroused by Oedipal Rivalry with His Brother*

The oedipal rivalry with the brother has become more manifest during treatment. Mr. H. claims that he was not fully aware of its intensity before. He recounted a recent incident when his brother paid the taxi for their mother to go from the hospital to her home. He felt the brother was "buying his way" at home; this was unfair because he cannot afford the money to do the same. At such moments he felt he could strangle his brother.

(iv) *As Shown in the Transference with Examples of Projection*

Frequently when Mr. H. feels annoyed or angry with the analyst he gets rid of the feeling by attributing it to the analyst. Thus, he finds that the analyst's face looks angry or his voice sounds angry.

Aggression has only rarely been expressed against the analyst. For example, the patient once stated in an angry voice that had he had the money, he might not have chosen me as an analyst. The sequence that followed is very illustrative of the type of conflict the patient has with his aggression and the type and form of defense activity that is called into operation. No sooner had he said this than he felt very perturbed because he had been offensive to me. A few seconds later he resorted to "projection" to dispose of what was obviously a very disturbing feeling. He started saying with much feeling that he felt that the analyst was trying to provoke him, but he would not be provoked at all, etc. (The analyst had been silent all this time.)

During treatment Mr. H. developed a fear of driving because he was afraid of having an accident in which he would smash a car. Soon Mr. H. connected this fantasy with his having noticed the analyst's new car and his feelings of envy. It was the analyst's car that he wanted to smash, the analyst having now become the successful brother, who can get a new car frequently and thus bid for the mother's admiration.

(v) *Aggression and Careless Driving, Death Wishes against Wife and Children*

In one of his sessions, Mr. H. told of a car accident, withholding a certain amount of information related to it because he thought the analyst would feel that he was a careless father who endangered the lives of his family. What he left out of his account was that his children were in the car when the accident took place. This accident seems one which, though the other party could be held responsible, really occurred because Mr. H. did not take the necessary steps or care to prevent it. It appears that it was due partly to his death wishes against his wife and children (the car was hit where they were sitting and then turned over). At this point Mr. H. talked with great distress about his many conscious death wishes toward his family.

He is in a way surprised that he is not more frequently involved in accidents since there are roads where he knows he ought to stop and does not; he just takes the chance.

(vi) *Death Fantasies Relating to His Brother-in-law and Mother, and Defense Activity of Turning Aggression against the Self*

Mr. H. frequently has fantasies about his brother-in-law's death, which he thinks will induce his wife's parents to turn their attention to her and himself. He will then be treated as a son and receive the benefits of their economic help that are at the moment given mostly to the brother-in-law.

Mr. H.'s abundant death wishes have always included his mother. When the seriousness of her illness became known and led to hospitalization and operation, Mr. H.'s guilt rose to a pitch, his death fantasies now having found support in reality. He started to turn them against himself and on a number of occasions was nearly run over by cars because he was distracted by thoughts and fantasies that interfered with his attention while crossing roads, etc.

(vii) *Conflict around Phallic Aggression*

One example of his conflict around phallic aggression could be observed when he was in the Army. He remembered "being in a panic and feeling sick" when there were exercises where he had to use the bayonet—body fights between two groups of soldiers, having to push the bayonet into the body of dummies, etc. The above material appeared in relation to a slip of the tongue. At the time his son wanted a penknife. This distressed Mr. H. greatly. He thought Joseph wanted it to fight with the other boys at the school: "I thought Joseph wanted it to fight with the other boys, *not to fight with the other girls."* The slip shows the unconscious link in Mr. H.'s mind of this type of aggression and phallic sexuality.

B. EGO AND SUPEREGO

(a) and (b) *Ego Apparatus and Ego Functions*

There are no known defects in this patient's ego apparatus and no primary deficiencies are observable in relation to his ego functioning.

(c) and (d) *Defense Activity* is used against libidinal and aggressive strivings as well as against certain painful affects (guilt, feelings of inferiority, etc.).

The patient tends to use a large number of defenses, including some rather primitive ones like denial and projection, which are used frequently and excessively. On the whole the defense organization is not successful in dealing with the many conflicts active in this patient and has led to a number of undesirable restrictions and faulty adjustments of the ego structure.

(i) *Withdrawal into Fantasy.*—He remembers that this tendency was already present and occupied a great deal of his mental activities when he was eighteen or nineteen years old. The patient feels that it was this constant fantasying that spoiled his academic efforts at the university. He remembers that he sat for hours with his book, but he could not concentrate. These fantasies seem to have taken the place of early masturbatory activities. He now has the same feeling of shame and guilt about them that he remembers having when he masturbated. Similarly, he feels that he now gets the same pleasure out of these fantasies that he did out of his earlier masturbation. Masturbation was always a tremendous conflict. He was always trying to stop himself from doing it but was quite unable to do so. This is what now happens with his fantasies.

(ii) *Identification with His Parents.*—(1) He has very high expectations of his children, but especially of his son Joseph. (2) Mr. H. still bathes Joseph, who is about seven years old, as his own mother and father used to do with him up to a very late age. (3) The patient recounted with guilt that on several occasions Alice actually walked into the room while Mr. H. and his wife were having intercourse. On many occasions his daughter has walked around the house in the middle of the night while they were having intercourse. Mr. H. seems to be forced to expose his children to the primal scene (sometimes look, more frequently listen), just as he was exposed to it himself.

(iii) *Identification with His Father.*—He never buys on Hire Purchase because that is against his principles. He does not remember his father buying anything through it. He cannot do it either.

(iv) *Passive into Active.*—Separation is difficult, even on week ends sometimes. He deals with this by turning passive into active. He felt he did not want to come one day and while he was on his way to the analytic session he made a mistake in the Underground and passed the right station.

Mr. H. reacts strongly to breaks in his treatment for holidays. At such points he feels he wants to stop coming to his treatment before the holiday arrives.

(v) *Passivity.*—He is extremely passive and leaves every decision, jobs at the house, etc., to his wife, who seems quite happy to take on these responsibilities.

(vi) *Displacement.*—This is frequently used to deal with aggression. The object to whom it is directed is thus frequently changed. At home aggressive feelings related to the wife are often directed to the children.

(vii) *Rationalization.*—For example, he makes all sorts of excuses to himself so that he can phone home two or three times every day and keep in control.

(viii) *Intellectualization.*—Included here and in the case of the previous defense is his use of analytic reading for defensive purposes.

(ix) *Externalization.*—At the time of the break for holidays Mr. H. externalizes his own fears and anxieties concerning the separation. He describes in great detail how upset his daughter is because of the coming holiday in her treatment.

Externalization of superego sometimes leading to projection is frequently observable. After a session when he talked about his sexual fantasies relating to a ten-year-old girl, his scoptophilia, and his death wishes, he said that he observed that at the beginning of that session my face was pale while at the end of it it was red. He attributed it to my having become very angry with him and my having to control myself in order not to recriminate him for his "thoughts," etc.

(x) *Intellectualization and Isolation of Affect.*—These two frequently combined defense mechanisms are used when he is talking about his sexual life or some other distressing event. He then sounds like a professor addressing his students in a cold fashion about sexual matters.

(xi) *Denial.*—He has to pretend to himself and others that he could not care less about getting in touch with his parents and especially his mother, when in fact he makes quite sure that his wife does so regularly and keeps him informed.

Denial was used as well to deal with his mother's illness and hospitalization (cancer operation). He constantly claimed that he did not care what might happen to her. In some cases the denial became a reversal of affects, Mr. H. claiming that he would be better off when she is gone, etc. At the same time he was obviously very disturbed because of his mother's illness and went to see her at the hospital practically every day. Interpretation of this denial and reversal frequently brought him close to tears.

At the time of the Profumo affair Mr. H. denied having any interest in it. In fact he says he has a rather "puritanical attitude" to these questions. He never buys or reads the *News of the World*, etc. Later it transpired that though he does not buy the paper himself, he regularly goes to his father-in-law's house, where *News of the*

World is available, and there reads it with great enjoyment. Moreover, he is frequently the one who starts discussion of this affair at work.

He has to deny any awareness or knowledge of the economic situation of his wife's parents in order to control the hate he would feel for his father-in-law if he admitted that the father-in-law is capable of helping him financially but never does so. He similarly attempts to avoid fantasies in which he takes the favored position of his brother-in-law after the latter's death, etc.

(xii) *Projection.*—Mr. H.'s mother-in-law likes to come down for a few days whenever the H.'s are on holiday. Mr. H. finds this unbearable. He thinks she comes because she cannot trust him at all. He thinks she feels he is not capable even of finding a *reasonably safe* and convenient place to take the family on holiday: that is why she really comes down, to check up that everything is all right. Mr. H. himself refers to this as being paranoid, but sometimes he feels convinced of the truth of such judgments.

Mr. H. said that he knew that in his first interview (facing the analyst) I thought he was a homosexual. He based this statement on my having asked twice during his interview whether he had three children. He interpreted this as my doubting his masculinity. (For another example, see under Aggression. After trying to be offensive to the analyst, he felt the analyst was trying to provoke him.) Similar examples are abundant and can be found in his relationship to colleagues and superiors. After having meant to be offensive to them, he begins to feel persecuted.

(e) *Secondary Interference of Ego Functions*

Mr. H.'s excessive use of denial and particularly of projection (the latter especially to deal with his aggression) frequently interferes with his reality testing and reality adaptation. These factors further complicate his relationship to colleagues and superiors and badly handicap his opportunities of improving his position in his firm.

Similarly, his excessive withdrawal into fantasy interferes with his ability to work. When he was at the university, it was partly the reason for his failure. It worries him that he can drive for long periods in this dreamy state paying no proper attention to conditions on the road.

(f) *Superego Structure*

Mr. H. has a well-developed superego structure and on the whole a rather severe one. Its severity seems partly the result of identifications with a strict mother, seen even stricter than she is in reality because of the projection of his own aggressive impulses onto her.

He reacts with extreme guilt to fantasies in which he sees himself married to rich women and consequently without any economic difficulties. Similarly, he shows great guilt and anxiety because of his aggressive fantasies and death wishes. He is very distressed that even in fantasy he can think such things, especially since he feels that whatever is wrong at home is largely his fault.

Mr. H.'s behavior at work is frequently aimed at showing himself in a bad light, as an extremely inefficient person. By such means he manages to keep isolated, never making any progress at work. By these and other similar mechanisms he seems to deal with intense unconscious guilt and need for punishment, thus being forced to make a failure out of himself in spite of his potentialities.

A great deal of this guilt comes from the oedipal rivalry with his father. His superego seems to demand that he must not outgrow or do much better than his parents did, especially his father. This is shown in the following two examples:

When he was about to buy a carpet for his bedroom, he talked about the unpleasant feeling he gets because his parents never had such a thing in their home.

Similarly, he cannot buy through the Hire Purchase because his father never did and doing so may bring material comforts that his parents never had.

C (A + B). REACTION OF THE TOTAL PERSONALITY TO SPECIFIC LIFE SITUATIONS, DEMANDS, TASKS, OPPORTUNITIES, ETC.

Mr. H. is unable to make full use of his potentialities at his work. He is reduced to the performance of activities well below his capabilities. His character difficulties make it difficult for him to relate to superiors, people in authority, and even colleagues.

He has very few friends, and at work he relates to a very limited number of persons.

Adaptation and capacity to enjoy his sexual life: As described elsewhere.

Capacity to enjoy leisure: Mr. H. finds week ends somewhat of a strain. It seems that at present this is due mainly to the fact that a week end implies many hours of close contact with the family and especially with his son Joseph, whom he sees as a rival and who tends to annoy and irritate him. Sometimes he finds it difficult to control himself in relation to the boy.

As for holidays, the only ones about which I have direct knowledge were not enjoyable for Mr. H. for a number of reasons. It is difficult to decide, on the basis of my scanty knowledge, how much his complaints are rationalizations or justified reality-adapted complaints about the places.

Capacity to enjoy companionship, social relationships, the ordinary pleasures of life, etc.: His capacities in these respects are limited by his conflicts in general and especially by those around aggression; the need for control and the type of his character disturbance further interfere here. Thus his ability to enjoy companionship and social relationships is limited, as is the case with the ordinary pleasures of life. He feels restless at the thought of having things easy or having more out of life than his very restricted parents did.

VI. Assessment of Fixation Points and Regressions

Mr. H. shows at present a great deal of drive activity pertaining to the anal and phallic-oedipal phases of drive development. There is very little, if any, relevant material that points to the oral phase. My general impressions through Mr. H.'s own description of himself, incomplete as it has to be, favor the conclusion that such activity is mainly the result of strong fixations acquired when going through such phases rather than the result of later regressive moves. This is based on the fact that his anal character traits have remained in the foreground, playing a most important role throughout his development up to the present. There are indications that a similar situation existed at the phallic-oedipal level and that the conflicts typical of this phase remained largely unsolved. These have shaped his personality and conflicts in their present form.

On the other hand, there are no indications in the history of this patient that conflicts in later life led to qualitatively relevant regressive moves to previously existing fixation points and earlier modes of drive gratification.

With this patient one has the impression that these early difficulties, especially the anal ones, found their way into the character structure, leaving a permanent imprint there in the form of an anal character of a not very desirable type or quality. Furthermore, the difficulties at the anal level have contaminated to some degree the phallic and genital levels of sexual development. Thus, sexual intercourse is somehow considered as a dirty activity.

A number of examples follow to show the indicators to fixation at the pregenital levels.

Anal

Mr. H. shows a clear-cut tendency to argue for the sake of arguing. This is a typical component of the transference relationship; every interpretation will at first be rejected. He can accept it only at a later stage and after satisfying the strong tendency to argue.

He needs to keep absolute control of what goes on at home. He has to be consulted about the most trivial things before his wife can make any decisions. Similarly, he phones home two or three times a day to arrange everything.

Some compulsive doubting is present, showing the strong anal components of his personality structure. This appears combined with strong ambivalent feelings as in the following example. He was trying to write a letter of thanks to his child's therapist because of her suggestion that he should come to treatment. He wrote several drafts of the letter and was never satisfied. Finally, he typed one of them, placing it in an envelope to have it posted. He did not send it and after some time had to open the envelope and type a different letter again. This behavior was repeated for several days. The compulsive doubting was related here to his ambivalence about treatment. This made him doubt that he expressed his thanks properly in the letter.

His ambivalence is clearly shown in most of his relationships, but especially in that with his brother. His anal ambivalent feelings in relation to him are exacerbated by his oedipal rivalry since the brother is believed to be more successful and admired by the mother. Mr. H. tries not to invite his brother to parties when the mother is going to be there.

Mr. H.'s attitude to money is very revealing. He is very secretive about it. At the time he was buying a carpet for his bedroom he hid from the analyst the fact that he had £80 to buy it. He pretended for some time that he had no money for it. Mr. H. connected this behavior with his need to keep this secret from his mother, who would otherwise want to *take this money away* from him. He also fears that his wife always wants to take whatever little money he has. He had similar feelings in relation to the analyst.

Anal provocative and teasing behavior is a characteristic trait of Mr. H.'s relationships to relatives, friends, bosses, etc. He will not come down for breakfast when called, forcing his wife to call and shout at him repeatedly that breakfast is getting cold. He knows this behavior annoys his wife very much.

His scholastic failure is partly a result of his anal defiant attitude against the parents' ambitions.

The relationship to the mother and others is still on a sado-masochistic level; if she says "white," he will automatically think in terms of "black" and the other way around. This is also observable in the transference, as described above. Further, he is somewhat stubborn and obstinate.

He frequently has a rather grubby and dirty appearance. His shirt, nails, and especially his suit were for many months somewhat dirty (now he wears a new suit).

Phallic-Oedipal

In the following fantasy Mr. H. sees himself as a prominent analyst who is consulted by two women from the Hampstead Clinic about a child. In the fantasy he was very pleased with himself because he was as good as I and was much admired by these two women, one of them being Alice's therapist (to make clear the oedipal connotation of this fantasy, see below the fantasy in which Mrs. X and I are a couple, have intercourse, and exclude him from the relationship). This fantasy is in fact one of a series in which he is admired by the mother and considered to be as good as the father.

Similarly, oedipal rivalry (related to both father and brother) is expressed in terms of colleagues who are preferred and promoted by "the firm" (mother). These people represent the father or brother who are admired and favored by the mother, while Mr. H. feels like a small child who cannot quite understand why the mother prefers the father, whom he envies and whose place he wants to take.

Fantasies of "having a successful business," "getting a better position," becoming "the head of an important firm," "getting control of the firm," etc., stand symbolically for taking his father's position in the relationship to the mother. His constant dissatisfaction is due partly to his oedipal rivalry and fantasies. The guilt and the fear of retaliation that go with it seem to interfere with his ability to make any actual progress in his work, as pointed out in the Superego section.

At a later stage in treatment Mrs. X and the analyst were made into the parental couple that excluded him from their sexual activities. He had fantasies that Mrs. X and I would meet during the holiday and have intercourse.

His son Joseph is seen as an oedipal rival competing for the favor of his wife.

Recently, his father showed some interest in a book Mr. H. was reading. The book is somewhat "sexy." He was very annoyed with his father and felt that he was watching his sexual activities.

At present Mr. H.'s oedipal rivalry is expressed mainly in the relationships to his son, his brother, superiors, etc. His father has so far largely been spared, partly because for defensive reasons Mr. H. shows strong positive feelings for him (partly perhaps as the result of his primary conflict around bisexuality, though it is not really possible at this time to point out with certainty what is primary and what defensive). In any case, for the moment the father has been rendered an inoffensive, weak, helpless creature. There are, nevertheless, a few indications that somewhere in Mr. H.'s mind there is the image—fantasied or real—of a violent, dangerous man. This could be seen in one or two recently recovered memories which showed that the father had been in quite a rage.

VII. Assessment of Conflicts

Conflicts in this patient are internalized. They involve id, ego, and superego structures, and concern both the libidinal and aggressive drives.

On the libidinal side they concern especially an insufficiently resolved oedipal situation and certain aspects of the patient's anal component instincts (other aspects having been taken directly into the personality structure in the form of character traits which, though perhaps undesirable, are not conflictive as far as the patient is concerned, e.g., his obstinacy).

On the aggressive side there is a massive conflict with practically all forms of aggressive expression. On the whole the conflicts described and the defense activity used in the attempt to cope with them have led to a number of ego restrictions, to an inability to utilize his full potential, and to certain character distortions, rather than to symptom formation of a more typical neurotic nature.

Similarly, there is abundant evidence of important conflicts of an internal nature such as unsolved ambivalence, active-passive conflicts and masculine-feminine ones. It is very difficult to say at this stage how much of the active-passive and masculine-feminine types of conflict is primary in nature and how much secondary and defensive.

As already described, he depicts himself as a very passive man, quite contented to leave every decision to his wife but at the same time insisting on being consulted. His passive-feminine and passive-active conflicts showed themselves clearly in the transference relationship in which he falls into a passive submissive position; he then feels compelled to reject all of the analyst's interpretations, though he admits that with a part of his mind he fully agrees with them. On the other hand, he wants the analyst to do everything for him, to love and to admire him, "to be on top of him."

His fantasies of occupying the position of a woman during intercourse while making his wife into a man lying on top of him have already been referred to. Other examples have been referred to elsewhere.

As to ambivalence, several examples have been given under Section VI, Assessment of Fixation Points and Regressions.

VIII. ASSESSMENT OF SOME GENERAL CHARACTERISTICS WITH A BEARING ON THE NEED FOR ANALYTIC THERAPY AND THE ABILITY TO PROFIT FROM IT

On the positive side:

—whether there is insight into the detrimental nature of the pathology, including the desire to be cured

This patient has always had some awareness of being in need of help but would not have looked for it himself at this stage. Particularly during adolescence and early adulthood, he was fully aware of how his conflicts and marked withdrawal into fantasy ruined his chances at the university. It was then that he started reading psychological books and articles in an attempt to understand and solve his problems. As already mentioned, he came to treatment through his daughter's treatment and the daughter's therapist's advice. He did not experience neurotic suffering or anxiety but instead had an awareness of the limitations and restrictions in his character and personality.

—whether there is ability for self-observation, self-criticism, and capacity to think and verbalize

The patient has given signs of a reasonably good capacity for self-observation. Self-criticism may be somewhat exaggerated, especially in relation to certain aspects of his personality or fantasy life. He can verbalize a good deal of his inner life without showing any marked tendency to act out.

—whether the patient has a sufficiently high level of object relationship, and a sufficient quantity of free object libido to establish a meaningful transference relationship to the analyst, and whether this relationship will serve also as a treatment alliance and withstand all the ups and downs of the resistances

The patient has reached the necessary level in terms of object relationships so as to make the type of transference relationship that he can be expected to establish during the analytic procedure a potentially useful one for therapeutic purposes. In other words, it can be expected that the object-constancy quality of his potential relationship to the therapist will be largely predominant since there are few signs, if any, of his having to use his object on a need-satisfying basis. Furthermore, there is every evidence that there is enough free object libido available at the present time to make it possible to expect the establishment of an appropriate transference relationship. There is no evidence of depression, ongoing intense mourning, etc.

*—whether there is enough frustration tolerance to cope with the
necessary restrictions on wish fulfillment in the transference
setting*

There was nothing in this patient's history to make us doubt
his ability to tolerate the frustrations and anxieties involved in the
analytic treatment.

*—whether there is enough tension tolerance to cope with the
additional anxiety likely to be released by exposing conflicts
and weakening defenses during the analytic process*

During the few months he has been in analysis he has shown
himself able to cope in these respects.

*—whether the patient has on previous occasions shown ability to
persevere in the face of difficulties*

This patient has the capacity to persevere. His failures are due
rather to the nature of his character and conflicts which interfere
with the achievement of positive results, sometimes in spite of strenuous efforts.

*—whether there are (past or present) areas of established sublima-
tions which attest to the patient's capacity to displace and neutralize energies and to accept substitute satisfactions*

His achievements in terms of actual sublimations, etc., are somewhat limited. The patient's situation is that so far he has not fulfilled his potential, being in fact very critical of himself for it. The
solution of his oedipal conflicts and especially of the conflicts around
aggression may lead to a better utilization of this energy for constructive and sublimatory activities with an over-all improvement of his
performance. There is no doubt that he has a potential capacity to
accept substitute gratifications and once the situations of conflicts,
fixations, etc., are helped by analysis, we can expect this to come to
the foreground.

*—whether in the absence of established sublimations there is evi-
dence of a sublimation potential which is interfered with by
pathology*

Mr. H. has a reasonably good potential for sublimation. At present his capacity to make use of it is very much interfered with by the

nature and content of some of his early neurotic conflicts, e.g., guilt about doing better than his father, etc. Similarly, some undesirable character traits (themselves an attempt at solution of some of his early neurotic conflicts) further interfere with the use of his sublimation potential, for example, his extreme obstinacy, stubbornness, and negativism.

—*whether there is flexibility of libido (as contrasted with adhesiveness)*

On the whole he shows no tendency to an excessive adhesiveness of the libido. He is most probably within the limits we observe in the large majority of cases.

—*whether there is a positive, optimistic general outlook on life (as contrasted with a crippling pessimism)*

Mr. H. is the sort of man who has a mainly positive constructive outlook, in spite of obvious handicaps, shortcomings, and past failures. He has come to analysis to improve his relationship with his family and the handling of his children, especially with the hope of being able to do better for himself in the future.

On the negative side:

In the case of this patient, there are no important secondary gains to be renounced. There is the question, already posed at the diagnostic interview, of the impact which important changes in the patient's personality and character structure might have on the patient's wife. The limited treatment period here covered has confirmed the fact that certain changes in the patient's attitudes and behavior brought about by the analysis are reacted to by the patient's wife with anxiety, aggressive outbursts, and depression. The patient himself has a distinct fear of changes that may interfere or create difficulties in his family relationships. Finally, though there is some evidence of self-punishing, self-destructive, and masochistic attitudes, they do not appear to be excessive or extreme and there is no reason to assume that they will tend to interfere unduly with therapeutic progress or lead to negative therapeutic reactions.

FREQUENCY OF PSYCHOTHERAPEUTIC SESSION AS A FACTOR AFFECTING THE CHILD'S DEVELOPMENTAL STATUS

CHRISTOPH M. HEINICKE, Ph.D. (Los Angeles)

With the assistance of

Joseph Afterman, M.D. (San Francisco), Marian Bradley, B.A. (Berkeley), Leah Kaplan, M.S.W. (Palo Alto), Anneliese F. Korner, Ph.D. (Palo Alto), and Jean Moore, M.S.W. (San Francisco)

The primary purpose of this publication is to present a series of hypotheses relating to the differential status (outcome) at the end of treatment, and at two points following treatment, of children seen once a week as opposed to those seen four times a week. The hypotheses are derived from the results of a pilot study exploring the effect of frequency of treatment in psychoanalytic child therapy. Future publications will attempt to clarify the differences in the therapeutic process of the two groups.

Despite much clinical experience indicating the importance of the frequency with which a child is seen, there are few studies which explore the differential outcome of children seen at varying frequencies. Arthur (1952) deals mainly with process considerations, but does suggest that the less frequent treatment is not likely to

This study was planned while the author was a Fellow at the Center for the Advanced Study in the Behavioral Sciences, and was initiated at Mount Zion Hospital, San Francisco, under grants from the Rosenberg Foundation and the National Institute of Health, Grant M-2948. It is being completed at Reiss-Davis Child Study Center, Los Angeles, with the assistance of a grant from the Grant Foundation.

We particularly wish to express our gratitude to Rocco L. Motto, Norman Reider, Anna Maenchen, Barbara Carr, Elise Greenhouse, and Dorothy Habben for their generous help in carrying out this project. Without the support of the school systems involved this study would not have been possible. Finally, we are much indebted to Sheila Speilman, Rosemary Ginn, Diana Hager, and Roselyn Katz for their devoted assistance.

reach the fundamental sexual conflicts and is thus likely to be "ineffective in a symptom formation which is based exclusively on a primary sexual fantasy."

The effects of frequency of treatment on adults has been investigated (Imber et al., 1957; Lorr et al., 1962; McNair et al., 1964), but these studies are limited in that twice a week represents the most frequent treatment studied.

Starting with a given theoretical and technical approach to child therapy, namely, that associated with Anna Freud's teachings, one group of seven to ten-year-old boys was seen once a week and another group was seen four times a week. This variation in frequency cannot be considered a simple independent factor. Despite the use of the same general technical approach, the nature of the material produced is soon different; therefore, the utilization and assimilation of this material are different. This in turn leads to variations in the further emergence of material, etc. (Bibring, 1954). Yet it was felt that the characterization of the cluster of independent process variables associated with differences in frequency and its effect on outcome was the first step in a long-term research strategy. It was anticipated that examination of the differences in the process could then suggest which are likely to be the most significant correlates of variation in frequency. For example, it has been hypothesized that the specificity, affect intensity, and variety of the transference phenomenon may well be one such significant correlate.

The findings of this study are based on the experience with ten children. Four of these were seen four times a week and six once a week. Two of the once-a-week children moved from the area, leaving four in each group. Two psychoanalytic child therapists trained at the Hampstead Child Therapy Clinic in London treated the children. One therapist saw three pairs of children and the other one. Both had had four years of child psychotherapy experience with children seen on a once- and five-times-a-week basis. All the mothers were seen once a week by a psychiatric social worker or other therapist, and where appropriate the fathers also were seen.

The children were all judged to be suitable for psychoanalytic treatment in that permanent and severe symptom formation of a predominantly neurotic character and the retardation of ego and libidinal growth were associated with permanent regressions and fixations (A. Freud, 1962).

Cases were assigned so as to insure that one group was not over-represented by the more severely disturbed or by certain qualitative constellations (for example, a defensive organization subject to deadlock versus lability). Individual variations are likely to defy matching of groups of cases; as demonstrated elsewhere (Heinicke, 1965b), however, the two groups of children did not differ at the beginning of treatment on any of 45 clinical dimensions which do differentiate them after treatment.

The two samples of four boys are also characterized *and do not differ* in regard to the following:

1. They were between the ages of six years, eight months and ten years, five months.
2. The main reason for referral was a learning disturbance linked to a psychological disturbance.
3. Their difficulties could not be readily linked to the influence of organic impairment or psychotic process.
4. They were either threatened with being held back or had been held back in school.
5. Their rate of academic growth in reading, spelling, and arithmetic was below the national average.
6. They scored a Verbal I.Q. of 91 or better.
7. They came from intact business or professional families.
8. All treatments were terminated at the request of the parents and with the consent of the therapist.
9. The length of the therapies ranged from one and a half to two and a half years, the mode being two years for both groups.

The subsequent sections of this presentation are organized to describe the following: (1) the assessment of each of the children at the beginning, end, one year and two years after treatment; (2) the use of the Developmental Profile (A. Freud, 1962) to integrate the information derived from these assessments; (3) an example of a set of three Profiles from the case of Steven; (4) the generalizations describing the hypothesized differential development of the two groups.

The Method of Assessing the Child's Developmental Status:
The Profile as an Indication of Psychotherapeutic Outcome

Anna Freud (1962) has suggested that Profiles drawn up at various junctures can among other things serve "as an instrument to measure treatment results, i.e., as a check on the efficacy of psychoanalytic treatment." Comprehension of what is to follow requires familiarity with the Profile (A. Freud, 1962, 1963; Nagera, 1963). Characteristics which make it especially suitable as an indication of therapeutic outcome should be highlighted. Most important, any indication of child psychotherapeutic outcome must deal with the fact of the child's potential for development. Although it is meaningful to study changes in the latency child's adjustment to school and peers, these diagnostic signposts are not as stable as the adult's capacity for work and love. The Profile is based on the assumption that "the capacity to develop progressively, or respectively the damage to that capacity, are the most significant factors in determining a child's mental future" (p. 150).

Previous experience suggests that it is essential to base the assessments of therapy on a variety of sources of information (Cartwright et al., 1963; Rosenfeld and Novick, 1964). By providing a common framework and language, and by insisting that all inferences are made within the context of all the material, the Profile makes the integration of descriptions as well as case comparisons both possible and clinically meaningful.

It is further assumed that to arrive at an adequate assessment of the developmental point that the child has reached, and what his growth potential is, the total diagnostic material must be formulated from different metapsychological points of view: dynamic, structural, economic, genetic, and adaptive. An assessment based only, for example, on the child's ego strength is likely to be misleading.

The Procedure for Obtaining the Information

The procedure used to gather the diagnostic information has been essentially the same throughout our work, but the experience did suggest slight changes which have in fact been incorporated into a second project.

Following an initial Clinic intake interview with the parents, at which time a preliminary assessment of the suitability of the case for psychotherapy was made, the mother began seeing the therapist assigned to her, and Joseph Afterman saw the child in two psychiatric interviews. The contact with the parent initially provided an elaboration of the statement of the problem, further developmental history, and the collection of information on the family and other aspects of the environmental situation.

At the end of his contacts with the child, the psychiatrist prepared him for the testing to follow, and certain tentative recommendations were made to the parents.

The battery of tests administered by Anneliese Korner consisted of: The Revised Stanford Binet, Form L; the Wide Range Achievement Test; the Rorschach; parts of the T.A.T. and Michigan Picture Test; and the Draw-a-Person Test.

To provide yet another independent source of information, visits were paid to the school for lengthy discussions with the teacher and related personnel. These interviews were structured to the extent that an effort was made to gather detailed information on the child's academic achievement, his relationship to peers, and his behavior in the classroom.

If after these various assessments the child and the family were felt to be suitable for the services offered by the Clinic, then the child began seeing the child therapist, and the parent or parents continued to see the therapist who did the intake interview.

After a year of treatment the tests of reading, arithmetic, and spelling were again administered by A. Korner, and a school visit was once more made at this point. Immediately after the end of treatment the child was first seen by J. Afterman, and then given the total test battery by A. Korner. A school visit was again arranged and the parents were seen at least once by their child's therapist to discuss the findings of the terminal assessment.

A year after the end of treatment the child's therapist saw the child at least once, the parent or parents were seen by their therapist, the total test battery was again administered by A. Korner, and another school visit was made. At the end of the assessment the child's therapist again met with the parents to discuss the findings.

The procedure for the second follow-up, two years after the end of treatment, was the same as for the first follow-up, but this time it was felt that the children would not be sufficiently motivated to take the tests. Reading test scores comparable to the Wide-Range Achievement Test were, however, available from school records.

Methods of Recording the Information

The method of recording the various diagnostic clinical interviews was essentially the same as that used to describe the therapeutic sessions with child and parent. Immediately following each session the clinician dictated the following into a tape recorder:

1. A description of the patient's general mood, appearance, and approach to the session.
2. A detailed chronological account of the session, including a careful description of the nature of the therapist's interventions and the patient's reactions to them.
3. The therapist's over-all understanding of the session: how the session relates to previous sessions and what he anticipates in the future.
4. The therapist's personal feelings about the session and the patient.
5. A summary of the changes observed in the patient.

In regard to the school visit, a detailed account of what transpired was given as well as some evaluation of this information.

All the data from the psychological test situation were recorded as suggested by the instructions accompanying the test.

Modes of Data Analysis: Interpretations by the Psychiatrist and Psychologist

In addition to providing a process account of his contacts with the child, J. Afterman prepared the following for each child at the beginning and end of treatment:

1. A running interpretative account of each of the significant items in the sequence of the diagnostic interview.
2. An integrated evaluation of each diagnostic contact, which considered both the child's history and certain salient facts known about the child's present circumstances. As it turned

out, the theoretical guide lines developed for this purpose were very similar to those suggested later by the Profile.

For the beginning of treatment, J. Afterman also ranked the children in terms of the level of ego integration exhibited.

A. Korner summarized her psychological findings for the beginning, end, and year after the end of treatment in an extensive report which included the following subheadings: an evaluation of cognitive functioning; an evaluation of scholastic skills; separate sections on the interpretation of the Draw-a-Person Test, the Rorschach, and the Apperception tests; a series of general comments; and finally a diagnostic summary.

Using the assessments based on the psychologicals, A. Korner also rated the children in terms of the following dimensions: the level of ego integration, progress as opposed to regression in phase development, and the over-all capacity for forming object relationships. Her rankings on the first of these correlated perfectly with those made by J. Afterman on the basis of his findings and also correlated significantly with the rankings made independently by the therapists. Although it was planned to repeat these ratings at the end and after treatment, limitations in resources confined us to the write-up and interpretation of the test results.

Integrating the Total Findings: The Profile

The Profiles for the beginning and end of treatment were constructed by the therapist some time before the first follow-up took place;[1] those based on the follow-ups were done soon after those assessments were made. The primary focus of these Profiles was to derive a cross-sectional and integrated statement of the child's developmental status and potential. It was assumed that at this point in research the most reliable and valid conclusions about a child were based on all the material available at a given point in time.[2] This approach would point to the essential variables and change in variables. It is then possible to develop ways of assessing a certain

[1] The Profile was not available when the project being reported on was begun. The procedure in the current project is to have both therapist and diagnostic psychiatrist write a Profile shortly after each assessment point.

[2] The reliability of the Profile construction and ratings based on them has been studied in a variety of ways and found to be satisfactory (Heinicke, 1965b).

function and changes in it by using one source of information or test.

Having formulated all the Profiles, it was possible to compare those for the children seen once as opposed to four times a week and to formulate hypotheses reflecting the differences in developmental status and potential at a given assessment point.

As will be seen, few striking differences were noted at the end of treatment, but the children seen four times a week did show a greater spurt in their growth during the two years after treatment. Before turning to these group differences, the Profiles written for a nine-year-old boy, Steven, are given below. He was seen four times a week for a period of nineteen months. His mother was seen once a week, and his father also had some contact with a therapist.

Steven's development illustrates well both the general and specific hypotheses formulated on the basis of the group comparisons. This is not to imply that the development of the other children was identical; very important variations did exist.[3]

THE PROFILES ON STEVEN: A CHILD SEEN FOUR TIMES A WEEK

REASON FOR REFERRAL

Steven's family was referred by a private psychiatrist following the parents' request for help because of Steven's failure to progress in school. Aged almost nine, he was at the time in the low third grade; although he had repeated half a year, he was a year behind in reading and spelling, and somewhat behind in arithmetic. In the classroom he was hyperactive, lacked self-control, had a short attention span, and was constantly seeking approval from the teacher.

DESCRIPTION OF THE CHILD

Steven is lightly built with dark, close-cut hair and slightly protruding ears. Appropriate boyish dress, a generally pleasant appearance, a shrewd, observing, intelligent look, and a warm smile together gave a likable impression. While he was at first solemn, his darting inquisitiveness anticipated the liveliness and movement which were to follow. His occasionally widened brown eyes and tentative explorations communicated fright, but a manly and seemingly confident approach was also apparent.

3 Copies of the set of Profiles formulated for Gordon, a child seen once a week, are available on request from the author.

FAMILY BACKGROUND AND PERSONAL HISTORY

Steven is the third child of a professional family. At the time of referral, his two older sisters, Jennifer and Barbara, were fourteen and eleven years old, and his brother, Michael, was five. The family lived in the suburbs of a large metropolitan area.

Some of the salient facts from his developmental history are as follows. The pregnancy with Steven was unplanned but an easy one; the mother felt good during the whole time. Steven was very active intra-uterine, and this excessive activity carried over into his babyhood. It made him a sharp contrast to the other children in the family, who were all very quiet. The mother nursed him for two months, but this proved unsuccessful because of her nervousness and his frequent spitting up. Because of his overactivity and his continuous vomiting she also found it very difficult to care for him and stressed particularly how difficult it was to keep him clean.

With the exception of a slow speech development, his second and third years were remembered by his mother as much more favorable. He walked at the usual time, but even though he could at one and a half years of age say simple sentences, he slurred them so badly that only his mother could understand them. It was not until the age of four that others could also comprehend what he was saying. Toilet training occurred "over night" when Steven was two and a half, and after it was completed, she took him everywhere with her. The mother reported she was very proud of her first son, thought he would be her last baby, and spoiled him a great deal.

The picture again changed during the third year. The mother first of all recalled that while she was giving Steven a bath, the father for some reason hit her. Steven, too, remembered this incident and later admitted that this was a great source of fear for him. At about three and a half when the mother was pregnant with the younger brother, Steven started to suck his thumb. Shortly after this he would sit or sleep on his hands to restrain himself from thumb sucking since this was strongly prohibited by the parents. It was also at about three and a half that his mother remembered getting very angry with Steven, screaming at him and hitting him because he misbehaved. She then begged him to forgive her by saying: "Help me be a good mummy by not doing these things."

When Steven was four and a half, the younger brother was born. Steven had been babied a great deal up until this time and now all this suddenly stopped. His father reported that while the mother was still in the hospital Steven told the neighbors that she was not going to bring the new baby home, and that the baby had died. Prior to the birth of the baby, Steven had had a room to himself. After the birth, he shared a room with Michael and about the same time became terrified of noise and cried a great deal. He was especially frightened by the street noises when put in the parents' bedroom in the front of the house for his nap. At about the same time he was put in nursery school, where he was a problem because of his overactivity.

In kindergarten Steven attempted to use scissors, broke out in a sweat, and was unable to do it. The teacher pictured him as being a very fidgety, active child who had difficulty listening and was unable to sit still. His speech was careless, his diction bad, and his homework poor. Toward the end of the term, he became more relaxed, more attentive, and a better worker, but then relapsed to a state of lack of self-confidence. He missed some school in kindergarten and the first grade due to tonsillitis. He missed much less school after the tonsils had been removed. Most important, despite being sent to bed at 7:00 o'clock, he seemed to be always tired.

The reports of his first-grade teachers indicate that he still could not use scissors and had difficulty writing. He dawdled and was disorganized. "He wanted to do a good job but just couldn't seem to concentrate," one teacher reported. He daydreamed, and chewed and dropped pencils frequently. His weakness was both in number work and in the recognition of written symbols. Beyond this, he was reported to be a good sport, friendly, and respectful of the rights of others.

Of particular significance in his seventh year was his having to repeat part of the first grade again and also being hit by a car. Although the car threw him some distance and he was unconscious for a few minutes, he was not seriously hurt. Almost exactly a year before this, his maternal grandfather had been killed in an automobile accident. Being held back in school depressed Steven because he wanted to continue to be with his five favorite friends. His second-grade teachers reported that he was still having trouble concentrating and still could not use scissors. He was reading in the low second reader, but had a small vocabulary, could not attack new words, and would skip over things. In contrast, it was reported that his number work was improving. It was during the second grade that he was referred for testing by the Guidance Service, but this was not followed up. Although Steven at times resented authority and criticism, he was never a behavior problem, and was well liked by his peers. By the beginning of the third grade he had become a little less popular, however, because he was pushing the smaller children around. The teacher felt that this was his way of trying to deal with the fact of being held back.

Just before the start of treatment, his mother reported that he was very high-strung, unable to sit still, but yawned a good deal when reading. He would know a word in the morning and forget it

by afternoon. The parents had stopped their unsuccessful attempts
to tutor him in reading, but the father would still sometimes sit for
two hours at a time and try to "drum arithmetic into his head." He
was still having trouble with fine skills, but rode his bicycle well
and had just passed his swimming tests.

Likely to be of significance in Steven's development were the
following past events:

1. The mother's inability adequately to feed a very active baby.
2. The mother's negative reaction to the messing associated with
   his feeding.
3. The father hitting the mother when Steven was three and a
   half; this was very likely representative of frequent parental
   conflict.
4. The mother's explosive outbursts at an uncontrollable child;
   these outbursts were very likely repeated frequently.
5. The excessive doting on and exhibition of her "last" son;
   i.e., Steven.
6. The birth of Michael and the impact of being "dropped" at
   the age of four.
7. Being held back in the first grade and the simultaneous loss
   of five friends.
8. Being hit by a car on the anniversary of the death of the
   maternal grandfather.

The rest of the Profile written at the beginning of treatment and
those formulated at the end and one year after the end of treatment
are given below. To emphasize the development over time, we present the conclusions drawn for each of the major subsections of the
Profile at each of the three time points.[4]

POSSIBLY SIGNIFICANT ENVIRONMENTAL INFLUENCES

At the Beginning of Treatment

The impact of Steven's parents overshadowed all other current
events. Mrs. A. was constantly impelled to intrude into Steven's
life. Angry at being treated like a stupid little girl and terrified
that her son would be found wanting, she burst into the therapy
room. Equally conducive to Steven's poor differentiation was her
constant push to organize. To deal with her feeling of hopelessness,
she insisted that Steven and her husband "get on the ball." She
said that they were alike in many ways and depreciated both with

---

4 Limitations of space have prevented presentation of the extensive descriptive material on which the Profiles are based.

accusations of their being "hopeless" when her attempts at organizing them had failed. This hopelessness was very likely linked also to previous feelings of hopelessness about her brain-injured younger brother. Her maternal organizing could, of course, be of great comfort; its sudden disappearance when her rushing literally exhausted her and she failed, for example, to pick Steven up on time led to serious disruption. Or turning the tables, she would plead with him to help her control herself and keep her from spanking him when he had been provocative and thrown his toys all over.

Threats of divorce and actual mutual attacks further challenged any anticipations of an "expectable environment." Neither the masculine nor the feminine model would appeal: the father was derided for not making enough money and had once been kicked out of the house. In turn he would suddenly hit his wife and call her stupid. Although Steven enjoyed being "her little man" and lying in bed with his mother, both her expectations and the threat of a father who actually hit him and cut his hair would be terrifying.

Yet, the father wanted his son to succeed, and thought he would, in fact, make it. Similarly, the mother's affection, caretaking, and feeding were clearly supportive. Her tendency to withdraw this support either because she was angry with her husband and displaced this anger onto Steven or because she unconsciously wanted to motivate him to "get on the ball" would, however, again lead to angry helplessness. Especially threatening was her tendency to give to Michael at the very moment when she was depriving Steven.

At the End of Treatment

Without underestimating the importance of factors like school environment, the nature of the impact of the parents on Steven again seems most important. The mother's need to intrude, to organize, and depreciate Steven had become less urgent. Able to perceive his increasing ambition, she could relax and instead encourage his independence by promising him a bicycle if he did all his work. The implicit supervision became more obvious as she tried "drilling him" to get even further ahead. This time she realized that too much pressure was useless. Many of her efforts to organize the best school experiences for Steven were also realistic. Most beneficial was her obvious pride in his achievement and her ability to encourage rather than curb his curiosity.

Still likely to be disruptive was the contrast between her organizing of his activities in response to his needs and the insensitivity shown when she would, for example, keep him waiting. This in turn was a function of her own disorganization. Although she had increasingly turned to pleasurable activities of her own and thus had less need to pressure her husband and son, she still had difficulty integrating her activities so as to avoid paniclike rushing or suddenly deserting others. While the father could still be provoked by Steven's "fooling around," he increasingly took pride in his son's successes.

Much of the open marital conflict had now ceased, so that the constant modeling of mutual denigration and victimization had lessened. A greater affectionate closeness allowed Steven to confess in their presence that his father had often terrified him.

A Year After the End of Treatment

Reports from the teacher and the material of the mother's interviews indicate that the mother had become even more aware of the futility of constantly pushing Steven. Interestingly, during the year she had been able successfully to resist the pushing of her own mother. She mentioned what great pleasure she took in Steven's achievement, did have realistic ambitions for his future education, and gave great support to a difficult project which Steven himself had decided to pursue.

There were still fights between the parents, but these were now more adequately resolved. During their joint interview with the child therapist they were more harmonious and affectionate with each other as well as the therapist.

As a model of organized ego functioning, the parents were still wanting. They arrived late for their interview because the mother had to finish the laundry. Many items of their clothes needed sewing, and the father several times got up to look out of the window at passing fire engines—like Steven, he could not sit still.

Otherwise benign trends in the parental impact as noted at the end of treatment continued in the year after treatment. Particularly noteworthy was the affection shown Steven by both parents.

ASSESSMENTS OF DEVELOPMENT: DRIVE DEVELOPMENT

At the Beginning of Treatment

Libido: Phase Development.—While Steven had reached the phallic phase, dominance on it had not been attained. He was chronologically in latency, but very little behavior appropriate to this phase was evident. His development had advanced sufficiently to take a positive oedipal stance; as Tramp (in the story) he had a secret love relationship with Lady. Yet these and other phallic advances were constantly subject to massive regression to earlier phases of development.

Libido: Distribution.—The quality and quantity of Steven's narcissism were such as to make a primary defect unlikely. Yet the quantity of the secondary narcissism was minimal. His tendency to split his body image best represented the lack of an integration necessary to experience a sustained self-esteem. In a moment of confidence he could challenge the therapist to a game of checkers and penetrate his "back line," but the least indication of possible defeat led to a fantasy of Humpty Dumpty. Unlike Humpty Dumpty, Steven's feet left him before "the great fall." His general ease in moving from aggressor to victim is also illustrated by the above. Similarly, he shifted from being clever to crazy, and boy to girl.

Given moments of sufficient integration to experience self-regard, the quantity of secondary narcissism derived from his ego achievements was nevertheless very limited and dependent on the reactions of others. He knew he could solve arithmetic problems, but even this skill was disrupted as he tried to demonstrate it to the diagnostic psychiatrist. All achievements were constantly subject to extremely sadistic external and internal evaluations. Without losing touch with reality, the constant shift in self representations offered a way out of this intense pressure.

The love reserved for the first son had, however, been sufficiently internalized to alleviate the above devaluation. In so far as this involved comparison with an encroaching younger brother and the retaliation of a jealous father, this source was again likely to be uncertain.

Object Libido.—Steven's ability to initiate object relationships represented his most advanced asset. He could express sufficient trust and affection toward both paternal and maternal figures to arouse the initial reaction of being likable. He was aware of his power to be his mother's little man and to elicit feminine reactions of "cute." Similarly, he expected that like his father, other men would be interested in promoting his development.

But if the above represented an advance to the oedipal level of object relationships, the regression to the preoedipal level was more impressive. As such it was consistent with the rest of his libidinal development. Any continuing relationships and particularly those involving passivity were likely to be flooded by monsterlike representations. Thus, he needed a mother who fed him good food and who provided the protective organization of daily life, but this was overshadowed by the representation of a devouring, intrusive, demanding, and overwhelming figure. Similarly, any competitive approach to a male was likely to be overwhelmed by representations of a hitting paternal monster. To this regressive construction of his object world, Steven reacted by passively complying or defying, by a variety of escapist tactics to keep from being tracked down, and by a magical longing for less monsterlike figures. Yet the most fre-

quent reaction to his expectations of being victimized was to provoke just this by unwittingly or purposely disrupting things through
his constant discharge. The teachers liked Steven, but they preferred to get rid of this uncontrolled, nonproductive "handful."

In contrast, his approach to his peers was accompanied by benign object expectations very likely modeled on his trusting relationships with his older sister, Barbara. But his younger brother,
Michael, and other younger children were viewed as an interference,
and had to be either denigrated (stupid, feceslike, etc.) or defensively
bossed around.

Aggression.—Initially inhibited and passive, Steven very quickly
expressed a great deal of aggression. Consistent with the regression
to all levels of libido development, its quality derived from all
phases. He was furious that he had been kept waiting by his mother,
was preoccupied with time-bomb explosions, and defensively enacted
how he would murder the therapist.

Although directed outward, the aggression initially tended to
be a part of a general explosion rather than taking the form of a
specific wish to injure; much of the aggression was also turned inward. "He invited murder." His feet were blown off by the time
bombs, and it was he who had lost so often that he didn't mind
anyway.

At the End of Treatment

Libido: Phase Development.—Steven (now ten and a half years)
had achieved dominance on the phallic phase and increasingly
showed behavior appropriate to late latency. A definite progressive
quality now characterized his libidinal development. Yet on occasions when his competence was threatened these advances were still
subject to regression to previous fixation points.

Libido: Distribution.—Steven's various self representations had
been sufficiently integrated to provide a stable focus for considerable
secondary narcissism. The tendency to split his body image was no
longer present. A feeling of having changed as a function of treatment was focused on feeling older, being different from his brother,
and no longer being the victim of family pressures.

It was particularly the feeling of making progress in reading that
would counter his previous "I can't make it." Yet if given difficult
problems he was still inclined to vacillate between "Am I not wonderful" and complete helplessness; too often the adult still had to
judge for him which of these self feelings he should accept.

His object relations also provided much narcissism. He had
shifted from being a victim to holding his own. He could compete
effectively with his father and could desire independence without
being motivated by a need to escape a devouring mother. When

confronted with the diagnostic psychiatrist he asked a number of challenging questions.

Least narcissism was still likely to be derived from superego sources. He still saw himself as one who "just can't help fooling around" (masturbating) and taking forbidden things (snitching cookies). To deal with his guilt he again had to be the feminine victim.

Object Libido.—Steven's ability to initiate and particularly to sustain a variety of object relationships had continued to develop and was now more consistent with the rest of his development. Although he was in some ways more reticent (and this was consistent with a move into latency), his capacity to express trust and affection was considerable. For the first time his teacher was experienced as an approving person; he tried hard to please her. He still viewed his brother and other young children with some contempt, but he tended either to overprotect them or leave them alone.

However, most important in accounting for the greater trust, as opposed to his previous need literally "to jump over the fence" and escape, was the change in his image of his mother. In fantasy it represented a change from a devouring monster tracking a small car to a normal-sized woman. He told of a boy who left his mother and went to camp because she insisted on treating him like a little baby. In another story a boy felt sorry he had broken a gift that his mother had given him. Both a greater independence of and sensitivity to the mother are implied by these stories.

Steven could now take a competitive stance, and the expectation of a castrating attack from the father was minimal. The former dread was further eased by Steven's ability to transfer the problems of oedipal rivalry to the boy-girl friend area. His stories reflected the acceptance of giving up the oedipal object and being chosen by a girl friend.

Yet there were still occasions when his inability to finish a school report gave him the feeling that he would never be able to succeed either in relation to the competition with the father or the oedipally tinged expectations of the mother. On these occasions he was forced to get the mother to coerce him and the father to shake (castrate) him in order to ease his guilt and depression.

Aggression.—Little aggression was now evident in the manifest picture. That seen took the form of provocative complaining and not doing his work in relation to specific people: his therapist, father, and mother. It was thus directed outward, but was also likely to incur punishment. As before, the content of these provocations derived from all three libidinal levels: the angry complaint of not receiving more help, the defiant failure to perform, and the fooling around linked to masturbation.

A Year After the End of Treatment

Libido: Phase Development.—Steven had achieved dominance on the latency phase and showed prepubertal interests. Signs of regression were temporary and were not likely to impede his further libidinal development.

Libido: Distribution.—Although there had been no striking qualitative changes in the integration and essential components of his total self representation, the quantity of secondary narcissism had increased further.

Although revealing less about his self feelings, and this would be consistent both with his age and the nature of the follow-up, what could be inferred indicated considerable change. He drew a picture of a boy approximately his age who was characterized as "building racers" and "doing well in his schoolwork." At the beginning of treatment he depicted a racing car escaping from a devouring feminine monster; during the follow-up interview he built a very fine, confident-looking racing car. The implication of an enhanced forward-moving body concept was supported by the fact that he had become a good runner and one of four team captains in his physical education class. Also new was the fact that he could tell a story about an eighteen-year-old boy who was considered "cute" by a sixteen-year-old girl. Other material supported the inference that Steven was increasingly aware of and accepting of his prepubertal status.

Similarly, being chosen by his class to decide questions of "the just punishment" would provide external support for his feeling "of being one of the boys." These "boys" included the five friends he had lost once because he had been held back.

In comparison with other sources of his narcissism, least was still derived in relation to superego sources. As indicated above, he could arbitrate in questions of fair play, showed the inner control necessary to be a captain, and did now finish all his academic work. Yet both in relation to the therapist and the mother his provocative "fooling around" suggested the previous image of: "I am a dirty boy who masturbates and doesn't work." The quantitative force of this fantasy was, however, greatly reduced.

Object Libido.—The progressive trends seen at the end of treatment had been consolidated further into normal object relationships. Fantasy material suggested that the mother was still seen as overpowering and demanding and the father as a forbidding as well as denigrated sexual rival. Such inner object representation could account for the need to "fool around" rather than work and succeed; but this provocation was now rare. Other observations pointed to his ability to withstand the mother's intrusion and depreciation and to his ability to reciprocate affection. This same affectionate charm was also seen in relation to his teacher. Similarly, a very realistic acceptance of his father's strengths and weaknesses had replaced the earlier image of a castrated yet physically explosive monster. Consistent with these changes was his tendency to distance himself and be independent of both his therapist and his parents. At the same time his observation of and sensitivity to the needs of others had also developed further.

His feelings for his brother continued to be both affectionate and defensively superior. He still had to tease and provoke "the little fellow" who had deprived him, but the nature of their fights was such that the mother did not feel impelled to punish Steven.

Underlining the progress in his object relations was his age-appropriate interest in the opposite sex. Although he still needed to keep his distance—and this is consistent with behavior seen in latency—his stories to the projective tests revealed a heterosexual interest: his boy and girl characters had amorous interests.

Aggression.—Manifest aggression had declined even further in the year after treatment. That directed toward peers appeared to be age appropriate. The re-emergence of occasional attacks on his little brother and the near emergence of anger toward the therapist's remaining patients revealed his former anger at not being the favorite one. It was in turn related to some evidence, on the fantasy level, of oral sadism.

Anger about not receiving more from the therapist and his parents could also be inferred, but the fate of this particular anger was now one of inhibition rather than explosion or turning it against the self.

Sadistic components could also be seen in his conception of intercourse. In occasionally provoking the parents by fooling around, he might have been inviting an attack, but, as indicated previously, these provocations were extremely limited.

ASSESSMENTS OF DEVELOPMENT: EGO AND SUPEREGO

At the Beginning of Treatment

Both the quality of his functioning (e.g., the hypermotility) and his development (e.g., the late onset of speech) suggested the diagnosis of some mild brain damage or a constitutionally based defect in the ego apparatus. Even the initial formulation did not, however, stress this explanation.

Rather, an emphasis was placed on the interruption of ego integration and differentiation. In all situations he moved rapidly from an initial inhibition to increasing motility expressed via gross and fine movements. This hypermotility was used for purposes of

discharge, as a defense, and as a symbolic expression of certain conflicts. Invariably he enacted what he talked about. As he put it: "I
can't sit still and think." When he spoke about a volcano, he made
explosive noises. Such heavy reliance on motility was not coupled
with a high degree of efficiency and differentiation of this function.
He misarranged picture sequences, even though he could verbalize
the solution correctly. His visual-motor deficiency was expressed
graphically through a WISC obtained at school on which he earned
a performance I.Q. of 79 as compared with a verbal I.Q. of 113.
Even his perceptions were mobile in that on the Rorschach he rarely
saw the same things twice. The constant shift in his thoughts and
feelings affected his orientation in space. At the Clinic he consistently went in the wrong direction. His time sense was also poorly
developed; he frequently had to ask what time it was. To avoid
being passively subjected to stress he substituted his own stimuli
for the ones offered. Since such defensive maneuvers are more difficult in auditory recall tasks, his extremely poor performance on
these tasks may in part be accounted for.

His vocabulary, verbal facility, and judgment were generally
above average. This could be associated with a generally effective
reality testing. However, by too often having to act out his thoughts
and by becoming what he talked about, he made a condensation
which blurred his differentiation of what is inside and what is external. At the beginning of his second session he could very accurately portray how like a sly fox he had outwitted his mother. The
observation of her weak points was most realistic. On the other hand,
as he enacted the military defense of a hospital containing one ill,
damaged, soldier, the enemy was suddenly everywhere.

While a variety of images and impulses were available, the pressure for discharge allowed little adaptive cognitive elaboration or the
adaptive use of a variety of specific affects. His capacity to bind tension was in general weak. His archaic fantasy in particular suggested
considerable primary-process intrusions in his mental functioning.
This fluidity could also be considered potentially consistent with
Steven's capacity for humor and his ability to observe his own predicament. About a drawing, undoubtedly a self-portrait, he remarked,
"If his eyes were not lopsided and his body not crooked, he would
look like a regular person."

Ego Ideal and Superego.—Behavior indicative of well-integrated
superego or ego-ideal representations and the associated appropriate
signs of guilt and shame were not in evidence; there was little consistent inner control. The operation of extremely sadistic injunctions could be inferred in relation particularly to academic failure,
aggression, cheating, and masturbation. To defend against his drives,

Steven relied heavily on the object world. He clearly wanted to succeed, but could not consciously experience either the intensity of his shame or show realistic concern about his academic retardation. Rather, responsibility for the initiation of academic or any other activity was left to the mother and teacher. Similarly, he depended on the adult world (parents and teachers) to stop his disruptive and provocative activities.

Defense Organization.—A great variety of defenses were apparent as Steven made an effort to deal with quantitatively overwhelming drives and internal and external demands. At best, their work resulted in a labile equilibrium; at worst, the primary process colored all expressions, and could result in further defensive steps leading to a fragmented body image.

Some defenses were age adequate: inhibition (of fantasy aggression), repression (forgetting the unpleasant), passive to active (keeping mother waiting), reversal of affect (he was glad, not sad, to miss a session), displacement (from person to toys), and identification with the aggressor (he beat up some kids at school). Although these defenses suggested normal functioning, they were unevenly deployed and appeared in the context of more primitive ones. Thus, the inhibition and repression represented an unstable hold and were overwhelmed by the excessive and primitive use of defensive identifications: Steven became, and motorically enacted, varying partial identities either to represent or to ward off. At times the connected discharge was directed at his own body image—suddenly he would hit his head; or it was projected outward (his parents became aggressive monsters). Obsessional ordering was attempted in relation to anger toward his mother. He hoped for magical solutions to his academic problems. When about to lose competitively, he could only disrupt the whole game and create a cloud of confusion. The pervasiveness of regression in all these defenses must be emphasized. Avoidance also played a key role in the equilibrium reached; he avoided discussion of his failure at school or denied that he cared.

The interference with ego achievements associated with the above defense constellation was extensive. The avoidance and his dependence on external control would make him unable even to confront the academic task. Even when he could be cajoled to initiate a task like reading, the pressure toward the use of defensive identifications, regression, and the associated defenses was such that he could not sit still, not take in, not remember, not think clearly.

At the End of Treatment

In contrast to Steven's initial status, gross signs of a lack of ego integration were now absent. The performance I.Q. rose 23 points to 102 and was thus less discrepant with the verbal I.Q. which remained essentially the same, 114, as opposed to the previous 113. With the exception of his drawing, his eye-hand coordination had improved greatly. There were many indications of a more orderly and consistent approach to tasks, but other observations pointed to the continued variability of cognitive functioning; e.g., although his visual memory had improved, he still had great difficulty with material presented orally.

The decrease in his hypermotility represented the most dramatic change and played an important part in improving the level of ego integration. In the test situation he worked with great persistence for more than three hours without getting restless. The teacher reported that for the first time he could sit still in class and attend; the gains he made in the five months before the end of treatment had brought him to grade level in reading and arithmetic. Thus, his verbal and conceptual facility was enhanced in part because he was no longer as frequently overwhelmed by a primary-process type of diffuse motility and fantasy discharge. He could reflect, ask very relevant questions, or just talk.

As this discharge and the associated pressure to avoid any type of passive experience became less intense, his ability to distinguish between inner experience and outer reality became more pronounced, and his orientation in space was much more adequate. His comments about school, treatment, and the nature of his own changes revealed his power to observe others, a considerable ability to observe himself, and the ability to seek information from others to confirm or disconfirm his observations. For example, he very pointedly asked the diagnostic psychiatrist why he had not continued working with him after their contacts at the beginning of treatment; or he could realize that not reading as a way of getting even with the parents was also self-punishing.

Consistent with the above was the greater ability to bind affects and to elaborate on ideas and fantasies. While the strong color cards could still arouse archaic imagery, secondary process now prevailed in that the images were elaborated on as part of a scientific-space theme. Similarly, his stories to the T.A.T. cards were longer, more complicated, and more interesting. The greater tension-binding capacities led to some suppression of affect, but this very fact made possible a shift from chaotic discharge to the adaptive use of a variety of feelings. As his therapy drew to a close, he could express sadness and anger at being left, disappointment that his wish for magic had not been fulfilled, and yet also gratitude.

Not perhaps surprising, regression to the previous level of ego functioning occurred as his adequacy was too overwhelmingly challenged. When tackling the I.Q. performance subtests, Steven once more became restless, and on occasion became what he was working on. Thus, when assembling a car, he seemed suddenly to become a "Dauphine" and made horn noises. These regressions were, however, limited in frequency and could in the context of sufficient integration conceivably become an asset in creativity.

Ego Ideal and Superego.—The evidence for integrated and benign inner controls was now considerable. Clear-cut internalized ambitions to get a college diploma were coupled with a high level of realistic concern and persistence. Although he was still more than usually sensitive to the possibility of being shamed academically, only occasionally was this associated with a chain of failure leading to further failure.

Signs of sadistic superego representations were no longer as obvious. Guilt about challenging his oedipal rival, about masturbation, and in relation to defying his mother by not performing academically could be inferred. At certain moments the only way for Steven to reach some sort of equilibrium was to have others push, punish, or discard him, but most of the time he had sufficient self-discipline to pursue his work at home and in school. The anger about not having been the therapist's favorite and not having received the magical gift also aroused his guilt, but these affects were again experienced in the context of the quiet functioning of other inner controls.

Defense Organization.—Regression to previous libidinal fixations was at the end of treatment still noticeable. Confronted with conflicts around object loss this tendency combined with other defenses: the need for the magical gift; the resort to passivity and its provision of food and sleep; a babylike crying appeal for help; provocatively inviting or doing the discarding; denial of all affect or the reversal of it; and turning the passive being left into active leaving.

Defensive identifications were also still evident, though greatly diminished. For example, in relation to conceptions of intercourse he was either the victim or the attacker. Similarly, the full implications of active masculine success were at times avoided. He provoked the adult to hit and push him and externalized: the therapist must choose the game during the last session just as his parents must make him do the homework. It was particularly this avoidance and provocation that still exacted a price in decreased adaptation and enjoyment.

Defenses of a most primitive sort diminished greatly or disappeared altogether: aggression to the self, a tendency to split the body representation, obsessional mechanisms such as doing and undoing, and crude forms of denial and projection. Most important, the defensive use of motility and a tendency to disrupt the total situation gave way to the age-adequate use of inhibition and conformity and resulted in an equilibrium which only occasionally was subject to regression and lability.

A Year After the End of Treatment

Although Steven's gain of 10 points on the verbal I.Q. and the maintenance of essentially the same level of performance I.Q. had resulted in considerable discrepancy (124 versus 99), there were no indications that the variability in his functioning had increased. Though by no means always predictable—and in this he fell below what would be expected for his age group—his total performance was more reliable than the previous year.

As at the end of treatment, there were no gross signs of a lack of ego integration. The level of tension-binding capacity continued to show gains and the mobility of images was not observed. There was no longer any evidence of confusion between what is inside and what is outside. The primary-process type of diffuse motility and fantasy discharge was now confined to a few instances: mouth noises, accidentally falling off a chair, and difficulty in handling a pencil.

There was instead much evidence of secondary-process functioning. His vocabulary was average. The quality of his thinking and judgment was realistic, though at times variable. He could sit still, attend, and perform verbally in front of the class. Although it was not evident in the psychological test situation, the teacher observed that he could remember material presented orally. Rather than dosing stimuli himself, he was more alert and thus more realistic.

Parallel to these signs of greater integration and efficiency were indications of greater inner freedom. His imagery was more lively and less pseudoscientific. The construction of a car during the follow-up interview with the therapist was based on a very creative plan. He could experience a greater variety of affects including sadness, enthusiasm, embarrassment, pride, affection, and disappointment.

New also was his clear-cut ability to plan, organize, and persist in relation to academic and other tasks. Having successfully completed his work he could take pride in it. The strength of his academic ambitions had definitely increased, but it had also become more realistic. He could accurately assess the extensive gains he had made in all three academic subjects, and was realistically planning his preparation for college.

His general self-awareness had definitely been advanced; at the same time he could more readily assume the other person's point of view. For example, he could empathize with the psychological tester in terms of the problems she was having writing down all his responses.

Ego Ideal and Superego.—Excessive guilt and the tendency to externalize control and provoke punishment had declined. There was still evidence in his fantasy expressions on the tests that he could be provocative about getting things done, and that he felt guilty when his sexual curiosity was aroused. Behavior with the therapist indicated a short-lived temptation to externalize and a tendency to provoke punishment for having indulged in masturbation, but there was no evidence of guilt about curiosity. On the contrary, it was openly expressed. Remnants of guilt in relation to anger about not "being the favorite" and not receiving sufficient oral supplies were still evident.

His total development was, however, suggestive of more benign inner controls. Illustrative was his ability to assume leadership in peer situations involving justice and fair play.

Defense Organization.—While a tendency to regress to mouth noises and passivity was still evident, the recovery was rapid. Similarly, he would express a wish for magical aid, but then dismiss it and proceed with the task.

Various passive to active maneuvers related to the loss of the object were still evident. His needing to know the time at the end of the session and some indication of having to run away suggested that he still had difficulty parting from significant objects. It was hard to evaluate at the time whether this was a specific residual in relation to the therapist or a more general problem with its associated defenses.

The defensive use of movement, various defensive identifications, provocative behavior, and the denial of affect, though once prominent, now occurred infrequently. In contrast, conformity with certain adult standards was observed more frequently. For example, Steven now tried to please the tester.

In summary, a balanced, age-adequate organization of defenses was operating effectively enough to lead neither to deadlock nor to lability. When regressions occurred they tended to be temporary and no longer resulted in the serious impairment of functioning seen at the beginning of treatment.

ASSESSMENTS OF DEVELOPMENT: TOTAL PERSONALITY

At the Beginning of Treatment

From Dependency to Emotional Self-reliance and Adult Object Relationships.—We have already cited Steven's dependence on external control to initiate any activity or to curb his instinctual life. In his move toward adult relationships he was still predominantly at the ambivalent anal-sadistic stage. Yet in his ability to find his way around his neighborhood and separate from his parents, he showed self-reliance appropriate for his age.

From Suckling to Rational Eating.—Although Steven had no feeding problem, there was evidence both of some irrational attitudes toward food and of battles with the mother. He reacted particularly strongly to her efforts to force him to eat foods reminiscent of the male genitals (e.g., two brussel sprouts).

From Wetting and Soiling to Bladder and Bowel Control.—Although complete sphincter control had been achieved, Steven had not internalized the standards of cleanliness usually found in his age group. He spilled food at the table, and often left his room in chaos.

From Irresponsibility to Responsibility in Body Management.—Given his very protecting father and mother, it was difficult to assess whether Steven had voluntarily endorsed the rules of hygiene, or whether he simply complied with requests made. Although he had at the age of seven been hit by a car, there was no indication that in health or safety matters he needed any particular protection.

From Egocentricity to Companionship.—Steven had had five good friends in his second school year, and related to them as partners. After he had been held back, the picture had changed. He still participated actively in games with his former friends, but with the younger children he was bossy, and was not liked because he was too loud and uncontrolled.

From Body to Toy and from Play to Work.—Least progress had been made in his capacity to work. There was little persistence and pleasure in the finished product. While he had made some academic progress, particularly in arithmetic, this was more a function of maternal pressure than of intrinsic interest. He had no hobbies, and even his play initially offered him little satisfaction. He could delay long enough to use material in the enactment of a fantasy, but the subsequent wild destruction left no finished product except discharge. Having carefully set up a fort, a wild car suddenly crashed through everything and left a shambles.

Although all aspects of Steven's development had been affected by his disturbance, there was considerable discrepancy between his ability to work and his development from egocentricity to companionship.

At the End of Treatment

From Dependency to Emotional Self-reliance and Adult Object Relationships.—Although Steven's general level of independence and quality of peer associations placed him well into latency, there were still occasions when he relied on the adult world either to initiate an activity like a report or to help him deal with his oedipal and masturbation guilt. Equally important, however, was the fact that he was actively attempting to move away from the constant protection of his parents.

From Suckling to Rational Eating.—Although the evidence for oral fixations persisted, indications of irrational attitudes toward food, battles over food with the mother, and unusual food habits were missing. His development in this regard was age appropriate.

From Wetting and Soiling to Bladder and Bowel Control.—In so far as his cleanliness habits were now well within the range of behavior expected for his age, Steven was progressing normally on this developmental line.

From Irresponsibility to Responsibility in Body Management.— There was no evidence that Steven was either excessively irresponsible or responsible in the care of his health and safety.

From Egocentricity to Companionship.—Both his old and new friendships were now characterized by partnership and by a considerable variety in the activities that were shared. On the basis of classroom observations, the teacher stressed that Steven was now capable of putting himself in the other person's place.

From Body to Toy and from Play to Work.—Steven had made the greatest progress on this developmental line. He persisted in his academic work and enjoyed the end result. Various classroom projects and peer games were approached with much enthusiasm. While he had no hobbies, he did now enjoy reading a book. His occasional need to be mobilized and limited has been mentioned previously, but even this deficit was not so great as to detract seriously from the general conclusion that the total congruence in development and functioning was now considerable.

A Year After the End of Treatment

From Dependency to Emotional Self-reliance and Adult Object Relationships.—Steven's self-reliance had in the year after treatment developed further. While the rare invitation to be coerced and the implication of dependency were still in evidence, indications of psychological independence were much more frequent. He could realistically criticize the father's efforts to help him, but at the same time he indicated very clearly that he intended to pursue the father's profession. He could not only resist the excessive help of his mother but in fact make suggestions which helped her. Taken together with his developing interest in the opposite sex, as well as slight indications of rebellion, these signs of psychological independence now placed him in the preadolescent phase.

From Suckling to Rational Eating.—Little change had occurred, but the previous progressive development was consolidated further.

From Wetting and Soiling to Bladder and Bowel Control.— Little change had occurred, but the previous progressive development was consolidated further.

From Irresponsibility to Responsibility in Body Management.— Little change had occurred, but the previous progressive development was consolidated further.

From Egocentricity to Companionship.—Little change had occurred, but the previous progressive development was consolidated further.

From Body to Toy and from Play to Work.—In what had always been the weakest area of his development, Steven had made more progress than might be expected in a year's time. Not only did he take responsibility for completing his work, but he clearly derived pleasure from being, for example, the best arithmetic student in the class and having gained more than a year in all subjects since last tested a year ago. There were instances when he would still get out of his seat or provoke the parents by not starting his homework until midnight, but these occasions were rare.

Given the above advances, and reviewing the absolute level as well as potential progress on all developmental lines, one can conclude that the congruence in Steven's total development was now considerable.

GENETIC ASSESSMENTS

At the Beginning of Treatment

Steven was both firmly rooted in the phallic phase of development and regressing to all previous libidinal levels. From his initial contacts conflicts around the activity of masturbation could be inferred. During his therapy session he played a solitary game of cards, built up and reduced the piles, and then suddenly noticed a gap in the card sequence. From this beginning his play soon revealed the tremendous regressive pull to earlier phases.

First to appear in the material and certainly central in emphasis were the intense conflicts around the birth of his brother and the regressively linked conflicts generated by feelings of deprivation. In an opening statement he told the psychiatrist that there are some things he does not know and other things he does know. He knows about borrowing, tried to subtract 9 from 5, but could not do so. The numbers were obvious references to how the birth of his brother (now five years old) had taken much of his mother's love away from him. Similarly, he was furious and became depressed because his mother could not get him to his hour on time. The emergence of intense death wishes and the return of thumb sucking at the time of Michael's birth as well as Steven's earlier overactivity and vomiting provided independent evidence for these fixation points. The constant mouth noises and vocalizations as well as the indistinct speech of his second year further underlined the importance of the oral fixation. While looking through a book on evolution he named words and filled the interstices between words with "dum-de-dum." An example would be: "There's a plant-eater—dum-de-dum—eats plants—dum-de-dum—bit one. . . ."

The repeated repetition in play of his being made unconscious in a car crash pointed to great anxieties about being the victim and the manifold meanings this had for him. In the context of a constant confusion about "he"and "she" and the associated intense castration and bisexual anxieties, the monsters (overwhelming forces) took different forms; regressive aspects as well as references to past trauma could often be inferred. A hurricanelike mother, looking more male than female, threatened to overwhelm and swallow everything. The mother's past appeal to Steven to help her control herself seemed relevant, but this overwhelming woman was herself subject to attack: "She is going to be blown to smithereens; a bomb goes right into her belly and she is going to die." In a different context, he recalled the father's attack on the mother while she was giving Steven a bath.

While anal regressive components were suggested by the overwhelming display of sadomasochism and the constant explosions, the evidence for regression to the oral phase was greater. The "sexual" cards of the Rorschach evoked associations suggesting oral-incorporative notions. Castration anxiety was largely experienced in archaic forms involving a fear of being devoured. For example, he saw a monster who would suck in and eat up anyone who came close to any of its orifices.

At the End of Treatment

As at the beginning of treatment, conflicts in regard to the activity of phallic masturbation once more constitute the starting point for the genetic assessments. While the quality of the fixation points preceding this developmental point was also similar to that seen at the beginning of treatment, the quantity of regression was greatly reduced.

Although he had made great strides in actively competing and being curious, there were other times when instead of confronting the task he again had to "fool around." This could consist either of actual masturbation or such derivatives as fooling around with his friends rather than working. The anal regressive component was suggested as he still was afraid of being tracked down for this "dirty" activity. Conceiving himself as "Bumface" he regressively invited the coercion of his mother to make him produce a school report.

Fooling around was also linked to cheating in the sense of depriving Daddy-O of his strength and thus becoming the "king around the house." While the various meanings and consequences of this wish had come up in treatment, the regression to a feminine identification still occurred and was associated with Steven's wish to incorporate the father's phallic-oral strength. The guilt deriving from both this biting wish and the positive oedipal one, as well as the longing for and dread of the passive feminine position still drove Steven actively to provoke the father. He told the therapist of accidentally coming across some of his father's M & M candies, and how he could not resist stealing some. The next day the father called. Steven had been "fooling around," refused to do his homework, and simply refused to understand the difference between M and N. In desperation the father had finally shaken him. Indicative of the potential for recovery from this crisis is the fact that not only did Steven finish the report, but in his contact with the psychiatrist immediately after treatment he had the letters of M and W upside down but then made the correction.

Without being able to see all the regressive links, residuals of the earliest fixations could be seen in his concern of why he was not the favorite son of the parents; the regression to passivity and oral noises also emphasized the earliest fixations, but, as indicated, these regressions were limited to stressful occasions, and recovery was adequate.

A Year After the End of Treatment

While both the regressive potential and the importance of phallic-oral fixations could once more be delineated, their force had further decreased and tended to be temporary in their effect. This is well illustrated by the hour held with the therapist.

After openly expressing his curiosity about the therapist's greatest secret, he momentarily began to provoke the therapist by "fooling around" with a microphone rather than dictating with it as he had done previously. He inhibited this impulse and a tendency to regress to the earliest phases appeared: he complained about the therapist's junk (toys) and then threw himself on the couch. Again, this was short-lived. The temporary nature of this regression to passivity could be inferred, but the evidence from the psychological tests indicated that a residual of sadistic conceptions of intercourse and the dread of femininity were also likely "to make him get up." Continuing with the sequence of the hour, after an interruption by the mother, Steven turned to building a racing car. He expressed the wish for help in designing it, indicated the tinker toy set was a gyp because there were not enough parts, but then quickly relied on his own resources. As he ran into difficulty in building a very masculine-looking car, there were other familiar signs of regression to the oral phase: he again made some mouth noises and talked of some pills that his father had given him; but the noises quickly stopped, and he expressed his independence of his father by saying (quite realistically so) that the pills had done no good. The positive progressive phallic move was once more underscored as he finished the car and took great pride in it.

Finally, the parting from the therapist once more stressed the regression to the earliest fixations as well as the ability to recover. Had the therapist fired his previous secretary? By implication he was asking why he had been fired and why was he no longer the parents' favorite? He took a gun off the shelf, but then returned it. The emergence of anger was this time inhibited. He clearly had difficulty ending the hour, but he could for the first time shake the therapist's hand.

DYNAMIC AND STRUCTURAL ASSESSMENTS

At the Beginning of Treatment

Steven was at referral subject to each of the three major types of conflict. The external conflicts can be related to the previous account of significant environmental events. Steps in the direction of autonomy were likely to be met by maternal organizing, depreciation, or intrusion. Moves toward phallic dominance encountered the physical blows of a jealous father. A constantly charged and disorganized family atmosphere did little to further Steven's internal integration.

Yet the internal conflicts were more prominent. In the previous section we have stressed the many regressive links between the phallic and oral phases. A hysteric structure is suggested. A phobia in relation to being in certain rooms had developed at one time, but neither this nor the signs of an obsessional solution were adequate to check the regressive force. Chronic defects in ego integration and differentiation had appeared early in Steven's development, and have been stressed in distinguishing his difficulties from a simpler neurotic structure.

In further trying to account for the failure of the above-mentioned neurotic solutions, one could emphasize the intensity of certain incompatible drive representatives: the intense ambivalence toward his mother and brother, the complete inability to balance passivity and activity, and the extensive fluctuation in age and sex identities.

Yet the sheer intensity and number of internalized conflicts were impressive. He showed great interest in the potential love relationship between Lady and the Tramp, but then became most concerned with the accident depicted in the story: Tramp is pinned down by the dogcatcher's wagon. He then told of a dog that was sent to the pound for fooling around. Fooling around referred not only to masturbation but also to not doing his homework and being restless. All were subject to injunctions analogous to the mother's hurricane yell of "Get on the ball," and the father's impulsive hit on his head. Any effort to move forward psychologically, that is, to achieve successfully or to compete, was thus likely to encounter such dangers. More specifically, to know or attempt to find out the adult secrets was clearly forbidden.

However, regression activated other conflicts. Salient were the injunctions against the oral sadism experienced toward his mother and that felt toward his brother, the intruder, who took away his favored position. When his mother brought him late for his first therapeutic hour he could at first only indulge in obsessional counting, but this soon gave way to a provocative messing; the invitation to be punished would help him with his guilt and also allow the forbidden wish to "kapuih" all over his mother.

Steven portrayed his dilemma dramatically when the hurt soldiers in a jeep could move neither forward nor backward; in front and in back they were hemmed in by monsters.

At the End of Treatment

In so far as the mother could be aroused to coerce him into performance and the father to shake him for cheating and fooling around, so Steven's conflicts clearly had an external component. Similarly, moments of family disorganization in basic routines would stimulate feelings of helplessness.

In delineating the structure of internalized conflicts and associated incompatible drive derivatives, those remaining at the phallic and oral phase of development were again central. If completing a school report still signified competing with a castrating father, then he still had to fool around so the father would be invited to turn him into a victim. In this way he controlled the powerful father by identifying with the masochistic rather than the sadistic partner in intercourse. To provoke the mother to coerce him into performance and punish him for his dirty masturbation again led to the unacceptable masochistic feminine position.

Regression from these phallic conflicts to earlier levels also activated conflicts, which, taken together with the above, would still give him the feeling of being hemmed in. An attempt to obtain oral strength from his father once more spelled femininity. To seek regressively the position of the favored son stimulated the ambivalence felt toward mother and brother and the guilt he experienced in relation to oral sadism and anal explosiveness. Rather than be the quiet, passive, little flower girl, he would still prefer to "jump over the fence," or fall off it as Humpty Dumpty.

While the potential for feeling hemmed in was still there, both the elaboration of the phallic derivatives and the lessening of the regressive forces were such as to allow a definite forward move. Internal regulators of his wish to take a competitive stand, of his active exploration of the adult secrets, and of the setting of his academic and other achievement standards were more benign and no longer of monster proportions. As he portrayed it: the army jeep could go back for (oral) supplies, but could then drive forward into the secrets of the night.

A Year After the End of Treatment

Conflicts with the external world would again be stimulated as the mother had to depreciate Steven by invidious comparison with his brother and to intrude into his private life, i.e., burst into his hour with the therapist. Yet she had become painfully aware of her actions, and the occurrence of these external conflicts was rare. The impact on Steven of the parental disorganization was now less clear, but it was still likely to have some effect.

Even though the major emphasis was now on the adequate resolution of internal conflicts, signs of inadequate resolution at both the phallic and oral level remained. A story told to the T.A.T. card showing a couple embracing best focused the residual of Steven's conflict. He identified the characters as a father telling a son not to go into the swamps. These details as well as the rest of the story suggested former conflicts around penetrating the secrets of the night. Not that his curiosity was inhibited, but the misidentification of the sexes was consistent with his anxiety around identifying with the active masculine role in intercourse for fear that he "might be sucked helplessly into a swamp" and again become the feminine cha-cha dancer. Whether the rejection of, as well as the obvious sexual interest in, the feminine was simply consistent with prepubertal developments or represented a deviancy beyond the normal could be determined only in further follow-up. Although the provocation to be turned into a feminine victim by the father or mother could well be related to the above anxieties, this provocation could no longer be considered deviant.

Such regression as occurred did stimulate conflicts related to the earliest fixations. Passivity had to be inhibited not only because of its feminine connotations, but because of its link to the residual of oral sadism. Similarly, his longing to be the favorite son could not be expressed because of the anger that would accompany it. By putting the toy gun away he was in a sense rendering himself impotent. On the other hand, he could express his oral longing by eating a considerable amount of food during the psychological testing.

While these observations again point to residuals of conflict suggestive of a hysterical character structure, the total resolution of conflict was now such as to allow for extensive libidinal and ego growth.

ASSESSMENT OF GENERAL CHARACTERISTICS

At the Beginning of Treatment

Given the impact of his frustrating and anxiety-provoking parents, it is not easy to evaluate Steven's own tolerance in these areas. Yet independently assessed, it was clear that he could not tolerate frustrations relating to any deprivation imposed by the mother: the absence of a favorite food, and favoritism toward his brother stimulated an intolerable anger.

Similarly, the anxieties stimulated by any phallic step forward were too overwhelming: curiosity, sexual possession, and any active approach to a competitive situation, but particularly the academic one, were intolerable.

If only by contrast, there did seem to be some potential for sublimation. He had been able to achieve in the motor area; he could swim and ride a bicycle. Furthermore, his arithmetic was nearly at grade level. Otherwise, the areas of neutralized adaptation were very limited.

Finally, although the regressive tendencies far outweighed the progressive forces, there was also no doubt that Steven wanted to escape from an intolerable situation. He wanted to catch up with friends, and expressed an intelligent interest in his therapy: "I guess I am not doing well enough and could improve."

At the End of Treatment

Both qualitative and quantitative changes had taken place in Steven's ability to tolerate frustration and anxiety. He still found it difficult to tolerate the loss of the object and to give up being the favorite son, and had difficulty with anxieties arising out of competition with the father. Not only did the evidence of inadequate tolerance tend to be confined to these areas, but Steven showed much greater powers of recovery: that is, the frustrations and anxieties were quantitatively less overwhelming.

The development of Steven's sublimations and particularly the acceleration of the turn toward neutralized gratification were impressive. He could now derive much satisfaction from age-appropriate attainment in academic subjects, sports, and friendships.

By implication the progressive developmental forces were in ascendancy. His wish to be free of treatment and to test his strength was not only defensive. Moreover, his perception of himself as having changed and his academic ambitions were realistic and reflected an active wish to grow up. Going to college had become one of his goals.

A Year After the End of Treatment

Qualitatively speaking, evidence of frustration in relation to losing the object, not being the favorite, and not receiving the magical gift could still be seen. Similarly, the idea of performing competitively aroused initial anxiety and withdrawal. Yet quantitatively, further shifts had taken place in that the lowered tolerance was momentary.

As at the end of treatment, the evidence of the increasing number of aim-inhibited activities was impressive. Aside from continued and considerable academic progress, he had become a team captain, was an excellent athlete, and actively participated in a summer camp which he attended.

That the progressive forces had further accelerated is indicated by the fact that the wish to grow up was no longer talked about but just assumed—he would be like the friends with whom he had now caught up.

DIAGNOSIS

At the Beginning of Treatment

It is clear that permanent regressions had led in Steven to permanent symptom formation, and to a standstill in libidinal and ego growth. Few progressive forces were in evidence at the time of referral, but the phallic development had definitely been reached, and a wish to move forward again was retained.

The conflicts associated with the main symptom, a learning difficulty, were predominantly neurotic in nature. Developmental deficiencies in the differentiation and integration of ego functions also contributed, however, to Steven's learning impairment.

At the End of Treatment

Although Steven still evidenced a considerable regressive potential as well as residuals of various types of conflict at all levels of development, their structural interrelation and quantitative force had been changed to the point where permanent symptom formation, impoverishing effects on libido progression, crippling effects on ego growth, and a lack of ego integration and differentiation were minimally present.

Projecting trends initiated during treatment, the therapist expected at the end of it that the predominance of the progressive over regressive forces in Steven's functioning would continue to increase in the year following treatment. It was anticipated that the conflicts specifically related to the terminal phase of treatment had been sufficiently interpreted so that their eventual resolution would aid rather than hinder the progressive forces. It was further anticipated that under pressure he would again tend to regress to crying or negative passive provocation, but that these tendencies would be temporary rather than permanent. It was realized, of course, that this would be possible only if his environment and particularly his parents were as supportive as was the case at the end of treatment.

A Year After the End of Treatment

Steven's functioning fell within "variations of normality." Permanent symptom formation, impoverishing effects on libido progression, crippling effects on ego growth, and evidence of a lack of ego integration and differentiation were quantitatively no greater than would be expected for a boy of this age.

It was anticipated, therefore, that Steven would continue to show the appropriate amount of progress in all areas of development, even though he was to be placed into one of the most advanced classes in his age group.

THE ASSESSMENT OF STEVEN TWO AND THREE YEARS AFTER THE END OF TREATMENT

Further follow-up evaluations of Steven and his family were done two and three years after the end of treatment. At each of these points the mother met with her therapist, Steven had a session with his therapist, a school visit was conducted, and finally the parents were seen jointly by the child therapist. While our formulations focused on Steven as evaluated three years after treatment, the information available from the follow-up two years after treatment was used in making these assessments. If previous assessments had been complicated by the reaction to termination and the accentuated repetition of material seen during treatment, in evaluating the assessments presented below it must be kept in mind that Steven was now thirteen and a half years old. Since in general the Profiles of the second follow-up confirm the results of the assessment done one year after treatment, only selected areas are discussed.

By three years after treatment Steven showed the beginnings of adolescent development. His wish to be independent in his choice of activities and an assertive defiance of his mother were differentiated from earlier behavior exclusively provocative in nature. The adolescent character of his object relationships was underlined by his great sensitivity to his peers. Although he knew he was well liked both as a companion and athlete, and had continued his ways of "fair play," he overreacted whenever one of his many friends left him. Here again one is reminded of his feelings of no longer being the favorite son, but once more we conclude that this type of depressed feeling falls within the normal range of adolescent object relations.

Examination of Steven's superego functioning best focuses both his strength but also potential deterrents to progressive development. He was consciously determined to succeed and there were many indications of the internalization of benign paternal expectations. He would train for the same profession as father, could identify with his religious values and yet compete with him in this area. Most important, he felt support from an inner feeling that the father wanted him to succeed.

While benign inner expectations would also derive from a devoted mother who had high hopes for her first son, there were still some indications that the severity of these demands (now internalized) could potentially hinder Steven's development. He had taken on a great deal of extracurricular activity; although he managed to cope successfully, the strain was considerable. Only a further follow-up could determine how the various components of his superego would be integrated, but the expectation was that the benign aspects would predominate.

THE DIFFERENTIAL DEVELOPMENT OF CHILDREN SEEN ONCE AND FOUR TIMES A WEEK

As the complexity of the case of Steven suggests, the number of different ways that the children seen four times and once a week could be compared is very great. Nor can a presentation of group findings do justice to the unique individual constellations. Considering each of the major sections of the Profile, it could, however, be determined which characteristics were salient in differentiating the two groups of children; those generalizations which could be derived despite important individual variations are stated in the form of hypotheses.[5] Thus the first of these is derived from the material available in the Profiles on phase development (A. Freud, 1962).

Because Steven has been presented in detail, and because he best illustrates the development of the children seen four times a week, the illustrations for this group will be drawn exclusively from his Profiles. The children seen once a week were Gordon, Robert, John, and Philip. At the end of their treatment they were twelve, eleven, ten, and twelve years old.

[5] Further substantiation of these hypotheses is provided by the analysis of the clinical ratings based on the Profiles (Heinicke, 1965b).

PHASE DEVELOPMENT

The children seen four times a week achieve dominance on a more advanced libidinal phase during the follow-up period.

At the risk of oversimplification, it can be said that at the beginning of treatment all children in both groups had achieved dominance on the anal phase and reached at least the phallic phase of development. Regression from this advance was, however, either massive (as in the case of Steven) or extensive. Needless to say, the specific fixation points and the quality and quantity of the regression involved differed a great deal.

By the end of treatment all children had reached at least the latency phase. This was judged by the fact that a considerable number of conflicts at the phallic phase had been resolved, some repression and neutralization of drive activity had taken place, and the extent of regression to pregenital levels had lessened.

That judgments of the phase *reached* do not differentiate the two groups is further supported by the fact that some signs of the pubertal and preadolescent development were seen in both groups. For example, there was some interest in the opposite sex and a growing rebellion and striving for independence.

Examination of the follow-up conclusions revealed, however, that for the once-a-week group this advance had been achieved without adequately resolving the libidinal conflicts of the previous phases. Thus, the once-a-week treatment is likely to facilitate an immediate forward move into latency, but the thrust is limited. In contrast to the four-times-a-week group, dominance in the latency phase had not been achieved at follow-up, and the regression to earlier phases was less likely to be in the service of the ego. Not that Gordon's turning to TV and the icebox after a challenging day at school interfered seriously with his school adaptations, but it was related to a disinclination to get involved in the complications of after-school peer relations. Furthermore, by the second follow-up this picture had changed little.

The lack of dominance in the latency phase was also further defined and characterized by the failure adequately to resolve certain components of the oedipal constellation. As already suggested, this in turn is linked to selected regressions to earlier levels.

Although very likely a function of the particular sample studied, this lack of conflict resolution was most readily seen in two areas. All children could by the time of follow-up assume a competitive stance, but the subsequent invitation to be the victim with its implication for unresolved bisexual conflicts was typically more pronounced in the once-a-week cases. Gordon would very effectively defeat the therapist in checkers, but then suddenly had to lose. In contrast, Steven's tendency to provoke his parents to turn him into a victim was by the second follow-up not only infrequent, but now mainly in the service of asserting his independence.

Another area of difference in the degree of conflict resolution and the associated slowing down of libidinal development involved curiosity and fantasies relating to intercourse and birth. Thus, Gordon could fully exercise his curiosity in many intellectual areas, and could even ask both parents and therapist direct sexual questions. Despite repeated explanations, however, his pregenital fantasies continued to have a disturbing influence on his reality testing and he would then out of embarrassment avoid the issue completely. In contrast, Steven had by the time of the second follow-up sufficiently resolved conflicts relating to these "sexual secrets" to be free both to have a realistic picture of adult sexual relations and to take the first adolescent steps toward participating in this pleasure.

LIBIDO DISTRIBUTION

The children seen four times a week show a greater growth in their over-all level of self-esteem during the follow-up period.

Even though the specific constellations vary a great deal, certain generalizations can be made concerning the children's quantity and quality of self-esteem. None of the children were at the beginning of treatment characterized by the type of defect in narcissism usually associated with psychotic process. Nor had any of them reached the point of depression associated with serious suicidal attempts. Some children's experience of narcissism was poorly integrated. Thus, not only was Steven's over-all level of self-esteem initially low, but his self representations fluctuated too frequently to allow for a feeling of some sustained competence and of a differentiated and relatively autonomous self. He shifted too quickly from boy to girl, clever to crazy, and proud challenger to amorphous Humpty Dumpty.

By the end of treatment none of the children showed this type of deficiency in the integration of self representations. It was, however, particularly the children seen four times a week whose libido distribution was characterized by the following: a feeling that they could attain age-appropriate goals by themselves; a feeling of having changed; a self-consciousness in relation to a total separate self; less reliance on the external world for support of their self-regard and a realistic hope which was most intimately related to a feeling of making progress. It was this *feeling* of making or not making progress *during the follow-up period* that most distinguished the two groups. Steven spontaneously spoke of how he was "doing well in my schoolwork" and already at the end of treatment indicated he felt that he "had changed." Although equally hopeful at the end of treatment, a year later and in a more despondent tone, Gordon felt he "was doing even."

In further assessing the children's self-regard, the experience of being the victim stood out at the beginning of treatment. This took many different forms. The children felt they might suddenly be abandoned; that they had deficient brains or bodies; that they were subject to constant control or intrusion, etc. Although the force of these self concepts had by the end of treatment declined for all children, residuals of feeling the victim were more pronounced during the follow-up period among the children treated once a week.

OBJECT LIBIDO

By the second follow-up contact the children seen four times a week more frequently show the capacity to form object relationships which are characterized by a gratifying libidinal exchange, a realistic give and take, and considerable autonomy.

In discussing the development of the children's object relations it must first of all be pointed out that the group differences are less striking and only emerged late in the follow-up period.

Although the nature of the children's object relationships initially varied greatly, two features were particularly striking: the intense longing to be gratified, which all expressed; and the extent to which they relied on the external object to turn them into the very victim they feared and yet also had to be. Because of their own inadequate ego and superego control, much energy was directed toward getting the externally perceived monsterlike objects to coerce or limit them.

Although all children could by the time of the second follow-up express more affection toward at least one parent, in the children seen once a week, both the longing and signs of ambivalence were more evident. When his family was contacted on the phone, Gordon screamed for his mother only to announce that she was not there; he knew this, of course, all the time. All four children in this group clearly expressed the feeling of things being "unfair" in relation to the teacher. Just as John had felt that his mother always favored his younger brother, so he thought that his teacher favored certain pupils and gave them better grades.

Several further phenomena were linked to the above and by the second follow-up characterized the object relations of the children seen once a week. All were still inclined to provoke a significant figure (mother, father, teacher) to coerce them into activity or limit their instinctual expressions. For example, in his anger that the teacher did not help him enough and yet demanded a great deal from him, Philip reflected feelings previously expressed toward the mother and provocatively got out of his seat until the teacher had to "freeze him" in it.

In contrast, the object relations of the children seen four times a week were by the second follow-up characterized by a greater give and take and a freedom from sadomasochistic involvements. Thus, Steven could accept the guidance and help of his mother, but also for the most part initiate and complete his academic work on his own. Also reflecting greater autonomy was his ability to criticize and even surpass his father without experiencing a retaliation of monsterlike proportions.

The children seen once a week also had developed greater autonomy in certain areas. Thus, Gordon could prepare his own meals and was now very capable of finding his way in the neighborhood. Robert and Philip showed their independence by very effectively serving as a focal point of peer feelings against an "unfair" teacher. As the examples indicate, however, the autonomy shown was at least in part likely to be defensive in nature. Gordon's self-care could be understood in relation to a frequently absent, very busy, "shadowy" mother. At the same time he still provoked her to "lower the boom" and force him to improve the Civics which he was in danger of failing. Similarly, Robert had come very close to being expelled from school.

AGGRESSION

The balance of effective assertion to defensive passivity is greater during the follow-up period for the children seen four times a week.

Despite the individual variation in the quality and quantity of aggression expressed at the beginning of treatment, certain conclusions can be drawn. Not surprisingly, it was initially predominantly related to the pregenital levels. If one thinks of the predominant sources, secondary sources, etc., then one can conclude that the children seen once a week showed little change in this hierarchy, while the children seen four times a week showed considerable change. Thus, although no longer openly expressed, and although the objects involved had changed, the aggressive derivatives that could be inferred from Gordon's behavior during the follow-up assessment were related to a constellation of conflicts very similar in structure to those seen at the beginning of treatment. Central at both points was the shift from an effective challenge of the male rival (at ping-pong or checkers) to the subsequent self-defeat. Similarly, at both points he could express his anal defiance (keeping his desk full of loose papers or not taking a shower after physical education) only to provoke coercion or further defeat. Too often he lost important papers, and his lack of cleanliness was responsible for a lowered grade. Finally, his oral sadism, and particularly his need to defend against it (are there muzzles for humans?), could be inferred from his mouth-opening, eye-widening gestures, and the passivity still present at follow-up.

In contrast, though the pregenital sources of the aggression were dominant in Steven's functioning at the beginning of treatment, by the second follow-up most of the aggression that occurred was related to the effective assertion of a preadolescent boy. He successfully maintained his academic progress in a highly competitive junior high school, and could successfully meet the challenge of a jealous bully in competitive basketball.

It is particularly this predominance of effective assertion and the implications for the neutralization of aggression that during the follow-up characterized the children seen four times a week. The level of effective assertion of the children seen once a week had also increased. Gordon's determined approach particularly in certain cognitive areas or in such matters as collecting and trading coins was impressive. However, the inhibition of aggression and the associated passivity were also prominent and more so than they had been at the end of treatment. He waited for others to initiate things, still expected his mother to get him to catch up in certain courses, and underlined the picture of passivity by feeding himself favorite foods, television, mystery books, etc.

In general, the children seen once a week could assert themselves in some areas more than they had at the beginning of treatment, but the continuance of passivity in other areas of adaptation and particularly those involving the academic challenge was also impressive. Philip could deal with mechanical problems and effectively defy the teacher, but he demonstrated little assertion in the academic area. Robert could by the follow-up play a good game of tackle football and could also effectively challenge the teacher's "fairness"; too often, however, he simply sat, still bit his knuckles, and, as could be determined in a further treatment, was consciously terrified he would explode and get into trouble with the school authorities. John could often actively approach both a sports situation (kickball) and the academic challenge, but on many occasions his parents had to "stand over him" to "get him going." Similarly, too often he simply sat in class and did nothing.

EGO AND SUPEREGO FUNCTIONING

The children seen four times a week make greater progress during the follow-up period in the level of ego integration, differentiation, and adaptation than do the children seen once a week.

If the above represents the most general hypothesis, a series of further hypotheses are given to specify the differences seen during the follow-up period. Before specifying these, however, similarities seen at the end of treatment should be stressed. While certain trends which were to be accentuated later could be noticed, there were few *striking* group differences at the end of treatment. The only exceptions were that the once-a-week children already showed a greater tendency to repress aggressive derivatives, whereas the four-times-a-week children were able to express a greater variety of affects and showed a greater ability to elaborate ideas imaginatively.

There were also a number of areas where striking group differences were not even observed during follow-up. Of these the following ego functions are of particular interest: the level of reality testing, the level of the visual and auditory memory, the quality of space and time orientation, and the level of the large and fine motor coordination. Although the quality of the auditory memory was often the poorest function in this group of children, in general the level of the above list of functions fell within the range of normal variations.

We turn then to a consideration of the dimensions in terms of which the two groups could be differentiated during the follow-up period.

1. *By the time of the first follow-up the children seen once a week show a greater imbalance in their defensive organization than the children seen four times a week.*

Early in our project we had been impressed by the fact that after treatment the underlying conflicts of even the most successful cases had not altered drastically, but the mode of coping with these conflicts had changed considerably. Similarly, it is the extent of balance in the use of defenses that differentiates the two groups being discussed. Rather than the defensive operations being silent and effective, or the child using a number of them flexibly, by the first follow-up the children seen once a week tended to use certain ones excessively. Excessive is judged here in terms of frequency and its nonadaptive consequences. Thus, John's continued tendency to turn the anger felt toward his mother inward could be associated, for example, with repeated accidents, one of which led to the chipping of his teeth. He now looked like the abandoned, starving, injured mouse that he had often felt he was.

Similarly, Gordon's turn toward passivity, indulging himself with food and avoiding the complications of more intimate relationships, was excessive and was associated with his impoverished object relationships.

Finally, Robert was by the follow-up isolating his anger toward an unfair, ungiving mother by experiencing these feelings in relation to the teacher and then provoking her until she had to kick him out of the room or even the school.

In contrast, though the exaggerated use of certain defenses had characterized Steven's functioning in the beginning of treatment— regression, avoidance, and the defensive identifications had been used excessively—by the first follow-up a variety of defenses were employed and none of them excessively.

2. *The defense organization of the children seen once a week as opposed to four times a week was by the first follow-up more dependent on the object world.*

Despite the expected individual variations within the two treatment groups, the children seen once as opposed to four times a week continued during the follow-up period to rely heavily on the intervention and guidance of the external adult objects. This was particularly true in terms of defenses relating to conflicts aroused by the academic challenge. Philip, Robert, and John all relied on the teacher to get them going in a task or to limit their provocations.

The greater level of assertion of the children seen four times a week has already been described. In the context of the present discussion with its implications for superego development, one can add that a more benign set of superego and ego-ideal representations could be inferred from these children's ability to initiate and guide the steps leading to successful academic achievement. They could remember the assignment, insist on doing their work in their own room by themselves, and be less dependent on immediate approval when they had achieved an "A" on a paper.

If the above is a reflection of certain essential differences in the defensive organization of the children, and this in turn can be related to the nature of the ego integration achieved, other dimensions can be thought of as relating to the child's inner differentiation.

3. *The children seen four times as opposed to once a week already by the end of treatment show a greater capacity to elaborate imaginatively.*

Judgments of the child's ability and freedom to elaborate certain ideas were based on such observations as his stories to T.A.T. cards, his play and other creative activities during his contact with the various clinicians involved. Could the child elaborate an extensive and yet coherent story? Could he create, enact, and bring to some kind of conclusion a dramatic sequence? Could he creatively plan a construction and carry it through? For example, during his follow-up hour Steven not only designed a very interesting car but completed it, responding flexibly to such changes as were dictated by the nature of the material. The greater ability to express themselves was also shown in other ways.

4. *The children seen four times as opposed to once a week could already by the end of treatment express a greater variety of affects.*

Although there would again be important differences within the two groups, the children seen once a week showed less feeling and such open feeling as was expressed was of limited variety. Thus, Gordon's disappointment was obvious in his whining though quiet tone, but he could show little open anger, little enthusiasm, little pride, little real pleasure. Even the anxiety about being attacked and scrutinized by the therapist could in no way be openly expressed.

In contrast, Steven briefly showed his anger with his brother, complained openly about not being the therapist's favorite, was obviously pleased to see the therapist, took pride in his achievements, and could laugh both at himself and his mother. This leads to another typical difference.

5. *The children seen four times as opposed to once a week by the first follow-up more frequently made use of a nondefensive form of humor.*

Although the predominantly nondefensive type of humor is not easy to define, judgments were based on whether or not it was used primarily in reference to the needs of the object and the social situation or whether its function was primarily determined by inner needs; for example, the need to express forbidden impulses. Steven's expression of his wish to continue his therapy by saying that it had not helped—he was sorry that the book saying that psychiatry did no good had already been written—was clearly defensive, yet it not only amused the therapist but was also an expression of gratitude. Finally, Steven's insight into his own wish to keep the therapist added a special quality to the humor.

6. *The children seen four times as opposed to once a week by the time of the first follow-up show a greater capacity to observe their own behavior and the motives underlying it.*

In attempting to judge the child's level of insight three factors were considered: (1) Does the child observe his own behavior? (2) Does he have any understanding of his motives for behaving in a certain way? (3) Is this recognition achieved in a context that lends conviction to it and is thus likely to lead to some alteration in behavior?

Steven again illustrates these distinctions. At the end of treatment he told the psychiatrist that he felt that he had changed; that he was older. This was in fact true and not only in the simple chronological sense. Moreover, Steven showed insight into his own motivations. Having been shown his anger about being kept waiting by his parents and how he could get even by keeping them waiting and not making any progress in his reading, he realized with surprise: "But then I would be hurting myself." There is little doubt that this type of insight did contribute to the very real progress he began to make in his reading.

Having given examples of specific hypotheses relating to the ego functioning of the two groups, we return once more to the level of ego integration.

7. *The children seen once as opposed to four times a week by the time of the second follow-up show a less adequate level of ego integration than the children seen four times a week.*

It will be recalled that the two groups did not differ strikingly in the level of ego integration achieved at the end of treatment.

Even at this point, however, the integration achieved by the children seen once a week involved greater strain; a greater quantity of countercathexes was involved. Although the previous signs of mobile discharge and unneutralized aggression were missing, these manifestations were associated even in the previously most labile children with a trend toward deadlock. This emphasis is supported by those differences that did emerge at the end of treatment: the children seen once a week were characterized by a greater repression of aggressive derivatives, less variety in the expression of affects, and less ability to elaborate imaginatively.

Given a quality of integration dependent on countercathexes against aggression and a restricted affect expression, one might expect that either the child's development would be restricted or that the aggressive discharge would again occur under certain circumstances. Both in fact occurred. Many of the findings presented demonstrate restriction in development during the follow-up period of the children seen once a week. With the exception of Gordon, all these children also were on several occasions overcome by uncontrolled aggressive outbursts. Robert once gave in to an urgent impulse to destroy a school wastepaper basket. A primary-process quality is suggested. The total evidence for this type of mental functioning was limited, but it was again more evident among the group seen once a week.

DEVELOPMENT OF TOTAL PERSONALITY

The children seen four times as opposed to once a week made greater progress during the follow-up period in moving from dependency to emotional self-reliance.

It was found that already by the first follow-up the children seen four times a week had made greater progress in moving along the developmental lines from suckling to rational eating, from egocentricity to companionship, and from play to work, as well as showing greater congruence in their total development. It was, however, their development toward self-reliance that seemed outstanding.

In judging the child's progress in this regard, considerations of the libidinal phase reached and the development of object relations are focused on the issue of self-reliance—on the extent to which the child can move from the mutuality in object relations characteristic of the oedipal phase to a sufficient lessening and transference of libido to the community (teacher, leaders, peers), impersonal ideals, and aim-inhibited, sublimated interests (A. Freud, 1963).

Previous findings anticipated the conclusion that the children seen four times as opposed to once a week showed greater self-reliance during the follow-up period. Several observations focused on this conclusion. Not only did the children seen once a week have a much more difficult time in independently coping with the academic challenge, but the evidence of the unresolved oedipal and preoedipal relationships with the parents was much more easily traced. Feeling that his mother had dropped her aspirations for him, Philip was likely to attribute similar characteristics to the teacher.

Although the difference in the development of friendships was not that striking, one example of independence occurred sufficiently often among the children seen four times as opposed to once a week at least to suggest a larger difference. When confronted with a domineering or insulting peer, these children were able to deal with the situation without giving in or becoming excessively belligerent. Although Steven was exposed to the jealous attack of a much larger boy, he nevertheless continued his very successful involvement in a basketball game.

GENETIC, STRUCTURAL, AND DYNAMIC CONSIDERATIONS

The children seen four times as opposed to once a week by the time of the second follow-up (1) show evidence of the previous fixations, but the regressive force of these is less; (2) are characterized by a more neutralized and adaptive form of derivative; and (3) are characterized by character traits which can be traced to previous fixations but which are adequately integrated into the child's functioning.

It is first of all important to note that no generalizations could be formulated about the specific nature of the fixations and the conflicts. The potential diversity may make this difficult in any case and this would be accentuated in turn by the considerable diversity among the children being studied.

Such hypotheses as could be formulated are again most easily illustrated by contrasting Steven and Gordon. It was possible once more to recognize derivatives of the most important fixation points in both boys at the time of the follow-ups. Steven's tendency to provoke his male rival to punish him both for his guilt about masturbation and his wish to defeat him were again evident. Similarly, the dangers of assuming the masculine position in intercourse were portrayed in terms of being "sucked into a swamp." Finally, his passive longing, wish to be the favorite, and the related oral-sadistic conflicts once more emerged. However, where regression to these fixations occurred, it was temporary. More important, not only was the interference of these derivatives with adaptation minimal, but the nature of the total structure was such (and this has been outlined previously) as to allow the inference of considerable neutralization of previous derivatives. By the second follow-up one could still readily observe character tendencies of being provocative and feeling depressed; but even these did not disrupt the general picture of sound ego integration.

At the same time it is clear that fluctuations in the nature of the external impact would either enhance or disrupt the adaptive function of the character traits of any of the children being discussed. Although Steven had by the second follow-up managed to integrate his superego demands for excellent academic performance into a realistic approach to his schoolwork, it was clear that should his mother from her own anxiety again "need to push him," then his adaptation might possibly yield to indications of "I can't make it."

In contrast to Steven and illustrative of the children seen once a week, the residual of Gordon's fixations and former conflicts could quite easily be observed during both follow-ups. His need to attack the therapist and the subsequent self-defeat revealed the active and nonadaptive struggle with the residual of bisexual conflicts. In contrast, his assertiveness on the mathematical subtests of the Stanford I.Q. was most impressive. Similarly, his effective verbal sparring with his father suggested the resolution of oedipal conflicts and the associated neutralization; but in the academic area closest to the father's occupation, the intrapsychic derivatives again interfered with adaptive functioning.

Finally, many of Gordon's character traits were not only related to previous fixations but were less well integrated into his total adaptation. Thus, his independence and inclination to "feed" himself provided a resolution of oral-sadistic conflicts, but because of its associated isolation also impaired the development of his peer relationships. Similarly, his persistent and meticulous saving and trading of coins absorbed derivatives of anal-explosive conflicts. Some aspects of this activity—dealing with the various officials, finding his way around town, learning the value of money—were likely to expand his capabilities, but the excessive concern with one activity and the intense interest in accumulating "piles of coins" were less well integrated and revealed the closeness of pregenital derivatives.

GENERAL CHARACTERISTICS

The children seen once as opposed to four times a week by the time of the follow-up period show less ability to resolve and thus tolerate instinctual residuals and in particular oral-sadistic derivatives.

Although all four indices from the section on the Assessment of General Characteristics—frustration tolerance, sublimation potential, attitude to anxiety, and the balance of progressive over regressive forces—favor the children seen four times a week, it was particularly the inability to resolve and thus tolerate residuals of a biting oral anger that characterized the children seen once a week.

Although one would conclude that the conflicts between the child's oral sadism and equally intense superego counterrepresentations were not completely resolved for any of the children treated, and this fixation point thus exerted a continuing force, its regressive force was more striking in the case of the children seen once a week. The child's total functioning was, of course, considered in judging his frustration tolerance; this characteristic could be observed in many situations. Yet various types of behavior particularly characteristic of the once-a-week children place the focus on the inability to tolerate the biting anger associated with earliest deprivation. In some instances the result was a break-through of aggression. John always felt that he might at a moment's notice be abandoned like a rat, and always experienced intense anger toward a younger brother who he felt was favored; the anticipation of another sibling brought on a renewed and extreme attack on his brother. These attacks were always timed so that he would be the subject of intense punishment. Among other ways, Gordon defended himself against the break-through of oral sadism by constantly "feeding" himself a variety of things from food to TV.

FURTHER CONSIDERATIONS RELATING TO THE DATA PRESENTED

Although it is felt to be an advantage to distinguish between the cross-sectional assessment of the child's developmental status and the study of his therapeutic experience, it is important to stress that the evaluation of the generalizations stated above is very likely to be influenced and possibly changed by the knowledge of the details of the therapeutic process. Findings on the differential development of the process in the two groups will be presented in future publication.

The method of constructing the Profiles and its relation to the generalizations derived also require further comment. During the hypothesis-making stage of a project, the therapist's extensive knowledge and capacity to integrate and highlight the findings are likely to be particularly valuable. Yet the therapist's involvement in the treatment can also be a source of bias. The first check on this bias was the great care taken to make cross-sectional assessments, to document the conclusions reached, and to integrate carefully the data from psychiatrist, psychologist, teacher, tutor, and parents.

Further support for the validity of the findings derived from the Profiles is given by the analysis of test indices derived independently of the therapist. The following indices have been used: the rate of improvement on academic tests of reading, spelling, and arithmetic; the Stanford Binet Intelligence Quotient, the vocabulary score on the Stanford Binet; and indices derived from the Rorschach. These results are presented in detail in another publication (Heinicke, 1965a). One example is given to support a general conclusion derived from the analysis of the Profiles, namely, that few differences in developmental status were noticeable at the end of treatment, but that the children seen four times as opposed to once a week did show greater developmental progress in the period after the end of treatment. The availability of test assessments of the child's academic progress made it possible to compute the rate of improvement during certain intervals of time for reading, spelling, and arithmetic. Comparing the trends for the children seen four times as opposed to once a week, it was found that the latter showed a significantly greater improvement in reading during the first year of treatment, that there was no significant difference during the last period of treatment, but that the children seen four times as opposed to once a week improved at a faster rate during the two years after treatment. (See Figure 1; the P <.01 indicates that the difference between the groups could have occurred by chance less than 1 in 100 times.) The same conclusions apply to spelling, but no significant differences were found for arithmetic.

A third major consideration in evaluating the generalizations takes the form of the following question: are the various Profile distinctions essentially governed by one conceptual dimension (e.g., mental health-sickness) and are the various group differences, there-

FIGURE I

SHOWING RATE OF IMPROVEMENT IN READING AS MEASURED BY THE
WIDE RANGE ACHIEVEMENT TEST

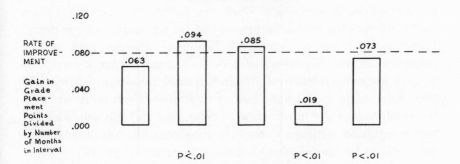

ONCE - A - WEEK - TREATMENT

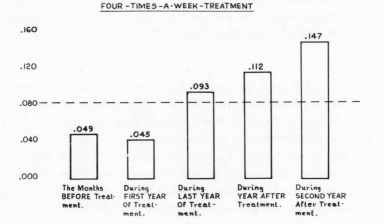

FOUR - TIMES - A - WEEK - TREATMENT

TIME INTERVAL

fore, essentially statements of one major group difference? The first answer is that even if this were so, the Profile does insure that all aspects of the child's functioning are considered in evaluating his over-all developmental status and potential. Moreover, various analyses do indicate that many more than one basic conceptual dimension must be postulated to understand the variation in the results presented (see Heinicke, 1965b).

DISCUSSION

As already indicated, the full understanding of the findings reported here will have to await the study of the differential therapeutic process experienced by the two groups of children.

Further limitations on any generalizations are imposed by the nature and size of the sample. There are, however, certain hypotheses which are very likely to be supported by future studies. Other things being equal, children seen in psychoanalytic therapy four or five times a week by comparison with those seen once a week are likely to give greater evidence of impending and important changes in their total adaptation by the end of treatment. Even more striking, the resolution of the termination of treatment and the nature of the new integration achieved in the two years after the end of treatment are likely to be associated with a more pronounced growth in adaptation. The clinical findings derived from the Profile, the analysis of the ratings based on the Profile (Heinicke, 1965b), and the analysis of the test results (Heinicke, 1965a) all support this general hypothesis.

This is not to imply that the children seen on a once-a-week basis in this or other settings derived little benefit from their treatment. It will be recalled that during the first year of treatment they showed a greater improvement in their reading than the children seen four times a week. In terms of the academic subjects they had by the end of treatment reached an average growth level; and in regard to the clinical indices derived from the Profiles, they differed little from the children seen four times a week. One of the children did return and made very good use of treatment two years after the end of his first one, but the other children have managed without further help.

It is clear, however, that any assessment of the outcome of treatment must include adequate follow-up contacts. The impression was that given the average age of these children at the end of treatment, that is, eleven, a two-year follow-up was likely to be a sufficient period of time for the most important effects of the treatment to be integrated into a new adaptation. This does not, however, take account of new and particularly challenging demands of the adolescent development. A further follow-up in early adulthood, therefore, seems necessary.

While the specific form of the accelerated adaptation of the children seen more frequently is likely to vary considerably as the nature of the samples being studied changes, a summary picture of the qualities which particularly differentiated the two groups being studied is of value.

This summary is attempted first in relation to Steven's development. Reviewing the Profile constructed for the first follow-up, it was clear that signs of pathology could still be detected. Many of these were further transformed and integrated by the time of the second and third follow-ups. However, it was particularly by comparison with the children seen once a week that certain positive qualities stand out. There is, first of all, the forward libidinal push as expressed in a sublimated form. The well-designed and executed car with a prominent antenna communicated the quality of ego integration and self-esteem. Where doubt occurred and regression set in, it could be overcome. The implied flexibility is supported by his ability to imagine such a car in the first place. The flexibility was further underlined by the variety of feelings expressed: from the angry complaint of "same old junk" to the pride in his achievement. This very ability to express his disappointment that he had not received the magical gift or was not receiving a "blue print" as well as the ability to tolerate this frustration and to recover from it characterized his functioning and that of the other children seen four times a week.

The nature of Steven's effective assertiveness and independence must also be underlined and may well be associated in part with the type of treatment he experienced. He could develop his own plan, he showed an active but not offensive curiosity, and he could withstand the intrusion of an overly concerned mother. Yet his independence and assertiveness were not associated with aloofness and a lack of humor, as they were in Gordon's functioning. He could express warmth in relation both to the therapist and his mother, and could achieve distance through an appropriate joke.

Once more summarizing, although the level of ego integration was not strikingly different for the two groups until the second follow-up point, by the first follow-up it had become clear that the integration of the children seen once a week was more dependent on the operation of countercathexes, particularly those directed at aggressive derivatives. The quality of the integration was further defined by an imbalance in the defensive organization. Passivity, the tendency to provoke punishment and to turn aggression against the self are outstanding examples of defenses used excessively. In general, these children were more dependent on the intervention and guidance of the adult to maintain their defensive organization. Nor did the resultant constriction in functioning guarantee a continued level of integration; by the second follow-up three of the children evidenced a breakdown in the control of aggression and some primary-process-like discharge.

In contrast to this picture of constriction, the ego integration of the children seen four times a week involved a more balanced use of defenses, indications of more benign superego functioning, and perhaps most important, such indications of flexibility and differentiation as the ability to elaborate an idea imaginatively, the capacity to express a variety of affects, the nondefensive use of humor, and the capacity to observe their own behavior and the motives underlying it.

Consistent with this more adequate level of ego integration, differentiation, and flexibility shown by the children seen four times a week were the increasing indications of sublimation and the neutralization of drive derivatives seen during the follow-up. The evidence here ranges from clinical judgments of the sublimation potential to the rate of improvement in reading and vocabulary.

In terms of their drive development, the children seen four times a week were characterized by a greater assertiveness, particularly in the academic area, and a generally greater progress in achieving dominance on the most advanced libidinal phase. The regressions and associated fixations observed in the children seen once a week were not of such force as to overwhelm the children; they were confined but were less often in the service of the ego. That is, these children neither regressed in an obvious way to former developmental stages nor were they as responsive to new developmental challenges as the children seen four times a week.

The children seen four times a week also showed a more favorable quantity and quality of self-esteem. They were particularly characterized by the feeling that they were progressing and that they could do things on their own.

In terms of the lines of development (A. Freud, 1963), it was the move to greater self-reliance and adult object relationships that differentiated the children seen four times a week. If only by contrast with the general pattern of differences found, in their peer relationships they did not differ strikingly from the children seen once a week.

In terms of certain general characteristics, their ability to tolerate frustration, particularly of their oral longings, and the general preponderance of progressive over regressive forces once more favored the development after treatment of the children seen four times a week.

Once more it must be stressed that the study of both the treatment process and the individual variations is necessary in order more adequately to evaluate the meaning of the differences found. Future presentations will include details of the therapeutic material which characterizes the two treatment situations.

BIBLIOGRAPHY

Arthur, H. (1952), A Comparison of the Techniques Employed in Psychotherapy and Psychoanalysis of Children. *Amer. J. Orthopsychiat.*, 22:484-498.

Bibring, E. (1954), Psychoanalysis and the Dynamic Psychotherapies. *J. Amer. Psa. Assn.*, 2:745-770.

Cartwright, D., Kirtner, W. L., & Fiske, D. (1963), Method Factors in Changes Associated with Psychotherapy. *J. Abnorm. Soc. Psychol.*, 66:164-175.

Freud, A. (1962), Assessment of Childhood Disturbances. *This Annual*, 17:149-158.

—— (1963), The Concept of Developmental Lines. *This Annual*, 18:245-265.

Heinicke, C. M. (1958), Changes in Children and the Intensity of Psychotherapy. NIMH Grant Proposal No. MH 02948-05.

—— (1965a), Frequency of Child Psychotherapeutic Session as a Factor Affecting Outcome: Independent Indices of Development (in preparation).

—— (1965b), Frequency of Child Psychotherapeutic Session as a Factor Affecting Outcome: Analysis of Clinical Rating (in preparation).

Imber, S. D., Frank, J. D., Nash, E. H., Stone, A. R., & Gliedman, L. H. (1957), Improvement and Amount of Therapeutic Contact: An Alternative to the Use of No Treatment Controls in Psychotherapy. *J. Cons. Psychol.*, 21:309-315.

Klopfer, B., Ainsworth, M., Klopfer, W., & Holt, R. (1954), *Developments in the Rorschach Technique*, Vol. I. Yonkers-on-Hudson, N.Y.: World Book Co.

Lorr, M., McNair, D. M., Michaux, W. W., & Raskin, H. (1962), Frequency of Treatment and Change in Psychotherapy. *J. Abnorm. Soc. Psychol.*, 64:281-292.

McNair, D., Lorr, M., Young, H., Roth, I., & Boyd, W. (1964), A Three-year Follow-up of Psychotherapy Patients. *J. Clin. Psychol.*, 20:258-264.

Nagera, H. (1963), The Developmental Profile: Notes on Some Practical Considerations regarding Its Use. *This Annual*, 18:511-540.

Rosenfeld, E. & Novick, J. (1964), Assessing Deviant Behavior. Presentation at Michigan State University Workshop on Assessment of Children.

ASSESSMENT OF ADOLESCENT DISTURBANCES

The Application of Anna Freud's Diagnostic Profile

MOSES LAUFER, M.Sc. (London)

The Diagnostic Profile prepared by Anna Freud (1962) for the assessment of childhood disturbances is based on a psychoanalytic theory of childhood development. This Profile, which is now used in all diagnostic work at the Hampstead Child-Therapy Clinic, enables the psychoanalyst to assess behavior in structural, dynamic, economic, genetic, and adaptive terms. Further, it enables the clinician to judge the available diagnostic observations as being part of a normal internal process, as a sign of psychopathology, or as indicating possible future vulnerability to mental disturbance.

When this Profile was used in the assessment of adolescent disturbances, it was found that some sectors of the Profile needed to be changed and expanded. These changes reflect the expected differences between childhood and adolescent development. Expressed more broadly, a Profile for the assessment of adolescent disturbances should reflect a psychoanalytic theory of adolescent development.

However, there is also a similarity between childhood and adolescence: both periods are developmental stages. In both instances, therefore, we may be observing either temporary manifestations of internal stress or signs of future pathology. Yet, the problems with

The author is a member of the Hampstead Child-Therapy Clinic where much of the material used in this study has been collected. The Hampstead Child-Therapy Clinic is maintained at present by The Field Foundation, Inc., New York; The Anna Freud Foundation, New York; The Grant Foundation, Inc., New York; The Estate of Flora Haas, New York; The National Institute of Mental Health, Bethesda, Maryland; The Old Dominion Foundation, New York; The Psychoanalytic Research and Development Fund, Inc., New York; The Taconic Foundation, Inc., New York.

Director, Young People's Consultation Centre, which is financed by the Youth Studies and Research Foundation of the Bernard Van Leer Trust.

A shortened version of this paper was presented at the 24th International Psycho-Analytical Association Congress, Amsterdam, July, 1965.

which the ego must deal in adolescence are qualitatively different from those which exist in childhood. These are related to

(a) the reaction to the physical primacy of the genitals;

(b) the changing relationship to the original objects;

(c) the finding of a heterosexual love object; and

(d) the integrating of preoedipal identifications, oedipal identifications, and present internal as well as external expectations of behavior.

At every stage of childhood the inadequacy of earlier conflict solutions makes itself felt as a distorting influence; but when these solutions are tested in adolescence in the context of the person's new sexual role, they may fail completely in crucial areas, and in this way they may hinder development to adulthood. Identifications which may have served their purpose well in the oedipal and pre-oedipal periods may be found to be inadequate in helping the person change the internal relationship to the oedipal objects or to take on the role as sexual partner. For example, the male child who, during the oedipal period, identified with a passive father may find that in adolescence this oedipal model is not only insufficient but may be a hindrance in his relation to a new love object.

Again, if we compare childhood and adolescence, we note that in childhood both the content and the functions of the structures are being determined. In adolescence, on the other hand, we observe mainly a change in the functions within each structure as well as a change in the relation of the structures to each other. In childhood, including latency, we are mainly concerned with the child's ability to progress further in both drive and ego development, or with interferences due to intersystemic or intrasystemic conflicts. The psychic structures are still incomplete in their development, and it is our task in diagnosis to see whether structuralization is proceeding or can be expected to proceed normally, or whether this process seems to be impaired. In adolescence we are examining something different. We no longer see structural development in the same way as in the child. Instead, what we observe is the *result* of either successful or faulty structuralization, which now, in addition, must be evaluated in the context of physical genitality. Changes may still take place, but they occur in the functions and the relation of the functions to each other, rather than in the content of the structures. The commonly held belief that adolescents easily give up old standards and earlier identifications and readily adopt new criteria upon which to base their present behavior refers to new ego identifications, and not to change in the content of the superego, which is determined at the stage of internalization (Laufer, 1964). These factors taken together imply that, in the assessment of adolescent disturbances, some areas of mental functioning must be viewed differently than they were in the child. Temporary id and ego regression, the use made of defenses, the role of the object world, extreme mood swings, must be seen not only structurally and genetically, but in relation to factors that are specific for adolescence.

These various new factors which affect behavior in adolescence are at the same time responsible for the fact that it is extremely difficult to distinguish between transitory disturbance and vulnerability to future pathology. The application of the Diagnostic Profile enables us to examine our observations more closely, and to organize the available data in such a way that we can be more precise about diagnosis and prediction.

Anna Freud constructed the Profile for the assessment of childhood disturbances. In adapting its use for adolescence several sections needed to be changed. These changes reflect our expectations of the normal development of each of the psychic structures in adolescence and highlight areas that are especially relevant in the assessment of adolescent disturbances. In what follows I have outlined the additional considerations and changes and I have also tried to show which sections coincide or differ in the Childhood and Adolescence Profiles.

For practical purposes, the Profile is a frame of reference which in many cases can be completed only gradually. Even though many of the answers may not be available at the diagnostic stage, the Profile presents those questions which are of special importance in assessment.

This article is a provisional draft, subject to amendment as its usefulness is tested against clinical data. At a later date, parts of this Profile will be elaborated to include a more detailed discussion of some aspects of adolescent development.

Provisional Draft of Diagnostic Profile

(Describe the material on which the Profile is based.)

I. Reason for Referral

In the Childhood Profile, the reasons for referral include arrests in development, behavior problems, anxieties, inhibitions, symptoms, etc.

It is always assumed that the referral of the child is initiated by the parents, the school, or social agency. However, in the referral of the adolescent, the family may or may not be involved or the adolescent may seek help on his own. His attitude to future help may depend on the manner in which the adolescent has first sought help. For these reasons, this section includes items which are not relevant for the child.

Note whether the referral is from the adolescent himself, or from parents, school, or other organizations. State the adolescent's *manifest* reason for seeking help, as well as the reasons given by those responsible for the initial referral. If the adolescent has referred himself, state whether his complaints are about himself or about the environment as the cause of the trouble.

State also the *latent* reason for the adolescent's attendance. (The latent reason for the child's referral could be related to factors not directly having to do with the child, e.g., parental problems, projection onto the child of a history of illness, etc. For the adolescent, the latent reason has often to do with his concern about his sexual role and development to adulthood, e.g., concern about homosexuality, impotence, inability to continue a love relationship, inability to change the relationship to the original objects.) Note also whether the adolescent sees the manifest difficulty as the main problem, even though there may be a much more serious latent problem.

II. Description of Child

This heading, used in the Childhood Profile, can remain the same for the adolescent. Note his personal appearance, moods, manner, etc.

While the child's external appearance reveals the way he is taken care of and cathected by the parents, the adolescent's appearance reveals his attitude to his own body. It is of diagnostic help to include here any observable incongruity in behavior, e.g., an inhibited manner compared to clothing which exhibits the body; a capacity for verbalization, but an inability to describe how he feels. The diagnostician should also include his own reaction to the adolescent.

III. FAMILY BACKGROUND AND PERSONAL HISTORY

The information available in this section of the Childhood Profile is generally quite extensive. Usually when the child is referred, it is possible (as well as accepted procedure) to obtain information about the child from a variety of sources—parents, school, social agencies, doctor, etc.

In the Adolescence Profile, however, this section may either contain a good deal of information or it may be very sparse. The amount of information depends partly on the manner in which the referral has taken place. Moreover, the possibility of obtaining historical data depends on whether the adolescent has sought help on his own or whether he has been referred in a formal way. Some adolescents find it easy to provide historical information, whereas others are quite unable to supply any at all. One should distinguish between those adolescents who do not wish to give historical facts and those who have little or no conscious recollection of them.

In some circumstances, it may be advisable to avoid collecting information in a set way from the adolescent. This section will then have to be completed at a later date. On the other hand, when it is possible to obtain information, a "Description of the Latency Period" should be included as part of the adolescent's personal history.

IV. POSSIBLY SIGNIFICANT ENVIRONMENTAL INFLUENCES

This section remains the same as in the Childhood Profile. We can, however, assume that the information about the child may well be more complete, simply because of the sources from which the material could be available.

Chronologically, one may note here which external factors may have had a special impact on the person's life, e.g., illnesses, hospitalizations, events which may have been traumatic, crises in the history of the family. What environmental influences does the adolescent himself emphasize? All *possible* influences should be included in this section, even if one is not able to state at this point whether these influences actually had a special meaning in the life of the person.

V. Assessments of Development

In the Childhood Profile, this section concentrates on the development of the psychic structures and functions within each structure. This is shown in the headings used. For example, the section dealing with "Drive Development" includes not only "libido" and "aggression," but libido is examined from the point of view of phase development and libido distribution (including cathexis of the self and cathexis of objects). "Ego and Superego Development" includes an examination of the ego apparatuses, ego functions, defense organization, and secondary interference with ego achievements. This is followed, in the case of the child, with an examination of the "Lines of Development and Mastery of Tasks." In this section of the Adolescence Profile, I have suggested a number of changes which will be described in what follows:

A. *Drive Development*

1. Libido

(a) Examine with regard to *phase development:*

In the Childhood Profile, there is an examination of the development of the libidinal phases to an age-adequate stage, especially beyond the anal to the phallic level. In this respect the Adolescence Profile is similar, with the emphasis now being on signs of puberty and adolescence. Therefore, state the signs indicating that the person has reached puberty and adolescence; whether he has achieved phase dominance; whether, at the time of assessment, he seems to have the ability to maintain the highest level reached, or whether there are signs of regression and to which level.

In adolescence, the drive organization develops progressively to the point where genitality serves as the most important means of gratification. Although phase dominance may not be established until the person is well into adolescence, there are earlier signs which enable the diagnostician to know whether preoedipal drive manifestations are such that they endanger the establishment of phase dominance. In the male adolescent, the physical ability to produce semen may act as an encouragement for further libidinal development. In the female adolescent, menstruation would be a sign of physical maturity, but it may be extremely difficult to judge the level of libidinal development reached until she has had sexual intercourse. The move from the clitoral to the vaginal stage may be accomplished easily, or it may be held up. In diagnostic assessments, one would have to differentiate between the level of drive development reached and drive development which is secondarily interfered with due to defense activity.

Phase dominance in adolescence does not mean that pregenital libidinal signs are nonexistent. Normally, the adolescent will seek satisfaction on a variety of libidinal levels, which he will give up for genitality only in late adolescence. Assessment of phase dominance must therefore be a quantitative one, i.e., whether genitality serves as the most important means of gratification. Temporary id regression results in drive expression characteristic of preoedipal libidinal levels, but this in itself is not a criterion for the assessment of the level of drive development which has been or is likely to be reached. However, the degree to which satisfactions from each level participate in his libidinal life can tell us whether phase dominance has been or is likely to be achieved, and whether this dominance can be regained following temporary regression. Such an assessment enables us to know whether satisfaction from any of the component instincts is interfering or will interfere with normal heterosexuality.

(b) with regard to *libido distribution:*
(i) Cathexis of the self

In the Childhood Profile, the main questions are whether the self is cathected, and whether there is sufficient narcissism (primary and secondary, invested in the body, the ego, or the superego) to ensure self-regard, self-esteem, a feeling of well-being. Does this lead to overestimation of the self and undue independence of the object, etc.? To what degree is self-regard dependent on the object world?

Although we need not raise many additional questions in the Adolescence Profile, the cathexis of the self may be affected by some specific factors that are relevant in adolescence but not in childhood. When the person reaches physical genitality, the role of the outside world takes on a different meaning. Demands and expectations of contemporaries become more important. Structurally, the superego is now a more defined system; therefore it may be helpful to see how each of the superego functions (conscience, ego ideal, self-criticism) participates in the cathexis of the self. Dependence on or independence of the object world has a different meaning now than during childhood. Is this related to oedipal objects, oedipal substitutes, or to contemporaries? Does it detach the adolescent from the outside world? Does his estimation of himself assist him in his relation to the external world? Does it result in withdrawal? If there is withdrawal, this should be examined as follows—is it to something or from something; is it from activity; is it into fantasy; is it into autoerotic activity? During periods of withdrawal, does the object world still remain important, or is the cathexis withdrawn from the object world?

(ii) Cathexis of objects

In the Childhood Profile, this section examines the level and quality of object relationships reached by the child; whether the highest level reached is being maintained; whether or not the existent object relationships correspond with the maintained or regressed level of phase development.

It is, of course, equally important in the assessment of the adolescent to enquire into the level and quality of object relationships, but at the same time there are some factors which are exclusive to adolescence. During this period, for example, a variety of object relationships can exist simultaneously, each having an important part to play in maintaining libidinal phase development and in assisting the adolescent to detach himself from the original objects. The object can act as a means of allowing for regressive manifestations and either help or hinder the libidinal detachment from the oedipal objects. In examining the level and quality of object relationships which exist, it is important to note not only the kind of relationships that exist but also which ones seem to be dominant.

The phases of adolescence should show alteration in cathexis of objects. The boy or girl who has just entered adolescence continues to have a variety of relationships serving different libidinal and ego purposes—including control of regression, overcoming superego demands, detachment from the oedipal objects. However, the late adolescent should primarily cathect those objects which can be instrumental in helping him to establish his sexual role. This means that the narcissistic type of object choice (including homosexuality) need not be a sign of pathology in the early adolescent, whereas a continuation of such an object choice in late adolescence may be viewed as a sign of failure to give up these earlier means of narcissistic supply and as a hindrance to further emotional development.

2. Aggression

The Childhood Profile examines the aggressive expressions (a) according to their quantity (presence or absence in the manifest picture), (b) according to their quality (correspondence with the level of libido development), (c) according to their direction, toward either the object world or the self.

For the adolescent, there is some slight change needed here to include the specific expressions which may be diagnostically meaningful. For example, in (c), when examining the direction of the aggressive expressions toward either the object world or the self, we should divide the object world into "within the family" and "outside the family."

In addition, for the adolescent, one should state whether there has recently been a change in the aggressive manifestations or whether the present picture seems to be similar to what existed before. One should also differentiate between physical harm to oneself and aggression which may be lodged in the superego and which may show itself in mood swings, etc.

One of the difficulties which may be encountered here is that mood swings need not be due to aggression lodged in the superego; they may be occasioned by other immediate problems which the adolescent is trying to solve. For example, the adolescent may go through a period of some withdrawal while he is trying to detach himself from the oedipal objects and has not yet been able to cathect other objects. The mood observed at such times would not necessarily be due to aggression. Furthermore, the adolescent must have some aggression available in order to free himself from the oedipal objects, and here too one should differentiate between this kind of aggression and that which is lodged in the superego.

B. *Ego and Superego Development*

In the Childhood Profile, this section includes an examination of (a) ego apparatuses, (b) ego functions, (c) defense organization, (d) secondary interference of defense activity with ego achievements.

For the Adolescence Profile, this section is divided into two separate sections, (1) *Ego Development* and (2) *Superego Development*. In addition, under "Ego Development," there are two new headings which do not appear in the Childhood Profile—"Affects" and "Identifications." These changes reflect a number of theoretical assumptions about adolescence which do not in the same way apply to childhood. They also show some of the specific demands made upon the ego during this period, and help us to assess the manner in which the ego deals with these demands. These points will be discussed in the relevant sections.

[1.] *Ego Development*

(a) There is no change in this section. Examine and state the intactness or defects of *ego apparatus,* serving perception, memory, motility, etc.

(b) The questions in the Childhood Profile relate to the intactness of *ego functions* (memory, reality testing, synthesis, control of motility, speech, secondary thought processes). Any primary deficiencies and unevennesses in the levels reached are noted. Intelligence test results are included.

For the Adolescence Profile, it is equally important to examine the intactness of the ego functions. But when we try to determine the level of development reached by the different ego functions, we have to begin by asking how the adolescent is dealing with the new age-appropriate demands. Our expectations of development vary with the age of the adolescent. Although the ego of the early adolescent and that of the late adolescent may be dealing with similar problems, the relative importance of these problems to the ego varies a great deal from one phase to the next. For example, although the adolescent of fourteen or fifteen normally chooses as friends contemporaries who can help him in establishing his sexual role, they may also have been chosen because they enable him to accept temporary regression or to find new ways of fighting old superego demands. The adolescent of nineteen will normally still have to deal with these same problems, but the relative importance of the problems has now changed. Regression, for example, will now mean something quite different to the ego; the superego disapproval will be much more severe; and the defenses employed may be aimed at avoiding any temporary regression or superego condemnation. Similarly, identifications will be used differently: now they are important for purposes of integrating the remnants of the positive oedipal relationship (through the elaboration of the ego-ideal content of the superego), whereas in early adolescence they were a normal means of defying the oedipal object.

This means that some ego functions in adolescence may be under greater pressure than others, and for this reason it is necessary to differentiate between levels reached and temporary regression of specific ego functions. Of special importance are reality testing, synthesis, and secondary thought processes. Although the other ego functions such as speech, control of motility, and memory should be examined as well, it may be that in assessment the latter should be given less weight than the former. At the same time, one should note the unevenness in development of ego functions.

Note also the signs of *secondary ego autonomy*. For example, has a disturbance affected the entire ego organization or only specific areas of ego functioning? Or, even though there is some disturbance present, has the adolescent been able to continue with his interests, or has he given up doing things? For example, a sudden severe drop in school functioning is usually taken as an ominous diagnostic sign.

(c) In the Childhood Profile, this section deals with the status of the *defense organization*. Here one considers:

whether defense is employed specifically against *individual drives* or, more generally, against drive activity and instinctual pleasure as such;

whether defenses are *age adequate,* too primitive or too precocious;

whether defense is *balanced,* i.e., whether the ego has the use of many of the important mechanisms or is restricted to the excessive use of single ones;

whether defense is *effective,* especially in its dealing with anxiety; whether it results in equilibrium or disequilibrium, lability, flexibility, or deadlock within the structure;

whether and how far the child's defense against the drives is dependent on the object world or independent of it (superego development).

In the Adolescence Profile, it is necessary to ask the same questions about the defense organization. At the same time, however, there exist a number of factors which are specific for the adolescent and therefore alter the manner of assessment. Although the adolescent uses every means available to him to assist the ego in coping with instinctual demands, with superego demands, and with what is experienced as the demands from contemporaries, we can learn a great deal about the capacity of the ego by examining the *hierarchy* of defense mechanisms used and the specific content against which they are directed. For example, the early adolescent normally uses primitive defenses without their affecting his relation to reality. However, if these primitive defenses are the only ones available in late adolescence, we may conclude that adolescence has brought about no significant internal change, and that there is now, or will be, deadlock in the personality. The adolescent who in situations of anxiety uses such defenses as projection, identification with the aggressor, or regression functions on a lower level than the adolescent who uses the more sophisticated defenses such as reversal of affect, intellectualization, displacement, or even reaction formation.

In assessing the adolescent, we would ask whether defense is used mainly against:

   (i) drive demand in general, or specific drives;
   (ii) superego demand, and which superego functions are felt by the ego as producing demand;
   (iii) demands and expectations of contemporaries;
   (iv) infantile object ties;
   (v) masturbation;
   (vi) fantasy content;
   (vii) specific kinds of object relationships.

We can assume that, normally, every adolescent tries to ward off superego demand, infantile object ties, and fantasy content from preoedipal and oedipal levels. Such defense activity is age adequate and serves the purpose of progression to adulthood. But if the adolescent wards off drive demands in general, demands and expectations from contemporaries, and masturbation, we can assume that his relation to his own body and to external reality is much more disturbed. If the defenses used are such that they do not allow for temporary ego regression, we may be able to conclude that he will solve none of his age-adequate problems, that there will be no significant structural changes, and that adolescence is merely another stage on the way to a mental disturbance in adulthood.

We know that a picture of equilibrium during adolescence is itself a sign of danger, and one should note the ego's general attitude to internal pressure.

Has the ego internal means at its disposal in dealing with anxiety and drive demand, or must the ego rely on external objects for this purpose? The adolescent may use one or the other of his contemporaries as an auxiliary ego or superego in helping him to cope with specific kinds of internal demands; or the adolescent may regard his contemporaries as an additional threat toward id and ego regression and may then withdraw from contact with them.

We should also inquire whether the current picture is a familiar one in the history of the adolescent, or whether a sudden change has taken place.

(d) This section remains the same as in the Childhood Profile. Note any *secondary interference* of defense activity with ego achievements, i.e., the price paid by the individual for the upkeep of the defense organization.

(e) *Affects.* (This section is added in the Adolescence Profile.) Examine the different affects available to the ego. Does a person respond to different internal and external situations with a variety of affects appropriate to them or is his response limited to a single affect, e.g., guilt, general anxiety, depression, feeling of shame, cynicism?

Although the availability of affect is a guide to the understanding of ego development at all stages of life, it is characteristic of the adolescent that he normally becomes able to express various kinds of affect much more easily than did the child. In addition, the adolescent becomes aware of his feelings and of their progressively becoming independent of the external world. This is in contrast to the child who normally feels that behavior and feelings are externally determined and who ordinarily is not expected to have some distance from his feelings.

In initial interviews with adolescents, a clear description of the availability and appropriateness of affect may give us a crucial clue to the underlying problem and can often be used by the diagnostician to decide which kind of help would be of greatest benefit.

Affects are one of the most certain indications of what parts of the personality are involved in conflict. At the same time, the range of affect available to the ego signifies whether it has one or many means of discharge for different internal and external situations. Affect differentiation also means that there is greater development from primary- to secondary-process thinking and functioning, that the ego is the master of affect rather than passive in the face of it. One should distinguish between mastering of affect and defensive control of affect—a distinction which constantly needs to be made in the assessment of behavior in adolescence.

For the adolescent specific affects may stand for a specific kind of danger situation. For example, a particular affect may represent his continued attachment to the oedipal objects, or it may be experienced as a sign of danger involving regressive manifestations. We should therefore distinguish between defense against affect and lack of availability of appropriate affect due to faulty structural development. The adolescent may use reversal of affect defensively, or he may try to present a picture of complete neutrality, as if affect did not exist. These methods may be a temporary means of dealing with specific kinds of anxiety, or they may be resorted to so extensively that they begin to distort the person's relation to the external world.

(f) *Identifications.* (This section is added in the Adolescence Profile.) Identifications in adolescence may either encourage progression or participate in pathology. They play a special part throughout adolescence, and their detailed scrutiny can significantly aid the diagnostician in determining which parts of the structure are under special stress. For example, does the adolescent identify mainly with oedipal substitutes, with contemporaries, or with impersonal ideals and ideologies? Does some of his behavior show us that identifications are now being used for the purpose of:

> (i) controlling regression;
> (ii) maintaining the repression of ego-dystonic thoughts and wishes;

(iii) detaching himself from the oedipal objects;
(iv) overcoming his awareness that earlier identifications (which helped to resolve the oedipal conflict) are now inadequate;
(v) dealing with the activity-passivity conflict;
(vi) coping with demands of the superego.

Which identifications are now most important—those which are used defensively, in a transitory way, or those which assist in structural rearrangement?

(Identification may be only one way of dealing with the activity-passivity conflict. More primitive means of handling the activity-passivity conflict would be by repetition of the event or identification with the aggressor. On a higher level, where there is more structuralization, the identifications would show up in sublimations.)

The part played by identifications should normally diminish in importance as the adolescent moves closer to adulthood. The early adolescent needs to use identifications as an aid in controlling regression and in dealing with superego demands, whereas the late adolescent may use them in his attempt to establish his sexual role.

One of the crucial problems with which the ego in adolescence must deal is the testing of earlier identifications in a new context. The behavior of the adolescent is often described as chaotic, unpredictable, infantile, adult, or both. Such manifest behavior may, to some extent, be indicative of the adolescent's efforts to close the gap between the earlier identifications and the more recent ego identifications related to demands and expectations of contemporaries (Laufer, 1964).

[2.] *Superego Development*

This heading becomes a separate section in the Adolescence Profile because the points included here are especially relevant to adolescence. They can help the diagnostician to see how much structural conflict exists and which functions are involved.

(a) Examine each of the functions of the superego (conscience, ego ideal, and self-criticism), stating which of the functions seems to be most highly cathected.

(b) Which of the functions of the superego seems most important in determining the superego's relation to the ego?

(c) Are the superego functions independent of the object world, or is the behavior partly a reflection of the effort to compromise between superego expectations and external expectations of contemporaries?

(d) Do the identifications act as an auxiliary to the superego? Which superego function utilizes identifications in this way?

(e) Does a change in the relationship to the oedipal objects bring with it an overthrow of superego demands and expectations and result in a feeling of loss of object and loss of earlier identifications?

C. *Development of the Total Personality* (Lines of Development and Mastery of Tasks)

This section in the Childhood Profile is used to determine the stages reached in the mastery of various tasks and to judge whether or not these stages are age adequate. Anna Freud (1963) states: "Whatever level has been reached by any given child in any of these respects represents the results of interaction between drive and ego-superego development and their reaction to environmental influences, i.e., between maturation, adaptation, and structuralization. Far from being theoretical abstractions, developmental lines, in the sense here used, are historical realities which, when assembled, convey a convincing picture of an individual child's personal achievements or, on the other hand, of his failures in personality development" (p. 247). Those lines of development which reflect the child's "gradual outgrowing of dependent, irrational, id- and object-determined attitudes to an increasing ego mastery of his internal and external world" (p. 246) are (i) from dependency to emotional self-reliance and adult object relationships; (ii) areas of ego development related to body independence—from suckling to independent eating; from wetting and soiling to bladder and bowel control; from irresponsibility to responsibility in body management; (iii) from egocentricity to companionship; (iv) from the body to the toy and from play to work.

Clearly, these developmental lines cannot in the same way be applied to the adolescent. We are no longer examining ongoing development of a child's personality; we are now looking at the *Functioning of the Total Personality*.

The diagnostician attempts to determine whether the adolescent can make the step to adulthood in an emotional sense and the extent to which such progress may be impeded. To get a complete picture of the total life of the adolescent, the following areas should be examined:

1. *Social Relationships.* The relations to the outside world, to adults, contemporaries, people in authority, etc., are of special importance in adolescence. Various kinds of relationships can exist simultaneously, but their quality and meaning should change as the person progresses through this period. For example, at the beginning of adolescence, the person may have a variety of relationships, each representing different needs at various libidinal and ego levels. As the person gets older, some of these relationships can be expected to lose in importance.

For this reason we should ask such questions as: are the relationships mainly narcissistic; anaclitic; to part or whole objects; related mainly to idealization; functioning as auxiliary ego or superego; on the preoedipal or oedipal level; on the genital level; a means of avoiding being alone, etc.? What part do social relationships now play in helping establish one's sexual role? Which kinds of relationships seem dominant?

2. *Frustration Tolerance.* How readily can the adolescent tolerate frustration? What kinds of frustration cannot be tolerated? Does frustration bring about regression and certain forms of defense activity?

The diagnostician should try to differentiate here between the inability to tolerate frustration and heightened anxiety due to this inability.

3. *Attitude to Anxiety.* Does the ego react to specific kinds of anxiety or to anxiety in general? Certain situations may induce special anxiety and be experienced by the adolescent as special dangers. Which are these?

Is there fear of the external world, or is the anxiety specifically related to internalized aspects? Is the ego active or passive in the face of anxiety situations?

4. *Sublimations.* In the child one can evaluate his potential, whereas in the adolescent one should be able to see the result, if any, of aim-inhibited and neutralized gratification.

5. *Attitude to School or Work.* How well does the adolescent function in these areas? Is there a discrepancy between performance

and ability? Has there been a recent change in attitude and performance compared to previously?

6. *Attitude to the Future.* Adolescence is a period of life in which
the "future" is of special importance. The child's concept of "future"
contains different expectations. They center on the oedipal objects;
approval from them for specific kinds of achievement; the wish to
take on a role similar to the parent of the same sex; the ego's ability
to control drive demand. To be "grown up" means for the child to
be like the parent of the same sex.

For the adolescent, the "future" is determined by different criteria. They concern his sexual role with real objects and his choice
of work. His attitude to the future must now take into account the
various superego demands, the oedipal and preoedipal identifications,
the fate of the earlier ambivalence, the internally determined reaction to success or failure, the internal reaction to one's adult sexual
role.

For diagnostic purposes it is helpful to trace the changes which
may have taken place in the attitude to the future. For example,
what did the child, in latency, want to be as an adult? How much
was this related to reality? Is the present attitude to the future the
same as existed in childhood, or is there a change which reflects specifically adolescent hopes, etc.?

7. *Attitude to Achievements.* Are achievements valued, and if so,
are they directed toward internal or external approval? Are they pur-
sued mainly for the sake of oedipal objects or for reasons of competition? On which level does the adolescent compete?

8. *Ability for Self-Observation.* Has the adolescent the ability to
observe his behavior, his difficulties, the impact he has on the object
world? Can his ego temporarily detach itself from the immediate
experience to see what is going on?

9. *Verbalization.* Is the adolescent able to express himself verbally (how he feels, what he thinks about)? Can he verbalize affect?
Or content?

10. *Comparison of the Various Sectors.* Comparison may show
whether there is balance or imbalance and in which areas. Is the
picture of balance or imbalance similar to what existed before adolescence, or has there been a sudden change in the personality?

VI. GENETIC ASSESSMENTS (Regression and Fixation Points)

In the Childhood Profile, the information collected here is meant to help the diagnostician locate the libidinal regressions and fixation points in the history of the child. Knowledge of these can be gained (a) by certain forms of manifest behavior characteristic for the given child; (b) by the child's fantasy activity; (c) by those items in the symptomatology where the relations between surface and depth are firmly established.

In the Childhood Profile Anna Freud (1962) stressed the need to distinguish between infantile regression and regression in the adult; ego regression "does not always require fixation points and it does not need to be permanent. As 'temporary regression' it takes place along the developmental lines mentioned before, and forms part of normal development as an attempt at adaptation and response to frustration. Such temporary regression may give rise to pathology, but the latter will be short-lived and reversible. For purposes of assessment the two types of regression (temporary or permanent, spontaneously reversible or irreversible) have to be distinguished from each other, only the former type justifying therapy" (p. 156).

Whereas preadolescence is normally characterized by massive regressions, i.e., repetitions of the past, adolescence should bring with it a change in the kind of regressions that take place. In adolescence, regression can serve a number of purposes: it may be a means of retreating from a danger situation and therefore a way of avoiding anxiety; it may be a temporary means of withdrawing from internal and external demands, but it is now undertaken with the ego's and superego's participation and mainly for purposes of temporary respite rather than to avoid anxiety; it may be the means of allowing for fantasy activity (which in turn can be used to avoid anxiety or as trial action to prepare the ego to handle new reality situations).

For the diagnostic assessment of adolescents, it is of utmost importance to determine both the quantity and quality of the regression; under which circumstances this takes place; whether it seems to be of a temporary or permanent nature; and whether the regression to pregenital fixation points offers so much instinctual gratification that the latter may override genital satisfaction as the main means of satisfaction.

Although this information often is not available at the time of diagnosis, we can gain some knowledge about these questions during the diagnostic procedure (as is the case in diagnosis of the child) without necessarily endangering the possibility of future work with the adolescent. In this respect the following items are significant:

(a) repetitive forms of behavior;
(b) withdrawal and certain kinds of activities which accompany this withdrawal;
(c) forms of impulsive behavior;
(d) daydreams;
(e) certain symptoms, which are independent of the adolescent process, and which analytically can be linked to specific fixation points—obsessional symptoms, obesity, etc.;
(f) addictions, food fads;
(g) overconcern about parents;
(h) masturbation fantasies, usually available only during treatment, would be our most certain way of knowing about regression and fixation points;
(i) the affect accompanying the above points may help us to decide whether the regression should be viewed as a sign of pathology.

Although instinctual regression in adolescence predictably takes place in the normal person and changes its quality as the adolescent gets older, there are nevertheless some genetic factors which could make the person more prone to pathology. We know that psychopathology (whether in the child, the adolescent, or the adult) always involves regression to fixation points at various levels. The strength of the fixation is therefore one factor that makes the person more prone to pathology. Another factor is the satisfaction or lack of satisfaction available through genital strivings. Still another is the ego's ability to cope with regression—to permit it but at the same time to have the means of re-establishing its more mature level of functioning.

VII. DYNAMIC AND STRUCTURAL ASSESSMENTS (Conflicts)

In the Childhood Profile, we ask whether conflicts are mainly externally or internally determined. Is the conflict between the ego and the object world; is it between ego-superego and id; is it related to internal conflicts?

In adolescence, too, there are demands from the external world, but we can say that behavior is determined primarily by internal factors. Development of the personality can no longer be considered in the same way as before adolescence. The content of the ego and superego as separate structures has already been established, although final structuralization may take place only during adolescence. The object world is still of crucial importance, but it may now be used as a means of strengthening the structures, or it can be experienced as an additional demand for specific forms of behavior. In whichever way the object world is used, the diagnostician must weigh the part played by each of the structures in determining behavior, but he must also take into account that the adolescent has to cope with society as well as with himself. Therefore, conflicts should be classified as follows:

(a) Conflicts which are felt to be between the ego and object world. Although the superego may play an important part here, the conflicts may be felt to be with oedipal objects, with external demands, etc. One should also take into consideration that the adolescent may be exposed to such real external pressures that to be in conflict with them is a sign of ego strength.

(b) Internalized conflicts between ego and superego. From the material available, is it possible to determine on which level the earlier internalized conflicts are being repeated; e.g., is the conflict related to the oedipal level; attachment to mother; sadomasochistic aspects?

(c) Internal conflicts (activity-passivity; masculinity-femininity; unresolved ambivalence).

VIII. Assessment of Some General Characteristics

Included in this section are (a) the child's frustration tolerance; (b) the child's sublimation potential; (c) the child's over-all attitude to anxiety; (d) progressive developmental forces versus regressive tendencies. These points are meant to assist the diagnostician to predict the chances for spontaneous recovery and reaction to treatment.

These "General Characteristics" cannot in the same way be applied in the assessment of the adolescent because during this developmental phase the entire personality structure is in flux: we simply cannot distinguish between what is permanent and what is transitory. In the Adolescence Profile, the points mentioned above have therefore been included under "Functioning of the Total Personality" (Section V, C), in addition to some items which are specific for assessment in adolescence, e.g., attitude to the future, attitude to achievements, self-observation, and verbalization. The inclusion of all these points under "Functioning of the Total Personality" gives the diagnostician a picture of how the adolescent reacts to specific stresses and what part the ego plays in solving them.

IX. Diagnosis

The first important diagnostic conclusion about both child and adolescent is the distinction between transitory disturbance and pathology. When we are dealing with the adult, we assess the outcome of internalized conflict (Anna Freud et al., 1965). With the adolescent, in contrast, we try instead to examine the interaction of the forces which are creating the disturbance; we try to determine whether there already is a deadlock or whether the disturbance represents a temporary defensive measure. In this sense, the psychiatric categories used to describe adult pathology are not suitable in the classification of adolescent disturbances. The diagnostic categories used in the Childhood Profile are based on metapsychological concepts; they reflect the degree of disturbance and enable us to decide whether outside intervention is required. The following categories are distinguished: (i) behavior which falls within the wide range of "variations of normality"; (ii) pathological formations which are a reflection of the developmental process and are transitory in nature; (iii) behavior which reflects permanent regression and results in ego and superego damage; (iv) primary deficiencies of an organic nature or early deprivations which distort development and structuralization; (v) destructive processes (of organic, toxic, psychic, known or unknown origin) which have effected, or are on the point of effecting, a disruption of mental growth.

The fact that we encounter such great difficulties in distinguishing between transitory disturbance and pathology in adolescence means that we are still unsure how to assess various forms of behavior or what criteria to use to reach a diagnostic conclusion. It is also an indication of the unknown factors which can influence the outcome. Therefore, although the categories used in the Childhood Profile can, with only slight change, be directly applied to diagnosis in adolescence, I suggest some amplification.

All our observations must first be viewed in relation to the ego's ability to deal with the new internal demands (changing the relationship to the oedipal objects, and establishing one's sexual role). Therefore, with regard to the drives, we would have to assess whether the satisfaction from any of the component instincts interferes or will interfere with normal heterosexuality. Although the fantasies can supply some answers, they should themselves be viewed as participating in future pathology only if they interfere with heterosexuality and with ego achievements.

Furthermore, we need to assess whether the present disturbance affects the entire ego organization or whether it is confined to isolated areas. Although there may be temporary regression of some ego functions, the function of reality testing remains crucial. Is there the ability to continue to distinguish between internal and external reality? The degree of distortion of external reality should be assessed; e.g., what is the adolescent's image of the parents and how does this compare to the real parents; how does he view his contemporaries and their expectations? The availability of affects and their appropriateness provide clues enabling us to assess the degree of structural conflict and to predict whether the adolescent will be capable of dealing with the immediate developmental problems. The way in which he uses identifications can tell us whether there is the possibility of structural rearrangement, or whether internalized conflict is so rigidly fixed that there is already a deadlock which makes further progressive development impossible. Vulnerability to narcissistic injury would reflect the degree to which narcissistic equilibrium depends on external objects as well as the extent to which achievements are independent of the object world.

A description of the latency period could help to establish whether interference with ego functions and achievements had existed at that time. We could then distinguish more clearly between behavior which is a continuation from the latency period and will change little during adolescence and behavior which is due to adolescence and will result in structural rearrangement. In some persons, when they reach adolescence, the new demands seem to have almost no impact on their ego. While there may be some slight outward changes in the personality, these adolescents have in fact found no new means of dealing with the heightened anxiety that we expect to occur in this period. The rigidity and limited availability of defenses have created some kind of deadlock long before adolescence, with the result that adolescence does not contribute to maturity but is another stage on the way to a character disturbance in adulthood. At the other extreme, there are persons who, when they reach adolescence, change beyond recognition. This change may be due to the person's ability to use earlier identifications and various defenses in such a way that he can give up the earlier means of narcissistic satisfaction. Ego achievements and superego expectations and ideals now become more important sources of self-esteem. On the other hand, a complete change in adolescence could also be due to the person's inability to give up precisely these earlier means of narcissistic supply. It is as if the adolescent tries, by overthrowing the superego demands and expectations, to disprove the existence of the emotional tie to the oedipal objects. Adolescence can be described as a period of narcissistic crisis, and our inquiry should enable us to find out how the adolescent deals with this crisis.

X. RECOMMENDATIONS (Including Initial Aims of Treatment)

(This is a new section, added to the Adolescence Profile.)

A number of special factors should be taken into account when we consider any recommendation for the adolescent. There are times when the adolescent experiences what seems to be a transitory problem and when help of some kind is advisable. There are other circumstances in which treatment at the present time is not advisable, even though we have no difficulty in diagnosing the existence of a pathological condition.

Similarly, considerations concerning the intensity of treatment at this period should take into account not only the degree and nature of psychopathology and the adolescent's attitude toward it, but also his ability to cope with the demands of treatment—the ego's capacity for insight, his ability to participate in a treatment alliance—as well as the cooperation that can be expected from the family, and the external pressures existing at that time.

The recommendations for treatment should include a statement about the aims of treatment. For example, if analysis is recommended, what structural changes should one expect or aim for; should we prepare for a long introductory period and why; will there have to be any variation in classic technique; should the family be involved or not? Or will help offered be mainly supportive, without intending to bring about much insight into the disturbance? Should we encourage changes in the environment, so that the adolescent will be in a better position to deal himself with his internal demands?

The aims, as stated, may have to be reformulated at a later date, but they should at this point reflect what we consider to be the major areas of the adolescent's personality which require help, as well as the limitations that exist because of either internal or external factors.

BIBLIOGRAPHY

Freud, A. (1962), Assessment of Childhood Disturbances. *This Annual,* 17:149-158.
—— (1963), The Concept of Developmental Lines. *This Annual,* 18:245-265.
—— Nagera, H., & Freud, W. E. (1965), Metapsychological Assessment of the Adult Personality. *This Annual,* 20:9-41.
Laufer, M. (1964), Ego Ideal and Pseudo Ego Ideal in Adolescence. *This Annual,* 19:196-221.
Nagera, H. (1963), The Developmental Profile: Notes on Some Practical Considerations Regarding Its Use. *This Annual,* 18:511-540.

THE IMPULSIVE PSYCHOPATHIC CHARACTER ACCORDING TO THE DIAGNOSTIC PROFILE

JOSEPH J. MICHAELS, M.D. and
IRENE PIERCE STIVER, Ph.D. (Boston)

Anna Freud's recent publication of a Diagnostic Profile (1962) represents a landmark in psychoanalysis and psychiatry. Psychoanalysts in particular have long been dissatisfied with diagnostic labels based on the Kraepelinian system, and there has been a growing demand for a more meaningful classification of the various personality disorders and defects. A recent Panel (1963) devoted to the nosology of childhood psychic disorders relied heavily on the propositions concerning the assessment of normality and pathology elaborated by A. Freud (1963).

In addition to offering a more dynamic approach to diagnosis, the developmental scheme which provides the framework for the Diagnostic Profile makes possible the application of an integrative conception of personality organization. By recognizing dynamic, economic, genetic, structural, and adaptive factors in personality development as well as the importance of their interaction, we can formulate a more organized and meaningful description and understanding of a particular personality disturbance.

While the concept of integration has frequently been employed in the writings of psychiatrists and psychologists, it has seldom been found as a prominent consideration in the body of these writings. In a sense, the concept of character structure adopted by the psychoanalyst involves an integrated view of the total personality in that defensive styles, developmental considerations, ego functions, and the energy principle are all implied, but a systematic and unifying framework of organization has been lacking. Adolf Meyer stressed

From the Harvard Medical School and Boston Psychoanalytic Society and Institute; and Harvard Medical School and Director, Psychology Department, McLean Hospital.

the necessity of having an integrated approach to personality (see Lief, 1948), but because his theoretical perspective was lacking in the psychoanalytic orientation, it did not acquire sufficient depth. On the other hand, some psychoanalytically oriented psychiatrists, for example, F. Dunbar (1943), published a number of papers of various profiles of personality, but these were of a relatively superficial nature. French (1941, 1952) entitled some of his works the "integration of behavior"; Brierley (1951) explicitly elaborated the application of the concept of integration to psychoanalysis and published a paper on "Some Problems of Integration in Women" (1932); and Hoffer (1949) confined himself to a limited segment of integration in relation to mouth and hand. Still, in the final analysis, the content of these papers was not systematically concerned with developing a broader integrated point of view.

A significant study of a normal developmental crisis, i.e., pregnancy, presents a profile of a particular phase of development. Some of its features are similar to those outlined by A. Freud in the Diagnostic Profile, but the pregnancy study conducted by Bibring, Dwyer, Huntington, and Valenstein (1961) was of necessity confined to one specific developmental phase, which was regarded as a period of normal, developmental crisis. For this research, a systematic and comprehensive set of variables was developed, to allow for the organization of large amounts of data around the significant categories of family background, personality development and structure, and current functioning. This system of codifying data facilitates the greater understanding of questions concerned with signs of crisis and signs of maturation found during pregnancy and the early mother-child relationship. It also facilitated a comparison of changes over time.

In contrast to the over-all approach in psychoanalytic writings, the concept of integration has long been a fundamental keystone in the fields of biology and neurology. The conception of hierarchy of levels in particular has led to a recognition of a pattern of dissolution with regressive features when there is a lesion at a higher level (Sherrington, 1911). More recently, however, L. Frankl (1961) published an article on the significance of evaluating the integration in a child's development. With the emphasis on research at the Hampstead Clinic, more and more attention is now being given to diagnostic problems, which in turn leads to an attempt to define and integrate psychoanalytic ideas. The question might be raised why the recent expansion and application of the concept of integration in psycho-analytic theory are at present of such interest. Ever since the struc-tural point of view was introduced in 1923 by Freud, increased attention was paid to functions of the ego and later to the autono-mous functions of the ego; hence a broader, more inclusive frame-work seemed essential. This extension of the framework facilitated the assimilation of findings by psychologists and sociologists and also focused more specifically on levels of personality organization.

This increased attention to the concept of integration in person-ality development has been paralleled by greater interest in synthe-sizing the principles of biology, neurology, and sociology with those of psychoanalysis. Thus there has been growing recognition that an understanding of personality depends in part on formulating prin-ciples of organization which take into account the many facets of development (dynamic, economic, genetic, structural, and adaptive), and in part on taking into consideration the interaction of biological, neurological, social, psychological, and psychoanalytic influences.

One of the authors (JJM) having entered the field of psycho-analysis from neuropsychiatry was influenced by the basic biological principles of integration as well as malintegration, and in his early work with delinquents was impressed by the importance of synthe-sizing biological, social, and psychological principles in an under-standing of character structure. In 1939 Michaels and Goodman reported the empirical finding of the high incidence of persistent enuresis in severe delinquents, which they regarded as a reflection of a disturbance in the psychobiological integration and maturation with psychosomatic manifestations. Through the subsequent years, further investigations led to the hypothesis that delinquency reflected a disturbance in the cultural-personality integration and maturation, with biosociopsychological manifestations (Michaels, 1940, 1955, 1958a, 1958b). In proposing a psychobiological interpretation of delinquency, it was suggested that "there is a concordance of vari-ables from the various disciplines which would indicate that the delinquent who has been persistently enuretic has a psychosomatic structure which is disharmonious and poorly integrated" (Michaels, 1940).

With regard to the impulsive psychopathic character, Michaels

(1959) stated, "From the standpoint of the total personality, this type has a unique malintegrated configuration of personality, the malintegration being manifested at the various levels of the personality, biological, neurological, psychological, and sociological." Later in an attempt to synthesize previous studies on persistent enuresis, juvenile delinquency, and psychopathic personality, which came to be considered disorders of character, Michaels delineated a broad general profile of the impulsive psychopathic character. Based on biopsychosocial interpretations, the following categories were elaborated: Primitiveness of the total personality—lack of control; Libido—persistent enuresis, urethral zone, and impulsiveness; Latency period—concrete and abstract thought; Persistent Enuresis and instinctual renunciation; Ego, superego and conflict; Identification and object relations; Psychosomatic disturbance of enuresis. In further descriptions of the impulsive psychopathic character (1959), the impression was strengthened that in a primitive personality organization there exists a form of ego disturbance which resembles an arrest in the development of some ego functions.

It was further suggested that if the impulsive type of character, in which the urethral zone is given a more prominent place, were added to the three types proposed by Freud (1931), a much broader area in characterology would be encompassed. The impulsive character might be divided into two types: (1) the impulsive psychopathic, and (2) the impulsive neurotic. The impulsive psychopathic character is more alloplastic, the conflicts are externalized, the ego-superego disturbances are less serious in nature than those found in psychosis but lead to more impairment than in neurosis. The impulsive neurotic character is more autoplastic, the conflicts are internalized, and the neurotic mechanisms are of the compulsive form.

Since these investigations of the impulsive psychopathic character have been directed toward developing an integrated picture of this type, Anna Freud's Profile seems to be a most appropriate vehicle for synthesizing the observations gathered to date. We recognize that the Profile was originally designed for use with individual cases and for the purpose of arriving at meaningful diagnoses, but it may also be of significant theoretical value as a means of describing the various diagnostic groups and explicating character typologies. While Anna

Freud's use of the Profile was directed primarily at prediction, the use of the Profile in this paper might be considered an instance of postdiction. The impulsive psychopathic character is proposed as a type and a diagnostic entity in which there is interference in mature development and malintegration of personality, and which therefore may be particularly helpful as a starting point in testing the value of the Profile for typological considerations. Thus, in addition to its practical usefulness in the individual case, the Profile may be of important theoretical value as a means of describing systematically the various diagnostic groups.

We shall start with a brief summary of the character configuration of this disorder, which will be more fully elaborated in the Profile itself. The structure of the impulsive psychopathic character is immature, simple, relatively primitive, and undifferentiated. There is a high degree of narcissism with faulty identifications, and the libidinal organization is primarily pregenital (oral-urethral); with the large amount of uninhibited aggressiveness, there is a lack of fusion of the libidinal and aggressive drives. The simplicity and lack of differentiation in the ego and superego systems are shown in the difficulty in control, in a disturbance in inhibition, and in an impaired capacity to delay action so that aggression is more easily expressed. The defense mechanisms are primitive (projection, introjection, and denial); there is a minimum of conflict and little capacity for feelings of shame, guilt, and for sublimation. The characteristics of the ego are probably related to the type of ego encountered in borderline conditions. It is not well equipped to bind tension and anxiety, which accounts for the low threshold to internal and external stimuli. The superego may be malformed, indicating an incomplete development. There is a disturbance in object relations in that the impulsive psychopaths are much more oriented to the need-satisfying phase (i.e., pregenital). Things are more cathected than persons, and there is a language retardation which may be accompanied by a reading disability. Concreteness takes precedence over abstraction. There is probably a special kind of psychosomatic disposition revealed in a history of persistent enuresis, a high degree of irritability, explosiveness, and uninhibitedness which permeates the whole personality.

Draft of Diagnostic Profile
of the
Impulsive Psychopathic Character[1]

I. REASON FOR REFERRAL

Behavior problems, lying, truancy, stealing, sexual promiscuity, misconduct, disobedience, recidivism.

II. DESCRIPTION OF CHILD

Usually well built, often mesomorphic (as reported by S. and E. Glueck, 1956), coarse features, restless, easily provoked, excitable, emotionally labile, sullen, belligerent, impatient, aggressive-masculine bravado.

III. FAMILY BACKGROUND AND PERSONAL HISTORY

Emotional disequilibrium in the home, low socioeconomic class, broken home, foster home placement and adoption; parental discord; abusive father, sometimes alcoholic; desertion; mother goes out to work. Fluctuation in upbringing (permissiveness, overindulgence to strictness and deprivation). Persistent enuresis; low tolerance to pain, anxiety, and frustration. (In recent years, there seems to be a greater incidence of this character type cutting across a broader socioeconomic range; thus middle and even upper-middle socioeconomic classes may be the background from which impulsive character disorders emerge. In these family backgrounds there also seem to be relatively high rates of adoptions, broken homes, parental discord, and absence of one parent during the formative years.)

IV. POSSIBLY SIGNIFICANT ENVIRONMENTAL INFLUENCES

Neglect, significant losses (see III above).

[1] In what follows the Diagnostic Profile as outlined by Anna Freud (1962) is applied to the impulsive psychopathic character. It has been necessary to select an extreme example of the impulsive psychopathic character as a prototype, although it is clearly recognized that the individual case may fall somewhere along a continuum within each of the following categories.

V. Assessments of Development

A. *Drive Development*

1. Libido—Pregenital

(a) *Phase development:* The predominant phase is oral-urethral, which colors and pervades subsequent developmental phases; thus, while the anal-sadistic and phallic phases may be reached to some degree, they tend to be dominated by the oral-urethral fixation. Because persistent enuresis occurs so frequently associated with lack of control, the urethral zone is especially significant. In view of the general primitive nature of the character, fixations are more prevalent than regression. The severe impulsive juvenile delinquent seldom reaches age-adequate stages.

(b) *Libido distribution*—pregenital: The self is primarily cathected with intense narcissism. Self-esteem is low, narcissistic supplies must always be acquired and generally a poor sense of self is indicated.

(c) *Object libido:* The object cathexes are preoedipal, narcissistic, need-fulfilling, and anaclitic. The world is highly somatized so that things are much more important than persons. The tactual sphere is also highly cathected. Objects are essentially interchangeable, and relationships are organized around sado-masochistic patterns. The peer group is viewed as an extension of the self and serves omnipotent and protective functions.

2. Aggression

(a) *Quantity:* There is a high amount of aggression in the form of hate, which is freely expressed and discharged in fighting the outside world. There is a constant battle with figures of authority.

(b) *Quality* of oral-urethral phase, and to some extent, anal-sadistic: defused, unneutralized, relatively undisguised, and manifested in behavior.

(c) *Directed to external objects:* There is defusion of libido and aggression. Antisocial behavior of lying, stealing, fighting, truancy are general expressions of unneutralized aggression.

B. *Ego and Superego Development*

(a) *Ego Apparatus*[2]

Just as the total character structure is primitive and undifferentiated, so there is lack of differentiation of ego and superego. There is little separation between observing ego and acting ego. Impulses are ego syntonic and autoplastic. The ego is fragile with a thin protective barrier in which capacity to bind anxiety and the thresholds to external and internal stimuli are low; there is a marked tendency to respond with action with a low degree of inhibition and a high degree of impulsivity. There is interference with ego and superego development, so that the ego remains primitive and undifferentiated; it is unclear whether this is due to a primary disturbance based on an ego defect or whether there is a developmental disturbance with an arrest in ego development.

Responses may be diffuse and of a global nature, suggestive of mass-reflex character. Brain damage (blindness, physical-motor disabilities) might interfere with the integration of neurological functions resulting in a disturbance in inhibition, hyperkinesis, etc. There is short-circuiting in a neurophysiological sense and acting out in a psychoanalytic sense. Acting out is of a different quality than the usual meaning of the term. There is action of a functional nature in the living out of impulses; acting upon impulses is described as "primary" acting out (Michaels, 1959). (See Glover's concept of "functional" or psychosomatic delinquency [1950].) Behavior has a repetitive quality.

---

[2] In view of the primitive organization of this type of character structure, it is difficult to differentiate between function and structure which then reflects itself in making it difficult to differentiate between Ego Apparatus and Ego Functions. There is a mutual interaction between these factors.

(b) *Intactness of Ego Functions*

Strong preverbal emphasis: Since energies are so readily discharged, certain autonomous functions do not fully develop; e.g., in the language area, there is a predominance of concrete thinking with little facility for abstract thinking and problem solving.

Some ego functions are on the side of impulsivity and perform most efficiently in attaining satisfaction of needs.

Perception: Only the immediate environment is perceived and perception is directed to objects which bring satisfaction; the low tolerance for anxiety precludes "looking" at the environment.

Memory: Traumatic interpersonal events are poorly remembered and/or altered by denial; unpleasant events are easily forgotten and not recalled. If impulses are immediately discharged, there is less energy available for substitute gratification in the form of "hallucinatory images" or fantasy—and thus there is less motivation to "remember." Dreams are infrequent or less accessible.

Reality Testing: There are no gross distortions as to immediate time, place, or person; the world is interpreted in somatic, concrete ways. An inability to learn from experience is indicated. "Behavior" can be inappropriate and "bizarre" (without clear evidence of a "thought defect"). A strong reliance on denial and projection contribute to poor judgment and distortions.

Synthesis: There is malintegration and impaired inhibition. There is difficulty in dealing with more than one portion of the world at a time—part of experience is accepted and taken for the whole. An inability to organize time in past-present-future continuum and an almost exclusively present-oriented attitude are evident. A difficulty in developing inner controls is reflected in a history of persistent enuresis (sphincter "immorality").

Control of Motility: Poor control of impulses. Impaired inhibition, action-oriented.

Speech: There is language retardation, manifested in

reading disability. Speech is concrete, inarticulate, often with an easy flow of four-letter words.

Secondary-Thought Processes: Thinking is greatly oriented to senses and the concrete with a minimum of abstraction. There is little use of similes and metaphors, little imagination, low level of creativity, and poor capacity to sublimate. Many aspects of thought resemble primary-process thinking, e.g., magical thinking, ideas of omnipotence. There is difficulty in anticipating the consequences of action and in learning from experience.

Intention (Conation): There is a low level of awareness for general behavior concerning time and place of initiation and choice of direction to a goal.

The unevenness of cognitive functions is most apparent in the discrepancy between skills (heightened motility, retardation in language). On intelligence tests, scores are higher on Performance than Verbal tasks. Perception, thought, and memory remain quite global, diffuse, and undifferentiated.

Impaired sense of social morality: A superego defect is apparent in that there is an interference in the fusion of self image and object (ego ideal) and an acceptance of parental prohibitions.

Self Boundaries: There is an impairment of boundaries with poor differentiation between self and object and between inner and outer stimuli and there is a propensity to externalize conflicts. Peer groups are seen as extensions of self.

(c) *Status of Defense Organization*

  (i) There is a paucity of defenses against drives since the ego accepts most impulses; but the defense is against arousal of painful affects (anxiety and depression)—if one can consider "action" as a defense. Impulses: ego syntonic. Most common defenses: denial, projection, introjection.

  (ii) The defenses are not age adequate but primitive (denial, projection, introjection), unstable, and

poorly organized, contributing to emotional lability and erratic behavior (e.g., unpredictable shifts
may occur from projection to introjection).

(iii) Defenses are limited since behavior is ego syntonic
and those employed are used excessively and rigidly.

(iv) Effectiveness of defense: The adequacy depends
on the extent of frustration encountered in the
environment, in the form of obstacles and limits
to immediate gratification; as long as impulsivity
is not limited by external factors, the defenses can
effectively forestall arousal of anxiety. Appraisal
of environment and impulse expression result in
difficulties with society—and in this respect defenses are ineffective. Also, since behavior is often
dictated by omnipotent fantasies and the limits
of reality are not accepted, confrontation with
reality and "failure" may lead to marked disappointments and contribute to cynicism and underlying depression. There is some speculation that
if action is curtailed, psychotic symptoms would
emerge. Furthermore, since defense mechanisms
are limited, they perpetuate action orientation and
the inability "to take in" aspects of behavior and
environment which would allow for "learning"
and future modification of behavior; thus a disequilibrium continues between action and thought.
Only a few defenses are used and one would therefore expect high emotional lability and motility.
There is a low tolerance for delay and frustration
and all events have a high potential for trauma;
since the ego is undeveloped, attempts to master
such trauma are relatively ineffective. Defenses
against drives are almost completely dependent on
the object world—with respect to external opportunities for or obstacles against impulse expression. There is minimal superego development to
prohibit impulse expression.

(d) *Secondary Interference of Defense Activity with Ego Achievements:*

   (i) The defense of action constantly avoids confrontation with environmental stimuli; as energy is always discharged, little is available for developing ego functions of learning, perception, memory.

   (ii) Denial interferes with the ego's full capacity to appraise reality.

C. *Development of Total Personality*

Biopsychosocial Aspects of Development, Psychosomatic Flavor

(Lines of Development and Mastery of Tasks)

Both drive and ego development follow parallel lines and remain at infantile levels; this is particularly apparent in the symptom of enuresis in which mastery and drive remain at an infantile level. Defusion of instincts is suggested; the ego remains relatively undifferentiated and global in structure. There is retardation in language which is consistent with low frustration tolerance of drives. While motor action tends to be normal or accelerated in rate of development, verbal skills and ideational features tend to be underdeveloped and/or retarded. Since the ego is on the side of impulse expression, the emphasis on action may be highly developed. A precocious motor development (perhaps at the expense of the development of verbal skills) may contribute to good motor dexterity and performance skills. However, the ego is not well developed and cannot effectively master anxiety, so that there is minimal ability to develop patience and to persist at a task, even when it depends on these highly developed motor skills.

Developmental Lines[3]

1. FROM DEPENDENCY TO ADULT OBJECT RELATIONSHIPS

"The part object . . . or need-fulfilling, anaclitic relationship, which is based on the urgency of . . . body needs and

---

[3] The section inserted here (in the Diagnostic Profile) is based on a further elaboration of the concept of developmental lines by Anna Freud (1963).

drive derivatives and is intermittent and fluctuating, since object cathexis is sent out under impact of imperative desires, and withdrawn again when satisfaction has been reached" (A. Freud, 1963, p. 247f.).

There are ambivalent relationships of the pregenital, anal-sadistic stage which are characterized by ego attitudes of torturing, dominating, and controlling the object.

2. BODY INDEPENDENCE

From Suckling to Rational Eating, from Wetting and Soiling to Bladder and Bowel Control, from Irresponsibility to Responsibility in Body Management

No specific developmental history of eating, bowel and body management training is apparent. Problems in early feeding are suggested by oral fixations. The high incidence of persistent enuresis points to the likelihood of continued difficulties in bladder control.

The narcissistic investment in the body may contribute to the attainment of a higher level of responsibility about body care than the over-all developmental level might suggest. Irresponsibility about body management may be more evident in the taking of risks which endanger one's well-being and body integrity, based on a bravado of fearlessness and omnipotent fantasies.

3. FROM EGOCENTRICITY TO COMPANIONSHIP, FROM BODY TO TOY AND FROM PLAY TO WORK

Egocentricity: Others are related to as lifeless objects or things, to be manipulated, sought out, and discarded as the mood and needs demand.

Role play characterizes play-work activities, with masculine behavior exaggerated and with difficulties in applying oneself with persistence and foresight to a work situation. There is a refusal to take tasks seriously due to a constant avoidance of external difficulties and responsibilities and the anxiety which might thereby be aroused. A poor ability to sublimate interferes with a successful work adjustment.

There is minimal evidence of participation in games

(which requires impulse control, cooperation, and controlled competition) or of the development of hobbies. Interests seem transient and easily discarded.

VI. GENETIC ASSESSMENTS (Regression and Fixation)[4]

Although later developmental stages are reached to some degree, it is likely that early fixations do contribute to a vulnerability to regress, particularly when confronted with any frustration or delay of need gratification. Thus it is often difficult to distinguish between arrest in development and regression.

(a) Manifest behavior is usually a direct expression of underlying id processes and impulses since they do not undergo sufficient repression and modification.

(b) Fantasy activity is low, impulses are lived out. Primary-process fantasy is expressed in action (e.g., "time" sense remains essentially at primary-process level and is expressed in immediacy of reactions, without ability to contemplate future; little fantasy is used to master future events).

(c) Relations between surface and depth (that is, certain invariant and fixed relations between surface behavior and underlying id impulses) more apparent: one sees a direct expression of impulse. Aggressive energy and libido are essentially nonneutralized.

The simplicity of the structure of the impulsive psychopathic character and its lack of differentiation would seem to make it possible to predict the behavior of these individuals. Waelder (1963) suggested that predictions can be made in two marginal cases. The impulsive psychopathic character would be the type of case in which "the wealth of determinants of human behavior is diminished." He also quoted A. Freud to the effect that "predictions are possible in the many instances in which the two ingredients, primitive inner forces and the sense of reality, are mixed in a characteristic and stable proportion."

4 We are now returning to the categories contained in the Diagnostic Profile.

VII. DYNAMIC AND STRUCTURAL ASSESSMENTS (Conflicts)

Difficulties are externalized and alloplastic, and the conflicts are primarily with external forces.

(a) External conflicts are between the id-ego agencies and the object world. The limits of reality are not accepted.

(b) Internalized conflicts: Interference with internalization.

In so far as the ego represents to the id the demands of the external world, the conflict is to some extent between id and ego—since there are superego lacunae. Because of the weak superego, there is little conflict between ego and superego or between id and superego. The superego is characterized by lacunae on the one hand and archaic punitive attitudes on the other, which tend to be externalized. Thus behavior is dictated more by fears of external punitive agents than by internalized restrictions. Conscious guilt is minimal.

(c) Internal conflicts are between incompatible drive representatives, since aggression and libido remain essentially unneutralized.

The predominance of conflicts between (1) id-ego agencies and (2) object world suggests, with regard to:

(1) level of maturity: dependence of personality structure on object world;

(2) degree of disturbance: severe;

(3) choice of therapy: an educational procedure aimed at bringing about internalization of conflicts, a more neurotic autoplastic adjustment, and the development of ego-alien impulses. Resistance to more traditional psychotherapeutic methods can be expected because of an anti-introspective attitude, poorly developed verbal skills and abstract thinking, action orientation, and low anxiety tolerance.

VIII. ASSESSMENT OF SOME GENERAL CHARACTERISTICS

(a) Frustration tolerance: Low; there is flight from anxiety-arousing situations; drives are ego syntonic.

(b) Sublimation potential: Low, in view of its dependence on secondary-process development and ability to anticipate via language. Impulses are discharged so that little energy is aim inhibited and displaced and there is no need to compensate for frustrated drive fulfillment.

(c) Attitude to anxiety: Very low tolerance since the ego is not equipped to bind anxieties; low conscious anxiety and flight from situations which might arouse anxiety.

(d) Progressive developmental forces are minimal because of the reluctance to renounce passive pleasures of infancy.

IX. DIAGNOSIS

(1) No demarcation between symptom and personality.

(2) Configuration of character traits: aggressive, acting on impulse, persistent enuresis, reading difficulties, language retardation, with a greater predominance and incidence in males than females.

(3) The impoverishing effects on libido progression and the crippling of ego growth are the result of immediate impulse discharge and biosocial defects in ego functions of perceiving, remembering, intending. The superego defect is also related to poor ability to cathect objects, so that "interpersonal" memories are minimally cathected and internalized.

(4) There is a question concerning the possibility of organic involvement and psychosomatic disposition in view of the existing disorder of excitation and discharge. In this respect suggestive features are the long history of difficulties, hyperactivity, abnormal EEG, persistent enuresis, and possibly reading difficulty.

CONCLUSIONS

The application of the Profile in this paper is in effect a reversal of its use by Anna Freud. That is, while she stressed the ongoing and incomplete development which is not readily predicted, we focused on the outcome of the early developments which manifested very little modification or change in adult years. It is important to note that although it was possible to identify early ingredients in the developments toward the impulsive psychopathic character, it is not possible to identify specific cause-and-effect relationships. While we are in the advantageous position of "knowing" the end result, as opposed to predicting an unknown future, it remains in doubt whether or not one can single out specific causes leading inevitably to a particular result.

We did not encounter any difficulties in describing the main characteristics of the impulsive psychopathic character in terms of the headings of the Diagnostic Profile, although there were some categories which seemed to overlap. However, the relative ease with which the Profile could be adapted in this way would indicate its applicability as well as its validity. We were also struck by the fact that no significant categories had to be added. The fact that the impulsive psychopathic character probably represents disturbances in early development rather than later adult modifications of personality may have contributed to the ease with which the Profile could be applied to this character type. Perhaps when an attempt is made to apply the Diagnostic Profile to individual adult cases or to other diagnostic groups, other categories may be required.

The attempt to fit a broad category of a type into a scheme which was intended for individual case analysis has many pitfalls. First of all, there are no pure types; there is only a theoretical construct of a type subsuming the many common denominators which experience has taught us are associated. We realize that the richness and variegation and uniqueness of the live individual case are sacrificed for a drabness and commonality of a class, which nevertheless may have heuristic value for diagnosis and nosology.

From our experience in "fitting" the impulsive psychopathic character to the Diagnostic Profile, we believe that the Profile lends itself to typological considerations, particularly since various levels of personality organization are considered in the context of the developmental process, which allows for a more holistic view of the character structure. It is our hope that this Profile will be applied to other diagnostic groups and typologies as a means of developing a more integrated approach to and conception of adult personality and psychopathology in general.

BIBLIOGRAPHY

Bibring, G. L., Dwyer, T. F., Huntington, D. S., & Valenstein, A. F. (1961), A Study of the Psychological Processes in Pregnancy and of the Earliest Mother-Child Relationship. *This Annual*, 16:9-72.

Brierley, M. (1932), Some Problems of Integration in Women. *Int. J. Psa.*, 13:433-448.
—— (1951), *Trends in Psycho-Analysis.* London: Hogarth Press.
Dunbar, F. (1943), *Psychosomatic Diagnosis.* New York: Paul B. Hoeber.
Frankl, L. (1961), Some Observations on the Development and Disturbances of Integration in Childhood. *This Annual*, 16:146-163.
French, T. M. (1941), Goal, Mechanism and Integrative Field. *Psychosom. Med.*, 3:226-252.
—— (1942), Some Psychoanalytic Applications of the Psychological Field Concept. *Psa. Quart.*, 11:17-32.
—— (1952), *The Integration of Behavior.* Vol. I: *Basic Postulates.* Chicago: University of Chicago Press.
Freud, A. (1962), Assessment of Childhood Disturbances. *This Annual*, 17:149-158.
—— (1963), The Concept of Developmental Lines. *This Annual*, 18:245-265.
Freud, S. (1923), The Ego and the Id. *Standard Edition*, 19:3-66. London: Hogarth Press, 1961.
—— (1931), Libidinal Types. *Collected Papers*, 5:247-251. London: Hogarth Press, 1951.
Glover, E. (1950), On the Desirability of Isolating a Functional (Psychosomatic) Group of Delinquent Disorders. *Brit. J. Delinqu.*, 1:104-112.
Glueck, S. & Glueck, E. (1956), *Physique and Delinquency.* New York: Harper.
Hoffer, W. (1949), Mouth, Hand and Ego-Integration. *This Annual*, 3/4:49-56.
Lief, A. A. (1948), *The Common-Sense Psychiatry of Dr. Adolf Meyer.* New York: Basic Books.
Michaels, J. J. (1940), Psychobiologic Interpretation of Delinquency. *Amer. J. Orthopsychiat.*, 10:501-509.
—— (1944), A Psychiatric Adventure in Comparative Pathophysiology of the Infant and Adult: With Some Theoretical Suggestions in Regard to Regression in Somatic Visceral Functions. *J. Nerv. & Ment. Dis.*, 100:49-63.
—— (1945), The Concept of Integration in Psychoanalysis. *J. Nerv. & Ment. Dis.*, 102:54-64.
—— (1955), *Disorders of Character: Persistent Enuresis, Juvenile Delinquency and Psychopathic Personality.* Springfield, Ill.: Charles Thomas.
—— (1958a), Character Disorders and Acting upon Impulse. In: *Readings in Psychoanalytic Psychology*, ed. M. Levitt. New York: Appleton-Century-Crofts.
—— (1958b), The Management of the Juvenile Delinquent: A Point of View. In: *Emotional Problems of Childhood*, ed. S. Liebman. Philadelphia: Lippincott.
—— (1959), Character Structure and Character Disorders. In: *American Handbook of Psychiatry*, 1:353-377. New York: Basic Books.
—— & Goodman, S. E. (1939), The Incidence of Enuresis and Age of Cessation in One Thousand Neuropsychiatric Patients: With Discussion of the Relationship between Enuresis and Delinquency. *Amer. J. Orthopsychiat.*, 10:501-509.
Panel (1960), An Examination of Nosology according to Psychoanalytic Concepts, rep. by N. Ross. *J. Amer. Psa. Assn.*, 8:535-551.
—— (1963), Psychoanalytic Contributions to the Nosology of Childhood Psychic Disorders, rep. by P. B. Neubauer. *J. Amer. Psa. Assn.*, 11:595-604.
Sherrington, C. S. (1911), *The Integrative Action of the Nervous System.* New Haven: Yale University Press.
Waelder, R. (1963), Psychic Determinism and the Possibility of Predictions. *Psa. Quart.*, 31:1-15.

ASPECTS OF NORMAL AND PATHOLOGICAL
DEVELOPMENT

THE INITIAL STAGE OF MALE ADOLESCENCE

PETER BLOS, Ph.D. (New York)

Before taking up the subject matter of my presentation I shall stake out the conceptual dimensions within which my observations are to be formulated in psychoanalytic terms. This seems desirable because it relieves me of the constant reference to modulating notions of those issues which I shall discuss and places them once and for all into the context of a broad point of view. It should be made explicit at the outset that I conceive of "individual" and "environment" as complementary operational abstractions whose mutual influence on each other is a continuous process. Usually one side or the other of the total process, namely, either "social man" or "instinctual man," is described at crucial points of their intersection. The total process is best studied in terms of interaction systems or in terms of projective-introjective processes which find a documentation, as it were, within the ego or, to be specific, within the ego's object- and self-representational world.

I view adolescence in its broadest terms as the second individuation process, the first one having been completed toward the end of the third year of life with the attainment of object constancy. Both periods have in common the vulnerability of personality organization; furthermore, both periods have in common the urgency of changes in psychic structure in consonance with a maturational forward surge, and a specificity of deviant development (psychopathology) which embodies the respective failures at individuation. What was in infancy a "hatching from the symbiotic membrane to become an individuated toddler" (Mahler, 1963) becomes in adolescence the shedding of family dependencies, the loosening of infantile object ties in order to become a member of the adult world, of society at large. Putting this process into metapsychological terms, we would say that not until the close of adolescence do self and object representations

145

acquire firm boundaries, i.e., at this point they become resistive to cathectic shifts, with the result that constancy of self-esteem and inner regulatory controls for its maintenance or recovery are successfully established (Jacobson, 1964). Adolescent individuation can also be described as a progressive disengagement from primary love objects, i.e., from the infantile parental figures and their substitutes (A. Freud, 1958).

Through ultimate "object removal" (Katan, 1937) the advance to adult object relations is opened up. This achievement remains, however, a Pyrrhic victory, if it is not complemented by the emergence of a distinctive social role, a sense of purpose and of fitting in (positive or negative), which secures an anchorage in the human community.

The finding of new identifications, loyalties, and intimacies outside the accustomed family dependencies permeates adolescent progressive development all along, but is most urgent at the closing stage of adolescence, which, indeed, is characterized by these very achievements. What we witness is an extraordinary spectrum of idiosyncratic accommodations within the realm of what can be called normality or adaptiveness. The crosscultural approach to the study of adolescence as well as the research into the historical morphology of adolescence have taught us a lesson in the enormous plasticity of drive and ego organizations of adolescence in conjunction with the formation and buttressing influence of social roles and social institutions (Muchow, 1962).

As a closing remark to this introduction I want to point to the fact that adolescence is composed of distinct developmental phases which are not as narrowly time fixed as those of early childhood, but both periods of development share the characteristics of following a sequential pattern of distinct phases. Each adolescent phase can be described along three lines, namely, in terms of typical drive and ego modifications, of an integral conflict to be resolved, and of a developmental task to be fulfilled (Blos, 1962; Deutsch, 1944). In other words, each phase makes its singular contribution to personality development or, conversely, its failure initiates a deviate course of development which can be understood in terms of adolescent fixation points. A bisexual orientation, tolerated within certain limits during childhood, comes to an end with the advent of pubescence, with sexual maturation. More accurately, one should say that it is the task of adolescence to render bisexual propensities innocuous through drive and ego accommodations which attain their definitive form during the consolidation period or the terminal phase of late adolescence. The adolescent progressive development which the boy and girl follow is neither similar nor parallel, but it does share the poignant differentiation of qualities which in our minds are associated with being a man or a woman. While certain social roles contribute to the sense of self and transcend the gender condition, every analysis reveals that the basis of the sense of identity is to be found in the clarity with which sexual identity is reflected in the self. A major contribution to this formation—in fact, the final and decisive one— is made during adolescence (Blos, 1962; Greenacre, 1958).

These introductory remarks summarize the conceptual perspective against which the study of a part aspect of adolescence is carried out. While this broad point of view is constantly and implicitly present in what follows, the circumscribed subject under study will be clearer to the reader if the general assumptions as outlined are thought of as the ground on which this investigation stands.

There remains one anticipatory hint to be given to the reader before I present the substantive material on male adolescence. Although the manifestation of aggression constitutes one of the most formidable and dramatic aspects of male adolescent behavior, it has not been satisfactorily traced within the adolescent process or in terms of psychic restructuring. I hope to show that the study of the initial phase of male adolescence will throw light on the vicissitudes of the aggressive drive by elucidating one particular component of it. This component, namely, phallic aggression and phallic sadism, stands out in great clarity at the phase of preadolescence when the genital phase asserts itself anew after its temporary decline during the interposing period of latency.

MALE PREADOLESCENCE

Let us start at the beginning of adolescence and turn our attention to the phase of male preadolescence. The most remarkable observation about the preadolescent boy is his decisive turning away from the opposite sex as soon as the first strivings of puberty increase drive pressure and upset the balance between ego and id that prevailed during the latency period. In fact, object-libidinal gratifications appear blocked and are indeed often violently resisted. The aggressive drive becomes pervasively dominant and finds expression either in fantasy, play activity, acting out, or in delinquent behavior.

You will recognize this kind of boy if I remind you of the many therapy hours you spent with him while he was playing with, drawing, or impersonating battleships and bomber planes, accompanying their attacks with a gunfire of onomatopoetic noises in endless repetition. He loves gadgets and mechanical devices, he is motorically restless and jumpy, usually eager to complain about the unfairness of his teacher, assuring us that the lady is out to kill him. In his behavior, language, and fantasies, the resurgence of pregenitality is easily recognized. An eleven-year-old boy who had started analysis at ten illustrated this development aptly by saying: "My favorite word now is 'crap.' The older I get the dirtier I become." At age fourteen the same boy made the following retrospective comparison: "At eleven my mind was only on filth, now it is on sex. There is a great difference."

The behavior which I have described conceals only thinly the ever-present fear of passivity. As the object of this fear, I came to recognize the archaic mother, the preoedipal active mother who is the prototype of the witch in folklore. The fear revolves around surrender to the archaic mother, and the wildly aggressive impulses are directed toward the ominous woman giant. On the genital level of prepuberty this constellation is experienced as castration fear in relation to the woman, the preoedipal mother. The erect penis cathected with aggressive impulses evokes at this stage the fear of reaching uncontrollable destructive dimensions. The counterphobic role of physical daring and accidents is often clearly recognizable as an effort to assuage castration fear. It is surprising to see how little of this fear is related at this phase to the father; in fact, the boy's relationship with him is often surprisingly good and positive. Even if it is not personally close or congenial, it is usually neither fearful, nor competitive, nor hostile.

In a child psychiatric clinic in Sweden where I recently (1963) discussed these problems I was told in strictly descriptive, i.e., statistical, and by no means dynamic terms that boys of eleven to thirteen show predominantly problems of aggression against their mothers, while among boys of fourteen to seventeen the aggression shifts toward the father. This observation fits well into my theoretical formulations which are based on a comparatively small sample of adolescent boys. The preadolescent boy perceives the often aggrandized father, or other men for that matter, as an ally rather than a rival. The discrepancy between a weak father and his son's perception of him is often quite startling. Only after the defensive idealization of the father has crumbled do we come to realize that the boy drew enormous reassurance in face of castration anxiety from an apparently strong father who had not been weakened or degraded or dominated, i.e., not castrated, by the mother witch. The boy of this phase has no use for female sentimentalities; in fact, he would rather die than surrender his feelings and consequently his bodily self to the tricks and traps of female intrigues. He rather remains a man among men. A delightful account of this stage in a boy's life is given by Lincoln Steffens (1866-1936) in his *Autobiography* (1931, p. 77):

> One of the wrongs suffered by boys is that of being loved before loving. They receive so early and so freely the affection and devotion of their mothers, sisters, and teachers that they do not learn to love; and so, when they grow up and become lovers and husbands, they avenge themselves upon their wives and sweethearts. Never having had to love, they cannot; they don't know how. I, for example, was born in an atmosphere of love; my parents loved me. Of course. But they had been loving me so long when I awoke to consciousness that my baby love had no chance. It began, but it never caught up. Then came my sisters, one by one. They too were loved from birth, and they might have stayed behind as I did, but girls are different, my sisters seem to have been born loving as well as loved. Anyhow, my first sister, though younger than I, loved me long before I can remember even noticing her, and I cannot forget the shock of astonishment and humiliation at my discovery of her feeling for me. She had gone to Stockton to visit Colonel Carter's family, and in a week was so homesick for me that my father and mother took me with them to fetch her. That was their purpose. Mine was to see the great leader of my father's wagon train across the plains and talk livestock with him. You can imagine how I felt when, as we walked up to the house, the front door opened and my little sister rushed

out ahead, threw her arms around me and cried—actually cried—
with tears running down her cheeks, "My Len, my Len."

I had to suffer it, but what would Colonel Carter think, and
his sons?

The many sadistic fantasies and actions of preadolescence are
clear reverberations of the infantile sadomasochistic struggles in
which mother and child are normally engaged during the pregenital
phases of learning body controls. In the case of the boy preadolescence opens the door to a regression to pregenitality and to the actu-
alization of its modalities on the genital level. By virtue of this fact
delinquency threatens to become virulent at this phase. Whether
this will be a transient or a permanent social deviancy depends first
and foremost on the proclivity toward acting out. The precondition
for acting out is not to be found in adolescence; it is anchored in an
incomplete separation of child and need-satisfying object, the latter
being later replaced in delinquency by the always available environment as a tension-relieving part object.

The girl appears to the preadolescent boy as the incarnation of
evil; in his eyes she is catty, bitchy, double-crossing, possessive, or
downright murderous in her intentions. When we listen to the tales
of boys at this age, we detect the theme of the mean and dangerous
female woven with such realism into the recounting of daily events
that fact and fiction are often difficult to sort out. The preadolescent
boy's tendency to give credence to his inner experience by laminating
it to reality, namely, perception, cannot simply be relegated to the
defense of projection. Of course, there is no doubt that the often
almost delusional quality of his experiences attests to this mechanism. At the same time one must acknowledge an adaptive effort,
namely, to come to terms with infantile anxieties or fantasies by
keeping them reality-bound so they can be tested and mastered. This
very fact presents an obstacle in treatment, because it works against
the accessibility of fantasies as well as against the awareness of affects,
especially if they are of an infantile, dependent or passive nature.
This condition has led many therapists to assume a direct and active
role in the treatment situation and to deviate by dire necessity from
the psychoanalytic therapeutic model. We came to see that modifications of treatment technique during adolescence are based on the

"working conditions at hand" which are dictated by the dynamic constellations of this developmental period.

One well-protected fantasy, preserved from the age of about five years and used again at the age of eleven to arouse genital stimulation, was revealed in installments by a boy in analysis. He did not reveal the accompanying sexual sensation until two years later, when he spontaneously corrected his earlier denial. The fantasy was this: "I always thought girls are wound up with a key which was stuck into the side of their thighs. When they were wound up they were very tall; boys in proportion were only one inch high. The boys climbed up the legs of these tall girls, got under their skirt and into their underwear. In there were hammocks hanging down from nowhere. The boys climbed into the hammocks. I always called this to myself 'riding the girl.' " We recognize in this fantasy the overpowering largeness of the female, the phallic mother, who has robbed the boy of his masculinity. Furthermore, we recognize the passive, reclining, blissful state of being an appendix to her. A fixation on this level will render the boy's later object relations immature and frustrating.

The above fantasy contains typical elements which I have often come to recognize in the analysis of older adolescents as a fixation on the preadolescent phase. In a case of this kind a male college student related two alternating fantasies which he had entertained since early puberty: (1) to be stroked on the genital by an older woman who is dressed while he is naked and who sits beside him while he is lying down; (2) to be loved, admired, and aggrandized by a very beautiful and highly intelligent girl who possesses firm and protruding breasts. However, the thought of finding himself in the company of such a goddess (the archaic mother) made him feel weak and small ("a nothing"), it made him literally tremble with fear. By sharing in the grandeur of an unattainable girl the patient expected to restore the sense of infantile completeness, power, and safety which he once possessed when he was a part of the mother. In such cases castration fear in relation to the archaic mother becomes absorbing to such a degree that any resolution of the oedipus complex is precluded. The frequent outcome of this impasse or preadolescent fixation is recognized in a homosexual orientation (latent or manifest) which at the terminal stage of adolescence has usually entrenched itself and has become more or less conscious. The drive pathology slowly permeates ego functions and a condition of failure or dissatisfaction prevails. This, then, brings many such cases to our attention. As a warning against sweeping generalizations we should keep in mind the fact that treatment, by its very nature, attracts more boys with passive trends. The aggressive drive in these cases is usually inhibited, relegated to fantasy, or bound in symptom formation.

As always in maturational crises, when dangers alert the ego to extraordinary measures in order to secure the continued integrity of the psychic organism, the ego in turn advances in its mastery of anxiety and gains greater independence from primitive helplessness. Therefore, after a lengthy account of the regressive drive organization of male preadolescence I must emphasize that the ego normally emerges strengthened from the struggle with the archaic mother. Ego growth is particularly evident in the realm of social competence, of physical prowess in team-oriented combat, in aim-inhibited competition among boys, in an awareness of tested body skills which allow freedom in action, inventiveness, and playful adventure, in short, in the emancipation of the body from parental, especially maternal, control, care, and protection. From these various sources accrues a sense of total ownership of his body which the boy has never before experienced to this degree.

In order to approach an elusive aspect of preadolescence I shall now embark on a *tour de force*. It is not necessary to belabor the point that delinquency during puberty commonly shows an arrest of emotional development or a fixation on the preadolescent level. This is equally true for boys and girls. I now want to call attention to a clinical fact which is familiar to everyone working with adolescents, namely, the observation that male delinquency is manifested primarily in an aggressive struggle with the object world and its representative authority figures, while female delinquency always tends to take the form of sexual delinquency (Blos, 1957). The universality of this clinical fact is impressive; on a recent study trip I found it confirmed by every observer in the field of delinquency from Oslo across the continent to Jerusalem. In the most commonly heard explanation of this clinical fact it is simply the result of the double standard or is due to the absence of any legal protection of male virginity, but both these arguments beg the question. Similar reasoning can certainly not be adduced to render a related clinical fact more intelligible, namely, the relatively frequent occurrence of father-daughter incest as contrasted to the almost nonexistent mother-son incest during the adolescent years.

Observation forces us to conclude that the delinquent boy possesses a greater capacity for the psychological elaboration of his sexual drive than the delinquent girl. Consequently, in the case of the boy we witness symbolic actions replacing direct genital expression as tension-regulatory behavior. I attribute this to the easier availability or regressive cathexis of pregenitality which endows male delinquency with a far richer and colorful repertoire than we are accustomed to find in female delinquency, which presents a monotonous, almost monosymptomatic picture. The girl, in contrast to the boy, resists with far greater determination the regressive pull to the preoedipal mother. She takes flight from a surrender to primal passivity into heterosexual acting out, which at this stage might more appropriately be called "cuddling" rather than referred to by the adultomorphic term of heterosexual relations. It seems that in the case of the boy regression to pregenitality is neither as dangerous to his sex-appropriate development nor as violently resisted as we are accustomed to observe in the case of the girl. While the preadolescent boy's regressive behavior is there for the world to see, the girl's, in contrast, is shrouded in secrecy and kept behind closed doors.

Sexual excitation in the pubertal boy manifests itself in genital sensation, erection, and orgasm with ejaculation. Orgasm at this stage contains the threat of an uncontrolled and uncontrollable state of psychomotor excitation and confronts the ego with the danger that primitive aggressive impulses will break through. There are indications which point to a process of defusion of instincts at this phase. Be this as it may, we observe that the boy seeks with ingenuity and persistence substitute discharge channels for his aggressive drive by displacement or substitution. A similar situation does not exist for the girl delinquent, who never experiences orgasm in her regressed sexual relations, i.e., "cuddling." She finds ample outlets for her aggressive impulses in the provocative, seductive, fickle, and demanding behavior which is characteristic of her general conduct and in particular of the relationship to her partner.

For the boy there exists no passive modality of somatic drive discharge which remains in consonance with his sex-adequate masculine functioning. The phallus serves at the dawn of adolescence as a non-specific discharge organ for tension from any source and in this phase is cathected with aggressive energy reflected in wildly aggressive, i.e., sadistic fantasies. Genital sensations and sexual excitation, including orgasm, can derive at this early pubertal stage from any affective state (fear, shock, anger, etc.) or fierce motor activity (wrestling, chasing, climbing, etc.); often it is a combination of both. The aggressive or, rather, the sadistic drive associated with the phallus inhibits its heterosexual employment through the rise of retaliatory anxiety. It must be remembered that at this stage of adolescent development the male genital has not yet become the bearer of specific sensations that are part of postambivalent interpersonal emotions. Only through the gradual involvement in an affectionate-erotic relationship, real or imagined, will the aggressive admixture of the sexual drive be tamed and domesticated. Only then will the libidinal aim, the preservation and protection of the love object, restrain the aggressive drive from pursuing directly its primitive aims; thus a mutuality of gratification is obtained. Before this stage is reached the boy normally elaborates symbolic representations of his sexual drive which indeed involve active as well as passive expressions of instinct gratification. In their various and exaggerated forms they are recognizable in delinquent behavior. The overwhelming role which sadism plays at this age needs no elaboration because it is well known from the behavior of the preadolescent boy and, for that matter, of the male delinquent.

The emotional proximity of libidinal and aggressive impulses and their rapid change from one to the other are constantly displayed in the treatment sessions of young adolescent boys. A typical incident in therapy will briefly illustrate the abrupt shift from sexual preoccupation to the arousal of aggressive-destructive fantasies. Chris, a boy of thirteen, in psychotherapy for exhibitionistic behavior and social immaturity, was talking with his therapist about "wet dreams" and about his infantile sex theories, which had survived behind a façade of factual enlightenment. While discussing intercourse in terms of "the man urinating into the vagina" he ventured to ask whether women actually possess testicles and a penis. At this point his mounting excitement became suddenly shrouded in silence until it burst forth in his vivid description of a new gun "which would not disintegrate a person, but would set fire to a person's clothing, his body, and could even blind a person." Restraining his aggressive fantasies he abruptly shifted to the suggestion that scientific efforts should be directed toward peaceful goals, such as the invention of an X-ray machine that could tell immediately after conception whether the baby will be a boy or a girl.

The violence of the sadistic phallic impulses of this phase can best be investigated in their unmitigated nature in older male adolescents who are fixated on the preadolescent level and continue to be engaged in the relentless struggle with the preoedipal mother. We commonly discover in such cases fantasies of rage often elaborating the destructive and mutilative aggression against the body of the woman whose protection is desired and whose domination is feared. We recognize in this rage the remnants of oral and anal sadism which at the genital phase of preadolescence and under the impact of sexual maturation appear in the modality of phallic sadism. As a positive aspect we recognize in it an effort which is familiar to us from earlier stages and which often has been only partially completed, namely, the effort to establish autonomy over that erogenous zone which has risen to dominance at the respective stage of psychosexual development. The conflicts, drive propensities, and ego efforts of preadolescence are only dimly apparent when this phase is traversed smoothly, but they represent the phase-specific sources of anxiety which we shall recognize whenever a failure occurs at this stage of development.

The Case of Ralph

Before I continue to trace the next phase of adolescent development, it might prove useful to illustrate the conceptualization of preadolescence with clinical data. Besides illustrating theory, the case material also serves as a convenient bridge, leading us to the phase that comes after preadolescence but is still part of the early stage of male adolescence.

Ralph is a twelve-year-old boy with a chronic chip on his shoulder. He says of himself: "Trouble follows me like a shadow." He feels victimized. He complains that the world is unfair to him, that everybody abuses his kindness and gets him into trouble by accusing him unjustly for misdeeds he has never committed. He is a sensitive boy who cannot tolerate the slightest criticism. He bullies his peers and he controls his parents with a dramatic show of his moods. He has an unsatiable hunger for recognition and power over people. Over the years he has perfected two social roles: the teaser and the trickster. He uses both activities compulsively and indiscriminately to control others and to attract the limelight of attention. In school he is a serious behavior problem, totally indifferent to punishment or kindness. Needless to say, he arouses the wrath of his peers when his tricks become sadistic. On one occasion he was ignored by a boy who sat next to him on a public bus; Ralph thereupon put a match to the newspaper his schoolmate was reading and thus forced his attention toward himself. On the other hand, the tricks he plays on the teacher often find the acclaim of his peers as, for example, when he introduced a topic in which he knew the teacher was personally interested and thus cleverly managed to waste class time and to avert a dreaded test. Ralph is fascinated by fire, by firecrackers, and by gory traffic accidents which usually involve a victim to be ripped open or maimed. He would never, so he protests, go for tricks like putting firecrackers into the mouths of frogs or burning cats' tails. The sadism in Ralph's teasing and playing tricks is obvious and so is his fear of attack, of bodily injury, of being overpowered and controlled. These fears are particularly intense in relation to his mother and to his women teachers. The fantasies of his retaliation on women are made up of sadistic, bloody tortures such as scalping them or drawing blood by punching their hands. During this stage of fighting off the castrating archaic mother in the substitute figures of his present life, Ralph made his father an ally in the struggle by insisting that he is a strong and clever man, which, indeed, he is not and certainly not in the eyes of his wife. Ralph justifies the father's shady deals, such as buying and selling stolen goods, as remarkable feats of shrewdness and courage. Identification with him made Ralph a delinquent who, for example, forged with extraordinary skill a bus pass to which he was not entitled. The boy was unable to see his father realistically or critically until the conflict with the preoedipal mother became resolved; then and only then did Ralph's delinquency become dispensable and fade away.

The therapeutic approach to this problem centered around the boy's complaints about his body intactness. An early childhood trauma had become the experience around which castration anxiety and ambivalence toward the mother had become organized. Ralph introduced the trauma by referring to a big scar on his lower abdomen and thighs which were the result of a third degree burn he had sustained when left sitting on a radiator at the age of fifteen months. This account proved to be factually correct. Ralph concluded his story by saying that he had a "hole in his leg" which was caused by the burn and he assured the therapist that his "skin was left sizzling on the hot radiator." He would now constantly cut his fingers accidentally, tear scabs of healing wounds, and make them bleed again. "Where was my mother when I burned?" he asks in rage and anger. When he finally revealed the fact that his mother forbade him to eat sugar in order to prevent him from becoming a diabetic, the scene was set for acquainting Ralph with the fact that his mother had bizarre ideas, that these ideas had become his reality, and that he defended himself against her influence, her distortions, and her morbid fears. He came to see his mother as strange and mentally ill, which, indeed, she was. The unmasking of the witch mother facilitated the investigation of the boy's distortions of reality as well as of the catastrophical dangers by which he felt surrounded in a hostile world, namely, the world of an ungiving, destructive mother image.

Two changes became apparent in therapy after the fear of the woman (castration fear and wish) was traced to its central core: he became critical of his delinquent father and he became an accomplished magician, having a card printed and performing as a pro at social occasions for a fee. The teaser and trickster had become socialized. The use of his hands was conspicuous also in his new interest in jewelry making, in which he became skillful—to the scorn of his father who wanted him to "work with his brains and not with his hands." He defied his father's dictum, which amounted to a masturbation prohibition, but he could neither succeed nor gain real satisfaction from his accomplishments as a craftsman. Ralph condemned his father's moral corruption and shoddy values and put himself in angry opposition to him in thought and action. But his father seemed unwilling to reform and live up to his son's ideal. For this reason Ralph became repeatedly depressed, experiencing the father's refusal of his wishes as deliberate disappointment, as being neglected, ignored, and not loved by him.

After four years of psychotherapy, it became clear that a delin-

quent career had been averted, that a sense of body intactness had
been restored, that the fear of the female had been appreciably reduced, and that progressive adolescent development had been kept
in motion. However, the disappointment in the father remained a
source of dysphoria and discouragement; the son's attempt at con-
verting the father to his way of life remained a futile but insistent
wish, making the prospect of achieving maturity a doomed and hopeless endeavor.

EARLY ADOLESCENCE

A review of this case in terms of the sequence of clinical manifestations and their changes leaves little doubt that the cathexis of
the "good father" image—the aggrandizement of the father and the
accompanying ebb of conflictual strife with him—represents a typical
defensive operation of male preadolescence. In this context we can
speak of an oedipal defense or, if you will, of a pseudo-oedipal formation. We came to realize that an oedipal constellation is not the
substantive content of this conflict despite the clinical picture which
resembles it. The confusion stems from the manifest behavior,
namely, the boy's admiration and envy of his father while seemingly
warding off the love for the oedipal mother. By misjudging the essence of this conflict therapy finds itself in a stalemate. We have seen
in the case of Ralph that with the resolution of the conflict in relation to the archaic mother a progression to the oedipal father became
apparent. This development proceeds in continuation of the preadolescent phase but moves gradually into the ascendancy of the
passive position of the negative oedipus complex. This drive constellation in its course leads to the central conflict of the phase of
male early adolescence. We shall now turn our attention to the vicissitudes of drive and ego typical of this phase.

At the turning point of early adolescence Ralph's progressive development had come to an impasse because he was unable to sustain
the discord with and estrangement from the father on the level of an
ideational, moral, attitudinal, and vocational approach to life and
action. He was unable to form an ego ideal that could exist and
function independent of the love object in the outer world. Ralph
endeavored to shape his father into his ideal partner in real life. To

say it differently: Ralph failed to detach narcissistic object libido from the oedipal father. Consequently, the ego ideal never became consolidated as a psychic institution. Reflections of this failure were clearly visible throughout his efforts at psychic restructuring. A fixation in early adolescence is responsible for the specific aspect of psychopathology which in the case of Ralph remained unresolved. The therapeutic progress described above is often all that therapy can accomplish at this stage of adolescence. We might ask whether it is our knowledge of theory and technique that confronts us with the same limitations which child analysis has demonstrated or whether these limitations are not an integral aspect of treatment whenever it is carried out during a phase of ongoing development. Experience tells us that a large proportion of children terminate analysis only to continue it at a later age, usually in late adolescence or postadolescence when a new wave of insurmountable emotional difficulties again threatens to engulf their lives. In cases of prolonged adolescence, therapy itself easily becomes a holding action because it represents a promise that the fulfillment of narcissistic fantasies can indeed become a reality through the magic of treatment, namely, through benign parental volition (Blos, 1954). The stalemate in Ralph's adolescent development will no doubt require treatment to be resumed. It seems to me that the time for the resumption of therapy will arrive when the failures in his relationship to both sexes as well as the aimlessness and frustrations in his vocational and social life have mobilized a crisis of more than usual severity in late adolescence or soon thereafter. Due to therapy in the initial stage of Ralph's adolescence he will no longer be able to fall back on acting out; conversely, a condition for internalization has been established, laying, so to speak, the foundation for a continuation of therapeutic work in the future.

We are now well prepared to turn to the phase of early adolescence, which is initiated on the drive level by certain characteristic changes (Blos, 1962). One of these changes concerns the shift from a merely quantitative drive increase (preadolescence) to the emergence of a distinctly new drive quality. A retreat from the preadolescent regressive position becomes apparent. Pregenitality loses increasingly, often slowly and only gradually, the role of a satiatory function. By becoming relegated to a subordinate or initiatory role—mentally and physically—it gives rise to a new drive modality, namely, to fore-pleasure. This shift in drive organization eventually elevates genital-ity to a place of dominance. The hierarchical organization of drives and its definitive and irreversible character both represent an inno-vation which decisively influences ego development. The ego, so to say, takes its cue from the shifts in the instinctual organization and it elaborates in its own structure a hierarchical organization of ego func-tions and of defensive patterns. I shall return to this point later and describe the typical ego development of this phase.

Early adolescence initiates the protracted attempt at loosening early object ties. It is no surprise, then, to see the rise of a series of predicaments over object relations and, in fact, an ever-narrowing concentration on these transactions. We expect this development to follow the ontogenetic lines of object relations which we encountered previously in preadolescence, when the boy's ambivalence to the preoedipal mother became the source of anxiety and the focal con-flict to be mastered.

Pubertal maturation normally forces the boy out of his preado-lescent defensive self-sufficiency and pregenital drive cathexis. We come to realize that the forward movement of object libido leads in its initial form to an object choice made according to the narcissistic model. This choice can be paraphrased by saying: "I love whom I like to be." The individual history of object relations calls to mind immediately that aspect of the oedipal constellation which falls un-der the most powerful repression in the male child, namely, his pas-sive attachment to the father, the negative oedipus complex. The stage of "I love whom I like to be" is only gradually, seldom com-pletely, replaced by the alternative of: "I will become whom I envy and admire." This latter step leads to the resolution of the positive oedipus complex and consolidates the superego precursors in the for-mation of the superego as a psychic institution.

It has been my experience that the drive development of early adolescence reflects an effort on the part of the boy to come to terms with the father as his oedipal love object. In my analytic work with adolescent boys I find this theme an ever-present source of conflict requiring the most laborious effort to make it accessible to thera-peutic investigation. I am inclined to say that the unfolding of object libido in male adolescence meets its first and often fatal impasse when the recrudescence of the passive attachment to the oedipal father dominates the emotional scene. Of course, we immediately recognize in the excessive exacerbation of this predicament the incomplete resolution of the preadolescent phase which culminated in the resistance against regression to primal passivity. Should this regressive trend be followed, it will add its share to the conflicts and impediments which under these circumstances become evident in the clinical picture of early adolescence.

The study of adolescence demonstrates with abundant clarity that the final decline, the mastery or resolution of the positive and negative oedipus complex is not totally accomplished in early childhood but is the task of adolescence, i.e., the genital phase. The intervening latency period plays an important economic role which is decisive for the outcome. The enormous gains in ego expansion and autonomy which accrue from the latency period ultimately furnish the structural resources that are essential for the encounter with puberty. An abortive latency period precludes the unfolding of adolescence and results in an unmitigated reactivation of infantile sexuality. It is obvious that these drive modalities manifest themselves on the corresponding level of physical maturation, namely, puberty, and in seeking drive gratification usually have at their service those resources which have accrued from ego development in the intervening years.

To summarize: after the regressive position of male preadolescence the forward movement of object libido leads in its first step to a narcissistic object choice. That this choice remains within the confines of the same sex should be no surprise to us. The phase of early adolescence is the time of friendships with unmistakably erotic overtones, either attenuated or more or less consciously experienced. Mutual masturbation, transient homosexual practices (i.e., fellatio), mutually granted scoptophilic gratifications, shared transgressions or crimes, idealizations, feelings of bliss and elation in the presence of the friend—these are the experiences in which the narcissistic object choice is manifested. Furthermore, these are the experiences which bring about the sudden termination of friendships whenever the intensity of the instinctual drive arouses homosexual panic or, to be specific, mobilizes passive wishes. A fixation at this phase is familiar to us from the analysis of older male adolescents whose object relations are disturbed and who will "fall in love" (often only in a fleeting fantasy) with every male peer or male adult whose mental or physical faculties are momentarily envied. What should interest us here is the course this development follows, namely, the accommodations of drive and ego which facilitate or preclude progressive development. Specifically, we would like to be able to see clearly the drive and ego alterations which in their mutual interaction bring about the resolution of a dilemma or conflict that is typical of the boy at the phase under discussion.

It is my contention that the phase of narcissistic object choice is brought to a settlement by a process of internalization giving rise to a new institution within the ego, namely, the ego ideal.[1] The ego ideal, as discussed here, is the heir of the negative oedipus complex. Transient identifications of the adolescent period play a major part in giving the ego ideal additional content and specific direction. Of course, the ego ideal can be recognized in prestages reaching back into early childhood. However, its consolidation as a psychic institution is not accomplished until early adolescence. With the decline of this phase narcissistic and homosexual object libido becomes absorbed and bound (neutralized) in the formation of the ego ideal. From this source it derives its inexhaustible vitality and strength. Submission to or, rather, affirmation of the ego ideal makes any suffering, even voluntary death, a matter of uncompromising choice. The establishment of the ego ideal attenuates the dominance of the superego by the reliance on an implicitly ego-syntonic guiding principle without which life loses inner direction, continuity, and meaning. Violations of the two institutions are followed by either guilt (superego) or shame (ego ideal). Any discrepancy between the ego ideal and the self representation is felt as a lowering of self-esteem or as shame, which is warded off by "paranoid" defenses, typical of adolescents at this stage (Jacobson, 1964). The fact that the ego ideal embodies not only an individual but also a social component, as Freud (1914) indicated, makes the ego ideal a controlling agency particularly well suited for the process of disengagement from family dependencies in adolescence.

In my study of ego-ideal formation during the phase of male early adolescence and especially of ego-ideal pathology I came to realize

[1] For a more extensive discussion of this topic see Blos (1962, Chapter V).

that Freud's formulation (1914) of the ego ideal is of particular relevance for an understanding of adolescence. The passage which I have in mind reads as follows: "In this way large amounts of libido of an essentially homosexual kind are drawn into the formation of the narcissistic ego ideal and find outlet and satisfaction in maintaining it" (p. 96). "Where no such ideal has been formed, the sexual trend in question makes its appearance unchanged in the personality in the form of a perversion" (p. 100). In other words, the forward movement of object libido to heterosexual object finding is precluded by a perseverance of the early adolescent position. In that case the next phase of adolescence proper is never reached; however, by imitation of social and experiential forms of behavior a more mature position can—at least for a while—be simulated.

Ego-ideal pathology—foreshadowed by antecedent conditions, to be sure—reaches a stage of dynamic specificity at the phase of early adolescence. The case of Ralph afforded us a glimpse into the pathology of this phase. The specific aspect that is due to the failure of ego-ideal consolidation does not always become readily apparent within the total clinical picture. In fact, it is my experience that it is often blurred and pushed out of sight by a pseudo-oedipal maneuver, by a defensive preoccupation with heterosexuality, by a professed impatience to grow up and do important things in life. Put to the test, such aspirations always collapse like a house of cards as the case of Ralph has demonstrated. The adolescent caught in this impasse searches desperately for a meaning in life, or he tries, at least intellectually or through acting out, to keep the outcome of his impasse within the bounds of his own powers, of his decision, and of his choice. My experience with cases of prolonged adolescence has taught me that the male adolescent crisis which we witness so frequently in late adolescence is rooted in arrests and incomplete resolutions of those developmental tasks that belong to the initial stage of adolescence.

This brings me to the end of my effort to delineate within the initial stage of adolescence the phase-specific conflicts, tasks, as well as failures in terms of drive and ego organizations. If we view these failures and their catastrophic impact on development as fixation points, their reflections can be recognized in the psychopathology of many late adolescent boys or young men who were not able to bring

the adolescent process to a close. We recognize in most cases the ongoing struggle within the initial stage of adolescence and come to
realize that this stage contained obstacles which proved to be unsur-
mountable, constituting consequently a permanent barrier to progressive development. The study of this stage, then, makes its contribution to an understanding of the developmental failures in the
young adolescent boy; furthermore, it throws light on a larger problem pertaining to the vicissitudes of the aggressive drive which usually plays a prominent part in the clinical picture of the male adolescent.

BIBLIOGRAPHY

Blos, P. (1954), Prolonged Adolescence. *Amer. J. Orthopsychiat.*, 24:733-742.
—— (1957), Preoedipal Factors in the Etiology of Female Delinquency. *This Annual*, 12:229-249.
—— (1958), Preadolescent Drive Organization. *J. Amer. Psa. Assn.*, 6:47-56.
—— (1962), *On Adolescence*. New York: Free Press of Glencoe.
Deutsch, H. (1944), *The Psychology of Women*, Vol. I. New York: Grune & Stratton.
Freud, A. (1958), Adolescence. *This Annual*, 13:255-278.
Freud, S. (1914), On Narcissism: An Introduction. *Standard Edition*, 14:67-102. London: Hogarth Press, 1957.
Greenacre, P. (1958), Early Physical Determinants in the Development of the Sense of Identity. *J. Amer. Psa. Assn.*, 6:612-627.
Jacobson, E. (1964), *The Self and the Object World*. New York: International Universities Press.
Katan, A. (1937), The Role of "Displacement" in Agoraphobia. *Int. J. Psa.*, 32:41-50, 1951.
Mahler, M. S. (1963), Thoughts about Development and Individuation. *This Annual*, 18:307-324.
Muchow, H. H. (1962), *Jugend und Zeitgeist: Morphologie der Kulturpubertät*. Rein-bek-Hamburg: Rowohlt.
Steffens, L. (1931), *Autobiography*. New York: Harcourt, Brace & World.

ON THE DYNAMICS OF NARCISSISM

I. Externalization and Early Ego Development

WARREN M. BRODEY, M.D. (Boston)

The disturbances to which a child's original narcissism is exposed, the reactions with which he seeks to protect himself from them and the paths into which he is forced in doing so—these are themes which I propose to leave on one side, as an important field of work which still awaits exploration.

—FREUD (1914, p. 92)

THE FAMILY STUDY

This paper has its beginning in a study (Brodey, 1959) of fourteen families, each having a schizophrenic young adult member and most including father, mother, and siblings. These families were observed in their daily living in residence in a research hospital, the period of residence varying from six months to two and a half years.

A subsequent four years of clinical work with other family units treated for a variety of problems, together with the study (Brodey, 1962) of a group of families, each stressed by the birth of a blind child, has inspired critical elaboration of the themes presented originally. What follows rests on a correlation of these clinical observations.

What is special about the operations of these families? This question arose every day for two and a half years as I worked with the hospitalized families. I attempted to develop concepts with which to begin to map this new territory. Fully aware of the bias and distortion introduced by the hospitalization, I valued the opportunity to explore families in a way never previously attempted.[1] My efforts

[1] The project was made possible by the support of the National Institute of Mental Health. I am indebted to the Director of the Family Study Project, M. Bowen, M.D., and to my colleagues, B. Basamania, M.S., and R. Dysinger, M.D., who developed this project. We shared in making many trial formulations. We often did not agree, but we listened, and talked, and learned from each other. The responsibility for what follows is my own.

were directed to integrating commonly known clinical information (the products of many different techniques of observation) with what I observed daily in these families. I hoped to find a simple and useful formulation and looked for the words that would encompass the outstanding special features of what I saw. It seemed to me that many variables depended on two major characteristics:

In each member of these families, there was *extreme individual narcissism*. This was expected; but it was not anticipated that such narcissistic people could be so powerfully bound together within the family unit. This *extreme intensity of relationship* required explanation.

The Narcissistic Way of Relating

The term "narcissism" is now a part of the common language; in its wide usage it has acquired many meanings. But the roots of the idea "narcissism" are epitomized in Milton's *Paradise Lost*.

> As I bent down to look, just opposite,
> A Shape within the watry gleam appeerd
> Bending to look on me, I started back,
> It started back, but pleasd I soon returnd,
> Pleas'd it returnd as soon with answering looks
> Of sympathie and love, there I had fixt
> Mine eyes till now, and pin'd with vain desire. . . .[2]

Narcissus is not aware that he is looking at his own image. To *him*, his love has an external object; it is *answering* looks of sympathy and love that lead him to pine with vain desire.

An intense relationship exists between Narcissus and his distanced reflection. This is not a relationship with another—it is interpersonal *only* as described by Narcissus. Narcissus can love only him-

---

[2] Thus far, Milton's lines echo the earliest stage of narcissistic development. The lines that follow make clear Eve's progression beyond this stage:

> Had not a voice thus warnd me, What thou seest,
> What there thou seest fair Creature is thy self,
> With thee it came and goes: but follow me,
> And I will bring thee where no shadow staies
> Thy coming . . . .

self. The image of himself seen reflected at a distance is called *an as-if other*.[3]

Externalization is a defense of the narcissistic, preobject period of ego development. It makes possible a way of life based on relationships with unseparated but distanced aspects of the self. What is perceived as reality is an *as-if* reality, a projection of inner expectation. The senses are trained to validate; the intense searching for what is expected dominates and forces validation. It is difficult not to validate an unquestionable conclusion. Each validation makes the conclusion even less questionable. The restricted reality perceived is experienced as though it were the total world. A special kind of learning is needed to hold this restricted world intact. The narcissistic person learns to manipulate reality to conform with his projection. His experiments are designed to make prior conclusions inevitable. Within this framework his world is reasonable. This way of life becomes a system of survival.

EXTERNALIZATION

Working with a family unit makes it possible to observe directly a way of family life that holds—indeed clutches—at its very core the function of *externalization*. Externalization is a mechanism of defense defined by the following characteristics:

1. Projection is combined with the manipulation of reality selected for the purpose of verifying the projection (Brodey, 1959).

2. The reality that cannot be used to verify the projection is not perceived.

3. When this mechanism is prominent in a stable group where people are learning from each other (as in a family), information known by the externalizing person but beyond the *Umwelt*[4] of the others is not transmitted to these others except as it is useful to train or manipulate them into validating what will then become the real-

---

[3] Freud's (1914) discussion of the narcissistic object choice does not reveal the *as-if* quality of the preobject relationship. For the first lucid description of this process we are indebted to Helene Deutsch (1934). *As-if*, in this paper, will be used to mean "involving an error of perception." At the heart of externalization we find not mere misnaming, not conceptual or symbolic error, but perceptual constraint in an extreme form.

[4] This term is used by von Uexküll (1934) to refer to the world available to the perceptual apparatus of a particular creature.

ization of the projection (Brodey, 1961).[5] Reality testing is subverted in this process. Interlocking systems of externalization shared in a family potentiate disturbed ego development.

As may be the case with other defenses, externalization so extreme as to fix the cathexis and prevent energy from flowing to later defense structures becomes a way of life. The budding narcissism of the child and thus his earliest movement toward a beginning of self-other separation are destructively disturbed by this way of life.

Externalization is more easily defined by the observer of the family unit, though it is equally significant in individual psycho-analytic therapy.[6]

TRANSFERENCE AND EXTERNALIZATION

The difference between transference and externalization becomes apparent to the expert therapist as he comes to realize that for the patient he has no meaning beyond the patient's expectation. What is left out has never been cathected and thus is not repressed. The full power of the problem envelops him as he feels the intensity of his patient's effort to manipulate him into validating projections. He feels the conflict as he struggles against this manipulation. But behavior that will be used as validation seems the only way to gain relationship.

The manipulation of the therapist into behavior that is symmetrical with the projection is different from the transfer of feelings to a therapist. The transference object has an existence to the patient beyond the transference. The therapist as a narcissistic extension has no other existence to the patient; the therapist must match the expected answering looks—otherwise, to the patient, he does not exist. Even if the therapist does not wish to conform, he still finds himself conforming to the narcissistic image. For no matter what he does, pieces of the therapist's actual behavior irrelevant to the therapist's self-identity are seized on by the patient, to whom they are predominant *as-if* characteristics. The identity that the patient sees may

---

[5] I am grateful for the assistance of Dr. Edith Jacobson in making similarities and differences between externalization and denial and projection clearer.

[6] This same process has been observed in child analysis (Anna Freud, 1960).

be unknown to the therapist (although it holds a kernel of truth [Freud, 1911], which is usually disturbing to the therapist). The therapist's active denial of the patient's presumption may serve as confirmation of the *as-if* identity, particularly because the patient, constricted to his own externalized image and expectation, does not perceive the context of other characteristics.

But if the therapist gives back only what is expected, he is merely a reflection. Although the patient's relationship with his own reflection in its *as-if*-therapist manifestation may be intense (Searles, 1963), he is out of contact with the existent therapist (that is, the therapist seen without the errors introduced by narcissistic perception). Therefore, the therapist of the ego-disturbed patient must become skilled at managing his congruence with the patient's projected image. This management is often intuitive and usually very demanding emotionally. Being a distorted object is much easier than being nonexistent.

A Genetic Approach

The Narcissus myth provides a poetic analogue useful in describing the original self-other separations and their later repetitions.

Freud (1914) conceived of the original process of separation in intrapsychic terms. He speaks of the gradual movement of energy from mouth to intrapsychic percept of the breast as the early paradigm of the movement of narcissistic libido to object libido. He describes the hallucination and the wish as mediators in this process.

The intrapsychic genetic approach, when combined with interpersonal family observations, leads to the dynamic formulation of one form of altered ego development commonly seen in those unable to establish adequate object relationships. These dynamic considerations extend theory to catch in its net clinical data which, although felt to be important, have previously not been structured.

To build this approach I shall begin with the child's maturing relationship *toward* his differentiating percept of the parent, then proceed to the parents' unfolding relationship *toward* their percept of the child. Finally, I shall attempt a conceptualization of the mutual relationship *between* child and parent in the family unit.

STAGES OF EGO DEVELOPMENT

The infant at first does not distinguish between stimuli perceived in his internal and external environments. Narcissus, too, does not realize that he is in love with his extension; he does not know inside from outside. This differentiation and separation must be learned (Bruch, 1945). This process of differentiation, which I have called developmental learning,[7] takes place, I believe, as follows:

1. In the first or *differentiated tension* stage of ego development,[8] instinctual energy is directed only by the differentiation of pleasant and unpleasant states of being. It does not differentiate in terms of aim and object. Outside experiences remain diffuse except as they are experienced in terms of total tension level.

Distance and time are not patterned into information. "Nipple" is a tension-change memory. Absent "nipple" wished for is "unpleasant."

The experience of undifferentiated tension-tension release is gradually defined by the mother's response as she answers the infant's activities—grasping of the nipple, sucking, digestion, and snuggling. The child and mother's patterning of these activities in relation to the child's pleasure-pain experiences moves the differentiation toward including specified aims in the next phase.

The rhythms of this physiological experience are patterned into the sense of time, and the tensions become localized in separate focal body areas where there has been more defined sensation. This body separation—fingers from mouth, for example—provides a beginning sense of distance. The activity center of this period is the mouth, in terms of which tension and tension release are most easily represented.

2. In the second or *differentiated aim* phase of ego development, energy is differentiated in terms of aim but not yet of object.[9] Feed-

---

[7] The term "developmental learning" emphasizes the *activity* of the process.

[8] No effort is made to ascribe a specific duration of time to each stage. Ego development, like learning itself, is an organizing process; all stages are represented throughout life as new data are assimilated and the old ones are reintegrated. The stages conceptualize a predominant sequence most easily observable in early infancy.

Furthermore, the word "undifferentiated" is chosen with the qualification that it is used relatively.

[9] In "Instincts and Their Vicissitudes" (1915), Freud distinguishes the aim from its object. The aim is the direction of the instinctual energy as it moves toward a specific

ing, not the feeder, is the point of view. Distancing occurs without separation. This is the stage of externalization. "Nipple" is gradually defined by the infant as distanced from the mouth, though not yet separated from it. The mouth seeks the specific gratification of being fed, but not an object.

In this phase, the "existent nipple"[10] is attended to only as a special, localized, patterned *experience of the mouth* influencing the state of oral tension. The pattern has become organized beyond *diffused* continuousness of tension and tension release.[11] Skin and mouth sensations become differentiated. Holding and feeding are experienced as separate. The mother's responses may reinforce the child's own knowledge of his needs or confuse this differentiation. The "nipple" now is perceived as a specific kind of tension releaser. This tension release is actively sought. That which resembles the "nipple" is similarly perceived and explored, but only in terms of this specific function of abolishing tension at its source. For example, the mouth is used to explore what it senses in terms of its feeding potential rather than as an object in itself.

Function or aim is the essence of identity rather than who or what performs it. The clinician working with the ego-disturbed patient knows what it means to be just a feeder and not a person. At this function stage, *what is not directly related to a specific kind of tension building or tension release is not perceived.*

Time and space are experienced only as the energy rhythm felt when the aim is achieved or disappointed. Crying for milk or for holding is not crying for mother. Gradually, functional parts of mother join in a mosaic, but the differentiation of aim does not yet lead to the discovery of object—for example, another person. The organization of time and space, being predicated on specific kinds of tension and its release, follows rules of consistency quite different from those prevailing in the phase of object relations. The discovery of others brings with it the discovery of their distance, their space

satisfaction, by abolishing the condition of stimulation at its source. The object is that through which the aim is achieved. I have broadened the concept "object" in this presentation.

10 By "existent nipple" is meant the mother's nipple as it exists within, but also beyond, the infant's experience.

11 Those who wish to translate this presentation into Pavlovian terms, or into learning-theory sequences, will find ample points of juncture with these other ways of describing what is happening.

and time coordinates. Later on, tension based on inner time and movement is integrated with that of the accepted cultural patterns learned through family teaching.

A clinician working with a patient fixated at this second stage is familiar with these time and space characteristics: time flow is changed by tension level; such a patient's lateness is different from neurotic lateness, for there is no common clock, just an inner sense of time which, though based on personal tension, becomes the world clock.

In this second phase, the wish is supreme, and the only issue is whether or not the wish is answered. Narcissus does not move to discover new sources of supply, nor can the young infant. His cry indicates a wish that needs fulfillment, but there is no intentional communication to another.

The wish when thus uncombined with the capacity for effective action becomes simply an attempt to revive the memory of a percept, to recreate the sensation of the earlier known fulfillment. The wish at this stage carries an unqualified power of expectation.[12] This self-fulfilling expectation is unsubstantial in its gratification except as mother makes it substantial by her comprehension of the need.

In this second stage, the "absent nipple" does not extend to an awareness of mother's other activities outside the child's immediate aim. The wish at first is not that her nipple return; there is simply a sense of the absence of gratification of the wish at its physiological source.[13] This genetic statement helps differentiate externalization from denial and projection.[14] In externalization, the absence of grati-

---

[12] The repetition of former behavior without regard to present reality, in the sure expectation of complete functional fulfillment, is a powerful manipulating force. The more reality-oriented person is easily seduced into believing that there must be a valid reason for the certainty of the ego-disturbed person. Like the proverbial one-horse shay, this certainty may disintegrate all at once. We are not used to dealing with this negative hallucination phenomenon as an everyday life occurrence.

[13] In the narcissistic family, the internal wish is experienced as a narrowly constricted necessity arising from outside. The hallucinated wish fulfillment is a preoccupation with a function, such as being loved. The function "being loved" is unrelated to a lover or to acts and happenings that could produce a lover. The narcissistic person is preoccupied instead with the absence of loving.

[14] In An Outline of Psychoanalysis, Freud (1940) states that the "claim from the external world which [the ego] experiences as painful" is warded off "by denying the perceptions that bring to knowledge such a demand on the part of reality," whereas "undesirable instinctual demands [are disposed of]" by means of . . . repressions" (p. 118).

fication does not stimulate an advance beyond the sense of absence. The world beyond the felt sense of absence is not a world that contributes information to be denied—it has no existence. That the hungry infant is narrow-minded comes as no surprise. That the child of this stage dreads abandonment is appropriate to survival. The child's cathexis of the mother's functional capacity to relieve his tension at its source ensures her ability to *teach* as she patterns her responses. She is not yet his object.

How does the movement toward an object relationship take place? The progression is most familiarly symbolized in terms of mouth and nipple.

When the "existent nipple" moves into congruence with the hallucinated nipple, the existent nipple fulfills the wish, and it is perceived and cathected with the energy attached to the wish. Thus begins the cathexis of the primordial other—at first without separation.

The condensation of this dynamic in the Narcissus myth begins to become manifest: the cathexis of a self which is at once distanced and yet unseparated is a stage in separation. The Narcissus image is the wish transported to a distance. The vicissitudes that occur during the movement to the differentiated object phase are the theme of this paper. Externalization mediates this progression. Let us first sketch the third phase and then return to the dynamic work that *either* makes separation possible *or* develops an ego that can manage without separation (at a price).

3. In the third or *differentiated object* stage of ego development, distancing gives way to self-other separation. Externalization gives way to techniques of reality testing that extend beyond the wish to negotiations with what is objectively available.

How does this take place?

DISTANCING AND SEPARATION AND LEARNING

The movement through the first two phases described above and toward the third can be elaborated in terms of the Narcissus analogy. Distancing and separation progress as the work of these three phases of ego development proceeds.

The beginning differentiation of self and not-self is first experienced by *distancing an as-if separate self*. Distancing precedes true separation. It precedes the cathexis of other human and nonhuman realities beyond one's self-control (Searles, 1960). But allowing the image of the nipple to become actually discontinuous is necessary before it is possible to be fed by another: *only as separation takes place does one receive milk that is not a function of one's own narcissistic creation*.

The mother uses her relationship to help the child from distancing toward separation. She cathects the child's beginning capacity for communication. As the child's wish ceases to be the only control, knowledge of the environment becomes useful. The aim now elaborates its object as learning extends beyond the wish to include what was not known and so not wished for—the unexpected.

Mother and child at first communicate by such simple expedients as responsiveness to timing. A full breast at a time when the infant is not hungry is an unexpected intrusion. The existent breast presented just at the moment when tension is not quite high enough to bring a preoccupying wish can induce a more neutral wish to feed.[15] The mother keeps moving just enough, first within, then beyond, the child's expectation, to make him aware of herself as another who, in fact, can supply his wishes even before his own attention has been turned to them. There is a critical timing (which most mothers sense) that allows her to move close enough to catch the child's narcissistic interest even as it makes him stretch to learn her separateness. This learning facilitates separation, which in turn enhances learning. The physiological communication loop mother-child is not cut with the cord—it is gradually altered as new forms of communication are patterned[16] and, being self-reinforcing, grow.

The same loop extends to basic emotional learning.[17] This learning builds upon the child's responsive imitation of the parent, who imitates in return. This imitation process takes place largely outside

[15] The term "exocrine" (cf. endocrine) has been used in the literature to emphasize the physiological nature of this process, which is only gradually lifted to more abstract, nonverbal and verbal coding.

[16] Just enough randomness consolidates the developing pattern as the child's own solution to his problem of prediction. There are critical points at which just the right amount of background noise (confusion) makes the message (pattern) stand out. In the degree to which mother becomes predictable, she begins to take form.

[17] Even early emotions are experienced differently in different cultures and so must enter the learning pattern (Bateson and Mead, 1942).

awareness and is exemplified by the change in a mother's gesture when she is near her baby. This change is just enough more than an imitation to build more differentiated learning. As the child imitates the body attitudes and muscle-tension patterns of his siblings and parents, he experiences nonverbally the emotions that these imitations evoke in him. He begins to match these subtleties of emotional expression to his own more physiological experience and to pattern a common code of emotional language long before he learns the common code of words. He thus physically incorporates within him a pattern of himself and the other that he seeks at first to control. He approximates these behavioral patterns to fit his imitation of the other to what he feels. As he imitates with his own behavior he predicts what his learned behavior will bring as response. Separation is made possible by accurate prediction. His crying is no longer always an expression of crude unpleasure. He is more able to communicate his own person, that is, to communicate himself as an object. He is said by the parents to have become a little person. This learning development builds upon the use of aggressive and libidinal energies in the service of the ego.

DEVELOPMENTAL LEARNING

Wishing, learning, discovering, testing—these are words for simultaneous aspects[18] of the expenditure of energy for the purpose of working out a pattern called normal development. Developmental learning and teaching are so fundamental to the progression to and within the third phase that they require too much data exchange to be managed in awareness. A child is taught with every breath and glance.

As the child progressively develops, he learns to signal his changing need for vital attention with increasing specificity. As his learning grows, his energies and concern can be devoted to issues less vital than learning for immediate survival. He turns his energies from serious concerns to curiosity and play.

The child's skill in recognizing change requires learning a mode of reality testing that recognizes the unexpected and then reduces

[18] By learning I do not necessarily mean "good" learning. Altered ego development that may lead toward psychosis is also learned.

the fear of unexpected experiences arising both from within and from outside his *Umwelt.*

The mode of reality testing learned as an aspect of object relationship can appropriately be called the object mode. It stands in contradistinction to the image mode, which is characteristic of the first and second phases. The image mode, described above, is an aspect of the preobject forms of relationship. As will be seen later, both object and image techniques of reality testing persist. In some families, however, the children are taught by their family experience to use the image mode predominantly. The way a child learns how to learn is different from one family to another, depending on the degree to which externalization is built into the family structure.

Using the object mode of reality testing characteristic of the third phase, the child continually redesigns the inner expectation in terms of objects observed to exist substantially. Exploring behavior no longer has as its sole purpose the finding of a new way to gain satisfaction of the feeding-fed need. The jump from instinctual wish to perceiving more of what actually happens is reduced by this learning design; much more can be experienced as this integration expands. This is an open learning system. The remnants of unintegrated inner wish and awareness of satisfactions available if one wished are used as memory, fantasy, and the idea of what might be. The omnipotent continuousness with the distanced feeding image begins to be replaced by skills, knowledge, and confidence that life support can be separate yet will not fail. The term "organismic terror" may be used to describe the fear of *prematurely* losing (without replacement) the unseparated continuousness reminiscent of life within the life-giving mother. Energy from this period may serve to reinforce later fears of mutilation.

The mother who knows her child is able to *titrate the experience of their separation, conforming with his wish just enough to allow the distancing of his wish to neutralize his fear of abandonment. This conforming is more than just satisfying—it is more than meeting his expectation. It is a part of teaching him to learn. She gauges his tension level so that overwhelming unpleasure will not interfere with the tender growth of investment in a separate outside world.* She introduces him to the unexpected. The child's actual and immediate behavior, particularly as it is then also unexpected, is used by the mother to correct her own predictive patterns based on previous responses. As mother tunes into his developmental learning, the child is gradually weaned from the power of his own expectation. His world broadens to include more that is unknown. The child becomes an explorer.

PARENT-TO-CHILD OBJECT RELATIONSHIP

The mother's capacity for object relationship to the child is one medium within which the abandonment-separateness conflict of the child's first extra-uterine attachment is solved. The mother purposively relates herself to the child's tension system as expressed by his spontaneous action and by his actional response to her intervention. She uses the behavior that she did not predict to correct her responses as well as to search out those unexpected messages he sends that indicate his rhythmic and continuous changing. She critically moves between responding just as he would like and introducing and responding to variations that will build new patterns. Mother and child come to know each other with a depth that allows more precise information exchange. Her image of him is constantly reformed in terms of his unique responses. She feels him with her body imitation, without losing her own identity. The mother learns to know the child in a way that the father cannot easily understand. She experiences a closeness that goes beyond receiving back what she has given. The mother's gratification is from outside her sphere. Her *Umwelt* is enlarged, as is the child's, by their shared experience.[19]

With skillful sensitivity developed out of objective awareness of the child's communication, the mother further alters congruence with his immediate internal demand by substituting a comforting acknowledgment. By her responsive action she rewards the child's developing skill at patterning a communicative action code and, later, symbolization. She reinforces growth by acknowledging slight change in the direction of maturation. The excellence of this preverbal teaching sets a foundation for integrated use of inner drive in behavior. The child's energy is acknowledged.

---

[19] The need for father to be a person who can also make contact is evident, particularly as mother changes with the birth of each child.

The mother teaches communication. As distancing is replaced by separation, communication maintains contact.[20]

At first, with hypercathected listening, mother leaves other interests to come to her child with his food. She responds at first to the unintentional, and then she increasingly demands more intentional signals of discomfort. As each more distant communication succeeds,[21] the child lets slip the milk supply hallucinated as immediate, breast-in-mouth, and flesh-continuous. Mouth, impulse, and wish are patterned in the context of a feeding and teaching nipple at first continuous with the wish, then a little separated, now timed as if controlled by the wish, then gently moving outside the child's wish and performing the pleasantly unexpected—and the child learns. As the child learns *this* kind of reality, the hallucinated wish or image is decathected. It remains as the precursor of imagination and of the mental representation process. The capacity to omit the unexpected is likewise decathected as the fear of abandonment is reduced. The beginnings of fantasy work develop as the child comforts himself by limiting his attention to the mother's tension-relieving and functional presence even as he perceives that she has left the room. She knows his needs by her accurate prediction, which is based on last-minute information; each distancing step of a mother who carries with her an accurate image of her child brings renewed confidence for both.[22] She knows when he needs her. He responds. He is comforted and enjoys his verified imagination-wish that she is still present: *now separate but within responsive communicative distance.* This is the togetherness of the tender experience.

As the child allows distance and separation to proceed, that which floods his body with sensation does not flood his total world. He begins to organize and structure tension into attention.

---

[20] I have elsewhere (1962) discussed the difficulties arising out of a sensitive mother's inability to be aware of her blind child's natural development, which is different from her own.

[21] The psychological delivery from the mother's body image is not as precipitous as the birth process. The channels for communication are hypercathected at first by the secondary narcissism of pregnancy, which, a few days after delivery, moves out to cathect the newborn as an outside object. The newborn draws this upon himself by his unintentional activity and, being outstandingly different from the mother's internal image, gains her cathexis as an object.

[22] Unfortunately timed absences, such as hospitalization, during this period can prolong this process (Bowlby, 1951).

As he attends to his mother as an objective other, he is more able to send signals to her according to her response; his signals then become more specific, rendering her awareness of his specific needs and his specific individuality less difficult. Receiving his more intentional communication, she can relate to him more objectively. And so the interpersonal dialogue grows.

His tension system becomes progressively neutralized by a broader percept. This percept is progressively organized and refined as the child is thus taught to learn by using the object mode of reality testing (Hartmann, 1939).

As the mother becomes less the wordless, undifferentiated rage-gratification of the first stage of ego development and less the feeding mother of the second period, she comes to exist beyond the mothering function. In the latter part of the third phase, she is an existing person, attended by the child even as her behavior is totally unrelated and neutral to the child's own expectation.[23] Awareness of incongruity, of absurdity in terms of previous expectation, sows the seeds of growth and change. The child laughs with pleasure as he explores.

The object mode of reality testing operationally defines the *object relationship*. In the object relationship, the inner image of the object is constantly being redesigned to fit with the experience of the existing other: *unexpected experiences are utilized for their corrective potential, broadening the relationship.*

When the mother cathects the child with object libido, the child is actively taught by her example and learns the object mode of reality testing. The control gained reduces externalization and makes possible the separation necessary for further growth of the object relationship.

PARENT-TO-CHILD IMAGE RELATIONSHIP

Parents who have not resolved their own earliest fear of abandonment and who themselves have not gone beyond the function stage of ego development cathect their child as a distanced part of themselves, *not* as a separate other (Burlingham, 1935).

---

[23] The analyst and patient may experience each other more and more in this manner toward the end of therapy.

Consider again Narcissus and his reflection: the not-self that is set at a distance for relationship exists only as a *relocation of a part* of "I." The reflected image of Narcissus has no separate existence. It is perceived outside of the self but is continuous with the self; *it owes its existence to the primary self image rather than to the transfer*[24] *of energy to the perception* (or misperception) of an existent other. The existent child is not libidinized. He is responded to by his mother as an *as-if* child—that is, responded to *only* when he validates his mother's projection. It is the experience of existence itself that is altered by the narcissistic relationship. This is at the heart of the intensity of the relationship.

The image relationship of this parent to the child, well known clinically, is poignantly described in Milton's poem:

> . . . I started back,
> It started back, but pleasd I soon returnd,
> Pleas'd it returnd as soon with answering looks
> Of sympathie and love, there I had fixt
> Mine eyes till now, and pin'd with vain desire . . . .

The image in the pool, having no separate existence, is wholly governed by expectation and can never be spontaneous. It can give nothing.[25] The relationship will be reported to be intensely interpersonal, but it is an *as-if* relationship nonetheless. *When, like Narcissus, a distanced self reflection is cathected as an existent other, this is delusion* (Deutsch, 1934). The narcissistic parent, trained to validate delusions from childhood, may so skillfully cover them that the process is not socially apparent. The altered ego development that has as its primary skill manipulating reality to conform to expectation is most evident when it is in the process of decompensation.

The following clinical illustration describes the regression of a mother's relationship to her child as her effort to validate her delusion breaks down. The mother fails in her effort to protect herself from psychosis by distancing her hypochondriacal preoccupation onto her child. Her validation of this distancing breaks down when her

---

24 Anna Freud (1960) has pointed out that a true transference requires some modicum of object relationship.

25 The child therapist knows the emotion that one experiences when one sees parents who relate in this way to their child. This makes the work with ego-disordered children technically more difficult. The child patterned to the mother's image expectations will not easily relate to a therapist who rejects these.

child is put (through her husband's efforts) in a situation where he is diagnosed as healthy. This story will not be unfamiliar—it caricatures a common clinical theme.

Mrs. Compton complained that she was afraid something dreadful was happening to her five-month-old boy. "He cannot burp," she said. As she proceeded to tell her story, the pediatrician became aware that too much energy was invested in this symptom. He was alerted by the mother's fixed belief in the child's symptom and by her urgent need to prove *her* diagnosis that the child was sick. The over-all picture indicated that it was the mother who was ill—moving rapidly into a psychotic episode.

Observed playing with her child, Mrs. Compton appeared aware only of those movements in the child that she herself had initiated. If he smiled in response to her smile or chuckling, the mother responded; if he smiled of his own accord, she was entirely unresponsive. Although desperately and completely focused on "the child," she was obtusely unaware of his autonomous smile; its presence did not even alter the rhythm or timing of her frantic efforts to *make* him smile. Time was a function of her inner feeling—thus her urgency. Her movements were awkwardly out of touch with his; her muscles could not conform to his natural postures in a relevant movement. He was held like a doll. Her teaching was quite unlike that of an ordinary mother.

Using the construct previously discussed, we would say that Mrs. Compton was relating to the infant within her, now distanced. Her system of logic made reasonable her inner determined expectation. She was blind and deaf to the noncongruent objective experiences. She could not discover her child as he existed.[26] What she perceived and organized into meaning led her to the conclusions that brought her to the pediatrician: "Since I have not seen him burp, he did not burp; he must be full of gas." She did not see the child's healthy appearance; the energy available for observation was devoted to her wish. Her hypersensitive ear listened only in order to match anticipation.

In the narcissistic predicament, the therapist of a child who has

[26] Hoffer (1952) discusses the importance of the negative hallucination that raises the physiological threshold of stimulation. He states: "Negative hallucination means that stimulus does not reach the sensory system." The existing child is not perceived by the mother's sensory apparatus and so does not exist within her *Umwelt*.

begun to improve knows the danger—the child will be withdrawn from treatment if his illness does not continue to externalize the parents' conflict. The experienced therapist uses the parents' anxiety about the child's improvement as a diagnostic criterion. He knows that this is pathognomonic of the narcissistic process.

Mrs. Compton's pediatrician knew the pattern. She had been taken by her husband to a children's hospital where psychiatric consultation was quickly available. The pediatrician called the psychiatrist for the mother, although he was aware that the mother had diagnosed the symptom as being located in the child.

The child was hospitalized for two days. On the third day the pediatrician (against the psychiatrist's advice) insisted to the mother that the baby was completely well. She was sure that he was wrong; but she shifted her preoccupation. She relocated her concern to her knees, claiming that the extreme pain had begun when she knelt down to feed the baby. Several days later she disappeared. She was located by the police in a neighboring town where her mother lived. Mrs. Compton was found lying curled in her absent mother's bed— stuperous and overtly psychotic.

Like the reflection of Narcissus in the pool, this parent's child existed for her only as a distanced part of herself, a projected image, a *hypochondriacal delusion* that fixed her vision so that she was unaware of his objective existence. Her wish-expectation energized and directed the image that she libidinized as an outside *as-if* object —her existent child. The child within, now distanced but not separate, could give nothing to her from outside herself, though her need was desperate.

What if mother had not become overtly psychotic, thereby signaling her disorder and allowing others to take over? What is the effect of such a delusion if it is chronically superimposed on a real but vulnerable existent child? Had the tension in the mother-child relationship produced a severe feeding disorder and verified the mother's projection, her internal conflict would have been perceived as between her (feeder) and her child (feeding) or as a problem exclusively within the child.[27]

[27] If the child later developed anorexia nervosa, the mother's psychosis would have been successfully transmitted, and the mother's preoccupation would be completely verified. The mother then would not socially be called psychotic.

The child who must conform to expectation to prevent severe psychological decompensation in the parents validates his early megalomanic and unbounded expectation that his behavior determines the existence of the world.

By validating or not validating the parents' projection, the child does hold power. Skill in using this power is one factor in the intensity of relationship that facilitates manipulation by the child and by the parents—they care so much. This kind of caring by parent and child is different from the kind in the object relationship. It is the caring of the infant in the second stage of ego development, whose functional aim is unmodified by belief in the existence of a separated object.

The clinical statement of this theoretical construct is simple and heart-rending to the clinician. We know it as pathognomonic of severe ego disturbance. "I live for him." "He couldn't live without me." "I feel his pain and joys." "He has become such a problem. I can think of nothing else." Or, in Milton's words:

> . . . there I had fixt
> Mine eyes till now, and pin'd with vain desire . . . .

Like a butterfly pinned to its own picture the child must conform to his parents' images. Nonconforming behavior is punished by real or threatened abandonment. If the child initiates nonmirroring, spontaneous action, he produces disturbing ripples on the pool, and the Narcissus image is confused. Mother experiences separation anxiety, she clutches her own image, she withdraws from such object relationship as does exist,[28] and her delusion becomes more intense and frightening to the child.[29]

ABANDONMENT AND LEARNING

For the child, the mother's deafness and blindness to his spontaneous, noncongruent behavior verify his terror of abandonment.

---

[28] The father at this time may become intensely jealous of the attention given "the child" and may attack the mother as he accepts her image, or, as his anxiety mounts, he may become depressed and suffer a decrease in his own capacity to relate with an object relationship, thus reducing the possibility of the child's escape from the narcissistic system.

[29] In later analysis she may be conceptualized as a crazy witch.

He disappears from her *Umwelt* when he does not conform to her expectation. Searching only for what she expects, she cannot find the existent child.[30] He must validate or he cannot gather to himself the distanced narcissistic libido that gives him a pattern within her differentiated aim-energy system, which operates without true objects. The child maintains his more primitive control—the hallucinated breast—as long as his pattern of hunger conforms to the mother's. The sensitive mediation necessary for teaching the infant how to learn objective reality testing and skillful communication is gone. The child may help the mother learn to go beyond her narcissism if he can get through.

The mother feeds the child when the child within her is hungry (or lonely). Mother's time is organized as a function of her tension. The child's time pattern and the mother's are not responsive to each other. To the mother, past behavior of the child is experienced as in the present. Serious long-term concerns—for example, about the child's problem—leave no room for the mother's timely curiosity and playful delight in momentary behavior. The child's necessity is patterned into an *as-if* necessity, designed from her wish. Mother relates to the way the child should feel and manipulates the child to conform with her aims, not his. Mother's externalization remains to conflict with the child's. There is no delicate learning of the kind that the child of the object-relating mother has. He is induced into retaining the system of learning natural to the preobject stage of ego development.

For the child, externalization does not mediate the conflict between separation and abandonment. Instead, his fears are made real. The second or functional stage of ego development remains the organizing force. The person who feeds continues to exist only as feeder-nonfeeder. The image mode of reality testing is taught, and the child's ego development is altered. It is not surprising that the parents' unresolved conflicts at this level interfere with the child's natural progression through the same stage.

---

30 As I have stated (1959), the way a particular child and his temporal circumstances match the externalized projection as well as the presence of object-relating others determines the effectiveness with which parents teach the child to follow in their footsteps.

The Unseparated Image

The clinician is familiar with the situation in which the child is omitted except as a maternal tension releaser. In the evaluation interview, the child is described by the mother only in terms of how well or how poorly he does his job of developing "for her." Mother does not recognize that she has trained the child to fulfill her expectation.

The child's development is basically altered, but mother has skill in manipulating a context that will make reasonable the developmental lag. She may use a physician or a book or an "unfailing" sense of intuition or a birth injury or an early illness to make natural the child's peculiarities.

Eating habits not based on one's own hunger are more likely to be peculiar. His period of waiting (for mother's action) has been randomly related to the child's own hunger. His stomach patterns, as they change from day to day, are irrelevant[31] to the pattern set by his training. He will not be fed except when the mother feels he should be hungry (when she herself feels inner hunger). He literally eats "for her."

And mother feeds her own distanced image of her as-if child. If the child conforms, the process of building a pseudo ego is begun. The clinician will recognize this kind of pattern. It is usually covered by the presentation of peculiar but valid hyperrealistic explanations.

The mother and child do not grow a living communication system that they can share and use for developmental work. This situation is not symbiotic in the spirit of that word: sym, together, and bios, life. This is more akin to death: the child the mother nurtures does not exist. The existent child feeds off her projected image, set before his birth. This child exists as a supposed-to-be, a masquerade, an image. He is split off from himself.[32]

---

[31] The word "irrelevant" is used in distinction to "opposing the child's pattern," which implies objective recognition.

[32] In the Schreber case, Freud (1911) refers to Schreber's use of the term "soul murder." This is an epithet that catches the feeling of this process.

Splitting and Altered Ego Development

Only those aspects of the child's inner environment congruent with his mother's cathected hallucination will be organized into his percepts and refined into culturally ordered ways of expression.[33] The pseudo ego is that organization which validates the parental projection. It is cathected by energy that aims to prevent abandonment and the threat of its own dissolution.

The movement from first to second stage of ego development will be limited to those energies acknowledged by the mother's responsive patterning. The energies of the existent child irrelevant to the experience acknowledged by the mother as the *Umwelt* of the child are not organized by contact with parental relationship. They remain random, unorganized, and split off from the pseudo personality, which is structured to match either negatively or positively the parents' projection. Information that enlarges the *Umwelt* of the child is supplied only as it makes logical the manipulation. The child's reality and his mode of organizing reality are altered. This is the path into which the child is forced. An identity grows that is unsupported from within. The process of externalization verifies this pseudo identity, this *as-if* total person.

The child is taught by his experience to learn (Bateson, 1942) to give preference to his (i.e., mother's) inner expectation. To prevent abandonment he learns to manipulate this reality to validate his (i.e., her) wish. He omits from cathexis what is not congruent. His instinctual energies are not patterned by acknowledging experience into sublimated skills and objective learning (Hartmann, 1939). One part of his energy is used to keep reasonable the *Umwelt* he knows. The remainder is untouched by ego work: it is a vague, intense fear, a sense of inner wildness, which is used to fortify the need to hold onto the defenses. The inner wildness—a remnant of the first stage of ego development—is not a source of information about the unexpected self.

---

33 The objective parents' responsive echoing and selecting for response also teaches the child not to use those sounds and movements which are not a part of the natural language of the parents. Inept and unresponsive selection increases the socially peculiar. This is different from inner-supported and broadly integrated originality. The peculiarity is not acknowledged by the pseudo ego.

The identity that is conceived is not continuously reworked. The meaning of any newness that seeps in is retranslated to fit the closed system. Sensations from within or responses from outside that would make the pseudo identity an obvious fiction are not skillfully received. They do not refine the image of the self according to the rules of the object mode of reality testing. As the unexpected and the absurd are increasingly omitted, the self becomes a concrete abstraction. Self becomes a single symbol or role that the child's life verifies.[34]

This pseudo identity is self-generating. Being seen as sickly by others, the child is not asked to use his muscles. He does become sickly as he is told that he must take care not to become sick (as is expected). He grows to be inexpert with his body. This is a self-reinforcing and progressively constricting process.

Even when mother is more able to use the object mode of relationship to her child, she will not be acknowledged: the child has learned to attend only to that which fits the earlier formed projected expectations. Ego energy exists only in the service of validating the expected tautology. Inertia in a closed system is high.

Ego libido does not become object libido. Instead, it invades the object world, working to keep the (mother's-child's) unbounded megalomanic or hypochondriacal delusions appropriately verified. This becomes the work of the ego that has no true object relations. The ego operations become hypercathected to a preoccupation—in a hypochondriacal way.[35]

There develops a hyperrealism which, unbounded, encompasses a world unmodified by fantasy or humor or awareness of multiple points of view.[36] When hyperrealism fails, perplexity develops.

The continued energizing of this altered reality testing alters the ego structure. Escape is easier when the child is in proximity to others who are not caught up in the network. Marriages based on

[34] The family drama enacted by the families observed in the hospital setting (Brodey, 1959) may be likened to a morality play, each family member becoming the embodiment of a dramatic role.

[35] "An internal cathexis could only have the same value as an external one if it were maintained unceasingly, as in fact occurs in hallucinatory psychoses and in hunger phantasies, which exhaust their whole psychical activity in clinging to the object of their wish" (Freud, 1900, p. 566).

[36] Again the reader will be reminded of the symptomatic fear of world destruction when the hold on reality of such persons is threatened.

this way of life propagate ego disorder and, in the extreme, psychosis. The process becomes more extreme as it passes from generation to generation of families organized around externalization as a way of life.

MUTUAL EXTERNALIZATION

The family who is unable to find a way out uses its energy[37] for what the scientist would call "starting with the answer." Energy is not used for discovering a more detailed and accurate image of self, other family members, or society. The family's hyperrealism has the neatness of a cultist's certainty—"the nonbelievers purposely cause that which does not fit the expectation."

The family caught in this way of life is not unfamiliar to the clinician. The whole family together reads a repetitious script—each validating the other's projected wish. The family's acknowledged reality is more rational and stable than life can be—until it breaks down. This is clinically familiar especially to those who have experienced the family with a schizophrenic member; it is also seen in other common ego disorders.

To this point I have spoken of the narcissistic process as the projection of the total wish. Projection is more commonly a means of distancing conflicting parts of self. These are reified in the process of mutual externalization. They are stereotyped into part images seen as distanced from each other. Each of the family members gathers to himself parts of the others, which he constructs into a single stereotype or role. These roles, then, are crudely concrete and hypercathected. Often mutually contradictory, they are used as though they included all data. Though reasonable within the world that the family defines, they provide the clinician with a psychological caricature.

This family tautology, together with the work needed to maintain it, is an identifying feature of the family held together by the narcissistic way of life. As the clinician is aware, it is the capacity to verify each other's projection that cements the narcissistic marriage; this gives it the stability that perpetuates its teachings. The

---

37 This use of energy is a characteristic of the externalizing family, but is here being diagramed in terms of the mother-child relationship.

matching roles, like master and slave, are intensely related to each other and cannot exist apart without the terror of dissolution-abandonment.

NARCISSISTIC INTENSITY AND ABANDONMENT

Terror of abandonment and the intensity of narcissistic relationship must both combine to train the child of such a marriage to an altered ego development.

The child from birth is allowed to face abandonment and rejection in terms of his needs while he is simultaneously coddled because his *as-if* screaming is a validation of what his mother thinks he ought to be crying about. She acts on these suppositions, not seeing or hearing their effect.

Unwittingly, the conflict of no-separation-without-abandonment is *used* to transmit the terror of abandonment. When the mother of the preobject-level child is absent, she no longer exists to the child. The mother who is capable of object relationships does not allow this abandonment to reach beyond the child's toleration—she does not allow him to become so overwhelmed that he disorganizes. The preobject mother, when she leaves the child, may literally be unaware that he is not with her. Existence is threatened by even brief separation from each other in a family joined by narcissistic grasping.

Terror is behaviorally transmitted in the family. This terror of separation is congruent with the mother's expectation learned from her own early experience. The mother's anticipation is now projected and validated by the child, and mother handles her terrors as existing all within her *as-if* child. The narcissistic intensity is a part of this process.

Terror of abandonment must be trained into the child if he is to develop the modes of ego functioning found in severe ego disturbance. A child who is only abandoned or rejected without at the same time being bathed in the intensity of narcissistic relationship develops a different variety of disorder.

The narcissistic intensity and its corollary abandonment become an important prototype. The child's mode of structuring experience parallels this intrapsychic organization. It is repeatedly reinforced—reaching out to discover the unknown is penalized; fear of separation is extreme in the child who is specifically trained *not* to find his way beyond the family circle. The struggle is to hold onto what is known. Nothing must be lost or abandoned except by *complete* loss of cathexis. There is no mobility in these relationships—one is either continuous or abandoned.[38] Under extreme stress, the experience of reality itself may be suddenly lost in this way.

THE IMAGE MODE OF REALITY TESTING

All symbolizing and abstraction require the loss of information. One cannot see or hear everything. There is always that which remains to become known if one can change one's vantage point. In the image mode of relationship this loss is denied. The world is the product of one's own conduct. It is held rigid, concrete, as though one's point of view was the only one. The world does not grow except as expected. Time is denied and stretched and used to manipulate. Other persons' time is not acknowledged. Life is confused with its words. What is learned is not integrated in an ever-expanding reworking of new sensory and labeled experiences (Luria, 1959). Knowledge does not integrate to wisdom.

Reality testing is always taught in the context of the family of significant others. Its prototype is the reality testing that is the most predictive of the infant-parent relationship. The skill necessary to the image mode of reality testing is skill in manipulating the world to fulfill conclusions.

This skill can grow best if not paralleled by skill in the object mode of reality testing. This may be taught concurrently by the other parent or siblings, or by the nursemaid or family friends.[39] Both these modes can coexist and have their functions.

The two techniques of reality testing having been described, it must now be stated that it is the quantitative matching of each that is important.

The image mode of reality testing is useful in proper proportion.

38 The storminess of such relationships is well known to the analyst.

39 The heterogeneous family, where externalization of one family member is managed objectively by another, will be discussed in future reports. Coexistent concepts of reality, formed by these two modes of reality testing, may sharply shift their balance as their relative cathexis is altered by the expectation of an explorative or restrictive environment.

It carries continuity with the past, organizing the future in terms of the past. The object mode is important to the discovery of what was not expected. The object mode is more important in a time of rapid change when the capacity to contact change is the only stability.

The extreme form of each mode of reality testing is problematic. These extremes sometimes seem confusingly similar. But the "creative person's" periods of vague ambiguity, when he has taken in more data than he can cope with, are quite different from the ego-disturbed person's explosion from restricted pseudo identity into periods of perplexed confusion.

The fantasy life of a person using the image mode is different from that of a person using the object mode. In the image mode, fantasy is more available and less diffusely cathected. It is not richly developed. Imagination and the dream are replaced[40] by selecting and manipulating reality so that the dream is validated by the reality that is attended. Even the dream is used as a way of validating what was expected. Its content has no novelty or freshness. Thus, in the image mode of reality testing, fantasy *does not* provide a means of exploring what seems irrelevantly fantastic. The dream is subverted, for its wish is a reality prediction. Ego work turns manifest reality into the reification of what, in the neurotic, would be the latent wish. Those who have experienced working with a severely ego-disturbed family that uses the image mode will know the horror of seeing this happen. What one expects to be in the unconscious is validated into a superrationality, which has, to the observer, the feeling of a dream.

THE NARCISSISTIC RELATIONSHIP

The narcissistic relationship is a reciprocal image relationship between two or more people who join in externalizing each other's projections. They marry a person with the ego-dystonic aspect of their conflicts. They are attracted because the narcissistic intensity is released with another who conforms to the projected expectation.

---

40 In the borderline families being described, the life situations that the clinician first believes to be delusional are often found to be actual events. The sense of horror that may develop in the clinician is much like that experienced in having a nightmare.

This may seem too simple, but the world *is* simplified by the image mode of reality testing. The husband and wife and then the children have a restricted reality, built to join conflicts unmodified by a richness of integrated experience. The hyperrationalism of each is displayed in the repetitious logic of their way of life. They care more about who is "right" than about what happens—to a bizarre degree (Brodey, 1959).

The narcissistic family cannot see the fallacy intrinsic in the fact that their logic works too well. The family lives in a narrow corridor of reality that they manufacture for each other to share. The reasonableness of the reality goes far beyond what ordinary reality can produce, but then—their reality is made to order. The energy normally available for free exploration is sapped by this process. Explorations beyond the family corridor of accepted reality are not admitted to any response from the other family member, except as they undergo reduction to the usual family metaphor.

Escape from these operations of the narcissistic system of multiple pseudo relationships becomes more difficult as the reciprocities and stereotypes become more exacting and the exploratory action of the family becomes increasingly closed, allowing less and less incongruity with their predetermined reality.

SUMMARY

The observation of families has led to some questions that may elucidate the dynamics of the developmental work necessary for passing beyond the stage of primary narcissism. Family observation provides a point of view which directs attention to this work as a family function. The conceptualization presented has grown out of observing many kinds of families. This concept is used in describing the organization of families in which the preobject mode of relationship is a primary way of life. A family system of behavioral transmission of this way of life is proposed. Continued exploration of this area holds promise of revealing pertinent information about the ways children in ordinary circumstances are taught to learn.

BIBLIOGRAPHY

Bateson, G. (1942), *Social Planning and the Concept of "Deutero Learning."* New York: Harper.
—— & Mead, M. (1942), *Balinese Character: A Photographic Analysis.* New York: Academy of Science.
Bowlby, J. (1951), *Maternal Child Care and Mental Health.* Geneva: World Health Organization Monogr. 2.
Brodey, W. (1959), Some Family Operations and Schizophrenia. *A.M.A. Arch. Gen. Psychiat.*, 1:317-402.
—— (1961), Image, Object and Narcissistic Relationships. *Amer. Orthopsychiat.*, 31:69-73.
—— (1962), Normal Developmental Learning and the Education of the Child Born Blind. *Gifted Child Quart.*, 6:141-149.
Bruch, H. (1945), Psychosomatic Approach to Childhood Disorders. In: *Modern Trends in Child Psychiatry*, ed. N. D. C. Lewis & B. L. Pacella. New York: International Universities Press.
Burlingham, D. T. (1935), Die Einfühlung des Kleinkindes in die Mutter. *Imago*, 21:429-444.
Deutsch, H. (1934), Some Forms of Emotional Disturbance and Their Relationship to Schizophrenia. *Psa. Quart.*, 11:301-321, 1942.
Freud, A. (1960), Four Contributions to the Psychoanalytic Study of the Child. Papers delivered in New York.
Freud, S. (1900), The Interpretation of Dreams. *Standard Edition*, 4 & 5. London: Hogarth Press, 1953.
—— (1911), Psycho-Analytic Notes upon an Autobiographical Account of a Case of Paranoia. *Collected Papers*, 3:387-470. London: Hogarth Press, 1925.
—— (1914), On Narcissism: An Introduction. *Standard Edition*, 14:67-102. London: Hogarth Press, 1957.
—— (1915), Instincts and Their Vicissitudes. *Standard Edition*, 14:105-140. London: Hogarth Press, 1957.
—— (1940), *An Outline of Psychoanalysis.* New York: Norton, 1949.
Hartmann, H. (1939), *Ego Psychology and the Problem of Adaptation.* New York: International Universities Press, 1958.
Hoffer, W. (1952), The Mutual Influences in the Development of Ego and Id: Earliest Stages. *This Annual*, 7:31-41.
Luria, A. (1959), *The Role of Speech in the Regulation of Normal and Abnormal Behavior.* New York: Pergamon, 1961.
Rosenblueth, A., Wiener, N., & Bigelow, J. (1943), Behaviour, Purpose and Teleology. *Phil. Sci.*, 10:18-24.
Searles, H. F. (1960), *The Nonhuman Environment.* New York: International Universities Press.
—— (1963), Transference Psychosis in the Psychotherapy of Chronic Schizophrenia. *Int. J. Psa.*, 44:249-281.
von Uexküll, J. (1934), A Stroll through the Worlds of Animals and Men. In: *Instinctive Behavior*, tr. & ed. C. H. Schiller. New York: International Universities Press, 1957, pp. 5-80.

SOME PROBLEMS OF EGO DEVELOPMENT IN BLIND CHILDREN

DOROTHY BURLINGHAM (London)

When blind children are compared with their seeing contemporaries with regard to their development (A. Freud, 1963), the nature and range of their achievements tend to be underrated. Observers usually emphasize—as we have done in earlier papers (Burlingham, 1961; A.-M. Sandler, 1963)—the slow rate of forward moves after the first weeks of life; that blind infants need more than the usual stimulation from the mother to respond to her; that the acoustic and tactile sensations do not seem to have the same arousing effects (Greenacre, 1959) on the infant as the visual ones; that they do not impel him to reach out, do not excite his curiosity or, later, his urge to imitate in the same manner. Above all, the impression is created that in addition to the lack of vision itself, there is also the lack of stimulation which vision normally exercises on the other senses, i.e., a contributory or synthesizing factor without which the blind child cannot make full use of hearing, touch, etc. Among the children under our observation, it was not uncommon, especially among the backward ones, to find a second sense, usually touch, employed so little that for all practical purposes it had to be considered out of action.

Due to this general slowing up of progressive processes, it is easily overlooked how much ingenuity the blind child actually expends at every stage. A mother or nurse may use endless patience or may despair while trying to teach a blind child some simple task such as fetching a toy, tying a shoelace, stringing beads; she may

The work with blind children is part of the Educational Unit of the Hampstead Child-Therapy Course and Clinic and as such is maintained by the Grant Foundation, Inc., New York. The research work with the blind is assisted further by the National Institute of Mental Health, Bethesda, Maryland.

easily be oblivious to the fact that at the same time the blind child is busy attempting to master different experiences (Hendrick, 1943) through which he goes on his own and for which he receives neither acknowledgment nor praise.

For example, both normal and blind toddlers have the same awkwardness when learning to walk: they stumble, fall over obstacles or steps, have to hold on to keep balance, etc. With the aid of vision, however, this phase is overcome in a few weeks. Without it the blind find it a formidable task, dominating their childhood and extending through their entire lives.

Watching our blind chlidren, we cannot but be impressed by the variety of capabilities which they bring to bear on this task: they *remember* the position of stable fittings in their environment to avoid running into them; they *listen* acutely for sounds or echoes to tell them what has been moved from its accustomed place; they *take note* of sidewalks and fix them in their minds; later on they *count* steps; above all, they constantly control their desire for quick movement. While normal children learn about the dangers of fire, water, heights, guided by adults who have passed through the same experience in their own lives, the blind learn to protect themselves from harm in ways which are basically unfamiliar to their custodians and which are therefore not taken over by identification with them but acquired painfully, and independently, by methods of individual trial and error.

THE PROBLEM OF MOTOR RESTRAINT IN THE DEVELOPMENT OF THE BLIND

The Achievement of Motor Restraint

Once we have learned to understand that control of free movement is an essential mode of self-protection adopted by the blind, it also becomes easier to grasp the degree of determination and will power exerted by them from a very young age for intentionally closing a pathway which, under ordinary circumstances, constantly serves for discharge of the boundless energy which is present in the young and which, we may assume, normal blind children have in common with the seeing.

While the seeing child hops, skips, runs or jumps, is almost always in motion and is almost invariably discontent and irritable when made to sit quietly (for instance, at mealtimes) or to lie in bed (for instance, when ill), the blind child walks quietly and carefully, holding on to somebody's hand, picking his way attentively among obstacles. In the seeing child, thoughts and desires are short-circuited from moment to moment into one or the other form of action, while the blind child contains them in immobility. Throwing, hitting, kicking, which are all children's normal aggressive outlets, are automatically checked by the blind as too risky because without vision the consequences of such hostile acts cannot be assessed realistically and are overrated. While pupils in a normal nursery school are invariably active and spontaneously occupied, the children in the Nursery for the Blind, if not compelled otherwise, will sit, motorically idle, on the floor, in a corner, often with their heads on the table.

On the other hand, it is not difficult to demonstrate that both the motor impulses and the potential pleasure in motor discharge are present but are in fact rendered ineffective by the child's own control. As soon as conditions of absolute safety are provided, the blind child too will hop and jump eagerly (for example, on the trampoline), or run and dance (when held by the teacher's hands), or even ride a bicycle (in a cleared area). The child will gladly "let go" of his own controls as soon as he is fully confident that danger arising from motility is controlled by the environment.

That self-restraint of motor activity is responsible for much of the depression, boredom, lack of spontaneity which we have learned to equate with the notion of a blind child is borne out by the changes observed in our nursery school after such opportunities for free movement were introduced: formerly sober, pale, subdued, and restrained children acquired a sense of well-being, healthy pink cheeks, and glowing vitality. When for some reason attendance in nursery school ceases and activity is curtailed, the child adapts once more to the altered circumstances, returns to the former mastery of his desires and, with it, to his slow, sedate, deliberate, "dull" behavior.[1]

[1] In the "Sunshine Homes" and other residential schools for the blind, the need for muscular activity is fully recognized and much scope is given to it by means of climbing frames, bicycles, etc. See also Mittelmann (1957).

The Consequences of Motor Restraint

It is unfortunate for the blind children that a major achievement such as their sensible motor control has outwardly nothing but negative results. Immobilization is displaced from the motor area to other ego functions. The energies which are held off from their normal outlet into constructive activities flow backward and find expression in rhythmical movements, repetitiveness, and use of the musculature for other than active purposes. Since such regressions are characteristic of the mentally retarded, blind children are often classed with them even when their intelligence is basically normal.

Blindisms

A regressive intensification of *rhythmical* movement is observed also in seeing children whenever they are unduly deprived of free motility by parental restriction or are partially or wholly immobilized in illness or after surgical procedures. In the blind these rhythmical movements appear so regularly and extensively that they are regarded as characteristic behavior which is referred to as "blindisms." This term is used for their rocking, swaying from one foot to the other, waving of the arms, twisting and turning the body, all of which take place not only when the child is unoccupied but also as an interruption of any occupation.

Doubtless, these rhythmical activities serve a dual purpose for the blind: on the one hand, as in the seeing, as sexual, autoerotic practices with the whole body and especially the musculature used as a source of pleasure; on the other hand, as their special outlet for general energy blocked otherwise. Which of the two aspects of the matter begins first and gives rise to the other, or whether they appear simultaneously, merely strengthening each other, has not yet been determined and needs further study. What is obvious, however, is the enormous effort demanded from the blind child to suppress the blindisms, which are offensive to the seeing world and do as much as anything else to set the child apart from his seeing contemporaries. It is even more difficult for the blind child to suppress blindisms than it usually is for any individual to break with autoerotic habits or their substitutes such as thumb sucking, masturbation, nail biting, etc. No wonder, therefore, that they last far into the latency period and occasionally even through adolescence.

Repetitive Behavior

Repetition of specific actions serves the purpose of learning in all children and is normally given up when one particular activity has become thoroughly familiar and its performance mastered. Repetition of the familiar by the young is also known as a pleasure in itself, as shown by the demands to be told the same favorite story over and over again, in the same words, etc. Since in the absence of vision mastery of performance is delayed and familiarity acquired more slowly, repetitive behavior inevitably lasts for longer periods.

Quite apart from this persistence which is explained by slowed-up progression to a new function next on the program for mastery, repetition of familiar (and therefore safe) actions is adopted by the blind as a welcome motor discharge and, for this reason, adhered to tenaciously.

This particular characteristic brings with it its own special difficulties for the program in the Nursery School for the Blind. In the usual nursery schools for the sighted occupations are chosen to meet the children's insatiable curiosity and hunger for new experience, a method of selection which cannot in the same way apply to the blind since neither of the two incentives is available in them to the same degree. This leaves the teachers guessing. Left to their own devices, the children tend to "play safe" by repeating the familiar, such as opening and shutting doors, turning switches on and off, playing with the water faucets, letting water run over their hands, or filling and emptying containers, all of them actions suited to much younger children. Again, like much younger children, they cannot be coaxed away from repetition to constructive progress by a specific game or by offering them a toy; the achievement of this purpose has to rely on their personal attachment to the teaching adult. They do not progress without individual help and are at their best not in the group but alone with the teacher; in an individual person-to-person relationship they function surprisingly well.

Use of the Body for Nonactive Purposes

While blind children, apart from uncontrollable rhythmical movements, keep their bodies immobile much of the time, bodily sensations and perceptions and other than active body uses are of the greatest importance to them. In playing with insets, for example, body contact with the cup takes precedence over the purpose of fitting it into its appointed place. A child (Winnie, 3;6) may be seen, for instance, feeling the inset cups with her head, her forehead, her ears, her mouth, before placing them into each other; another one (Sammy, 4;8) puts the ring on his finger each time before placing it correctly on the pegboard. Altogether, the children are concentrating primarily on their inner bodily sensations, including those derived from sound and touch; cues should be picked up from those areas to lead them from such preoccupations to interest in the surrounding world. But such cues are not easy to pick up, and the seeing world must learn to be more alert to them.

The blind child uses his body and musculature further to express pleasure, again in a manner which is more appropriate for the toddler stage, before communication of affect is confined to facial expression (E. Kris, 1939). When pleased, our children jump up and down on the spot, clap their hands, etc. One boy makes a funny little hop whenever he succeeds in putting a peg into the right hole, following this with handclapping and the words, "I've done it." Another child, though completely underdeveloped, used to dance up and down with peculiar body movements and wave her arms frantically for no obvious reason; when, under guidance, progressive development was initiated, these body movements were restricted to the expression of pleasure after successful achievements or while hearing music to which she was extremely sensitive.

ORIENTATION AND RECOGNITION OF OBJECTS

For a lay person, the obvious way to judge a blind child's alertness is on the basis of his orientation in space and his ability to recognize objects in his environment; nevertheless, both proficiencies are complex ones and it is easy to go astray in their assessment.

One source of error is the fact that, for the sighted adult, orientation in space as well as object recognition are taken for granted. Therefore the blind child's successes in this respect are also taken for granted, even though they represent outstanding achievements in synthesizing the remaining senses with memory, judgment, and other ego functions; his failures, on the other hand, strike the observer forcibly since a blind child groping helplessly, searching for a door or a toy in the wrong direction with hands outstretched, is a pitiful and impressive sight.

Another difficulty in assessment is that the child's potential competence in orientation and his actual performance are often wide apart. Because of the very intricate interaction of functions which underlie it, the child's effective orientation depends not on his intelligence but on the equilibrium or disturbance of the state of his emotions. Any unexpected happening, any increase of stress, excitement or anxiety can overthrow the balance and result in complete lack of orientation.

Thirdly, successful orientation is as much a function of the desire for an object or of the wish to reach a certain place as it is an ego function.

Sammy (4;6), who otherwise gave no sign of being able to orient himself, could always find his way to the trampoline, which he loved.

July (6) was backward in all respects and was never able to locate a toy on the shelf. Yet she had no difficulty in finding a sweet in the same place.

Joan (7), usually slow to find her way, when she heard a child say to the teacher, "Let me turn the light on," rushed from the other side of the room and got there first to turn the switch.

If the desire is great enough, it seems that memory, concentration, and the ability to move combine quickly in order that the wish can be fulfilled.

As mentioned elsewhere (Burlingham, 1961) we often have occasion to observe the children's complete inability to locate a fallen toy. Again, we would be wrong to ascribe this to a basic incapacity. On the contrary, what impresses the observer at first sight as indifference, lack of attention, lack of understanding, etc., reveals itself on closer inspection as a complicated mixture of very different emotional attitudes: blind children hate to be reminded of their defect and their limited capacity, as they are in this situation. They realize that the sighted accomplish easily what is endless trouble for them and therefore "do not bother." They may even control the instinctive movements of their bodies toward the fallen object. Sometimes a stillness can be observed in them at such times, a holding of the breath in listening, a blankness of expression, but more often it is impossible to find a clue to the child's feelings.

On these occasions too it is not difficult to prove that this reaction is determined by control of feelings and not lack of intelligence. It becomes obvious later that the child has been fully aware of all the happenings and has stored them in his memory: where the fallen toy has rolled to, who has tried to retrieve it, whether a broom has been used to reach under the furniture, etc. Often, as soon as the child thinks himself alone, and if his desire for the lost object is great enough, he begins to use his intelligence and, taking things in his own hands, takes appropriate action.

The following example, taken from one of our highly developed blind children, illustrates clearly how intelligence, ambition, disappointment, a sense of failure and futility, anger, pent-up rage, etc., combine in the child and determine his behavior. It also shows how easily the whole turmoil of emotions is overlooked and the child's strenuously kept-up façade of indifference and lack of involvement taken at its face value.

Richard (4;10), using little wood blocks, had built a village with a street running down the middle, an attempt much praised by the teacher. The next day, while he was again playing with the blocks, he was pleased to find and recognize the church by the steeple. He then held up for verification an object which he called a tree. The teacher corrected him and told him its shape was like a tree but it was supposed to be a little man. A few seconds later this figure was dropped on the floor as if by accident, and soon all other objects not recognized by Richard found their way there as well. Encouragement to play as on the previous day was not accepted. Seeing him sit back idly in his chair, an adult in passing remarked how bored he looked, whereupon Richard promptly swept the remaining blocks and shapes from the table to the floor.

But even if, in this particular example, disappointment and stress had become too great to permit continuation of the action, there are many other occasions in the children's lives when frustration itself serves as a stimulation to thought, action, and further effort. In fact, closely observed, our blind children can be seen to be constantly involved in problem solving and they come up all the time with their own solutions, which are often bizarre enough—not unlike the bizarre sexual theories of infancy, which reflect a seeing child's attempt to answer questions that age-adequately are beyond his understanding.

VERBALIZATION AS A PROBLEM FOR THE BLIND

While speech comes naturally to the sighted child, in contact, communication, and identification with his first love objects, for blind children learning the language of the sighted is an intellectual feat, comparable in its formidableness to the other tasks of adaptation to a sighted world such as motor self-control, orientation in space, object recognition. The driving force behind the learning process is the wish to communicate and share experience with the object world, i.e., to arrive at mutual understanding, an ambition which is not always realized. Far from simplifying matters, learning to speak adds further problems to the blind child's life. To bridge the new gulf which opens up between him and the sighted world, the blind child once again has to take recourse to his own ingenuity and to use ego resources such as denial, pretense, withdrawal. Success or failure in this particular respect, more than in any other area of life, will be decisive for his further course in life, his schooling, his professional training, in short, his acceptance as a member of the sighted community.

When describing speech development in blind children in former publications, I stated that the beginning of verbalization is delayed and that later there is a dramatic forward spurt; that by the time they enter nursery school, they speak fluently and have a good vocabulary; that they use many words which are meaningless to them, in imitation of the sighted; that they build up their own concepts gradually; that they use verbal contact in order to orientate themselves in space; that they collect information by means of questioning; finally, that verbalization of thought has a liberating effect on their development (A. Katan, 1961) (as it has for the sighted). Keeping these points in mind should help as a starting point from which to probe further into the intricacies of the language of the blind.

At the time of life when normal infants make visual contact with their surroundings, learn to distinguish between people, and familiarize themselves with things by means of sight, blind infants listen to the sounds in their environment and become knowledgeable about what is going on around them, such as approaching and receding footsteps announcing the coming and going of the mother; the noises made by other family members or by strangers; things hitting against each other in the kitchen; movement in the street. There is, though, no justification for equating the two experiences. Vision brings into the infant's orbit a variety of figures and impressions. While some of them disappear and reappear periodically, others are permanent fixtures in his orbit.

Above all, during the child's waking time there is *always something or other to be seen;* so long as there is light, the field of vision is never empty. In the absence of light, fear of the darkness characteristically takes over in the seeing child, i.e., the mere absence of visual impressions creates fear. In contrast, sound is by nature intermittent, and silence, i.e., absence of acoustic impressions, is frequent in the infant's waking time. At best, there are more or less constant background noises; but if they remain meaningless, they do not fill the vacuum as visual impressions do. Moreover, visible objects are, for the most part, tangible, i.e., capable of being touched, grasped, investigated, understood, while noises are more often intangible, ephemeral, not to be contacted by any of the other senses. It is a big experience for a blind child to be able actually to reproduce a noise which he has heard (by banging things together, etc.); much more often the noise "escapes him," i.e., remains outside his jurisdiction, something which comes and goes and cannot be brought back at will. Very often, explanations from the sighted are needed to give the sightless clues to the meaning of a noise. With practice and time the blind children develop acute hearing and learn to unravel and solve the mysteries of the acoustic impressions to which they are exposed. Until that happens the blind child has every right to be fearful when he is confronted by a strange noise or silence, just as sighted children are fearful when confronted by unfamiliar visions or the dark.

There is, thus, a comparative void left in the minds of those who have to build up their world image without visual impressions, from tactile perceptions of the nearest objects and acoustic perceptions of those that are farther removed. From our observations of the blind it appears that this void is filled in part by the child's attentiveness to the sensations arising from his own body. While these do not as such differ from those in all normal children, the blind are less distracted from them by events in the external world, concentrate more on their content, and are consequently more under their dominance. Blind children are often called "withdrawn" (Klein, 1962), overinvolved with their own bodies, apparently more given to autoerotic indulgence. I believe it is more correct to say that the blind child makes use of his own body and its experiences to compensate for his lack of experiences in the external world. A child whose attention is turned in this direction cannot help but register the stirring of impulses, the changing sensations derived from affects, long before they are conceptualized psychologically.[2] Such physical representations of what will later be called love, hate, sexual desire, etc., are stored away somewhere in the memory of all children, ready for later reinforcement, but more vivid, more important, and probably more accessible in the blind than in the sighted.

Quite apart from these specific residues of prepsychological experience, what is stored in the memory, regardless of its source, is particularly important to the blind and in their case outweighs the impact of new impressions. Possibly, vision keeps the mind more firmly tied to external reality, while hearing, through its connection with verbal residues, has more links with the internal world. However that may be, we have little doubt from our close contact with blind children that they are oriented toward their own inner world and that their minds are constantly preoccupied with going over past experiences.

In lay opinion blind children are often thought of as endowed with unusually acoustic and tactile capacities, which are at their disposal to compensate for the lack of vision. In fact, this is not so. As mentioned before, in the blind child the other senses work less efficiently in the beginning since stimulation from the side of vision is missed. It is only when stimulation of other kinds is given and

[2] According to a helpful verbal exposition by Dr. H. Nagera.

inhibitions removed that hearing and touch are sharpened and placed more fully at the disposal of the ego.

On the other hand, what blind children really possess to an extraordinary degree is an excellent memory made more and more efficient by constant inward looking. During observation in the nursery school, we are constantly surprised by its scope and availability. The children not only soon know the teachers, helpers, visitors, and where the furniture and toys are placed, but remember cracks and unevennesses in the wall or floor. Every sound, once noted, whether understood or not, is remembered, to be referred to later. This attention to detail has some similarity to what happens in analysis when certain highly cathected unconscious material is uncovered, and details appear with photographic exactitude, their significance probably heightened by the emotional cathexis displaced onto them from the main events. Blind children seem to possess such "photographic" (phonographic, tactilographic) memories, the displacement in their cases being a consequence of cathexis not being needed for the world of sight.

To return to verbalization and its specific problems in the blind:

Normally, speech begins after the initial vocalizations, which are the same for all children, by the child finding words (or being given words) for the people and things most highly cathected with libido; i.e., finding expressions for the parents and naming desired and familiar things in the environment. Following this pattern, by rights, the blind child should begin to verbalize (after the usual *ma ma* and *da da*) by giving words to his world of sounds, tactile perceptions, and body sensations. This is what does not happen, and the lack of it distorts the further course of events. No words are found at this juncture for his important experiences, since no help or pattern of identification is offered by the adults in this respect. Since they are sighted, such words are used less often, while verbal expression of visual experience abounds. What the child picks up and appropriates as his own speech is therefore a mixture of words which are meaningful to him as verbalization of his personal experience and words which are meaningless, since they refer to visual experience; the latter are nevertheless important bcause they are offered by the parents, hold out the hope for verbal communication with them, and because their use becomes a means of giving pleasure to the parents. From then onward, the advances of speech in the blind seem to proceed on two lines: one which is their own and which they develop on their own, guided by their own intelligence and inventiveness, finding words for their own affects and body feelings and things heard, more readily than the sighted; and a second one which is personally strange to them but also highly cathected as being the speech of the seeing world, i.e., the type of verbalization shared with the parents.

As the vocabulary of the blind child increases, it contains more and more words which are essentially meaningless to him. Since the intelligent blind child's wish to communicate is great, this increases his effort to understand, to clear up confusion, and not to appear stupid. Unavoidable frustration merely spurs him on to solve the riddles which are contained in the language of the seeing, a language that constantly refers to things of which he has no knowledge. In this impasse his extraordinary powers of memory are summoned to his help. It is true that many words of the seeing are meaningless in so far as they do not refer to anything in the child's experience, and that no other facts or impressions can be associated with them to explain their symbolic content. But they are still words, i.e., things heard and as such cathected, taken note of, stored; these words have been spoken by people important to the child and are cathected from that source. For this reason the blind child also appropriates words of this kind and treats them as his own, though on a different basis. He likes to use and repeat them (for which the derogatory term of parroting = speaking without understanding is used) even though they are likely to cause confusion. And he does his best to clear up confusion by attempts to digest them, to associate past experience with them, as if he asked himself: "Where have I heard this before?" "Who used this word?" "In which context?" "What did I feel at the time?" His ability to recapture internal experience thus helps him to place things, often correctly, where missing external experience leaves him guessing and confused.

In observing the speech development of our nursery school children, we find it useful to disentangle the mixture of the two divergent derivations described, i.e., to separate the expressive elements based on their own sense experience from the borrowed (parroted) ones which are filled with experience only with the help of extraneous memories. As development proceeds the difference between the two kinds tends to be obscured. What usually remains in the language of the adult blind is a certain lack of individuality, some traces of borrowed experience, and in extreme cases some phrases creating the impression of insincerity.

The following are some examples of speech observed in our nursery school.

Words Acquired Normally on the Basis of Sense Experience

A record of "Little Jack Horner Sat in a Corner" was being played when Richard (4;1) was asked what corner meant. He explained and showed how the two adjoining walls made a corner.

Caroline (4) was helped to acquire the new word "oblong" while using a construction toy. She was heard to whisper the word many times looking very pleased with her ability to use the new word. Six months later when she felt the street sign on Maresfield Gardens by stretching up her arms to feel it, she announced correctly: "This is an oblong."

Verbalizing by Sense Association

Caroline (4;6) was asked whether she would like to touch the guinea pig. Caroline backed away and said: "No, I don't like it, it feels like a horse."

Using Words of the Sighted World

Richard (4;3) built a tall tower and called out to the teacher: "Come and see my tower." The teacher said she could see it from where she was. Richard corrected himself: "I mean come and feel my tower." "See" instead of "feel" is almost constantly used by all our children.

Associating from Memory to Unknown Words

Sammy (4;8), on learning that the window he was hitting was made of glass, murmured: "Glass, glass of milk."

Caroline (4) was putting the bricks back in a corner of the shelf and said: "It is a girl in a corner in school."

Confusion between Word and Thing

Judy (4;6) screams "off, off" whenever anything unpleasant or frightening is mentioned. If her anxiety increases, she crouches in a corner, repeating: "Turn off."

Sammy (4;10) shows fear whenever the word "hole" is mentioned. However, he has no difficulty in touching holes. The teacher learned that the mother, in Sammy's presence, had burned a hole in a tablecloth and had been upset and excited over the incident.

Undigested Parroting

Judy (6;10): "Once upon a time there is a bird, he has nice wedding boots, so he can put his shoes on. The fishes come along, the dogs are barking, the kittens are crying, they found their mittens." Knowing Judy, it is possible to disentangle even here the elements picked up and repeated from nursery rhymes, talk of a wedding heard at home, the expectation of some happy event as in fairy tales, and the expectation of a new outfit given to her. In her case, though, parroting speech, which encourages rambling associations, is still more prominent than the normal purposeful speech which aims straightforwardly at communication and which by now she can use in other moods.

BIBLIOGRAPHY

Burlingham, D. (1961), Some Notes on the Development of the Blind. *This Annual,* 16:121-145.
—— (1964), Hearing and Its Role in the Development of the Blind. *This Annual,* 19:95-112.
Freud, A. (1963), The Concept of Developmental Lines. *This Annual,* 18:245-265.
Greenacre, P. (1959), Play in Relation to Creative Imagination. *This Annual,* 14:61-80.
Hendrick, I. (1943), Work and the Pleasure Principle. *Psa. Quart.,* 12:311-329.
Katan, A. (1961), Some Thoughts about the Role of Verbalization in Early Childhood. *This Annual,* 16:184-188.
Klein, G. S. (1962), Blindness and Isolation. *This Annual,* 17:82-93.
Kris, E. (1939), Laughter as an Expressive Process: Contributions to the Psychoanalysis of Expressive Behavior. *Psychoanalytic Explorations in Art.* New York: International Universities Press, 1952, pp. 217-239.
Mittelmann, B. (1957), Motility in the Therapy of Children and Adults. *This Annual,* 12:284-319.
Sandler, A.-M. (1963), Aspects of Passivity and Ego Development in the Blind Infant. *This Annual,* 18:343-360.

ON THE DEVELOPMENT AND FUNCTION OF TEARS

PHYLLIS GREENACRE, M.D. (New York)

For the stimulus to present the considerations offered here, I am greatly indebted to L. Börje Löfgren. His most interesting paper "On Weeping" (1965) was the catalyst for me to bring together and reformulate thoughts of my own. The subject has preoccupied me in a peripheral fashion for nearly twenty years, since I observed and reported two patients whose weeping was extreme and dramatic (1945a).

While in ordinary parlance the words *weeping* and *crying* are used practically synonymously, Löfgren pointed out that crying may but does not always involve the production of tears, whereas in weeping they are the prominent feature. In crying, the wailing, moaning or some form of *crying out* occurs with or without tears, and in weeping the excessive lacrimation is generally associated with crying sounds, but these are not the salient characteristic. Facial changes (grimacing, dilatation of the veins of the face, and sometimes edema of the tissues) may occur, but are marked in weeping, especially when it is severe. Löfgren also thinks that weeping is always associated with mood change, and that lacrimation without mood change is generally on a purely physiological basis. The essential point here seems significant. But one must take into account the pathological weepers in whom the disturbance of mood is not subjectively felt or expressed in overt behavior other than tears. This may be true, for example, in cases of hysterical repression of depressed angry states as in the various forms of missed mourning.[1]

Löfgren was particularly concerned with the relation of weeping

---

This paper is based on and expanded from my discussion of L. Börje Löfgren's paper "On Weeping," read at the Congress of the International Psycho-Analytical Association, Amsterdam, July, 1965.

[1] Löfgren has referred to this in another form when he says that in pathological weeping the situations to which the patient is reacting appear to be ego alien or nearly so to the weeping person himself.

to aggression, and postulated the central thesis that "weeping is an act whereby aggressive energy is dissipated by secretory behavior." He sees the secretion of tears as the essential neutralizing process dissipating the internalized aggression occurring after a loss, which the sufferer has been unable to discharge in any direct way, or through a motor storm in which he regresses to a quasi-helpless state and beats himself in lieu of beating a real or hypothetical enemy. It seems to me that this may be substantially true, and certainly that weeping occurs most frequently associated with some internal change in psychic attitudes coincident with a beginning change from hostile aggression to the use of its energy in a positive and nondestructive way.

But the secretion of tears is a moderately complex biological phenomenon in the service of both physiological and psychological needs. In addition, the show of tears (which is what we usually mean when we speak of weeping) is neither always commensurate with the secretory activity nor dependent on it alone. Further, weeping can secondarily assume hostile aggressive significance, just as screaming or sobbing does. Consequently in considering the relation of weeping to aggression one has to think both of primary and secondary defensive functions involved. In some instances the dissipation of the hostile aggression may simulate a disappearance of it, and be the result rather of the change in the objects toward which it is directed, as multiple minor objects become substituted for the major object which was its original focus. In such cases there is the appearance of a less severe mood change than occurred or might have been expected to occur immediately after the loss. This kind of displacement may be prolonged and possibly become permanent even when its source and its nature are obscured.

Löfgren's postulation in regard to weeping would place the basic neutralization in a physiological process, rather than, as it seems to me, in a metapsychological one with which the physiological is most intimately associated. Weeping is a situation in which it is peculiarly difficult to separate the metapsychological from overt physiological activity, and the total process might rather be referred to as a psycho-biological one. At this point my interest must be directed not so much to the place of weeping in accordance with the structural theory as in its development and functioning. It is from these angles that I would look at the symptom or syndrome of which it may be a part. As already intimated, the question arises whether it is the secretions of tear fluid per se which is primarily the initiator of the change from the original focus of disturbance and produces the relief from the pressure of the hostile aggression,⁻ permitting the reinvestment of this energy in more constructive pursuits. It seems rather that the tears come insidiously as part of a change in the individual's attitude toward his modified external reality usually with a reciprocal change in his self appreciation and even in his self image. This usually involves some degree of renunciation, and the resultant relaxation and the tears express and help along such an internal change.

Simple lacrimation may occur in animals in response to irritation or trauma to the eye or to the tissues around it.[2] This may also occur in human beings. Lacrimation itself is a silent affair; weeping is rarely so. The latter occurs only in human beings in a state of affective distress, and the lacrimation is most often associated with some display of activity of the general body and facial musculature as well as with disturbed respiratory and vocal activity. The extent of the body-activity involvement is commonly greatest in infancy and childhood but diminishes as better bodily control and more economical ways of communicating are established. (All of this paragraph has been admirably brought out in Löfgren's article—and I am here only paraphrasing, for the sake of the continuity in my own observations and suggestions.)

The most common situation in which affective distress with weeping occurs is that following a loss: whether this be the loss by death or by alienation of someone to whom the weeper has been closely attached; or there may be the loss of some material object, or the withdrawal of something promised, or the loss of a body part or possession; or even—and not infrequently—the loss of esteem for a

---

[2] Among the conditions in which frequent lacrimation occurs without crying or apparent affective change as a symptom is Sjörgen's disease. This is usually considered to be entirely independent of psychological causes. I have twice had patients, however, with persistent lacrimation which was diagnosed as Sjörgen's disease by competent ophthalmologists. Both were women who had had severe affective disturbances following conditions of missed mourning in the loss of a mother relatively early in life—with an early history of extremely severe castration problems. In both women, there appeared to have been permanent marked changes in the character, which were not, however, of a nature to be apparent to the ophthalmologists. Vision was highly libidinized and the eye was the site of old conflict.

friend or of self esteem, resulting then in a diminished self image. In any of these situations the first reaction may be one of anger and the wish to attack either the person who has gone away (deserted) or someone who is blamed for the loss, or the self for in some way, either actually or in feeling, being responsible for it. Anger with hostile aggressive impulses then is associated with a variety of muscular responses. But it is usually after the anger is spent in fatigue, or in other ways has proved ineffective, that the weeping sets in. This may be the faint dawn of renunciation, or of stubborn repression and other defensive maneuvers.

Now as weeping is an affair of the eye, it is worth while to examine the relation of weeping to looking and to seeing, or to looking and not seeing. Let us take the example of mourning and assume the situation of the loss of a friend to whom the bereaved person has had a strong and relatively unambivalent attachment. If the death is sudden and the friend has been very recently at hand, then there is at first a state of some shock which is superseded either by tension (blocked aggressive feelings) or open resentment; and wishes to deny the loss, un-believe it or undo it by dwelling on events before death occurred. Resentment is greater if the death might conceivably have been avoided or even delayed. Children not infrequently are angry at the deceased person for disappearing and so deserting, and adults tend to blame Fate, God, or the attending doctor.

The bereaved person may find himself actually expecting to see the lost loved one, and will accordingly be startled by seeming resemblances in strangers. All these reactions go on for some time, are usually fluctuant, but are interspersed with periodic weeping. This may be quite solitary and occur when the mourner is actually beginning to realize the loss, to give up the deceased person, and to know that he will not find him again in the expected or unexpected place. This begins very much as in the child who weeps when left by the mother or when an unexpected and strange person appears in her place to take care of him. I have known instances where weeping occurred during sleep; and it is not very rare that someone waking with such sensations in the face and around the eyes is convinced that he has been weeping.

The weeper weeps because he does not see the person or the object which he has lost and must gradually accept the fact that his looking is in vain. The steps of establishing the reality of his loss must then be gone through as a kind of retracing of the steps originally involved in establishing the reality of the separate object. The eye is the most important sensory object in establishing a loss, though other senses participate according to the nature of the life contact which has preceded.

In cases of missed mourning, the relationship to the lost person has generally been more than ordinarily ambivalent. Consequently the loss arouses especially strong guilt feelings which would contaminate or threaten to overcome feelings of sorrow. The awareness of both feelings may then be repressed and the repression maintained with the aid of various other defensive mechanisms. Tears may come rather tardily and even then may be displaced either as to the object or situation which elicits them or appear as edematous effusions in the should-be weeper's own body. Or, as has already been mentioned, they may appear during sleep, without the accompanying affect becoming conscious. It is interesting how relatively infrequently tears appear in an undisguised way in the content of dreams. But their appearance at all is an indication, I believe, of the activity of the internalized conflict.

But what seems to me most interesting about tearfulness is that the disappointed eye, failing to find the lost object, behaves very much like the physically irritated or traumatized eye which defends itself with the soothing tear lotion. Weeping is distinctly a human talent. Although other vertebrates, especially terrestrial ones, have the equipment for lacrimation, it is used by them not in the interest of emotion but only as a means of keeping the surface of the eye well lubricated and in order. It is not always essential even for that. The tear fluid may be described as a built-in substitute in land animals for the ocean which they have lost. In humans the lacrimal glands produce tear fluid in very small amounts, less than 1 c.c. a day in the absence of irritation. Most of the tear fluid which is mixed with mucus secreted by scattered glands in the conjunctiva is disposed of by evaporation. With a marked irritation of the eye the excess fluid usually is drained through the lacrimal sac and into the nasal cavity. But when the irritation is extreme or during a marked emotional state, fluid may spill over and appear on the cheeks as tears. This is the lacrimal component of weeping. The essential factor in emptying the sac is a pumping action by the orbicularis oculi. This in turn may be increased by rapid blinking and the appearance of the tears of weeping thereby prevented. It is in this way that tears may be held back or "swallowed."

It is worth noting, then, that weeping as it is observed by the onlooker obviously is somewhat under the control of the weeper. It follows also that the amount of observable weeping is not always directly proportionate to the amount of secretory activity. But weeping itself, being visible, has a communicating function as well as the soothing reparative one. The fact that it is under some control by the weeper increases its susceptibility to suggestion and to auto-suggestion and means that it can be exploited for secondary values, especially those of an exhibitionism serving sadomasochistic ends.

The basic use of tears in uncomplicated physiological lacrimation is to clean and wet the cornea. Their overproduction when there is an irritation of the cornea or the conjunctiva is often sufficient to wash away the irritating substance or particle. It is possible that the evaporation of tears has some local cooling effect. In addition, the tear fluid contains enough sugar and protein to have some nutrient value for the corneal epithelium. Further tears contain a special antiseptic ferment, lysozyme, and are appreciably bactricidal. It is indeed apparent that lacrimation offers a primitive physiological local defense with valuable healing, nourishing, and soothing functions. It is only in humans, however, that this defensive reaction is combined with other reactions and utilized in emotional states of distress. This may be related to the greater importance of the eye (and of visual functioning) due to the upright position of man with the eyes more forward-looking.

Other observations indicate further how much the capacity to shed tears is associated with visual activity in humans. Although lacrimation in animals is part of a reflex response to irritation of the eye, in many animals lacrimation is not essential to keep the eye in order, sufficient lubrication being obtained from mucous secretions. Even in human beings sufficient lacrimal fluid for lubrication and protection of the eye is maintained without participation of the main lacrimal glands as is evidenced in cases in which these glands have been extirpated (Mutch, 1944).

This finding harmonizes with the observation that although the lacrimal glands are well developed and capable of secretory functioning at birth, tears do not become evident until one to three months later. They first appear rather scantily when the infant is in pain or other bodily distress. Their earliest emergence in emotional states (not dependent on physical distress) occurs at four to six months and corresponds to the early intrusion into the oneness of the mother-infant relationship, as this is permitted and mediated through vision. In the first weeks after birth the relationship to the mother has been in the more immediate form of oral and general body contact, with smell, touch, body pressure, and warmth playing their parts.

As vision develops it extends the distance of contact and sometimes substitutes for these earlier forms. The development of focusing and the ability to look in one direction or another seems to proceed parallel in time and be interdependent with general muscular development. Thus the infant's gradually increasing ability to control hand-arm movements and at about six months the ability to sit up greatly increase the range of vision and add a more differentiated category of contact. It is my impression that weeping then develops as part of the emotions connected with seeing the strange or missing the familiar. As already emphasized, seeing may become the most sensitive axis of the reaction to loss.

In connection with the relation of the lacrimation of weeping to visual functioning, the interesting question arises whether weeping (as distinct from crying) is any less frequent in blind children than in sighted ones. In the literature on the development of blind children which was available to me, I could find no special focusing on this question. Certainly there are tantrums and many bouts of crying described, but the special question of tearfulness is not isolated or specially emphasized. It had been my impression that in her "Notes on the Development of the Blind," Dorothy Burlingham mentioned tears in the case of a partially blind child, but in a rereading of her discussion I failed to find it (1961). In an article by Segal and Stone (1961) on "The Six-year-old Who Began to See," there is a reference to the child wiping tears from her eyes on one occasion, which occurred after sight had been restored. But there is no indication whether this capacity for tearfulness represented a change. In the article by Omwake and Solnit (1961) having to do with the vicissitudes of treatment and development in a blind twin, whose sister could see, there was an interesting and dramatic event. Then at the age of eight, following a lifelong and very sensitive kind of therapy and teaching, the child had actually grasped something of what vision really meant to others. This was accompanied by an effort to deny that she herself was blind, followed by a correcting insistence that the therapist should undo this denial by telling her that she (the blind child) could *not* see with her eyes. In this setting the child replied with affect, "The eyes are for tears," and added, "And now I can cry." The phrase "The eyes are for tears" was one which four years earlier, i.e., when she was four years old, she had repeated without show of affect during a time when with the aid of her therapist she was building an image of her own body through the discussion of various organs and parts. This then was an extremely poignant and significant situation: she really grasped something of the meaning of tears at a time when she had become aware of vision and inevitably also more fully of its absence in herself. It would be so helpful to know whether she wept tears at this particular time, whether she had wept earlier, and even whether she has wept since. When I asked Dr. Solnit about this, he was unable to say definitely about this particular point. It was his impression that there might have been some tears earlier, but he could not recall clearly. Certainly the significant connection of tears with seeing seems here to be indicated, however.[3]

In a very comprehensive, rich, and careful study of ego development in two children blind since birth, by Fraiberg and Freedman (1964), it is noted that the developmental defects are based not only on the blindness but on the combination of this with the varying degree and nature of the mother's own difficulty in accepting the child and forming a relationship with him in the very earliest weeks and months of his life. One child, a boy suffering from retrolental fibroplasia and from severe lack of maternal stimulation, had begun

[3] Since the preparation of this article for publication additional information has been received concerning the child whose case was reported by Solnit and Omwake. This child did weep before the experience at eight and does weep now when she is disappointed, frustrated, and resentful, but not when she is in a temper tantrum. Eveline Omwake who has had considerable experience in work with blind children found that they weep, but rather less than sighted children. She states, further, that children who have even a fraction of their sight intact tend to weep more than those who are totally blind. It seems that sighted adults become especially uncomfortable at seeing tears come from the eyes of totally blind children, and tend to ward off recognition of this weeping.

treatment only at about the age of nine. He was then in a very inactive state, undernourished, uncertain in his walking, delayed in any responsiveness to others than his nurse, and then responding with an excessive clinging and clawing, seemingly unaware of pain or giving pain. Much of his activity was mouth-centered. He "had no concept of an object that existed independent of his perception of it." Consequently he showed no reaction to the loss of an object and did not search for it. At one time fairly early in the treatment, when the therapist had succeeded in teaching him to find her through tracing her voice, she varied the teaching exercise by walking away from him making a clicking sound with her heels as she walked. When after a considerable effort of search, he was unable to find her and had gone into another room, he was found lying on his mother's bed, "his shoulders heaving convulsively and a look of mute terror on his face. He could not cry in those days, he could only go through a kind of motor parody of grief." The therapist tried to explain and to put his experience into words. But he refused to resume the hide-and-seek teaching game for some time.

It is noted that at some later time when the therapist and the boy's mother had succeeded in teaching him more about the permanence of objects which might be lost and then found again, he would ward off feelings of grief with heaving movements of the shoulders and ticlike grimacing of the mouth. When encouraged to cry, the muscles of his face would react and he appeared as though "on the verge of tears," but suddenly would come forth with repetitions and monotonous asking for some relatively indifferent object, and would keep this up for ten to fifteen minutes in a mechanical way. He seemed to substitute the idea of something which he could readily have but did not care especially about for the lost object he was grieving for, and his request became mechanically repetitious,[4] but

4 The authors see this device as a distraction and liken it to the defensive action of the dentist's patient who, by counting the squares in the ceiling and thereby focusing on a neutral object, disconnects himself from the experience of pain. It seems to me that it may be a little more than this. The example given is that the boy asked for triangle crackers, but did so in such a mechanically repetitious way that it was the mouthing of the words which was conspicuous rather than the actual demand for the cracker. This suggests to me, that the cracker—or even the mental representation of the cracker—may have become a compromise and a step in the direction of relinquishing the lost therapist. It is in such a situation that tears might have come. But there is a hint further of a regressive autoerotic substitute, not only in the idea of the cracker, but in the rhythmic mouthing of the words themselves.

he did not weep tears. I have seen this same device used by adult patients whose acceptance of mourning was prevented by the distress of their ambivalence to the lost person. The authors state that when grief in the blind boy emerged again it came as an "emotional storm" with the fear that his mother would go away and be "all gone." But there is no mention of weeping.

To return to the subject of the relation of tearfulness in weeping to hostile aggression, one must realize that it is a very complicated problem, especially as our evidence of tearfulness is dependent on the show of tears rather than on a direct observation of the process of lacrimal secretion. Since the show of tears is under some control by the weeper, the tearfulness, which is probably basically a part of the feeling of helplessness and resignation before a situation about which one can no longer expect to do much actively, may secondarily take on further aggressive significance. This is to express reproach against another as though to say "See what you have done to me," or as a demand for help or restitution. In the two cases of my own reported years ago, the continued tearfulness seemed to carry aggression largely from this secondary source.

The whole consideration of tears in weeping presents many interesting facets. In addition to those mentioned, it is a situation in which the nucleus of a primitive physical defensive activity is later used in a much more complicated situation and assumes the role of a quasi-psychic defense. There are questions also regarding the relationship of tears and tearfulness to disturbances of other fluid discharges of the body such as sweating, urinating, or the periodic appearance of fluid in body tissues in response to psychological as well as to physiological irritations, as in urticaria and recurrent bursitis. The extraordinary susceptibility in some women to accumulate fluid in body tissues in connection with the menstrual rhythm, and even for the rhythm itself to be disarranged by emotional causes may have elements that belong in any general consideration of the body's use of fluid in psychosomatic defenses. But these are general interests which need further investigation and cannot be developed here.

BIBLIOGRAPHY

Burlingham, D. (1961), Some Notes on the Development of the Blind. *This Annual,* 16:121-145.
Fraiberg, S. & Freedman, D. A. (1964), Ego Development of the Blind. *This Annual,* 19:113-170.
Greenacre, P. (1945a), Pathological Weeping. *Psa. Quart.,* 14:62-75.
—— (1945b), Urination and Weeping. *Amer. J. Orthopsychiat.,* 15:81-88.
Löfgren, L. B. (1965), On Weeping. Presented at the Congress of the International Psycho-Analytical Association, Amsterdam.
Mutch, J. R. (1944), The Lacrimation Reflex. *Brit. J. Ophthalmol.,* 28:317-336.
Omwake, E. & Solnit, A. J. (1961), "It Isn't Fair": The Treatment of a Blind Child. *This Annual,* 16:352-404.
Segal, A. & Stone, F. H. (1961), The Six-year-old Who Began to See. *This Annual,* 16:481-509.
Walls, G. L. (1942), *The Vertebrate Eye.* Bloomfield Hills, Mich.: Cranbrook Institute of Science.

REFLECTIONS REGARDING PSYCHOMOTOR ACTIVITIES DURING THE LATENCY PERIOD

ELIZABETH BREMNER KAPLAN, M.D. (Philadelphia)

When I think of elementary school children, I see them rushing and tumbling at recess, balancing on railings, climbing, sliding, swinging with zest, chanting their rhymes, sucking lollipops, comic books in their hands, tearing around chasing one another. I hear the sound of roller skates on the pavements, hopscotch chalked on the sidewalks, the girls skipping rope to chants such as

> Teddy bear, Teddy bear,
> Turn around.
> Teddy bear, Teddy bear,
> Touch the ground (Magran, 1964).

Eager-faced boys are off to high adventure and explorations, with canteens dangling from their belts, some of the more fortunate ones proudly clutching fishing poles. Amid the sounds of laughter and shouting they are seemingly oblivious to the adults around them.

These images lead me naturally to considerations about the activity of the latency child. The topic of activity covers such a broad range that I shall focus on the perceptual-motor activities of latency children. I shall try to exemplify some of the ways in which motility affects the ego and superego operation and the vicissitudes of the drives in the so-called normal latency period.

Psychoanalytic literature has covered extensively the subject of motility in the preschool child (infancy to five and a half years) and has traced its course through the oral, anal, and phallic phases. Among the eminent contributors to this subject are Anna Freud, Sigmund Freud, Hartmann, Loewenstein, Kris, Mahler, and Mittelmann.

The motility of the latency period, as well as the psychomotor activities in all other developmental phases, cannot be understood without the background of the development of the perceptual-motor organizations, including such basic patterns as posture, walking and speech, during the pregenital period. Although we are familiar with the theoretical formulations, a brief review would seem to provide the appropriate background for a discussion of the psychomotor activities of the latency child.

MOTILITY IN INFANCY AND EARLY CHILDHOOD

Hartmann (1950) proposes that ego functions related to motility, perception, and the like have a primary autonomy and normally belong to the conflict-free sphere of the ego. Speech and walking, once established, become automatic and are a part of the conflict-free organization of the ego. One of the first signs of the developing ego is the ability of a three-month-old baby to follow moving objects with his eyes. The psychologists would call this the beginning of intelligence. We analysts see this as a budding ego functioning; i.e., we see the part that motility plays in it, the degree of motor control present in the ability to get the hand to the mouth for sucking. As described by Hoffer (1949), perceptual activity and the rudiments of reality testing are present in the baby's choice of what he wants to put into his mouth.

Through motility and perception the infant learns about his body and outside world. In this way the concept of body image develops. Hartmann, Kris, and Loewenstein (1949) have pointed out that "Musculature and motility, apparatuses for the discharge of aggression, contribute decisively . . . to the differentiation of the environment itself" (p. 23).

The first distinction between what belongs to the self and what belongs to the outside world is learned on a sensorimotor basis. By three to four months the baby finds his hands and learns that they stay with him, unlike other objects which come and go; this self discovery is paramount to the task of differentiating between inner self and outside world. Another such opportunity for the baby, aside from visual and tactile-motor activities which lead to exploration by the mouth, the baby's major zone of gratification and knowledge, lies in his increasing ability to get things for himself, to grasp, to manipulate, and to learn what is self and nonself.

According to Piaget (1923, 1937) and other observers, at around nine or ten months the infant, by his active searching efforts, demonstrates the concept of object permanence. He pulls off whatever hides the searched-for object; he is pleased when he finds the lost object. As his visual-motor coordination increases, he drops or throws things and then delights in retrieving them. His delight in the return of the lost object is almost insatiable (Kessler, 1964). With the recognition of familiar persons and places and the establishment of the permanence of persons and things, the child is able to form a lasting attachment to the mother.

Freud (1905b) demonstrated that we continuously identify ourselves unconsciously, below the threshold of perception, with the movements of objects which we notice in the outside world. Imitation is a precursor of identification. Gradually, through his senses and motility, the baby automatically behaves like his mother. We say that he has incorporated her, and this incorporation results in identification with her. Through sensorimotor elements, he has identified with the beloved active mother, a tremendous advance in ego development. Later identification with the aggressor (A. Freud and D. Burlingham, 1944) and its motoric elements will contribute to superego development.

Speech emerges from the spontaneous diffuse motor activity of the infant. First, we have the child's preverbal signals to the world in the form of cries and gestures, and on the expressive side of speech there is the child's babbling, which is an oral pleasure. It is an expressive function which appears initially as the direct discharge of tension in the neonate. Later, the infant's ego organization progresses so that the infant connects his crying with tension relief offered by the environment. The response of people to his various vocal signals leads to the infant's recognition of language as a communicative device. Development of speech is decisive in the establishment of secondary-process thinking.

Besides speech, the other great maturational feat of the toddler is posture, standing and walking. Anna Freud and Dorothy Burlingham (1944) have this to say about the toddler's ego development and intense id gratification:

The great event in the child's life is his new ability to move freely and to control his movements, an ability which progresses quickly from crawling to walking, running, climbing, jumping, and is continued with the handling and moving of objects, as pushing, pulling, dragging, carrying, etc. . . . Some children at this period for a while disregard all toys and show little interest in their companions; they behave as if they were drunk with the idea of space and even of speed; they crawl, walk, march and run, and revert from one method of locomotion to the other with the greatest of pleasure [p. 14f.].

All of us have observed that children use their skeletal muscles for the discharge of aggressive and libidinal drives. Freud (1905b) related skeletal musculature to the discharge of aggression. Loewenstein (1950) says:

On the side of instinctual drives, we might say that learning to walk must have considerable influence on canalization of aggressions into co-ordinated actions. It is certainly accompanied by libidinal gratifications. On the side of the ego phenomena, it may be said that it produces gratification of the pleasure of functioning (*Funktionlust*) and of mastery of bodily movements. It obviously brings about a changed relationship to objects, the ability to reach them, and a change from passivity to activity, thus an increased mastery of the object and increased security against the danger of helplessness [p. 51].

Always we are aware of that integral part of ego maturation, the myelinization of the corticopyramidal part of the central nervous system. This takes place gradually throughout childhood and makes possible the dominance of the cortex over neuromotor subcortical organization. Repeatedly we come back to Freud's dictum (1923): "The ego is first and foremost a bodily ego" (p. 26).

Ernst Kris (1939, 1951) and Lourie (1949) have written about the rhythmic movements prevalent in infancy and early childhood. The motility patterns in the first months of infancy are diffuse and rhythmical. During the first two years rhythmical motor activities such as rocking, head banging, bouncing, swaying, and whirling reach their peak. In this rhythmic motility kinesthetic, tactual, and visual sensations are integrated. Their organic basis is in the subcortical central nervous system; they are automatic.

Rhythmic, repetitive motor patterns tend to occur in the transitional maturational periods between sitting and crawling, between standing and walking (Lourie, 1949). In these periods learning occurs through repetition (so well demonstrated in the development of language, such as the repetition of babbling).

That these rhythmic, repetitive motor patterns subsume autoerotic activities is well known. The satisfaction and absorption which the child finds in such activities are striking. Gratification in rhythmicity and repetition is observable in the infant's sucking and pleasurable feeding experience. Fries and Woolf (1953) emphasized the adverse effect on development when the infant's motility pattern differs from that of his mother. Gesell and Amatruda (1941) term the reciprocal basic rhythm between mother and child in child care "the relaxational expedient."

The motivations for these rhythmic motor patterns are exceedingly varied. My focus is upon the manifestations of rhythmic, repetitive activities, which are transitional, rather than upon the pathological, which have permanency and rigidity. Examples of normal activities are bouncing, swaying and rocking to music, transitory rocking, and rhythmic body activities at transitional stages of maturation and development. Examples of pathology are established tics, postural rigidity (both functional and organic), inhibition of movement, motor incoordination, primitive discharge movements, persistent rocking and head banging.

The autoerotic, affectomotor release in these transitional, normal, rhythmic, repetitive activities seems to me to be a forerunner of and preparation for the genital activities appropriate in the phallic phase of psychosexual development. In the first two years of life the avenue for gratification of erotic and aggressive drives should *not* be the genital but the sensorimotor activities, and the tension discharge should be through the musculature. I want to stress this point in the discussion of the motility of the latency child.

The ego, through the development of the reality principle and the secondary process, gains increasing control over motility. Its physiological concomitant is the maturation process of the corticopyramidal tracts. Motility becomes more purposive, intentional, and voluntary. Automatic rhythmic discharge movements such as hand flapping and rocking disappear by the age of three to four. They recur as regressive phenomena when the child's ego organization is weakened by fatigue and stress and is overburdened with tension.

One of the diagnostic criteria of ego deficit is its poor integrative control over motility. This deficit can be due to organic brain damage, such as cerebral palsy, perceptual defects, illnesses that restrain motility, and many other conditions. In blind children, such rhythmic, repetitive activities are known as blindisms.

Analysts recognize that one of the major areas of ego expansion in latency is cognition. Cognition, the learning process, has its origins in the perceptual-motor learning of the first three years. Psychological tests of intelligence in the infant and child are based on patterns of perception and movement. Because of the significance of the body image in latency activities, I repeat an earlier reference to the way this body image develops in the first three years. It is the result of the infant's (or child's) observation of the movement of the parts of his body (his hands, for example) and the relationship of the different parts of his body to one another (finger to finger, hand to mouth), as well as their relationship to objects in his environment (Kessler, 1964).

Schilder (1935) has written: "When the knowledge of our own body is incomplete and faulty, all actions for which this particular knowledge is necessary will tend to be faulty too. We need the body-image in order to start movements. We need it especially, when actions are directed towards our own body" (p. 45). Faulty body image, Schilder points out, shows up in faulty perception.

The importance of motility during the child's phallic phase should not be overlooked. During the phallic phase movement is coordinated under the control of the ego. Ernst Kris (1939) aptly describes this as the melody of movement.

Loewenstein (1950) says: "Phenomena of the phallic phase, identification of the body with penis, and of bodily movements with erections are built on traces of instinctual processes, and particularly on traces of ego changes acquired by learning to walk." The psychomotor activity of the latency child reflects the further development of these ego functions so important in learning and adaptation.

This review of the role of motility in the child's libidinal and ego development during the pregenital and the phallic years has treated this vast, complex subject very schematically. Its main aim was to emphasize its significance.

Just as the pregenital phase is a precursor of and preparation for the phallic phase, so the latency phase is a precursor of and preparation for puberty and genitality.

MOTILITY IN LATENCY

Berta Bornstein (1951), in her article "On Latency," convincingly described two phases of the latency period. Although Bornstein emphasizes that she is discussing primarily the neurotic child, neurological and physiological findings as well as observations of the normal child's personality in latency validate her division into these two periods. The first period covers roughly age five and a half to eight, and the second period covers age eight to ten and a half.

In early latency, as described by Bornstein, the defenses are directed against both genital and pregenital impulses, and reaction formations are prominent. The conflict between superego and id results in heightened ambivalence, which is expressed in alternating obedience and rebellion, usually followed by self-reproach. At this stage guilt feelings are not well tolerated and lead to identification with the aggressor and to projection. Phobias of animals are replaced by a wave of separation anxiety; and castration fear by the fear of death.

In the second phase, as Bornstein points out, the ego is less conflicted because the superego is less like a foreign body, is less rigid, and there are fewer sexual demands on the ego. The older latency child no longer believes in the omnipotence of his parents. He is influenced by children and adults other than his parents. This improves the relationship between his ego and superego. Between five and eight years of age, the conscious thought processes dip into the primary thought processes.

The principal task during both phases is "the warding off of incestuous fantasies and masturbatory temptations." Bornstein further states: "The ego during this period is engaged in deflecting the sexual energy from its pregenital aims and is utilizing it for sublimation and reaction formation. But in neither period do they fully succeed and a close-up of this period shows the child in a ceaseless, though quickly repressed, battle against the temptation to masturbate." Free association is a threat to the ego organization in both periods. Until prepuberty there is little capacity for introspection.

At the risk not only of being tendentious but also of paying more attention to the maturation of the ego apparatus than to ego autonomy, I shall try to correlate the motile activity of the normal latency child with the psychic structure as described by Bornstein in these two periods of latency. I shall first depict the psychomotor activity of the child from five and a half to eight years. This overall, general view is culled from observations of the early latency child made by members of our child analytic study group in the Philadelphia Association, and also from my own observations as well as those of Gesell and Ilg (1946).

None of us deny the importance of the neuromuscular development of the ego apparatus used in the latency child's motility, yet we sometimes overlook it. When it is awry, as in the brain-damaged child, we become painfully aware of its basic importance. By eight years myelinization of the tracts from the cortex to the thalamus is completed. Around this same age, the alpha wave pattern on the EEG stabilizes (Madow and Silverman, 1956). These neurological findings substantiate Bornstein's division of latency.

Laterality and directionality closely related to body-image formation are established in latency. The six-year-old can tell left from right on his own body, but not on others. By eight years of age laterality has developed. The child can distinguish left from right and left on others as well as on himself. Directionality is also maturing. With this orientation of body to side movement, the six-year-old can start to bat a ball. True, he is awkward, but by ten years of age such perceptual-motor ego activities as batting and catching, involving the body image, have become perfected. The maturational ability to throw a ball comes sooner than batting and catching, because the finer hand movements and eye coordination develop later. Sometimes fathers and interested relatives expect six- and seven-year-olds to have the physical perceptual-motor maturation to enable them to catch balls and bat, and to engage in other motor activities involving form and space discrimination that are beyond the physiological maturation present at this age. The child's affective reaction to these unreasonable demands can lead to ego restrictions that affect his motor development. The six- and seven-year-olds love to balance on railings, enjoy standing on their heads and turning cartwheels, try to walk on fences; they like the balance involved in bicycling as well as the gross motor leg activity; they like to climb, to skate, to do tricks on bars.

These activities are based on the developing perceptual-motor system which is steered by the autonomous ego and powered by unconflicted drive energy. Finer muscular movement skills, accessory muscles of fingers, and muscles of eye accommodation develop last. Thus we see six- and seven-year-olds struggling with writing and reading. It is hard for a six-year-old to grasp a pencil; not until eight do most children have a smooth release of their grasp on objects such as pencils. Nor are the eye movements of the average youngster sufficiently coordinated to scan a page of print before the age of eight. Yet the latency child does have sufficient ego development and neutralized energy to persist in, and to master through repetition, these finer motor activities for which the neuromuscular apparatus now has sufficiently matured.

After Tinker Toys for the six-year-olds come erector sets of increasing complexity which exercise these finer motor skills, as do the cutouts and paper-doll play of girls. Carpentry interests the boys in part because its exercise involves the organization of the finer accessory muscles. Sewing and handicrafts have similar appeal for girls.

The most conspicuous difference in the perceptual-motor patterns of latency-age girls and boys seems to be in muscle strength and endurance. This seems to be the *maturational* factor in the boy's increasing interest in physical prowess and activities. The difference between the way a boy throws a ball at this age and the way a girl does is readily observable. Whereas boys throw balls, girls tend to bounce them. It is perhaps banal to mention that there are constitutional differences both in the neuromuscular apparatus of children of both sexes and also between the sexes. It is well known that boys have a far greater number of gross disturbances of motility such as tics, stuttering, reading and writing disorders, and that these are most prevalent in latency.

The process by which the muscular system becomes the executor of purposeful action, in addition to being the organ of discharge, is a gradual one, involving, as I have emphasized, the physiological maturation along with the growing ability of the ego to defer to the reality principle. As we all know, repression inhibits the motor release of the aggressive and sexual drives. In early latency, repression is not as well established as in later latency, and we see the six- and seven-year-olds struggling with a wavering control over motility, sometimes too much and at other times too little. Adaptation to school and to community activities confront the early latency child with new tasks and problems: it is difficult for him to sit down to read and write; the six-year-old moves while he is sitting; he moves around the schoolroom, and frequently stands while writing. This early period of latency is a transitional phase, just as in the pregenital years there is a transition from crawling to standing to walking. In latency the transition is from the unrepressed, freer affectomotor expressions to the repressed, purposeful activities, such as the sedentary actions of writing and reading, which utilize the new capacity of the fine muscle organization.

We must keep in mind that in early latency the secondary process is not as well established as most adults are inclined to believe. Early latency is a period of transition. It is in early latency that we see again a flare-up of repetitive automatisms, just as we saw them in infancy and early childhood. These are the repetitious discharge phenomena: foot tapping, leg jiggling, finger movements of tapping, twisting hair or ears, nose picking, sniffing. Also particularly prevalent during latency are oral activities, such as blowing, lip licking, tongue protrusion and clicking, mouth grimaces, stuttering, finger sucking, nail and cuticle biting (chewing of pencils). According to the studies of Malone and Massler (1952), out of 4,587 children studied, 61.6 per cent bit their nails between six and eight years of age. There was no sex difference until age ten. Nail biting began to diminish in girls at age nine, and in boys at eleven.

Mahler (1949) stated that in the school-age child the motor system easily becomes involved in neurotic symptom formation, tics, impulsions, and hyperkinetic and dyskinetic behavior. She describes the genetic and structural differences between these motoric disorders and the tension-discharge movements I have mentioned, which are normally transient and semiautomatic. These aggressive discharge movements normally reach their climax in the early stage of latency and gradually cease in the second period as the ego and superego structures become well differentiated.

As emphasized earlier in this paper, during the pregenital years rhythmic movements, such as swaying, bouncing, and rocking, which have fluidity, repetitiveness, and transigence, play an important role in forestalling premature genital discharge patterns for which there is psychosexual and physiological readiness in the phallic phase. Rhythmicity and repetitiveness are also characteristic of the motility involved in the predominant play of children from six to eight. I shall now focus on their significance in the progression of psychosexual development.

Skipping, jumping rope, swinging, ball bouncing, hopping, and running games are often accompanied by chants with a cadence, such as the following:

> Hippity hop to the barber shop
> To get a stick of candy
> One for you, and one for me,
> And one for Sister Annie.

> There was an old man named Michael Finigin.
> And he grew whiskers on his chinigin.
> The wind came along and blew them in agin.
> Poor old Michael Finigin, begin agin.

> The grand old duke of York,
> He had ten thousand men.
> He marched them up the hill,
> And he marched them down agen.

The refrain in hide-and-seek, a game popular in early latency, is "Allee allee outs n' free ee."

Throughout the centuries these rhythmical motor activities have characterized the early latency child.. They are cathected with unconflicted drive energy and are ego syntonic; they absorb the interest of the latency child just as the transitional rhythmic activities interest the child in the pregenital period. It is generally agreed that the child's main task during latency is to ward off masturbation and its attendant incestuous fantasies. Libidinal aggressive gratification in latency is released normally through the perceptual-motor system, especially in the form of these transitional rhythmic motor activities.

These activities maintain the latency child's libido-economic balance until the secondary process is established firmly and safeguard the attainment of genital supremacy in puberty. My point of emphasis is that these progressive rhythmic activities are important in the normal psychosexual development of latency.

The ego's development is enhanced in many ways by these pleasurable rhythmical motor activities. Not only do they maintain the libido-economic balance and add new ego skills, thus augmenting positively the latency child's body image; they also contribute to the latency child's object relations with his peers. The child who does not hop, skip, jump, tumble, perform balancing tricks, rhyme, and shout is "out of it." The rhymes accompanying this active play are passed on by word of mouth to each succeeding generation of children. By means of these rhymes children take pleasure in communicating with other children, master speech, learn quantitative concepts by counting. In this way children can dip into the primary process without danger of ego disorganization. Carpentry (sawing, hammering), play with Tinker Toys, erector sets, and the many manipulative pursuits of latency by which the child builds up neuromuscular patterns of finer muscle movements are not only autonomous ego functions operative in these activities but also vehicles for the discharge of desexualized libidinal-aggressive drive energy. In those latency children for whom these pleasurable motor activities are conflicted or restricted, the genital can prematurely become the organ of discharging tension, which later becomes alloyed with sexuality.

Bühler (1930) indicates the close psychological relationship between space and time by pointing out the relationship between rhythm and melody in time perception and spatial form perception. In this connection the importance of melody and counting in the games of latency-age children should be noted.

The synthetic function of the ego, strengthened by repression, operates in these cadenced, pleasurable, sensorimotor games and stunts. Kinesthetic rhythms are integrated with tactual and auditory rhythms into a dominant rhythm pattern which manifests itself in the child's posture, gait, speech, and learning.

Free-flowing movements are more likely to be achieved if there is a gradual balanced amount of repression. It is the old story of trouble caused by too much or too little or too soon. Sudden repression, with overcontrol by a shaky ego and too much id frustration, leads to rigid, splintered movement patterns with inhibited motor activity. Insufficient repression contributes to poor control and poor integration by the ego, and shows up in hyperkinesias and dyskinesias.

The perfecting of free movements such as posture, begun in pregenital years, is one of the major achievements of latency. These movements are stabilized by their enduring cathexis with libidinal-aggressive and neutralized energy. The body image continues to evolve. Flexible body movement and body image are key factors in learning, especially in problem solving in contrast to rote memory learning. Free motor patterns are utilized by educational methods whereby youngsters in the primary grades are able to develop concepts of higher mathematics.

These free, flexible movement patterns are the basic preparation for satisfactory genital organization, the great achievement in the next psychosexual phase, puberty.

A study by Bricklin and Gottlieb (1963) seems pertinent to my thesis. This study is concerned with the prediction of some aspects of marital compatibility on the basis of human movement responses given on Rorschach tests. The authors conclude that the chances of marital compatibility are greater when the difference in the human movement response given by husband and wife is smaller and when the quality of each of the perceived human movement responses is similar. (The quality of a human movement response refers to the kinesthetic element of the figure projected in the Rorschach response.)

Another phenomenon of late latency which is repetitive and rhythmic extends into prepuberty and early adolescence. This is Rock 'n' Roll. At present I am especially aware of Rock 'n' Roll because I have in treatment a ten-year-old girl who is secretary to the vice-president of the Society for Prevention of Cruelty to the Beatles. When asked who was cruel to the Beatles, she replied, "Parents are Beatle beaters."

Even the name Rock 'n' Roll recalls the repetitive, rhythmic activities of infancy and early childhood. We are familiar with its simple, steady beat. Like the repetitive rocking and other rhythmic activities of infancy and childhood, Rock 'n' Roll normally occurs at a transitional phase of maturation and psychosexual development. Normally it has a transitory appeal. Interest in Rock 'n' Roll usually recedes when true heterosexual genitality is reached.

Case Illustrations

I want to stress that the following case presentations are over-simplified and extremely condensed. Also, I declare emphatically that psychotherapy is not accomplished on the playground, in the stadium, or in the "Y" gym. The objective of the case material is to illumine the points made in this paper.

Jerry's analysis began when he was eighteen years old. At the age of seven he had been treated at a child guidance clinic because of fears and lack of friends. He was a college freshman, who, though brilliant (I.Q. 160), was in danger of flunking out of college. Whenever Jerry experienced tension of any kind, he masturbated. His childhood and adolescence were lonely and friendless. He was a fearful boy and inept at all sports and childhood activities. Comic books and stamp collecting were his chief sources of pleasure and interest.

Jerry's father, a successful businessman away from home much of the time, was a tyrannical person, who, for example, would beat Jerry when he failed to empty the trash cans.

Jerry's mother, a sick woman, unhappy with her husband, was Jerry's chief companion. She confided intimacies to him, such as telling him about her extramarital sexual affairs. Her constant seduction interfered with repression in Jerry. He masturbated through the latency period, although he struggled not to do so. When he started analysis, Jerry began to have sexual intercourse. During the first three years of his analysis his erections were weak and difficult to maintain. He complained of feeling "tied" and longed for spontaneity and a feeling of freedom in his sexual activities.

As he progressed in analysis, Jerry went to the "Y" for workouts. He also played soccer and learned to ski. He no longer masturbated when tense. He was now assured of his masculine genital potency. He became engaged to a girl who seemed to be a suitable marriage partner for him. Whereas he had previously experienced unallevi-ated excitement, he now experienced fulfillment in intercourse.

Julie was seen for evaluation when she was eight years old. At that time she was an intelligent, serious child whose school adaptation and bed wetting concerned her mother. Julie, an avid reader, wrote poorly and found arithmetic incomprehensible. She did not skip rope, bicycle, skate, or join in any of the children's motor activities. There was a frozen quality about her. Shortly before Julie was brought for study, she had an acute febrile illness. At the peak of her fever she became delirious. In her delirium she excitedly called to her mother to see the children playing, pointing to the hallucinatory children swinging or skipping rope, all having a fine time. Julie's mother was, of course, alarmed by the child's delirium and unaware of the significance of its content. For various reasons Julie's family could not at that time follow up the recommendation of analytic treatment for Julie.

When Julie was twenty-three years old she herself initiated analysis. She was phobic and had many ego restrictions. She was noticeably awkward and clumsy. Reading was her sole recreational outlet. Although she had graduated from college and then had become an English teacher, she had never realized her intellectual potential. She related to a young man interested in her by means of her intellectualization. She had never had sexual intercourse, nor had she consciously masturbated.

Analysis soon revealed that Julie's mother had been a bed wetter, as was Julie. The mother intuitively associated this symptom with masturbation. Julie, as her mother had done, prayed obsessively to overcome the bed wetting. Her mother, also phobic, had restricted Julie's motility from infancy. The first steps Julie took led to a fall and she cut her face. Both mother and father feared that the child was maimed for life, an attitude that persisted with the mother. Early sexualization of thinking, along with bed wetting and prolonged nail biting, became libidinal-aggressive releases. Julie is still in analysis. Although freer, she remains sexually frigid and inhibited in motility.

Bruce, age nine, could not sit still, nor did he stop talking. His schoolwork was poor. He had had several cystoscopies for a ureteral constriction. His father had died in an accident almost in sight of the boy, who was then five years old. Bruce's castration fear was understandably intense and interfered with his motor development. During the first stages of his analysis, he stood while painting or making papier-mâché objects. He shunned motor activity with other children. Instead, he restlessly made his papier-mâché dolls in the company of his grandparents. He bit his toenails as well as his fingernails, wet the bed, and compulsively masturbated. At his insistence, Bruce's mother showed him her vagina.

Subsequent knowledge about Bruce, who finished his analysis at age eleven, was gained through a friendly telephone call from him (when he was sixteen and passing through town) and a later similar telephone call from his mother. Bruce, in the telephone call, told of his activities in the school band. Some years later his mother reported Bruce's interest in girls, which was reciprocated, and his forthcoming graduation from a school of landscape architecture.

CONCLUSION

The part that perceptual-motor behavior plays in the formation of the latency child's superego and ego ideal is readily discernible. Identification with the aggressor leads the six- or seven-year-old to strike out, to stamp and storm about like the Giant in Jack and the Beanstalk when he feels bad. He projects his own motor actions and identifies with this projection. At this age his morality is based on specific actions that are prohibited or sanctioned by his parents. For example, it is bad to throw and to tear things, to pull the cat's tail, to pinch and to hit brother Johnnie. It is good to turn off the TV, to go to bed when mother tells you to, to say thank you, to keep your clothes clean, to look before you cross the street. With the stabilization of the superego in the eight- to ten-year period, more verbalization of aggression takes the place of action.

Aided by progress in ego development, in identifications and in ego ideals, ethical standards of right and wrong gradually come to replace the bad and the good based on parental prohibitions of certain actions.

The various ideals of latency children have this common trait: their heroes do things, they are people of action. This is more obvious among boys, who admire the plumber, the fireman, the pilot, the sports hero. Yet latency girls also idealize the active, for example, the dancer. The girl, in her dramatic play, is the mother or the older girl who is "on the go" and constantly engaged in a multitude of adult pursuits.

Pearson (1949) deplores that most fathers today do not have to use the skills that were so necessary in our pioneer American past. As a result, he points out, the psychomotor need of the latency child for manual activity is deprived of its father-identification link. In its place, love for, and to some extent identifications with, adults in the teaching role, adults in sports, games and crafts exert a very positive influence upon ego development (see also Pearson et al., 1956, 1964).

Before ending this paper I would like to re-emphasize the importance of rhythmical repetitive activity in the early period of latency. This is a transitional period when the child's secondary process is still shaky. By age eight and a half or nine the secondary process, the total personality development, and physiological maturation are much more firmly entrenched. Competitive games and skills by and large have replaced these rhythmic, repetitive movements and activities.

We tend to overlook that in other phases of development we adults give help to the children in handling their instinctual urges, whereas we do not give the same help to early latency children. The children are left to their own resources with their genital drives. To me it seems that these rhythmic, repetitive games and activities are the children's solution which they have passed down via psychomotoric communication through multitudinous generations of children. Later in life, the repetitive, rhythmical movement is expressed psychomotorically in more secondary-process activity as in learning, in all forms of art, and in genitality and love and creative living.

It seems fitting to conclude with a quotation from a man who experienced the greatest triumphs and the severest tribulations in the perceptual-motor area, Beethoven. This quotation (Machlis, 1955) expresses beautifully the zest and urgency in the psychomotor activity of latency.

"You will ask where I get my ideas. I am not able to answer that question positively. They come directly, indirectly; I grasp them with my hands out amid the freedom of nature in the woods, on walks, in the silence of the night, early in the morning. Called forth by such moods as in the minds of poets translate themselves into words, but in mine into tones that ring, roar, storm, until at last they stand as notes before me." And to this I join in for the latency child, "To be alive!"

BIBLIOGRAPHY

Bender, L. (1938), *A Visual Motor Gestalt Test and Its Clinical Use.* New York: American Orthopsychiatric Assn. Research Monogr. No. 3.

Bornstein, B. (1951), On Latency. *This Annual,* 6:279-285.

Bricklin, B. & Gottlieb, S. (1963), The Prediction of Some Aspects of Marital Incompatibility by Means of the Rorschach Test. *Psychiat. Quart.* Suppl., 35:281-303.

Brown, D. G. (1959), The Relevance of Body Image to Neurosis. *Brit. J. Med. Psychol.,* 32:249-260.

Bühler, K. (1930), *The Mental Development of the Child.* London: Routledge & Kegan, 1949.

Erikson, E. H. (1950), *Childhood and Society.* New York: Norton, 2nd ed., 1963.

Fries, M. E. & Woolf, P. (1953), Some Hypotheses on the Role of the Congenital Activity Type in Personality Development. *This Annual,* 8:48-62.

Freud, A. (1962), Assessment of Childhood Disturbances. *This Annual,* 17:149-158.

—— & Burlingham, D. (1944), *Infants Without Families.* New York: International Universities Press.

Freud, S. (1905a), Three Essays on the Theory of Sexuality. *Standard Edition,* 7:125-245. London: Hogarth Press, 1953.

—— (1905b), Jokes and Their Relation to the Unconscious. *Standard Edition,* 8:3-236. London: Hogarth Press, 1960.

—— (1923), The Ego and the Id. *Standard Edition,* 19:3-66. London: Hogarth Press, 1961.

—— (1926), Inhibitions, Symptoms and Anxiety. *Standard Edition,* 20:77-174. London: Hogarth Press, 1959.

Gesell, A. & Amatruda, C. (1941), *Developmental Diagnosis.* New York: Hoeber, 2nd ed., 1954.

—— & Ilg, F. (1946), *The Child From Five to Ten.* New York: Harper.

Hartmann, H. (1950), Comments on the Psychoanalytic Theory of the Ego. *This Annual,* 5:74-96.

—— & Kris, E. (1945), The Genetic Approach in Psychoanalysis. *This Annual,* 1:11-30.

—— —— & Loewenstein, R. M. (1946), Comments on the Formation of Psychic Structure. *This Annual,* 2:11-38.

—— —— —— (1949), Notes on the Theory of Aggression. *This Annual,* 3/4:9-36.

Hoffer, W. (1949), Mouth, Hand and Ego-Integration. *This Annual,* 3/4:49-56.

Kessler, J. (1964), Mental Development. In preparation.

Kris, E. (1939), Laughter As an Expressive Process. *Psychoanalytic Explorations in Art.* New York: International Universities Press, 1952.

—— (1951), Some Comments and Observations on Early Autoerotic Activities. *This Annual,* 6:95-116.

Larner, J. (1964), What Do They Get From Rock 'n' Roll. *Atlantic Monthly,* August.

Loewenstein, R .M. (1950), Conflict and Autonomous Ego Development during the Phallic Phase. *This Annual,* 5:47-52.

Lourie, R. (1949), The Role of Rhythmic Patterns in Childhood. *Amer. J. Psychiat.,* 105:653-660.

Machlis, J. (1955), *Enjoyment of Music.* New York: Norton.

Madow, L. & Silverman, D. (1956), Child Analysis Seminar, Philadelphia Association for Psychoanalysis. Unpublished.

Magran, B. (1964), Personal communication.

Mahler, M. S. (1949), Psychoanalytic Evaluation of Tics: A Sign and Symptom in Psychopathology. *This Annual*, 3/4:279-310.

Malone, A. & Massler, M. (1952), Index of Nailbiting in Children. *J. Abnorm. Soc. Psychol.*, 47:193-202.

Mittelmann, B. (1954), Motility in Infants, Children, and Adults: Patterning and Psychodynamics. *This Annual*, 9:142-177.

Pearson, G. H. J. (1949), *Emotional Disorders of Childhood*. New York: Norton, 1949.

—— et al. (1956, 1964), Child Analysis seminars, Philadelphia Association for Psychoanalysis. Unpublished.

Piaget, J. (1923), *The Language and Thought of the Child*. New York: Harcourt Brace, 1932.

—— (1936), *The Origins of Intelligence in Children*. New York: International Universities Press, 1952.

—— (1937), *The Construction of Reality in the Child*. New York: Basic Books, 1954.

Rickers-Ovsiankina, M. A., ed. (1960), *Rorschach Psychology*. New York: John Wiley.

Schilder, P. (1935), *The Image and Appearance of the Human Body*. New York: International Universities Press, 1950.

A BOY DISCOVERS HIS PENIS

JAMES A. KLEEMAN, M.D. (New Haven, Conn.)

The drama implied in the title is in the mind of the adult[1] and the title actually refers to a rather undramatic moment in the first year of the male child.[2] Several authors (Spitz and Wolf, Lampl-de Groot) have stressed the limitations of studies to date in this area of autoeroticity and genital manipulation. Spitz and Wolf (1949) state: "A really unimpeachable study would have to offer continuous 24-hour observation of the infant during the whole of the first year of life." Longitudinal studies of individual children offer a partial answer to this problem. In this paper I shall utilize observations of a male infant throughout his first year to compare with certain general statements in the literature about autoerotic activity, genital play, and genital discovery and to illustrate certain specific items of interest about this child which the longitudinal case method makes possible.

SOURCE OF DATA

The author has undertaken the longitudinal collection of information about a small number of children where his own observations are greatly enriched by the daily recorded observations of the mother of each child. Part of the method is described elsewhere (Kleeman, 1964). Though, in general, the validity of child data collected by parents is "impeachable," the circumstances of the child to be de-

---

Assistant Clinical Professor, Department of Psychiatry, Yale University, New Haven, Connecticut.

[1] Cf. Freud (1905): "Among the erotogenic zones that form part of the child's body there is one which certainly does not play the opening part, and which cannot be the vehicle of the oldest sexual impulses, but which is destined to great things in the future" (p. 187).

[2] In Casuso's report (1957) the genital discovery was more dramatic because it was associated with anxiety.

239

scribed were fortuitous for obtaining information about genital self-stimulation. "Genital play" was only one of a number of behaviors studied, but other material about this child here reported will be limited to that necessary to clarify the focus of this paper.

This boy, William W., was nursed by his mother throughout the first year (weaning from the breast was completed late in his sixteenth month). Since he did not drink milk from a bottle or cup and was nursing three times a day at eleven months and two times a day at one year, his mother was out of the home without him at most only a few hours at a time throughout this year. Furthermore, since he was in diapers and rubber pants except during his bath and since the mother exclusively gave him his baths, we have available as complete a record of his exploration of his genitals as one could hope to obtain in a home setting. Mrs. W. was a sensitive observer of people, which enhanced the value of the material. Thus this method of data collection not only permits an exact dating of the first time William discovered his penis but also offers a record of essentially every time he did so during his first twelve months.

Mrs. W. was a well-educated woman. She and her husband were agreed that William's interest in all parts of his body was a normal evolution. She neither encouraged nor discouraged his genital manipulations and visual interest, but just observed their unfolding (with the exception of distracting his handling himself when he was being cleaned after a bowel movement).

Other than a skin condition and a gastrointestinal disorder, both detailed below, William in his first year was a healthy, large (9 lbs. at birth), alert, vigorous, active infant, advanced in social responsiveness, affectionate behavior, gross motor activity (he walked effectively at eleven months), and language development (in addition to *mama* and *dada*, at eleven months his vocabulary included sounds used meaningfully for no, yes, nice, car, bye, baby, ball, kitty, and thank you).

OBSERVATIONS

Observation 1 (0;8 + 0):[3] He was just eight months to the day. There he sat in the bathtub playing with the rubber mat beneath himself as the water ran out the tub. Looking down, he spied a small

---

[3] The observations reported here are only selected samples from a much larger total, and usually only fragments from a given observation are included for the sake of brevity.

object between his chunky, little thighs. He reached down and gently felt it in his fingers (his initial approach to anything new was usually a gentle one). He moved it and squeezed it with interest several times. He released his hand and reached again for the bathmat and then for the drain plug and, as if he were suddenly reminded, once again he lowered his eyes and put his hand down to discover anew his penis.[4]

Observation 2 (0;8 + 30):[5] After his bath William was sitting undressed on his mother's knee facing a mirror as his mother was putting on his shirt. He saw his penis in the mirror and looked intently at it. He made no movement to reach for it or touch it but stared with interest for about ninety seconds.

It seems reasonable to assume that William had essentially no established mental representation of his genitalia at this time. In contrast, he had a developed mental part image of his thumb, which he sucked vigorously to ease distress. Often he put his toes in his mouth and sucked them, "knowing" them, at least, as appendages.[6]

Between eight and ten months William was making a good start at self-sufficiency. In his bath he would suck on the rubber mat or a washcloth, splash, and "swim." His forefinger-thumb coordination had enabled him for some time to feed himself pieces of bread and other food skillfully; he could with great fascination open and close a doll's eye with his forefinger. At nine months he was a real explorer with curiosity and intrusiveness and a special mechanical bent. He made wheels spin and examined various protuberances— light switches, radio and phonograph knobs. He pulled out drawers, turned on radios, flushed toilets, and unscrewed tops of jars.

Observation 3 (0;10 + 6):[7] After nursing at the first breast and before starting at the other, William explored the nipple of his

[4] In this observation which gives the paper its title I have quoted the mother directly.

[5] Between the initial observation and Observation 2, William did not again direct attention to his unclothed genitalia.

[6] This was a baby who at a very young age was observed to be remarkably aware of form: he reached with his mouth for nipples, toys, mother's nose, fingers, breast, etc. When he began to utilize his hand at eleven and a half weeks, he then reached with his hand as well as his mouth for these positive forms. He would regularly grasp his mother's facial features and fingers.

[7] In contrast to his other two nursings, which preceded sleep, the initial nursing of the day was carried out in the light. The mother, hoping this might enhance a feeling of separateness and encourage weaning, permitted William to examine her breast sometimes at this feeding.

mother's breast with great interest. He held it between his fore-finger and thumb and squeezed it several times.[8]

Observation 4 (0;10 + 9): William played with his genitals again, for the first time in two months. It also occurred this time in the bath. He had an erection. I am not certain whether this preceded, or was the result of, his manipulation. He played with one hand and then with both, talking in a quiet jabber as he did. He then got on all fours and "peeked" as if to check if his penis was still there, but his pendulous belly made viewing difficult. He sat down and checked. He felt himself a little more. That was that![9]

This second occurrence of tactile genital self-stimulation was two months and nine days after the first. In the interval there was the single instance of visual interest in the mirror and a few occasions when he would clutch his genital area through his diapers, usually when they were wet or contained a bowel movement. Following this date, visual and tactile interest in his genitals was regular and frequent, though not daily.

Observation 5 (0;10 + 10): In the tub on this day William touched his penis with his forefinger. He rubbed his thighs together, which appeared stimulating to the genitals. He had an erection part of the time.

Observation 6 (0;10 + 11): Today in the bath, William did not touch his genitals. At one point he was on all fours looking back at himself. This was the third consecutive day he had an erection in the bath. It was clear this time it occurred spontaneously. He also paid special attention to his knee, touching and rubbing it.[10]

Observation 7 (0;10 + 14): William showed tumescence throughout the bath.[11] He examined his penis with his forefinger and then stroked it with his forefinger and thumb back and forth four times.

This kind of tactile genital self-stimulation was rather characteristic of what was observed during his eleventh month. It also resem-

[8] The quality of this fingering, its intensity, and his facial expression were reminiscent of his "discovery" and examination of his penis at eight months.

[9] This is again a direct quotation from the mother.

[10] The intensity of the interest in the knee seemed about equivalent to that shown for the genitalia or for certain external objects at this time and represented his increasing awareness of this sector of his body.

[11] The mother thought prolonged tumescence might indicate a full bladder. She stated that when changing him as a newborn, she would wait before putting on a dry diaper (but would keep him covered) when he had an erection. She said he usually would urinate if she waited a few minutes, and the erection was her clue.

bled his behavior at this time with the nipple of his mother's breast. The mother felt that the nipple was similar to the penis in color, temperature, erectile tissue, and, to the baby boy, similar in size. The day following this observation William began walking unaided.

Observation 8 (0;10 + 18): On the three previous days there was no genital touching in the bath. This evening William showed interest in his penis as soon as he was in the tub and remained interested throughout the bath. While sitting, he bent over trying to look at himself. He touched his penis with the thumb of one hand. Then with the other hand he held the penis with his forefinger and thumb. After additional clutching of the whole genitalia and squeezing of the penis, William started to get an erection. Near the end of the bath he was holding the penis between his thumb and forefinger. He began tugging at it back and forth in a more vigorous fashion than had previously been observed. After he stopped, he bent over again and tried to see.

Observation 9 (0;10 + 27): In the bath William approached his genitals with an open hand and partly enveloped his scrotal sac and penis together. Bending over, he looked at his penis, tugged on it, and continued to look at it off and on throughout the bath. While holding his penis, he looked up at his mother's face with a facial expression she interpreted as "Isn't it wonderful!" She responded, "That is your penis; you like that?"

In diapering William afterward the mother retracted the remnant of his circumcised foreskin to clean the area. He giggled as she did this.

It is fairly apparent that by this time the genital area had sensation of a special quality. However, it was not yet clear whether the degree of sensation was markedly different from the sensation that produced laughter when he was "tickled" in other sensitive parts of his body.

Observation 10 (0;10 + 28): As warm water came flowing in around William sitting in the bath, both testicles retracted upward and the penis seemed to bob up and become partially erect. At this point William grasped his penis in his fingers. The penis remained erect. He bent over, presumably to look at it.[12]

---

[12] Earlier the same day William had again fingered the mother's nipple during the nursing period in a way very similar to the above fingering of his penis. Though I have assumed that his bending over was always to look at his penis, the breast-penis equation here leaves open the possibility that bending over also involved a wish to suck on the penis.

Observation 11 (0;11 + 1): At the outset of his bath William looked down at the genital area, took his penis in his fingers several times, briefly, for not more than thirty seconds and then did not touch his penis the rest of the bath despite the fact that the penis was erect most of it. After his mother washed his legs, there was soap left on the right knee and leg. With his right hand he made a washing movement over the knee and part of the thigh and leg as the mother had done. It apparently felt good or he enjoyed doing it, for he smiled; he then repeated the stroking of the right knee, making six rotations. At the end of the bath when the soap had been rinsed away, he again carried out the motion over the right knee.

Though the recorded observations focus on the genital self-stimulation and activities, it is important to emphasize that they represent a very small fraction of his total daily interest in himself and his surroundings. In the bath itself the great majority of time was spent otherwise, getting up and down, splashing, trying to drink bathwater, patting the wall, opening and closing the drain, holding something, sucking on a washcloth, etc. He almost always wished to hold something in his hand during his bath, such as a washcloth, toothbrush, plastic bottle, or ball.

During the twenty-four days following his second genital self-stimulation there was some tactile self-stimulation of his genitals on fourteen days.

Observation 12 (0;11 + 8): William walked unclothed from his room to the tub. He touched his penis as he entered the bathroom (possibly in response to his mother's looking at his genital area momentarily). During most of the bath he played with a washcloth. As the water was draining out, William grabbed at his penis and held it with one hand. He released the penis shortly thereafter, and pressed his genitalia with a plastic bottle he was holding in the other hand. He rubbed the bottle against his penis. He again put his free hand back on his penis and pulled back and forth on the foreskin, in fine movements with his fingers. He squeezed the penis and testicles together and moved them around. The penis became erect. The mother (who frankly acknowledged her interest in his budding masculinity) said, "Do you like it, Billy?" Shortly he let go; the mother did not focus any more attention on his genitalia. The erection gradually subsided.

This incident had the quality of intent to excite by self-stimulation (in contrast to the wish to explore, with stimulation the inevitable result). There was nothing one could characterize as an orgasm.

Observation 13 (0;11 + 12): As the water came in, William was sitting on the rubber mat, mouthing a small ball. He had a spontaneous partial erection without touching or gazing at his genitals. When his mother washed the genital area and, on this occasion, retracted the foreskin, he immediately reached with his right hand to his penis and "washed" it in three rubbing motions. He looked as he did. He did not touch his genitals again during the bath, though a partial erection remained for awhile.

This seemed a clear-cut example of an active self-stimulation following the passive receipt of stimulation from his mother, although there were many occasions when her ministrations did not evoke such a response.

Observation 14 (0;11 + 16): During this bath William neither looked at nor touched his genitals; however, a variety of tumescences and detumescences and testicular movements were observed. The first tumescence occurred as William sat with his right foot tucked under his buttocks and genitalia. The added pressure of his foot against the genitalia as he moved his body or his foot seemed responsible for the erection.

Observation 15 (0;11 + 27): In changing his diapers, Mrs. W. noted that his knee was bent so that the heel of one foot was pressing his genitals. He rubbed the heel against the genitalia four times with a resulting increase of erection. At two other diaper changes, when his diapers were removed, William extended his legs and squeezed them together exhibiting total body tension. (It also seemed to involve genital stimulation via thigh pressure.) In the bath the degree of genital stimulation was greater than had been seen recently. At the outset, he lightly touched the tip of his penis with a forefinger. He explored his genitalia with his hand, squeezing and looking and stroking, all briefly, and then shifted the activity to the knee. His mother's washing did not renew the genital touching. As the water went out, he made his most active approach to his genitals. He looked down at his partially erect phallus, squeezed it, rubbed it back and forth, squeezed again, and tugged on the foreskin, lasting about fifteen seconds in all. He shifted his interest to the drain handle, and then got up on his feet and hands and looked backward at himself. As he was dried in his mother's lap, his thumb went into his mouth.

Observation 16 (0;11 + 29): At the beginning of his bath William grasped a toothbrush in his hand, and alternately banged it against the wall, sucked it or just held it. He had a 1+ erection at this moment.[13] Several times he lightly put both hands to his lap, perhaps touching his genitals. He then held his penis between his thumb and forefinger, squeezing it gently, as the water came into the tub. Shortly thereafter, he was observed to have a 3+ erection, and both hands dropped to his lap, one still holding the toothbrush. The hands lightly touched his erect penis but did not grasp it. (The movement seemed to be a response to the erection.) During the last part of the bath there was no (0) erection and no more touching of his phallus. He sucked his thumb actively in his mother's lap after the bath. She permitted him to play, unclothed, in his crib for a few minutes, which included his lying face down and rocking his pelvis on the crib sheet several times. This seemed pleasurable to him, though he did not reach for his genitals. In being diapered William squeezed his thighs together while extending his legs.

This observation brings us to the end of William's first year. He touched his genitalia on seventeen of the previous twenty-nine days and looked, without touching, on two additional days. His genital self-stimulation at one year appeared more complex than a month earlier and was associated with an interesting cognitive development in another mental sphere; his capacity for organizing percepts was now such that he made connections between parts. A simple example concerned a small plastic bottle and snap-on top. He knew how the two went together. He could remove the top, and attempted to replace it. Failing this, he would hand them to his mother, vividly indicating that she should and could do it. The process was then repeated a number of times.

The observations continued throughout his thirteenth and fourteenth months. They will be summarized. There was a definite increase in tactile self-stimulation and visual interest during the thirteenth month compared with the twelfth, but especially noteworthy was the prominence of bending over and looking at his genitalia, often with no touching. There were many more clear-cut occurrences where self-stimulation aroused an erection, although spontaneous tumescences were still in evidence. For this child the erections themselves were apparently not yet especially sexually exciting since they usually did not attract his attention when they arose

13 From this time for the duration of the observations a rough grading of the degree of penile erection was attempted: 0 for no erection, 1+ for slight, 2+ for moderate, and 3+ for full erection.

spontaneously. Whereas in the eleventh month his approach was often to the whole genitalia, progressively in the twelfth and thirteenth months the penis was singled out, undoubtedly because of its special sensation, for focused attention.

Self-stimulation through thigh pressure was frequent in the thirteenth month, but this and tactile self-stimulation decreased somewhat in the fourteenth month, possibly because of his focus upon apparent discomfort associated with prolonged upper respiratory infections. However, a good deal of bending and looking persisted in the bath. Four observations during these two months warrant special mention:

1;0 + 15: The mother put her hand inside his diaper to see if it was wet; her hand touched his penis. His immediate response was to stroke her cheek and say "Ni" (making nice). (This is a striking example of a passivity-activity connection and a reversal of the process whereby general affection from the mother leads to genital sensation [cf. Kris, 1951, p. 100].)

1;1 + 20: William had a 3+ tumescence in his bath which was followed immediately by detumescence (0) after urination.

1;1 + 21: William stood for quite awhile in his bath so that it was possible to observe without difficulty spontaneous tumescence and detumescence occurring without any tactile stimulation of the genitals.

1;1 + 25: After bending over on all fours to look at his genitalia three separate times, William was sitting in the bath. His mother named body parts, which he knew, suggesting he wash his knee. As she pointed to the knee, he stroked it with the washcloth. She encouraged him to wash his belly, touching it as she pointed to it. He did not acknowledge her but instead reached for his penis and tugged at it. She again pointed to the belly and suggested he wash it, and he repeated the same behavior. This time his tugging aroused an erection (3+).

Discussion

Freud referred to masturbation in many of his writings without exploring its genesis or manifestations exhaustively in any (Freud, 1912; Levin, 1963). He referred to masturbation in earliest infancy especially in two writings (Freud, 1905, 1912).

In reviewing the rest of the significant literature relating to the development of interest in the genitals during the first year of life, one finds the work of Spitz especially noteworthy and widely quoted. Several aspects of his writing on this subject (Spitz and Wolf, 1949; Spitz, 1962, 1952) stimulated reporting the above observations. Both he and Lampl-de Groot cite the limited data available on normal children and the need for twenty-four-hour observations throughout the year. Obviously that kind of observation of a normal child in the natural setting of the home is possible only through the mothering person and then only under unusual circumstances. Thus far information of a longitudinal nature is scanty.

Body-Image Learning

My primary intent was to make behavioral observations. Then secondarily, I wished to compare these data with existing psychoanalytic developmental propositions.[14]

In the papers of Spitz dealing most extensively with "genital play" in the first year of life he approaches the data from the standpoint of a selected aspect of existing psychoanalytic theory; i.e., he views the observations under the heading of autoerotism. While his work in this area has given us very valuable information, this method would obscure one of the more important findings derived from the observations of William; though his genital touching in the first year had a gradually increasing autoerotic element in it, the autoerotic did not seem the most significant aspect of the behavior. Rather the discovery of a part of his body and emerging delineation of it overshadowed the drive gratification or pleasure element (cf. Provence and Lipton, 1962). Several authors have criticized the tendency of psychoanalysts to stress autoerotism in the self-stimulation of the first year and to minimize body-image learning in this behavior (Kinsey et al., 1948, p. 498; Escalona, 1963).

A. Freud (1953), Kris et al. (1954), and Greenacre (1953, 1958) have emphasized the emergence of body image and the establishment of a body self through self-stimulation (see also Loewenstein, 1950, p. 48). For example, A. Freud (see Kris et al., 1954) states: "Here ap-

14 Hartmann, Kris, and Loewenstein (1953, p. 16) rightly raise a question about such an approach when they remind us that the collection of observable data is always influenced by explicit and implicit assumptions. However, it is also patent that too strict an adherence to a theoretical framework or segment of that theory can lead to minimizing certain aspects of behavior observed.

plies Dr. Greenacre's suggestion that the pain produced by head knocking may serve the purpose of establishing an otherwise missing body reality for the child. Perhaps the aim of establishing a closer relationship with one's own body underlies many of the autoerotic or autoaggressive practices as a secondary, subsidiary purpose" (p. 41). The observations of William suggest that for this normal infant during the latter part of the first year (when thumb sucking and a soft diaper pressed against the cheek, partly covering the eyes, were the dominant modes of self-stimulation of a comforting nature) genital tactile self-stimulation and visual exploratory behavior had the *primary* aim of establishing a closer relationship with his body and the erotic aim was distinctly secondary, in the sense that intentional self-arousal and self-absorption qualities were not prominent.[15] Two studies, in particular, have clearly brought out how self-stimulation tends to assist the infant in distinguishing between self and the outer world through the avenue of discovering body reality (Provence and Lipton, 1962; Escalona, 1963).

Degree of Eroticity of Genital Self-Stimulation

This leads us to the important question: How erotic is genital self-stimulation in the first year?[16] One can elucidate three positions in regard to this question. At one extreme are the statements of a number of analysts who attach great erotic significance to the "genital play," masturbation, or genital self-stimulation in the first year of life. An example of this point of view is from A. Balint (1954): "We know that genital erotism manifests itself even in babyhood, in infantile masturbation. . . . We may conclude that from the very beginning the genitals have this property of affording sensuous

[15] Data of A. Freud and Burlingham (1944) tend to support this idea. They noted that infants under conditions of maternal deprivation show an increased gratification from thumb sucking, rocking, and head knocking without any increase in baby masturbation (first and second years).

[16] Lustman (1956) described an experimental evaluation of sensitivity of erogenous zones in neonates. Though the lips represented the most sensitive erogenous zone, this was a relative, not an absolute primacy. There were striking individual differences in sensitivity among the babies, and there were infants who hyperreacted in all zones stimulated (including the genital), even though the lips were the most sensitive zone. This work has not been carried out by Lustman or others on older infants. Various data suggest to me that at one year the oral area is still the most sensitive zone for a majority of healthy infants represented by William, but certainly not for all (see the infant *Sybil* at twenty-eight weeks in Escalona, 1963), and certain infants at one year show marked genital sensitivity compared with other infants of the same age.

pleasure. . . . Infantile masturbation should be regarded in the same way as, for example, thumb-sucking. At this age it has no more, but also no less significance."

At the other extreme is the belief that the genital touching and stimulation in the first year are the equivalent of the discovery and play with a toe or knee. Spock (1946) records: "Babies in the last half of the first year discover their genitals the way they discover their fingers and toes, and handle them the same way, too."

My own experience favors a position midway between these. Several of the qualities which may characterize an erotic activity are an absorption of the attention by it and a mounting excitation. Mild pleasure rather than the prominence of these other two qualities marked William's tactile stimulation of his genitals in the first year. Among the writers espousing this point of view are Bender (1939), Engel (1962), Levine (1951), Murphy (1964), Provence and Lipton (1962), Ribble (1955), Spitz and Wolf (1949, p. 102), and Stone and Church (1957).

However, under certain circumstances a greater degree of genital sensitivity in the first year exists in individual infants: (1) One of the babies tested by Lustman (1956, p. 94) showed a hyperresponse to air stimulation of the genitalia at three to four days after birth, indicating an innate characteristic. (2) In some cultures mothers actively stimulate the children's genitalia either to soothe them or teach them to masturbate (Sears, Maccoby, and Levin, 1957). (3) In the case described by Sylvester (1947) excessive masturbation was a clinical symptom of an eleven-month-old boy. Maternal care consisted of nearly uninterrupted attention to and manipulation of him. Masturbation ensued whenever attention was discontinued, even briefly. It would seem that either innate or especially environmental factors can lead to heightened genital sensitivity in the first year.

Greenacre (see Kris et al., 1954) reports that situations of stress can lead to inappropriately precocious development resulting in genital orgasm in the first year, from about the eighth month on (see Townsend, 1896). Isaacs (1935) also makes a claim for genital orgasm in the first year. Spitz's impressive experience certainly makes the occurrence of orgasm in this age group sound rare indeed: "In all the series of over a thousand children I have seen and observed, of these four hundred long-term and continuously, I have never in the first

year seen an orgasm stemming from genital stimulation" (see Kris
et al., 1954, p. 54). Spitz's thorough review of the literature also left
him suspicious of the reports of orgasm in the first two years. There
was nothing in the observations of William approaching the excitement of orgasm or even the "acme" reported by Lampl-de Groot
(1950).

There are two facts of life about male infants which distinctly
make stimulation of the genitals different from stimulating the knee,
for example, and certainly suggest a greater erotic quality than knee
stimulation: (1) tumescence and (2) reflex movement of the testicles.

Relatively little has been written about the erections of boy infants in the first year (Halverson, 1938, 1940; Greenacre, 1941; and
Casuso, 1957). The observations of William in this area of tumescence are suggestive but are difficult to interpret because of the problem of accurate observation. Noting the degree of erection in an
active little boy through soapy bath water, without being too obvious
about the observing, presents obstacles, which are less in a younger
child lying nude in his crib. However, it can be said that erections
and partial erections were frequent (they could be seen either at
diaper changing or in the bath almost daily); more arose reflexly
than through genital stimulation. As Halverson (1940) pointed out,
there was often an association with micturition; i.e., tumescence
would occur as the bladder was full and detumescence followed
quickly after urination. On rare occasions the tumescence would
draw William's attention to his genitalia. His mother's cleaning the
area or his own touching would stimulate an erection more commonly later in the period reported than earlier (see Casuso, 1957).
By fourteen months it was very common.

We do not know how testicular movement feels to a one-year-old.
It occurs frequently during diapering, cleansing, and bathing, and it
seems reasonable to assume that some awareness of this is present
on some level and that the testicular movement confers on genital
stimulation an additional quality of sensation unlike any other body
part (see A. Bell, 1961).

The observations point to an increasing interest in visual exploration and tactile self-stimulation of the genitalia as the first year
progressed. There was a suggestion of increasing genital sensitivity,
particularly in the way the phallus became singled out for special

attention.[17] Most authors writing on the subject describe a progressive interest, but as Casuso noted, it is an interest with discontinuities. For example, in William's fourteenth month, he would frequently stare at his genitalia and check on them visually, but tactile stimulation was decreased. Greenacre (1958) and others have pointed to the increase in genital feeling late in the second year and into the third (when masturbation really deserves the name).

Significance for Future Development

A related question about which we can only speculate, because of the multiple variables, concerns the significance of genital self-stimulation in the first year for future personality and sexual development. Freud (1905) expressed the extreme view that the libidinal aspect is of great importance: ". . . it is scarcely possible to avoid the conclusion that the foundations for the future primacy over sexual activity exercised by this erotogenic zone are established by early infantile masturbation, which scarcely a single individual escapes" (p. 188). Others have re-emphasized this libidinal significance. The answer to this question depends to some extent on the earlier answer to: how *erotic* is the self-stimulation? The work of Escalona (1963) and Lustman (1956) and others suggests that no one answer describes all babies, and that the experience (innate characteristics interacting with environment) of individual babies varies tremendously. For many normal infants, of which William would be representative, I would shift Freud's emphasis. I believe that genital self-stimulation in the first year of a normal child takes its place among the many experiences contributing to healthy personality growth and sexual development. It is the beginning stage of later sexual activity, much as the saying of "ba, ba" is preparatory for later complex speech; rather than making a major contribution to sexual development, first year genital self-stimulation is an indicator of the quality of object relations (Spitz, 1962, p. 311), which is truly crucial for future sexual and libidinal development. From the standpoint of libidinal development genital self-stimulation in the first year does not, in most babies, have the importance of phase-specific oral ex-

[17] However, if one compares William's genital sensitivity as seen in the observations early in the fifteenth month with those at eight months or one year, the increase is striking (see observation on 1;2 + 5).

periences. Yet, "An infant learns by doing. The more he applies whatever he is capable of at the time by way of orienting and adapting his behavior to what he perceives, the more does the very act of practicing push him toward the next step" (Escalona, 1963, p. 219). In addition, the genital self-stimulation is an expression of the multiple factors of maturational processes, progressive awareness of one's own body, the quality of maternal care, and the interaction between the baby and the mothering person. Therefore, the genital self-stimulation both reflects and facilitates the development of the awareness of the body (Provence and Lipton, 1962, p. 119) and, to a lesser degree, libidinal development in general and genital sexual activity in particular.

Genesis of Genital Self-Stimulation

What is the genesis of genital self-stimulation? What factors contribute to its presence or absence? It is clear that maturational factors, such as a certain level of purposeful motor coordination and skill and of functional use of the visual apparatus, are essential. As discussed, innate variability of erogenous zone sensitivity might affect timing, preferred modes of self-stimulation, and interaction with the environment. Controversial is the degree to which mechanical stimulation, such as cleansing, powdering, and bathing by the mother, contributes to self-stimulation. Provence and Lipton (1962) list three key factors of adequate maternal care leading to optimal development of the body scheme: (1) the "dosage" of stimuli (particularly the tactile and kinesthetic); (2) the maturational phase in which the stimulation occurs; and (3) the emotional environment. They emphasize that ministrations of the mother are essential to the infant's awareness of his own body. Spitz and Wolf (1949) stress: " 'a close *and* balanced' mother-child relationship is an important prerequisite for the development of genital play during the first year of life" (p. 99). The observations of William do not conflict with this finding.

Unanswered is the question, raised by A. Freud (see Kris et al., 1954, p. 61), "whether autoerotic activities exist in their own right as the expression of the child's relationship to his own body, or whether the body is used only as a substitute for the mother, and has to fill the needs which have been frustrated by her." A. Freud (1953) writes extensively, expressing the feeling that autoerotic ac-

tivities increase and fill the void when gratification from the mothering person falls short of what the child normally experiences (see
also A. Freud and Burlingham, 1944). However, she notes, as mentioned above, that "baby masturbation" is not one of the activities
showing such increase, suggestive, at least, that first year genital self-
stimulation is more an expression of the child's relation to his own
body. The fact that autoerotic activity tends to replace what is missing from the mother is one form of the infant's expressing actively
what was formerly passively experienced. This and other forms of an
activity-passivity relationship have been applied to autoerotic activities by Freud (1905, p. 188), Kris (1951), Mahler (see Kris et al., 1954,
p. 66), Provence and Lipton (1962, p. 121), and Escalona (1963).
Although several observations of William (0;11 + 12; 1;0 + 15 and
1;2 + 5) illustrate this, under normal conditions the active carrying
out precisely what has been experienced passively does not seem to
contribute as much to genital self-stimulation as it does to some other
first year autoerotic behaviors. In the case of Sylvester (1947) an abnormal situation, a generalized overstimulation (without any specific
mention of genital stimulation or seduction), resulted in masturbation as a cause for referral at eleven months.

Spitz and Wolf (1949) make some observations relevant to this
issue, concluding: "There is further evidence that genital stimulation
in itself is not sufficient to provoke genital play . . . our material
shows that eczema and genital play are independent of each other. . . .
Thus we have at present no adequate explanation why a 'close'
mother-child relation, without particular genital stimulation should
result in genital play when local stimulation does not" (p. 101f.).

Kris (1951) directs himself to this very point: "The transfer from
general affection to the genital zone itself is a complex process; it
need not only come about by the direct contact of the mother with
the genital region of the child during her ministrations, an experience the child would repeat by self-stimulation. It may also arise as
consequence of the general bodily closeness to which, we assume, the
child tends to react with sensation in the genital region. . . . The
genital self-stimulation could then replace the more general stimulation which had produced the pleasurable sensation in the genital
region" (p. 100f.).

Based partly on observations not included here, I suggest adding to Kris's formulation that an early identification process is involved in the one-year-old's self-stimulation. His behavior toward his own body reflects in part his mother's behavior toward him. By acting himself in the mother's place, he simulates the whole experience with the mother, inclusive of the sensation she stimulated. Theoretically, after perceiving, representing, and organizing the mother's care, the one-year-old can then discharge maturational drive representatives in the activity of self-stimulation (see Lipin, 1963).

Referring again to A. Freud's question, I believe we can assume the position that genital self-stimulation represents an expression of the child's relation to his own body as well as an active and independent expression of what the infant receives from the mother's general care. This is supported by the thesis that genital self-stimulation in the first year is primarily a maturationally relevant exploratory activity (part of a normal infant's investigation of his own body and its boundaries), and only secondarily is an erotic activity. Related is the fact that severe deprivation of maternal care not only causes a stunting or absence of genital self-stimulation and autoerotic activities (except rocking) but also seriously impairs, to varying degrees, a whole array of ego functions, healthy drive derivatives, and later superego functions. "If essential experiences are not lived-through, regardless of cause, percepts and representations indispensable for discharge of related maturational drive-representatives are not available" (Lipin, 1963).

One way to test these hypotheses is by attempting prediction in longitudinal observations of individual children. I shall close this part of the discussion with some pertinent quotations from Escalona and description of an attempt at prediction concerning William.

Although genital self-stimulation was not part of Escalona's (1963) data (the babies described by her were only twenty-eight weeks old), several of her conclusions are applicable to the issue of the genesis of autoerotic activities with special focus on the activity-passivity question:

[1] One of the adaptive consequences of the entire process of ego formation is that the infant changes from primarily reactive patterns of behavior to active ones . . . this growing capacity to act upon the environment might be described as "behavioral autonomy" . . . this matter of behavioral autonomy is important as a

. . . component of the child's changing transactions with the physical environment, including the own body [p. 223f.]. [2] The data suggest that the same developmental transitions may be accomplished by different routes, depending upon the infant's established reaction propensities, and the mother's mode of dealing with the child [p. 241]. [3] Infants differ in the type of body stimulation[18] which they conspicuously show. The data suggest that infants provide for themselves the kind of bodily sensation which mothers have provided for them at moments of intense and pleasurable interaction [p. 241].

The point made under 3 was essentially what I had in mind when making a prediction about William when he was eight months. As an infant, he was unusually active, highly sensitive perceptually, and subject to an extraordinary kinesthetic experience when nursing at the breast (moments of intense and usually pleasurable interaction). Because of a peculiar gastrointestinal intolerance, he was subject to much distress during the day. He was able to tolerate very little solid food[19] and would interrupt nursing with crying, pulling away, and burps. His mother gradually found that motion seemed to relax him. It would keep him nursing at the breast with diminished discomfort. She provided this by remaining standing, while nursing,

---

[18] Patterns of bodily self-stimulation.

[19] The pediatrician, noting William's healthy appearance and development, approved the mother's trial-and-error method of diet selection in order to permit the baby the least fretful day. She gradually evolved a solid diet largely of bananas (in the form of banana flakes), supplemented by small amounts of applesauce, strained pears, oatmeal or cream of wheat in addition to nursing. Any attempt to expand this basic diet would result in what the mother described as a tense and bloated abdomen, fast thoracic breathing protective of the abdominal area, writhing, twisting, and disturbed naptimes and night sleep. She said, "His burps were more like the belches of an adult who has overeaten than like those of a baby having taken in air."

Extreme were his responses to animal proteins, including cow's milk. Thus, the nutritional aspect of nursing encouraged the mother to continue beyond ten months, although she was prepared and hopeful to begin weaning by that time. Mrs. W. describes another factor as follows, which she felt was prime in causing her to continue: "Although William showed only moderate interest in the breast, nursing seemed to offer a prolonged and intense positive relationship outside the baby that I had wished would counteract the prolonged and intense negative inner frustration, and hopefully secure for him a foundation of trust. I reduced his nursing one feeding at a time until we were down to one a day at thirteen months (which marked his beginning tolerance of whole cow's milk). When I weaned him completely at sixteen months, it was because he showed a greater tolerance for more foods and because, in a number of ways, he exhibited a new kind of separateness from me implying characteristics of an inner security I had wanted for him. I then felt satisfied that Billy was really beginning to know where Billy (cramps and all) ended and where mommy began."

so that she was able to walk, sway, hop, or dance to radio music. She would sometimes bump his buttocks against the wall lightly and rhythmically which enabled him, on occasion, to relieve himself of rectal gas. This truly exhausting procedure for the mother for a 15-20 minute nursing was greatly preferred to the interrupted feeding, crying, gastrointestinal distress, and frustration for mother and child that was frequent without it. This went on between four and eight months. When William was eight months, I made the prediction that at about one year, it would find expression in some rhythmic autoerotic activity. However, this did not occur, possibly because nursing continued through this period (much less kinesthetic activity was needed). William rocked some in his crib around nine months, but the dominant mode of self-stimulation was thumb sucking, sometimes with a soft diaper pressed against his face. There was occasional playful head banging at a year, but no significant rocking, head banging or other major rhythmic activity. Escalona anticipated the complexity of such a prediction. In conjunction with point 3 quoted above she added: "In this area, too, the facts are such that knowing how the mother tends to stimulate her infant does not predict the preferred modality for autoerotic activity in the baby. Nor is there a consistent relationship between that modality to which the infant proves most reactive and the modality he chooses for conspicuous self-stimulation" (p. 241f.). *Retrospectively*, it is not difficult to understand why this infant utilized thumb sucking and a soft diaper pressed against the face as his preferred modes of self-stimulation, expressing his experience (his innate characteristics and his mother's style of caring for him). In addition to the kinesthetic stimulation offered him, the mother was richly oral herself. She kissed him a lot, talked to him with the use of a variety of facial expressions, sang freely, and offered him the breast to satiety. She also exposed him to much tactile pleasure.

Below I discuss four items specifically derived from the observations of William:

Age of Onset

1. The age of onset of genital self-stimulation could be precisely stated. Two points are of interest, knowledge of the exact age of onset and the prolonged interval before it was resumed more con-

sistently. The first genital touching occurred on the day he was eight months old. This was not repeated until he reached ten months nine days.

Spitz, after extensive bibliographic research, comments: "In the literature on infantile autoerotic activities collected by us, references to exact age of the inception of genital play are almost absent" (Spitz and Wolf, 1949, p. 91). Spitz shows a chart of the age of onset in the twenty-one "institution" infants who showed "genital play," one beginning at six months and over 60 per cent starting after ten months. In children reared in families with "excellent" mother-child relations Spitz found that sixteen out of seventeen infants studied manifested genital play within the first year, at ages which were on the average two months earlier than those observed in the institution (p. 95). Bender (1939) declares genital play begins between the eighth and ninth month in normal children. The infant reported by Loewenstein (1950) was ten months old and so was the boy described by Casuso (1957).

Bornstein (1953) states that pleasurable self-manipulation may occur in the fifth or sixth month. Levine (1951) reports that between five and six months an infant rarely finds his genitals, but the fingering is not purposeful or continuous. After six months the fingering of genitals begins to occur with greater frequency. Bell (1961) notes an infant, at about six months, who, making random movements toward the genital, manipulated the scrotal sac as his first encounter with his genitalia; only later, when more directed movements had developed, did he reach for the penis. Her observation and the following one from Halverson (1940) are of a different order from the "discovery" at eight months by William and the genital play reported by Spitz; the latter involve coordination of purposeful hand and finger movements and visual focus. Halverson describes a fifteen-week-old infant: "M's tumescences were usually of long duration and the cause of considerable annoyance to him. He repeatedly reached for his penis and scrotum and grasped or clawed them violently."

Role of Trauma

2. It is well established in psychoanalytic theory that various pregenital experiences or traumata can precociously erotize a zone or organ (Greenacre, 1965), but it is still a task of infant observers of the

present and future to delineate which experiences in which infants produce such a result. A negative correlation of this sort emerged from the longitudinal study of William. At two weeks of age he was found to have a prominent communicating hydrocele, which persisted for about six months; a severe excoriation of the scrotal sac and tip of the penis of unknown origin developed at the same time. Both of these caused increased manipulation of and attention to his genitalia by the mother and pediatrician. The skin rash lasted three weeks, was quite painful to the infant for about one week, being irritated by urine and bowel movements, and required frequent wet dressings and the application of ointments.[20] There was no evidence that the pain or extra manipulation affected the normal emergence of his genital self-stimulation late in the first year.[21] Spitz and Wolf (1949) have several similar cases, especially case N 18, although the conditions they reported were more complex and subject to several possible interpretations.

Thigh Pressure

3. A number of times on his changing table William was observed stretching his legs and squeezing his thighs in a way stimulating to his genitalia. The pleasure he seemed to derive from this was moderate at most; it appeared to be a transitory and normal phenomenon in his total development. It was of about as much importance as his infrequent head tapping (part of his varied explorations and stimulations of his surroundings and himself). Freud (1905, p. 188) refers to this form of self-stimulation, and Greenacre (1941) discusses it (see also Levine, 1951, p. 120). In a rarely quoted paper Rachford (1907) described this in detail. He cited a number of cases, documented its occasional early onset in the middle of the first year, and noted its predominance in females.

---

[20] Frequent warm baths, the treatment which seemed to offer the baby maximal relief through relaxing him, were not specifically zonally directed.

[21] It is evident from the following observation that, because of the augmented genital sensitivity and conscious awareness of it, the same genital attention at fourteen months would have had a markedly different impact: 1;2 + 5: William had a slight irritation around the urethral meatus. His mother applied ointment to the spot three times during the day, and on each occasion this minimal stimulation aroused an immediate (3+) erection. At one of these times he pushed his mother's hand away and stared quite intensely at her. At another he responded to the tumescence by squeezing his thighs together.

Visual Component

4. The visual component of William's genital exploration not only was important, but actually tended to supersede the tactile in later observations. Because of their location, the genitals and back are the last major external areas of the body discovered. Apprehending any object (external or body part) simultaneously in various modalities, such as touching or manipulating it while also looking at it, promotes a more distinct awareness of the thing or its properties than is possible through a single modality (Escalona, 1963, p. 221).[22] In the case of a body part there is the additional sensation created by the stimulation in the part itself. Greenacre (1958, 1960) has written extensively about the role of vision in developing a sense of identity, as an indispensable adjunct in establishing the confluence of the body surface, delimiting the self from the nonself, and integrating body parts into an organized central image. She points out that for a girl touch and vision play less of a part in forming the image of her own genitals than they do for a male.

Concept of Autoerotism Re-evaluated

Although the subject cannot be elaborated adequately here, data from a variety of sources converge to suggest that the concept of *autoerotism* in infancy is not well defined and requires re-examination (Provence and Lipton, 1962; Kinsey et al., 1948; Rapaport, 1960; Kris et al., 1954; Wolff, 1964; Escalona, 1963).

Freud originally used the term *autoerotic* to describe a relation to an object and did not regard the genesis of the excitation as the essential point (1905, p. 181). However, the etymological character of the term has resulted in its being commonly used more broadly.

Spitz and Wolf (1949) under a title of *Autoerotism* consider together rocking, genital play, and fecal games. They state, "Like sucking, these three activities are characterized by their rhythmicity, their character of self-stimulation, and the fact that the child appears to derive some sort of pleasure while performing them" (p. 86). Though these activities are all autoerotic as Freud defined it, autoerotism does not seem a fitting generic term for classifying them. For example,

---

22 I would like to cite vision for its special place among the sensory modalities in this regard. The eye is experienced as a confirmer of truth. What it can't see cannot be known as well. What it can see cannot be doubted.

several investigators have shown that rocking in the first year can arise in a number of different circumstances expressing different meanings, and at times with very little pleasure apparent (Provence and Lipton, 1962; Kris, 1951; Kris et al., 1954; Wolff, 1964; Brody, 1960; A. Freud and Burlingham, 1944).

I believe that a future classification of the behaviors which have been subsumed under *autoerotism* will have to heed David Rapaport's warning (1960) that (1) psychoanalytic theory conceives of such a concept to explain *behavior;* (2) there has been a tendency to use explanatory concepts as though they referred to specific behaviors rather than to specific aspects of behavior. It is suggestive that one could and should describe genital touching, for example, theoretically in terms of the following propositions: dynamic (sexual or aggressive drive or both and tendency for excitation or discharge), economic (amount of pleasure or energy involved), structural and adaptive ("auto" aspect, reality testing, development of sense of self, etc.), genetic (regressive quality, history of the behavior), and psychosocial (the behavior will be subject to what the environment wishes to make of it and will be molded by the culture-bearing parents).

Future classifications should include the not yet adequately systematized suggestions of several writers:

Hartmann (see Kris et al., 1954) recommends the study of the pleasure potentialities in the three psychic systems and their changes on the different levels of growth and development.[23] (In this regard, William, in the first year, seemed to derive the ego pleasure of self-discovery, body reality testing, and the visual-tactile delineation of his penis more than the gratification of the sexual drive. At the same time his thumb sucking before bedtime conveyed the impression of

[23] After writing this I discovered that Nagera has made an initial effort of re-examining the concept of autoerotism (1964). Tracing the writings of Freud he distinguishes "autoerotism" (a phase in the development of object relations) from "autoerotic" (a term used to describe a specific type of sexual activity and gratification). He differentiates three levels or types of autoerotic phenomena corresponding to the level of ego and self development present in the phases of autoerotism, primary narcissism, and true object relationships. Ernst Kris (1951) encouraged such a view: "The psychoanalytic approach to an understanding of early autoerotic activities is bound to relate these activities to various overlapping aspects of the problem of growth, particularly to the sequence of maturational processes, the development of the ego as a psychic organization, and to development and vicissitudes in the infant's and child's relation to his love objects. In studying any concrete phenomenon we are faced with a merging or interacting of these and other factors" (p. 96).

providing him a lulling erotic satisfaction—the gratification of an instinctual drive primarily, with mild regressive implications prior to sleep.)

Greenacre (see Kris et al., 1954) differentiates two biological rhythms, pleasurable soothing and orgastic.

A. Freud (see Kris et al., 1954) distinguishes between autoerotic and autoaggressive elements[24] and between activities expressing the child's relationship to his own body versus activities serving as a substitute for the mother, the benign versus the malignant aspects, the activities which foster developmental progress and those which tend to interrupt it, phase-specific activities versus those which are not, and a functional differentiation, on the basis of efficiency in dealing with tension.

Escalona (1963; Kris et al., 1954) makes a distinction between self-arousal and discharge components, and such refinements as the dual role of oral activity, on the one hand in the service of mediating body sensations and excluding awareness of outer reality, and on the other hand in the service of a primitive and literal form of reality testing.[25]

Wolff (1964) recommends a new look at theory derived largely from verbal, symbolic communication data but applied to the pre-symbolic first year of life, *after* we have a sufficient body of information from direct infant observation to make such revision meaningful (see also A. Freud [Kris et al., 1954, p. 25]).

Conclusions

Opportunity for complete observation of a normal boy's genital self-stimulation during the first year reveals a rich and varied repertoire of activities. The observations combined with a study of the relevant literature suggest:

1. Under normal conditions a boy's genital self-stimulation in

---

24 Historically the term *autoerotic* was applied before our dual drive theory had evolved in its present form, but the term *autoerotic* has not similarly been kept up to date.

25 William exemplified the rapid alternation of the dual roles, observed at one moment with the bath-drain plug in his mouth (clearly primarily exploratory in meaning), and moments later sucking his thumb while in his mother's lap as she dried him (withdrawing interest from the outer world and soothing himself in preparation for sleep).

the first year primarily fosters discovery of a body part and helps the establishment of a body self. The erotic aspect is secondary.

2. Mild to moderate pleasure characterizes the activity as time progresses without self-absorption or mounting excitement. Orgastic intensity or masturbation are inappropriately precocious indications of disturbance.

3. Although there is great individual variation in erogenous zone sensitivity, the genitals do not usually have the pleasure potentiality of the mouth at the end of the first year; however, there is a gradual increase in eroticity. Self-stimulation of the genitals does not usually serve as an autoerotic activity substitutive for the mother's stimulation in the way that other means, such as thumb sucking, do.

4. The factors of tumescence and testicular movements add to the sensation differentiation of the genital area from other body parts.

5. Genital exploration of a meaningful kind, as opposed to random tactile contact with the genitalia, is a development relatively late in the first year (from eight to ten months on) *after* the infant has developed skills of manual-visual coordination and forefinger-thumb dexterity, and has used them on his foot and toes, his mother's body, and other objects in his surroundings.

6. Whereas tumescences are largely reflex throughout much of the first year (partly associated with the function of micturition), late in the first year and increasingly in the first months of the second year they can be aroused also by tactile stimulation of the penis.

7. Of the factors contributing to the genesis of genital self-stimulation in the first year maturational processes and good infant-mother relations seem to play a more essential role than the direct process of the infant's repeating actively the genital stimulation which he received passively from the mother. In addition, self-stimulation seems partly reflective of an early identification process. A slightly different way to conceptualize this is that good maternal-infant relations facilitate the discharge of maturational drive representatives in the form of self-stimulation.

8. In the case reported, focused stimulation early in the first year because of dermatitis did not appear to affect subsequent normal emergence of genital self-stimulation. Observation suggested that the same trauma in the second year would have a more significant impact.

Any assessment of this child's autoerotic activities must include recognition of his above-average oral experience, resulting from the combination of his food intolerance and gastrointestinal distress which prolonged nursing as an attempted compensation, and the mother's own orality.

The visual component of genital exploration was important and at times predominated over the tactile.

9. A review of this subject pointed up the need for a refinement of the concepts *autoerotism* and *autoerotic*.

SUMMARY

Utilizing the twenty-four-hour-a-day availability of the mother, longitudinal observations are presented of the genital self-stimulation of a normal boy during the first year from its inception exactly at eight months. The degree of eroticity of this behavior is discussed, and its primary exploratory aspect, important for discovery of a body part and delineation of the body self, is emphasized. Factors responsible for the genesis of genital self-stimulation are enumerated, and the need for a refinement of the concepts *autoerotic* and *autoerotism* is raised.

BIBLIOGRAPHY

Balint, A. (1954), *The Early Years of Life*. New York: Basic Books.
Bell, A. (1961), Some Observations on the Role of the Scrotal Sac and Testicles. *J. Amer. Psa. Assn.*, 9:261-286.
Bender, L. (1939), Mental Hygiene and the Child. *Amer. J. Orthopsychiat.*, 9:574-582.
Bornstein, B. (1953), Masturbation in the Latency Period. *This Annual*, 8:65-78.
Brody, S. (1960), Self-Rocking in Infancy. *J. Amer. Psa. Assn.*, 8:464-491.
Casuso, G. (1957), Anxiety Related to the Discovery of the Penis, an Observation. *This Annual*, 12:169-174.
Engel, G. (1962), *Psychological Development in Health and Disease*. Philadelphia: Saunders.
Escalona, S. K. (1963), Patterns of Infantile Experience and the Developmental Process. *This Annual*, 18:197-244.
Freud, A. (1953), Some Remarks on Infant Observation. *This Annual*, 8:9-19.
—— & Burlingham, D. (1944), *Infants without Families*. New York: International Universities Press.
Freud, S. (1905), Three Essays on the Theory of Sexuality. *Standard Edition*, 7:125-245. London: Hogarth Press, 1953.
—— (1912), Contributions to a Discussion on Masturbation. *Standard Edition*, 12:239-254. London: Hogarth Press, 1958.

Greenacre, P. (1941), The Predisposition to Anxiety. *Psa. Quart.*, 10:66-94; 610-638.
—— (1953), Certain Relationships between Fetishism and Faulty Development of the Body Image. *This Annual*, 8:79-98.
—— (1958), Early Physical Determinants in the Development of the Sense of Identity. *J. Amer. Psa. Assn.*, 6:612-627.
—— (1960), Considerations Regarding the Parent-Infant Relationship. *Int. J. Psa.*, 41:571-584.
—— (1965), Infantile Trauma. Abstract in *Psa. Quart.*, 34:148-150.
Halverson, H. M. (1938), Infant Sucking and Tensional Behavior. *J. Genet. Psychol.*, 53:365-430.
—— (1940), Genital and Sphincter Behavior of the Male Infant. *J. Genet. Psychol.*, 56:95-136.
Hartmann, H., Kris, E., & Loewenstein, R. M. (1953), The Function of Theory in Psychoanalysis. In: *Drives, Affects, Behavior*, ed. R. M. Loewenstein. New York: International Universities Press.
Isaacs, S. (1935), *The Psychological Aspects of Child Development*. London: Evans.
Kinsey, A., Pomeroy, W., & Martin, C. (1948), *Sexual Behavior in the Human Male*. Philadelphia: Saunders.
Kleeman, J. (1964), Optimal Sensory Opportunity in Infancy: A Review and a Case Report from a Longitudinal Study. Unpublished manuscript.
Kris, E. (1951), Some Comments and Observations on Early Autoerotic Activities. *This Annual*, 6:95-116.
—— et al. (1954), Problems of Infantile Neurosis: A Discussion. *This Annual*, 9:16-71.
Lampl-de Groot, J. (1950), On Masturbation and Its Influence on General Development. *This Annual*, 5:153-174.
Levin, S. (1963), A Review of Freud's Contributions to the Topic of Masturbation. *Bull. Phila. Assn. Psa.*, 13:15-24.
Levine, M. I. (1951), Pediatric Observations on Masturbation in Children. *This Annual*, 6:117-124.
Lipin, T. (1963), The Repetition Compulsion and 'Maturational' Drive-Representatives. *Int. J. Psa.*, 44:389-406.
Loewenstein, R. M. (1950), Conflict and Autonomous Ego Development During the Phallic Phase. *This Annual*, 5:47-52.
Lustman, S. L. (1956), Rudiments of the Ego. *This Annual*, 11:89-98.
Murphy, L. (1964), Personal communication.
Nagera, H. (1964), Autoerotism, Autoerotic Activities, and Ego Development. *This Annual*, 19:240-255.
Provence, S. & Lipton, R. C. (1962), *Infants in Institutions*. New York: International Universities Press.
Rachford, B. K. (1907), Pseudomasturbation in Infants. *Arch. Pediat.*, 24:561-589.
Rapaport, D. (1960), The Structure of Psychoanalytic Theory, A Systematizing Attempt [*Psychological Issues*, Monogr. 6]. New York: International Universities Press.
Ribble, M. (1955), *The Personality of the Young Child*. New York: Columbia University Press.
Sears, R., Maccoby, E., & Levin, H. (1957), *Patterns of Child Rearing*. Evanston: Row, Peterson.
Spitz, R. A. (1952), Authority and Masturbation: Some Remarks on a Bibliographical Investigation. *Psa. Quart.*, 21:490-527.
—— (1962), Autoerotism Re-Examined. *This Annual*, 17:283-315.
—— & Wolf, K. M. (1949), Autoerotism: Some Empirical Findings and Hypotheses on Three of Its Manifestations in the First Year of Life. *This Annual*, 3/4:85-120.
Spock, B. (1946), *The Pocket Book of Baby and Child Care*. New York: Pocket Books.
Stone, L. J. & Church, J. (1957), *Childhood and Adolescence*. New York: Random House.

Sylvester, E. (1947), Pathogenic Influences of Maternal Attitudes in the Neonatal Period. In: *Problems of Early Infancy*, ed. M. J. E. Senn. New York: Josiah Macy, Jr. Foundation.

Townsend, C. W. (1896), Thigh Friction in Infants Under One Year of Age. *Arch. Pediat.*, 13:833-835.

Wolff, P. H. (1964), The Pertinence of Direct Infant Observation for Psychoanalytic Theory. Paper presented at Fall Meeting of Amer. Psa. Assn.

ASPECTS OF THE CONTRIBUTION OF SIGHT TO EGO AND DRIVE DEVELOPMENT

A Comparison of the Development of Some Blind and Sighted Children

HUMBERTO NAGERA, M.D., B.Sc. and
ALICE B. COLONNA, M.A., B.A. (London)

This study is based on six blind children observed in our Unit for the Blind. It is an attempt to organize and describe by means of the Profile headings what was learned during "periods of observation," analytic treatment, and Diagnostic Profiles about this group of children. For each of the children a Developmental Profile[1] was prepared and discussed in the Profile Research Group at the Hampstead Clinic.[2]

At the time of the assessment the children ranged in age from four to eight and a half years; four of them were between five and six years; one was four, and the other was eight and a half years.

We are especially indebted to Anna Freud, Dorothy Burlingham, Ilse Hellman, Liselotte Frankl, Ruth Thomas, Joseph Sandler, John Bolland, S. Fahmy, Martin James, Moses Laufer, Hansi Kennedy, Doris Wills, Marion Burgner, Elizabeth Model, Pat Radford, Lily Neurath, and many others who either have greatly contributed to group discussions or have been responsible for the preparation of the Developmental Profiles of the cases selected for this study. Special mention is due to Dr. Ehud Koch who helped with the collection of material and its organization for a pilot study on the subject a year ago.

[1] See Anna Freud (1962) and Nagera (1963).

[2] This paper is the result of the group discussions of the case material presented there. "The Profile Research Group" is a working unit of the project "Assessment of Pathology in Childhood," supported by the National Institute of Mental Health in Bethesda. The Group consists of more than thirty members including psychoanalysts, psychiatrists, child therapists, psychologists, psychiatric social workers, teachers, etc. All members are also analytically trained. The specific observations included as illustrations in this paper were made by Alice B. Colonna, Marion Burgner, Hansi Kennedy and Barbara Bank.

A brief description of the children's history of blindness follows:

George (5;3 years).—Pregnancy was normal, born in hospital. Nothing was said to the parents about eyes at this time, though, according to the father, there was no pupil present in the left eye from birth. First seen at Moorfields in December, 1957 at age 2 months, when examination under anesthesia showed that he had a mass in the right fundus and the left eye was large and prominent with a raised intraocular tension and hazy cornea. It was thought that the right fundus picture was not that of a neoplasm but probably of developmental or inflammatory pathology. The tension of the left eye remained high and the globe increased; therefore, in March, 1958, the left eye was enucleated. Histology of the eye showed a chronic endophthalmitis. Since then, the right eye has been kept under observation regularly; the mass in the right eye showed no change in size and tension was normal. It is difficult to assess accurately George's visual acuity at present.

Joan (4;6 years).—Totally blind as a result of high concentration of oxygen. Born prematurely (thirty weeks). Retrolental fibroplasia.

Gillian (4;6 years).—Retrolental fibroplasia, blind from birth. Born by Caesarian section. Mother very ill during pregnancy, child's weight at birth 3 lbs.; spent nine weeks in oxygen tent. When the child was ten weeks old the mother was told that Gillian was blind.

Helen (4;6 years).—Helen was born prematurely (at twenty weeks), had little sight afterwards, remaining sight was lost when she had measles, at age of three. Mother had three miscarriages, but Helen was the first pregnancy. Weight 2 lbs. at birth in an incubator for 102 days, at which time she weighed 5 lbs. and was taken home. When she came home her mother went to a home for a week.

Winnie (7 years).—Congenital cataract. Born one month premature (weight 6 lbs. 1 oz.) (not in oxygen tent).

Janet (8;6 years).—Blind from birth, pseudoglioma, eyes removed at four months.

Speaking very generally, we have had the opportunity to observe two very different possibilities of development among children who are born blind (and we include here as well children who may have become blind very early in life, perhaps soon after birth). In a small number of such cases their development, in spite of their blindness, does not seem to lag much behind the development of sighted children. Their ego processes, their drive development, their object relationships are not too far behind those of the sighted of similar ages. In another very distinct group, one finds blind children whose developmental processes are atypical. They lag behind in different degrees in the different areas, giving in some extreme cases the impression of a marked mental retardation. These two types are the two extremes on a scale with all sorts of possible combinations in between.

The cases we are referring to in this paper belong mostly in the second group; they show a specific clinical and developmental picture which they have in common with many other blind-born[3] but which is by no means representative of the developmental possibilities of all the blind-born children.

We further believe that the study of these two different groups of children born blind may teach us a great deal about how and by what means some overcome their handicap and find effective alternative ways to a degree that brings them closer to the level of the sighted. Even when the blind grows up under the most favorable circumstances (which are rarely encountered) in terms of ego endowment, good early mothering, reasonable environmental conditions, favorable object relations, etc., there is a point at which the development of one or another ego function clearly requires a contribution from the side of vision. When that contribution is not available, a disruption in the development of a specific function ensues. In turn, the insufficiency of these functions or of other aspects of the ego leads to further developmental interferences in all areas in which such functions are a necessary prerequisite. A somewhat similar point of view was expressed by A.-M. Sandler (1963) and by Fraiberg and Freedman (1964). It seems to us that this state of affairs can be somewhat alleviated by the environment, its handling of and attitude to the blind and their problems. It can make a positive contribution to the blind child's development by teaching him directly and at the right points the suitable alternative ways and means of compensating for the lack of sight. Left to itself the ego of the blind may never achieve this or only through long and painful detours and at much later stages. It may well be that some of the differences in development of the two groups of

---

[3] See, for example, some of the cases reported in the recent literature by Omwake and Solnit (1961), Segal and Stone (1961).

blind we are describing are related to these very factors.[4] Thus, the observation of the means by which the blind child's ego finds alternative solutions can give us clues to the kind of teaching and handling required at the different development points at which help may be needed to stimulate further development.

In our study we have made special efforts to single out those aspects of development and personality of blind children which are specific to them, and those in which they differ somehow from sighted children. In this way we hope in time to be able to understand the nature of the contribution sight makes to normal ego development and how much blindness can distort it. Though our study is based primarily on the six children described above, we have also checked relevant material of a large group of other blind children to verify certain aspects of our formulations. These formulations are nevertheless to be considered as tentative. The study of more cases will either confirm or modify them. With growing insight into the developmental processes of the blind new formulations may become necessary.

As previously stated, we shall present our formulations in terms of the relevant headings of the Developmental Profile introduced by Anna Freud (1962).

The Drive Development of the Blind

Libidinal Development

All the cases studied show that the blind develop in this area at a much slower pace than the sighted child.

Helen's Profile at five years eight months showed that even at that age there were no significant signs of her being in the phallic phase and no indication of oedipal development. There is a great deal of oral activity that finds direct expression in the sucking of objects and in the way she devours food and drink. She sometimes spits them out. Drooling is still observable. Anal messy behavior is noted in her intense enjoyment in pouring water or powder on the floor in a provocative manner.

Janet, at eight and a half, showed no signs of latency. The material contained only tenuous indications of her having reached the

---

[4] We are planning a close study of the group of blind children that develops more like the normal in the hope of clarifying some of the problems here posed.

phallic phase, but oral and anal activities are still very prominent, including rinsing of her mouth and spitting; she does a great deal of mouthing (which is partly an ego exploratory activity); anal masturbation was noted during her analytic sessions.. She pulls at her knickers and skirt and places her index finger in her anus. She comments on smells and noises, frequently passes wind and once soiled herself in doing so. There are endless and repetitive games and fantasies of other children soiling and wetting themselves and having to clean up the mess. Water play is accompanied by fantasies of mother forcing her to defecate and of other children soiling and wetting and being smacked.

Even more striking perhaps is the fact that this group of blind children, in marked contrast to the sighted children, seems incapable of leaving behind the previous phases when a new developmental move occurs. The move into the phallic-oedipal phase does not at all imply that drive gratification and autoerotic activities pertaining to the anal and oral phase will tend to disappear or even to recede notably into the background. On the contrary, marked activity of the anal and oral stages is always observed simultaneously with the newly found phallic-oedipal forms of drive gratification. This can best be illustrated in the case of Winnie.

At the time she came into analytic treatment (at the age of three) there were clear manifestations of active libidinal interests on the anal and oral levels of libidinal development. After five months of treatment, Winnie progressed into the phallic-oedipal phase, as the following material illustrates. Envy of little boys made its appearance and began to be openly expressed. She made clear what she wanted to do to them by attempts at dismembering dolls with much giggling. The dolls previously called "girl doll" were now "boy dolls." On one occasion when her envy of boys was verbalized, she strutted around the room with a boy doll held between her legs, saying, "Look what I got stuck up my fanny." She expressed wishes to sleep with her brother-in-law, Martin. Nevertheless, and in spite of this move, there remained a great deal of anal and oral concerns which were expressed in her fear of messing, her discomfort due to constipation, her use of anal swearwords, and her attempts to seduce her therapist to "smell" her fanny. Similarly noticeable were her strong ambivalent (anal-sadistic) feelings toward objects.

It may perhaps be concluded that blindness can so much interfere with finding new means of gratification both in drive discharge and ego activities that any form of gratification once experienced is not easily abandoned or left behind, even when further developmental steps are taken by the blind child; all earlier forms of gratification remain ego syntonic. We shall come back to this point.

Cathexis of Self

Self-esteem Regulation. In this area our group of blind differs from normally sighted children in that the blind have a more marked and presumably longer period of dependence on the external world in order to maintain the cathexis of themselves at a level compatible with well-being. In many of the children we have studied and observed in our Nursery for the Blind, this extreme dependence upon the object world is further shown in an inability to maintain their own self-esteem and cathexis of the self when the object world withdraws cathexis from them.

When Winnie's mother was depressed, Winnie suffered a loss of the feeling of well-being and tended to become immobilized, particularly so at the nursery, where she also retreated from interaction with the other children. However, she showed very different behavior in the treatment situation, where she was able to enjoy a one-to-one relationship with the full attention of the therapist concentrated on herself. Thus, she was often verbal and active in treatment, while in school she appeared withdrawn and involved in manneristic gestures.

Cathexis of Object. It seems clear from our observations that even apparently retarded blind children can reach object constancy and can relate to the object world on that level. On the other hand, they may not completely leave behind the other phases and will sometimes relate to and use the objects on a need-fulfilling basis. Indeed, they tend to move forward and backward from the one to the other phase quite frequently.

They sometimes give the impression that they readily and easily exchange objects, even for unfamiliar ones, as if object constancy had not been properly established.

A more careful examination of the facts will support the view that, owing to the lack of sight, the blind child experiences extreme anxiety when someone is not nearby to protect him. The blind child, fully aware through experience of the very many dangers around and of his inability to care for himself in the absence of a protective object, tends to cling to anyone present when the familiar or dearest objects are not available, for whatever reason. It is presumably this attitude, which in fact serves self-preservation, that leads to the false impression that some blind children are not attached to their objects on the level of object constancy. We have noted that the blind group we studied shows a strong tendency to comply with the wishes of their important objects and especially with those of the mother. This is carried to extremes that are hardly observable in sighted children of the same age.

Aggression

We have formed the impression that these blind children show a tendency to inhibit any form of overt expression of aggression against those objects on whom they are dependent. The fact that they do inhibit aggression in this specific way may not be apparent to the casual observer who may easily gain the impression that the children's behavior is quite aggressive. This misunderstanding of the real circumstances is due to two factors.

First, many of these blind children are still largely at the anal-sadistic stage of libido development. Winnie, for example, was fully at the anal-sadistic stage and behaved accordingly; it is true that descriptively, i.e., to an observer, behavior of this type may seem extremely aggressive, but it is in fact the phase-adequate expression and type of relationship of children in that phase. The extreme ambivalence of the anal-sadistic phase allows us to see, for example, the child's expressions of love followed by violent biting. It may be profitable to distinguish this type of phase-adequate expression of the aggressive drive from aggressive behavior as a more organized type of response which is phase independent; the blind child's inhibition is of the second type.

The second factor concerns the child's relationship with other children. In Winnie's case one must take into consideration that on the line of development "from egocentricity to companionship" (A. Freud, 1963) she has not yet developed any empathy for other children's feelings; consequently they can be used freely for the expression of her strong ambivalence. This type of aggressive behavior must be distinguished from the later forms where the aggressive act is carried out with full awareness of its effect on the other child.

Although Winnie was able to express open aggression to the therapist in the "permissive situation" of the treatment, it was not quite the same in relation to other objects or in other environments. In the nursery, for example, Winnie rarely made aggressive assaults; during a period in which she was unusually destructive in her sessions (throwing bottles, breaking glass, lashing out at the therapist, etc.), she was described at the nursery school as moving less freely, with a bad posture, "as though she were carrying the cares of the world on her shoulders," and indeed she presented the picture of a depressed child. Similarly, she rarely expressed openly aggressive, hostile impulses toward her mother. On one occasion when she did, after playing out having been nagged by her mother for making too much noise, she said, "What have you done with your mummy, did you throw her in the muck bin?" The next day, she snuggled up to the therapist and said, "But I wouldn't really do that; I'm a helpful girl, I help mummy."

In this way, she behaved very much as other blind children do, that is, with a marked inhibition of the expression of aggression. This is due partly to the fear of losing the favor and love of the object, a fear that is immediately transformed into a fear of annihilation caused by the extreme dependence on objects for reasons of safety.

In Winnie's case we noted that it was important for her "to hear" the result of her aggressive actions (breaking objects, glass, etc.), but we have not been able to confirm that this applies generally to other blind children. Some instances of very disturbed behavior which takes place in moments of regression provoked by current difficulties at home, in school, etc., may be wrongly interpreted as object-directed aggression. In fact, some of these manifestations are the panic reactions of an overwhelmed ego; they lead to disorganized behavior and other primitive expressions of the infant stage such as crying, throwing things at random, etc.

THE EGO OF THE BLIND

The consistent and systematic study of the personality of a number of blind children, by means of the application of the Developmental Profile, has forced us to conclude that there is an unwarranted readiness to interpret their peculiarities of behavior, fantasies, symptoms, etc., in the same light and on the same basis as those of sighted, normal or neurotic children.

Thus, we proceed in our assessments as if the blind were ordinary children except for their lack of sight. This may be so when the loss of sight has taken place late in the child's life, when his development in every direction may have been fairly well advanced. Clearly, when the child's lack of sight dates from birth or early babyhood, drive and ego development proceeds in atypical and distorted ways. The correlations valid for the sighted between surface (behavioral material) and depth (unconscious determinants and meaning) are not directly applicable to the blind. Many of the pointers, indicators, clinical evaluations, etc., on which we can rely with a fair degree of certainty in assessing the sighted child's personality and neurotic conflicts are unreliable instruments in the evaluation of the blind.

Many of the blind children we have studied tend to show a marked fear of animals and noises. Helen feared dogs, horses, birds, and noises. Janet feared thunder, rain, wind, trains, drilling machines, dogs, etc. When these fears occur in sighted children of a comparable age, they can be taken as a sure indication of an area of disturbance, of specific conflicts, of clear defense activity and symptom formation. In the sighted child of a given age, the presence of fear or phobic avoidance of certain animals such as birds, horses, dogs, etc., entitles us to assume that the animal stands for the oedipal rival and that the fear of being attacked by it is the result of the child's projecting his own aggressive feelings onto the hated rival.

In the case of the blind it is frequently very difficult to determine how much of the above behavior or symptomatology is the result of defense activity against the drives, i.e., the result of conflict, and how much is in fact appropriate adaptive behavior (in terms of survival) in a child who lacks vision. Here one has to remind oneself that when a blind child hears a barking dog he cannot see whether the dog is big or small, whether it is playful or hostile, whether it intends to bite or not.

The same viewpoint applies to the blind child's unusual degree of clinging to and dependence on the object at an age when he would normally be expected to have outgrown this type of relationship. In the sighted of the same age such clinging constitutes a clear indication either of important fixation points at the oral level or of defense activity directed against certain specific conflict situations. In the blind this extreme clinging and dependence, as already mentioned, are characteristic for a long period of life. Rather than being the result of defense activity, they may be another sign of the complex pattern of ego adaptation to a sighted world.

Other pieces of behavior characteristic of the blind, like their withdrawal (into fantasy or otherwise), their passivity, etc., can be understood in a similar way.

The sighted adult who has learned to cope with the ordinary conditions of his immediate environment experiences "fear of reality" only in the face of true danger situations. For him, it is practically impossible to imagine the state of extreme helplessness and anxiety of the blind child, for whom a great deal of the external world represents dangers that he is ill equipped to master. The blind child is swamped by constant waves of anxiety derived from an unending variety of occurrences which are incompletely understood or wrongly interpreted.

This state of permanent alertness to external dangers which have to be mastered seems to occupy the child's mind to a degree which outweighs the importance of the internal dangers, represented by the impulses and other drive representatives. Compared with the dreaded hazards of the environment, the inner world is a source of safety and gratification to the blind child. It is this combination of factors (fear of the external, retreat to the internal world) which may explain the marked delay in the mastery and control of drive activity which we observe in our blind children.

On the other hand, the children's fantasy life seemed extremely limited in comparison with the richness of imagination and fantasy production of the sighted (either normal or neurotic) of similar ages, a fact which may be due, of course, to the comparatively low level of ego development of the group of children studied. Fantasy production, as a well-known prestage of neurotic symptom formation in children and adults, usually represents the withdrawal from an unpleasant external reality which interferes with processes of drive gratification. The blind children, in spite of their most unpleasant external reality, cannot afford to withdraw from it. Only constant surveillance, with the alternative senses at their disposal, will avoid unpleasant, hurtful experiences. Consequently many of their mental activities consist of attempts to master through repetition and in imagination the many painful situations which they have experienced.[5] No less important is the fact, mentioned above, that the blind child allows himself a great deal of direct drive gratification which may make the function of fantasy less vital for him.

As regards the development of certain ego functions in the blind, it is important to note that their ego performance can be extremely unreliable even in cases of reasonably well-established functions. Most important in this respect is the ease with which anxiety can become overwhelming and traumatic and result in the temporary collapse of otherwise well-established functions.

Thus it was frequently observed than when in distress, danger, or in extreme anxiety, many of the children would become immobile. Winnie, for example, became immobile to the extreme of being rigid. This immobility may well be a response learned very early in order to protect themselves from further pain, damage, or dangers.

Immobility in blind children was observed as well when they were introduced to a new environment. For a short while they tended to remain still in order to orient themselves, perceiving and collecting as much information as possible through the appropriate sense organs, especially the ear.

In the cases studied, walking started at any time between thirteen months and three years, the parental attitude to the child being a significant factor in connection with this function. Winnie started walking at thirteen months. She did not crawl but used to turn round and round on her behind, then pulling herself up. The father used to help her by walking alongside. Helen began walking at eighteen months without previous crawling. She was given a large doll to push and in this way began to walk. George walked by twenty months; Joan at two years without having ever crawled before; while Janet did not sit up until she was two years, crawled at two and a half years, and walked at three years of age.

---

[5] D. Burlingham (1964) has pointed to a piece of behavior that is often misleading. To the casual observer the blind children frequently appear to be fully withdrawn into passivity when in fact behind this façade there is an extremely active listening and a close attention to what goes on in the environment.

The following examples illustrate the blind child's use of ego functions in the service of adaptation to the world around him.[6]

Winnie relied on other sensory modalities to orient herself in and explore the environment, and for her own stimulation. Her reliance on tactile sensations was great (e.g., feeling the bumps on the windowpane, stroking a new object with her cheek). She also used her head as a drum knocking an object against her temples, which would seem to involve both tactile and auditory sensations. She enjoyed being barefooted and explored her environment in this way. Her awareness of surfaces was seen in her recognition of certain streets with cobblestones. Her hearing was most acute: she would aim objects correctly at the therapist when she wanted to throw them; she felt more at ease when she heard the therapist knitting and thus was assured of her awake presence; she derived much pleasure from hearing the sound of glass breaking; she would knock two objects together and listen for their sound. Smell was also important to her: she could locate the local bakery by means of the smells. Smell was at the same time sexualized as can be seen in her request to the therapist, "Come, smell my fanny." Throughout the treatment, she often sought close physical contact by sitting on the therapist's lap and asking for love, which suggests that the total surface of her body was a major receptor of stimulation.

Helen showed and made use of a very well-developed sense of hearing. She was able to tell when the paper boy was coming down the road long before her mother could hear him. She was also clearly attracted to her mother's powder and scent.

George compensated for his lack of vision mainly by means of auditory and tactile senses. In addition, testing, mouthing, and licking (very frequent in blind children) were used by him when he was five years old, in a manner similar to the ways of a sighted toddler.

Memory seems to serve the blind well. In practically all the cases studied and in many others observed, this function showed itself as adequate and helpful. Not infrequently it served purposes of orientation, as shown in Winnie's trips with her therapist to the local shops. Things recalled for such purposes were memories of smells experienced, of noises heard, of texture of surfaces felt (cobblestone surfaces, etc.).

[6] D. Burlingham's (1964) paper contains an interesting account of the development of hearing in the blind and the role of the relationship to the mother. See also D. Burlingham (1961).

Contact with the object world through words plays a particularly important role in the blind. In the cases here studied the acquisition of speech was not precociously developed and the timetable for the beginning of talking ranged roughly from eighteen months to three years of age. George began talking at eighteen months; Helen was fairly fluent by two and a half years; Winnie was talking by two years; Janet talked when she was three years.

It is a well-established fact that certain forms of thinking and the development of several other ego functions are dependent largely on the acquisition of a proper imagery, and of adequate symbols, on the basis of which thought processes of an ever-increasing complexity and quality are possible.

The synthetic and integrative functions of the ego are very dependent on the intactness of these processes, which are essential for the proper understanding and mastery of the world around us, making further ego development possible on that basis.

It is likewise well established that words are the essential units, the required symbols, on the basis of which the above-mentioned processes can take place. Quite clearly, whatever interferes with the child's ability to acquire such symbols may bring aspects of his ego development to a near standstill and be responsible for sometimes creating the impression of extreme backwardness. Extreme examples of such cases can be observed in children with congenital deafness. When they are taught to lip-read and to talk, dramatic improvements often take place in their ego development, and with it in their object relationships, in their understanding and mastery of the world. This happens because words as symbols have become available for thought processes and for the performance of functions which are contingent upon secondary-process thinking of a certain quality.

Although the blind child's disadvantages in this area is not on a par with that of the deaf, there is some evidence that lack of vision interferes with the ability to acquire and make use of words as symbols. Many essential elements of these "word symbols" can be contributed only by sight. For this reason the concepts abstracted by these words have no real meaning for children blind from birth. "Dark," "light," and the whole range covered by words describing "color," etc., belong in this category. No other sense can convey suitable alternative information to clarify these concepts and abstractions. It is not difficult to imagime how many limitations are thus imposed on the mental processes of the blind. A few observations from our Nursery for the Blind can exemplify some of these problems.

Gillian (six years) was in the lavatory. "Put the light on, it's dark."
Teacher: "What do you mean?"
Gillian: "You know, it is cold and horrible."

Matthew (age four), playing hide and seek in the cupboard, called out, "It's all dark in here." When asked what he meant, he answered, "Well you know, all cold and rainy."

In a still larger group of words the contribution of sight may not be as fundamental but nevertheless important enough to render these symbols somewhat insufficient when compared with the equivalent symbols of the sighted.[7]

Whatever ego functions are dependent on the availability of the right kind of imagery of symbols are thus limited in a proportional degree. The imagery of the world of sighted people is of necessity in many ways inappropriate for the blind. Nevertheless, it seems that in spite of the absence of the visual contribution to many of these "word symbols," alternative compensatory means are finally found so that these symbols become useful elements in the performance of the complex mental processes for which these basic units are required. This need not imply that they finally become identical with the same "word presentation" of the sighted. Experiments on blind adults (from birth) who have recovered sight in adulthood through certain operations have shown that they are unable to pick out objects by sight, to recognize or even name them, even though they know all about them and their names by touch. As Young (1960) points out:

At first he only experiences a mass of colour, but gradually he learns to distinguish shapes. When shown a patch of one

---

[7] "A word is thus a complex presentation . . . ; or, to put it in another way, there corresponds to the word a complicated associative process into which the elements of visual, acoustic, and kinaesthetic origin enumerated above enter together. A word, however, acquires its *meaning* by being linked with an 'object-presentation,' at all events if we restrict ourselves to a consideration of substantives. The object-presentation itself is once again a complex of associations made up of the greatest variety of visual, acoustic, tactile, kinaesthetic and other presentations" (Freud, 1891). The quotation appears as part of Appendix C, Words and Things, attached to Freud's paper "The Unconscious" (1915, p. 209), because the last section of that paper is based on these views expressed in *On Aphasia*.

colour he will quickly see that there is a difference between the patch and its surroundings. What he will not do is to recognize that he has seen that particular shape before, nor will he be able to give it its proper name. For example, one man when shown an orange a week after beginning to see, said that it was gold. When asked, 'What shape is it?' he said, 'Let me touch it and I will tell you'. After doing so, he said that it was an orange, when he looked again at it he said: 'Yes I can see that it is round'. Shown next a blue square, he said it was blue and round. A triangle he also described as round. When the angles were pointed out to him he said, 'Ah, Yes, I understand now, one can *see* how they feel'.

Further evidence supporting the limitations we are describing is presented by the indiscriminate use of words that can be observed in many blind children. They use words in a "parroting fashion" without having a proper understanding of their true and complete meaning.

For example, when Janet was nine she frequently used words such as "contradict" and "nuisance," without knowing their meaning, obviously having taken them over from her mother. Matthew (four and a half) was washing the stuffed bunny and said that at home in the bath when soap gets into his eyes its stings. "They are delicate," he said, adding, "I wonder what delicate means?"

The occurrence of word parroting long before the child grasps the corresponding abstract meaning of the words shows how much longer it takes the blind to assimilate many of the concepts symbolized by words.

Not all words represent the same level of abstraction; many are more concrete than others. The blind learn the concrete first and more easily than the abstract. Though there exist noticeable individual differences in this respect, in general the blind children show a certain tendency to concreteness in their verbalized thoughts and some difficulty in the formation of abstract concepts. Similarly, abstract concepts are readily concretized.

Wendy, for example, shows concern with the meanings of "wearing out" and "worn out" as used with regard to people, objects such as toys, feelings, etc. She worried whether worn-out people are discarded like worn-out music boxes.

Peter at around five years of age was gingerly fingering dough. He said, "Squeeze it; can he squeeze it? Will it hurt?" On another occasion he tried to open a peanut, saying, "That hurts it." He then stopped the activity.

Matthew (at around six years of age) heard at home the story of *Pinocchio*. He asked at the nursery what "conscience" is. "Can you really hear a little voice when you do something naughty? He decided to try it out and with a serious expression tore up a paper napkin. He then pushed over a chair and said, "I still can't hear it."

These limitations help to explain why, in many cases, the blind children are not able to master and fully understand the world outside; large areas of it remain sources of intense fear and anxiety.

Nevertheless, at some point of development, some of these limitations disappear or are reduced to a minimum compatible with performances on the ego side more similar to the level of performance of the sighted. We have no doubt concerning the usefulness of the close study of how, when, and through what means the ego finds alternatives and compensatory ways that finally to some degree help overcome its original limitations. Such a study will throw abundant light on many developmental processes undergone by the ego. It will also clarify and establish the essential elements that must combine to bring about the performance of more complex ego functions.

It is our belief that the ego of the blind must first find alternative means of coping with some of the problems described in this paper before it can turn to the rather primitive drive organization and establish appropriate controls over drive activity. In many blind this seems to happen at a much later stage than in the sighted. At this later point the ego can make use of alternative sources of gratification and find sublimatory outlets. Exactly when this happens should be determined by detailed study and analyses of blind adolescents and adults.

THE SUPEREGO STRUCTURE

The whole question of how the superego structure as a controlling agency develops in the blind deserves a study in its own right. We are limiting ourselves to highlighting some striking differences between sighted and blind.

First of all, in the group we have studied, it is very difficult to find signs of guilt when specific transgressions occur, even at ages when such signs are plentiful in the sighted. For example, the blind children engage freely in a great deal of autoerotic activity and drive gratification corresponding to all sorts of levels, as pointed out above. These activities are performed openly in the presence of adults; on the whole they seem to be ego syntonic and free of guilt.

It is also important to point to an apparent contradiction in these children's superego development. In the sighted child the process of internalization of external demands (leading to superego precursors and in due course to the final establishment of the superego structure) is assumed to start when the child's awareness of the importance of the object forces him to give up drive gratification, out of concern and fear of the loss of the love of the object. The blind children, in spite of their extreme dependence on their objects, do not seem forced (by fear of loss of the object's love when his disapproval is incurred) to internalize prohibitions and commands or to give up the multiple and primitive forms of autoerotic activities and drive gratifications to which they cling so tenaciously.

DEVELOPMENT OF THE TOTAL PERSONALITY
(Lines of Development and Mastery of Tasks)

A marked retardation and unevenness in the development of the total personality as shown on the Lines of Development seems to be the normal picture in this group of blind children. This is in part due to the lack of sight which implies interference with development in every area and in part to environmental interferences such as pity and overprotection. We anticipate that the study of the blind in terms of the "Lines of Development" (A. Freud, 1963) established for sighted children will throw some light on certain aspects of ego development, especially on the contribution made to that development by the organ and the function of vision.

It is also possible that for an independent assessment of their development we shall have to set up entirely new standards permitting us to explore the possibility of different interactions between the expressions of drives and the severely handicapped ego and superego structures.

REGRESSION AND FIXATION POINTS

This is another area where we have become aware of the fact that the behavior and symptomatic manifestations of sighted children, usually taken as indicators and pointers to the levels at which they may be fixated, are not always applicable to the blind.

Thus, the intense mouthing observed in most blind children up to a very late age cannot be taken as a sure indicator of a fixation on the oral level. Mouthing in the blind, quite apart from the oral drive gratification, must in some of its aspects be considered as an auxiliary exploratory ego function. A very similar situation exists with regard to the prominent use of the sense of smell. It is, of course, not an easy matter to distinguish between drive and ego activity in this respect.

We suggest that one should try to note whether an organ is used by the ego in a limited way to compensate for the lack of vision (as in the exploration of objects through mouthing). In this case the activity will cease when this purpose has been accomplished; otherwise it will continue well past the exploratory phase and show an impulsive, instinctual quality.

Another example is the frequent touching inhibition of the blind which as an indicator of fixation to the anal phase does not have the same value it has in the sighted.

There are many other important differences between blind and sighted children with regard to fixation and regression. For example, it is very difficult to establish where phase dominance lies in the blind, since drive activity remains spread through all levels of development and the ego acquiesces in this state of affairs. The picture is further complicated by the extreme readiness of the blind children to regress temporarily from higher to lower levels of gratification as soon as any difficulties arise. In fact, the group we observe gives the impression of moving backward and forward far more readily than sighted children would in similar circumstances.

On the other hand, it is not quite correct to refer to what we have been describing as "fixations" proper, since it may well be that the reluctance to give up earlier forms of gratification is due to the immense and constant frustrations experienced by the blind; these make the ego more tolerant to the obtaining of gratification by whatever means possible. In fact, we have the impression that if sight could be restored (which would lead at once to a better balance between pleasure and frustration, etc.), very many of these earlier forms of gratification would disappear, a development which could, of course, never occur in the case of true fixations.

The constant shift in functioning from the one level to another (with backward and forward moves), for example, in relation to external events, tends to support this view.

Dynamic and Structural Assessment (Conflicts)

External Conflicts

Owing to the extreme and very prolonged dependence of the blind child on his objects, the "external type" of conflict is perhaps more prominent than it is in the sighted. The blind need a longer period of time for internalization to take place and even then they seem to remain to some extent dependent on the approval of the outside world. They are more likely to have conflicts between the wish for independence and self-assertion and the ever-present realistic need for continuous support and protection from the objects. The outcome of such conflicts frequently seems to be extreme passivity and a readiness to comply with the demands of the object out of the fear of loss of love or fear of annihilation.

Internalized Conflicts

Blind children of the age group we have studied may show some superego precursors. They have internalized some of the environmental demands that have thus become their own. For example, they may take over from the environment the command to become clean and dry and make it into an internal concern. On the other hand, it has been noted that in blind children it is not easy to come across clear examples of "guilt" when transgressions of these or other commands do occur.

Although at the present time we cannot be more specific, there is no doubt that there are important differences between this group of blind and the sighted in the process of internalization as well as in the ego and the superego (or its precursors), as shown by the apparent "lack of guilt." On the whole internalization probably starts later and takes longer in the blind than in the sighted.

Assessment of Some General Characteristics

Frustration Tolerance

It is very difficult to evaluate the blind child's reaction to frustration. On the one hand, a great deal of direct drive gratification occurs all the time, a circumstance that would indicate low frustration tolerance; on the other, there is little doubt that in their dealings with the external world they are constantly exposed to and must tolerate excessive frustrations owing to their blindness and the resultant helplessness.

Sublimation Potential

It seems that the tendency to cling to any form of gratification that has been experienced previously, the general tolerance of the ego in this respect, etc., are factors working against whatever capacity or potential these children may have for sublimation. Moreover, the need for close bodily contact with the objects may further interfere with the blind child's capacity to sublimate or to accept substitute gratification.

These statements are true only up to a given age. Random observations of blind adults seem to point to the fact that at some stage there occur important economic and structural developments and rearrangements in the personality of the blind (partly described under the Ego section), which sometimes allow satisfactory sublimations to take place.

Over-all Attitude to Anxiety

This is an area of special interest in blind children (see under Ego Development).

Because of their readiness to develop anxiety to a traumatic degree in times of stress, the function of anxiety as a signal is frequently overruled. At such moments the children tend to look for very close bodily contact with the object. It seems that up to a comparatively late age the children's anxiety, as observed in our group, is aroused mainly by their inability to deal with, understand, and master the external dangers and the external world.

Progressive Developmental Forces versus Regressive Tendencies

In this group of blind children the material seems to point to a very marked backward pull exerted by the regressive tendencies. We have already mentioned the need to cling to old forms of satisfaction which does not make it any easier to take progressive steps into new phases. Although progressive tendencies are seen, development on the whole takes place at a slower and rather retarded pace; certain environmental attitudes, such as overprotection, etc., may further obscure the true state of affairs concerning the blind child's potentialities in this area.

BIBLIOGRAPHY

Burlingham, D. (1961), Some Notes on the Development of the Blind. *This Annual*, 16:121-145.
—— (1964), Hearing and Its Role in the Development of the Blind. *This Annual*, 19:95-112.
Fraiberg, S. H. & Freedman, D. A. (1964), Studies in the Ego Development of the Congenitally Blind Child. *This Annual*, 19:113-170.
Freud, A. (1962), Assessment of Childhood Disturbances. *This Annual*, 17:149-158.
—— (1963), The Concept of Developmental Lines. *This Annual*, 18:245-265.
Freud, S. (1891), *On Aphasia*. New York: International Universities Press, 1953.
—— (1915), The Unconscious. *Standard Edition*, 14:159-215. London: Hogarth Press, 1957.
Omwake, E. G. & Solnit, A. J. (1961), "It Isn't Fair": The Treatment of a Blind Child. *This Annual*, 16:352-404.
Nagera, H. (1963), The Developmental Profile: Notes on Some Practical Considerations Regarding Its Use. *This Annual*, 18:511-541.
Sandler, A.-M. (1963), Aspects of Passivity and Ego Development in the Blind Infant. *This Annual*, 18:343-360.
Segal, A. & Stone, F. H. (1961), The Six-year-old Who Began to See: Emotional Sequelae of Operation for Congenital Bilateral Cataracts. *This Annual*, 16:481-509.
Young, J. Z. (1960), *Doubt and Certainty in Science: A Biologist's Reflections on the Brain*. New York: Oxford University Press.

THE TEACHER GAME

HELEN ROSS (Pittsburgh)

This paper is an effort to bring the light of psychoanalysis to the teacher game. Though the doctor game has often been noted and scrutinized by psychoanalysts, the equally ubiquitous teacher game has received less attention.

Freud (1920) describes the first identifiable play activity of the infant as a defense against anxiety. This is the well-known throwing-away and bringing-back play of the baby in his crib who retrieves with pleasure the toy he casts out, a play interpreted as letting the mother go and then bringing her back. In this and in the peek-a-boo game, the child maintains control of the situation he has learned not to like, i. e., the disappearance of the mother. If the adult in the play makes it too realistic and disappears for a longer time than the child can sustain, the fun breaks down in excessive anxiety and sometimes he will refuse for long periods to engage himself with the parent or other adult who offers to play peek-a-boo. With repeated trials, he may give up his anxiety and rejoin the partnership, or with continued disappointment, suffer a blow to his object relationship.

Waelder (1932) in his psychoanalytic interpretation of play shows that play characteristic of the developmental phases is imbedded in the anxieties specific for the period: in the anal period, for example, concern with putting in and taking out (the dump truck is a favorite toy), giving and withholding, piling up blocks, pleasure in messiness and so on.

These activities are followed in the phallic-oedipal period with more elaborate acting-out fantasies, largely defensive against fear of castration. The child who plays out a painful dental experience on his teddy bear, the child who abreacts a motor accident in fantasy

---

Read before the Pittsburgh Psychoanalytic Society, March 22, 1965.

collisions, always coming out unhurt, the rescue games of sibling rivalry are examples of defense against fear of hurt or injury. To the clinician as well as to the nursery school teacher, these activities are familiar, and are helpful in divining the particular anxiety of the moment, if it is phase-specific or regressive. They also indicate the manner of the defense characteristic of the individual.

Erikson's early work (1937) makes vivid the use of play in diagnosis, showing the subtleties of the child's tacit communication.

Peller (1954) points out the meanings of dramatic play, and Alexander (1960) devoted a chapter to play in one of his late works.

In short, play as language has long intrigued the analyst, especially the child analyst, to the advantage of greater understanding of child development and child behavior, and at one period to the detriment of therapeutic technique. Therapy with children called "play therapy" misled some into thinking that play in itself was therapeutic, overlooking the necessity of the verbalization of insight.

No mention of play as a ubiquitous human activity, however scanty, should overlook Huizinga's *Homo Ludens* (1938). Huizinga sees practically all human activity as play—war, politics, religious observance, jurisprudence, etc., just as Lorenz (1952) interprets much of animal behavior in anthropomorphic play terms.

The intention of this paper is not to cover the subject of play, but rather to look particularly into the child's interest and pleasure in playing school, the teacher game.

This play normally begins when the child learns about school through observation of his siblings and older playmates. Though he may be fixated at an earlier level, and this may carry over into his motive for and manner of entering the game, playing school is an ego activity and corresponds to that phase on the developmental lines (Anna Freud, 1963) in which the child has achieved readiness to enter a group activity, willingness to cooperate, and ability to sustain interest.

Though the "doctor game" tries to unlock the genital secrets of the grownups, it is highly tinged with anal components according to the fixated interest of the individual players, as the young child's anal jokes and terms betray. Starting as curiosity, it finds masturbatory pleasure in this activity that takes sanction in the illusion that this is play, albeit not carried on in the presence of adults. It usually carries some sublimation in the form of examination of the patient, ministration of a "nurse," and a fantasied cure. A nurse's uniform and a doctor's kit are frequent "props." The game satisfies the voyeurism of the phallic period, both active and passive; it seeks to allay castration fears in both boy and girl (the game is usually coeducational), but this anxiety tends to repetition rather than abandonment of the play. Parental forbidding brings guilt, which may serve merely to drive the fun underground. While such prohibitions do not extirpate the need to learn by looking, they may serve so poignantly to make learning by looking a "bad thing" that a learning inhibition ensues, especially in the area of reading, as clinical material testifies.

The teacher game, in contrast, is in the open and looks like a fine ego activity, a preparation for school itself. In their eagerness to grow up and do what the older siblings do, those children about to enter formal school seem most to enjoy playing school. Nursery school and kindergarten, being so much play in themselves, seem not to promote the acting out of fantasies in school terms, though occasionally one hears a kindergartener say, "Now let's play real school."

The *dramatis personae* of the teacher play are a teacher, authoritative, usually harsh and demanding, and pupils, most of whom are troublesome and noisy. The less popular masochistic part may be played by a "teacher's pet," despised and picked on. There is also the dunce, a stupid one who gets his revenge as he pretends he cannot understand what the teacher says, a forerunner of the pseudostupid child who has been too much praised or prodded by the parents. In my day, he was made to wear a peaked dunce cap of paper and had to sit on a stool in the corner. He pays the teacher back for her pretended omniscience and for her nagging. For the rebellious and aggressive pupils, punishments are meted out by the teacher, who in the progress of the game is often deposed by the offended and a new teacher takes over, by sheer force of aggressivity. Understudies in this play are not necessary; the actors are always ready.

But playing school is not merely a sadomasochistic activity. The ego demands some serious semblance of a real school. Material is given out; monitors distribute paper and pencils for arithmetic, spelling, drawing, etc. Papers are collected and graded so long as the teacher can maintain enough order. Though the teacher is often self-appointed, she (more likely than he) is a somewhat older sibling or friend who can discipline the younger ones because they are now having the fun of going to school in fantasy. As a symbol of authority, the teacher wields a pointer or a ruler, which in itself becomes powerful, as Golding's children in *Lord of the Flies* demonstrated with a large sea shell. The one who held the shell held the authority.

With this description of the teacher game in mind, let us examine the inner motivation, the psychological springs of the play.

At first glance, we see models of common defenses, i.e., passive into active and reversal (the child afraid of the teacher may now become teacher and identify himself with the fantasied aggressor); projection (the child puts his own hostility into the authoritative person); introjection (the child takes over attitudes of the authoritative one); and, finally, sublimation.

It is precisely this look of sublimation that makes the teacher game seem primarily an ego activity, and this may explain why it has escaped closer psychoanalytic scrutiny. The defenses mentioned are characteristic of most of the play and fantasies of young children, who are in a developmental struggle to become independent of their parents. I want here to particularize what underlies the teacher-pupil role, interchangeable and mercurial.

Interestingly enough, the older players in this game, the ones who usually are the teacher, will sometimes take the part of the least mature, cry and annoy the others, and so on. This is not unlike the regression we note among our older students who return to the pupil role after some years and regress to earlier school behavior.

Bertram Lewin (1965), with his insight into the process of education, says that theory is the result of the "need to teach." We are examining here the need to teach.

The child's first teacher is the mother; she and later on the father become the all-knowing ones. Boasts overheard in nursery school and kindergarten and even in the lower grades attest to the child's belief in the parents' omniscience. To identify oneself with the parent, therefore, is to know what he knows as well as to do what he does. To become like the model, the child must have knowledge which he can pass on to others. Very early, however, he discovers that father and mother know more than they impart: there are secrets, hidden information he must possess in order to complete the fantasy of omniscience and omnipotence. Through the teacher game, he can act out this omniscience. From Jean-Paul Sartre's autobiography, *The Words*, I take the following:

> Worst of all, I suspected the adults of faking.
> The words they spoke to me were candies,
> but they talked among themselves in quite
> another tone. And in addition, they sometimes
> broke sacred contracts. I would make my most
> adorable pout, the one about which I felt the
> surest, and I would be told in a real voice:
> "Go and play elsewhere, darling. We're talking."

In the teacher game, the teacher can treat the pupils as he would be treated, or as he is treated. He can give information to the pupil (which is what he wants the parent to do) or he can withhold knowledge (which is what happens to him). In the teacher game, he is both parent and child according to that common mechanism of satisfying oneself during the painful process of growing up. He can be both passive and active; child and parent; pupil and teacher. He can gratify his sadism and his masochism. Economically, the teacher game serves him well. A passage from Little Hans (Freud, 1909) gives us an excellent sample (p. 89):

> *I* [the father]: "You'd like to be Daddy yourself."
> *Hans:* "Oh yes."
> *I:* "What would you like to do if you were Daddy?"
> *Hans:* "And you were Hans? I'd like to take you to Lainz every Sunday—no, every week-day too. If I were Daddy I'd be ever so nice and good."

Playing father or mother in the family game is as old as the process of identification. Dolls, pets, sticks, stones, anything can be made to serve the fantasy. The teacher game is a little closer to reality. It is a fantasy "screened live." The script makes use of ego activities, though the satisfactions spring from the unconscious.

The young child is constantly on the border between object cathexis and identification with the object and this may lead even to merging with the object, as we often see in borderline cases. The teacher game uses both tendencies, cathexis of the object and identification, and it employs these psychic mechanisms interchangeably. Perhaps this helps to explain the ubiquity of the game. It follows the child's need for equilibrium between these trends. It allows for regression and progression.

The young graduate from college often turns to teaching, though he may not remain in the field. We hear it explained: "He has not found himself yet" and that is probably true. It could be stated also: "His identification is with a loved and admired teacher, a love object from whom he is not ready to separate." In an ego way, he is playing the teacher game.

The child (teacher) introjects the parent and teacher and thus obtains narcissistic gratification. Their attributes are structuralized within the ego. I take here an excellent statement from Sandler (1960): "The construction of an introject is the sequel of a complete or partial dissolution of the relationship to the real object. Through introjection the *relationship* to the object is maintained and perpetuated, but the real object is no longer so vital to the relationship. It follows that what is introjected is neither the personality nor the behavior of the parents, but their *authority*" (p. 159). The same could be said of the teacher's authority.

If one listens to children playing school, one observes the pleasure in wielding authority, "Keep your seat"; "quiet, quiet" in loud tones. "I am the teacher and you must do what I say." It is obvious that the pupils enjoy this, though rebellion is always near the surface. The meaner the teacher, the wilder and more aggressive are the pupils. The teacher seems to know how far she can go in order not to disrupt the game entirely. Otherwise, she is replaced.

Huizinga (1938) notes that "every game has rules and restrictions which cannot be violated without destroying the playful character of its performance." Sometimes the pupils complain that the teacher is not telling them what they wish to know, and they demand a change in subject matter, a situation not unlike what happens occasionally in their more mature years. School rules on higher levels are often scoffed at, but when they are absent complaints may be heard. At Palo Alto in the Center for Study of the Behavioral Sciences, it was found that many advanced students in the younger group felt quite lost without structure; they needed some outline of activities.

But we are not finished with the need to teach. To teach in this game, one must have pupils just as to play the parent in the family game, one must have children. A child's wish to have children of his own is well known to child analysts. Little Hans gives us an example in his anal children: "This morning I was in the W.C. with all my children. First I did lumf and widdled, and they looked on. Then I put them on the seat and they widdled and did lumf, and I wiped their behinds with paper. D'you know why? Because I'd so much like to have children; then I'd do everything for them—take them to the W.C., clean their behinds, and do everything one does with children" (p. 97). It is to be noted that he had his pupils look at him, just as he looked at them.

The disappointed Schreber found no surcease from sorrow over his inability to have children. Perhaps this was rooted in his own father's sternness of discipline. His father devised various ways of child rearing, some of them tortuous (Schreber, 1865). Schreber never had an opportunity to act as father to those longed-for children he might have treated differently, even as he wanted to be treated; or perhaps those children he never had were spared a cruel revenge on on his exacting, sadistic father.

An eleven-year-old boy confided to his analyst his wish to have children, saying, "I would like a child of my own, all by myself with no other parent, so it would do just what I wanted." "What would you do with it?" asked the analyst. "I would bounce it on my knee and tell it what to do." This boy's identification was with his mother; the father had served a minor part in his emotional life until his castration fears were revitalized by his preparation for Bar Mizvah, when his father became the model by which to measure his own growth. "I'll know when my penis is big enough." In this way, his father was his teacher; the model in his textbook.

A boy patient, age ten, brought his toy rubber horses to the analytic hour. They were his children. One, called Frisky, his favorite, "understands everything." But Frisky became a delinquent girl and had to go to jail. "Understanding everything" is dangerous, and for omniscience, she had to be punished. This boy desperately was trying to master anxiety produced by congenital mild hypospadias for which he had repeated examinations.

An eleven-year-old girl patient in her first analytic hour enumerated her problems: "My mind wanders, I have bladder trouble, and can I have babies?"

Child patients in the beginning of treatment often see analysis as a school situation. The analyst is the teacher, therefore omniscient, and the patient begs to be told. One anxious child pleaded in these words, "Tell me, hypnotize me, kill me." When the analyst asks questions, he becomes the teacher; when he overdoes this, he destroys for the child the omniscience which the patient both wishes and fears.

Sartre gives a poignant variation on our theme. The death of his father, in his first year, brought him and his mother to live with the maternal grandparents whom he fused in the appellation, "Karlè-mami." In fantasy, his mother was his sister: Karlèmami referred to mother and son as "the children." Both grandparents lived with and among books, and books became the fatherless boy's transitional objects, his parents and his children, the source of all knowledge: "books were my birds and my nests, my household pets, my barn and my countryside." At about five, he writes, "I did not yet know how to read, but I was pretentious enough to demand to have *my* books."

Some books were brought to him by a friend of his grandfather, stories of folklore. Of these, he writes: "I wanted to start the ceremonies of appropriation at once. I took the two little volumes, sniffed at them, felt them, and opened them casually . . . making them creak. In vain: I did not have the feeling of ownership. I tried, with no greater success, to treat them like dolls, to rock them, to kiss them, to beat them. On the verge of tears, I finally put them on my mother's lap." He wanted to feel maternal. It was not long after this episode that the precocious child discovered he could create his own stories; he began to write.

The fact that the teacher in the teacher game is usually a girl may bespeak the greater concern of female children to possess children of their own, in competition with mother. Girls play with dolls more than boys do. Little boys play with dolls, too, and in nursery school often offer to play the part of the mother, but they give this up normally when their masculinity is questioned. The boy pupils usually give the play teacher a hard time. Defiance to authority satisfies their hostility toward father or mother, who as teachers are also disciplinarians.

The deep-seated wish to have children often takes on neurotic forms in later life, as one who has observed teachers in real schools knows. Some become highly possessive of their pupils and encourage acting out against the parents; they become competitive with mothers and with other teachers, types well known to the psychoanalyst. Because of the need to hold the children to themselves, they suffer when the child grows up into another grade. The year after year of having to give up beloved children they have patiently worked with may account for the great number of depressions seen clinically among teachers. The greater the possessiveness the more poignant is the mourning. Another common type is the teacher embittered in childhood because of competition with too many siblings; she wants children on whom to wreak her ambivalence, and many pupils suffer therefrom. Both these neurotic teachers are foreshadowed in the teacher game.

In the early years, the teacher, almost always a woman, is often the first parent surrogate, loved or feared. The child frequently calls the first teacher "mother" or "mama," and most adults can reproduce a vivid visual image of that first teacher, her looks, her voice, her clothes.

Teaching is the prescribed activity of both mother and teacher. It does not follow that the teacher must become mother, though she is at first just that in transference. The "good" teacher sticks to her realm: the child's ego primarily and the superego. The teacher in the teacher game, though imitating school on a realistic basis, indulges unconscious wishes and fantasies. Playing school like playing doctor is as old as the ages. The need to teach is as old as the need to learn.

Though the teacher game is well rooted in phallic curiosity, as we have noted, and its anal hostility clearly marked (the first maternal teaching is in matters of cleanliness), essentially it is an orally entrenched activity. The teacher, like the mother, gives or withholds; she demands that the child accept what she has to give; she differentiates between correct and incorrect information (good and bad food). She tempts with her kind of bribery, favoritism, and compliments. Candy is often the reward in the teacher game.

As Socrates well knew, the teacher is the seducer; the information imparted or sought springs *au fond* from sexual concerns. The teacher in the game sublimates the craving to know, to tell, and to show. It is not surprising that on the daily kindergarten program, a special time is devoted to "show and tell." Omniscience and exhibitionism are both gratified.

Perhaps at the deepest level of satisfaction in the teacher game lies the wish to have children. Not yet a procreative urge, it harks back to the wish to be fed and loved and guided by the parent. The game therefore needs objects in the parental image and in the child image at the same time.

Assuming that theory springs from the need to teach and the need to teach comes from the wish to have children, it follows that theorizing is an ongoing pursuit. When a new and startling and complicated theory, such as psychoanalysis, springs substantially from the head of one person, there ensues competition among the children as to who gets (learns) the most from the fountainhead. Since the pupils also wish to be teachers and to have pupils of their own to teach, new groups appear who take from and add to and elaborate the original learning, just as children do with their sexual fantasies. What they do not understand, they fill in with old fantasies; what they cannot accept (according to their own fixations), they change or deny.

There comes a time, however, when elaboration becomes tenuous and hence boring. Then there are cries for a unified theory, ecumenical efforts are inaugurated, and a plateau of mediocre thinking is leveled off, to await another eruption.

BIBLIOGRAPHY

Alexander, F. (1960), *The Western World in Transition*. New York: Random House.
Erikson, E. H. (1937), Configurations in Play. *Psa. Quart.*, 6:139-214.
Freud, A. (1963), The Concept of Developmental Lines. *This Annual*, 18:245-265.
Freud, S. (1909), Analysis of a Phobia in a Five-Year-Old Boy. *Standard Edition*, 10:3-149. London: Hogarth Press, 1955.
—— (1920), Beyond the Pleasure Principle. *Standard Edition*, 18:3-64. London: Hogarth Press, 1955.
Golding, W. (1959), *Lord of the Flies*. New York: G. P. Putnam's Sons.
Huizinga, J. (1938), *Homo Ludens*. Boston: Beacon Press, 1955.
Lewin, B. D. (1965), Teaching and the Beginnings of Theory. *Int. J. Psa.*, 46:137-139.
Lorenz, K. (1952), *King Solomon's Ring*. New York: Crowell.
Peller, L. (1954), Libidinal Phases, Ego Development, and Play. *This Annual*, 9:178-198.
Sandler, J. (1960), On the Concept of Superego. *This Annual*, 15:128-162.
Sartre, J.-P. (1964), *The Words*. New York: Geo. Braziller, pp. 44-45, 85.
Schreber, D. G. M. (1865), *Ärztliche Zimmergymnastik*. Leipzig: Fleischer.
Waelder, R. (1932), The Psychoanalytic Theory of Play. *Psa. Quart.*, 2:208-224, 1933.

THE FIGURE DRAWINGS OF
THREE-YEAR-OLD CHILDREN

A Contribution to the Early Development of Body Image

THEODORE SHAPIRO, M.D. and

JOHN STINE, M.D. (New York)

Figure drawings have been used as a clinical tool by psychiatrists and psychologists for the last forty years. In 1926, Goodenough demonstrated significant correlations between the level of complexity of such drawings and Stanford-Binet scores, thus furnishing a simple but effective means for estimating I.Q. levels of young children.

Figure drawings also achieved wide acceptance as a means of gathering insight into the body image of the individual. It has been hypothesized that such a drawing is, in effect, a projection of the postural, libidinal and interpersonal experiences which are then integrated as components of the body image (Schilder, 1935). Careful analysis of the figure drawn thus yields information on neurological maturation and integration (Bender, 1946; Cohen, 1953), on zonal and object-libidinal cathexis, and on the interpersonal preoccupations of both the adult and child (Machover, 1949).

Schilder (1935) maintained that the body image is not a given entity of psychology, but is rather the functional composite of a

Dr. Shapiro is Instructor in Psychiatry, New York University School of Medicine. Dr. Stine is Resident, Kings County Hospital; work done while a fourth year medical student at New York University School of Medicine.

The authors wish to thank Else Loewenthal, Research Psychologist, for her help in rendering the statistical analysis, and also Dr. Barbara Fish, Associate Professor, Psychiatry, New York University School of Medicine, and Psychiatrist-in-Charge of the Children's Services, Bellevue Psychiatric Hospital, for her helpful comments on the manuscript.

This work was supported in part by a contribution from the Harriett A. Ames Charitable Trust, New York City.

continual layering and integration of innumerable body experiences. Hence, a study of the sequential development of the figure drawings of children should offer a means of exploring at least one aspect of early ego development and integration of function, namely, the formation of body image.

Unfortunately, much of our knowledge regarding figure drawings has been derived from studying the productions of children over four years and adults (Goodenough, 1926; Terman and Merrill, 1937). For this purpose the projective hypothesis has been employed; it is summarized in Goodenough's statement: "The child draws what he knows, not what he sees." This does not take into account the important possibility that the body experiences which are expressed in figure drawings at an early stage may represent only a part of the total perceptual experience of the young child. His visual-motor abilities may be insufficiently integrated with other of his perceptual functions (tactile, kinesthetic, auditory) to allow him to depict graphically a composite body image. If this is so, then the projective hypothesis is only partially applicable to the drawings of young children; it is therefore important to establish which experiences are differentially tapped.

Studies of the sequential development of figure drawings of the young child repeatedly note, in the early stages, the absence of significant and important parts of the body which appear in the drawings of normal adults. The gradually increasing ability of the child to depict an increasing number of body parts in increasing detail has been found to correlate well with other measurements of mental age, and thus provides the basis for the Goodenough Draw-a-Man Test and the Picture Completion part of the Stanford-Binet test as measures of intelligence (Goodenough, 1926; Terman and Merrill, 1937).

Although psychoanalytic reconstructions and direct observations have emphasized the importance of orality in the mental life of children, one of the parts frequently missing in early drawings is the mouth. This has also been noted by one of the authors (T.S.) in many drawings of mentally defective and schizophrenic children. Kato (1936) reports the following sequence of appearance of differentiated body parts in the drawings of kindergarten children: ". . . first there comes the head, trunk and eyes, to which legs follow and complete the simplest form of man. Soon after this appear the eyebrows, nose, hair and mouth." In Goodenough's series of 3,593 children's drawings, she noted that at four years of age, 58 per cent included mouths in their drawings, while 80 to 90 per cent of five-year-olds and 90 to 96 per cent of six-year-olds included the mouth, thus indicating a steady increase in the frequency of its appearance with advancing age.

On the other hand, 81 per cent of her four-year group drew eyes, and 100 per cent of children five and over drew eyes, indicating the relatively early differentiation and constancy of this feature. Gesell's figures for the same age groups indicate that 52 per cent of the four-year-old group drew eyes and 32 per cent mouths (Gesell et al., 1940). From five years on, well over 80 per cent drew both mouth and eyes. Only 79 per cent of his four-year group drew heads, in contrast to 94 per cent of Goodenough's group. Detailed data on three-year-olds, however, are sparse. Since this is the earliest period in which the child's maturity is sufficient to produce a coherent figure beyond a scribble, such data are important for developmental considerations. Gesell offers detailed reports of seventeen three-year-olds, only four of whom drew heads; the remainder only scribbled. Half of these drew eyes and mouth, while in his four-year group sixteen of twenty-five who drew heads drew eyes, and ten drew mouths. Gesell does not offer detailed data on an additional fifty three-year-old children mentioned elsewhere (1925). Cohen (1953), reporting on 200 children between the ages of three and a half to five, gives no breakdown of his group by age, but in one drawing by a three-and-a-half-year-old (reproduced in the text of his report) the mouth is absent. The paucity of detailed information on the drawings of three-year-olds prompted the current study, in which the drawings of three- and four-year-olds are compared for sequential differentiation of parts.

By this means we may be able to detect some clue concerning which sectors of the three-year-old child's perceptual experiences are projected into his drawings. Moreover, this method might enable us to investigate the sequence of integration of his functionally discrete sensorimotor patterns. Such an exploration could elucidate the developmental basis of functional dissociations in the adult ego where scoptophilic impulses remain poorly integrated with other perceptual functions. Some voyeuristic perversions in which there is incomplete synthesis of component instincts under genital primacy could be related to events occurring in this developmental period (Fenichel, 1945).

METHOD

Sixty-one children between the ages of thirty-six and sixty-three months attending normal nursery schools in the Manhattan area of New York City were asked to draw "somebody" after initial rapport had been established between the examiner and the child. Although no sampling of representative socioeconomic strata was planned, one third of the children tested were attending a nursery school which is run for children of low and lower-middle socioeconomic status. The remaining two thirds were attending full-fee nursery schools serving upper-middle-class families.

If the initial request elicited no drawing, a second modification was offered in the form of "draw a boy or girl" as the case might be; if the child said, "I'll draw a Mommy," he was permitted to do so as long as he indicated that what he was producing was a human form.

The first production was put aside and the child was asked, "What is this?" as the examiner pointed to each part of the subject's own face, and, "What is it for?" If no mouth was indicated in the first drawing, the child was offered a piece of chewing gum or candy to create an additional kinesthetic or tactile focus on the missing part. Forty-nine children were asked to do additional drawings. An inquiry was made about each drawing with reference to what parts were represented and to each spontaneous production by the child. A dynamic inquiry was not specifically sought. Each child was then asked to copy the figures indicated in the Gesell developmental schedule (1940).

RESULTS

The first, and when present, the second and third figure drawings of each of sixty-one children were examined and compared for the appearance of eyes, nose, mouth, extremities, and body. The drawings of seven children were only scribbles and were rejected for purposes of analysis (see Table I). When the data were scanned, it was apparent that at forty-six months, the children began to include a mouth in their drawings more systematically than the younger children.

Twenty-two per cent of fourteen children under forty-six months who drew more than a scribble drew a mouth, while 75 per cent of the children older than forty-six months did so. Chi square analysis of the dichotomous groups indicates that the difference between the groups is significant at the .001 level (see Figure 1). A similar analysis of the difference between the same age groups with reference to the representation of the nose was at the .01 level of significance (see Figure 2). Moreover, there was a correlation between the presence or absence of nose and mouth together at well above the .01 level of significance (see Figure 3). The statistics indicate a greater than chance difference between the two age groups with regard to the appearance of these facial parts in the drawings. By way of contrast, chi square analysis showed that the representation of both the eyes and body did not differ significantly between the age groups designated, although for somewhat different reasons (see Figures 4 and 5). While the eyes appeared almost as frequently as did the head at every age tested (89% and 99%), the body appeared much less frequently in both age groups (33% and 36%). Finally, no significant relationship could be demonstrated between the presence of mouth or nose and either sex or Gesell pencil and paper scores (see Table I and Figure 6).

In comparing the drawings produced before and after attention was drawn to the face and mouth, it was found that of forty-nine children who produced two or more acceptable drawings, thirty-five showed no change between the first and second drawings, twenty consistently including the mouth and thirteen consistently omitting it. An analysis of this group in terms of age showed that only about 20 per cent of the children under forty-six months of age drew a mouth; but way of contrast, about 78 per cent of the children over forty-six months of age drew a mouth, thus emphasizing both the relationship between increasing age and the appearance of the mouth, and the relative fixity of the young child's depiction of parts of the face. The latter is further emphasized when one recalls the statistically established tendency toward simultaneous appearance or absence of the nose and mouth.

Of the remainder, seven children drew a mouth only after attention had been drawn to the face, and seven children drew a mouth originally but did not do so after the questions had been asked. These data do not permit us to designate what factors other than the mere visual-motor ability to depict the mouth were operative.

In comparing consecutive drawings of individual children, several observations were made. First, there was a striking sameness in the way some children would produce what were essentially replicas of the first drawing, though the children labeled them different people, often of different sexes. Many of these were drawn almost by rote, the child laboriously going through the same motions in each drawing, strongly suggesting a relative fixity of visual-motor patterns.

Second, a few of the children showed an extraordinary sequence of progression and regression in their drawings. One forty-four-month-old girl, for example, first drew a figure with no mouth. After questioning, however, she drew a figure with both a mouth and teeth; her third figure had a mouth only and the mouth was absent in her final drawing. Moreover, it was striking to note that her various figures were otherwise quite similar with respect to size, shape, body parts, and detail.

Finally, several of the children were asked why their second drawing did not have a mouth. One or two of them answered, "I forgot about it." One boy, however, volunteered the explanation that "Daddy" had taken it away because it had said "bad things." Another child, aged four and a quarter years, spontaneously noted that his drawing had no mouth or nose. When asked why, he said, "It was taken off because it hurts, because it talks horrible." He indicated on further inquiry that it said things that "bad people say." Although he would not indicate who such bad people were, he did draw another picture and said it was his sister. He again produced a mouthless, noseless image, stating that "Daddy took them away because he was angry with her because they hurt, because they were bad." He then became mute, and he proceeded to copy the Gesell figures only after much coaxing. The level of disturbance of this child was not assessed, however, because of the setting of the study, and we cannot make any generalizations from this anecdote.

Dynamic considerations of this sort were not as overtly or spontaneously in evidence in the majority of the subjects tested.

Discussion

Schilder suggested that the body image of an individual is the composite integration of neurological maturation, libidinal and interpersonal experiences. The examination of this rather gross conceptual function has been approached through many avenues, not the least of which and probably the best investigated is the figure drawing. The developmental sequence in which the figure drawing evolves is one of a progression from rather formless scribbling and vertical movements to gradually differentiated and recognizable head and other body and facial features which are reproduced on paper to the request "Draw a man," or "Draw a person." The evolution described corresponds to the idea that the body image of an individual is "built up," integrated, and differentiated, and is not simply a "given" of maturation (Schilder, 1935).

Although both Gesell et al. (1940) and Goodenough (1926) record the frequencies of body-part representations in their analyses of figure drawings, neither elaborates the significance of the sequences. Of Gesell's seventeen three-year-olds, only 24 per cent drew a head. The focus of our study, based on a detailed analysis of the drawings of thirty additional three-year-olds, should enable us to understand the meaning of the sequences of differentiation of parts tacitly indicated by Goodenough and Gesell et al. and directly stated by Cohen (1953) and Kato (1936).

In agreement with the data of these authors, we found that once the child is motorically able to manage a pencil and to draw an ellipse, he will also draw eyes and only later include the other facial features. The appearance of this Gestalt of oval with eyes, we believe, is developmentally significant and suggests that the earliest figure drawings represent only partial integrations of the child's perceptual experiences; that is to say, the earliest drawings resembling a human head are taken mainly from the visual experiences of the child, and tactile experiences are only later "projected" onto the figure drawings. The reasons for this hypothesis are two: first, the Gestalt of oval and eyes (in association with movement) is the first "sufficient stimulus" for the "smiling response" at six weeks of age (Spitz and Wolf, 1946). The earliest figure drawings offer a striking parallel in their resemblance in this Gestalt. This resemblance is probably not a developmental accident but seems to attest to the persistence of certain patterned responses which are ontogenetically earlier than others.

Second, the impact of "oral" and tactile experiences of the infant, as well as the kinesthetic ones, is certainly conspicuous both in direct observations of children and in reconstructions during psychoanalytic treatment of adults (Hoffer, 1949); yet the mouth (as well as other facial features) is prominently absent in the earliest spontaneous figure drawings. Rather than making suspect the significance of these oral experiences, we would suggest that they are often not represented in the three-year-olds' drawings merely because the earliest drawings are based primarily upon visual Gestalten, while the tactile and kinesthetic perceptions are only later integrated with the visual percepts to form a representation of the human body. Our data do not show complete absence of the mouth; therefore, we cannot state that this is a universal fact.

Independent observation, not recorded here, of a bright child's sequential figure drawings from age two to three revealed that this child included mouth representations as early as the eyes. It is likely that there are some children in whom the integration of these different perceptual areas occurs prior to their visual-motor capacity to draw a head. However, the data presented indicate that this integration usually occurs later.

Even the few children who after the first mouthless drawings responded to the oral stimulation of chewing and introduced a mouth in subsequent drawings lost the mouth again in the third or fourth drawings. We must, of course, consider the possibility that at age three there are dynamic factors which might cause the subjects unconsciously to project their denial of the mouth pictorially. This was suggested by the one youngster who said that "Daddy" had taken the mouth away because it said "bad things." The tendency to oral regression as a defense during the phallic phase has been noted in such phenomena as the fear of being eaten by animals who represent the father (Freud, 1909; Fenichel, 1945). Our study was not designed to tap such depth-psychological factors; but even if they were at play in every case, we would suggest that the form of the ego regression remains suggestive of perceptual regression to the appreciation of an earlier visual Gestalt.

The developmental implications of this rather late integration of the visual elements of experience into a composite body image has wide-ranging speculative implications concerning the relative independence, even in adulthood, of scoptophilic impulses. However, we shall leave such speculations to other experimental or clinical approaches.

TABLE I

DRAWING WITH FIRST RECOGNIZABLE HEAD

AGE	S	EYES	EARS	NOSE	MOUTH	BODY	ARMS	LEGS	GESELL
3^0	M	+	−	+	−	−	−	−	Circle
3^1	D	+	−	−	+	−	−	−	−
3^2	Di	−	−	−	−	−	−	−	Circle
3^5	El	+	−	−	−	−	−	+	Circle
	Je	+	+	+	+	−	+	+	Square
	Ed	+	−	−	−	−	+	+	Square
	Jo	Only scribble in three trials							−
	B	Only scribble in three trials							Circle
	Da	+	−	−	−	−	−	+	Square
	En	Only scribble in three trials							−
	Be	Only scribble in three trials							Cross
	M	+	−	+	−	−	−	−	Square
3^6	L	+	−	−	−	+	+	+	Cross
	Do	+	−	−	+	−	+	+	Circle
3^7	A	+	−	+	+	−	+	+	Circle
	S	Only scribble in three trials							Cross
	M	+	+	−	−	+	+	+	−
3^8	D	+	+	+	−	+	−	−	−
	J	Only scribble							Cross
	Fr	+	−	−	−	−	+	+	Square
3^9	J	−	−	−	−	+	−	−	Square
	Mi	+	−	−	−	+	−	−	Square
	Wm (2)	+	−	−	−	+	+	+	Circle
	Ni	+	−	−	−	−	−	+	Cross
3^{10}	Joa	+	−	+	−	−	−	−	Cross
	L	+	−	+	+	−	−	+	Cross
	S	+	−	+	+	+	+	+	Square
	Mit	+	−	+	+	−	−	−	Square
	Ly	+	−	−	+	+	−	+	Square
	Fr	+	−	−	+	+	−	+	−
	Pi	+	−	−	−	−	−	−	−

TABLE I (continued)

AGE	S	EYES	EARS	NOSE	MOUTH	BODY	ARMS	LEGS	GESELL
3¹¹	Deb	+	−	+	+	−	+	+	Square
	Jef	+	−	+	+	−	−	−	Cross
	Sh	Only scribble in three trials							Cross
	K	+	−	+	+	+	−	+	Square
	Cl	+	−	+	+	−	−	−	Square
	Bl	+	+	+	+	−	+	+	Square
	Nich	+	−	−	+	+	+	+	−
4⁰	Am	+	−	+	+	−	−	+	−
	Th	+	−	+	+	+	−	−	−
	Ma	+	−	−	−	−	+	+	−
	Dr	+	+	+	+	+	−	−	−
	Ki	+	+	+	+	+	+	+	Cross
	Mi	+	+	−	+	−	−	−	Square
	Ch	+	−	−	+	−	−	−	Triangle
	Deb	+	−	+	+	+	−	−	Square
	Den	+	+	+	+	−	−	−	Circle
	P	+	−	+	+	−	−	−	Cross
	R	+	−	−	−	−	−	+	Square
	T	+	−	−	−	−	−	−	Square
	K	+	−	+	+	−	−	−	Square
	Kar	−	−	+	−	−	−	+	Cross
4¹	A	+	−	−	−	+	−	−	Square
	S	+	−	+	−	+	−	−	Cross
	Ge (2)	+	−	−	−	−	−	+	Square
	B	+	−	+	+	+	−	+	Square
4³	R	+	−	+	+	−	−	−	Square
4⁵	Dav	+	−	+	+	+	+	+	Square
	Li	+	−	+	−	−	−	+	Cross
4⁹	G	+	−	+	+	−	−	+	Cross
5³	Am	+	−	−	+	−	−	−	Diamond

+ Part present
− Part absent

FIGURE 1

	Less Than 46 Months	More Than 46 Months	
No Mouth (−)	14	9	23
Mouth (+)	4	27	31
	18	36	54

P < .001 significance

FIGURE 2

	Less Than 46 Months	More Than 46 Months	
No Nose (—)	13	11	24
Nose (+)	5	25	30
	18	36	54

P < .01 significance

FIGURE 3

	No Nose	Nose	
No Mouth	16	7	23
Mouth	8	23	31
	24	30	54

P < .01 significance

FIGURE 4

	Less Than 46 Months	More Than 46 Months	
No Eyes (—)	2	1	3
Eyes (+)	16	35	51
	18	36	54

Not significant

FIGURE 5

	Less Than 46 Months	More Than 46 Months	
No Body (—)	12	23	35
Body (+)	6	13	19
	18	36	54

Not significant

FIGURE 6

	Mouth	No Mouth	
♂	17	9	26
♀	14	14	28
	31	23	54

Not significant

BIBLIOGRAPHY

Bell, J. (1949), *Projective Techniques.* New York: Longmans, Green, pp. 350-398.

Bender, L. (1946), The Goodenough Test in Chronic Encephalitis in Children. *J. Nerv. Ment. Dis.,* 91:277-286.

Cohen, R. (1953), Role of Body Image Concept in Patterns of Ipsiliateral Clinical Extinction. *A.M.A. Arch. Neurol. & Psychiat.,* 70:503-509.

Fenichel, O. (1945), *The Psychoanalytic Theory of Neurosis.* New York: Norton.

Freud, S. (1909), Analysis of a Phobia in a Five-year-old Boy. *Standard Edition,* 10:5-149. London: Hogarth Press, 1955.

Gesell, A. (1925), *The Mental Growth of the Pre-school Child.* New York: Macmillan.

—— et al. (1940), *The First Five Years of Life.* New York: Harper, pp. 148-149.

Goodenough, F. (1926), *Measurement of Intelligence by Drawings.* Chicago: World Book, p. 72.

Hoffer, W. (1949), Mouth, Hand and Ego-Integration. *This Annual,* 3/4:40-56.

Kato, M. (1936), A Genetic Study of Children's Drawings of a Man. *Jap. J. Exp. Psychol.,* 3:75-85.

Machover, K. (1949), *Personality Projection in the Drawing of the Human Figure: A Method of Personality Investigation.* Springfield, Ill.: Thomas.

Mott, S. M. (1945), Muscular Activity as an Aid in Concept Formation. *Child Develpm.,* 16:97-109.

Schilder, P. (1935), *The Image and Appearance of the Human Body.* New York: International Universities Press, 1950.

Seeman, E. (1934), Development of Pictorial Aptitudes in Children. *Charact. & Pers.,* 2:209-221.

Spitz, R. A. & Wolf, K. (1946), The Smiling Response. *Genet. Psychol. Monogr.,* 34:57-125.

Terman, L. M. & Merrill, M. A. (1937), *Measuring Intelligence.* New York: Houghton Mifflin.

VICISSITUDES OF THE NEED FOR TACTILE STIMULATION IN INSTINCTUAL DEVELOPMENT

HOWARD SHEVRIN, Ph.D. and POVL W. TOUSSIENG, M.D.

(Topeka)

The mystery of early childhood experiences is deepened and its understanding made more difficult by efforts to impose adult modes of thought upon the totally fresh events of infancy which, rather than being explained by the ideas of maturity, are their progenitors. Yet, if we are to achieve a scientific account of psychic development and the pathology of childhood, we must venture to use tools fashioned by necessity in an adult mold. If the child is father of the man, it is also true that a wise father *can* know his own child. In a previous paper (1962), we have discussed the little-understood and infrequently considered role of conflict over tactile stimulation in the etiology of severe childhood disturbances. When we further examined the reasons for the importance of tactile experiences and their unique place in psychic development, we found it necessary to reconsider some aspects of psychoanalytic instinct theory. These reconsiderations will be presented in this paper. Although the reader is referred to our earlier paper for a full account of the clinical relevance of conflict over tactile stimulation, we shall summarize the main points from our previous presentation.

At the heart of our proposal was a clinical and developmental model based on the assumption that infants have a need for optimum tactile stimulation.[1] When they receive too little or too much such

From the Menninger Foundation, Topeka, Kansas.

We would like to thank Dr. Cotter Hirschberg, Dr. Richard Siegal, and Dr. Robert Switzer for careful reading of the manuscript and many helpful suggestions.

[1] For us tactile stimulation includes not only stimuli emanating from receptors in the skin but also from deeper tissues giving rise to proprioceptive and kinesthetic sensations.

stimulation in the early months of life, the ensuing conflict appears to interfere seriously with psychic development. The course of this conflict can be traced in the thoughts and actions of severely disturbed children of all ages. Rather than using repression or other psychic defenses directed at ideational derivatives of instincts, the main ways in which these children cope with tactile conflicts is either by a defensive raising of thresholds for all stimuli emanating from the environment or from inside the body, or through protective fluctuations in the physical distance between themselves and other people. The conflict can also be observed in their fantasy productions, usually in the form of an elaborate denial of the need for closeness. Despite these efforts the need for tactile stimulation persists. We have hypothesized that certain rhythmic behavior, such as rocking, often observed in severely disturbed children, is used to prevent a total loss of tactile stimulation resulting from excessive raising of thresholds.

This model made it possible to explain many otherwise puzzling phenomena occurring in the treatment of some severely disturbed children. We refer here to instances in which these children display an inordinate fear of being touched, while revealing in their behavior a great yearning for contact. One child, for example, would at times move within a hair's breadth of his therapist, yet when he was touched he would flee in terror. These children are often preoccupied with the texture of surfaces: another child complained that her skin was rough when she was born and therefore it was an annoyance to her mother. These children often experience periods of numbness, which we have explained as resulting from the raising of thresholds. This absence of sensation may be related to the frequent preoccupation with death found in these children. Lastly, in various metaphors they use time and distance as ways of denying the immediacy of human contact. We were able to postdict from current clinical material that there had been severe disturbances in physical contact between these children and their mothers in the early months of life. Such major disturbances were found in the history of all the children we have studied so far.

Our suppositions concerning the vital role of tactility in early development which were based on clinical data from older children have received support from an unexpected quarter. Bronson (1963), in his review of Conel's morphological study of the infant cortex, remarks: "From neurological data the infant in the first weeks following birth must be largely dependent on innate reflexes mediated at lower neural centers, and would be primarily responsive to internal stimuli (pain, hunger) which have little direct representation in the neocortex. *With maturation the increasing responsiveness to the external environment is mediated through tactile and, to a lesser extent, auditory and visual input. One would predict therefore that tactile experiences during these earliest months would be particularly salient"* (pp. 57-58; our italics).

In what follows we shall first define a number of terms which will be used in delineating the nature of the need for tactile stimulation and the threshold mechanism we have postulated and their relationship to psychoanalytic instinct theory. We shall then be in a position to describe the character of tactile conflict in more precise terms than we have previously. In the concluding section we shall adduce evidence from recent clinical research done by others who were unaware of our hypotheses. Their findings support the implications derived from our conception of tactile conflict.

DEFINITIONS

We have been careful to use the concept of "need" with regard to tactile stimulation, a concept which leaves open whether this need is to be classified as a "drive," an "instinct," or perhaps is to be viewed in other ways. For the purpose of our discussion five terms will be provisionally defined: stimulus, need, craving, threshold, and defense.

Stimulus. Osgood has defined a stimulus as "that form of physical energy that activates a receptor" (1953, p. 12). If we keep in mind that there are receptors deep within the body as well as on its surface, we can see that the use of the term stimulus is limited only by convention to sources outside the body.

Need and Craving. Stimuli arising from inside the body range across a wide spectrum. One category is of special interest to us: the stimuli produced by deficits. The term *need* is often used to refer both to the deficit itself (hunger) and to the stimulus arising from the deficit (hunger pangs). This equivocal usage creates difficulties because there are deficits that are unaccompanied by stimuli and inner stimuli that are not related to deficits. Those deficits without associated stimuli, no matter how serious they may be, remain mute as far as the mind is concerned. For our purposes, we shall use the term *craving* to refer to the stimulus produced by a deficit and the term *need* to refer to the deficit itself.

Threshold. A stimulus is defined in terms of the availability of a receptor. There are many more forms of energy both within and outside the body that are outside of psychology because no receptors have been evolved which these forms of energy can activate.[2] For each receptor there is a limited range of a given energy to which it can respond. These thresholds determine what will prove effective as a craving, but they cannot in any direct way influence the need which gives rise to the craving. In so far as an insistent, strong craving may overload a receptor or create distraction and confusion at higher levels of thought organization, these thresholds protect the integrity of the perceptual organs and the efficiency of the central organs of cognition.

It would be important to bear in mind that the danger which the organism must guard itself against at this point is primarily a danger to its psychic integrity, although there is also a danger to its somatic intactness. By this we mean that once an insistent craving is permitted to enter higher levels of psychic organization, it would completely dominate the organism's actions and feelings, thus making it almost impossible for other needs and adaptive requirements to be met. In Hartmann's terms (1939), the synthetic functions of the immature ego would be sorely pressed. A helpful analogy is to compare this psychic danger with the actual circumstances of a drug addict whose entire life is controlled and dominated by one insistent craving.

---

[2] The possibility must also be kept in mind that there may be more receptors than we have discovered. The work of Richter and Eckert (1937) has shown that the rat will respond to a calcium deficiency by preferring calcium-rich food, which suggests that there may be a craving arising from this metabolic insufficiency and a receptor for this craving. Recent work has strongly indicated that the rat may have a special sensory receptor at the spinal level for X-ray radiation (Odum et al., 1964). The existence of unsuspected sensitivities is not limited to rats. Two women with remarkable sensory responsiveness have been reported in the literature: one can hear electrical impulses, the other can discriminate colors on the basis of touch (Amrine, 1964).

A threshold works to render a potentially effective stimulus ineffective, thus making mute an otherwise articulate deficit. As long as the receptor remains refractory to the craving the underlying need has little opportunity for being satisfied. The height of a threshold must be attuned to the degree of need: if the threshold is too high, then the growing deficit may result in danger to the person even though the receptors and higher cognitive centers are protected. This outcome would result from a strategy comparable to protecting the highways, railroads, and capital of a nation while permitting the countryside to be ravaged. If the thresholds are too low, then the arteries of communication and the centers for integration would be clogged with trivial messages. A threshold, then, is a protective measure which by controlling the cognition of a craving permits or does not permit action aimed at relieving the related deficit. In the light of this definition a threshold follows an all-or-none principle.

Defense. There are certain protective measures, however, which do permit some partial relief while maintaining higher cognitive processes at a relatively efficient level. The basic restriction imposed by these protective measures is that the psychic representative of the underlying deficit not advance as high as the organs controlling consciousness. Cognition of the stimulus at the level of consciousness would bring about some critical degree of disorganization. We have avoided talking about cravings at the level of psychic defenses and have used instead the term psychic representative because it is likely that some significant change in the organization of the psychic stimulus has taken place in the shift from a lower to a higher level of cognition. We thus distinguish a psychic defense from a threshold on three grounds: (1) whether or not partial satisfactions are possible; (2) the level of functioning in the psychic apparatus; (3) the type of psychic representative of a need against which the particular protective measure is taken, a point to be developed later in the discussion.

With the help of these definitions we can now discuss the mechanism of raising of thresholds and its role in conflict over tactile stimulation.

Raising of Thresholds as a Protective Device in Relation to Cravings and Impulses

In our previous paper we presented clinical evidence indicating that many disturbed children deal with an unresolved conflict over tactile experiences by the raising of thresholds. We are now in a position to consider in more precise terms the three aspects of this threshold mechanism which we discussed in our previous paper:

1. With respect to its protective function, the raising of thresholds is related to Freud's idea of the stimulus barrier in so far as a threshold keeps potentially overwhelming stimulation from harming the organism, although Freud had in mind primarily the protection against *external* stimulation. By postulating that a similar barrier may be present with respect to *internal* stimulation, or cravings, we may be aligning this concept with the neurological notion of inhibition. This comparison is little more than an analogy because we do not know the exact nature of either mechanism.

2. With respect to its role in conflict resolution, the raising of thresholds may persist in some individuals as a protective measure at later points in life. As an age-appropriate protective measure, however, it is probably most prominent during the first year.

3. With respect to its structural role, the raising of thresholds can be differentiated from repression and other psychic defenses because it is directed at stimuli rather than at the psychic representative of instincts. This distinction between inner stimuli and the psychic representative of instincts needs further elaboration, which we shall now undertake.

On the basis of Freud's conception of instinct (1915), three related problems can be distinguished which have direct bearing on our effort to contrast cravings and instincts: (1) What relationship can be said to exist between instincts and stimuli—the former in their special psychoanalytic usage and the latter in their broadest psychological and physiological significance? (2) What function is served by defining instinct as the "psychical representative of the stimuli originating from within the organism and reaching the mind" (Freud, 1915, p. 122)? (3) How are different qualities of instinct distinguished by the individual (e.g., oral from anal, libidinal from aggressive)?[3]

Instincts and Stimuli

Freud (1915) considered the concept of instinct from a broad biological perspective and identified the specific way in which the term instinct would be applicable to psychoanalytic phenomena. From a biological standpoint, Freud considered an instinct to be any persistent, genetically given internal stimulus which required some effort at mastery on the organism's part. However, not all such internal stimuli were to be considered as instincts from a specifically psychoanalytic point of view. Only those persistent internal stimuli which become psychically represented were to be defined as psychoanalytically relevant instincts. This definition left a broad category of persistent internal stimuli, instinctual from a biological point of view, beyond the scope of psychoanalytic theory.

At the same time, Freud contrasted stimuli from *within* the organism with stimuli originating from *outside* the organism, for he suggested that avoidant movements of the body help the organism to distinguish external from internal stimuli: if a body movement effectively terminates a stimulus, then it is external; if it does not, then it must be internal. However, this criterion does not cleanly separate internal from external stimuli: sound is an external stimulus that at least early in life cannot be avoided by movement; proprioceptive stimuli constitute an even clearer exception to this rule. Within the body certain stimuli emanating from the lower colon are effectively handled from the start of life by reflex contractile movements. Were we to apply this criterion of body movement with rigid logic, then sound and tactile stimuli would be "internal" while the stimuli prompting such actions as defecation and urination would be by definition "external" to the organism.

Avoidant muscular movement is an inadequate criterion for distinguishing internal from external stimuli. Some other basis will need to be found for the early adaptive functioning of the infant which Freud ascribed to the "original reality ego." The criterion

3 In much of the discussion that follows, our thinking has benefited from a study of the issues and problems clarified by Rapaport (1957, 1959) and his students in their consideration of Freud's "Instincts and Their Vicissitudes."

based on body movement can at best be considered as attempting unsuccessfully to distinguish *external* from *internal* stimuli but cannot be relevant to the distinction between instinctual and noninstinctual stimuli which Freud attempted on this basis. Although all external stimuli are noninstinctual, not all internal stimuli can be instinctual. Any transitory condition producing internal stimulation, such as colic, or pain in general, can hardly be considered instinctual. We are confronted with the difficulty of dealing with two incoordinate categories. There is a group of internal stimuli, not mentioned by Freud, which are not necessarily instinctual in nature in the specific psychoanalytic sense. We are referring to proprioceptive and interoceptive stimuli, of which the craving for tactile stimulation is a prime example. The problem would still remain, however, to determine on what basis one can distinguish between instinctual and noninstinctual groupings of internal stimuli.

Instinct as the Mental Representative of Some Internal Stimuli

One of Freud's most intriguing and puzzling notions is the suggestion that an instinct be defined as a *psychically represented* stimulus to the mind. This form of psychic representation must be distinguished from ideational representations which are later derivatives from this fundamental form of mental representation. Freud may have made psychic representation a part of his definition of instinct in order to work within an entirely psychological model.

In the *Three Essays on the Theory of Sexuality* (1905), Freud traced the development of sexuality from its early primitive component instincts to their final synthesis in adult genitality. Later in "Instincts and Their Vicissitudes" Freud observed that the earliest instinctual components are *"auto-erotic;* that is to say, their object is negligible in comparison with the organ which is their source, and as a rule coincides with that organ" (Freud, 1915, p. 132). Despite this difference, we must assume that these "auto-erotic" impulses are instinctual and therefore psychically represented and thus on a par with later libidinal component instincts. Although Freud strongly implied in the *Three Essays* that instincts not only suffer vicissitudes but undergo development, it is not clear in what way other than through combining with other instincts (through synthesis or fusion) instincts change and mature. In the previous section in which we considered Freud's handling of instincts and stimuli, we noted that he apparently ignored a large group of internal stimuli deriving from deficits which are not necessarily instinctual in nature, such as the need for tactile stimulation. To these stimuli we have given the name craving because of their insistent, unmodifiable and pre-emptory character. Since our main concern is with the craving for tactile stimulation, we shall use this one craving as a model for what may be a class of noninstinctual—or, as we shall subsequently explain *pre*instinctual—stimuli. We shall suggest that at least some instincts may have an earlier stage of development in which they function as cravings.

We would like to propose that at the beginning of life the im-maturity of the infant is manifested not only in the negligible role that objects play in drive satisfaction (autoerotic versus alloerotic), or in the absence of drive synthesis (isolated libidinal components versus genital synthesis), but in the sheer level of drive organization within the psychic apparatus itself. In order to distinguish at least two levels of drive organization we suggest that a craving may under-go a critical development as a result of which it *becomes* psychically represented and assumes the status of an impulse (or instinct in the psychoanalytic sense). Prior to this significant transition the craving was, in actuality, no different in relation to the psychic apparatus than any purely external stimulus such as light or sound: the organ-ism must rely on some form of threshold against topologically exter-nal as well as topologically internal stimuli in the absence of means for diminishing stimulus intensity. The topological references of outside and inside may now be redefined in functional terms: when a craving has become psychically represented, it has been raised to a new level in the psychic apparatus where it is now subject to pro-tective measures based primarily on displacement mechanisms which can successfully provide a variety of quiet, efficient avenues for stimulus control without disrupting other adaptive requirements. These displacement mechanisms are the psychic defenses which make possible partial satisfaction while maintaining control over impulses. But psychic defenses cannot be effective against cravings—it would be like attempting to control the wind with a network of irrigation ditches: the means would not match the task and the wind would blow right over the most elaborate system of canals. "Inside" describes what has been psychically represented; "outside" describes what has failed to become psychically represented or has not yet achieved that status, but exists as an insistent stimulus nonetheless.

This redefinition has one important implication with regard to Freud's concept of the "purified pleasure ego" to which Freud ascribed the function of "projecting" unpleasant *inner* (from a topological standpoint) stimuli onto the outside, and "introjecting" pleasant *outer* (from a topological standpoint) stimuli inside itself. In so far as cravings are not psychically represented and thus not subject to the moderating influences of psychic defenses, they are functionally *outside* the higher reaches of the psychic apparatus and are experienced as in the same category as those external stimuli whose intensities would be disruptive if they were not blocked by threshold mechanisms. There is thus no need to postulate an additional mechanism of projection; whatever suffers the same fate is by that reason in the same category. We need only add that these stimuli dealt with by thresholds would tend to fuse or condense in the infant's experience due to the immature condition of the mechanisms underlying cognition.

This cognitive factor is of special importance when we consider introjection. For with introjection a similar fusion is undergone by stimuli because they have resulted in *satisfaction*, whether their sources were inside or outside the body. Thus two separate groupings of experience would emerge in the young infant: (1) one class of stimuli with sources both outside and inside the body which are held together by being excluded from full participation in the infant's experience by thresholds. If one wishes to look at the matter solely from the viewpoint of *internal* sources of stimulation, they may be said to have been "projected"; (2) a second class of stimuli with sources both inside and outside the body which are unified by providing satisfaction. If one wishes to look at the matter from the viewpoint of *external* sources of stimulation, they may be said to have been "introjected." In addition, within each grouping the representations of these different stimuli tend to fuse because of cognitive immaturity.

Introjection can be given still another meaning with reference to the transition undergone by cravings as they become impulses. We may say that the craving has been "introjected" or made part of a higher level of psychic functioning. The reference points for this use of the term introjection are certain specifiable levels of psychic functioning rather than the loci of need-satisfying stimuli. An additional advantage of this reconsideration of projection and introjection is that we can avoid assuming that the young infant possesses well-established reference points for self and nonself.

In our use of the terms introjection and projection it is clear that we feel it necessary to distinguish the processes so designated in infancy from their later analogues in the older child and adult. Projection in the adult paranoid is not simply based on a resort to threshold mechanisms: what is "projected" is based on complex processes involving psychic representation and such relatively late-forming structures as the superego. The purely formal cognitive property of fusion and condensation may be present, but in no sense can we speak of a full regression toward an early infantile condition such as is reflected in projection and introjection as we have discussed them.

Qualities of Instincts

One of the most perplexing problems in psychoanalytic theory is the one posed by drive quality. On what basis can the different instincts be distinguished? Freud (1915) appeared to be of two minds: at one point he argued that only differences in *quantity* of excitation differentiate drives, and he maintained that impulse sources cannot be used as a basis for differentiation because they belong to physiology and are beyond the purview of psychology; at another point in the same paper he appeared to change his mind and offered *sources* as a criterion for distinguishing impulse qualities. It may seem as if we have further complicated the matter by proposing another category, cravings. We would like to suggest, however, that cravings, unlike impulses, do not possess quality. We can liken the different ways in which cravings and impulses are related to quality to the scrambled and unscrambled messages in telephonic communication. In order to insure privacy in transmission, some telephonic messages are scrambled so they cannot be overheard; before the message reaches the receiver it is unscrambled and thus becomes intelligible to the listener at the other end of the line. A craving is a sensory message without a clearly definable quality other than that of "demand-for-reception"; in this respect cravings are indistinguish-able from each other. Once a need is signaled by an impulse, how-ever, the message has become *unscrambled* and the quality of the deficit is self-evident, for example, as a need for sexual release. We suggest that by becoming psychically represented the craving can be experienced as qualitatively distinct and thus achieves the status of an impulse. The problem for future investigation then becomes focused on the nature and development of psychic representation.

The view that the instinctual life of the infant is different from the instinctual life of the older child and adult, though by no means a thoroughly explored issue, is not new. Anna Freud (1936) implied a distinction similar to our own when she suggested that denial and mechanisms related to denial so often found in young children ought not to be considered as psychic defenses because they were directed at reality dangers rather than the dangers emanating from impulse. Her position is that denial is solely aimed at *external* dangers, as can be judged from the following excerpt:

"The defensive measure [denial] to which the ego has recourse is not aimed against the instinctual life but directly at the external world which inflicts the frustration. Just as, in the neurotic conflict, perception of a prohibited instinctual stimulus is warded off by means of repression, so the infantile ego resorts to denial in order not to become aware of some painful impression from without" (p. 96).

We would add to this formulation that at the beginning of life *all* stimuli, from inside as well as from outside the organism, poten-tially represent real dangers to the child and are dealt with by a protective measure, raising of thresholds. We have suggested in our previous paper that denial may be related to the raising of threshold mechanism. When a person denies reality, he is in effect saying no to an actual event and thus refusing to grant its existence although he *may be conscious of the reality*. In repression, however, the exist-ence of a painful reality is accepted, but its *access to consciousness is barred*. Denial is on a much more primitive level of reality testing than repression because it involves accepting a blatant contradiction. It is likely that when the raising of thresholds fails to keep insistent cravings from consciousness the overloaded ego is reduced to denial. To limit denial to external dangers only, however, runs the risk of reintroducing the ambiguities present in a formulation based on reference points outside and inside the infant at a time when this differentiation can hardly be made. Anna Freud speaks of id anxiety, the ego's fear of impulses, as representing for some people a real, albeit internal, danger and that this fear is unanalyzable because it is based on reality rather than neurotic distortions. Thus, the reality danger *can be* "inside" a person. We would add that when the very young child is coping with insistent cravings, he is in the same position as one who fears his impulses.

More recently, Jacobson (1954), Schur (1958), and Fisher (1965), each from different vantage points, have felt it necessary to assume that instincts in the strictly psychoanalytic sense have a prehistory in the individual. Because of her dissatisfaction with Freud's concepts of primary narcissism and primary masochism, Jacobson suggested that at the beginning of life there is an *undifferentiated drive energy* which only later (at roughly three months of age) becomes differentiated into libidinal and aggressive energies. Prior to this differentiation, the infant's instinctual life is dominated by a diffuse "silent" physiological discharge of this undifferentiated drive energy. There are two difficulties with this position which make it hard for these ideas to be translated into workable hypotheses:

1. Energy is a quantity which can be greater or smaller; it is not a substance which can have one or another quality such as libidinal or aggressive. By *electrical* energy, for example, we refer not to a condition of the energy itself but to certain quantitative relationships existing in a special system. The structure of the system and its various interrelationships determine the amount of energy in it; but it is the nature of the system itself that defines the energy as electrical rather than mechanical or hydraulic. If Jacobson is following the same shorthand as in this physical illustration, then she should specify what structures determine that energy at the start of life is "undifferentiated" and what structures later in life determine energy to be "libidinal" or "aggressive." It is necessary to conceptualize the nature of the structure through which the force acts as well as the force itself. This we have tried to do in suggesting the concepts of craving and threshold, on one level, and impulse and defense on the other.

2. The mingling of physiological and psychological concepts

results in unclarity. At one point Jacobson stated that "a continuous, 'silent' discharge of small amounts of psychic energy can occur mainly through 'inside' physiological channels" (p. 79). Unless carefully delimited the statement would be comparable to saying that one could connect a light bulb to a waterfall. One can of course light an electrical fixture through water power, but first one must discover the structures through which the energic transformations can be achieved. The search for such transforming structures may be unnecessary because the psychological and physiological structures may parallel each other throughout development. We have suggested that deficits, or needs, relevant to psychic development give rise to stimuli which at the beginning of life are cravings and that cravings are later transformed into impulses acting at a higher level in the psychic apparatus.

In a careful systematic comparison of instinct in man and animal, Schur (1958) suggested that three aspects must be considered: instinct, instinctual drive, and drive. By *instinct* Schur referred to the organized stereotypic behavior of lower animals in the service of biological needs. In man, instincts in this sense do not exist because man's behavior, although prompted by needs, changes with experience and is not fixed. By *instinctual drive*, Schur referred to what prompts man's malleable behavior and in this respect *instinctual drive* is comparable to Freud's *"Trieb."* By *drive* Schur referred to the somatic source which energizes the *instinctual drive*. Of particular interest to us is Schur's assumption that at the beginning of life only *drive* as such exists which through the maturation of the psychic apparatus becomes psychically represented in the form of a wish, defined as the "impulse to obtain satisfaction" (1958, p. 203). The concept of drive as used by Schur is made to do the work of two concepts: it refers both to the deficit or need itself and to the stimulus arising from the deficit. In our view there are parallel physiological and psychological functions or else the deficit would remain mute and of no direct consequence to the psychological development of the individual, as is true for fluoride or iron deficits. When Schur talks about "diffuse discharge phenomena, both in the vegetative and in the motor spheres" (1958, p. 205) he may be bypassing important issues with regard to the psychological *means* used to cope with drives, or, as we would prefer to call them, cravings.

We have proposed that thresholds be considered to perform this protective function of coping with cravings. If these thresholds fail, then the cravings are transmitted upward in the psychic apparatus. This process may precipitate a crisis in a young organism which does not yet have available the means for stilling the craving itself. The "diffuse" behavior of the infant is thus not necessarily a "discharge" of physiological energy but may represent the limited actions of an immature organism attempting to cope with a situation beyond its capacity.

As a result of recent research on the dream-sleep cycle, it has become evident that the pattern of physiological activation accompanying dreaming is present from birth. This pattern includes rapid eye movements, widely varying rates of autonomic activity, erection, and the apparent blocking of gross muscular movements. In an examination of this literature, Fisher (1965) asserts: "There is no doubt that the biological processes described have priority over the psychological process of dreaming. The biological cycle, that is, the Stage I REMPs [rapid eye movement periods], is present at birth at a time when it is inconceivable that dreaming is taking place because psychic structure has not yet developed" (1965, p. 272). He then draws upon the thinking of Jacobson and Schur to help provide a genetic account for the emergence of dreaming as a psychological event out of a physiological matrix. He proposes that "dreaming as a psychic event . . . cannot occur until the emergence of the 'wish,' until psychic structure formation advances to the point of memory trace development of sufficient stability that traces of past events can be aroused to hallucinatory intensity during dreaming sleep" (1965, p. 273). Fisher cites the observations of Wolff on neonates as supporting this view. Wolff has noted two phases of sleep in neonates: irregular sleep marked by variability in respiration, among other things, and regular sleep marked by regular respiration. In irregular sleep a variety of motor patterns were observable, such as smiling, sucking, and erection; in regular sleep these motor patterns were infrequent but an increase in startle responses was observable. Wolff postulated that during regular sleep "neural energy" accumulated which was only partially discharged by the startle responses but was more fully discharged during irregular sleep by way of the greater number of motor channels then available. On the basis of Wolff's observations Fisher proposes that "Sleep is characterized by alternating REM [rapid eye movement, dreaming sleep] and NREM [nonrapid eye movement, dreamless sleep] periods, or alternating periods of energy discharge and build-up. In the early neonatal period we are dealing only with neural energy discharge. At some unknown point in infant development, psychic structure develops, memory trace formation becomes possible, physiological 'drive' discharge is in part replaced by 'instinctual drive' discharge through the psychological process of dreaming. It is at this time that dreaming as a psychic event takes on its function of discharging instinctual drive tensions through hallucinatory wish fulfillment" (1965, pp. 274-275).

The same considerations with regard to the energy concept and the mingling of physiological and psychological concepts in Jacobson's and Schur's use of the terms apply to Fisher's suggestions. It would be consistent with our theoretical formulations to view Wolff's observations in another light: it could be assumed, for example, that the thresholds for cravings may be lower in irregular sleep than in regular sleep. In irregular sleep individual cravings would activate related consummatory mechanisms (e.g., sucking, smiling, erection), while in regular sleep the way to activation would be blocked although there may be alerting responses to persistent cravings as well as to other internal and external stimuli. We have suggested that displacement appears later in psychological development and is associated with an impulse-defense level of psychic organization. From this point of view, the ready displaceability of "neural energy" in the neonatal period postulated by Fisher and Wolff would be open to question. It is more likely that certain fixed relationships exist initially between cravings and consummatory mechanisms which are made more fluid in the course of development allowing for increasing amounts of displacement. In an article cited earlier in this paper, Bronson (1963) has interpreted recent physiological evidence to suggest that cognitive functioning in the neonate is based on qualitatively different mechanisms from those present in the older child.

As a way of summarizing these reconsiderations we may attempt to see how a complex problem like primary masochism can be restated in the terms we have proposed. Freud assumed that at the start of life the forces of the death instinct could destroy the infant unless they were either neutralized by libido or directed outward in the form of sadism. There would seem to be little doubt that the organism is in greatest danger during birth and in the first hours and days afterward. If there is any psychogenic component in this danger, Freud's explanation may be one way of accounting for it. We would like to propose another: at the start of life, the stimuli created by certain deficits can create a crisis in the primitive ego's capacity for synthesis which may eventually disrupt autonomic functioning. The danger may then be real, but it may derive not from the death instinct but from competing cravings inundating an immature organism. Unless these cravings are checked by thresholds and diminished by gratification the infant may indeed find himself in a dangerous position. In place of neutralization of the death instinct by libido, we suggest that thresholds perform this same function of keeping cravings in check. In place of a sadistic turning outward of aggression, we suggest that the organism makes an optimum demand of the environment to relieve not just its physiological deficits but to still the clamor of its cravings.

In actual fact the neonate, if he can be said to be concerned with anything, is concerned with stilling his cravings rather than with relieving his deficits. Only an adult or older child knows that he must eat to live. Young (1943) has shown that in rats appetite may work against the relief of physiological deficits. Thus, a rat with a calcium deficiency will ignore calcium-rich foods in favor of a nutritionless saccharin solution and will drink inordinate amounts of the unnecessary fluid. In the absence of a saccharin solution, however, it will prefer foods containing the physiologically required substance. Furthermore, cravings are adaptive, in Hartmann's phrase (1939), only in a certain average expectable environment which stills the craving by satisfying the underlying deficit rather than by simply diminishing the craving. In an unusual environment, such as one in which sweet foods are plentifully available to the rat, cravings may work at cross-purposes with real needs. If the environment fails to provide optimum relief, then some pathological response is the outcome, among which aggression may be one possibility.

THE ROLE OF THRESHOLDS AND CRAVINGS
IN TACTILE CONFLICT

In our previous paper we attempted to demonstrate that conflict over tactile stimulation is one important factor in severe childhood disturbances. With our new definitions and on the basis of our discussion of the raising of thresholds we can now reconsider the three conditions giving rise to conflict over tactile stimulation in early life and the nature of the possible pathological response to them: (1) tactile understimulation, by which we refer to the absence of relief for the tactile deficit or need; (2) a constitutionally high need for tactile stimulation, by which we refer to the existence of a relatively high tactile deficit from birth; (3) tactile overstimulation, by which we refer to a surplus of external stimulation relative to the actual tactile deficit.

Tactile Understimulation

When tactile gratification is insufficient in the first weeks and months of life the craving created by this deficit will become more insistent. When the insistence of the craving reaches some critical point, the receptor threshold for the craving will be raised to a high enough level to protect against receptor overloading and central disruption. Once this point is reached a seemingly anomalous situation is created; its clinical manifestation is a condition in which any amount of tactile gratification is reacted to as if it were a danger. This clinical anomaly can be explained by recalling that a threshold obeys an all-or-none principle so that once partial relief of the need would begin to occur the threshold would be totally removed, which would then make effective an overwhelmingly strong craving. The organism must guard itself against this possibility by imposing a compensatory threshold against gratifying tactile stimulation. For example, the infant is observed to go limp when held. The stimulation provided by the mother, which might relieve the tactile deficit, is kept from doing so by a new threshold resulting in hypotonia. It would be analogous to an older child tightly compressing his lips when he does not want food even though he may be hungry. Once this new threshold is imposed the possibility for tactile relief is severely reduced and the organism is faced with an insistent craving with the additional burdensome task of guarding itself against any relief, for relief itself is now a threat.

Constitutionally High Need for Tactile Stimulation

This condition in its end result does not differ from the first. The only difference is that the child at birth has a great tactile deficit and consequently a strong craving arising from this deficit, so that right from the beginning a modest amount of such gratification would pose the same threat as for children who are understimulated.

Tactile Overstimulation

Persistent and chronic tactile overstimulation would present the immature organism with the very same problem with regard to mastery of insistent stimuli that its own inner stimuli or cravings would. There is the further complication, however, that when the infant responds to the threat of external overstimulation by raising of thresholds for such stimuli, this would also make the possibility of relieving his tactile deficit less likely. If this were continued long enough, the infant would arrive at the same point as in the first two conditions. Because he could not abide or tolerate overstimulation from without, his response would result in increasing his own internal deficit; finally, even a modest amount of stimulation would pose great internal difficulty.

As a result of any of these three conditions a situation would be created in which the child would become excessively dependent on thresholds for maintaining himself. If no corrective experience supervenes early enough, we would anticipate that the child would encounter difficulty in reaching and maintaining an impulse-defense level of psychic functioning.

CLINICAL EVIDENCE

The differentiation and narrower definition of commonly used psychoanalytic concepts which we have attempted remain a type of intellectual gymnastics if it cannot be shown that these steps can make clinical research data more intelligible. We have come across several impressive studies of infants and young children which have yielded data pertaining to tactility, although the investigation of the role of tactile experiences was not a specific goal in any of these studies. The data support and illustrate the model we proposed in our previous paper. We hope to show further that the concepts we have discussed in this paper will help us relate seemingly disparate and incidental research observations to each other in a predictable and new way.

In a study comparing seventy-five institutionalized infants with seventy-five infants reared in families, Provence and Lipton (1962) observed that institutionalized children: (1) reacted peculiarly to being held; (2) engaged in much rocking behavior; and (3) were unusually quiet and slept excessively. In what follows we shall comment on how these three observations relate to our model and in the course of discussing these points we shall introduce additional data from other sources pertinent to them.

Reaction to Being Held

Provence and Lipton report that by the second month of life all of the institutionalized children reacted abnormally to being held: "They did not adapt their bodies well to the arms of the adult, they were not cuddly, and one noted a lack in pliability . . . . they felt something like sawdust dolls; they moved, they bent easily at the proper joints, but they felt stiff or wooden" (1962, p. 56). This odd response to holding was the first notable symptom Provence and Lipton found in institutionalized infants. It is important to note that feeding disturbances or intestinal upsets were rare. The tactile modality rather than orality as such was thus most sensitive to revealing the effects of maternal deprivation, which is consistent with our expectations and accords well with Bronson's conclusion based on neurological data that tactility is the most salient sensory channel in the first three months of life. Provence and Lipton suggest that these infants responded like "sawdust dolls" because they lacked the opportunity for experiences in mutual adaptation with a mother and had thus failed to learn to respond adaptively to being held. However, Patton and Gardner (1963) in a clinical study of severe maternal deprivation have demonstrated that some infants and children even after many months of deficient mothering can surprisingly rapidly change their response to physical care once they receive better *emotional* care. This would suggest that we may be dealing with dynamic functions, involving protective reactions to stress, rather than with a primary deficiency in practice. These infants probably suffered from tactile understimulation which would eventually result in an abnormal raising of thresholds with regard to the tactile craving and to the offer of tactile gratification. The peculiar hypotonia of these infants may be the outcome of this condition of raised thresholds.

Yarrow (1963) offers several striking examples of children who react primarily with disturbance in tactility to any difficulty in the mother-child relationship. Yarrow had the rare opportunity of studying two infants of the same age and sex placed in the same foster home. The one infant, Jack, was reported to have shown a low activity level and low level of responsiveness from birth on. In contrast, George was a responsive, cuddly, vigorous active infant. It was found that George consequently appealed much more to the foster mother and the rest of the family than Jack. While George received a great deal of physical stimulation, Jack demanded very little and received very little stimulation, mostly lying in his playpen in an isolated corner of the dining room. When the infant was three months old, the foster mother was consciously aware of her feelings of rejection toward Jack. She complained about his excessive sleeping, lack of interest in his environment, and his restlessness and discomfort at being held. This restlessness and discomfort would suggest to us that Jack constitutionally was oversensitive to tactile stimulation. He thus had to respond with raised thresholds to the normal maternal care he was receiving, which would explain his excessive sleeping, low activity level, and low responsiveness. This also would have left Jack without means of satisfying his tactile cravings and would create a vicious spiraling process resulting in increasing withdrawal from the environment.

Ray, another case reported by Yarrow, left a foster family to enter an adoptive home at eight months of age. In the foster family Ray had been the object of constant warm affection and stimulation. His adoptive mother, however, found it difficult to develop warm maternal feelings toward this large and husky baby. Ray, too, reacted negatively to the new mother, in that he "literally withdrew from her touch, ignored her when she spoke to him and seemed in effect to be denying her existence" (p. 112). We would expect that by eight months of age Ray had established a close tie with his affectionate foster mother and had begun to pass from a *craving-threshold* psychic organization to an *impulse-defense* organization but that the higher level had not yet stabilized. The trauma of loss resulted not in excessive fear, not in an acute anxiety reaction typical of some eight-month-old infants, not in physical difficulties, not in tics—but in a literal refusal of contact. This symptomatic response would indicate that the child had slipped back into a condition in which cravings and thresholds reasserted their primacy. He could only withdraw; the withdrawal could only result in increased cravings and higher thresholds. The vicious spiral might result in a severely disturbed child unless the adoptive mother could respond correctively to this apparent rebuff on the part of her newly adopted child.

Appearance of Rocking

Provence and Lipton report that rocking appeared in most institutionalized infants by the age of five to six months and was universal by eight months. They also report that the infants did not seem to be emotionally involved in the rocking and that they were quite ready to respond and stop rocking the moment an adult approached: "Behavior suggestive of excitement was extremely rare; no curve of mounting tension and discharge could be identified, in contrast to the rocking of infants reared in homes which often clearly has these characteristics. We also observed no autoaggressive component in their rocking" (p. 106).

Provence and Lipton describe four types of rocking: (1) transient rocking seen as a normal reaction to frustration in some children; (2) rocking as an autoerotic activity in children who have suffered from some degree of maternal deprivation; (3) rocking of children diagnosed as suffering from infantile psychoses, accompanied by withdrawal of attention and an extreme degree of preoccupation; and (4) the rocking observed in their study, which was in their view neither autoerotic nor accompanied by withdrawal and preoccupation. Provence and Lipton speculate that the rocking they observed "served some purpose of discharge or even of self-stimulation of a primitive and global sort, but it was difficult to see any clear differences in intensity or any evidence of self-comfort, pleasure, or satisfaction" (p. 109). Provence and Lipton suggest that the absence of excitement or pleasure may be due to these infants' lack of "investment of the own body . . . as a reflection of the degree of deprivation [they had suffered]." This "investment of the body" is a function of impulse development permitting partial and differential influence of an impulse upon consciousness and providing certain means for satisfaction. The normal infant who rocks when frustrated may be substituting pleasure for pain; but the deprived infant who rocks because of abnormally high thresholds does so in order to maintain a thread of continuity in his experience of himself.

It is more difficult for us to account for the readiness with which institutionalized infants give up their rocking on the approach of an adult. We would have predicted that they would be particularly unresponsive upon being approached. The only explanation we can offer of this observation is that the children Provence and Lipton studied were *environmentally* deprived but very likely did not suffer from congenital deficits.[4] The origin of the deficit may make a difference in that environmentally understimulated babies may be able to take advantage of whatever stimuli are made available to them, meager as they may be, and that this may retard or slow down the development of thresholds as we have described in more severely disturbed children, many of whom are reported to have difficulty with stimuli very soon after birth, sometimes from the very first day of life. If this is true it could also explain why the institutionalized infants appeared to be able eventually to respond favorably to the affectionate care of foster mothers.

Excessive Sleeping

The infants cared for in the institution slept "longer hours and with fewer interruptions than babies in families" (p. 44). When babies from the institution were moved to a foster home, they would sleep excessively during the first several weeks: "a reduction in total hours of sleep accompanied the general improvement in the infant's

---

4 It is explicitly stated that children included in this study were "free from congenital handicaps, neurological disorders, and acute or chronic illness" (p. 5).

development in response to an improvement in nurturing care" (p. 44). When thresholds are raised excessively so that the child is spending considerable time sleeping, an impoverishment of inner stimulation occurs which sooner or later is matched by a withdrawal from external stimuli as more and more potential satisfactions become a threat and require compensatory thresholds. The child can respond either with rocking or with sleep as the ultimate consequence of a summation of thresholds. Consequently, when these babies are moved to foster homes and have access to more adequate tactile stimulation, they initially maintain all the thresholds at a high level until patient, sensitive care by the foster mother gradually helps the infants to tolerate tactile gratification with a gradual diminishing in the height of the thresholds and an eventual decrease in the total of daily hours of sleep.

The dynamic, protective function of sleep in infants is beautifully illustrated in a report by Brazelton (1962a) on an experiment conducted while a neonate was receiving an EEG and EKG. The baby was screaming when brought in and failed to respond to lactose feeding. Tight elastic bands were placed on the head, one ankle, and both wrists. Brazelton reports: "Within a matter of one to two minutes, the baby's crying ceased entirely, he assumed a rigid, flexed, restricted posture with eyes tightly closed. He maintained this posture through a forty-minute period of stimulation [involving strong light stimuli and loud banging on a metal bell] with no observed spontaneous activity or startles, rare whimpering, high-pitched cries, but little other perceptible movement" (p. 56). The EEG suggested spontaneous sleep. When the restrictive bands were removed, the "inert, quiet, 'asleep' baby 'woke up' with a piercing scream and screamed continuously thereafter. He did not accept a bottle again, and thrashed constantly for the many minutes that remained" (p. 56). Brazelton thought that this spontaneous sleep might be a possible mechanism of adaptation with "usefulness and meaning as a stimulus barrier," and wondered about "its meaning as an Anlage of future mechanisms of defense" (p. 56). We fully agree with this speculation and want to point to the remarkable similarity between this baby's reaction to tactile overstimulation and the "comatose state" spontaneously induced in a severely disturbed boy described in our previous paper when he was being held firmly by attendants after an attempt to throw himself out of a window (Shevrin and Toussieng, 1962, p. 582).

Elsewhere (1962b, p. 104), Brazelton added that babies who were given repeated light stimuli went into a state of nonresponsiveness. At the end of the stimulus period they showed the same type of motor discharge as in the baby just described. Again we see here a marked raising of thresholds with a total disappearance of the threshold when the stimulation ceases.

Bridger, another investigator of neonate behavior, has studied the effect of varying intensities of stimulation on young babies: "we found that by producing a strong stimulus we easily produced sleep, and by decreasing the intensity we reach a point where the baby awakens and we would not produce this sleep. The effect is therefore definitely correlated with the intensity of the stimulus. We also found that at a certain point at which the stimulus was strong enough to produce sleep but not very strong, babies have different abilities to break out of sleep and start responding again" (1962, pp. 102-103).

These findings reported by Brazelton and Bridger accord well with recent discoveries in the neurophysiology of sleep and waking nota-bly by Hernández-Peón (1962). On the basis of these neurophysiologi-cal investigations sleep emerges as an active process rather than as a passive response to monotonous or diminished stimulation. Hernán-dez-Peón and others have isolated a "sleep center" in the midbrain which when stimulated results in spontaneous sleep in animals. Thus, we can see a completely alert animal suddenly falling asleep when the midbrain sleep center is stimulated electrically. This response closely resembles what Bridger and Brazelton have reported with neonates after they have administered intense amounts of stimulation. It would seem then that the sleep center can be activated by external stimulation or by internal stimulation, the important similarity be-ing the sheer amount of such stimulation the organism is called upon to deal with. These behavioral observations in neonates and physio-logical investigations of the sleep center support our hypothesis that the raising of thresholds constitutes an important early protective measure taken by the young organism to preserve some modicum of intact functioning.

These new findings extend our speculations into the realm of neurophysiology and suggest something of the nature of the underlying mechanism involved in this primitive protective device. It may very well be that these discoveries have a direct bearing on the experience of psychotic children who suffer from periods of numbness and anesthesia which we have reported in our previous paper. As we have suggested, severely disturbed children may regress to a mode of protection involving the raising of thresholds against stimuli. In this process they surrender a good deal in the way of realistic adaptation to the environment, but it enables them to maintain some level of organized functioning. We can speculate that the recourse to raising of thresholds has the important role of preserving autonomic balance. Were the threshold mechanism to be disrupted we might expect to find an infant who was in danger of dying because of improper autonomic functioning.

It is a common observation that an infant will "cry himself to sleep" if not attended. Our reasoning would lead us to believe that the child is not simply falling into an "exhausted" sleep, but rather that the intensity of whatever craving is causing the discomfort as well as his own self-stimulation in the form of loud crying and vigorous movement at some point activate the sleep center. A protective raising of thresholds then brings temporary peace to the distraught child. Once the self-stimulation decreases, we would expect the child to reawaken, thus initiating a cycle of crying and sleep well known to mothers who have tried to follow a rigid feeding schedule. Cravings persist during these bursts of sleep, but they are not permitted access to consciousness or expression. It has also been reported that adults under conditions of intense, inescapable stimulation will fall asleep. Soldiers under constant, heavy fire on D Day placed themselves in even greater danger by dozing off to the point at which they could not easily be aroused.

Three lines of investigation converge upon the use of sleep as a protective measure: (1) our own thinking with regard to the raising of thresholds in severely disturbed children which traces its lineage back to Freud's stimulus barrier; (2) observations of spontaneous sleep in neonates following intense stimulation; and (3) neurophysiological investigations showing that sleep is an active process whose functions are localized in a specifiable part of the brain.

It now becomes possible to formulate the hypothesis that in some severely disturbed children the protective use of thresholds against

intense stimuli inside and outside the body persists beyond infancy
and may account for such symptoms as apathy, withdrawal, ignoring
of reality, depersonalization, and fear of death. Moreover, the physiological counterpart of this threshold mechanism may be found in the
sleep center. Fortunately we can detect the activation of the sleep
center independent of behavioral sleep, which may be feigned or due
to a variety of causes, especially in older children. Recent work on the
sleep cycle permits an accurate estimation of different levels of sleep
on the basis of electrocortical activity. We may find, as Brazelton
(1962a) reported with neonates, that some severely disturbed children
would respond to an intense stimulus with a synchronized EEG typical of Stage IV sleep, a condition of physiological quiescence.

We have had the opportunity of conducting a pilot experiment
with a six-year-old boy who appeared for evaluation at The Menninger Clinic. What especially attracted our attention to the boy was
his remarkable response to touch and to being held. Several members
of the evaluation team reported that by simply grasping the youngster
by the arms or by holding him firmly in their lap he would abruptly
halt the most violent physical activity and become limp and flaccid.
When the psychiatrist would firmly grasp the patient by the arms to
arrest a violent assault on him, the patient would fall limply to the
ground with his eyes closed. Occasionally the psychiatrist noted a
smile on the patient's lips so that it was hard to say conclusively
whether the boy was really temporarily asleep or engaged in a childish game. There seemed to be enough material in these observations
relevant to our hypothesis to warrant observation of the patient's
EEG response to intense stimuli. Would we observe a transitory
sleep EEG as a given stimulus intensity would increase, as others had
found with neonates?

We investigated the patient's response to sounds at two different
frequencies (1,000 and 8,000 cycles) of steadily increasing and decreasing intensities as well as his response to touch stimulation.[5] Our first
anticipation was that we would observe a synchronized EEG pattern
typical of sleep associated with physiological quiescence. Due to many
artifacts in the record created by the patient's unwillingness to shut
his eyes and to his intermittent restlessness, it was hard to determine

[5] We wish to thank Dr. Clyde Rousey for his help in supervising the administration
of the auditory stimuli.

whether the slow wave activity of Stage IV sleep occurred. However, a noteworthy feature in the record was the disappearance of eye movements in response to sounds at an intensity level of 90 to 100 decibels. He assumed a quiet, restful posture when such stimulus intensities were presented to him. At one point, an observer noted that the patient's eyelids drooped as if he were falling asleep which would be consistent with the absence of recorded eye movements. The patient was able to tolerate intense auditory stimulation for two minutes, which is well beyond normal endurance. These observations would be consistent with our hypothesis that a threshold mechanism was at work. The outcome of this exploratory study is all the more significant when seen in the light of this patient's reported hypersensitivity to all qualities of sound. He could by sound alone identify all the lawnmowers in the neighborhood. The patient responded with a similar absence of eye movements to intense touch sensation produced by pinching the skin on the back of his hand. We may summarize these initial findings by saying that this youngster responded with an anomalous quiescence to stimuli which would have caused a normal child to demand relief. The results obtained from this one subject thus are in the direction we would expect and suggest that a more systematic experimental investigation is feasible and desirable.

Summary

We have discussed the vicissitudes of certain internal stimuli related to deficits. We have called the deficit itself a need and have called the stimulus arising from the need a craving. These cravings initially are kept from upsetting the organism's psychic integrity through variations in the height of threshold mechanisms. Certain cravings eventually achieve psychic representation and then become impulses which can be dealt with through psychic defenses based on displacement mechanisms. Cravings are different from impulses on three counts: (1) they are protected against by thresholds rather than psychic defenses; (2) they lack quality which impulses possess; (3) because of the all-or-none basis on which threshold mechanisms operate, once insistent cravings gain access to consciousness they are likely to disrupt the immature ego's fragile synthetic efforts.

We thus have postulated that there are at least two levels of drive organization: craving-threshold, impulse-defense. In order to demonstrate the usefulness of this model we have applied it to the need for tactile stimulation which in a previous paper we have discussed as being an important craving particularly in infants. The development of cravings into impulses may at times fail to occur, so that the growing organism must rely on threshold defenses abnormally long. This can have serious consequences for psychic development and may be one important factor in many severe childhood disturbances. Certain symptoms in these disorders can be made intelligible through the use of our model. We have also examined a number of research findings derived from the observation of neonates and infants and found that many of these findings can be related to each other by application of our model.

BIBLIOGRAPHY

Amrine, M. (1964), Psychology in the News. *Amer. Psychologist*, 19:217-218.
Brazelton, T. B. (1962a), Observations of the Neonate. *J. Amer. Acad. Child Psychiat.*, 1:38-58.
—— (1962b), Panel discussion: Symposium on Research in Infancy and Early Childhood. *J. Amer. Acad. Child Psychiat.*, 1:92-107.
Bridger, W. H. (1962), Panel discussion: Symposium on Research in Infancy and Early Childhood. *J. Amer. Acad. Child Psychiat.*, 1:92-107.
Bronson, G. (1963), A Neurological Perspective on Ego Development in Infancy. *J. Amer. Psa. Assn.*, 11:55-65.
Fisher, C. (1965), Psychoanalytic Implications of Recent Research on Sleep and Dreaming. *J. Amer. Psa. Assn.*, 13:197-303.
Freud, A. (1936), *The Ego and the Mechanisms of Defense.* New York: International Universities Press, 1946.
Freud, S. (1905), Three Essays on the Theory of Sexuality. *Standard Edition*, 7:130-243. London: Hogarth Press, 1957.
—— (1915), Instincts and Their Vicissitudes. *Standard Edition*, 14:109-140. London: Hogarth Press, 1957.
Hartmann, H. (1939), *Ego Psychology and the Problem of Adaptation.* New York: International Universities Press, 1958.
Hernández-Peón, R. (1962), Sleep Induced by Localized Electrical or Chemical Stimulation of the Forebrain. *Electroencephalog. Clin. Neurophysiol.*, 14:423-424.
Jacobson, E. (1954), The Self and the Object World: Vicissitudes of Their Infantile Cathexes and Their Influence on Ideational and Affective Development. *This Annual*, 9:75-127.
Odum, E. P., Rogers, D. T., & Hicks, D. L. (1964), Electroencephalographic Desynchronization in Irradiated Rats with Transected Spinal Cords. *Science*, 143:1039-1040.
Osgood, C. (1953), *Method and Theory in Experimental Psychology.* New York: Oxford University Press.
Patton, R. G. & Gardner, L. I. (1963), *Growth Failure and Maternal Deprivation.* Springfield, Ill.: Thomas.
Provence, S. & Lipton, R. C. (1962), *Infants in Institutions.* New York: International Universities Press.

Rapaport, D. (1957, 1959), *Seminars on Elementary Metapsychology*. New Haven: Western New England Institute for Psychoanalysis (mimeographed), Vol. II, pp. 249-290.

Richter, C. P. & Eckert, J. F. (1937), Increased Calcium Appetite of Parathyroidectomized Rats. *Endocrinology*, 21:50-54.

Schur, M. (1958), The Ego and the Id in Anxiety. *This Annual*, 13:190-220.

Shevrin, H. & Toussieng, P. (1962), Conflict over Tactile Experiences in Emotionally Disturbed Children. *J. Amer. Acad. Child Psychiat.*, 1:564-590.

Yarrow, L. J. (1963), Research in Dimensions of Early Maternal Care. *Merril-Palmer Quart. Behav. Develpm.*, 9:101-114.

Young, P. T. (1943), *Emotions in Man and Animal*. New York: Wiley.

INNATE INHIBITION OF AGGRESSIVENESS
IN INFANCY

BENJAMIN SPOCK, M.D. (Cleveland)

Observation of babies suggests to me that their potential hostile aggressiveness toward other people is initially under a strong innate inhibition and that they have to be taught to release it. Lantos (1958), in discussing the genetic derivation of aggression, expressed this same view in regard to the devouring energies of the carnivora: "These archaic oral energies are, in the human being, under primary repression."

In the early months of infancy there is what we are accustomed to call rage, in the sense that the baby, when hungry, hurt or tired, cries furiously; his involuntary body movements are violent, and his facial expression reminds us of anger. Nevertheless, there is no indication that there is an objective focus for his feelings.

Teething appears to be the stimulus for the biting of suitable objects. Though the infant is apt to be irritable during phases of active teething, he does not appear to be expressing any feeling of hostility toward the objects, but only relieving the tingling of his gums.

The average age for the eruption of the first tooth is seven months, but there is wide variation among individuals. More significantly, those babies who are made uncomfortable by teething (and some do not seem to be uncomfortable at all) show evidence of this discomfort for two or three months before a tooth appears. They are fretful, they drool profusely, and they chew on whatever suitable object is available. The intensity of the discomfort appears to vary somewhat from day to day.

Though the average baby will frequently bite hard with his gums

From the Child Rearing Study at Western Reserve University Medical School, supported by the Grant Foundation.

on his teething ring or toy from four or five months onward when his teeth are bothering him, he will be careful at most times, when his mother is nursing him, not to bite her nipple. Some mothers report never having been bitten, others say biting occurs only occasionally. When it does occur the mother involuntarily startles or cries out. This appears to impress the baby and to reinforce the inhibition, usually for a number of days or weeks. Some mothers report that when they startle or cry out, the baby begins to wail as if frightened or ashamed.

A sense of shame during the first year may sound implausible. Yet, some mothers are convinced that a baby of eight or ten months may hang his head and cry with shame when scolded with unusual suddenness and sharpness. I have seen the same phenomenon and believe it is shame. An occasional baby at this age will also cry when laughed at.

In the last third of the first year it is fairly common to see a baby, tired and cranky in his mother's arms at the end of the day, experiment cautiously with biting her cheek or pulling her hair. Characteristically he advances his face to her cheek in slow motion, or tugs very gradually at her hair, keeping his eye carefully fixed on hers all the time, as if to be guided by her reaction. The sensible mother anticipates the intended hurt and wards it off, or protests promptly afterward and firmly avoids the next attack with words or action. However, it is surprising to a pediatrician to see that a fair number of mothers are unable to rise to the occasion with a parental type of control. One will resentfully bite the baby back and ask the pediatrician later whether this was not the right method. Another will unhesitatingly turn the situation into a sadomasochistic game: with a half-whimpering, half-playful manner she complains to the baby that he has hurt her, but makes no effort to protect herself; this provokes him to further gleeful attacks, until the game eventually becomes too rough even for her.

In the second year almost all children have a few temper tantrums when frustrated by the parent, as they inevitably must be. They hurl themselves on the floor and beat it with their fists and kick it with their feet, crying loudly. However, I do not recall any mother ever telling me that her child attacked her in an angry spell at this age, even if she was a tactless or provocative parent.

Parents of the polite, self-controlled type are likely to complain, when their first child is about two years of age, that he seems unable to defend himself or his possessions from other children. If they grab his toys or hit him, he looks bewildered or runs crying to his mother. By three years, if he has had opportunities to play regularly with others, he will probably have overcome this disadvantage. In marked contrast is the second or subsequent child. He has usually taken a certain amount of abuse from his jealous older sibling almost from birth. Despite this, for most of the first year, he appears delighted to see his persecutor approach, even more delighted, a mother may emphasize, than he is to see her. (Does this enjoyment of a sometimes mean sibling more than of a loving mother indicate that even in the first year a baby's striving for autonomy makes his mother seem slightly oppressive compared to another child?) By a year of age the baby is wiser, and winces when his persecutor comes close. By a year and a quarter he has usually learned to fight vigorously for his rights. He begins to yell when the sibling starts toward him—not so much in fear but apparently to try to discourage him and perhaps to alert the parents. He hangs onto his toy with determination or he may use it freely as a weapon. He may bite. Some mothers report that their second child can regularly defeat the first, despite his disadvantage in size, because the older one is inhibited by guilt.

Puppies and kittens demonstrate a similar initial inhibition against biting their mothers, their litter mates, the people who tend them. Later they play at mock oral ferocity with each other, and their mothers teach them how to hunt and attack in earnest. In the book *Born Free* (1960), Joy Adamson describes how a lioness brought up from infancy by people showed no hostile aggressiveness toward them or other animals and was only with difficulty taught by the people to attack other animals.

These observations of the development of humans and other mammals suggest to me several conclusions:

The impulse to bite anything that is in the mouth is probably under strong innate inhibition in human and other mammalian infants from birth, at first to permit nursing, but later to avoid intrafamilial and intraspecies carnage. It is stimulated in the human by teething and thereby released in respect to inanimate objects; but is easily kept under inhibition in regard to the mother's nipple by means of her disapproval.

In humans the impulse to bite with the deliberate intent of hurting a person does not show in behavior until about eight or ten months. Even then it is still under enough inhibition to make the infant distinctly cautious in releasing it, and the inhibition is easily reinforced by parental disapproval. Sharp disapproval evokes what appears to be a shame reaction.

(If there are impulses to hurt the mother by the end of the first year which are held in check by an inborn inhibition, and if this inhibition is effectuated in part by a sensitivity toward or anticipation of disapproval, could this not be related to the depressive position postulated by Melanie Klein [1935]?)

Early in the second year, when the child develops a clearer sense of his identity and his rights, he can be taught to feel, release, and focus a hostile aggressiveness by another child who persecutes him. Otherwise his readiness to fight may lie dormant for another year or more. When a mother frustrates her child in the second year, his anger is aroused, but he takes it out on the floor and on himself not only because he loves and depends on her but also, I believe, because an innate inhibition against attacking her has not been sufficiently released.

BIBLIOGRAPHY

Adamson, J. (1960), *Born Free*. New York: Pantheon Books.
Klein, M. (1935), A Contribution to the Psychogenesis of Manic-Depressive States. In: *Contributions to Psycho-Analysis, 1921-1945*. London: Hogarth Press, 1948.
Lantos, B. (1958), The Two Genetic Derivations of Aggression with Reference to Sublimation and Neutralization. *Int. J. Psa.*, 39:116-120.

SOME OBSERVATIONS ON BLIND NURSERY SCHOOL CHILDREN'S UNDERSTANDING OF THEIR WORLD

DORIS M. WILLS (London)

It has been said that "Every handicap is connected with a greater or lesser detachment from the environment, depending on the degree and kind of handicap" (V. Lowenfeld, 1952), and it is reasonable to suppose that a child lacking a major sense such as vision would understand his world later than a child with full sensory equipment.

Intelligence and Social Maturity Scales constructed for the blind tend to support the idea that, compared with sighted children, blind children are slightly retarded in certain areas when they are very young, though this may change later on. However, such evidence should probably be treated with caution because of the difficulties of getting an adequate sample. We have relatively few children in the Hampstead study and therefore cannot draw conclusions about the developmental level of blind children in general; but we can look at our children with the help of the new insights that psychoanalysis can give us.

It is also reasonable to assume that a child lacking vision will understand his world in a manner different from that of the sighted child, that he will have to circumvent his handicap. Comparatively little attention has been paid to this problem, which has proved a

The work with blind children is part of the Educational Unit of the Hampstead Child-Therapy Course and Clinic and as such is maintained by the Grant Foundation, Inc., New York. The research work with the blind is assisted further by the National Institute of Mental Health, Bethesda, Maryland.

I am very grateful to D. Burlingham, A.-M. Sandler, and H. Kennedy, for many helpful suggestions, and would like to thank members of the Research Group on Blind Children at the Hampstead Clinic for the majority of the observations.

difficult area of study, but here the reconstructions that can be made in psychoanalytic treatment of blind children, such as those of Om-wake and Solnit (1961) and Fraiberg and Freedman (1964), are at last giving us a much needed key.

Both problems (retardation and differing development) can, how-ever, be attacked from another angle, that of trying to understand the comments and behavior of blind nursery school children who are not in analysis. Such an approach will concentrate our attention mainly on ego functions and, though we shall miss the understanding in depth that analysis would give us, we can then endeavor to link the children's behavior with what we learn from analytic and other sources. While careful studies such as those of Norris et al. (1957) help to delineate a picture of the normal blind nursery school child and his difficulties, there is still very little "natural history" of such children, perhaps because, at this early age, their thinking is often hard to understand and so goes unnoticed.

With this end in view we have been gathering observations on the blind children in our day nursery school in the Hampstead Clinic. These observations have suggested certain hypotheses about the chil-dren's difficulties in understanding their world. In her paper, "Some Notes on the Development of the Blind" (1961), Dorothy Burling-ham commented on some of the ways in which our blind children try to conceptualize the world around them, and on their drive to know and understand. In this paper I shall present more observations to illustrate this and to show that these young blind children are behind in understanding their world, and that their understanding some-times follows a different course from that of sighted children: in other words, that they show difficulties and differences in relation to reality testing and that this affects their general development.

The material used is drawn largely from observations made in our nursery school group for blind and partially sighted children (where the ages range, or have ranged, between three and seven years), and observations made in intelligence test interviews with these children. For what such figures are worth at this early age, the six children quoted have I.Q.s ranging from 94 to 127.[1]

The following is a brief description of each child's eye condition

1 Williams Intelligence Scale for Children with Defective Vision.

and amount of sight as far as we have been able to ascertain it by observation:

Matthew was born without eyes and is, therefore, totally blind.

Joan's and Judy's blindness is due to retrolental fibroplasia; both children possibly have some light perception.

Winnie's blindness is due to congenital cataract; she also has some light perception.

Caroline's blindness is due to buphthalmos; she has some color perception and some very slight discrimination of figure and ground.

George, the least blind, has chronic endophthalmitis, and has more discrimination of figure and ground, e. g., he can say if there is someone outside the window, but he cannot say whether it is a man or a woman; he has no color perception.

As far as we know, none of these children had more sight in earlier life than they had at the time of the observations. With their current degree of sight all will have to learn Braille when they reach school age.

The observations that follow and the conclusions drawn from them are borne out by analytic material on blind children also available in the Clinic. I am well aware that any conclusions based on such a small group with such a mixed etiology should be viewed with caution.

DIFFERENTIATION OF THE INNER AND OUTER WORLD

The Children's Difficulty in Distinguishing Reality from Make-Believe

Many of the observations used in this paper are reminiscent of the way a sighted child understands his world at a younger age, and our blind children's occasional doubt as to whether something is real or "pretend" is no exception.

Caroline (4;0) was playing with a little figure about five inches long which George had given her, and which squeaked when pressed. She called it Winnie, the name of another nursery child, and played for a long time pretending it was a baby. She tucked it up skillfully and talked to it lovingly. Then she said to the observer, "You know, it's not really Winnie, it's a birthday present from George."

The pretense was, of course, initiated by Caroline herself. Two months later, Caroline behaves in a way which probably indicates a similar difficulty. The observer wrote:

Caroline (4;2) was playing with dough, making different kinds of food—potatoes, meat, etc. She then got a plastic bowl and put them in it and wanted to show them to me. The meat was in a big piece, and I said it was enough for a big family, and then asked her who cut the roast at home. "Daddy," she said. I then described how I imagined the meal at home, Daddy putting meat on each plate, etc. When I suggested cutting up the piece of dough (meat) she had made like at home, she said, "It's pretend." This surprised me. It was as if she had imagined the situation so vividly that to pretend was unacceptable, or as if she was not sure any more whether the dough was real or not.

A sighted child might show somewhat similar behavior, but there is a difference in the half-playful way a sighted four-year-old would say "It's pretend" of such a game and in Caroline's sudden anxiety, which came as a slight shock to the observer. It seems that Caroline's mental representation of the dough was so uncertain that it was easily shattered. Such uncertainty must delay both the cathexis of the object, in this case the dough, and any displacement onto it.

These observations are supported by our analytic material on blind children. It was found that interpretations suitable for sighted children sometimes confused a blind child at first. For example, a child whose urethral games were interpreted touched her knickers and said, "They're not really wet." Such behavior indicates the blind child's need to check the difference between reality and make-believe, reality and fantasy, owing to the constant danger of falling into confusion with its attendant anxiety.

In this connection, Helen Keller's autobiography (1905) supplies another example of how a greater degree of sensory handicap made it difficult to distinguish the inner and outer world. She was, of course, both blind and deaf from the age of nineteen months. She wrote a story when she was twelve years old which was good enough for publication. Later it proved a plagiarism. She must have been told the story at some point, though she could not remember this. She was very greatly upset by this episode, and said that, a year later,

"The thought that what I wrote might not be absolutely my own tormented me."

The confusion between reality and make-believe introduced by giving blind children toys which represent in miniature only the visual aspects and shape of an object is hinted at by George (5;3) when he was playing with a "soldier." George asked, "Does the soldier talk?" as if he were thinking of a real soldier. Here, however, it is the conventions of the sighted world which cause the difficulty. Model toys, based as they are on the visual aspects of the object, rarely give blind children the same sensory experience as the thing they represent. A lead horse, for instance, does not sound, smell, feel, or taste like a real horse, nor can one sit on its back. The question of toys suitable for the blind is a topic in itself, and needs much further study.

Break-through of Fantasies

The mistakes the children make often show a break-through of their own fantasy and preoccupations in quite unexpected everyday areas, a break-through which a sighted child cannot allow himself because of his visual perception of the facts. In the sighted such break-throughs usually occur only at the limit of knowledge (or in cases of severe psychopathological disturbance), and the fact that they occur so easily in our blind children suggests how low the limits of knowledge are for them.

Matthew (3;11) had a snowball and the teacher suggested he should put it in a bowl and see what happened to it. He did this, and expected it to explode like a firecracker. Eventually when it had melted he asked what had happened. After quite a long time and much encouragement he was able to say that it had become warm water, but he still expected that what would happen would be something in the nature of a noisy explosion. (We know that Matthew at this particular time had problems around aggression, and these he externalized onto the snowball.)

Here again we can point to more extreme examples of the same tendency to externalize fantasies when sensory stimuli are greatly reduced: we know that adults with normal sensory equipment who are deprived as far as possible of perceptual input tend to hallucinate (Heron, 1961).

Omwake and Solnit (1961), describing the treatment of a disturbed blind child, Ann, suggest that the disturbance in reality contact interfered with secondary-process thinking. They quote Goldberger and Holt (1961) who contend that "the functions of the secondary process depend for their maintenance on continual contact with reality," and add: "From our treatment of Ann we can suggest that the development of the functions of the secondary process and the ego's defense against intrusions of primary-process drive derivatives into consciousness are dependent on adequate and well-balanced perceptual contacts with reality—the external world—via the exteroceptors" (Omwake and Solnit, 1961). I would like to revert to this point later.

To come back to the nursery children, their difficulties in distinguishing reality and make-believe, reality and fantasy, have to be borne in mind in considering their further difficulties in understanding the world.

Approach to the Understanding of the Outer World

The Tie of the Previous Experience and Failure to Generalize

The following observations have a common factor in that the children refer back to an actual experience and show how their understanding depends largely on this, probably because of the rarity of highly cathected experience. This means they have little basis on which to generalize.

There are "books" in the nursery school, especially made for the children, where an actual object is attached to each page with some writing around it which the teacher can read to them:

Caroline (4;4), when feeling the stone in the book about the garden, says, "It's a bit of wall." She always calls it this.

Caroline's mother says that there is a flint wall near her home that Caroline very frequently feels. A sighted child of this age would see stones almost daily and be able to say "a stone."

George (5;1), when asked what cardboard was, replied, "To throw balls over." George is referring to a nursery school game.

In the following Winnie confuses sugar and sand. George corrects her, but, instead of saying, "It's sand," he recalls a previous experience of sand:

Winnie (6;4) and George (4;8) were playing in the sand and pouring it over their arms. Winnie said, "Look there's sugar over my arm." George answered, "No, it's not sugar, it's sand just like at P——" (a seaside place he recently visited).

These examples suggest that our children are going through a learning phase which is largely preverbal in sighted children, who begin to understand their world through single experiences of common objects, but who quickly add further experiences through vision, and so lay the beginnings of generalization. These blind children probably have heard the words "stone," "cardboard," and "sand" at least as often as sighted children, but in these examples it is perhaps significant that it is the situations in which they have been active, not merely listening, which are recalled.

Partial Understanding of Common Objects

The paucity of our children's direct experience of things easily apprehended by sighted children may lead to a partial understanding of such objects. This is indicated in a variety of ways.

Occasionally a child will make a mistake in naming or describing something, showing the nature of his understanding:

Joan (4;9) asked for "a chair with handles." She meant the visitor's chair with arms. She pulls this about the nursery by the arms. She has probably never sat in it because the seat is rather high; she therefore experiences the arms as handles.

George (5;3) referred to snowflakes as "snowdrops." His experience of snow is probably of something wet on his hand like a raindrop. He cannot of course see the flakes.

More frequently a child will identify something wrongly on an insufficient cue and so indicate how far his understanding goes:

George (4;9) was doing the washing up and investigating a milk jug which he called a cup. His teacher suggested he try again. He lifted it to his mouth, tasted some of the milk left in it, and said,

"It's a little milk bottle." His teacher then told him it was really a jug, and gave him a milk bottle, cup, and jug. He felt them carefully several times and said: "It's a jug! It's a jug!"

George must have been guided in the first place by the texture, handle, and general shape of the jug when he called it a cup. When asked again he tried its contents which provided an additional but insufficient cue, and this led to "milk bottle." He did not make any differentiation on the basis of shape, the most important cue, and had to be helped to do this.

In the next example, Matthew confuses the heat of the sun with that of a fire:

Matthew (5;8) seemed fearful of going near Pat, the gardener, remembering the bonfire Pat had made several weeks previously. Pat reassured him there was no fire that day and Matthew then said, "Is it the sun?"

Matthew had not yet learned the other cues to a bonfire—sound and possibly smell—nor did he differentiate between a near and distant source of heat. How far his own anxieties facilitated such a mistake can only be guessed at, but a sighted child has so many more cues to the real situation, i.e., he sees that there is no bonfire, that he could not have fallen into the same error.

In the following examples the children do not make mistakes on the basis of incorrect or insufficient cues but show their partial understanding more directly:

Winnie (6;0) was polishing the table. When it was suggested she should also polish the table legs, for a very short moment she stopped all activity, apparently surprised and puzzled. Then she muttered, "Yes . . . the legs." She went on polishing the top of the table and made no attempt at doing the legs. It seemed that for Winnie the table was essentially a flat surface.

George (5;2) knew a chair had four legs but thought a table had two. On investigating a table (about two feet square), at first he found only the front two. He had made this investigation before, but his teacher observed that when the children could not reach all the legs at once the concept was difficult for them.

While reading a story well known to Matthew (6;1) and Judy (6;9), the teacher misread "duck has four legs." She immediately stopped and asked the children how many legs a duck has. Both children replied "four."

Children with sight would not, of course, fall into such errors about tables and ducks because of knowledge gained through vision.

Comparisons

The comparisons our children use often give indications of how they weight the understanding they have. Naturally many are based on sound and are sometimes very precise indeed.[2] The sighted observer has to put on one side his normal associations to the object if he is to understand them:

Judy (7;1) was dropping a ball into a Tate sugar box with a little sand on the bottom. She said, "It's like cooking," and indeed the movement of the sand as she dropped the ball onto it sounded like something boiling.

George (5;3) was expelling the air from a large plastic ball near his ear. He said, "It's like thunder." He was referring to the very faint crackle of the plastic as the ball collapsed, which sounded precisely like very distant claps of thunder. The ball had to be held right up to the ear before the comparison to thunder could be understood.

Our children sometimes also note differences in sound ignored by the sighted. Caroline (4;4), e.g., during an intelligence test, noted that three cardboard boxes of similar size, containing wooden objects, all made a slightly different sound when rattled.

If we are to help these children develop and enjoy this type of listening, we have to try to develop and enjoy it ourselves. Many teachers of the blind do this to some extent intuitively. It is, however, only through study of children at this early age that we can learn to appreciate their listening potentialities to the full, since later on habits of listening acquired from contact with sighted people tend to be superimposed. Brodey (1962) raises the interesting question whether "all small children have perceptive skills that only the blind are motivated to develop," and adds, "Are humans using their

2 Blank (1958) states that hearing is the predominant sensory modality in the dreams of the congenitally blind.

perceptual potential, have we trained out—extinguished—all but a small fraction of human perceptual potential?"

Comparisons are sometimes based on texture and, like those based on sound, are frequently unexpected to the sighted observer:

Caroline (4;0) was feeling a large plastic ball very carefully. When asked what it felt like, she said, "A lady's dress." In fact, the ball's surface did feel like marocain.

Caroline (4;0) was waving some newly peeled eggshell and said, "It's like tea leaves." The membranes attached to the shell were still damp so that the feel resembled wet tea leaves.

Here again we have to develop and enjoy a greater appreciation of texture if we are to enter into the way these children are thinking.

Children do, of course, make textural associations which are more familiar to us; e.g., when Winnie was playing with the sand for the first time, she let it run through her fingers and said "sugar." This association is easier to follow because sand looks a little like sugar as well as feeling like it. It suggests that textural associations made by sighted people, and associations based on sound (and maybe others also), are often heavily conditioned by the visual aspect of the object.

Comparisons are, of course, often based largely on shape and size and "feel":

Caroline (4;1) was threading beads and called one "a dice." When told it was a bead, she said, "But it is like a dice, isn't it?"

George (5;0) felt a coffee bean very sensitively between his thumb and forefinger and said, "This is like a nut."

Matthew (5;2), while eating pineapple cubes at lunch, said, "They are like bricks, little bricks and big bricks . . . juice in the bricks for lunch."

Caroline (4;5) was pasting a piece of corrugated cardboard onto a bigger piece. She said, as she felt it, "This is like an accordion."

On several occasions we observed, the children associated things to mouths. The oral phase is, of course, prolonged in our children; they mouth objects, partly in order to recognize them, all through their nursery school years. Though the following examples can be looked at from several angles, they do suggest that our children may be attempting to understand shape, a particularly difficult concept for the blind, in terms of their mouths. In the first example, the association to a mouth is based mainly on shape:

Matthew (6;4) eats potato crisps, one of which is curved. He says, "It is like a mouth."

In the following three examples, shape is not the only determinant, because the comparison is to objects which to some extent can open and shut:

Caroline (4;4) agreed that she had very nice pockets on her dress. She then put her finger in her mouth and said: "This is a pocket in my face, and it has a tongue inside and I can put sweets and biscuits in," and she laughed.

Judy (6;8) closed the lid of her Braille board, saying, "I've closed its mouth."

Matthew (6;2), after telling of a bad dream, said when he woke from such dreams he always felt in his bed to see if he was "in the mouth or not," adding that "under the covers it's a bit like being in a mouth, isn't it?"

These three observations suggest that the children may understand certain shapes by reference to their own bodies (in this case, the mouth) long after the sighted child has largely abandoned it in such areas, and has come to use other more neutralized points of reference (for example, a sighted child would be more likely to compare a curved potato crisp to the moon than to a mouth). If this is true, it again suggests that the absence of visual cues to objects in the external world makes the child's mental representation of them uncertain and so hinders displacement of bodily ideas.[3] This would, on the one hand, tend to keep the blind child's body cathexis at a comparatively high level, which in turn may increase his proneness to anxiety. It may, on the other hand, cause a delay in the repression of the bodily ideas and fantasies attached to the learning process in these areas (in this case, the learning of shape), a repression so necessary for autonomous ego functioning.

This tendency to understand the world in bodily terms can be further illustrated from the drawings of the partially sighted. Viktor

---

[3] See Caroline's uncertainty about dough (p. 347).

Lowenfeld, in *The Nature of Creative Activity* (1952), shows a picture drawn by such a child of a figure who is stretching up for an apple. The arms are greatly elongated, and, incidentally, the apple is greatly enlarged also. (We are reminded of exaggerations in modern art, some of which also appear to have a somatic basis.) Lowenfeld comments, ". . . our investigations have clearly shown that in the pictorial art of the weak-sighted, bodily experience is an integrating factor among the various instinctive creative components, whilst in the drawings of children with normal vision it plays a more subordinate part in the totality of their creative work."

Reverting to our nursery children, similes used by sighted people sometimes confuse them because of their lack of basic knowledge:

George (5;1), when asked the difference between a bird and a dog, replied, "Birds fly, dogs crawl."

This response is based on a game played in the nursery where the children crawl "like dogs" to a record which suggests this. Such a simile would not mislead sighted children.

The comparisons our children use, and their difficulty with those made by the sighted, raise the query how children with other sensory handicaps react to this problem. For instance, deaf children's natural associations to objects to which sound is a major cue must often be quite different from those of the hearing. It is likely that, left to themselves, such children would evolve systems of classification which in certain areas differ from the systems evolved by those with full sensory equipment.

Reasoning

If we understand reasoning in its simplest terms as "mental exploration," we can sometimes observe this in our nursery school children, though our understanding of it is often hampered by the difficulty some of them have in verbalizing their experience. Caroline, however, very much enjoys putting new knowledge into words:

Caroline (4;0) felt a lettuce and said, "It's a cabbage." She was told that it was a lettuce, but that it was a *sort* of cabbage. Meanwhile Katherine, who is sighted, said, "Look, there's a tomato." Caroline then said, "A lettuce is a *sort* of cabbage, but not a *sort* of tomato."

On another occasion (at the same age), there was a new book with three buttons on the page, one large, one medium, and one small. Caroline said, while she was feeling them, "That's funny, the medium one is in the middle," making it quite clear that she has some concept of "in the middle" and also of the fact that "middle" and "medium" both start with the same sound.

Caroline (4;5), while urinating, said, "Water comes out of my bottom when I do wee wee." After a few minutes, while washing her hands, Caroline commented, "Wee wee is not really water—it has a nasty smell." She cannot of course see the difference in color.

Her mother reports that any new word Caroline hears in conversation she tries to understand and use herself, almost at once. She heard the word "orphan" recently (4;5) and had subsequently decided that a child with only one parent must be "half an orphan." Sighted children will talk about new words in this way, but they rely far less on the verbal cue. Such children see not only their own mothers and fathers; they constantly see children with mothers and fathers when out walking, etc., an experience blind children cannot share.

The following question, which was asked by Matthew (6;3), indicates reasoning peculiar to a blind child:

While walking along Maresfield Gardens, the teacher said they were going to climb up a hill. This reminded Matthew of something about the car, and he asked, "Is there a hill in the road as well as on the pavement?"

It was, in fact, difficult to find very many examples of reasoning among our observations on these blind nursery school children, a difficulty one would not have encountered had they been sighted nursery school children of similar age.

Faulty Reasoning (Including Animistic Thinking)

As mentioned earlier, our children have difficulty in being sure of the difference between reality and make-believe, reality and their own fantasy, much longer than sighted children. It is therefore not surprising that we have observations showing a tendency to animistic thinking about things in their immediate experience, long after sighted children have been forced to abandon it because of observation. In the following two examples the children's animistic thinking is linked with their concern about their aggression:

George (5;0) was trying to cut with scissors. He said, "Can I cut the beads and really hurt them?"

Judy (6;11) was having difficulty in hammering one of the pegs through the hammer-peg toy. She changed to another peg, saying, "It's hearing a lot of hammering in its head." When asked, "Do you think the peg can feel?" Judy said, "No," rather doubtfully, but she appeared to be giving this peg a rest from time to time.

The next observation shows that Caroline thinks slippers grow, but we do not know whether she gives them any further attributes of life:

Caroline (4;1) was feeling the different sizes of slippers and dis- covered one of the teacher's slippers. She said, "These must be very old—they are the biggest." Katherine asked, "Why are they old?" Caroline said, "My daddy is the biggest and he is old."

It will be seen that, because of difficulties in reality testing, our children's animistic thinking is both more extensive and lasts longer than it does in sighted children.

Helen Keller reported: "I only know that after my education be- gan [at eight years] the world which came within my reach was all alive. I spelled to my blocks and my dogs. I sympathised with plants when the flowers were picked, because I thought it hurt them, and that they grieved for their lost blossoms. It was years before I could be made to believe that my dogs did not understand what I said, and I always apologised to them when I ran into or stepped on them." Helen Keller's deafness (in addition to her blindness) must have put an additional difficulty in the way of reality testing, but she appears to have had difficulties very similar to those observed in our children.

Animistic thinking is only one area where reasoning is based on the wrong analogy; the child treats inanimate objects as if they had life. Our children use wrong analogies in other aspects of their rea- soning about everyday objects and one of the problems in trying to classify such observations is to decide how much weight to give to the subjective aspect of such mistakes, how much to the objective aspect, because each can be looked at from two sides. The example of Matthew, who thought a snowball would explode (mentioned above), suggests to the therapist mainly concern about aggression, but the mistake has an objective, cognitive aspect: some round things, such as balloons, do blow up. The fact that Matthew found difficulty in believing the snowball would not blow up in the face of actual experience suggests, however, that we are right in seeing this mistake as based mainly on some externalization of his own aggression. The following examples have a different slant:

George (5;3) was interested in the snow, so a piece of it was put in a bowl, and he put it on the radiator. When it had turned to water, he kept saying, "The snow's all gone out." He emptied the bowl, refilled it from the tap, replaced it on the radiator, and admitted he was thinking it would turn back into snow. On encouragement, he put it outside to freeze.

Here George, like Matthew, uses a wrong premise, but his lack of knowledge, rather than the projection of aggression, is what stands out. The following mistake in reasoning also suggests lack of knowledge. Matthew assumes that wood can be used like clay:

Matthew (5;0) brought back the car he made of wood last week, having pulled off three of the wheels. He said he wanted to make it into something else—a cup with a handle. He was encouraged to feel a cup and compare its shape with the very different shape of the wood. He had been using clay recently in the nursery, and expected wood to have the same malleable properties.

Of course one needs to know the child and his environment before making a judgment on whether his behavior shows lack of knowledge about the world or distortion through fantasy, but it seems important to try to understand which is the main reason for the mistake since it has implications for the nursery school regime.

CONCLUSION

Similar observations were made on older blind children in analysis, some of whom showed an impressive verbal fluency which proved to be largely parroted from adults around them. It was not supported by any genuine understanding of the everyday world about which they were talking. Further work needs to be done, but such observations do suggest several points.

1. Our blind nursery school children need much more time than sighted children to gain a working knowledge of the world around them, knowledge which must provide the basis for later learning.

2. Since their method of comparing and associating everyday objects and reasoning about everyday experiences often differs quite markedly from that of sighted children, they may need help in establishing their own way of thinking, which is based on their own sensory experience, at the same time that they learn about the associations, comparisons, and reasoning of the sighted world, some of which must always remain artificial for them. Though a blind child must, by the time he is grown up, adapt as fully as possible to the sighted world, he may be able to do this with more satisfaction both to himself and the outside world if he is helped to develop his own methods of understanding and adaptation, and then to integrate them with those of the sighted world around him.

DISCUSSION

By looking at these observations from a different angle, can we infer anything about the early ego development of blind children?

While of course no broad generalization can be drawn from such a small blind group, these children's difficulties may throw some light on the difficulties which other blind children surmount, or retreat from, in the course of their development. We know that many blind children go on to gain university degrees, but also that an unusually large proportion of them show withdrawn behavior. Assuming these withdrawn children have had average mothering (which all our children have received), so that body boundaries, etc., are established, it may be that there is some hurdle in their development which they are unable to surmount (with or without any brain damage in addition); for example, it may be that there is some critical period when they fail to cathect and organize their external world because of the many difficulties it presents, and that they subsequently withdraw from the attempt.

What then is the history of the ego development behind the picture our nursery school children now present? Can we make some formulation with the help of analytic and other material already available? Anne-Marie Sandler (1963) described the break in the sequence of the blind baby's development because sound cannot further his grasping in the way that sight can, and showed that this hinders the integration of his sensorimotor experiences. She also commented on the difficulty which the transition from mouth grasping to hand grasping poses for these children and on the danger that the hand, when it does learn to grasp, will be used for direct bodily gratification rather than for exploring the world, and so hand autonomy, which involves neutralization of the drives, will not be reached.

Assuming the baby surmounts this hurdle and learns to use his hand for exploration of inanimate objects, he must then organize— mainly on the basis of sound—that part of the world which is out of range of his hand and not in immediate contact with his body. This is a very difficult task. As Gesell and Amatruda (1960) stated, "Sounds do not acquire objectivity, localization and distance meanings except through long and tedious training via the tactile route."

The danger here is that the child will gain little pleasure from the world around him which he has such difficulty in organizing and manipulating, and will fall back on deriving it from his own and his mother's body, and those of his immediate family. Fraiberg and Freedman (1964) cite observations of a congenitally blind baby girl, Toni. At nine months Toni had no interest in inanimate objects other than the bottle, a spoon, and a dummy, but during this period when she had no interest in inanimate objects her discrimination of human objects had achieved a high level: "She discriminated mother from a stranger, she recognized each of her [five] siblings and responded selectively to them . . . absence of interest in inanimate objects in a sighted child of Toni's age would indicate grave deficiencies in object ties. Evidently, for Toni, the path from human objects to inanimate objects was slow and circuitous compared to that of the sighted child. . . ."

This suggests that the mother of the blind child might have to perform two distinct roles: she has on the one hand to establish a good bodily relationship with her blind child through her handling and care, but she also has to provide the right kind of auxiliary ego for him, not in the usual sense of supplying control, but in the sense of giving him meaningful experiences of the world, something that the mother of a sighted child can do automatically on the basis of her own experience. We do not yet know exactly how she can best do this. She will have to pick up cues from her child as to his interests, many of which will be auditory, help him to organize and explore his world, and allow him to share the ups and downs of family life.[4] While doing this she will always have to combat the blind child's tendency to revert to direct bodily gratification. It may be that the withdrawal seen in some blind children stems from the mother's failure in her second role, as auxiliary ego, so that the children are unable to cathect and organize their world, and that these mothers do not necessarily fail in their first role, the immediate relationship with the child. This would account for the comparatively good object relationship made by some of these withdrawn blind children in treatment: they have cathected the human object, their mother, but this cathexis has not spread automatically to the inanimate objects on her periphery and to the external world, as it appears to do with the sighted child. For the blind child the absence of this step may be roughly equivalent to a deprivation of experience.

Turning to the animal world, we know that if young mammals are deprived of the opportunity to move about and to enjoy a variety of experience, they are later less intelligent (in the areas of problem solving and learning new tasks) than they would otherwise have been, and, once youth is past, lost opportunities cannot be fully made up (Barnett, 1962). While it is always dangerous to draw parallels between man and animal, it may be that if a blind child's mother cannot help him to make this step from her to the world at the right time, he does not make up the deficit; in other words, it would seem, as other workers have surmised, that this may be in fact a "critical period."

Supposing the child is helped to overcome this hurdle and cathect his world, he will still depend on his mother to help him to some kind of synthesis through the experiences she provides. Otherwise he

---

4 Provence and Ritvo (1961) have suggested that certain discomfort-comfort experiences in very early life facilitate the laying down of memory traces of (human) objects and allow of their permanent cathexis, which is then displaced onto inanimate objects. Whether or not all cathexis of inanimate objects is derived from displacement, it will in any case be necessary to continue giving the blind child such experiences throughout his early life, both in terms of people and things, so that he realizes he can act on the environment both to relieve discomfort and to gain satisfaction.

will be flooded by a wide range of perceptions from his different senses; and, without the aid of vision, he will not know which to attend to and so will have difficulty in organizing them into concepts. This in turn will hold up secondary-process thinking. It appears that our nursery school children are showing vestiges of these earlier difficulties in their imperfect understanding of the world and in the poverty of their reasoning about it.

What is the prognosis for these children? Will even the brightest of them, such as Caroline, be able to catch up or surpass the average sighted child? What can ultimately take the place of vision in binding perceptions into concepts? It seems to be language, but only if it is based on and linked with a great deal of highly cathected and meaningful experience. Even then the speech acquired from the sighted is often short of words which the blind child needs.[5] The importance of basing language on a wide range of experience cannot be overestimated since blind children fall all too easily into parroting the speech of those around them without understanding its implications. Meaningful language may at last give the child without vision a chance to organize his understanding of the world that does not immediately impinge on his other senses, and help him to differentiate between this outer world and his inner world of feelings. Meaningful language may enable such children as Caroline to overcome early difficulties in reality testing, and allow them to go on to considerable later achievement in direct competition with sighted people.

This whole topic of blind children's difficulties in ego development and the way they overcome them needs much further study, for its own sake, and for the light it may throw on "silent" areas in the development of normal children and on the development of children with other perceptual anomalies.

SUMMARY

The supposition was made that a child lacking a major sense such as vision would understand his world later and in a different way from a child with full sensory equipment. With this in mind, observations made on the blind nursery school children in the Hamp-

---

5 E.g., to describe certain textural experiences.

stead Child-Therapy Clinic were examined. These children showed some difficulty in distinguishing reality and make-believe, reality and fantasy, a somewhat partial understanding of some common objects, and certain differences in the way they compared and reasoned about them. This is discussed in the light of other work. While no general conclusion can be drawn on the basis of this very small group, the study raises certain queries concerning the hurdles other blind children may surmount or retreat from in the course of their development, and concerning the importance of the mother not only in her nurturing role, but more particularly as the child's auxiliary ego helping him to cathect and organize his world without the aid of sight.

BIBLIOGRAPHY

Barnett, S. A. (1962), Attitudes to Childhood. In: *Lessons from Animal Behaviour for the Clinician*, ed. S. A. Barnett. London: Heinemann.
Blank, H. R. (1957), Psychoanalysis and Blindness. *Psa. Quart.*, 26:1-24.
—— (1958), Dreams of the Blind. *Psa. Quart.*, 27:158-174.
Brodey, W. M. (1962), Normal Developmental Learning and the Education of the Child Born Blind. *Gifted Child Quart.*, 6:141-149.
Burlingham, D. (1961), Some Notes on the Development of the Blind. *This Annual*, 16:121-145.
Drever, J. (1955), Early Learning and the Perception of Space. *Amer. J. Psychol.*, 68:605-614.
Fraiberg, S. H. & Freedman, D. A. (1964), Studies in the Ego Development of the Congenitally Blind Child. *This Annual*, 19:113-169.
Gesell, A. & Amatruda, C. (1960), *Developmental Diagnosis*. New York: Hoeber.
Heron, W. (1961), Cognitive and Physiological Effects of Perceptual Isolation. In: *Sensory Deprivation*, ed. P. Solomon et al. Cambridge: Harvard University Press.
Hoffer, W. (1949), Hand, Mouth and Ego-Integration. *This Annual*, 3/4:49-56.
Katan, A. (1961), Some Thoughts about the Role of Verbalization in Early Childhood. *This Annual*, 16:187-188.
Keeler, W. R. (1958), Autistic Patterns and Defective Communication in Blind Children with Retrolental Fibroplasia. In: *Psychopathology of Communication*, ed. P. H. Hoch & J. Zubin. New York: Grune & Stratton.
Keller, H. (1905), *The Story of My Life*. London: Hodder & Stoughton.
Klein, G. S. (1962), Blindness and Isolation. *This Annual*, 17:82-93.
Lowenfeld, B. (1956), *Our Blind Children*. Springfield, Ill.: Thomas.
Lowenfeld, V. (1952), *The Nature of Creative Activity*. London: Routledge & Kegan Paul.
Maxfield, K. E. & Buchholz, S. (1957), *A Social Maturity Scale for Blind Pre-School Children*. New York: American Foundation for the Blind.
Norris, M., Spaulding, P. J., & Brodie, F. H. (1957), *Blindness in Children*. Chicago: University of Chicago Press.
Omwake, E. G. & Solnit, A. J. (1961), "It Isn't Fair": The Treatment of a Blind Child. *This Annual*, 16:352-404.
Parmalee, A. H. et al. (1962), The Development of Ten Children with Blindness as a Result of Retrolental Fibroplasia. *Research Bulletin*, No. 1. New York: American Foundation for the Blind.

Provence, S. & Lipton, R. C. (1962), *Infants in Institutions.* New York: International Universities Press.

—— & Ritvo, S. (1961), Effects of Deprivation on Institutionalized Infants: Disturbances in Development of Relationship to Inanimate Objects. *This Annual,* 16:189-205.

Sandler, A.-M. (1963), Aspects of Passivity and Ego Development in the Blind Infant. *This Annual,* 18:343-360.

Segal, A. & Stone, F. H. (1961), The Six-Year-Old Who Began to See: Emotional Sequelae of Operation for Congenital Bilateral Cataract. *This Annual,* 16:481-509.

von Senden, M. (1960), *Space and Sight.* London: Methuen.

Williams, M. (1956), *Williams Intelligence Test for Children with Defective Vision.* Birmingham: University of Birmingham.

CONTRIBUTIONS TO PSYCHOANALYTIC THEORY

THE EFFECTS OF EARLY OBJECT RELATIONSHIPS
ON SEXUAL DEVELOPMENT

Autistic and Symbiotic Modes of Adaptation

IRVING HANDELSMAN, Ed.D. (Forest Hills, New York)

Helene Deutsch and other participants of the Panel on Frigidity (1961) have raised the question of why it is that the very disturbed person is sometimes capable of achieving orgasm even though his or her psychosexual development is on a pregenital level, whereas less disturbed persons, whose ego and sexual development are more advanced, are unable to achieve a climax. As indicated in that panel, as well as in most of the psychoanalytic literature, there is considerable disagreement and confusion regarding the definition of orgasm. Therefore, for the sake of brevity I shall omit the biological, physiological, and some of the psychoanalytic definitions and descriptions of orgasm and refer to Keiser's (1952) description. He attributes a certain type of preorgastic anxiety to "apprehension of the physiological, momentary unconsciousness that accompanies a healthy orgasm, which is comparable to death or to falling asleep—all accompanied by withdrawal of cathexis from the body ego" (p. 154). He regards the momentary loss of consciousness as a *sine qua non* of normal orgasm.

This definition includes the word "healthy"; we can therefore infer that there is an unhealthy orgasm. It is my belief that in the healthy orgasm there is a regression in the service of the ego (Kris, 1934), that is, an adaptive type of regression. The orgasm is characterized by a temporary dissolution of the boundaries of the self and the object, there is a feeling of fulfillment and pleasure in the drive discharge and in the sense of merging with the partner, after which the individual is able to recover the self representation, reestablish the self boundaries, and recathect the love object. In con-

367

trast, in the unhealthy orgasm the regression is not in the service of the ego and therefore is maladaptive in nature. It is a partly satisfying experience which does not lead to a full re-establishment of the boundaries between the self and the object. Since the individual does not experience the permanent fusion which he seeks, there is a lack of fulfillment which leads to chronic object hunger. Thus the sexual partner is not necessarily recathected after the drive discharge, and consequently there is no object constancy in the sense of mature constant object relations. The result may be an unrelenting need to reunite with the lost symbiotic partner.

The purpose of this paper is to discuss sexuality by considering only the factor of object relations and specifically those difficulties which arise when there is some ego modification as a consequence of unresolved problems in the autistic, symbiotic, and separation-individuation phases of ego development. It is my contention that disturbances in any of these *specific phases* will result in a certain type of sexual adaptation which may manifest itself in orgasm in the pregenital character, frigidity, impotence, homosexuality, and masturbation, the outcome being dependent upon the nature of the parent-child relationship during the child's development in the early years. The hypothesis set forth in this paper is not an attempt to negate classic psychoanalytic theory, but it is offered as an additional theoretical consideration. It is in line with the principle of multiple functioning (Waelder, 1930) which occupies an important place in the structural theory. Briefly stated, it holds that the id, ego, and superego, as well as external reality, affect human behavior.

Review of the Literature

Since the concepts of ego, self, self and object representations, and symbiosis are relatively new in psychoanalytic theory, a brief review of the development of ego psychology is in order. As early as 1895, in his "Project for a Scientific Psychology," Freud introduced the concept of the ego; and in 1900, he described the contributions of the ego to dreams. However, for the next twenty years the study of the ego, as a psychic structure, was neglected. During the period in which the concept lay dormant, Freud's clinical writings and observations centered on the libidinal development of the individual. He established the basic model of the libidinal phases (1905) and described psychosexual development in terms of the oral, anal, phallic, and genital phases. Nevertheless, Freud's writings and clinical observations demonstrated the presence of defenses, even though he did not explicitly state that they were ego activities. Hartmann (1956) points out that in Freud's discussion of the Schreber case (1911) there are interesting insights into the interactions of libido and ego. Hartmann states, "At one point in this paper he noted, in addition to the possible effect of libido disturbances on ego cathexes, the secondary or induced disturbance of libidinal processes *as a result of abnormal modifications of the ego*" (p. 284; my italics).

During the second decade of this century the role of the ego as an independent agent had reached its nadir; however, in the latter part of the second decade Freud published his papers on metapsychology and finally, in 1923, *The Ego and the Id*, in which he outlined the tripartite division of the psychic structure. At first Freud stressed the biological functions of the ego, but he also recognized the importance of the environment and its impact on the development of the ego. Freud (1926) emphasized the value of object relations in ego development. Some of the statements made by Freud may be at the root of what we now refer to as symbiosis, the early tie between mother and child.

In 1930, Freud stated that at the height of being in love the boundary between ego and object threatens to melt away: "Against all the evidence of his senses, a man who is in love declares that 'I' and 'you' are one, and is prepared to behave as if it were a fact" (p. 66). He then reflects upon the fact that this state of adult ego feeling must have gone through a process of development which he could only reconstruct. He postulates that an infant at the breast does not yet distinguish his ego from the external world. However, he gradually learns to differentiate the self from the object world. This fact is suggested in several of Freud's papers (1895, 1900, 1915, 1925). Freud (1930) describes the earliest feeling of oneness as the "oceanic feeling," which is an indissoluble bond of being one with the external world as a whole. The place of early object relations in the theoretical development of ego psychology became increasingly important. Hartmann (1956) states that "This conception of ego development is at the origin of much of what Ernst Kris (1950) has called 'the new environmentalism' in psychoanalysis. It is the theoretical core for the turning to a closer scrutiny of the impact of object-relation on development, and of the ego-aspect of object-relation, in addition to the earlier consideration of the developmental significance of the libidinal phases" (p. 292).

In contrast to Freud's use of reconstructive methods to conceptualize early childhood development, child analysts have in the last two decades turned to direct observations of behavior. Mahler et al. (1949), Kanner (1943), A. Freud, (1945), Geleerd (1946), and others have contributed greatly to the literature on childhood development, both normal and pathological. Just as Freud used his observations made on patients suffering from hysteria and other mental disturbances to formulate his theories of normal development, i.e., the model of the libidinal phases, analytic observers of child behavior are contributing to present-day knowledge of the formation and development of the ego and object relations.

A. Freud (1936) systematically studied the ego and its mechanisms of defense. Hartmann (1939) described the ego as a partly independent entity, not *solely* related to the environment or drives, a structure that can be partly autonomous and need not originate in conflict. He introduced the concept of an undifferentiated phase out of which the ego and id become differentiated. There are primary and secondary autonomous ego functions, the primary functions being part of the inborn ego apparatus and therefore present at birth, while the secondary functions, related to maturational and environmental factors, may become autonomous in the course of development. Hartmann views the ego as man's special organ of adaptation. This more definitive description of the ego and its functions helped facilitate the work of direct observation. Hartmann (1950) further refined the structural concepts by making a distinction between the *ego*, which represents a psychic system in contradistinction to other substructures of personality; the *self*, referring to one's own person, including the body as well as the psychic organization; and the *self representation*, which is the psychic image (as opposed to the object representation) of the self within the ego. Jacobson (1964) uses the term self to distinguish the person from the surrounding world of objects. She further states that "I shall employ terms such as a person's 'body self' or his 'physical self' or his 'psychophysiological self' or his 'mental self' or 'psychic self.' To distinguish the concept 'self' from its ordinary usage, I have omitted the customary hyphenation of all compound nouns with self" (p. 6).

As stated in the introduction, it is the aim of this paper to employ the observations made by Mahler in her studies of the autistic and symbiotic child psychoses to establish a developmental model which might enable us to explain some of the problems in adult sexual adaptation. In other words, by combining the methods of reconstruction and direct observation of infants, some new conclusions about adult sexuality might be drawn.

Mahler's (1952, 1960) observations of children suffering from autistic and symbiotic psychoses have led her to postulate three normal phases of ego development: the *autistic period,* from birth to three months; the *symbiotic phase,* from three months to the twelve- to eighteen-month period; and the *separation-individuation phase* which follows the symbiotic phase and lasts approximately until thirty-six months of age. Mahler considers the latter phase a second birth experience. While events in each or all of the specific stages will affect the ego development of the individual, his sexual adaptation, as well as his pathology, the outcome will rarely be as extreme as that observed in the autistic or symbiotic psychoses. These terms are therefore employed in a more general way, and serve to depict a modification of the ego which may have been a consequence of a difficulty in one or more of the stages. Pollock (1964) states that fixation at or regression to particular stages may lead to symbiotic neuroses, which are an attempt to relieve anxiety and deal with conflict. Symbiosis is a general term and there are many stages of normal symbiosis along a developmental axis. However, it is my belief that the autisticlike or symbioticlike adaptation is a result of a phase-specific problem.

Since these phases constitute the specific model of ego development upon which this paper is based, it is necessary to describe them in detail. Mahler (1952) acknowledges the existence of a rudimentary ego at birth. She states that "the intra-uterine, parasitic host relationship within the mother organism must be replaced in the postnatal period by the infant being enveloped, as it were, in the extra-uterine matrix of the mother's nursing care, a kind of social symbosis" (p. 286). The first orientation to external reality arises when the infant becomes aware of the fact that his satisfaction depends upon a source outside of his body. Within the state of somatopsychic symbiosis bodily contact with the mother is a prerequisite for the demarcation of the *body ego* from the *nonself*. As the mother is left outside "the omnipotent orbit of the self of the child," and as the process of endowing the mother with object-libidinal cathexis develops, there is a separation of the self from that of the mother. Mahler and Gosliner (1955) feel that the period from twelve or eighteen to thirty-six months is crucial for the development of the ego. Mahler (1958b) pointed out that in the case of normal development, the presymbiotic, normal autistic phase of the mother-infant unity gives way to the symbiotic phase proper. The experiences in the symbiotic phase must be adequate and enable the child to make the next step —gradual separation and individuation (Mahler and Furer, 1963). The stable image of the self depends upon successful identifications and the distinction between object and self representations.

In contrast to the normal resolution of the symbiotic and separation-individuation phases, Mahler and Gosliner (1955) describe the pathological results of unhealthy parent-child relationships during these crucial phases of ego development. Although Mahler and Gosliner (1955) attribute infantile psychosis to a hereditary Anlage, an inherent ego deficiency, there is sufficient evidence in the literature to support the view that parental attitudes contribute to the problem of ego development, especially in the case of symbiotic neurosis as described by Pollock (1964). Studying the mother's relationships to the psychotic child (autistic and symbiotic), certain problems peculiar to the mother were observed (Mahler, 1961; Mahler and Furer, 1963). In some cases the mothers were not attuned to the needs of the child and in some way there was a breakdown in the communication between them. On the one hand, the child may have been overstimulated by the mother; on the other hand, there may have been a lack of contact with the child. In other words, the mother was unaware of the child's stimulus barrier as described by Bergman and Escalona (1949). Mahler and Furer (1963) make the point that these mothers might have been more successful in mothering other children whose requirements would be less overwhelming than the needs of psychotic children. In some of her other papers Mahler describes instances in which the mother prematurely terminated the symbiotic relationship as a reaction formation to her having to give up her child, thus thrusting the child into the separation-individuation phase without proper resolution of the symbiotic phase. In contrast, there were mothers who were unable to accept the separation of the child from them and consequently perpetuated the symbiotic phase by not allowing the child's individuation or by discouraging it. The pathological results of such disturbed relations are described in several papers on the autistic and symbiotic psychotic child (Mahler and Gosliner, 1955; Mahler, Ross, de Fries, 1949; Mahler, 1952; Mahler and Elkisch, 1953).

The autistic child is described as one who emotionally never perceives the mother as a representative of the outside world. She is not cathected, not distinguished from inanimate objects, and is at best a part object. There is no affective awareness of other human beings, and there is an inherent lack of contact with the human environment. The instinctual forces, aggressive and libidinal, exist in an unneutralized form, due to the absence of the synthetic function of the ego. The state of autism is viewed as a basic defense against the outer world.

In the symbiotic psychotic child, the early mother-infant symbiotic relationship is marked but does not progress to the stage of object-libidinal cathexis of the mother. The mental representation of the mother *is not* separated from the self. There is little evidence of this in the early years of life; however, with maturation the ego disturbances become apparent as separation and individuation become imminent. The illusion of symbiotic omnipotence is threatened and severe panic reactions occur. Attempts at restitution are made in order to restore the delusions of oneness with the mother or the father. Boundaries of self and nonself are blurred.

The Symbiotic Mode of Sexual Adaptation

It is my impression that the sexual life of a person may indeed be symptomatic of the symbiotic conflict. The consequences may manifest themselves in two forms of sexual adaptation. In the one case there is a constant seeking of sexual union and orgasm; and in the other, there is complete withdrawal and abstinence with the concomitant symptoms of frigidity or impotence. In this conception, the sexual act and the orgasm come to represent a person's wish for reunion with the mothering figure for the purpose of restituting or restoring that period of life in which mother and self existed in an omnipotent and single orbit. Promiscuity, compulsive sexual activity, "people addiction" may be symptomatic of the search for the mother who failed to allow the symbiotic phase to run its full course or to be resolved. The behavior of such persons resembles that of children who have suffered an object loss and who indiscriminately seek substitute objects because they have not yet been able to establish mental object representations. Consequently, there is a constant seeking and need for the presence of and union with an object in order to maintain the omnipotent system. Such persons are making an effort to achieve a corrective symbiotic experience. In adults, this behavior is maladaptive in nature; and since there is no resolution, it leads to a compulsion to repeat behavior resembling that observed in the repetitious acts and dreams of persons suffering from a traumatic neurosis (Freud, 1920).

Secondly, the person who has not successfully resolved the symbiotic phase has a dim awareness of the contours of his self and is unable to distinguish the boundary of the self from that of others. He lacks a feeling of separateness; does not sufficiently cathect his body image or body self; and cannot find adequate resolutions in the separation-individuation phase. The consequences of such a defective ego development are manifold. In the first place, the choice of object is dominated by primary-process activities in which there is little or no discrimination of the qualities of the object. A specific object is not cathected. The response to objects is based upon nonverbal memory traces and is part of a person's unconscious sensory experiences during the nonverbal period. Thus, the sexual act may be the result of a lack of ego autonomy. The wish to merge is based upon the need for oneness as well as upon a lack of self boundaries. Without the latter, there is no integrity of the body self and the ego's capacity to say "no" is impaired. In either case, there is no true self representation and such a person's image of himself and his sexual activities are of the field-dependent type as described by Witkin (1962).

Lewin (1950) quotes a psychotic patient's description of coitus with a superego figure. "I melt into the other person. It is hard to describe, but there is a certain oneness, a loss of my body in the other person, as if I were part of him without my individual identity, yet in him part of a larger whole. At other times, I am the dominant individual and he the lost one, so that I become the perfect whole ..." (p. 148). While Lewin is primarily concerned with documenting his hypothesis of the oral triad, this description might well be applied to the phenomenon of symbiosis as discussed by Mahler and even earlier by Freud (1930). It can be assumed that this psychotic patient had a poor ego structure, no sense of body self, and was seeking a corrective symbiotic experience which would be restitutive or restorative in nature. Obviously, this patient had not reached the genital level of development; and the union of the two, the feelings of oneness, and the loss of the sense of self can be viewed as pathological forms of regression. There was no object constancy, drive fusion was unsatisfactory, and the ego identification was fluid. The regression of functioning was not in the service of the ego. In the situation described by Lewin, the ego abandoned its supremacy and the primary process obtained control. This may be a good illustration of the difference between healthy and unhealthy *orgasm.*

Eissler (1958) suggests that "possibly Ferenczi (1924, p. 379) is right to attribute to male intercourse the meaning of a return to the mother's womb. It is feasible that under normal circumstances, orgasm might affirm that the very first frustration man has suffered, the greatest grievance he has to complain of, namely his separation from the maternal organism, has never occurred. (Cf. also Nunberg, 1947, p. 17 and Freud, 1923, p. 249.)" (pp. 241-242).

Homosexuality

The literature on homosexuality is very extensive and will not be reviewed in this paper. I shall confine my discussion to those aspects of homosexuality which may be related to the autistic and symbiotic modes of adaptation. In the research study of Bieber et al. (1962) as well as in other papers on homosexuality, it is a recognized fact that many male homosexuals had a "binding-intimate" relationship with their mothers. Secondly, the fathers are described as distant, uninterested in their sons, and are frequently hostile. Mahler and Gosliner (1955) emphasize the important role of the father in helping the infant separate from his mother. If there is no partial decathexis of the mother, and a partial cathexis of the father, individuation does not take place and the symbiosis with the mother is not resolved.

If we assume that resolution of the symbiosis with the mother is one of the prerequisities for experiencing healthy orgasm, then it follows that such orgasm cannot be experienced by the homosexual. Nevertheless, homosexuality is a form of adaptation which may be explained by the hypothesis of this paper. First, the homosexual defends himself against making a transition from his mother to another female object; thus merging with a partner of the opposite sex does not take place and consequently the tie with the mother is never severed. In other words, there is only a partial giving up of the mother figure and the primary identification with her continues. On the other hand, there is a part-object relationship with the homosexual partner. If a permanent type of homosexual relationship develops, then we can say that there is an accommodation to the symbiosis by remaining loyal to the mother while at the same time having a part-object relationship with someone outside the mother-child orbit. It is as if the male partner were the father to whom the son is looking for salvation from engulfment. In the homosexual who has transient or temporary relationships, the symbiotic tie is so strong that he cannot even partially cathect an outside object; therefore his ephemeral affairs lack constancy because he is still in the throes of a more primitive relationship. He remains entirely faithful to the mother, but his object hunger, because of the absence of the mother, drives him to seek the penis as a substitute for the breast. Such behavior could be explained in innumerable ways. One plausible way is to interpret this type of behavior as a means of maintaining the symbiotic relationship with the mother, whereas the permanent type of homosexual relationship is a compromise solution with remnants from the symbiotic phase and the separation-individuation phase. In any event, it is possible to hypothesize that in homosexuality there is evidence of strong symbiotic ties to the mother.

The Autistic Mode of Sexual Adaptation

In contrast to the persons seeking restitution or restoration of the symbiotic phase, there are others who resort to an autistic mode of adaptation to sexuality in order to safeguard the self representation.

The consequences of such adaptive measures may be frigidity, impotence, and homosexuality. This mode is essentially a negative adaptation to life and may also result in other types of behavior. Some of these autisticlike persons may have fairly well-developed ego structures, some feeling of a sense of self and the body self, while others do not. Mahler (1952) describes autism as a *basic defense* against the outer world because of a lack of emotional ties to the mother; consequently the child cannot tolerate external stimuli or inner excitation. The fear of engulfment may lead to a partial regression to or to a fixation at the autistic phase in order to ward off the feeling of dissolution of the self representation. Mahler (1958a) states that "infantile autism is a somatic defense against impingement of an incomplete internal maternal milieu" (p. 137).

Anna Freud (1951) described some cases in which she found that surrender to the love object is experienced as a return to primary identification; these patients fear and defend themselves against the regressive dissolution of personality by a complete rejection of all objects. Spitz (1957) maintains that negativistic behavior may be an attempt at individuation. Hartmann (1939) states that the fear of "ego loss" in orgasm is a familiar form of pathology. Discussing the problems of virginity, Freud (1918) pointed to defloration in marriage as leading to feelings of both "bondage" and hostility to the husband. Granted that the act of defloration per se may lead to hostility, he also cites examples of women who are able to achieve climax in either clandestine extramarital affairs or in second marriages. Could it be that the narcissistic wound of penetration of the body self as well as the feeling of bondage result in frigidity in marriage, while the woman's freedom of choice may give her a feeling of a sense of self? Freud states: "The woman only recovers her susceptibility to tender feelings in an illicit relationship which has to be kept secret, and in which alone she knows for certain that her own *will* is uninfluenced" (p. 203). In a fragment of a case cited in this paper Freud (1918) describes a woman who loved her husband very much, used to demand intercourse herself, and unmistakingly found great satisfaction in it. Yet, after each instance, the woman expressed unconcealed hostility toward the man, abusing him, raising her hand against him, or actually striking him.

While there are multiple reasons for such behavior, it is my impression that in some instances the person seeking intimacy might at the same time fear engulfment. In the attempt to effect distantiation between the self and the object, physical or verbal aggression may be resorted to, in order to safeguard the boundaries of the body self or the self representation. There are innumerable situations where couples engage in heated arguments or physical fights prior to sexual relations, while others have violent arguments following sexual intercourse. Could this be explained as a symbiotic mode or autistic mode of adaptation depending upon whether the person is seeking intimacy or distantiation? The autistic mode of adaptation is basically a result of a person's determination to maintain his or her ego identity or self image at the cost of libidinal gratification or object relationships. There is a hypercathexis of the boundaries of the self; and the person constantly observes the line of demarcation between the self and the object lest there be any encroachment by the latter.

Impotence and Frigidity

Freud (1905, 1912) discusses impotence in men and explains this psychic phenomenon as being the result of castration anxiety (the unconscious idea that the penis might be injured while in the vagina), a fear of one's own excitation. He also noted that some men were impotent with one type of woman and not with another. In the last instance Freud's basic assumption is that the male is suffering from guilt because of the incestuous nature of the sexual act. My impression is that in addition to the incestuous guilt which causes the impotence, another factor could be that the impotence is a result of an autistic mode of adaptation. First, the act of intromission may be fraught with anxiety because the male is fearful of losing or having part of his body self damaged, namely, the penis. Secondly, the fear of one's own excitation implies fear of loss of ego control. Thirdly, the need to find a woman different from one's mother may certainly be due to a fear that the partner is similar to the maternal object. On the other hand, the fear of fusion with or engulfment by the substitute mother may cause the male to retreat from heterosexuality or from a particular type of woman.

I refer the reader to Moore (1964) for a comprehensive review of the topic of frigidity in women. At this point I would like to discuss some of the ego aspects of frigidity as related to the autistic mode of adaptation. It is my belief that many women are unable to respond sexually because of their fear of ego regression. These women fear that such regression may result in their being overwhelmed by their impulses and consequently there may be a loss of ego control. Furthermore, they are anxious that they might lose anal sphincter and bladder control. Secondly, the penetration by the penis is perceived as a violation of the body self. Finally, the sexual act is experienced as a surrender of one's self to another person.

Keiser (1952) stated that the fear of death that accompanies frigidity is a mobilization of anxiety to prevent loss of the primitive ego which threatens a total annihilation of self. Anxiety is created when destruction of the body is anticipated. Keiser believes that the body ego based on oral gratification is too weak and insufficiently differentiated from external reality to achieve genitality because the normal loss of ego boundaries during orgasm is too great a threat. Although the emphasis is on the oral phase, the autistic phase is held to occur at the same time. It is my impression that the autistic, symbiotic, and separation-individuation phases, though focusing primarily on object relations, can easily be related to the psychosexual phases of development.

In conclusion it may be said that impotence and frigidity can be an autistic mode of adaptation designed to protect the self from being engulfed, damaged, or penetrated. In order to insure the integrity of the self, the individual is willing to forego libidinal pleasure.

Masturbation

In a discussion of masturbation Lampl-de Groot (1950) mentions that "In 1912, the Viennese Psychoanalytic Society published a symposium on the topic of 'Onanism.' . . . Professor Freud concluded his own contribution with the statement: 'We all are of the same opinion, that the subject of onanism is inexhaustible.' Today, after a lapse of thirty-eight years, I think this statement is still valid" (p. 153). This opinion encourages me to add still another observation.

A rather strange phenomenon can be observed in a certain type of person employing the autistic mode of adaptation. Although these persons have a problem in engaging in sexual intercourse or in achieving orgasm, very few of them deny autoerotic behavior. In fact, climax during masturbatory activity is not uncommon. Perhaps this type of behavior may be explained as an autistic defense against the dangers of heterosexual relations, which are perceived as being of an engulfing nature. Therefore the individual derives gratification from the self and his own fantasies, without having to cathect or enter into a union with another person. Obviously, the libidinal drive is present, but again the preservation of the self image is the foremost aim.

Fantasy

In their article on the metapsychology of fantasy, Sandler and Nagera (1963) summarize the literature on this topic. However, they specifically refer to Freud: "The function of fantasy, says Freud as late as 1930, is to help make make oneself independent of the external world by seeking satisfaction in internal psychic processes" (p. 166). Thus fantasy may be another form of autistic withdrawal which helps a person in gaining distance from the object. Some persons have active fantasy lives during sexual intercourse. This type of mental activity may be explained as a means of creating distance between the self and the object, thus precluding the "danger" of completely merging with the partner, psychically and physically, during sexual union. Consequently, the psychic separation between the partners is upheld though there is physical union. The integrity of the self representation is maintained.

PATHOLOGICAL TYPES OF LOVE

To close this discussion without making reference to the subject of love would be remiss, although volumes have been written on this subject. Freud (1921) states that the label "love" is given to a great many kinds of "emotional relationships." In one type "We see that the object is being treated in the same way as our own ego, so that when we are in love a considerable amount of narcissistic libido overflows on to the object. . . . *The object has been put in the place of the ego ideal*" (pp. 112, 113). Freud then distinguishes between identification and such extreme states as fascination or "bondage." In the former case the ego has enriched itself with the properties of the object; in the latter, the ego is impoverished, it has surrendered itself to the object, it has substituted the object for its own important constituent. There is a hypercathexis of the object at the ego's expense. It is my belief that the person who complains of his inability to "fall in love" perceives a relationship as implying entrapment, engulfment, or a loss of one's ego identity; consequently, he defends himself against such a fear by autistic withdrawal. It follows that pathological love leads to either of two choices—symbiotic union or autistic withdrawal, the choice depending upon the level of object relationships and ego development reached.

CONCLUSIONS

Freud noted that psychic activity can be understood best by studying pathological extremes. In this paper Mahler's studies of psychotic children were employed to establish a model of development wherein the autistic, symbiotic, and separation-individuation phases are used as a basis for understanding the role of the ego in sexual adaptation. Healthy orgasm is distinguished from unhealthy orgasm. In the former, there is a regression in functioning in the service of the ego and of adaptation. The boundaries between the self and the object are temporarily dissolved; however, the boundaries are re-established after full gratification is experienced. The object is then recathected. In the unhealthy orgasm, in contrast, regression is pathological and maladaptive. The ego abandons its supremacy to the primary process and the boundaries between the self and the object are not firmly established or fully recovered after the unhealthy orgasm. Satisfaction is not complete and consequently recathexis of the object does not occur.

In persons employing a symbiotic mode of adaptation, sexuality is a means of fusing with the lost symbiotic partner. It is a restitutive or restorative process for the object-hungry person who is seeking a corrective symbiotic experience. In view of the fact that the psychosexual development of such persons is on a pregenital level, orgasm of the unhealthy type is experienced. Those individuals whose mode of adaptation is autisticlike in nature either avoid sexuality completely or are frigid or impotent. In any case, the attempt is to defend the self representation from being engulfed by the object. In pathological love relationships, the mode of adaptation may be either symbiotic or autistic. The parent-child relationship during the autistic, symbotic, and individuation-separation phases may be indicative of the adult's adaptation to sexuality.

BIBLIOGRAPHY

Bergman, P. & Escalona, S. K. (1949), Unusual Sensitivities in Very Young Children. *This Annual*, 3/4:333-352.
Bieber, I. et al. (1962), *Homosexuality: A Psychoanalytic Study*. New York: Basic Books.
Deutsch, H. (1961), Panel: Frigidity in Women, rep. B. E. Moore, *J. Amer. Psa. Assn.*, 9:571-584.
Eissler, K. R. (1958), Psychoanalysis of Adolescents. *This Annual*, 13:223-254.
Freud, A. (1936), *The Ego and the Mechanisms of Defense*. New York: International Universities Press, 1946.
—— (1945), Indications for Child Analysis. *This Annual*, 1:127-149.
—— (1951), A Connection between the States of Negativism and of Emotional Surrender. Abstr. *Int. J. Psa.*, 33:265, 1952.
Freud, S. (1895), Project for a Scientific Psychology. In: *The Origins of Psychoanalysis, Letters to W. Fliess: 1887-1902*. New York: Basic Books, 1954.
—— (1900), The Interpretation of Dreams. *Standard Edition*, 4 & 5. London: Hogarth Press, 1953.
—— (1905), Three Essays on the Theory of Sexuality. *Standard Edition*, 7:125-243. London: Hogarth Press, 1953.
—— (1911), Psycho-analytic Notes upon an Autobiographical Account of a Case of Paranoia (Dementia Paranoides). *Standard Edition*, 12:9-79. London: Hogarth Press, 1958.
—— (1912), On the Universal Tendency to Debasement in the Sphere of Love. *Standard Edition*, 11:179-190. London: Hogarth Press, 1957.
—— (1915), Instincts and Their Vicissitudes. *Standard Edition*, 14:117-140. London: Hogarth Press, 1957.
—— (1918), The Taboo of Virginity: Contributions to the Psychology of Love. *Standard Edition*, 11:193-208. London: Hogarth Press, 1957.
—— (1920), Beyond the Pleasure Principle. *Standard Edition*, 18:7-64. London: Hogarth Press, 1955.
—— (1921), Group Psychology and the Analysis of the Ego. *Standard Edition*, 18:69-143. London: Hogarth Press, 1955.
—— (1923), The Ego and the Id. *Standard Edition*, 19:13-56. London: Hogarth Press, 1961.
—— (1925), Negation. *Standard Edition*, 19:235-239. London: Hogarth Press, 1961.
—— (1926), Inhibitions, Symptoms and Anxiety. *Standard Edition*, 20:87-174. London: Hogarth Press, 1959.
—— (1930), Civilization and its Discontents. *Standard Edition*, 21:64-145. London: Hogarth Press, 1961.
Geleerd, E. R. (1946), A Contribution to the Problem of Psychoses in Childhood. *This Annual*, 2:271-292.
Hartmann, H. (1939), *Ego Psychology and the Problem of Adaptation*. New York: International Universities Press, 1958.
—— (1950), Comments on the Psychoanalytic Theory of the Ego. *This Annual*, 5:74-96.
—— (1956), The Development of the Ego Concept in Freud's Work. In: *Essays on Ego Psychology*. New York: International Universities Press, pp. 268-296.

Jacobson, E. (1964), *The Self and the Object World*. New York: International Universities Press.

Kanner, L. (1943), Autistic Disturbances of Affective Contact. *Nerv. Child*, 2:217-250.

Keiser, S. (1952), Body Ego During Orgasm. *Psa. Quart.*, 21:153-166.

Kris, E. (1934), The Psychology of Caricature. *Psychoanalytic Explorations in Art*. New York: International Universities Press, 1952, pp. 173-189.

—— (1950), Notes on the Development and on Some Current Problems of Psychoanalytic Child Psychology. *This Annual*, 5:24-46.

Lampl-de Groot, J. (1950), On Masturbation and Its Influence on General Development. *This Annual*, 5:153-174.

Lewin, B. D. (1950), *The Psychoanalysis of Elation*. New York: Norton.

Mahler, M. S. (1952), On Child Psychosis and Schizophrenia: Autistic and Symbiotic Infantile Psychoses. *This Annual*, 7:286-305.

—— (1958a), In: Panel on Problems of Identity, rep. D. L. Rubinfine. *J. Amer. Psa. Assn.*, 6:131-142.

—— (1958b), Autism and Symbiosis: Two Extreme Disturbances of Identity. *Int. J. Psa.*, 39:77-83.

—— (1960), Perceptual De-Differentiation and Psychotic Object Relationship. *Int. J. Psa.*, 41:548-553.

—— (1961), On Sadness and Grief in Infancy and Childhood: Loss and Restoration of the Symbiotic Love Object. *This Annual*, 16:332-351.

—— & Elkisch, P. (1953), Some Observations on Disturbances of the Ego in a Case of Infantile Psychosis. *This Annual*, 8:252-261.

—— & Furer, M. (1963), Certain Aspects of the Separation-Individuation Phase. *Psa. Quart.*, 32:1-14.

—— & Gosliner, B. J. (1955), On Symbiotic Child Psychosis. *This Annual*, 10:195-212.

—— Ross, J. R., Jr., & de Fries, Z. (1949), Clinical Studies in Benign and Malignant Cases of Childhood Psychosis (Schizophrenia-Like). *Amer. J. Orthopsychiat.*, 19: 295-303.

Moore, B. E. (1964), Frigidity: A Review of Psychoanalytic Literature. *Psa. Quart.*, 33: 323-349.

Pollock, G. (1964), On Symbiosis and Symbiotic Neurosis. *Int. J. Psa.*, 45:1-30.

Sandler, J. & Nagera, H. (1963), Aspects of the Metapsychology of Fantasy. *This Annual*, 18:159-194.

Spitz, R. (1957), *No and Yes*. New York: International Universities Press.

Waelder, R. (1930), The Principle of Multiple Function. *Psa. Quart.*, 5:45-62, 1936.

Witkin, H. A. (1962), *Psychological Differentiation*. New York: Wiley.

A CONTRIBUTION TO A PSYCHOANALYTIC
THEORY OF WORK

DOUGLAS HOLMES, Ph.D. (New York)

It is the purpose of this paper to investigate the concept of work and the role it plays in personality development. Specifically, an attempt is made to demonstrate how, as a function of early social experience, an individual will tend to invest work with varying amounts of drive energy or neutralized energy. Corroboratory evidence is drawn from both clinical experience and the findings of experiments in social psychology. Suggestions are made for a research strategy with which to evaluate the theoretical position taken.

One of the few theories of work, and certainly the most inclusive one, was suggested by Freud (1930):

> No other technique for the conduct of life attaches the individual so firmly to reality as laying emphasis on work; for his work at least gives him a secure place in a portion of reality, in the human community. The possibility it offers of displacing a large amount of libidinal components, whether narcissistic, aggressive or even erotic, on to professional work and on to the human relations connected with it lends it a value by no means second to what it enjoys as something indispensable to the preservation and justification of existence in society [p. 80].

It is necessary to note in this passage that Freud differentiates between two psychic functions of work. The first provides for a discharge of libidinal and aggressive impulses; the second provides a means for "binding the individual more closely to reality." Both may or may not be a result of conflict. With regard to the latter function, Freud would appear to have allowed for the existence of a mechanism neither directly caused by nor dependent upon drive, a position agreeing with that of ego psychology. As Hartmann (1939) noted:

The close connection between theory and therapeutic technique so characteristic of psychoanalysis explains why the ego functions directly involved in the *conflicts* between the mental institutions commanded our interest earlier than others. It also explains why other ego functions and the process of coming to terms with the environment—except for a few pertinent problems which played a role in psychoanalysis from the beginning— did not become the subject matter of research until a later stage of our science. . . . *We must recognize that though the ego certainly does grow on conflicts, these are not the only roots of ego development* [pp. 7-8; my italics].

Many analysts and other writers appear to have accepted this differentiation, and consequently to have confined their investigation to one or the other imputed work functions, i.e., as a means of drive reduction or as a means of binding the person to reality. Pederson-Krag (1951), for example, notes that to a degree which increases as a function of the increased utilization of mass-productive techniques, the individual relies upon work not as a "reality-binding" agent, but rather as an avenue for the expression of sublimated libidinal desires. Pederson-Krag also notes that if such avenues of sublimation are blocked, the individual will regress further, exhibiting such symptoms as withdrawal and aggression. Another example of the emphasis placed upon the drive-reduction function of work is that of Sachs (1933) who stated: "We have long known that the tools which enable man to accomplish his work more successfully . . . without achieving independent and automotive existence of their own are mostly phallic symbols. Their employment . . . was originally, according to Sperber's theory, a substitute for a sexual act" (p. 415).

Ginsburg (1942), on the other hand, reports a study in which he demonstrated that an individual deprived of work lost his sense of status, his sense of identification with society, and apparently the very basis of self-evaluation. Whereas Pederson-Krag and Sachs attributed to work the function of drive reduction, Ginsburg has suggested that we depend on work as a source of self-evaluation and the basis upon which to pattern modes of adaptive or reality-oriented behavior.

Such a theoretical dichotomization between the two functions of work appears neither necessary nor fruitful. It would seem that, for a given individual, work fulfills both functions, to varying degrees. Thus, for one individual work may serve primarily as a means of expressing drives and as such will be invested with drive energy, whereas for another individual, work may be invested with neutralized energy and may serve primarily a self-evaluative, planning, and reality-orienting function. In line with current views regarding finite amounts of available psychic energy, it is further suggested that these two functions of work exist, within a given individual, in a complementary relationship: the greater the investment of drive energy, the less neutralized energy is available for investment in work activity. Furthermore, as will be developed below, it seems most probable that the proportion of each function is related to the individual's whole developmental history and as such remains relatively stable within a given individual. Thus, if one were to posit a dimension, which might be termed conflict-conflict-free, any individual could be placed somewhere along this dimension or continuum, in terms of the degree to which work is invested with neutralized or drive energy. An attempt will now be made to identify this continuum and to identify those factors in the individual's developmental history which determine his position on the continuum.

Hartmann (1939) stated that "though fantasy always implies an initial turning away from a real situation, it can also be a preparation for reality . . . [it] may fulfill a synthetic function by provisionally connecting our needs and goals with possible ways of realizing them" (p. 18). Thus, fantasy plays an important role in childhood ego development, since manifest replication or veridical imitation of the behavior of those who constitute social reality, especially in the family group, is to a great degree impossible. It is then the function of fantasy to permit enactment and development of the reality-orienting processes that are momentarily thwarted by developmental limitations. For example, in a community in which work is a major criterion of status and of the efficiency of social organization, the child must engage in work-related fantasies in order to develop some appropriate mode for dealing with his immediate reality.

Rapaport (1951) has summarized certain of Kris's formulations as follows:

> . . . differences in cathexes are responsible for the difference between the two roles of fantasy, the one being reflecting, planning, and the fostering of reality-adaptation, and the other the expressing of id-wishes. The former uses neutralized energic-cathexes,

while those of the latter are libidinous or aggressive cathexes, little or not at all neutralized. It may be conjectured that the maturity of the ego and the strength of its tie to reality are reflected in the kind and amount of energic-cathexes that the ego has available for use [p. 372].

In general, it can be said that of the two courses of fantasy adaptation, the former, being more directly concerned with reality, will involve the introjection of the manifest work-related cues afforded by the environment at an early stage. This introjected model will then form a basis for ego adaptation and future work behavior. Thus, the very development of reality ties through fantasy will culminate in the existence of this model in the conflict-free sphere of the ego. Consideration of the latter course, in which fantasy is used primarily as a vehicle for the expression of id wishes, suggests that the individual will invest the work reality with his own libidinal or aggressive needs, reality thus becoming invested with drive energy. Therefore, given the case of fantasy being used in the service of the expression of id wishes, reality will be impressed *upon* fantasy; on the other hand, if fantasy is used in the fostering of reality adaptation, the sense of reality develops *through* fantasy. Development manifesting use of only one type of fantasy activity could be considered as one end of a continuum of which the other end would represent development comprised solely of the alternative course of fantasy. In the rest of this paper, that end of the suggested continuum which has been identified as development *through* reality-based fantasy will be termed the "integrated" end; that end which represents reality impressed upon fantasy will be termed the "imposed" end.

Piaget (1937) outlined a theory of the development of logical thought in children which is analogous to certain of the present theoretical formulations. He suggests that the initial relation between the child and the external world is egocentric. To use Piaget's terms, the child *assimilates* reality, a stage in which "the universe consists in mobile and plastic perceptual images centered about personal activity" (p. 351). Soon, however, through the process of assimilation, relationships between various phases of activity and between the activity and the external objects central to the activity are established. As this occurs, *accommodation* of self to the external reality must occur; thus again, in Piaget's words, "Assimilation and accommodation are therefore the two poles of an interaction between the organism and the environment" (p. 353). Initially, the two processes of assimilation and accommodation are relatively undifferentiated, and the ego boundaries between the external world and the self are unformed. Piaget notes that appearance is taken for reality; e.g., "It is the mountains which are moving, not I," until relatively late in development; and that "thought in all realms starts from a surface contact with the external realities, that is, a simple accommodation to immediate experience" (p. 383). At this stage, a point in time where the relationships existing between the infinite dimensions of external reality have yet to be established, it is necessary for the child to be presented with a consistent view of any reality area. The discovery of the relations among external objects and the relation between the external world and the self are otherwise made much more difficult; an inconsistent view might lead the child to rely on egocentric, drive-involved fantasy, in which emphasis is placed upon assimilation of reality to self.

It is important to make note here of several points. First, an individual's reality is not monolithic. There are many divisions or areas of reality, depending, at least in part, on the function each of these areas serves for the individual. There may exist, in any one individual, a number of such "reality areas," each invested, perhaps, with differing proportions of drive and neutralized energy. These qualitative differences in psychic investment might account for differential coping ability in various areas, e.g., the psychotic who can function at work compared with the neurotic whose functioning is inhibited at work. It is to be expected that relatively few of the areas reach a position of ascendancy in reality adaptation. That is to say, as a function of the culture in general and the family values in particular, certain culturally valued "reality areas" will be especially important and particularly salient in determining individual status. Second, the course which the individual utilizes in adapting to reality in any given "reality area" will be a direct function of the individual's early perception of the parents' mode of dealing with this particular reality area.

Before discussing work as one of the most potent "reality areas," it is important to suggest two situations which could culminate in an individual being represented at one of the ends of the "integrated-imposed" continuum. If the child perceives conflict in parental values and psychic investment in work, it becomes difficult for the child to relate the self to reality even on the most basic level, and he will then retreat into a fantasy life which is constituted primarily of id wishes. If, on the other hand, the child's family environment is such that he can introject clearly defined value concepts, his adaptation will tend to be of the "integrated" type. That is to say, if the family recognizes, accepts, and adheres to a certain set of values and norms as a basis for the determination of status, success, or growth and if these values or norms involve reality-based criteria which can be met during growth, the child will accept, and in fantasy elaborate on and develop through, these valued activities. For example, if the family views work as a major reality area, and if immediate day-to-day discussion of the actual family work not only exists but also agrees with the imputed cultural value of work, the child will be able to form a more veridical picture of work and utilize it without investing it with idiosyncratic, probably libidinal or aggressive, meanings of his own.

I have suggested above that a great number of "reality areas" may exist in an individual; however, due to the particular mode of relationship between the individual and his environment, only a few of these reality areas are important in the process of individual reality adaptation. In the earlier stages of development, this narrowing of the field of primary reality areas is, except in the case of individual pathology, prescribed by the environment. It is a set of culturally valued activities transmitted by the parents, who to a great extent determine the child's first social reality. It is generally accepted that a given culture traditionally attaches importance to certain values; it is to be expected that these values become most relevant in the most general overt activity of a culture. In American society, possibly as a function of the dominant Protestant ethic, evaluation of the individual tends to be in terms of his relative success at work. In terms of both actual practice and ideological tradition, work is a most important reality area for evaluation of the self and for the transmission of cultural values. It is therefore reasonable to assume that the primacy of work as a reality area will be made abundantly clear to the child early in his life; the ultimate use the maturing organism makes of work will then be a function of the parental experience with, attitudes toward, and use of work.

For these reasons, work plays an important role in the adaptation of the ego to reality, and this development may be represented by any point on the continuum of fantasy adaptation. Hence, work can be invested with neutralized energy or with drive energy; it can serve as an agent in binding the individual more closely to reality and as an avenue for the discharge of drive energy.

What then is the evidence supporting these contentions? A full corroboration of Kris's suggestion with regard to the role of different cathexes and mine with regard to the two general types of fantasy in the course of reality adaptation would require extensive longitudinal study; at this time it is possible to offer only isolated instances of corroboratory evidence.

The first such evidence comes from clinical experience. Children do engage in different general types of fantasy, along the dimensions I have suggested; some children, for instance, will build elaborate structures with blocks and imbue them with various properties, such as "this is the house that Daddy is building"; others will build the same elaborate structures, repeatedly, only to destroy them just as repeatedly. Similarly, in play therapy, we see, on the one hand, the child who invests the "Momma" and "Papa" dolls with culturally prescribed adult social roles. On the other hand, we see the child manipulating the dolls and explaining that "This is Mommy and this is Daddy . . . he sticks his sword in her and she dies. . . ." Such observations suggest the existence of the two quite different roles of fantasy, one the reality binding, the other the vehicle for expression of drive energy.

Various studies conducted by social psychologists on the effects of social deprivation have established that: (1) isolation from perceptual cues will make a subject more susceptible to propaganda (Scott et al., 1959), i.e., an apparent readiness to accept and elaborate upon any cues despite a disparate frame of reference; (2) social reinforcement is more potent when a subject is kept, for brief periods, in social isolation (Gerwitz and Baer, 1958); (3) child subjects are more susceptible to the autokinetic effect after social and sensory deprivation (Walters and Quinn, 1960); (4) subjects after prolonged sensory and social deprivation will engage in primary-process thought, and reality-testing processes will be temporarily affected (Goldberger, 1959). These findings, taken together, have the following implications: when "social reality" is undefined or when social and sensory cues are removed, the individual will (a) be increasingly willing to accept any available cues even if they result in a formulation which does not constitute "reality" in the normal situation, and (b) tend to engage in autistic logic and poor reality testing. These experimental situations can be considered to parallel the situation in which the child is deprived of consistent environmental cues with regard to any of the reality areas. These two areas of findings, from clinical and social psychology, afford some corroboration of the hypotheses that (a) individuals' fantasies differ as a function of the kind of energy invested in external situations; and (b) the energy invested in any "reality area" depends, at least in part, on the number of cues afforded by the environment; i.e., the number must be sufficient to permit an evaluation both of the environment and of one's position relevant to that environment.

As previously stated, the kind of energy an individual invests in his work is a function of childhood experience. As a means of both operationalizing the theoretical position taken and conducting an objective evaluation of this position, the following outline for a research strategy is offered. This strategy would make it possible to demonstrate whether it is possible to predict, on the basis of the child's early perceptions and experiences with regard to work, both the nature of the child's current work fantasy and the eventual position of the individual on the "integrated-imposed" continuum.

The research evaluation will be made on the basis of data collected through the use of four instruments or techniques:

1. A projective device (similar to the TAT but involving work-related pictures), through which the child can express his or her fantasy relating to work.

2. An objective questionnaire, with which the child can describe perceived parental work roles and attitudes.

3. An objective questionnaire, with which parents can describe their perceived work roles, their experiences, and their general attitudes toward work.

4. The same projective device as in #1 above with which, at a later date, the original child subjects can be retested to determine their position on the "integrated-imposed" continuum.

The subsequent analysis of data collected through initial presentation of instruments would provide the following measures of relationship.

1. The relationship between the child's fantasy and the parental description of work role and attitude (Measures 1 and 3, above). Here the general prediction would be that the more consistent the parental attitude toward work, the greater the degree to which the child's work-related fantasy is reality-oriented.

2. The relationship between the child's work-related fantasy and the child's perception of parental work roles and attitudes (Measures 1 and 2, above). Here the prediction would be that the more clearly and consistently the child perceives parental work roles and attitudes, the more the work-related fantasy will tend to be reality-oriented.

3. The relationship between the child's work-related fantasy, on the one hand, and the child's perception of parental work roles and attitudes, and the parental description of work roles and attitudes, on the other hand (Measures 1, 2, and 3 above). Here the prediction is that the degree of similarity between the child's perception of work roles and attitudes and the parents' perception of work roles and attitudes will have an effect on the nature of the child's work-related fantasies. Although, as predicted above, the nature of the child's fantasy is expected to vary primarily as a function of the consistency of parental feelings about work, the congruence of the child's and the parents' perceptions may act to weaken or strengthen this relationship.

4. The relationship between the child's work-related fantasy and the eventual position on the "integrated-imposed" continuum (Measures 1 and 4, above). The prediction here is that the greater the degree of original reality-oriented fantasy pertaining to work, the nearer the individual will be, at a later date, to the "integrated" pole of the continuum.

It is hoped that the foregoing will serve as a contribution to a psychoanalytic theory of work. There are many problems which remain unanswered; for instance, it is quite apparent that a question remains with regard to the relative consequences of drive, as contrasted to neutralized, investment in work. That is, although it might appear desirable to have work invested with only neutralized energy, it is equally possible that some jobs are filled, and provide satisfaction to the incumbent, just because they permit the discharge of drive energy.

A related question is that of matching work characteristics with the level of psychosexual organization, particularly among those at the "imposed" end of the continuum. For instance, whereas phallic-assertive behavior might be of definite advantage to the aspiring executive, a primarily oral organization would be more appropriate for a nurse. Here, an ultimate question is whether the greatest productivity is to be obtained through such a matching of work characteristics and psychosexual organization, or through an individual's being near the integrated end of the continuum. Questions such as these can be answered only through further theoretical development. This theorization must be accompanied by empirical evaluation, perhaps along the lines suggested above as a research strategy.

BIBLIOGRAPHY

Freud, S. (1930), Civilization and Its Discontents. *Standard Edition,* 21:59-145. London: Hogarth Press, 1961.

Gerwitz, J. S. & Baer, D. M. (1958), The Effect of Brief Social Deprivation on Behavior for a Social Reinforcer. *J. Abnorm. & Soc. Psychol.,* 56:49-56.

Ginsburg, S. W. (1942), What Unemployment Does to People. *Amer. J. Psychiat.,* 99:439-446.

Goldberger, L. (1959), Experimental Interference with Reality Contact (Perceptual Isolation). *J. Nerv. Ment. Dis.,* 127:99-112.

Hartmann, H. (1939), *Ego Psychology and the Problem of Adaptation.* New York: International Universities Press, 1958.

Pederson-Krag, G. (1951), Psychoanalytic Approach to Mass Production. *Psa. Quart.,* 20:434-443.

Piaget, J. (1937), *The Construction of Reality in the Child.* New York: Basic Books, 1954.

Rapaport, D., ed. (1951), *Organization and Pathology of Thought.* New York: Columbia University Press.

Sachs, H. (1933), The Delay of the Machine Age. *Psa. Quart.,* 2:404-411.

Scott, T. et al. (1959), Cognitive Effects of Perceptual Isolation. *Canad. J. Psychol.,* 13:200-209.

Walters, R. & Quinn, M. (1960), Effects of Social and Sensory Deprivation on Autokinetic Judgments. *J. Pers.,* 28:358-367.

NOTES ON PAIN, DEPRESSION, AND INDIVIDUATION

W. G. JOFFE, M.B., B.Ch., D.P.M. and
JOSEPH SANDLER, Ph.D., D.Sc. (London)

I

The Depressive Reaction

In a previous study of depression in children (Sandler and Joffe, 1965), based on material from the Hampstead Index, a picture which was called the *Depressive Reaction* was isolated. It was characterized by a mood which was variously described by therapists as "sadness," "unhappiness" or "depression." This mood had both mental and bodily components. The child looked unhappy, had little interest in his surroundings, and appeared withdrawn, bored or listless. He had a feeling of discontent with what was offered to him and showed little capacity for pleasure. He communicated a sense of feeling rejected or unloved, and showed a readiness to turn away from disappointing objects. He was not prepared to accept help or comfort readily, and if he did respond at all, his underlying disappointment and dissatisfaction would re-emerge. He showed a tendency to regress to passive oral attitudes and behavior. Insomnia

The material used has been collected at the Hampstead Child-Therapy Clinic, a therapeutic and research center financed by the following foundations: The Field Foundation, Inc., New York: The Anna Freud Foundation, New York; The Estate of Flora Haas, New York; The Old Dominion Foundation, U.S.A.; The Psychoanalytic Research and Development Fund, Inc., New York; and the National Institute of Mental Health, Bethesda, Maryland.

This investigation was supported (in part) by Public Health Service Grant M-5683, MH (L) from the National Institute of Mental Health.

Particular acknowledgment is due to E. Dansky, S. Baker, I. Elkan, and members of the Depression Research Group of the Hampstead Psychoanalytic Index, for their collaboration in the work which led to this paper; and to Anna Freud, James Strachey, and A. J. Solnit for helpful suggestions.

and various other sleep disturbances were noted, and autoerotic or repetitive self-comforting activities described. A general feature was that the therapist reported difficulty in making sustained contact with the child at this time.

The depressive reaction, which could be transitory or of long duration, intense or mild, occurred in different personality types and clinical conditions. It was seen at all stages of development and could be found in association with a variety of other symptoms. It was a reaction which, it seemed, can potentially occur in any child.

The clinical picture described as the depressive reaction consisted of a number of components, *having at its core a basic depressive affective response.* It was also associated with features which could be understood as representing attempts to deal with the existence of this affect *or to prevent its development.* It seemed that undischarged aggression played a significant role in its genesis, and derivatives of or defenses against aggressive manifestations were also part of the picture.

While the depressive reaction, as described in our earlier study, referred to a clinical constellation, the terms *depressive response* and *depressive reaction* will be used in a restricted sense in the present paper, denoting the basic affective response which formed its core. This affect was thought to represent a fundamental psychobiological response which could be conceived of as being as basic as anxiety. It has its roots in a primary psychophysiological state which is an ultimate reaction to the experiencing of helplessness in the face of physical or psychological pain in one form or another. It occurs in babies who suffer from nutritional deficiency diseases, and in infants who are deprived of adequate psychological stimulation (Provence and Lipton, 1962). The basic response was considered to be one which could occur at any time in the individual's life span. It ought not to be confused with those forms of depressive illness which can be considered to be the consequence of further defensive and restitutive processes, and in which pathogenic introjections and identifications occur (Bibring, 1953; Jacobson, 1953; Zetzel, 1960).

Depression, Pain, and Well-Being

The basic depressive response was regarded as representing a state of helplessness, hopelessness, and resignation in the face of mental pain.[1] It is not the only possible response to pain or to the anticipation of pain, but a *particular* one, in which there is a feeling of being unable to restore a wished-for state, accompanied by an attitude which is essentially one of capitulation and retreat. The healthy response to the experiencing of pain is protest, "fight" rather than "flight." Many children who are called "unhappy" are not in fact manifesting a depressive response. They have not "capitulated," but rather show varying degrees of discontent and resentment, and their aggressive response to pain is much more directly manifest.

Biological separation of the young infant from his mother is one source of pain, as is separation in the somewhat older child in whom the mother image has been differentiated from the self representation. The child's reaction to pain brought about by separation, as to pain brought about from any other cause in reality or in fantasy, may be that of the basic depressive response; on the other hand, it may not. Our nodal concept in this connection is not the factor of object loss per se, but rather the subjective state of pain and a depressive response to it.

Freud considered mental pain to be a phenomenon which paralleled physical pain. The painful place (in Freud's example [1926, Addendum C] the missing lost object) receives a hypercathexis of longing which mounts to an intolerable level. Although Freud conceived of this in the context of loss and mourning, his statements on the subject can be generalized in such a way that the loss of an object need not be seen as the only precondition for the experiencing of mental pain. When an object is lost and its representation receives a libidinal hypercathexis, this means that the cathected internal image of the object is not met by a corresponding perception arising from outer sources. Thus the painful hypercathexis can be taken as indicating a state of discrepancy between an existing state of the representational world (Sandler and Rosenblatt, 1962) and a wished-for, so-called ideal state. We would suggest that it is precisely such a discrepancy which reflects mental pain, and that, more specifically, it is a discrepancy between the actual state of the self on the one hand and an ideal state of well-being on the other.

[1] There are different degrees of pain, and even qualities of pain. The relationship of pain to the spectrum of unpleasures, although touched on by Freud (1926, Addendum C), merits further investigation.

The term "ideal state" needs some explanation. "Ideal" in this context refers to a state of well-being, a state which is fundamentally affective and which normally accompanies the harmonious and integrated functioning of all the biological and mental structures (Sandler, 1960). The striving toward the attainment of an ideal state is basic in human development and functioning. It represents the feeling component which is attributed to the state of primary narcissism (Freud, 1914). Much of the dynamics of ego functioning can be understood in terms of the ego's striving to maintain or attain a state of well-being, a state which even in the child who has been unhappy from birth exists as a biological goal. Freud put it: "The development of the ego consists in a departure from primary narcissism and gives rise to a vigorous attempt to recover that state." The ideal state of well-being is closely linked with feelings of safety and security. It is the polar opposite of feelings of pain, anxiety or discomfort, and bears the same relation to these as the state of physical satiation and contentment in a small infant bears to the unpleasure of instinctual tension. The attainment of this state may follow or accompany successful drive discharge, but there are circumstances in which drive satisfaction does not lead to the development of well-being, but rather to the experiencing of its opposite, as in states of mental conflict.

In this there is a qualitative difference between the systems *id* and *ego*. The drives are characterized by states of tension and demands for discharge (and the body pleasures associated with such discharge) which change in the course of development. The dynamics of ego functioning appear to be much more related to the maintenance of affective states of well-being which do not change as grossly in the course of development (although the ideational content associated with the ideal state may change markedly). In what follows we shall use the term *ideal state* to refer to the affective state of well-being, and the term *ideal self* to denote the particular shape of the self representation at any moment in the individual's life which is believed (consciously or unconsciously) to embody the ideal state. As the representational world of the child becomes increasingly structured, his system of self representations includes images which reflect affective states of well-being. The "ideal self" derives its content not only from affect representations, but also contains ideational components which may originate from various sources.[2] These sources include memories of actual states of well-being previously experienced, or of fantastic and symbolic elaborations of such states. The elaborations in fantasy may subserve defensive functions, in which case we may get magical and omnipotent components in the ideal self. The specialized form of ideal which ensues when the child needs to aggrandize himself for the purpose of defense can be referred to as the "idealized self," but it should be borne in mind that idealization is only one possible source of the content of the ideal self. Similarly, where the ideal self is based on identification with an admired object, we can distinguish between qualities which the child attributes to the object because of its infantile perception of the object at the time, and those which are attributed to the object representation in fantasy (usually resulting from ambivalence conflicts).

The Role of the Object

We saw the role of the object as being that of a vehicle for the attainment of the ideal state of well-being. While this is perhaps obvious when object relationships are of the anaclitic, need-fulfilling (part-object) type, it is not so obvious when the state of object constancy has been reached. It could be argued that love for the object can be truly altruistic, that the object can be loved for and in itself. Yet we believe that this is never entirely true, and that the value which any object has is directly connected with its genetic and functional relation to the self. This would appear to be so even after the attainment of object constancy, when the object has developed "uniqueness" and has become an indispensable key to states of well-being. The subject was explored by Freud in his paper "On Narcissism" (1914) where he traced the development of object love from primary narcissism. Object love, like the whole development of the ego, can be seen as a roundabout way of attempting to restore the ideal primary narcissistic state. The perception of the presence of the love object when its presence is expected is, moreover, a source of feelings of well-being and safety (Sandler, 1960). And this is true

---

[2] We have related the ideal state of well-being to the dynamics of ego functioning rather than to the gaining of pleasure associated with instinctual drive discharge. This will be the topic of a later study.

even when the object is fulfilling no drive-reducing role.[3] It is clear that if the presence of the object is a condition for a state of well-being in the self, then loss of the object signifies the loss of an aspect of the self, of a state of the self. One might say that for the representation of every love object there is a part of the self representation which is complementary to it, i.e., the part which *reflects the relation to the object,* and which constitutes the link between self and object. We can refer to this as the object-complementary aspect of the self representation.

We have suggested that even if the highest level of object love has been reached, the object is ultimately the means whereby a desired state of the self may be attained, in fact or in fantasy. This does not imply any degree of undervaluation of the role of object relationships in development and in mental life in general; the object is, after a certain point in development has been passed, unique and essential for the maintenance of well-being in the self. When a love object is lost, we not only have the loss of the object in its own right, but also the loss of the object-complementary aspect of the self and the affective state of well-being which is intimately bound up with it. In such a state of object loss, the affective value cathexis of the object is greatly increased, and attention is focused almost exclusively on the object because it is the key to the reattainment of the lost state of the self. This displacement is biologically conditioned, because of the long period of dependence of the human infant on its biological object.[4] In the case of the toddler, the mere presence of the mother in the nursery may be sufficient for him to play happily, all but ignoring her presence. His state of well-being

[3] The transition from anaclitic relationships to those characterized by object constancy reflects changes in the child's ego rather than in his drives. From the point of view of the id, objects are, in a sense, the means whereby the drives attain discharge. The relationship of the ego to objects, in the anaclitic phase, is determined by the requirements of drive discharge. The transition to the state of object constancy implies that the child's needs have become more complex, and now reflect not only the requirements of the drives, but also secondary needs related to the maintenance of states of safety and well-being. Object constancy, therefore, reflects not only the drive cathexes of the id, but in addition implies the existence of a secondary (ego) need for the *particular* object.

[4] The infant has a biological object relationship to his mother from conception. This is quite different from the psychological object relationship which develops as the child gradually constructs a differentiated object representation from the initially inchoate mass of pleasure-pain sensations.

may be quite obvious from his contented play. If she leaves the room without his noticing her departure, he will go on playing happily, until he notices her absence. His perception of this may precipitate a disruption of his well-being and a state of distress. All his attention and activity will be directed toward restoring her presence. What he feels is lost is the mother; what is actually lost is not only the mother but also the well-being implicit in the relationship.

II

The material in the previous section represents a summary, and to some extent an elaboration of the views on pain and depression presented in our previous paper. There we introduced briefly the application of the concept of individuation, a topic which will be taken up more fully in Part IV. Individuation was related to normal development and referred to a process whereby the ego's striving to attain past ideal states was changed and new, ego-syntonic, and more reality-adapted ideals constructed. But before we proceed to a more detailed discussion of individuation and its relation to depression, it is appropriate to summarize and comment on the work of a number of authors in Great Britain whose contributions are relevant to the present topic.

Melanie Klein

Basic to Melanie Klein's theory of depression (1948) is the notion that the infant experiences a "depressive position" in the first half year of life. Before this, the child suffers multiple primordial anxieties from birth due to the conflict between the life and death instincts. In the first few months, when only part objects can be distinguished, the infant attempts to deal with his anxieties by splitting of the part object (breast) into "good" and "bad" parts, with a corresponding splitting of the ego into loving and hating parts. Projective and introjective processes are said to occur, which bring about, in favorable circumstances (when good experiences predominate over bad ones), a degree of integration and a capacity for love, stemming from the life instinct. In this period (the paranoid-schizoid position) the splitting of the object into good and bad parts can serve a valuable function in that the good object is preserved and the security of the ego enhanced (1957). These processes may follow a different course if, for various reasons, the "bad" experiences predominate over the "good." Persecutory anxieties may be more intense, confusion between self and object occurs, and defensive idealization indicates the strength of feelings of persecution. This is an unsatisfactory basis for the development of security.

The paranoid-schizoid position is normally followed by the depressive position in the second quarter of the first year. The child recognizes the mother as a whole object and begins to relate to it as such. Good and bad experiences are now felt to arise from the same object, and as a consequence the child experiences conflict based on ambivalence. The integration of the good and bad parts of the mother, as well as those parts which have been separated by splitting, is accompanied by a corresponding integration of the various aspects of the child's own ego. In contrast to the anxieties of the paranoid-schizoid position (where the child feels that his ego is attacked by his own projected hostility), the main anxiety is now that the infant will destroy the object he loves and upon which he is dependent. The child is at the mercy of feelings of despair, guilt, and hopelessness when he feels that he has destroyed his external or internal mother. The conflict in the depressive position is thought by Melanie Klein to be mainly between the infant's destructive impulses and his love for, and wish to make reparation to, the object. If he can feel that reparation has been achieved, then this contributes to the "working through" of the depressive position. The infant begins to distinguish between himself and his objects, and to distinguish between fantasy and reality. The infant's belief in his own omnipotence becomes modified, and his relationship to reality becomes established. The ego is strengthened on this account, as well as by the further introjection of good objects into the ego. Concurrently the superego becomes more integrated, and with time resembles more the good parents than the persecuting ones.

Melanie Klein saw the depressive position as being a crucial and fundamental stage in the child's development. Much of the pathology seen later is thought to result from a failure to work through this "position," and a degree of success in its resolution may come only through repeated working over of the depressive position or through analysis. The depressive position implies a "pining" for the loved good object, and the ego may develop methods of defense, particularly *manic* defenses, which are specifically directed against the pining for the lost object.

Hanna Segal (1964) comments as follows:

> The depressive position is never fully worked through. The anxieties pertaining to ambivalence and guilt, as well as situations of loss, which reawaken depressive experiences, are always with us. Good external objects in adult life always symbolize and contain aspects of the primary good object, internal and external, so that any loss in later life reawakens the anxiety of losing the good internal object and, with this anxiety, all the anxieties experienced originally in the depressive position. If the infant has been able to establish a good internal object relatively securely in the depressive position, situations of depressive anxiety will not lead to illness, but to a frutiful working through, leading to further enrichment and creativity.

Melanie Klein makes little or no distinction between the dynamic, structural, economic, genetic, and adaptational points of view, and her theories represent a sort of condensation in concrete terms of all these approaches, allocated, moreover, to the very earliest months of life. In spite of this her work has drawn clinical attention to certain aspects of the processes whereby the child and adult establish secure feelings of well-being and a stable state of the self which is relatively independent of the objects. These processes, as she sees them, involve the development of the ability to tolerate painful feelings of loss, a view which is consonant with our own. The link which she made between these processes and depression is important, although she viewed the child's experiences of pain and depression as identical with those which can be seen in later psychotic illnesses. We would approach the subject rather from the point of view of more basic and elemental instinctual and affective processes, and distinguish as Bibring (1953) and Zetzel (1960) have done, between depressive affect and depressive illness. However, in so far as what Melanie Klein has called "working through the depressive position" is related to the process of individuation, it reflects an important aspect of clinical psychoanalytic work with both children and adults. We would add that although Melanie Klein formulated successful working through of the depressive position in terms of the establishment of the primacy of the good object, it could be inferred that she is also referring to the establishment of a "good" state of the self, in spite of the fact that she considers the development of the self to be based primarily on object incorporation. It might follow, as a corollary of her views, that loss of a good object could also be seen as the loss of a good part of the self.

Winnicott

Winnicott's work is difficult to translate into metapsychological terms partly because of the richness of detail and the highly personal language he uses. His views are not identical with those of Melanie Klein, but he also conceives of the attainment of a state in early development in which the whole infant relates to the whole mother in an ambivalent way (1954). This phase is described as one of "concern for the object," and although Winnicott regards the term "depressive position" as a "thoroughly bad name for a normal process," he believes that no better one has been found. If all goes well with weaning, the depressive position should occur in the second half of the first year, but he suggests that it often takes much longer to be established, and some people never attain it. Winnicott regards the depressive position not as a phase but rather as an *achievement,* a position reached, and the earlier this occurs, the better the outlook for the child. The attainment of the depressive position signifies a development from the stage of ruthless demandingness to a state of concern for the object and, in particular, of concern about the effects of the infant's instinctual demands on the mother. The mother has been the object of "assault" during the phase of instinctual tension. During "quiet" phases the mother is loved as the one who has been adapting to the infant. The coming together of these two functions in the mind of the child initiates the beginning of guilt feeling. This is an intrinsic personal source of the sense of guilt. Subsequent processes enrich the inner world, and ultimately the child builds up a store of "good" memories "so that the experience of the mother holding the situation becomes part of the self, becomes assimilated into the ego. In this way the actual mother becomes less and less necessary."

Winnicott suggests that if the individual has attained the depressive position, his reaction to loss is one of grief or sadness; if the depressive position has failed, if the processes in it go wrong, the child "wet-blankets" the whole inner world, functions at a low level of vitality, and the mood is one of depression. He points out that this type of failure and recovery differs from the manifestations of depressive illness seen in clinical psychiatry, is associated with depersonalization, hopelessness in respect of object relationships, and the special type of futility seen in the development of a false self (1956). These illnesses relate, he believes, to a developmental phase preceding the depressive position.

The depressive mood is distinguished from the anxieties associated with the depressive position. Winnicott details many of the defense mechanisms which are employed against depressive anxiety. The depressive mood is in itself seen as an over-all control which is gradually lifted. This is a major defense through the relative inhibition of the instinct, so that all the consequences of instinctual experience are correspondingly diminished. Other defenses include the negation of everything serious (the manic defense) and various forms of projection, introjection, etc.

Winnicott's position in this connection is clarified to some extent in a recent paper (1964), in which he discusses the value of depression for individual development. He describes the way in which objects and the environment are differentiated from the self, and the processes of integration which accompany this. A "good enough" environment is essential for the inborn maturation processes which underlie these developments to occur (Winnicott, 1958).[5] When the child has developed a sense of identity, has gained a degree of ego strength, and can contain the stresses and strains which arise in his inner personal psychic reality, he becomes able to be depressed. Winnicott sees the depressed mood as evidence of the existence of a mental organization sufficiently strong to be able to control otherwise disrupting tensions, in particular those associated with hate. Crises which may arise later and which create a depressed mood are brought about by "a new experience of destructiveness and of destructive ideas that go with loving. The new experiences neces-

5 While Winnicott clearly states his views on the relation between environment and ego maturation, he does not formulate as explicitly his views on the dependence of maturation on drive stimulation.

sitate internal reassessment, and it is this reassessment which we see as depression." If the depression is free of "impurities," the individual will recover and may be "stronger, wiser and more stable" than before. The "impurities" of which Winnicott speaks are, for example, failures of ego organization, delusions of persecution, hypochondriacal tendencies, manic defenses, and so forth.

Winnicott concludes by remarking that depression belongs to psychopathology, and may range from being severe and crippling to a passing mood in a relatively healthy person. At the normal end of this continuum, depression "is a common, almost universal, phenomenon [which] relates to mourning, to the capacity to feel guilt, and to the maturational process."

Balint

Balint's work over the past thirty years relates to the problem of individuation, although he approaches the subject mainly from the point of view of the changes which occur in the patient during the course of analysis. He has progressively refined his views over the period between his papers on "Character Analysis and New Beginning" (1932) and "The Benign and Malignant Forms of Regression" (1963). In 1952, in a paper specifically relating his view of the new beginning to Melanie Klein's work, he formulated his ideas in a way which is particularly relevant to our present topic. He points out that, in favorable cases, the analytic patient relinquishes his accustomed and automatic forms of object relationship, and makes tentative attempts to try out new ones. During the analysis he regresses to a pretraumatic, undefended state, begins anew to love and hate in a primitive way, and then develops mature and well-adapted ways of loving and hating.

Balint suggests that "The original and everlasting aim of all object relations is the primitive wish: *I must be loved* without any obligation on me and without any expectation of return from me. All 'adult' ways of object-relations, i.e. of loving and hating, are compromise formations between this original wish and the acceptance of an unkind, unpleasant, indifferent reality." It is this point which he believes is reached in the type of regression which he describes, and from which the "new beginnings" take their origin.

In the period preceding the new beginning, the patient's attitude is characterized by deep suspiciousness. "Everything, the most every-day happening, will inevitably be referred to the patient's own person." There are certain patients who can be successfully helped through this phase, which Balint links with Melanie Klein's paranoid position (although he does not accept her view that it constitutes the first phase of extra-uterine existence). These patients then experience a state of depression (which has a different mechanism from the melancholic depressions discussed by Abraham and Freud). The essence of the depression is the feeling of being worthless and unlovable, and a belief that change for the better is impossible. There follows a hard and painful fight to give up "parts of ourselves as unlovable and unacceptable to our fellow men." During this struggle, these patients show dejection, loss of interest in the outside world, loss of the capacity to love, inhibition of activity, and a lowered self-esteem.

Balint points out that everyday adaptation to reality means the sacrifice of wishes which constitute part of the personality. Adaptation, together with mourning and all forms of depression, implies the acceptance of unpleasure. The narcissistic wound which results brings about responses which show both paranoid and depressive mechanisms. In the type of depression which is involved in the new beginning, the patient's aim is different from that which he has in other depressive states, in that it is now to enable the patient to be at one with himself.

"New beginning" thus implies, first, the abandonment of a paranoid attitude, and secondly, the acceptance of a certain amount of depression as "an inevitable condition of life." With this is coupled "the confidence that it is possible—nay certain—to emerge from this kind of depression as a better man."

Balint remarks later in his paper that real adaptations, which mean the acceptance of unpleasure, are possible only if depression can be faced without undue anxiety. Every line of development must pass through this focus.

Balint has always been an uncompromising opponent of the theory of primary narcissism. As a consequence he has suggested that the wish "I want to be loved" is the final goal of all erotic striving (1937). This view is unacceptable to us, as it seems to be based on a confusion (which he shares with Melanie Klein) between the roles of the biological and psychological objects of the instinctual drives. Balint does, however, refer to the outcome of gratification as being a quiet, tranquil sense of well-being, and with this we would fully agree. We also find ourselves in agreement with his view that adaptation to reality always implies the acceptance of unpleasure and the relinquishing of certain valued parts of the personality, although we would formulate this in terms of acceptance of pain, the giving up of the striving toward infantile ideal states of the self, and all the sacrifices which have to be made in the renunciation of infantile modes of instinctual satisfaction.

Curiously enough, although Balint's "primary love" is conceptualized in terms of an object relationship existing from the beginning, many of his formulations are couched in terms which refer to states of the self; depression (not melancholia), for example, is related to "a deep, painful, narcissistic wound."

Recently Balint (1959, 1963) has modified his views on early development, and described a phase before that of the emergence of primary objects, one which he refers to as that of the "undifferentiated environment." While Balint still insists on putting his thesis in terms of relationships (in this phase an interpenetrating relationship with primary substances), he is clearly concerned with the infant's feelings before objects have been differentiated in the psychological world of the child. He has also qualified (1963) his use of the term "regression," and has expressed the view that "new beginning" is not a true regression, or a repetition of a previous experience, but a new discovery, leading to a different, more satisfactory relationship to an important object. We would suggest that Balint has in fact described a process of individuation occurring as a special experience in the analytic situation.

Bowlby

Over the past decade Bowlby has contributed substantially to the literature on separation and mourning (1954, 1960a, 1960b, 1960c, 1961a, 1961b, 1962a, 1962b). He has taken the view that the occurrence of separation anxiety (the fear of loss of the object) plays a crucial part in normal and pathological development, and although much of his work is not directly connected with our present topic, we shall comment briefly on those aspects which relate to individuation. It is important to note that the research strategy followed by Bowlby is to study the effects of object loss occurring at different ages and in different conditions; the depressive reaction is only one of many possible outcomes of object loss. Nor does Bowlby necessarily relate depression only to the specific event of object loss, and he does not attempt to construct a theory to account for all depressive reactions (Bowlby, 1965).

Taking into account observations made by Robertson (1953a, 1953b; Robertson and Bowlby, 1952), three phases in the child's reaction to gross separation (e.g., hospitalization) have been described. The initial phase of *protest* is one in which "the instinctual response systems binding the bereaved to the lost object remain focused on the object, because during this phase yearning and an angry effort to recover the lost object seem to be the rule" (Bowlby, 1962a). We would see this as a phase of anger and discontent prompted by the changed state of the self arising, in this case, from the disappearance of the object. The child in this phase is certainly an unhappy child, reacting to pain with protest. We take the view that this particular type of response occurs frequently as a reaction to all states of mental pain, however determined.

The second phase is that of *despair,* described by Bowlby as follows (1960a): "The active physical movements diminish or come to an end, and he may cry monotonously or intermittently. He is withdrawn and inactive, makes no demand on the environment, and appears to be in a state of deep mourning." This would appear to correspond to the depressive affective response which we have described. However, Bowlby's interpretation of the child's behavior in this phase as *mourning* can, in our view, be questioned. He sees mourning as the set of psychological processes which are initiated by the loss of the love object, and which usually lead to relinquishment of the object. We find this definition too general, and suggest that it is valuable to differentiate pain (whatever the cause) from the depressive response as such, and from mourning. In the depressive response the yearning for the lost state is suppressed through a generalized inhibition of function, without modification of the content of the ideal self. Mourning, in contrast, can be regarded as involving a continual facing of the painful situation, a gradual acceptance of the fact of the unattainability of the lost ideal state through a continual contrasting of the lost and wished-for state with present reality. This leads to a gradual recovery of hope through the creation of new ideals.

Bowlby's third phase is that of *detachment*. The child "no longer rejects the nurses, accepts their care and the food and the toys they bring, and may even smile and be sociable. When his mother visits, however, it can be seen that all is not well. . . . So far from greeting his mother he may seem hardly to know her; so far from clinging to her, he may remain remote and apathetic; instead of tears there is a listless turning away. He seems to have lost all interest in her" (1960a). We would suggest that the basic process in this phase is an attempt to restore a minimum level of well-being and feelings of safety. Whereas in the phase of despair we can discern a general inhibition of both id and ego functions, in the phase of detachment we can postulate a partial lifting of the generalized inhibition which is characteristic of the depressive response. This is made possible by a form of ego restriction, in particular a restriction of attention and a flattening of feelings. It shows itself in a devaluation of the unique affective importance of the mother or indeed of any object. The child settles, so to speak, for its actual state of the self. It is a type of resignation which can be seen as an attempt to do away with the awareness of the discrepancy between actual self and ideal self, and in this sense it is a form of adaptation which stands in contrast to processes of mourning.

Although Bowlby's three sequential phases may be an appropriate description of the reactions of children to gross separation experiences under unfavorable conditions, they do not necessarily occur as a response to painful states of the self in general. We can discern all the elements of Bowlby's phases as isolated responses to pain, or combined in a variety of different ways. Some children react with a state of unhappiness and discontent, in which much hostility is evident. We can also see states of despair and responses of depression with or without a previous phase of "protest." And, of course, there exists the whole gamut of defensive operations directed either against the experiencing of pain or against the emergence of depressive affect. One particular defensive operation (among many) is "detachment," a reaction which is not an inherent response to a separation experience but rather one fostered by deficiencies in the supporting environment. We believe that "detachment" may occur even in situations where there is no actual separation, but rather chronically inadequate mothering.

The processes which Bowlby has studied relate to gross separation experiences, in which the attention of both child and observer is focused on the loss of the object. Starting from such observations as these it would seem, on the face of it, to be understandable that so much emphasis has been placed on the state of object loss as such. Although Bowlby has elaborated what is essentially an object-oriented psychology, he does not believe, as Melanie Klein and Balint do, that psychological object relationships exist from the beginning. He says (1965):

> In an infant's behavioural equipment there is a built-in bias, genetically determined, that in the ordinary expectable environment leads to the development of object relations. The built-in bias is there from the first: the actual development of object relations takes time. The same is true of arms and legs. In the fertilised ovum there is a strong predisposition to develop arms and legs; but they take time actually to develop and, as the thalidomide story illustrates, they only do so if the chemical and physical environment is within certain limits.

Our own view in this connection is that psychological object relationships cannot start until a sufficient degree of perceptual differentiation has occurred, although when they have developed they come to play an increasingly important role in the life of the child. They are crucial to the maintenance of well-being, which is, psychically and biologically, a state of the self. Object loss may bring about acute mental pain through creating a "wound" in the self. This view coincides with what Abraham and others have described as the "severe injury to infantile narcissism" which object loss entails. And although Bowlby has maintained (1960b) that such a statement misses the true significance of object loss, we take the view that it contains its essence.

III

Some Further Comments

Both Winnicott and Melanie Klein assume that the depressive reaction can occur only when a certain stage of development, characterized mainly by the capacity for "whole object" relationships and associated ambivalence toward the object, is reached. Both assume the depressive response to be a much more integrated one than the response characteristic of the preceding developmental stage.

The notion of a point in early development when a variety of highly complicated psychological changes take place almost simultaneously (as embodied in the theory of the depressive position) is one which we do not find convincing. What Melanie Klein sees as a "position" seems to us to be an oversimplified condensation of a number of different facets of development which extend over varying lengths of time. These developmental processes include the emergence of social responses (as distinct from purely drive-satisfying behavior), the development of the capacity to recognize specific objects, the capacity to visualize the object in its absence (and to distinguish such visualization from perception), the development of ambivalence, the need to make reparation, the development of an internally structured superego, and so on.

Central to the theory of the depressive position is the role of aggression and ambivalence. While we would agree that conflict over ambivalence is an important source of pain, and therefore also a possible source of the depressive response, we consider it to be only one of a number of possible sources of pain, and the depressive response is by no means specifically and uniquely related to it.

Although Freud saw the painful state of longing in terms of the libidinal aspect of object relationships (1926), there is little doubt that the role of aggression is vitally important. As Freud put it in "Instincts and their Vicissitudes" (1915):

> It is noteworthy that in the use of the word 'hate' no . . . intimate connection with sexual pleasure and the sexual function appears. The relation of *unpleasure* seems to be the sole decisive one. The ego hates, abhors and pursues with intent to destroy all objects which are a source of unpleasurable feeling for it. . . . Indeed, it may be asserted that the true prototypes of the relation of hate are derived not from sexual life, but from the ego's struggle to preserve and maintain itself.

We can add that just as the child's love for the object has its counterpart in feelings of well-being in the self derived from the object relationship, so is there a state of the self which mirrors a *hostile* relationship to the object. If the object were only hated, loss of the object would tend to restore well-being, and the loss would be accompanied by relief because of the lessening of unpleasure in the self, and the resulting approximation of the self to an ideal state. Here again, the feelings of unpleasure may be related by the child to the object representation which is felt to be the source of the existence of the undesired, painful, state of the self.

If the object were only loved, regaining of the lost object would equally restore a sense of well-being. However, once the child has achieved a degree of object constancy, once so-called whole-object relationships have been established, no object is only hated or only loved. In simple ambivalence there is, on the one hand, the wish to maintain well-being in the self by ensuring the object's presence; on the other, there is a wish for it to disappear because it arouses feelings of unpleasure or pain in the self. This creates a state of conflict, and there are a variety of ways in which attempts may be made to deal with this conflict. There can be, for instance, the splitting of ambivalence, so that either the loved or hated aspect of the object is displaced onto another person who is treated accordingly; or one facet of the ambivalence may simply be denied or repressed. There can be identification with some attribute of the object. There are the various forms of externalization of an aspect of the self representation (more commonly the aggressive aspect) as in projection ("I do not hate him, he hates me"); and, indeed, all the defense mechanisms can be called into play to deal with the conflict situation. The child may also attempt to control his environment by clinging or other methods of manipulating the object, but if his ambivalence is intense, no state of his environment will be felt to be satisfactory to him, i.e., will be capable of producing feelings of well-being in the self.

It is self-evident that the situation of ambivalence which we have described is a painful one. The child cannot in reality approximate the actual state of his self to that of an ideal state, because the ideal object (which would only be loved and only love in return) and which would create a state of perfect contentment in the self does not exist in reality. It is here that the child so often turns to idealization and compensation in fantasy.

It seems obvious that pain is in itself not the depressive reaction. If the internal or external situation can be successfully defended against, the pain will lessen or disappear. If the child reacts to the experience of pain by an increase in his discontent, and, in particular, if he regresses to an oral demanding attitude, he becomes the typically unhappy and complaining child with whom we are all familiar. In such cases one often sees an inner source of discontent, one which may have a long history in the development of the child, displaced onto the external environment, so that nothing really satisfies, nothing pleases. Children defend against the recognition of an inner source of pain, and find it more comfortable to blame an object for it.

This brings us to a further important point. If a state of pain is experienced in the self, then the actual self may become an object of the child's anger or even hate. It is an unsatisfactory self, and will be invested with aggressive cathexis. *The child may experience a state of ambivalence toward his own self.* This is quite distinct from the phenomenon of aggression directed toward the self on the basis of identification with an ambivalently loved object. Unless this is successfully dealt with by some externalizing mechanism, the child may become the victim of a circular process, in which ambivalence toward the self increases the degree of pain and discontent.

Important sources of pain are external authority figures (or the superego, once it has been established). Anger felt toward the object world (and the introjects) may be inhibited because of the fear of retaliation. Fear of punishment and guilt are themselves sources of pain; but, in addition, if the ego deals with these feelings by directing aggression against the self, then this too will result in pain. Aggression may be turned toward the self by a process of displacement from the object or via identification with the hated object.

The condensation of pain and depressive affect evident in the writings of Melanie Klein may perhaps have come about because of a tendency to confuse the depressive response with those feelings of misery and unhappiness which constitute a patient's inevitable response to successful analytic confrontation with the narcissistically painful state of his self. This unhappiness is not the same as the specific type of adaptation to pain which is the depressive response. The quality of the patient's response to the painful state will depend, to a very large degree, on the extent to which he is able to express and discharge the relevant hostile and aggressive feelings toward (what he regards as) the source of his pain.

The failure to distinguish between pain and depression lends itself to the elaboration of misleading and stereotyped links between the wide field of disturbance of narcissism and the specific affective response of depression. An individual may, for example, react to a painful discrepancy between the ideal self and his actual self by a response of angry resentment, or by overcompensation in fantasy, or by exhibitionistic behavior. This does not imply that he is either experiencing a depressive response or defending against one. What we can say, however, is that if he could, in some way, be prevented from using such defenses against the painful state in the self, and then reacted with a feeling of hopelessness and helplessness, he would become depressed. Thus, whereas Winnicott and Melanie Klein might see, for instance, phallic overassertiveness as a specific defense against depression, we would say that it can be more fruitfully considered to be, for example, a defense against a painful narcissistic wound. Only if the individual abandoned his existing adaptive and defensive measures, felt helpless and lost hope, would he then become depressed.

One of the effects of the development of the depressive reaction is a lowering of the level of drive activity and an inhibition of ego functions (Bibring, 1953). This is very much like a process of hibernation, or what Winnicott (1954) describes as "wet-blanketing." While it would appear that such a lowering of the level of mental functioning provides a breathing space which may, in certain cases, allow processes of recovery to occur, we do not believe that the experience of depression is a necessary precondition for recovery. It may, of course, ultimately prove to have been of value to the individual if he successfully recovers from it and if it does not become a habit. We deplore the tendency among some analysts to elevate depression to the status of a virtue without regard to the distinction between the mastery of pain in an adaptive way, the depressive response, and melancholia.

IV

Individuation

In our previous paper on this topic it was suggested that in the course of normal development the child constantly experiences discrepancies between actual and ideal states of the self. His progressive movement toward the appreciation of reality involves the relinquishing of previously experienced satisfactory states of the self. In the child's early years these satisfactory states have been felt to be magical and omnipotent. We said: "this is a spur to adaptation, and the attractions offered by the child's new potentialities and experiences enable him to withdraw cathexis from the lost ideal states with the minimum of pain, cathexis which can be invested in new ideals created by processes of maturation and the move forward into a fresh developmental phase."

The picture of a smooth move forward conveyed by this statement is an optimal one, never occurring fully in reality. Conditions of frustration and suffering will bring about a turning toward the attainment of previous infantile ideals which can be reached in fact or in fantasy. This is probably the essence of the processes of temporary regression which we see in the course of normal development. The regression may in fact function as an attempt to stave off helplessness and its possible sequel, the depressive response. The overcoming of regression and the subsequent move forward must inevitably be linked with some degree of suffering, however small, and it follows that a process in some way analogous to processes of mourning must normally occur. The mourning is,[6] in this case, associated with the pain of giving up infantile ideal states of the self (but not necessarily with depression). This process is among those which have been referred to as individuation by Jung, Erich Fromm,[7] and

---

[6] The relation between mourning for a lost object and adaptation has been extensively discussed by Pollock (1961). His emphasis is, however, on adaptation to a changed external reality, while our own is related to adaptation to a loss of an ideal state of the self.

[7] The dictionary definition of the term "individuation" is the action or process of individuating, i.e., the process leading to individual existence, as distinct from that of the species. This usage dates at least from 1628. It also means the condition of being an individual, individuality, personal identity (1642). The biological meaning of the term is the sum of the processes on which the life of the individual depends (nineteenth century). For Jung (1923), individuation "is the process of forming and specialising the individual nature—in particular, it is the development of the psychological

Margaret Mahler. We shall adhere to the same term, meaning by it the gradual development of increasingly reality-adapted ideals for the child,[8] with the associated giving up of infantile aims and dependence on external objects for supplies of well-being.

This relates closely to the ideas expressed by Margaret Mahler (1952, 1957, 1958, 1961, 1963; Mahler and Furer, 1963). She has, over a number of years, elaborated her concepts of normal developmental phases in terms of *autism, symbiosis, and separation-individuation.* The separation-individuation phase is one in which the infant develops into a toddler, delimiting his own individual entity from the primal symbiotic mother-infant unit. It is in this phase that he separates the mental representation of his own self from that of the mother, and it occurs simultaneously with the consolidation and maturation of autonomous ego functions. The development of locomotion allows the child to separate from the mother, and he will then show pleasure in his new independence and mastery. He may, however, show anxiety at this separateness. Mahler emphasizes that such anxiety occurs even in the presence of the mother during the "separation-individuation" phase (in contrast to situations of traumatic separation of the type described by Bowlby). Mahler (1963) speaks of the "minimal threats of object loss which the maturationally predetermined ascendance of autonomous functioning by necessity entails." She makes a valuable point when she emphasizes that the development of autonomous functions itself constitutes a threat of some sort to the child. But whereas she sees the danger, however slight, in terms of threats of object loss, we would

---

individual as a differentiated being from the general, collective psychology. Individuation, therefore, is a *process of differentiation,* having for its goal the development of the individual personality." A discussion of the Jungian view has been presented by Fordham (1958).

Erich Fromm (1941) regards the process of individuation as the emergence of the individual from his original ties. He has discussed the process primarily in terms of the relation of the individual to society, pointing out that the individual pays the price of "growing isolation, insecurity . . . and a growing feeling of one's own powerlessness and insignificance as an individual." As this process occurs it may result in anxiety and insecurity or in a new relationship with others if the child has been able to build up the necessary inner strength and productiveness. Fromm's view of this process is, in one sense, close to Jung's; but in so far as he deals with the growing individual's attempts to cope with pain through the development of new ideals, his view is related to ours. Tomkins (1963) has recently discussed the relation between what he refers to as "distress-anguish" and individuation, and has related many aspects of progressive development to the mastery of unpleasant affect.

[8] Identification plays an important role in this connection.

stress the painful necessity for the child to give up *ideal states of the self* previously experienced during the "symbiotic" phase. The mother representation is, of course, after a certain level of development has been reached, the prime perceptual key to states of well-being. In addition, the substitution of what might be called "pleasure in function," for libidinal gratifications through the object, is an important element in the formation of new, reality-adapted ideals for the child (Hendrick, 1942, 1943).

In addition to obtaining "pleasure in function" and "pleasure in mastery," the toddler attaches a "cathexis of value" or "value accent" (Hartmann, 1947) to his newly acquired achievements, and the alteration in his ideal self which ensues is one which enables him to achieve unity of actual self and ideal through his independent activities. The effective operation of this process minimizes the pain involved in the abandonment of previous mother-dependent ideal states of the self. Erikson (1946) describes this: "To be 'one who can walk' becomes one of the many steps in child development which through the coincidence of physical mastery and cultural meaning, of functional pleasure and social recognition, contribute to a more realistic self-esteem."

It follows that individuation involves not only the giving up of the wish for past and inappropriate ideal states and the acquisition of new phase-specific reality-adapted ideals, but also the gradual attainment of pleasure in function and mastery (in addition to the gratification afforded by direct drive discharge).

In contrast to those who see such processes as occurring in a specific developmental phase, we consider individuation to be a line of development which continues throughout life. While it is true that failures in early development may later make individuation difficult, and conversely, that adequate early individuation lays the foundation for more successful individuation later in life, the growing individual is constantly confronted with situations which require further processes of individuation. Anna Freud (1963a) has described, in another context, certain developmental tasks which occur in the life of the child.[9] These situations confront the individual, we be-

[9] For example, separation from the mother; birth of a sibling; illness and surgical intervention; hospitalization; entry into nursery school; school entry; the step from a triangular oedipal situation into a community of peers; the step from play to work; the arousal of new genital strivings in adolescence; the step from infantile objects within the family to new objects outside the family.

lieve, with important individuation tasks and extend into adult life in such situations as university entrance, taking a job, engagement and marriage, parenthood, mid-life crises, menopause, bereavement, adaptation to retirement and old age, and so on. In each of these there is the necessity to relinquish not only earlier modes of drive satisfaction, but also previously satisfying or secure states of the self, in the service of adaptation. When individuation proceeds smoothly, the positive gains in well-being outweigh any pain which might accompany the loss of a previous source of satisfaction and states of the self.

The specific tasks and crisis situations which we have mentioned may exist as external sources of pain in their own right. The recognition of such situations forms a basis for the clinical approach of many practitioners in social and preventive psychiatry. However, it is common analytic experience that such tasks or demands are significant to the extent to which they are involved in the individual's unconscious inner conflicts.[10] What may appear as an external crisis may be predominantly an internal one, but we can distinguish between those situations which are created entirely by the repetition compulsion or by the need to externalize inner conflict and those which stimulate and intensify existing conflicts (either by disrupting the defensive organization or by reinforcing repressed infantile wishes or fantasies). Some individuals can deal with the painful state which arises only by attempting to reapply past solutions, while others may be able, under the pressure of the need to adapt to the new situation, to relinquish the tie to previous ideal selves in the process of individuation.[11]

The turning toward new, more reality-adapted ideals in the interest of pain avoidance does not necessitate a slavish acceptance of culturally determined norms. The important point here is that

[10] The significance of external situations may be greater for the child before external conflict has been fully internalized. However, he constantly experiences internal developmental crises (e.g., the threats to security brought about by the realization of the failure of his omnipotence in the anal phase; by the need to reconcile himself to the unattainability of his oedipal objects, etc.).

[11] In this paper we are dealing with the problem of individuation in fairly general terms. It is not our intention to discuss here the question of the role of the superego introjects and the whole problem of individuation from the infantile ideals which they sustain. This topic, crucial to the analytic process, will be discussed in a later communication.

the new ideals, if individuation is successful, diminish, by means of their conflict-reducing character, the possibility of the individual's paralysis through intolerable feelings of ambivalence and envy. On the contrary, they permit progressive personality development to take place. We have stressed the construction of reality-syntonic ideals as an essential aspect of the process of individuation. It is clear, however, that these new ideals must have conflict-reducing properties. They may be regarded as ego-syntonic compromise formations, compounded of both external and internal reality.

Although we have spoken of the "giving up" of earlier ideals in individuation, what is given up is the pursuit of these infantile ideals by the ego in relatively unmodified form, through the establishment of appropriate countercathexes. These ideals are given up as unrealistic, although the fantasy content of previous ideals may show itself in the compromise formation which has become the new, reality-adapted ideal.

If we consider the relation of pain to depression and individuation, then a particular statement made by Melanie Klein is of some interest. In her paper on "Mourning and Its Relation to Manic-Depressive States" (1948) she remarks: " . . . any pain, caused by unhappy experiences, whatever their nature, has something in common with mourning. It reactivates the infantile depressive position; the encountering and overcoming of adversity of any kind entails mental work similar to mourning." This statement has something in common with what we have described as individuation; but we do not believe it necessary to evoke an infantile "depressive position" to explain adaptive responses to painful adversities. Nor do we consider that the loss entailed in "the encountering and overcoming of adversity of any kind" is always object loss, be it in the present or in the past, in reality or in fantasy, or of an internal or an external object. Further, we do not believe that we should take it as axiomatic that the "working through" involved in overcoming adversity is always accompanied by depressive affect, consciously or unconsciously.[12]

12 It has been suggested that there is a possible link between our views and Melanie Klein's idea of the infant's need to make reparation. There may indeed be a common element in the notion of "restoring the wished-for state" and the process of reparation referred to by Melanie Klein in connection with the working through of the depressive position. In making this comparison we should bear in mind that there are

In this paper we have viewed the process of individuation predominantly from the side of the ego. Yet it represents, in a sense, a line of development which includes changes on the side of the drives, particularly as drive and ego development normally go hand in hand. What we have viewed as the state of well-being is genetically linked with the attained state of drive satisfaction (but not necessarily with the pleasures which arise during the course of drive discharge). During the course of development the individual may retain ideal self representations which reflect earlier states of instinctual satisfaction, even though the drives may have proceeded further along their developmental path. Normal individuation will therefore include the changes in the ideal self which are appropriate to drive progression.[13]

Conclusion

We have defined mental pain, whatever its cause and extent, as reflecting a discrepancy between an actual state of the self and an ideal wished-for state. This can be based on the memory of a pre-

---

two sides to the process of reparation as described by Melanie Klein. The first aspect relates to the *restoration* of a previous state, and the second to the need to *make amends* because of guilt about the effects of sadistic attacks on the love object. While the dictionary definition includes these alternative meanings of reparation (i.e., restoration and making amends), the two are not always the same. In so far as Melanie Klein uses reparation in the sense of repair or restoration, we could find ourselves on common ground with her. But we do not believe that the motive for restoration is always to make amends for a sadistic attack on the object. In order to avoid misunderstanding we would like to say at this point that we recognize that fantasies of sadistic attacks on the object can be an important source of pain (or the special form of pain which may be found in guilt) and that making amends to the object may be one form of dealing with such pain. However, what we refer to in our paper in this connection is a functional process in the ego whereby the ego attempts to maintain a state of maximal well-being. We have put forward the view that in painful states, whatever their cause, there is, of course, a loss of well-being, and that the ego may strive in many different ways to restore the ideal affective state. This may be attempted by defensive maneuvers of one sort or another, through attempts to recreate regressively past ideal situations, or through the progressive creation of new ideals (which we have called individuation). We do not subscribe to the view that it is always and only guilt about destruction of love objects which is the primary motive for restoration in the sense in which we use the word.

13 The whole topic of the discrepancy between drive progression on the one hand and changes in content of the ideal self on the other requires much further study. For example, we have the very interesting situation in certain individuals in whom changes in the ideal self occur in advance of drive progression. Perhaps we can include in this broad group the case of the highly gifted person who has achieved an apparently successful adaptation through what might be termed *pseudo individuation*, based on a massive magical identification with an idealized object.

vious state of satisfaction or on fantasies which may have multiple determinants.

From the point of view of the drives, the normal response to pain is aggression, directed at whatever is considered to be the source of the pain. Projective, identificatory, and displacement processes enter here, in both normal and pathogenic development. Particularly after object constancy has been attained, the object representation comes to be an essential component of ideal states of well-being. Although clinically we may deal with states of object loss, we would stress again that what is lost in object loss is ultimately a state of the self for which the object is the vehicle. A failure to defend against pain, to discharge aggression adequately, or to reduce an intolerable "cathexis of longing" may be followed by a depressive response.

From the point of view of the ego there are many possible responses to pain. Prominent among these is individuation, a process which involves "working through" in a manner analogous to mourning. It involves the adaptive abandoning of the pursuit of lost ideal states and their replacement by new ideals which are both ego and reality syntonic. Individuation occurs as a process throughout life, and in particular is associated with typical developmentally and culturally determined tasks and crises. It can fail for many reasons and such failure may be followed by maldevelopment or a depressive response.

The depressive response has previously been described in some detail. It represents a capitulation in the face of pain, a capitulation which involves a generalized inhibition of drive and ego functions. While this may blunt the pain and provide time for recovery, *it is not aimed at recovery*. It may be followed by individuation, but it may also be followed by other defensive measures which do not result in individuation; nor is depression an essential prerequisite for individuation.[14]

14 We want to emphasize this point, for we believe that the association of depression with that individuation which occurs during the course of analysis is, to some extent, imposed by the analytic process itself. If a patient is confronted with a painful state which he has been defending against, and if all his further defensive attempts are aborted by interpretation, depression may follow as a natural consequence. Recovery from this depressive response may be associated with gradual working through and individuation with the help of the analysis. The occurrence of the depressive response *may indicate* that other defenses against pain are no longer effective. It is an aspect of correct analytic technique that it promotes conditions which facilitate progressive

Theoretically, optimal individuation could be regarded as a relatively painless, depression-free process. In reality it is never seen without some degree of pain. In addition to this, there is often some degree of temporary regression to early ideal or idealized states, regression of the sort which is found in the course of normal development (Anna Freud, 1963b).

There are many factors which influence and determine the outcome of the individual's struggle to master pain and depression, and we should be wary of regarding any one specific cause, or a failure in any one developmental phase, as being the sole factor in determining the outcome of such a struggle. We can recognize, to mention but a few, the influence of constitutional factors (including the predisposition to use particular defenses, frustration and discharge thresholds, differences in the apparatuses of primary autonomy, and variations in drive endowment), the nature of the holding environment at various times in the person's life, the intensity of phase-specific anxieties, the influence of drive fixation points, and all the vicissitudes of superego formation.

BIBLIOGRAPHY

Balint, M. (1932), Character Analysis and New Beginning. In: *Primary Love and Psycho-Analytic Technique*. London: Hogarth Press, 1952.
—— (1937), Early Developmental Stages of the Ego. In: *Primary Love and Psycho-Analytic Technique*. London: Hogarth Press, 1952.
—— (1952), New Beginning and the Paranoid and the Depressive Syndromes. In: *Primary Love and Psycho-Analytic Technique*. London: Hogarth Press, 1952.
—— (1959), *Thrills and Regressions*. New York: International Universities Press.
—— (1963),The Benign and Malignant Forms of Regression. In: *New Perspectives in Psychoanalysis*, ed. G. E. Daniels. New York: Grune & Stratton.
Bibring, E. (1953), The Mechanism of Depression. In: *Affective Disorders*, ed. P. Greenacre. New York: International Universities Press.

individuation. This is especially important in ·the case of those patients who cannot individuate without a measure of depression. The view expressed by Winnicott that depression contains a "built-in" therapy reflects a view which we do not share. We know that depressions tend to lift, particularly if, as Winnicott has put it, they are not contaminated by "impurities." We would correlate this, however, with the ego's recovery, and it does not imply that the painful state of affairs which prompted the depressive response has been resolved. In many instances the lifting of the depression is associated with nothing else but the bringing into play of more effective defenses, and the subsequent failure of these may be the reason that so many depressions tend to recur. The aspect of recurrence should always be considered when the aspect of remission is considered.

Bowlby, J. (1954), Psychopathological Processes Set in Train by Early Mother-Child Separation. In: *Infancy and Childhood*, ed. M. J. E. Senn. New York: Josiah Macy, Jr. Foundation.
—— (1960a), Separation Anxiety. *Int. J. Psa.*, 41:89-113.
—— (1960b), Grief and Mourning in Infancy and Early Childhood. *This Annual*, 15:9-52.
—— (1960c), Ethology and the Development of Object Relations. *Int. J. Psa.*, 41:313-317.
—— (1961a), Separation Anxiety: A Critical Review of the Literature. *J. Child Psychol. & Psychiat.*, 1:251-269.
—— (1961b), Processes of Mourning. *Int. J. Psa.*, 42:317-340.
—— (1962a), Pathological Mourning and Childhood Mourning. *J. Amer. Psa. Assn.*, 11:500-541.
—— (1962b), Loss, Detachment and Defence. Unpublished manuscript.
—— (1965), Personal communication.
Erikson, E. H. (1946), Ego Development and Historical Change. *This Annual*, 2:359-396.
Fordham, M. (1958), *The Objective Psyche*. London: Routledge & Kegan Paul.
Freud, A. (1963a), The Concept of Developmental Lines. *This Annual*, 18:245-265.
—— (1963b), Regression as a Principle in Mental Development. *Bull. Menninger Clin.*, 27:126-139.
Freud, S. (1914), On Narcissism: An Introduction. *Standard Edition*, 14:69-102. London: Hogarth Press, 1957.
—— (1915), Instincts and Their Vicissitudes. *Standard Edition*, 14:111-140. London: Hogarth Press, 1957.
—— (1926), Inhibitions, Symptoms and Anxiety. *Standard Edition*, 20:77-174. London: Hogarth Press, 1959.
Fromm, E. (1941), *Escape from Freedom*. New York: Rinehart.
Hartmann, H. (1947), On Rational and Irrational Action. *Essays on Ego Psychology*. New York: International Universities Press, 1964.
Hendrick, I. (1942), Instinct and the Ego during Infancy. *Psa. Quart.*, 11:33-58.
—— (1943), Work and the Pleasure Principle. *Psa. Quart.*, 12:311-329.
Jacobson, E. (1953), Contribution to the Metapsychology of Cyclothymic Depression. In: *Affective Disorders*, ed. P. Greenacre. New York: International Universities Press.
Jung, C. G. (1923), *Psychological Types*. London: Kegan Paul.
Klein, M. (1948), *Contributions to Psycho-Analysis, 1921-1945*. London: Hogarth Press.
—— (1957), *Envy and Gratitude*. London: Tavistock.
Mahler, M. S. (1952), On Child Psychosis and Schizophrenia. *This Annual*, 7:286-305.
—— (1957), On Two Crucial Phases of Integration Concerning Problems of Identity: Separation Individuation and Bisexual Identity. Abstr. in Panel on Problems of Identity, rep. D. Rubinfine. *J. Amer. Psa. Assn.*, 6:131-142.
—— (1958), Autism and Symbiosis: Two Extreme Disturbances of Identity. *Int. J. Psa.*, 39:77-83.
—— (1961), On Sadness and Grief in Infancy and Childhood: Loss and Restoration of the Symbiotic Love Object. *This Annual*, 16:332-351.
—— (1963), Thoughts about Development and Individuation. *This Annual*, 18:307-324.
—— & Furer, M. (1963), Certain Aspects of the Separation-Individuation Phase. *Psa. Quart.*, 32:1-14.
Pollock, G. H. (1961), Mourning and Adaptation. *Int. J. Psa.*, 42:341-361.
Provence, S. & Lipton, R. C. (1962), *Infants in Institutions*. New York: International Universities Press.
Robertson, James (1953a), Film: *A Two-Year-Old Goes to Hospital*. London: Tavistock Child Development Research Unit.

—— (1953b), Some Responses of Young Children to Loss of Maternal Care. *Nursing Times.* 49:382-386.

—— & Bowlby, J. (1952), Responses of Young Children to Separation from Their Mothers. *Courrier de Centre International de l'Enfance,* 2:131-142.

Sandler, J. (1960), The Background of Safety. *Int. J. Psa.,* 41:352-356.

—— & Joffe, W. G. (1965), Notes on Childhood Depression. *Int. J. Psa.,* 46:88-96.

—— & Rosenblatt, B. (1962), The Concept of the Representational World. *This Annual,* 17:128-145.

Segal, H. (1964), *Introduction to the Work of Melanie Klein.* London: Heinemann.

Tomkins, S. S. (1963), *Affect, Imagery, Consciousness.* Vol. II: *The Negative Affects.* New York: Springer.

Winnicott, D. W. (1954), The Depressive Position in Normal Emotional Development. *Collected Papers.* London: Tavistock, 1958, 262-277.

—— (1956), On Transference. *Int. J. Psa.,* 37:386-388.

—— (1958), Psycho-Analysis and the Sense of Guilt. In: *Psycho-Analysis and Contemporary Thought,* ed. J. D. Sùtherland. London: Hogarth Press.

—— (1964), The Value of Depression. *Brit. J. Psychiat. Soc. Work,* 7:123-127.

Zetzel, E. R. (1960), Introduction to the Symposium on 'Depressive Illness'. *Int. J. Psa.,* 41:476-480.

NOTES ON OBSESSIONAL MANIFESTATIONS
IN CHILDREN

JOSEPH SANDLER, Ph.D., D.Sc. and

W. G. JOFFE, M.B., B.Ch., D.P.M.

In collaboration with S. Baker and M. Burgner

(London)

I

In surveying the psychoanalytic literature on the obsessive-compulsive disorders one cannot fail to be impressed by the fact that there appears to be a continuing need to re-examine this topic. Yet, in spite of this, over the years little essential change has occurred in our views on obsessional phenomena. There is no doubt that Freud's ideas on the subject have stood the test of time and of clinical experience, and the fact that so many authors have arrived at formulations which are fundamentally identical with Freud's testifies to this; at the same time, their very need to explore and re-explore obsessional disturbances bears witness to a feeling that the subject is still far from being well understood; a feeling which has found its expression in the main topic of this Congress.

In the present paper we want to examine one or two facets of what is certainly a complicated subject, and we should like to begin by considering some of the manifestations of obsessive-compulsive

Presented to the 24th International Psycho-Analytical Congress, Amsterdam, July, 1965.

The material used has been collected at the Hampstead Child-Therapy Clinic, a therapeutic and research center financed by the following foundations: The Field Foundation, Inc., New York; The Anna Freud Foundation, New York; The Estate of Flora Haas, New York; The Old Dominion Foundation, U.S.A.; The Psychoanalytic Research and Development Fund Inc., New York; and the National Institute of Mental Health, Bethesda, Maryland.

This investigation was supported (in part) by Public Health Service Grant M-5683, MH (L) from the National Institute of Mental Health.

disturbances as they occur in children. The study of cases referred for diagnosis to the Hampstead Child-Therapy Clinic, as well as those cases taken into analytic treatment, has made it clear to us that there are a number of different, but in some ways very similar clinical pictures normally designated as obsessional, not all of which can be labeled "obsessional neurosis."

In considering these we need to bear in mind the fact that the term "neurosis" must to some degree be qualified when it is applied to childhood disturbances. While it is true that, from a descriptive point of view, many of the symptom constellations which present themselves during the course of development resemble the more stable adult syndromes, they are not all necessarily carried on unchanged into adult life, and they often represent solutions which become modified during the course of development. The differences between adults and children in this respect have recently been discussed in some detail by Anna Freud (1965).

The true obsessional neurosis seen in children resembles its adult counterpart very closely. Its development follows what Anna Freud has called the "classical etiological formula" for neurosis in general:

> [There is] initial developmental progress to a comparatively high level of drive and ego development (i.e., for the child to the phallic-oedipal, for the adult to the genital level); an intolerable increase of anxiety or frustration on this position (for the child of castration anxiety within the oedipus complex); regression from the age-adequate drive position to pregenital fixation points; emergence of infantile pregenital sexual-aggressive impulses, wishes, and fantasies; anxiety and guilt with regard to these, mobilizing defensive reactions on the part of the ego under the influence of the superego; defense activity leading to compromise formations; resulting character disorders or neurotic symptoms which are determined in their details by the level of the fixation points to which regression has taken place, by the content of rejected impulses and fantasies, and by the choice of the particular defense mechanisms which are being used [p. 150].

The obsessional neurosis is characterized by a drive regression to the anal-sadistic level, with heightened ambivalence. The drive impulses show the characteristic changes attributed to "drive defusion." On the side of the ego we find an increase in magical thinking, with a heightened sexual and aggressive cathexis of thought. There is a prominent use of the defense mechanisms of displacement, reaction formation, isolation, and undoing, together with the excessive use of intellectualization and rationalization. Object relationships show regressive alterations, although residua of phallic-oedipal types of relationship may be discerned. Indeed, we hardly ever see a complete and simple regression to the anal phase but rather see a regressive analization of oedipal relationships and conflicts, so that masturbation conflicts, for example, may be a dominant feature of the clinical picture.

The obsessional disturbance is marked by a tendency of the conflict to spread, with no stable compromise solution appearing as we see it in the classic hysterical symptom. There is a high degree of superego conflict, and the superego introjects show primitive features, with a reinforcement of their aggressive qualities. The form taken by the symptoms bears an intimate relationship to anal drive characteristics.

In a number of cases an obsessional neurosis which develops in childhood continues into adult life, although there may be developmental fluctuations in the intensity of the disturbance. In other cases obsessional neurotic symptoms may be transient, the regression to the anal-sadistic level being of a more temporary nature and representing a greater or lesser degree of developmental disturbance. These obsessional manifestations can occur both during childhood and adolescence, and range from an exaggeration of the type of normal ritual found in children's play, thoughts, fantasies, and general day-to-day activities, to gross symptoms which may, on the surface, appear to be indistinguishable from those of the more enduring obsessional neurosis.

A number of children show symptoms which resemble in form and content those of an obsessional neurosis, but which occur during the anal phase of development (Anna Freud, 1965). These are not, strictly speaking, neurotic in nature because they occur during the course of progressive development rather than as a consequence of regression. In these cases the ego is relatively intact, and what we see are exaggerations of the normal modes of functioning characteristic of the anal phase. In other respects, development seems to be phase-adequate. The appearance of preoedipal obsessive-compulsive manifestations has been related to precocious ego development (Wulff, 1951), a factor which Freud (1909, 1913) considered to be of importance in creating the disposition to obsessional neurosis proper. We shall return to the question of precocious ego development later.

Obsessional manifestations in the borderline child often represent attempts on the part of the child's ego to deal with threats of annihilation or disintegration which are a consequence of the borderline pathology. The child's anxiety is not primarily derived from conflict, and the symptoms may take the form of what has been described as a "pseudo neurosis." They may constitute an attempt to achieve by magical means (by excessive controlling and ritualistic behavior) a degree of security and safety (Sandler, 1960).

Obsessive-compulsive symptoms have been seen to play the role of preventing or retarding personality disintegration in adult schizophrenics (Stengel, 1945). This has been confirmed in a comprehensive study by Ismond Rosen (1954, 1957), who examined the development of obsessional symptoms (occasionally going back to childhood) prior to the onset of a schizophrenic illness. Anna Freud (1965) also drew attention to the significance of obsessional manifestations in very young children as possible indicators of "splits and disharmonies within the structure, severe enough to lead later to a psychotic total disintegration of the personality" (p. 153).

We also see the development of behavior which resembles the compulsions and rituals of obsessional neurosis in a number of children who are neither borderline nor psychotic. Among these are children who have suffered severe traumatic experiences and who attempt to deal with the aftereffects of these by a form of "mastery through repetition" which may show itself in compulsive behavior. Obsessional manifestations can also be the outcome of the ego's struggle to control and to regulate phobic anxieties. Another group of children whose narcissism is constantly threatened (this includes many children with real deformities) resort to what appears to be obsessive-compulsive behavior in an attempt to regulate their self-esteem in a magical way.

In addition to all of these, obsessional character traits and symptoms occur in a wide variety of other contexts and associated with other clinical manifestations.

II

It is convenient to begin with a discussion of the nature of the regression which we know takes place in obsessional neurosis. Classically, this has been seen as a drive regression to the anal-sadistic phase, a regression which is facilitated by the existence of strong anal fixation points on the side of the libidinal and aggressive drives, and which occurs under the influence of intense oedipal conflict. Although much is known about fixation and regression when viewed from the side of the instinctual drives, the picture is not as clear when we come to examine the topic from the point of view of the changes which occur in the ego. These have for the most part been assumed to reflect drive regression, but it has been more or less taken for granted that it is not necessary to evoke the concept of ego regression to explain the phenomena which occur. This latter concept has on the whole been reserved for structural changes which occur in organic and psychotic pathologies.

In the development of the obsessional neurosis, as in all neuroses, we find a state of conflict in which the structure of the ego remains intact, the ideals held up by the superego introjects persist, and the defensive struggle is carried on against the drives and their derivatives at the drive-regressed level, with the resulting formation of neurotic symptoms. Changes in the severity of the superego are thought to be due more to economic changes consequent on the drive regression than to structural changes per se.

This view, correct as it is, does not help us a great deal to explain the ego changes which occur in obsessional neurosis. We know that different neurotic conditions are, to some extent, distinguished by differences in the defensive activities of the ego, defenses which appear in some way to have a special link with the fixation points on the side of the drives. Thus we assume that there is an association between drive regression to anal-sadistic fixation points on the one hand and such defense mechanisms as isolation, undoing, and reaction formation on the other; and that it is this association which results in typical obsessional symptoms. The changes which occur on the side of the drives and those which occur in the ego are by no means randomly related. Indeed, we would be extremely surprised to find, for instance, regression to predominantly passive-oral drive fix-

ation points associated with the type of ego functioning and the defensive constellation which we find in obsessional neurosis. It is obvious that there is an intimate connection between the path of drive
regression and the changes in function which we see on the side of
the ego.

Although we can postulate a relationship of this sort between
drives and ego, we know that a drive regression of exactly the same
order as that which we see in obsessional neurosis need not necessarily lead to the development of obsessional symptoms. We can find,
for example, the appearance of such symptoms as soiling in children.
We also find nonobsessional anal-reactive characters as well as certain
forms of homosexuality in adults. In the past attempts have been
made to explain these clinical differences on the basis of the relative
strength of the sadistic components, the degree of instinctual defusion
involved, etc., but such notions seem to be rooted in a prestructural
emphasis on drive transformation. Today the all-important role of
the ego in determining the outcome of drive regression is obvious.

If we accept this statement, we are faced with the following problem: on the one hand a change in the ego enters into determining the
neurosis, and on the other hand its structure remains essentially un-
altered. This problem can be clarified to some extent by postulating
a distinction between ego structure and ego function.[1] This distinction is related to one which we have previously made between structural and functional autonomy of the ego (Sandler and Joffe, 1964).
We now propose to make a further distinction between structural
and functional regression of the ego, and to suggest that we see, in
the obsessional neurosis, a disturbance which is the outcome not only
of drive regression but also of functional regression of the ego. The
latter shows itself in changes in the mode of ego functioning and in
the evocation of specific defense mechanisms. The changes brought
about by the functional regression of aspects of the ego may in turn
secondarily interfere with other aspects of the ego.

We shall postulate a link between the evocation of specific defense
mechanisms and functional regression of the ego, and this point de-

---

1 The work of Hartmann (1964; Hartmann, Kris, Loewenstein, 1964) on these and
related topics is directly relevant to all the arguments in this paper. A full discussion
of the links between our own views and those of these authors is in the course of
preparation.

serves some amplification. Defenses in general can be taken to be special adaptations of normal ego functions, from which they do not essentially differ except in their application. For example, we can associate repression with the normal processes of clearing the perceptual field and separating present perception from memories of the past.[2] Denial is linked with a particular use of processes which are involved in normal concentration and attention. The defensive use of displacement can be seen to be a special application of a normal ego process which enters into such activities as symbol formation and sublimation; similar processes can be shown in all the mechanisms of defense.

It is likely that drive regression is always accompanied by some degree of functional regression in one or another area of the ego. When we come to examine the functional changes in the ego which accompany the development of obsessional disturbances, we shall see that they can be considered to be particular types of distortion or exaggeration of aspects of the ego's normal activities and functions; in particular those processes of control and mastery which are essential ingredients of secondary-process thinking. And we can add that this will occur only if the ego has specific characteristics and potentialities, i.e., if it is a particular type of ego.

Let us examine this a little further. The predisposition to a specific form of neurosis, determined as it is in part by particular drive fixation points, requires in addition that there be a correlated pattern of ego functioning which provides the appropriate matrix for the development of the specific pattern of defensive activity and the specific neurotic symptomatology. This is not to be equated with relatively macroscopic character traits, nor can we speak in general terms of intelligence and intellectual precocity in this connection. We would suggest that what is significant in the ego of the individual who may develop a particular neurotic symptomatology is (in addition to the specific drive fixation) his potentiality for using a particular type of defensive organization. This does not necessarily mean that he will have shown a disproportionate use of the defense mech-

---

2 Freud has referred to this aspect of normal mental functioning in his gem of a paper on "A Note upon the 'Mystic Writing-Pad'" (1925). The existence of a relationship between the specific mechanisms of defense and particular ego functions has been suggested and discussed by Lampl-de Groot (1965).

anisms which we know to be characteristic of specific neuroses prior
to the development of his disturbance. What he will have shown,
however, is a particular mode of perceptual and cognitive functioning. In this we are suggesting that the particular type of defensive
organization employed by the individual in situations of neurotic
conflict is as crucial to the form of his illness as is fixation and regression on the side of the drives. Further, that *this defensive organization is latent and inherent in his particular mode or style of perception and cognition.*[3]

We may now legitimately look for those factors which enter into
the development of the particular type and style of ego functioning
that forms an integral part of the predisposition to obsessional neurosis. In this we make a distinction between character structure and
style of ego functioning because we know that there is no direct correlation between the so-called "anal" character structure and obsessional neurosis. There is evidence (e.g., Sandler and Hazari, 1960)
that patients who have, for example, a reactive anal character do not
have a special tendency to develop an obsessional neurosis if they
break down.

We have spoken of the notion of a functional regression of the
ego which parallels drive regression. The question now arises whether
processes occur in the ego which are the counterpart of instinctual
drive fixation. We usually understand drive fixation in terms of
quantities of drive cathexis which remain at particular points in
psychosexual development, but it is clear that any explanation or description of drive fixation must include a consideration of the attrac-
tion of particular forms of drive discharge and the particular pleasure
qualities associated with them. There seem to be good grounds for
assuming that something similar may occur on the side of the ego
functions.

Ego functions can be viewed as the operation of the ego apparatuses of primary and secondary autonomy. But much more can
be said about them. In a previous study (1964) we have taken the
view that the functioning of the ego apparatuses is accompanied by
pleasurable experiences of a particular quality. We would say no
more here than that these experiences relate to what has been called

---

[3] We shall make no attempt to review, in this short paper, the extensive and pertinent literature on "cognitive style."

"function-pleasure" (Bühler's *Funktionslust*), pleasure in mastery and "work-pleasure" (Hendrick, 1942, 1943). These (largely precon- scious) pleasurable feeling tones accompany effective functioning of the ego, over and above any more sensual pleasures which may be generated when the ego apparatuses operate in the service of direct drive discharge.

We suggested that in the course of normal development the ego apparatuses (whether apparatuses of primary or of secondary auton- omy) gradually show some of the characteristics of modes of instinc- tual drive discharge. The prototype of this is the way in which hand grasping gradually becomes a partial substitute for grasping with the mouth, and in the same way the eye also becomes a grasping organ. In this process the ego is able to bring about a reduction of the de- mand for work imposed on it by the oral drives, but the reduction in instinctual tension in hand and eye grasping is now accompanied by pleasures in functioning, mastery, and achievement, pleasures which are considerably less sensual, less somatically based, and of a lower intensity than the affective accompaniments of primitive instinctual discharge. We put forward (1964) the notion of "affective distancing" as a correlate of autonomous ego development; however, as a conse- quence of the genetic link between specific ego apparatuses and the drives which stimulate their development, the characteristics of the original somatic drive discharge are reflected in the functioning of these ego apparatuses, even though, from a maturational point of view, they may be apparatuses of primary autonomy in the sense of Hartmann's description (1950).

It follows from this that the ego apparatuses which develop dur- ing the oral phase will show something of the qualities of the passive and active oral aims which characterized the drives operating at that time. Equally, with the move of the child into the anal phase, the various aims of the anal component instincts leave their stamp on those ego apparatuses and functions which develop during the anal phase.

It seems very likely that the quality of the so-called "distanced" ego pleasures which arise at any developmental phase bears a relation to the qualities of the somatically based pleasures associated with the direct discharge of the dominant part instincts at that time. In this sense, the id is reinstated in the ego. The pleasure in the act of grasping, for instance, is probably in some way related to the much cruder and primitive pleasures which accompanied mouth activity. Similarly, the "ego pleasures" involved in much secondary-process thinking may have something in common with the pleasures derived from direct anal discharge.

Because of the pleasurable qualities associated with particular ego functions we can assume that experiences which bring about drive fixation may also leave their mark on the ego in the form of a fixation to particular modes of ego functioning. If this view can be accepted, we are in a position to understand more of the nature of regression in general and that which occurs in obsessional neurosis in particular; and also to comment further on the question of the preconditions for the development of an obsessional neurosis.

The anal phase of development is characterized by vast strides forward on the part of the ego. The way in which ego functions develop and operate during this phase bears a close resemblance to the mode of functioning of the somatic apparatuses which subserve drive discharge in this phase. We see the development of a whole hierarchy of discharging, delaying, and controlling functions. Some of these relate to the control of feces, to their retention and expulsion, others to the control of motility and action, and still others to the control of internalized action in the form of thinking and fantasying. In the development of verbalization, speech, and thinking we can discern the general characteristics of the phase in the way in which words and thoughts are formed and their expression controlled. Further, we can see the way in which words, actions, and thoughts have to be released at appropriate times and in appropriate circumstances. In the process of thinking and speaking there is a delay in discharge, and inappropriate elements have to be held back. The child shows the beginnings of organized memory and voluntary recall.

In recent years a number of psychoanalytically orientated psychologists have done important work on the interrelation between cognitive and perceptual controls, adaptation, mechanisms of defense, and the discharge of the instinctual drives (e.g., as reported by Gardner et al., 1959).

We have spoken of the hierarchy of id and ego functions which develops in the anal phase. This hierarchy of functions is associated with a hierarchy of feelings which show greater or less distance from the sensual feelings accompanying direct somatic drive discharge. Pleasure obtained through uncontrolled discharge may then be partially replaced by pleasures derived from delaying, postponing, and fashioning products in reality or in thought.

The essence of the view put forward at this point is that the functional characteristics of the ego in the anal phase bear a close resemblance to the mode of functioning of the somatic apparatuses which act in the service of anal drive discharge.

Of special interest in the present context is the development of those cognitive and perceptual processes which find expression, when they become exaggerated, in the defense mechanisms characteristic of obsessional neurosis. We have alluded to the "clearing of the perceptual screen," and the parallel between this and more directly instinctual anal activities needs no elaboration. But it is a form of discharge which makes use of maturationally predetermined apparatuses, and the pleasures associated with perceptual functioning are of a more highly refined and nonsensual form than the affective feeling accompaniments of more direct anal activities. The obsessional neurosis is characterized by a prominent use of such defenses as isolation, undoing, reaction formation, intellectualization, and rationalization, coupled with such features as omnipotence of thought and magical thinking. All of these can be considered to be an exaggeration of normal cognitive and perceptual processes, and in particular, of cognitive and perceptual control. The particular ego processes which form the basis of the specific defenses we have mentioned are those which came into being or were extensively employed during the anal phase of development. If we think of the defense mechanism of isolation, for example, we can see it as a hypertrophy of the normal ego processes used by the ego to prevent the ideational content of thought from becoming too affect-laden for efficient secondary-process functioning. Undoing, in its turn, represents a caricature of the normal ego processes of trial thought and trial action.

We know that drive fixation points and regression to them may find expression through the ego in the form of character traits. These show classically the influence of both a particular component drive and the ego's defensive struggle against it. Thus, in the ego-syntonic traits which distinguish, for example, the anal-reactive character, we can discern disguised forms of anal-sadistic drive discharge as well as the operation of the mechanism of reaction formation. While it appears that character traits may reflect particular ways in which the ego mediates drive discharge, it may be that what has been referred to as cognitive and perceptual style is rather a reflection of fixation to the particular ego pleasures in functioning which we have discussed earlier.

The implication of all that we have said is that drive regression to the anal-sadistic phase is an essential ingredient in the genesis of an obsessional neurosis; but even with the addition of the particular character of the superego, of particular types of object relationships (involving a high degree of ambivalence), and with the increased sadism consequent on the drive regression, this is not enough. We suggest that a particular type of ego organization is an essential component. This is not necessarily reflected in what we usually call traits of character; it is reflected rather in a particular style of the perceptual and cognitive functions of the ego, a style which indicates a functional fixation of the ego to the anal phase.

The precocious development of the ego which is so often thought to be an important feature in the development of obsessional neurosis can now be understood, more specifically, in terms of an early or developmentally premature "distancing" of the ego functions from the drives. This may show itself in a premature "intellectuality." We would suggest that fixations which occur at the anal phase of development need not influence drive and ego functions equally, and that a fixation of the sort which we have described in connection with ego functions need not be accompanied by a fixation of equal degree on the side of the drives, and vice versa. However, both drive fixation and functional fixation of the ego may occur at the anal-sadistic phase; and we would suggest that this is the case which obtains in the individual who is prone to develop an obsessional neurosis.

III

We can now return, very briefly, to the question of the applicability of the ideas which have been put forward to the clinical manifestations of obsessional phenomena. As far as the syndrome of obsessional neurosis proper is concerned, we may simply add to the classic formulation the notion that the ego changes which occur are attributable, in part at least, to a functional ego regression which accompanies the drive regression so prominent in this disturbance. The functional ego regression involves those ego functions which showed their most prominent development during the anal phase—particularly those functions which relate to cognition, perception, and to control in general. The functional ego regression brings into operation the defense mechanisms which are characteristic of the neurosis and which represent a natural development of the individual's particular style of ego functioning.

Those disturbances which occur in childhood during the anal phase itself need offer us no difficulty. Here we see an exacerbation of features of the normal developmental conflict, and we would suggest that in these children a premature turning against direct instinctual drive discharge has taken place. We may assume that there has been a stronger-than-usual tendency for the replacement of direct drive gratification by pleasures in functioning, mastery and control. On the other hand, perhaps even because of the premature affective distancing, the mode of functioning of the rapidly developing ego apparatuses is closer in form to the anal pattern of drive discharge. The modes of ego control, for instance, are probably patterned to a greater degree on the somatic sphincter-involved modes of discharge. All of this results in a tendency to use the particular methods of cognitive and perceptual control which we have discussed, and the emergence of the characteristic defense mechanisms is an inevitable consequence of this.

With progressive drive development this "anal" style of ego functioning may alter. This is probably what happens in the case of the transient obsessional phenomena which occur during the anal phase, but which disappear with its passing. However, drive progression may take place without substantial alteration in the "anal" style of ego functioning, and we have suggested that those individuals who have such a style possess, from the side of the ego, the propensity for the development of a later obsessional neurosis. This may be the case, even though their anal phase of development was not necessarily characterized by the development of significant obsessional manifestations.

Finally, we come to those obsessional phenomena which do not emerge as a consequence of the classic obsessional psychopathology.

These occur in many different circumstances and conditions, and range from the mildest and most transient to gross controlling mechanisms which constitute strenuous attempts to stave off threats of catastrophic disintegration. Their emergence is not primarily linked with drive regression to anal fixation points, but they indicate a functional regression to an "anal" mode of ego functioning. They are mobilized by the urgency of the need to control, and we would suggest that the likelihood of their appearance bears a relation to the degree to which an "anal" style of ego functioning has persisted.

BIBLIOGRAPHY

Freud, A. (1965), *Normality and Pathology in Childhood*. New York: International Universities Press.
Freud, S. (1909), Notes upon a Case of Obsessional Neurosis. *Standard Edition*, 10:153-318. London: Hogarth Press, 1955.
—— (1913), The Disposition to Obsessional Neurosis. *Standard Edition*, 12:311-326. London: Hogarth Press, 1958.
—— (1925), A Note upon the 'Mystic Writing-Pad.' *Standard Edition*, 19:227-232. London: Hogarth Press, 1961.
Gardner, R., Holzman, P. S., Klein, G. S., Linton, H., & Spence, D. P. (1959), *Cognitive Control: A Study of Individual Consistencies in Cognitive Behavior* [*Psychological Issues*, Monogr. 4]. New York: International Universities Press.
Hartmann, H. (1950), Comments on the Psychoanalytic Theory of the Ego. *This Annual*, 5:74-96.
—— (1964), *Essays on Ego Psychology*. New York: International Universities Press.
—— Kris, E., & Loewenstein, R. M. (1964), *Papers on Psychoanalytic Psychology* [*Psychological Issues*, Monogr. 14]. New York: International Universities Press.
Hendrick, I. (1942), Instinct and the Ego during Infancy. *Psa. Quart.*, 11:33-58.
—— (1943), Work and the Pleasure Principle. *Psa. Quart.*, 12:311-329.
Lampl-de Groot, J. (1965), *The Development of the Mind*. New York: International Universities Press.
Rosen, I. (1954), The Clinical Significance of Obsessions in Schizophrenia. M.D. Thesis, University of Witwatersrand. Abridged version, *J. Ment. Sci.*, 103:773, 1957.
Sandler, J. (1960), The Background of Safety. *Int. J. Psa.*, 41:352-356.
—— & Hazari, A. (1960), The 'Obsessional': On the Psychological Classification of Obsessional Traits and Symptoms. *Brit. J. Med. Psychol.*, 33:113-122.
—— & Joffe, W. G. (1964), Hobby, Skill and Sublimation. Read at the Fall Meeting of the American Psychoanalytic Assn., New York.
Stengel, E. (1945), A Study on Some Clinical Aspects of the Relationship between Obsessional Neurosis and Psychotic Reaction-Types. *J. Ment. Sci.*, 91:166-187.
Wulff, M. (1951), The Problem of Neurotic Manifestations in Children of Preoedipal Age. *This Annual*, 6:169-179.

CLINICAL CONTRIBUTIONS

PUPPET PLAY OF A PSYCHOTIC ADOLESCENT GIRL IN THE PSYCHOTHERAPEUTIC PROCESS

RUDOLF EKSTEIN, Ph.D. (Los Angeles)

The play has been considered the royal road to the unconscious conflict of the child. While one may suggest that the neurotic child weaves in his play—as Waelder (1932) phrases it—fantasies around external objects, Ekstein and Friedman (1959) characterize the play of psychotic children as weaving hallucinatory and delusional fantasies around external objects. They stress the child patient's unstable capacity to differentiate objects which serve as play material from internal objects. The psychotic child's play represents the ceaseless struggle between the forces of individuation and identity formation on the one hand, and those which aim toward symbiotic union or symbiotic conflict on the other, a struggle which has been elucidated by Mahler and her coworkers (1952, 1955).

In an earlier paper (Ekstein and Friedman, 1957), it was suggested that the play of children, neurotic, borderline, or psychotic, can be understood in terms of different maturational stages of play activity, along a developmental axis of thinking, the end points of which are impulse release and secondary-process reality-oriented thinking. We referred to Freud's (1911) famous dictum according to which thinking is trial action, and suggested that acting out be considered a form of trial thinking, a form of experimental recollection. We related the different forms of play to action and acting out, to a form of unconscious trial thinking. The attempts to resolve unconscious conflicts can be ordered along the above-mentioned

Presented at the San Francisco Psychoanalytic Society on January 8, 1962, and at the American Orthopsychiatric Association on March 23 and 24, 1962.

Coordinator, Training and Research, Reiss-Davis Clinic for Child Guidance, Los Angeles.

axis, which leads from impulse release, a kind of thoughtless act, to secondary-process reality-oriented thinking, an actless thought.

In the clinical presentation which follows these ideas have been applied to elucidate more fully the meaning of the puppet play of a psychotic adolescent girl. The use of puppet play is, of course, not new in work with children, has been mentioned frequently in the literature, and has received special consideration in Rambert's *Children in Conflict* (1949). Piaget, who introduces her work, suggests that "It is many years since such specialists in child psychoanalysis as Anna Freud, Melanie Klein, Susan Isaacs and others have employed techniques founded upon spontaneous games of children in the same way as the analysis of dreams is employed in the case of adults. . . . But Mlle Rambert has to offer an original innovation, a technique of her own in the form of puppet games of such a kind that the standardization of the material and the motif-types which it elicits permit the comparison of one case to the next and yet allow each patient to unfold his own personality." Rambert utilizes the insights of analysis as well as those of Piaget into the development of thinking. She offers fascinating clinical examples which show the differing uses that children of different ages make of puppets. The puppets taken up by the child usually represent forbidden wishes and activities which the child cannot readily accept as his own and which he has displaced onto the puppets. In using the puppets the child guardedly conveys to the analyst not only the nature of his wishes but also that he is only playing with the forbidden thought; he may not yet be fully aware of it or he may feel that it is permissible to play-act the thought rather than to act and live it out in reality, to fantasy about and verbalize it. Erikson (1940) has shown that if the play brings the conflict too close to consciousness, or if the play is in danger of becoming a realistic act, we will frequently find a "play disruption" in the therapeutic situation. This is true, of course, for puppet play as well, since it is only temporarily suitable as an appropriate distance device (Ekstein and Meyer, 1961).

The puppet play to be described differs from Rambert's material in that the play was the spontaneous invention of a child who was struggling with a psychotic disorder.

The material to be presented was obtained in the 60th and 130th treatment hours. It consists of two kinds of data: the therapist's process notes and summary and electric tape recordings of the hours. The latter raises many questions in terms of scientific methodology.[1]

The analyst's notes were taken immediately after each session and contained his attempt to remember what happened, what he thought the happenings meant, his own reactions, and whatever else he deemed important in order to recapture the spirit of the hour. These notes are supplemented by the electric tape. There are several reasons for making this attempt at integrating these two kinds of data rather than relying exclusively on the usual methods of the analyst, that is, to use his own recollections and interpretations. The techniques used in the treatment of psychotic children and adolescents have not yet been consolidated and need to be investigated from case to case. Apart from the fact that we do not yet have a reliable body of techniques for this category of patient, we are constantly trying to use theoretical concepts which are derived from our basic experience with neurotic patients and which are not completely applicable to the new situation. Moreover, the rapid give and take in work with these severely disturbed borderline and psychotic patients, who usually arouse strong countertransference reactions, does not readily permit the therapist to give as reasonable an account of a process as is true for other types of analytic work. In an earlier communication (1963a), I was able to document that some of the oversights of which I was unaware while dictating my own impression at the end of each session could be rectified through comparison with the electric tape.

In this same paper I have reported much of the diagnostic work of Teresa Esperanza. For the purpose of this communication an abstracted summary of the mental examination may suffice:

Teresa is a fifteen-year-old girl who seems quite immature and of dull-normal intelligence. Basic comfort areas are related to her infantile anaclitic relationships and her constant feeling of being threatened and endangered by the loss of objects. Her chief defense mechanisms are those of projection and flight, and her chief defense against anxiety lies in her attempt to receive love as an assurance of being wanted and of maintaining the relationship with a love object. The basic conflicts are related to her intense infantile, oral

---

[1] For different opinions of such methods, see Melanie Klein (1961, pp. 11-12); David Shakow (1962, pp. 146-161); Kenneth Colby (1960, pp. 28-29).

demands and her fear that she would be rejected and cast away because of her excessive needs and demands. What seems to be a hysterical character formation is a disorganization and loosening of thought processes suggesting a thought disorder related to the fusion of past and present, and to the absence of adequate boundaries and isolation mechanisms making for adequate intellectual integration and separation of functions related to adequate reality testing. She was diagnosed as suffering from a "schizophrenic reaction, childhood type, with hysterical personality features."

By the time of the 60th hour, the patient, now about sixteen years old, had been in treatment for about half a year. During the first few months of treatment she was involved in play with small objects which she obtained as gifts from the therapist or from other sources. Her life reminded one of the *Glass Menagerie*. There was a complete absorption in these little objects, which she used in order to fantasy about the past, which was fused with the present. Much of her symptomatology centered around the constant need to be gratified with such objects, candy and food of all sorts, and an insatiable appetite for outer stimuli of this type; however, these always proved almost useless in the attempt to re-experience actual events in her life. Frequently she would ask for a special object which she would describe in detail. Whenever she would receive it, she would discover that it was not exactly what she had had in mind. She reminded one very much of a person who wants to play; who wants to weave fantasies, delusions, and hallucinations around some kind of object, but cannot find the object which could serve as the crutch either for recollection or for trial thinking in the play activity. She could not maintain a cathexis of an external object, which instead immediately triggered off and became fused with inner stimuli. Neither her internalized objects nor her external objects were stable. She is presently the victim of insatiable object hunger, but whatever she swallows, whatever she attempts to introject seems to be devoured by an empty void and becomes useless again. At the same time she struggles desperately to maintain a façade of normalcy, trying to meet the external demand as much as she can, and giving one the feeling that all her play is an attempt to move toward a position in which rather than "playing crazy" (Cain, 1964), it could be said that she is attempting to play normal, but cannot truly think or act normal. Her play reveals the attempt at a hopeless flirtation with normalcy, and the dim awareness that this goal is unreachable; that she is caught in a dilemma for which there is no way out. The notion of normalcy is borrowed, of course, is imitation rather than identification with the adult world, is a flirtation with a new identity, behind which lurks the inability either to maintain or to abandon earlier positions.

This struggle, her play with normalcy, as well as her play with the therapist, who has not yet become an external object for her, but is at best a crutch, a dehumanized mechanical object, is beautifully illustrated in the hour to follow. At first I shall present my own recording at the end of this particular session, my summary of the event as well as my understanding at that point of what went on between me and the patient.

Today a rather charming hour with Teresa. She was at first somewhat delayed and asked whether she could go to the toilet before she came in, but then when the session started she soon brought out the puppet that she had made at school, an Easter bunny by the name of Lizzie, with black eyebrows to remind one of the movie actress, Liz Taylor, and practically the whole hour was spent in a conversation that I carried on with Lizzie the puppet, while Teresa listened in. It was a conversation which helped us to establish a collaborative relationship between two aspects of Teresa, the sick Teresa and the healthy Teresa, Lizzie somehow representing the helper who understood Teresa very well and serving as a kind of interpreter between the different aspects of Teresa, who described during the hour that she wanted to be many contradictory things, such as a movie actress, a puppet maker, a candy maker, a teacher, a sales person, a married woman, a child, etc.; in this attempt I constantly tried to bring about a collaborative relationship. The Easter bunny was, as it were, the healthy part of the child who tried to understand and work with me in order to help the sick child to keep from stuffing, to grow up, to clear up the confusion, etc. The device of the puppet served marvelously to bring indirectly into the situation a variety of treatment goals such as the desire to grow up, the desire to work well with the school, to do junior high school work rather than grade school work and to make an adjustment.

The hour would be typical perhaps of an eight-year-old child, but nevertheless I felt that I had much better and constructive contact than in previous hours; and Teresa herself expressed her delight about Liz, whom she considered to be an excellent collaborator, somebody who was trying to help her, somebody who ought to come back.

I am reminded of the kind of hours that Rambert described in *Children in Conflict* where ample use is made of puppets. The only difference is that this puppet device, rather than being suggested by me, was brought in by the child and was the spontaneous and creative contribution of the patient who in this way found a new bridge for communication.

We also talked about the Easter gift that ought to be brought tomorrow; the main version was one in which the puppet, as it were, would help Dr. Ekstein to help Teresa. I felt that in this case the puppet was not so much the expression of the id wish but was rather the expression of the reflecting ego, the part that was successfully identified with the psychotherapeutic process, with maturation and development. The puppet in that way became the projected replica of the psychotherapist, that part of Teresa's mind which can fully collaborate with the therapeutic process but is still, as it were, a puppet in the hands of the illness.

What follows is the transcript of the electric tape. This transcript will permit a more exact study of the interplay between therapist and Teresa, or rather, between that part of her which is projected onto the puppet, Lizzie the Bunny, and that part of her which she maintains for herself. The typed transcript, of course, while going much further than the therapist's own summary, does not quite allow us to gain insight into the emotional quality of the interview, the artistry of the interplay between Teresa and her puppet. We miss the inflection of the voices of patient and therapist, the whole range of emotional subtleties, the laughter, the giggles, the pauses and interspersed remarks in English or Spanish which could not quite be caught by the transcriber. Even the spoken word makes one aware of the many ingredients still missing: the visual representation, the actual activity and acting going on during this interview, types of observation so important in a psychotherapeutic contact. The meaning of the spoken word is but one aspect of the total meaning which is carried through play acting, through the change of voices, the acting out of voices, the handling of the puppet, as well as the movements of the therapist, who sometimes addresses himself to the puppet and does not look at the child, and vice versa. Nevertheless, the transcript, whether heard over the loud speaker or read in print, does permit us to gain insight into the actual therapeutic situation.

T.: I'm sorry I took a lot of your time—I took a little longer, I guess (breathlessly). I told you that I would bring a puppet now that I would show you. These are the puppets we made at school. (The Dubnoff School?) Yes, umhmm—it's a bunny. Look, you handle her like this—you put your finger here and she starts talking.

E.: Starts talking, opens the mouth, has two long ears, beautiful black eyebrows.

T.: Isn't she pretty?

E.: Very nice. Make her talk.

T. (falsetto voice): Hello doctor. (T.'s voice:) You know what her name is? Wait. (Puppet:) Guess what my name is?

E.: I'd like to know. Tell me.

T.: My name is Lizzie.

E.: Is your name Lizzie?

T.: Yes.

E.: Now, tell me, what kind of bunny are you, Lizzie?

T.: Well, I'm an Easter bunny.

E.: Oh, and tell me, what are you going to do at Easter time this year?

T.: Well, I'm gonna help T. take the children some Easter eggs and give away Easter eggs.

E.: Are you a friend of T.'s?

T.: Yes, I'm her pet, we're pals, aren't we? (T.:) Umhmm.

E.: Well, tell me what about T., what's T. doing these days?

T.: Well, I'm gonna tell you something she's been doing, but I'm gonna tell you the truth, I can't lie to you about it.

E.: Okay, go ahead.

T.: She's still been stuffing herself.

E.: Oh, is she doing that?

T.: Wait, she just feels she can't help it, that she oughta keep on doing it.

E.: What do you think about it, Bunny?

T.: Well, what I think about it is that . . . she's still harming herself by doing it, it's not healthy for her body, it's unhealthy. . . .

E.: Do you really think it's. . . .

T.: It makes her sick, it gives her tummy aches, she's stuffing herself with too much junk. Yesterday she did it. . . . I'm gonna tell you all the things she stuffed herself with, doctor, so that you know.

E.: Tell me, bunny, what can we do to help her?

T.: Well, doctor, I'm gonna tell you something she tells me. Can I tell you? (In T.'s own voice, "Yes, go on, Lizzie.") Well, she told me to tell you, this is very important, I want you to listen carefully.

E.: Well, bunny, go ahead and tell me, I'm gonna listen.

T.: She said that when she stuffs herself she feels she has a need to do it. It's a sickness, not really, because if she were cured and she would see things the way they are, do you think she would feel like doing it? She wouldn't.

E.: Why do you think that she has that need?

T.: Well . . . she has that need . . . because . . . uh. . . .

E.: It's hard to think, bunny, isn't it?

T.: Yes. Well, I'll tell you right now. She has the need to do it because she feels that in her sickness she's . . . she's supposed to do it, like if somebody tells her "do it, do it, you're supposed to do it, you should do it. . . ."

E.: You mean she thinks that someone makes her do it.

T.: Yes, that's right. She knows that nobody makes her, but she feels it that way, it's part of her sickness, believe me it's not a lie, it's the truth.

E.: Tell me, Lizzie, how do you think we can help her?

T.: We-e-ll. . . .

E.: Maybe you and I can think something out that helps T.

T.: Well, you know the only way I think that we can help her because she feels that she's gonna keep on doing it all the time and she might still do it forever.

E.: Umhmm. Do you think we can do something to help her?

T.: If she can't do it, yes.

E.: What do you think we can do to help her?

T.: Well, let's see, I'll stop and think of something. (In her own voice:) She's thinking (giggles).

E.: A very thoughtful bunny.

T. (laughing and in her own voice): Isn't she cute?

E.: A very cute bunny.

T. (in her own voice): Yah. Miss Jayne made her for me. Emily sewed the eyelashes. Miss Jayne sewed the mouth . . . the only thing I sewed the . . . the. . . .

E.: Ears?

T.: Ears. And Miss Jayne stuffed them up. And Miss Jayne sewed the rest of her. (Reverting to puppet voice:) Well, let's see. . . .

E.: She's a very, very nice bunny.

T.: Thank you, doctor. (Bunny voice:) Is it true that I have beautiful eyelashes because that's what my mommy says, she says that I'm beautiful, that what she likes best in me are my eyelashes, that I sort of resemble Liz Taylor a little. That's true?

E.: That's right, you got eyelashes like Liz Taylor's.

T.: Well, that's why she named me Lizzie.

E.: I wonder what Liz Taylor would think if we would hear that she looks like a bunny.

T.: Oh no . . . you think she would want to look like a bunny, she wouldn't even dare. . . .

E.: She might love to look like an Easter bunny.

T.:   Well, I think she's too old for that. When she was a little girl that would be fine.

E.:   Well, Easter bunnies are nice people.

T.:   Yes, that's true, they are very nice, they're the ones that bring the children Easter eggs in the baskets and candy. . . .

E.:   Tell me, Lizzie, I want to ask you something.

T.:   . . . and candy eggs. Yes, go ahead.

E.:   Will you listen to me, Lizzie?

T.:   Yup, any time.

E.:   Tell me, did you notice, Lizzie, that T. has a new hairdo?

T.:   Oh yes, well . . . doll . . . you didn't say nothing about it, why didn't you say something?

E.:   Well, I wanted to ask you first whether you noticed it, Lizzie.

T.:   Sure, sure, I noticed it. . . .

E.:   You like it, Lizzie?

T.:   Very much, I think she looks lovely, she looks beautiful.

E.:   Tell me, since when did T. do this, Lizzie?

T.:   Well, yesterday, last night my . . . her aunt fixed up her hair in curlers and this morning, and she slept all night with the curlers on—but she sleeps in the rug, you see, because that's healthy for her, and her aunt prefers her to sleep in her rug than the bed, but she's seldom comfortable without a pillow, 'cause she always sleeps without a pillow 'cause that's the best thing you can do, you know, because if she sleeps with a pillow it's bad for her, she gets neck aches, you know, her neck, her neck starts aching terribly. . . .

E.:   Oh, she's so used to just sleep on the ground, without a pillow.

T.:   Yes, you know her neck starts aching terribly, so she felt she needed a pillow. (In her own voice:) I wish she would really talk and I wouldn't talk for her (giggles). I love her so, doctor.

E.:   But you do pretty well talking for her.

T.:   I do?

E.:   Yes.

T.:   But if I wish that she would talk instead of me making her talk, that really gets me more sick than what I am, doctor.

It seems appropriate to interrupt at this point to make two observations. The first concerns the fact that the voice of the puppet, while representing the voice of health, as it were, the voice of the adult world which puts realistic demands on the child, actually does not represent the therapist to any large degree. The words of the puppet are primarily the injunctions of the aunt who constantly tries to keep Teresa within limits, who forbids her the senseless devouring of food, and who constantly threatens her that the overeating will lead to illness and must be stopped. We hear therefore that the puppet calls the therapist's attention to the child's eating difficulty, and does very much what Teresa has done in the past, when she informs the therapist that her aunt had told her to speak to him about having again been caught overeating, stealing from the refrigerator, etc. The puppet then voices the educational goals of the aunt; inasmuch as these repressive goals are voiced through the puppet, the mechanical extension of the child, the sick child, the injunctions are nothing but hollow imitations of orders from the outside which can be ignored in the name of the illness.

What will happen during the interview is reflected in the change in the puppet. The puppet will take on more and more the qualities of the therapist. Instead of a forbidding puppet who has educational goals, and who speaks of limits, the puppet will become a reflecting puppet, will make efforts at explaining, at creating a rationale for the difficulties of the child. One can literally see how the image of the forbidding aunt disappears and is slowly replaced by the image of the therapist, but also how both are kept at a distance since they gain entrance into the child's mind only via a well-controlled puppet which is in her hands and cannot get out of hand, as it were.

Teresa's last comment shows that the influence of the therapist is in ascendancy; that she plays with the idea, so to speak, of permitting the controlled extension, the puppet, more freedom. The child wishes that the puppet should really talk, should become alive, and that she, Teresa, should not talk for the puppet. She flirts with this change of roles, with the idea that the controlled voice of the puppet, still an extension of the psychotic child, should become the uncontrolled and spontaneous voice of an independent function, an independent ego. But as she seems to choose this new situation, in which the puppet becomes alive like Pinocchio in the story (which she will quote later), she also becomes frightened.

Since the puppet actually represents the increasing influence of the therapist, she cannot help but try and ward off this influence; she expresses the fear that if the puppet actually were to talk independently, she might become sicker. She is afraid of the overwhelming power of a fantasy which is to lead toward normalcy, toward health, toward self-control, and she sees a danger in becoming well.

The fear that the puppet might become alive, might gain power over her, in the projected fear that the therapist might gain power over her, that his interpretations or interventions, understood by her as injunctions, might be an evil influence and lead to the giving up of the quasi individuality which she retains in her illness, which is her defense against the symbiotic position. As we follow the transcript, we shall see that the puppet no longer stresses the goal of control but turns more and more to reflection. The contact with the therapist becomes more meaningful, and much of what the puppet says seems to be the working through of earlier interpretations, but on a level which permits the sick child to retain control. Beginning reflection should be associated with identification rather than mere imitation mechanisms.

E.: You mean if you would really think that that thing's alive.

T.: Umhmm, that's right, that would get me worse than what I am, and I might really see it, and I don't want to see it, I would be frightened, and that's why I shouldn't even think of it. It's something to see even a cartoon, you know, funnies, talking cartoons, like Donald Duck, you know—at least I can make her move as if she were alive, she seems to be alive, see. (Reverting to puppet's voice:) Well, so she felt uncomfortable to sleep without a pillow because all her curlers were bothering her and were aching her head and she couldn't just sleep well, so she asked her aunt if she could let her sleep with a pillow, so she slept with a pillow in the night and she slept comfortably and everything and next morning she, well, well, she fixed her hair nice and everything and now she has this nice hairdo—what do you think of it?

E.: Very nice hairdo—grownup girl hairdo.

T.: Thank you. Yeah, that's what I think. But, you know, the poor thing she always feels she's a child, you know, and . . .

E.: Suddenly she has a big girl's hairdo.

T.: Well, you know, she's mixed up, she's in between the two, this is something hard to explain, but I'll explain it to you at one time. She acts both ways—sometimes she acts like a grownup and sometimes like a child, and she doesn't know which to choose, which of the two, she's mixed up, you know—it's something like if, let's say, you go to a store, and you see two dresses, let's see—this girl sees a very pretty dress, and she sees a beautiful dress, and they're both so pretty she doesn't know which one to choose, she gets mixed up, you know, it's the same way with her. You understand what I mean, doctor?

E.: Yes, I understand that very well. I just wonder why she doesn't want to choose the one or the other, Lizzie.

T.: Well, it's—that's a part of her sickness, don't you understand? 'Cause if she were cured, she would choose one of the two dresses.

E.: She sure would.

T.: Of course. But the reason why she doesn't is she gets mixed up about it and starts saying, "Well, I want this one or this one." She goes for the two, but she doesn't know which. one, she gets mixed up, confused, it's in her sickness, you should know that, I'm sure you know it, don't you?

E.: Sure. But tell me, what would be the trouble if she were to choose one part, just leave out the other.

T.: Well, um, uh, let's see, let's see.

E.: Oh, Lizzie, you gotta do a lot of thinking.

T. (giggles): I know what you're saying.

E.: Yah, well, if you can think that out, you've got a good thought.

T.: Well, what do you think would be the best thing? Which of the two dresses would you choose? (Lizzie addresses T. here, who answers, "Well, I think I would choose if I were cured, I would choose the beautiful more than the pretty one.") See? She would choose the beautiful one.

E.: She'd rather be the grownup woman.

T.: That's right. Well, that would be both for a grownup woman and girls, you know, but she would choose the beautiful one, you know what I mean? You understand me, don't you?

E.: Yes, she would want to be the beautiful woman.

T.: Yes, that's right. See? You like my voice, isn't it sweet?

E.: It's sort of like a bunny's voice.

T. (giggling): Oh, Thank you. You're very nice (giggles).

E.: Tell me bunny, what are you eating for breakfast? Are you stuffing yourself the right way?

T.: No, I'm eating Easter eggs right now and carrots. My aunt—my mother—gives me carrots, celeries, this morning I had two carrots for breakfast and a celery.

E.: That's healthy food.

T.: Oh very, it's better than eating Easter eggs and chocolate and all that because that's, I have that for dessert, you know. For breakfast sometimes I have two carrots, and for lunch a carrot and a celery and for dinner carrots and celeries and for dessert chocolate eggs, chocolate Easter eggs, you know.

E.: Tell me, do you and T. eat the same things?

T.: No, she eats different from what I eat, but she also eats carrots and celeries and chocolate eggs and Easter eggs. . . .

E.: She does.

T.: Of course, but not exactly as much as I do because she's not a bunny, I'm a bunny and she . . .

E.: You mean you stuff more than she?

T.: Well, of course, I think bunnies . . . no, no, no, we both stuff ourselves the same way, don't we, T.? (In her own voice:) Yes (giggles).

E.: Liz, you got a big mouth, if you start to eat with that mouth, you sure would stuff yourself.

T.: Oh, thank you, thank you. I wish you had a little mouth, you know, T. was gonna make me a little mouth, first Miss Jayne asked her, "What kind of a mouth would you like in your Easter bunny in your puppet, a big one, a little one or a medium one?" And she first told her, "A little one," then she said, "No, a medium one." This isn't a big mouth, doctor, this is a medium mouth.

E.: Oh, that's just a medium mouth.

T.: It's not big, not little, just the way it should be.

E.: Sure. If it were a big mouth, it would be as big as a crocodile's.

T.: Yah, and I don't wish to have a mouth as big as a crocodile, worse if it were like a hippopotamus.

E.: Well, it isn't really a small mouth of a birdie either.

T.: Well, it's just the way it should be, you know.

E.: It's like a big Easter bunny's mouth.

T.: That's right, it's the way it should be, not little, not big, just the way it should be, you know.

E.: Well, you would be very nice in a puppet show, Lizzie.

T.: Oh, thank you, thank you.

E.: Children would love to watch you.

T.: Oh—I love children, don't you?

E.: Oh sure, and you could tell them a story about T.

T.: Oh, any time. I think she told me once that she's gonna get me in a puppet show, didn't you? (T.'s own voice says, "I think I did.")

E.: She might even help you make up the story.

T. (in her own voice): I must have, did I tell you that? I think I did, I'm not sure, I don't remember, did I, Lizzie? (Reverting to Lizzie's voice:) Well, well, I think she must have anyway.

E.: And if she didn't, she will later.

T.: Yah, but I think that she told me that one time she was gonna put me in a puppet show so that kids would watch me, and I said, "Oh, I'd love to be in one."

E.: Well, what kind of show would you put on, Lizzie?

T.: Well, an Easter bunny show or fairy tales of bunnies or remember when the children are asleep and the bunnies go and hide their Easter eggs?

E.: All around the place.

T.: That's right and then when they wake up and go hunting for their eggs—or, also, a parade, an Easter bunny parade, a puppet show, the bunny family.

E.: One after the other marching up and down.

T.: That's right. Or, also a story of bunny, of bunnies, of parents, of the mommy, the daddy, and the kids, the granny, the grandpa, the uncle, the aunt, and all the family. You know what I mean, don't you?

E.: Umhmm.

T.: And the bunny family, you know. Well, I would also like to be in a bunny family, you know. You understand what I mean, no?

E.: Yes, I do, I certainly do.

T.: Well, you see, that's what I mean.

E.: Well, what would it be, dear bunny, if T. would grow up and when she would be a grownup woman she would have nice, beautiful puppet shows for children, and in that way she wouldn't have to give up all the lovely things of her childhood. But she still would be a grownup woman, she would become a puppeteer.

T.: Well, that would be wonderful. But, you know, doctor, this is something I want to tell you. She wishes she could become many things, not only that, she wishes she could become a movie star, a nun, a nurse, a doctor, a lady that sells in a toy store, that sells toys for children or that sells nice things, jewelry or perfume or, you know, things for the ladies that they use, you know, or also, a cake store, she wishes, what she would like the best to be, to become if she's big and . . . that, that she would make cakes herself, and she would sell them. She would make pies, cakes, you know, donuts and all sweets and she would sell them and have her own sweet store, you know like in Mexico those stores. (Talks in Spanish:) You know, that's the way they call them in Spanish—I know how to talk in Spanish also, she taught me, didn't you, T.? (In her own voice: "Umhhmm.") She taught me how to talk in Spanish.

E.: So you're a Spanish bunny too.

T.: Yup. So what I'm telling you is that, um, let's see, for example, well those stores that are in Mexico where they sell wheat bread, you know, and she would be working in one of those stores and she would sell wheat bread, she would make them herself, cakes, pies, donuts and all kinds of sweets and sell them. Or she would also love to be a toy maker, she would like to have her own toy store, like Giuseppe—did you see the story of Pinocchio where Giuseppe was a toymaker and he used to make his toys and sell them? He had all kinds of toys, cuckoo clocks, and the cutest things, he made them himself, he used to be really a good toy-maker.

E.: Well, she will have a very rough time, won't she, to make up her mind which one of these things she wants to be.

T.: Yah, you know the poor thing is confused. I'm gonna help her, really, I'm gonna try and see what she would really. . . .

E.: Gee, the poor thing, she can't do all these things, she can't do all these things all at once.

T.: Pardon?

E.: This poor thing, she can't do all these things all at once, she can only do one thing at a time.

T.: Well, yes, of course, but I'm gonna help her to try and see which of all the things she would really like to become to be.

E.: What do you think, Lizzie, you would want her to be? If you could make her?

T.: Well, let's see, I would . . . let's see . . . that's hard for me to think of also. I'll see.

E.: A rough question.

T.: Umhmm. Yup.

E.: Gee, you're a great thinker.·

T.: Thank you (giggles). For an example, I think I would like her to be . . . well . . . I have an idea . . . she could make . . . she could be, she could become to be a toymaker, you know, and sell.

E.: Like Pinocchio's daddy.

T.: That's right. But look what kind of a toymaker, she would make puppets and, you know, all kinds of toys, and she would sell these puppets and all these toys in her own toy store, she would have her own toy store and she would sell them. That's what I would like her to be. Wouldn't you think that would be fine?

E.: I believe it would. It would. So that's what you would want her to do: to make toys and sell them to children.

T.: Yup. And puppets also and sell them.

E.: So she would be a grownup but she would always make children happy.

T.: Sure. She likes children, she loves them, she would never say she hates them, 'cause she loves them all.

E.: She would never pull them by their hair.

T.: Oh, no, even her own·children if she would get married and have her babies. She said, you know what she said? That every time they would behave bad and, and, and, you know.

E.: They would be naughty. What would she do?

T.: She would punish them, she wouldn't hit them, she wouldn't hurt them, because she'd feel that she wouldn't like to harm her own children, she would just punish them, you know.

E.: But not very strongly, not very badly.

T.: No, because she would love them so much that she would just be too delicate with them, you know, she would have so much love for them that she would treat them as if they were little angels.

E.: Would she take candy away from them?

T.: No, she would always give them everything they wished for if she had the money. She would give them all the toys in the world, all the candy, clothes and everything.

E.: Would she help them not to stuff?

T.: Oh, that's right, that's the trouble, well, that's what she's mixed up in, you know.

E.: Gee, but she doesn't want to mix up her own children with that stuff.

T.: No, but that's something else that she's mixed up in, you know. (To T.:) Aren't you? (T.: "Umhmm.")

E.: Well, you know, Lizzie, as long as we are fond of T., it's all right if she's a little mixed up.

T.: Well, yah, at least we know why.

E.: You still like her, don't you.

T.: Sure, I love her.

E.: Even if she's mixed up.

T.: Sure, I love her very much.

E.: That's good of you, have you ever been angry at T.?

T.: No, never, we get along very nice, don't we?

E.: You would even get along with her nicely if sometimes she is not so nice to you?

T.: Well, yah, sure. You only should be careful when she gets in a bad humor because she really gets like a bad humor, you know.

E.: What would . . .

T. (interrupts): If you just get calm and listen to what she says and that's all. Because look, doctor, just hear me in this, every time she gets in a bad humor just stop and say, "Well, the reason of why she gets that way is because that's a part of her sickness, that's an attack that comes to her, that's something, an attack that gets her in a bad mood, see?" So every time that happens just think of that and you, you know why it happens.

E.: But, Lizzie, if she would have a bad humor about you?

T.: Oh. Well, then I'd just accept it, that's all. But if it's about something else. . . .

E.: You would just accept it if she has a bad humor about you?

T.: Yep, yes, I would.

E.: I hope she doesn't have a bad humor, because you're a very nice bunny, nobody should be angry at you.

T.: Well, well, just very little times she's been in a bad humor of me, because I'm always nice to her and I always behave good, and she loves me very much, believe me, she likes me, since she made me and she created me, she likes me very much.

E.: Well, she most likely thinks that you're very much like her.

T. (to T.): Do I look like you? (T.: "Yah. Well, then her eyebrows are brown.") See, she says my eyebrows are brown.

E.: Just like yours, just like T.'s.

T.: Umhmm. Yup. And my eyelashes are black, like Liz Taylor's. Because she has brown eyelashes, you know.

E.: So between T. and Liz Taylor.

T.: Hu huh, yup, you know, I wish I looked like T., completely like T.

E.: Of course, who wants to look not completely like T.? T.'s . . .

T.: Well, of course.

E.: T.'s a very . . .

T.: Well, tell me one thing, doctor, who is more pretty, who do you think is more pretty . . . because to me Liz Taylor and Tammy and her . . . I don't know, they're both so pretty, I mean, they're both so pretty, which of them do you think is the nicest?

It seems that the puppet is trying to reconcile the interest of Teresa and that of the therapist. Teresa, through the mouth of the puppet, plays with a variety of identifications, a variety of roles which are to make her acceptable in this world, and she tries them on for size. As a matter of fact, she even tries to make up roles which would permit her to continue to live in part in the world of childhood, in the world of the puppets, in the world of fantasy, but in the service, as it were, of helping other children. It is almost a role which could be compared with the role of a therapist who can indulge in metaphors and similies, work with fairy tales, and continue with puppets in the service of the therapeutic ego. As she continues to make these compromises, she starts to offer herself to the therapist as a more acceptable love object, and she tries out whether the changes she promises are sufficiently attractive for the therapist. It is true these promises are—to use a phrase of Schlesinger's (1964)— "primary promising," a kind of promising which is not meant to be kept, but is meant to solicit love from the adult and to stop his anger. The puppet's name is Liz, a reference, of course, to the movie actress Liz Taylor, a movie idol of the child, a reminder of the movie career which failed for her once so beautiful but schizophrenic

mother, and her present notion of what mature and desirable woman-
hood may lead to.

The puppet's question whether the therapist could make a choice
by comparing Liz and Teresa raises a technical problem because the
answer gives the patient a cue to what the conditions of acceptance
are. When the choice is directly between the rabbit puppet Liz and
the patient Teresa, the therapist decides here (as well as at a later
point) in favor of the child. He feels that as long as the healthy
aspects of the patient's ego organization are merely rudimentary
formations which can at any moment be upset by new regressions, he
will do better to ally himself with the dominant forces rather than
to choose or identify with the puppet. In showing his preference for
Teresa, the therapist seems to maintain a contact which permits the
child to express, via the puppet, her actual concerns about the problem of getting well. She offers a rationale for her illness, for her
unwillingness to identify with the forces of growing up, and eventually she describes her dilemma by comparing it to a dream from
which one cannot wake up. One might well say at this point that the
playing with normalcy, as expressed through the investment she
makes in the puppet, could be compared with a dreamer who starts
to become aware of the fact that the nightmare is but a dream, that
he should wake up, that a part of him knows better, but that nevertheless he cannot wake up and must continue with the experience of
terror. The puppet—Teresa's nascent ego—knows better, but cannot
yet wake her up.

E.: Well, I think T. is much nicer than Liz Taylor.
T.: You think? Because Liz Taylor is the beautifulest, you know.
E.: Well, yes, for the movies. But T. is a nicer person.
T.: Oh, oh. Well, she would also like to become to be a movie star,
     you know.
E.: Well, you think she should, Liz?
T.: Well . . . sure, any time she wants to.
E.: Well, I think so too, but once she worried about becoming a
     movie star, Liz, you know, she told me that maybe if she wanted
     to become a movie star that might make her sick. What do you
     think about it, Liz?
T.: Oh yah, just like her mother got sick.
E.: You think she's right on that or is that just sort of a worry that
     she could throw out?

T.: No, that's a worry she has in her mind. But it wouldn't happen if she. . . .

E.: No, it wouldn't happen because if we make her well, she could be a movie star as much as she wants to.

T.: That's right, she just worries about things and that's a worry she has, you know.

E.: That's right. Well, I guess you can't blame her to worry. She saw that happen in her family.

T.: Yah. Poor thing, really, that's the sad thing about her.

E.: Well, you know, you can tell her, Liz, that she didn't get sick, I mean her mommy didn't get sick because she wanted to be a movie star, that just happened to be that way, but there's no connection.

T.: Well, what I think is it wasn't her, it was her father that got her that way. Her father was always so mean with her mother, he used to always slap her in the face, he used to be the meanest father one child could have ever had.

E.: Oh gosh, well that mommy sure didn't choose right when she chose that man for a husband.

T.: Yah, she chose the wrong one.

E.: That wasn't a very reliable man.

T.: Umhmm. That's right.

E.: He was a mixed-up guy.

T.: Yah. Alice in Wonderland, I guess.

E.: He wasn't Alice in Wonderland.

T.: Well, something like that, lost in between Wonderland and other places, you know.

E.: You mean mixed up because Alice in Wonderland, you know, she liked it there most of the time.

T.: Yah, but she was lost, didn't you know that? One thing she was dreaming.

E.: That's right, but she woke up.

T.: Umhmm, and good thing she did because that nightmare she had was just too painful.

E.: That's right, nobody likes painful nightmares.

T.: That's right.

E.: She woke up and what pleasure it was to realize that it was all but a dream.

T.: That's right, and maybe with her she feels that she's dreaming also, that all this is a dream, a nightmare she has, but it's not that, not really, I mean it's a nightmare in her sickness that she sees things this way, she sees them, she dreams them.

E.: She really wants to wake up more and more.

T.: Yah, it seems as if she's dreaming . . . but you know that she's not dreaming, you know that it's true, you know? You understand?

E.: Oh yah, sure, we do quite well. I guess as T. watches us she must have fun. You think we should get T. into this conversation, or should we just continue talking and leave her out?

T.: Well I don't think it's bad really, we can get her into this.

E.: Lizzie, I'm just sort of a little worried that if we leave her out she might feel offended, you know, or she might think we don't like her any more, and really we do like her.

T.: Of course we do like her.

E.: So maybe you tell me what you think whether we should leave her out and just let her watch us or whether we should invite her to become a part of the conversation.

The puppet here displays some insight: in comparing the patient's experience with that of a dreamer, and in suggesting that the therapist knows, as does the puppet, that Teresa actually was not dreaming. The therapist takes this as a cue that Teresa is ready to listen to the puppet, as it were, to permit the therapist more influence and to join the conversation as an active partner. He invites a conversation between the three of them, Teresa, the puppet, and himself. The *folie à deux* turns into a *folie à trois*.

T.: I'm gonna ask her, wait. (To T.:) Would you like to be with us or just hear us or what? (T.'s own voice answers: "Well, I'd like to join you.") Well, she says she'd like to join us.

E.: Oh sure, well, you tell T. to come right in and join us.

T.: Yah. Come on right in and join us.

E.: Now we're three people, Liz, Dr. Ekstein, and T. Hi, T., are you awake.

T. (in her own voice): Yup, hi, how are you? (Giggles.)

E.: How have you been passing these last two days?

T.: Oh fine.

E.: You did fine. You know, I had a very fine conversation with an old friend of yours.

T.: Lizzie. You like her? Isn't she nice?

E.: Lizzie the bunny is very, very nice, a real pleasure.

T. (giggling): I think she's the cutest thing.

E.: Didn't we do well? She and I did very well together, we talked a lot of good things, and she's a bright kid, a very good observer, she starts to get to know you very well.

T.: Sure.

E.: Yah, even though she has eyelashes like Liz Taylor. She's got also, I suppose, brown eyes, like T.

T.: Well you know something, she wishes she had eyes like Liz Taylor. She wishes she had long eyelashes.

E.: Oh, you mean T.

T.: Yah.

E.: Oh, you tell T. she's pretty enough.

T.: Oh, really?

E.: Oh, yah, she's a very pretty girl, she doesn't need to be any prettier.

T.: Oh, thank you. (To T.:) See? You heard what he said? Tell him thank you very much. She said thank you very much.

E.: Delighted, delighted.

T.: (Oohs and aahs.)

E.: Well, Lizzie, what will we get T. for Easter?

T.: For Easter, well, now let's see.

E.: Should she get tomorrow some surprise.

T. (screams delightedly): Oooh, she can't even imagine it! Will I get something? Oh, please, please! Look, give me carrots or celery for Easter, candy carrots and celery.

E.: Oh, T. gives you plenty of that.

T.: Oh well, Easter eggs, oh please, oh please!

E.: Well, wait a moment, I was just asking you what to give T., now you want something yourself. How can you be so greedy?

T.: Ohhh . . . I'm sorry.

E.: Why don't you think of T.?

T.: Oh, well, for both of us, no?

E.: Oh, for both, I see. Now, okay, what do you think we should get T. and you?

T.: Well, oh look, she's excited, she's excited!

E.: Who, you or T.?

T.: T., and I'm excited also, aren't we? (In her own voice, as T. giggles: "Uh huh.")

E.: T. likes Easter, as a matter of fact, T. likes all the holidays.

T.: Oh, she gets excited about things like that, you know. Well, you know what the best thing we could give her. . . . Well, tell me, for example, give me an example of what you got for her.

E.: Well, I haven't made up my mind yet, you know, because if I tell you everything, then you might go and tell T., and I don't trust you, you know?

T.: Oh.

E.: You might whisper it into T.'s ears. You might . . .

T.: I wouldn't, I wouldn't dare.

E.: Oh, but look I know you like T., so you would tell her.

T.: Oh, well come on, I won't tell her, I promise you I won't, I give my word.

E.: You promise?

T.: I promise.

E.: Well, I thought to get her something that really has to do with Easter, you know.

T.: Yes?

E.: Exactly with Easter time.

T.: Oh goodness. Give me an example of like . . . what?

E.: Well, it will be something that is filled up with something, but it won't be stuffed, it will be just filled up.

T.: Filled up?

E.: Filled up, yes.

T.: Will it be to eat? Or just toys?

E.: Well, I think . . . usually it is to eat, you know.

T.: Oh.

E.: Because Easter time is an eatup time.

T.: Yah, that's right.

E.: Not only a happy time, but an eatup time.

T.: Oh.

E.: And it's a time where all of us are allowed to stuff a little bit.

T.: Oh, goodness, Ohh (excitedly).

E.: A little stuffing time. You think T. likes that?

T.: Of course. She'll bring you something else that she has for you tomorrow.

E.: That's great. But tell me, maybe T. will get upset about stuffing?

T.: No. She'll eat it little by little, she promises. Don't you promise? Now, I'll try to stop her, believe me, I'll help her in that, I'll be her companion.

E.: All you need to do is to keep her, you know . . .

T. (interrupts): That little devil is just attacking her too much, and she needs a little guide from heaven, she needs a little angel or something.

This statement is an excellent example of insight, expressed through the voice of the puppet, into the shifting fortunes of the different introjects as well as into the need for external help, the angels, who are to struggle against the forces of the devil. We are of course aware of the fact that at this point the therapist is in a precarious position because the very problem of psychotic transference is that his influence too fluctuates. In most phases of therapy he is experienced not as a real and full object but rather in terms of ever-changing, fragmented introjects, good ones and evil ones. In a similar fashion, the patient experiences the environment's demand for health and adulthood sometimes as temptation, as seduction, as evil action, and at other times as positive and desirable forces.

E.: Little by little. Well, what you do is you give her the food . . .

T. (interrupting): And I'll be her little angel and I'll guide her to good ways.

E.: Excellent, you give her little by little, and when that devil comes you snap at him.

T.: That's right, that's what I'll do, I'll. . . .

E.: You got a nice big mouth.

T.: I'll spit him in the face and blow your horn, get out of here.

E.: Exactly, that's what you'll tell him.

T. (giggling): Yah.

E.: The old devil will run so fast that he won't know what his club-feet are doing. Oh, will he be frightened.

T:. He sure will.

E.: He sure will. Because now that the devil has found out, you know, that T. is not alone any more, T. has friends, she's got you, she's got Dr. Ekstein, and between the two of us she'll be stronger than the devil.

T.: That's right. And she has God, her best friend.

E.: That's right, and the poor old devil, he will say, "Oh . . ."

T. (interrupting): He's just gonna cry to the full moon.

E.: That's right, that's good for him, because maybe some day he will turn into a good guy. Then we eat him.

T.: That's right.

E.: When he's a good guy we eat him, if he's a bad guy, we spit him out.

T.: That's right.

E.: Okay? We only eat good guys, no bad guys.

T.: That's right, eat only the good guys, not the bad guys.

E.: The bad guys we spit out.

T.: See? The bad guys we spit out.

E.: And the good guys we swallow and keep.

T.: Umhmm. . . .

E.: That's what we'll do.

T.: Well, that's the best thing we can do really, there's nothing else you can do but that . . . you're a very wonderful doctor, really, that's all I can say.

E.: Thank you, Lizzie.

T.: You're welcome.

E.: I guess we understand each other.

T.: Sure, that's all I can say, that you're wonderful, you know, you're marvelous.

E.: Well, I hope, Lizzie, that T. understands that too, but if T. doesn't know it, then it doesn't help me to be marvelous; you think T. understands it too?

T.: Oh, she knows it, sure she knows it.

E.: Well, if she doesn't know it, we're gonna help her find it out.
T.: Aw, don't worry, she knows it, she knows exactly all about it.
E.: I think she's a pretty smart girl, that T., don't you think so?
T.: Yah, she's very smart. She's bright.
E.: Well, even though she's sometimes such a confused little girl. Tell me, Lizzie, I want to ask you something, you know, behind the back of T., don't tell her.
T.: No, I won't.
E.: Tell me, Lizzie, how is she doing in school right now?

It is at this point that the therapist wishes to test whether this play with normalcy can be translated into normal action. Could he press the collaboration between himself and the puppet (the auxiliary ego) to a point at which Teresa will face some of the tasks of growing up such as her schoolwork? Will this encounter then be more than a playing at normalcy? Will it be true trial action, or will it prove that the puppet is actually well controlled by the child; that Pinocchio is still but a wooden figure instead of a live person; that the healthy part of the child is still "dead" and only the psychosis lives? The puppet in the hands of the child represents inverted psychotic omnipotence, comparable to the megalomania of the infant who is helpless but "controls" the mother. The Negro spiritual about Him who has the whole wide world in His hands touches upon the problem of utter helplessness and omnipotent trust.

In the ensuing conversation the puppet seems to give the answer. The puppet asks again on whose side the therapist is. The original choice was between Liz Taylor, the beautiful actress, and Teresa the patient. This time the choice is more direct: who is prettier, the puppet or Teresa? Whom does the therapist elect as true collaborator, as true friend, as his choice? Does he side with the forces of insight, the forces which are to meet real tasks, or does he side with the forces of regression? Realizing the extent to which the collaboration can be maintained, he chooses Teresa, although giving some credit to the puppet.

T.: Well she's doing very well, she's cooperating with the teacher, everything that her teacher gives her she does it, well, only some things that Miss Jayne gives her she doesn't know how to do them she doesn't do them.
E.: Does she get easily discouraged when she gets some harder work?

T.: No, she doesn't, she just doesn't do it, she says, "I don't know how to do this." She just does what she can do, but she's cooperating and is doing very well.

E.: Do you think, Lizzie, that she will soon be able to do some more advanced work?

T.: Well, I have a feeling she will.

E.: You know that all the children do. Because I think, Lizzie, I wanted to ask you whether that's true, I sometimes think that she does sort of third grade work, fourth grade work, when really she could do junior high school work.

T.: Yah, she does, that's right. She's doing second or third grade work right now.

E.: Uh huh, so tell me, do you think we can get her to do junior high school work?

T.: Yah, sure, we can help her.

E.: Uh huh. But why do you think that she gets so easily, you know, thinks that she can't do it. She's such a bright kid, you know, I think she can.

T.: Sure, she can, oooh, if she really tried.

E.: Tell me, Lizzie, how long does she sit still there when she does her work?

T.: Well . . . well . . . an hour, I think?

E.: A whole hour? That's pretty good.

T.: Yup. Till twelve, because she gets to school at seven, at eight, and at twelve she leaves and goes home, but sometimes at one or at two when she stays for lunch. . . .

E.: Do you think she's gonna be able to stay with her work a little longer?

T.: Yah, sure.

E.: Because you know what I think, Lizzie, between me and you, we want to make a high school girl out of her. Or are we wrong?

T.: No, no, we should make a high school girl out of her, yes.

E.: She's pretty enough to be a high school girl.

T.: Oh yes, sure she is, of course.

E.: But don't tell her too often, because, you know, if we tell her too often that she's pretty, she would just be full of vanity, you know.

T.: Oh! No, never!

E.: We want her to be a modest girl even though we know she's pretty.

T. (sort of a half giggle): Oh, yes, sure, thank you anyway for saying that. Now, am I pretty?

E.: You're not talking about T. now, you're talking about yourself.

T.: That's right.

E.: Well, Lizzie, I tell you a secret. You're very pretty, but you're not as pretty as T. I hope that you don't mind that I tell you that.

T.: Oh no! Oh no! I'm not, it doesn't hurt my feelings. Yah, I know that. . . .

E.: You know why it doesn't have to hurt your feelings? Because, look, T.'s older than you. When you will be her age you will also turn to be prettier. When people grow up, when you will grow up too, they become prettier and prettier. So you don't worry, you know. But right now, T.'s prettier than you. Oh, she sure is. Don't you admire her? Just don't tell her too much, you know, because if she thinks that she's so pretty she'll be conceited.

T.: (Punctuates the above with "ohs" and "very much," etc.) (Giggling:) No, I won't.

E.: And you know, we want her not only to be a pretty person, we want her also to be one that isn't confused, that does well in school and does well with people and enjoys life, and you and I are going to do this together. You are from now on my helper. You know what I want to tell you, Lizzie? You are going to be on the staff, you know, you are going to be employed by Reiss-Davis Clinic for Child Guidance to help T.

T.: Oh, oh, doctor, that's nice, I'd love to.

E.: You're my helper, and I don't mind if you tell T., because I don't want to do anything behind her back, I want her to know that you and I are going to be assisting each other.

T.: Oh, sure, sure, no, she doesn't mind, it's okay.

E.: Why should she mind?

T.: It's okay, go on.

E.: Well, you know, I want to tell you something, Lizzie. I brought something tiny for T. today. Do you think we should give it to her?

T. (considering): Well . . . yes . . . really, doctor, I'm gonna tell you something—if you don't hear this . . . if you don't give it to her . . . she feels heartbroken. . . .

E.: Oh, she does?

T.: Yes, she feels terrible, she feels very painful in her sickness.

E.: But, Lizzie, doesn't T. know by now that even if I wouldn't give her anything I'm just as fond of her?

T.: Yah, sure, but she still feels that she needs a little present.

E.: Isn't it funny that she needs that?

T.: Yes, she does, it's part of her sickness.

E.: Maybe some day she will know that people like her without ever getting anything.

T.: Yah, she will, she will notice it.

E.: You know, I brought her a little telephone book to put in telephone numbers . . .

T.: Oh, isn't that nice?

E.: . . . so that she can put in Dr. Ekstein's number in case she needs him. . . .

T.: Oh. (To T.: "You heard what he got you, how do you like it?")

E.: And then I brought her a few little·tiny toy charms, so she will have more charms. Do you think she will like that?

T.: Oh, oh!!! Sure, she would love it!

E.: I tell you what I'm going to do, I'm going to stick it in your mouth, and then you give it to T.

T. (giggles delightedly): Oh!! Okay, I'll take it. Okay, come on! (Giggling happily:) She's not gonna look, don't look, huh? I have my mouth open. . . .

E.: Don't let T. look. Here's one, snap it, and then I have to find the others. Well, here goes! Okay, snap it. Wait a minute, open your mouth, okay, snap it. Wait a minute, open the mouth again, you didn't do right. Okay. Wait a minute, wait a minute, okay.

T. (all through this T. is giggling delightedly): Isn't this cute? (In her own voice: "Oh, Lizzie, tell Dr. Ekstein that this is awfully pretty.") Oh, she says this is very nice, she says she liked it very much and thank you very much for it, she's very happy with it.

E.: Very pleased, Lizzie. Lizzie, will you come tomorrow again?

T.: Sure.

E.: You know, we had such a pleasant hour with you, a very pleasant session. Will you tell T. now that we have about come to the end of the session and tomorrow is Easter Friday.

T.: Yah, that's right, she has to— (not understandable).

E.: So please, will you tell her not to forget to come tomorrow? It's important.

T.: Okay, I'll tell her.

E.: If she forgets tomorrow, what would I do with the surprise?

T.: She won't forget, she'll promise, she knows she has to come.

E.: She knows it.

T.: She will come, don't worry.

E.: And some day she might even come if she doesn't get anything, because she would know that she gets her health here, that's even more important than little things.

T.: That's right, yup, to be sure, that's the best thing.

E.: Did you see the telephone book that I gave her? It has an alphabet, where she can put under each letter the people whom she knows and to put in the little . . .

T.: It's very nice.

E.: . . . and the phone numbers.

T.: Yah, it's a very cute telephone book. She's happy with it, you should see how glad she is, she has a beautiful smile on her face, a big one. Aren't you happy, T.? (In her own voice: "Umhmm.")

E.: Yes, sort of a grown-up child smile.

T.: Yes, she feels painful, you know, once in a while she gets a pain. She gets, well, you know, she gets sort of mixed-up things, and terrible misery that come into her life and they're painful and make her suffer and a lot of things, you know. Well, something, doctor, I'm gonna tell you, this is very important, I'm gonna help her, and please, you give me a little power to help her.

E.: Exactly. I will.

T.: Look, she feels that since tomorrow you're gonna bring her her Easter things she wishes that she, she wishes, and she feels even that she's gonna try hard not to stuff herself because she still— yesterday she thought to herself that yesterday is gonna be the last day that I'm gonna stuff myself, and I'll never do it again. But she feels like doing it again today.

E.: Lizzie, tell her this, tell her that you're gonna watch over her so that she only stuffs herself a little bit, and only little by little, then she won't have to be unhappy, but around Easter time everybody stuffs a little, just a little, and you see to it that she won't stuff more than little. Okay?

T.: All right. Okay. I will. I'll take good care of her.

E.: Okay. You take your T., pack her up now.

T.: Okay. And see you tomorrow. Happy Easter. It was very nice talking to you.

E.: Happy Easter.

T. (in her own voice, giggling a little nervously): I'm gonna put her back in the bag. Bye!

E.: Bye-bye.

T.: Oh, Lizzie, come on, go in, say good night to Dr. Ekstein, we're leaving. Ooh, can't go in this way. Well, doctor, it was very nice seeing you. Did you like my Lizzie?

E.: Well, you saw, you heard me, no doubt about it. Lizzie and I got along beautifully. If you and I get along always as well as Lizzie and I, we'll do fine.

T.: She's my best pal I ever had, believe me, she's wonderful.

E.: I'll see you tomorrow.

T.: Okay. It was very nice, uh, talking to you, and I enjoyed talking to you. Happy Easter. (She seems a little upset, giggles nervously, finds it hard to leave.)

E.: Sure.

The interchange could be maintained as long as the therapist again made concessions to the child, who wants gifts and food, who must satisfy the object hunger, and who feels she has done all she could by offering a pseudo act, a microcosmic stage play of inner forces at work. This conflict was staged in such a way that health was confined to the little bunny-puppet, who on the one hand aspired to look like Liz Taylor and on the other shared with Teresa her main preoccupations, the love of carrots and gifts and the fear of stuffing herself with too many things given by objects who can turn into evil forces. Both Liz and Teresa struggle for mastery through maintaining the distance from outer forces, namely, the parental figures and the therapist, who at times of stress are experienced as evil creatures trying to enter her mind and destroy her.

This play with normalcy is a desperate one. It constitutes her attempt to "wake up" as well as her struggle against it—a struggle between the tendency to turn imitation into identification and the fear of becoming a victim of devouring outer forces. The primitive projective-introjective mechanisms threaten to wipe out the precarious individuality of the delusional world which permits the maintenance of a sort of private world but at the same time constantly undermines the search for human objects. This endlessly repeated struggle, which goes on week after week, month after month, which at times spells hope and frequently desperation, nevertheless permits one to discern an upward spiral. This progressive trend can perhaps best be demonstrated if we turn to an hour, some eight months later, in which the child again, for the second time, made spontaneous use of puppet play.

In this 130th hour Teresa had some difficulties in establishing contact with the therapist as well as in describing her own problem. She turned from toy to toy and somehow none seemed to allow her to develop what she wished to convey.

I quote from my summary prepared at the end of that session:

Finally, she took the puppet and here, for the first time, a sort of fantasy dialogue developed inasmuch as she assigned the puppet the role of Suzie Wong, a movie role, which she knew only from magazine descriptions. She did indicate, though, that Suzie Wong stood for the beautiful girl who loved many men, attracted many men, and was loved by many. She was a sort of mature fantasy of a world of promiscuous love, and Suzie Wong now had, as it were, a talk with Teresa. Somehow, with occasional questions from me, directed primarily to Suzie Wong, Teresa developed with Suzie Wong the theme of Suzie Wong's being interested in an adult love life, as defined by the role of Suzie Wong. Teresa seemed to indicate that marriage was a rather dangerous thing and that one could be a lovely beautiful girl and grow up without marrying. I intervened to have Suzie Wong ask her whether it wasn't perhaps true that she liked to think of herself as a person who would never marry because of the hard fate of her mother as well as the decision of her aunt not to marry. Both seemed to believe that men were dangerous. Suzie Wong took this up with Teresa, who was trying to explain. I had Suzie Wong ask Teresa whether there would not always be a conflict even if one did not marry, that one would have to choose between adulthood and childhood anyway. At this point the situation became too dangerous for Teresa, even though she had Suzie Wong try to pose the question.

Putting pressure on Teresa via the puppet, which she handled herself, about the choice between childhood world and adult world, I also remarked that the puppet, that is, Suzie Wong, was from the world of the movies and Teresa was from the world of fantasies; I wondered how they would get along with an adult person who was mature. Teresa let Suzie Wong say that she knew of a man on television who had a puppet and that this man and the puppet talked to each other, and that was exactly what Teresa and Suzie Wong were doing. It was her way of saying, I thought, that what I was doing with Teresa was, in a way, a method of talking with the puppet and therefore she identified with that method and did the same thing with Suzie Wong. I said that I realized that there was such a man, after which the play deteriorated. It had become dangerous. Teresa became restless, seemed to look more disturbed, and suddenly apologized for having to go to the bathroom.

After she returned from the bathroom, the session proceeded in terms of "what should we talk about now?" She took up the question of what gift she might expect me to bring her for Christmas. I said that just as she was wondering about Christmas, I had been wondering about December 31, the date that she had set for herself when "things will have passed once and for all" (her reference to the promise to give up delusions, come New Year). Teresa wondered what sense there was to my wondering since I knew the answer anyway. The answer was that she would have passed things once and for all by that time. Actually she felt she was well by now. Nobody had helped her. I did not help her even though I was a wonderful doctor. She had helped herself completely and alone. She would simply have passed things once and for all by New Year's. She would be a different person, and that was that. I said I understood that, but

I was wondering what kind of a different person she would be, because when one thing ends something else starts. What would come then? This question, of course, could not be answered and was deeply disturbing to Teresa; she tried to direct the conversation to something else, as if to say that she did not want to have that issue raised. Then she chose to take a piece of chewing gum and recognized the flavor; as the end of the hour had come, she said loudly, "So long," packed up all her books, and took her leave.

I shall again present the transcript of the recorded 130th hour, but only the part that deals with the Suzie Wong puppet episode.

E.: Your time is running out, you told me you will have it passed once and for all by December 31.

T.: Well, you know that I'm doing it right now, you've seen me do it these days. (Changes voice:) Hello, my name is Suzie Wong.

E.: Suzie Wong, I'm glad to meet you, you are one of those dolls that the boys like.

T. (Suzie's voice): Oh, thank you.

E.: Have you seen the movie, T.?

T.: The movie?

E.: Suzie Wong.

T.: No, oh yah, it was a movie, yah.

E.: Yes, there was a movie about Suzie Wong.

T.: Oh yah, Suzie Wong.

E.: Did you see that?

T.: No, I saw it, I saw parts of the movie in a magazine, yah, I saw pictures of the movies in a magazine, I saw Suzie Wong, she. . . .

E.: She's quite a girl, that Suzie Wong.

T.: Is she pretty anyway?

E.: A very pretty girl.

T.: Is she beautiful?

E.: Yes. She's a Chinese girl, you know.

T.: But is she beautiful?

E.: I think so, yes. She lives in Hong Kong in that story. A Chinese town.

T.: See, the world is full of pretty girls, see how many pretty girls there is in the world? There's too many pretty girls, yeh?

E.: That's right, some are real girls and some are just movie projections.

T.: Yah, like this one is a doll, kind of. . . .

E.: A puppet.

T.: A little puppet. (Changes voice:) Hello, hello, hello. My name is Suzie Wong.

E.: Glad to meet you, Suzie Wong.

T.: No. (Changes voice, screams:) Hi!!

E.: Hi, Suzie.

T. (Suzie's voice): Hi!!!

E.: Suzie, what's new?

T. (Suzie's voice): What's new? Well (sings), wake up, Little Suzie, wake up in the morning, wake up, Little Suzie, wake up in the morning . . . wake up. . . .

E.: Yes, wake up, Suzie.

T. (continues with song, unaware of Dr. E.'s interruption; giggles): Isn't she cute?

E.: Sounds like Suzie wants to keep on dreaming.

T. (giggles, pays no attention to Dr. E.): What's your name, Suzie? (Suzie's voice:) Suzie, that's my name, Suzie Wong, haven't you seen me in the great picture, Suzie Wong? (T.:) No. (Suzie:) Well, when they give the picture, I'll tell you and you can go and see me, okay? (T.:) Okay. I promise. (Suzie:) You promise you'll go? (T.:) Yeh. (Suzie:) Or if not I won't tell you. (T.:) I promise you I'll see you. (Suzie:) Okay. Then, then, then I can tell you. Whenever they get it, they start getting it, I'll tell you where they give it and you can go and see it. (T.:) Okay.

E.: Suzie?

T. (Suzie): Yes?

E.: What kind of picture is there about Suzie Wong?

T. (Suzie): Well, it's about a Jap . . . Chinese girl, she's a very pretty girl, and she acts very well. It's a story of her, see? She falls in love, she finds many men in the story, she dances in that story and she sings, and you know what Japanese girls do, you know, that's the story.

E.: What do they do?

T. (Suzie): Well, they sort of do what American girls do, only that in their type they also kiss boys, they fall in love, they sing, they dance.

E.: Exactly. These Japanese girls do just like our American girls do.

T. (Suzie): That's right, that's what they do, exactly. So what's the big idea? What's the big idea, Curlie? What's the big idea, what's the big idea? (Giggles; her own voice:) What's the big idea? What's the big idea, so what's the big idea?

E.: Well, the big idea is that Suzie Wong is interested in boys.

T.: Are you? (Suzie:) Uh huh. And I have many loves. (T.:) You know, Suzie has many loves in that picture, didn't she? All the boys used to see her and just fall in love with her because she was so lovely that they couldn't resist her. She couldn't resist them either, because she just liked to have so many loves.

E.:   That was one of her troubles, that she couldn't resist.

T.   (Suzie): Yah, yah, naturally.

E.:   So that was the tough thing with Suzie Wong.

T.   (Suzie): Uh uh, that's right. (T.:) See, Suzie Wong liked to be kissed by boys and liked to have them as sweethearts. She, she, she even liked, they liked to date her and take her out for dates and all that stuff, and all those things, you know. Oh, look at the little ball, oh, this is a little goat, oh, it's a dog, yah, it's a German shepherd.

E.:   It's a war dog.

T.:   Yeh, it's a beautiful. . . . (Changes voice:) Hello, hello, beautiful, beautiful, you heard what Suzie Wong said: Beautiful Suzie Wong, she's a beautiful gal, you should go and see the beautiful Suzie Wong in her picture, you know, beautiful, beautiful, beautiful Suzie Wong. (Sings:) Cuddle up a little. (Deep sigh:) You should see Suzie Wong, believe me, she's a precious child on earth. No matter how many beautiful girls in this world there could exist, but she's one of the most beautiful, Suzie Wong, so why don't you go and try and see her? See the angel, Suzie Wong, in her great picture Suzie Wong.

E.:   Is Suzie Wong an angel?

T.   (Suzie): Well, that's how beautiful she is dear. I said she's one of the most. . . .

E.:   Well, but then she was running around . . .

T.   (interrupts): Like, she's not the only beautiful, dear, this gal here is beautiful too, the one you're seeing, hah?

E.:   Who's beautiful?

T.:   Well, T., isn't she beautiful?

E.:   Oh, T. too?

T.   (Suzie): Well, aren't you seeing her, don't you think she's beautiful? Or don't tell me she's ugly?

E.:   Oh, is she also one of those girls who likes all the boys?

T.   (Suzie): Well, let's see, I'll ask her. Do you like boys? (T.:) Sure, I do, I didn't used to like boys, but I do. I'm like any other girl is, so, what's something different about me? (Suzie:) Well, you have loves? (T.:) No, I had one when I was a little girl, I had many loves, you know, the little boys used to go lalala, bother me too much. (Suzie:) Well, do you like to have loves, would you like to have loves? (T.:) Would I like to have loves? Uh huh. Well, sure, all the loves I . . . no . . . I'd rather not get married. I just want to be without marriage, I want to live my life alone. (Suzie:) You wouldn't like to get married when you grow older?

E.   (interrupts): Who is that, Suzie Wong or T.?

T.: No, she talking to me. (Suzie:) You mean you wouldn't like to
     get married? (T.:) No, no, uh uh. I want to live my own life
     happy when I grow older. (Suzie:) Really? (T.:) Yah, I don't
     want to get married, if you get married you get into trouble,
     that's all, your husband later doesn't love you, he just fooled
     you, you have to be sure whom you marry first, anyway. (Suzie:)
     Oh yah, that's right. (T.:) But Suzie Wong got married at the
     end of the picture, I think, I don't remember.

E.: Suzie, Suzie.

T.   (Suzie): Yeh?

E.: Tell T. that the reason she doesn't want to marry is because she
     thinks her aunt feels it's wiser not to marry, and not to have
     trouble, like mama.

T.: Because what?

E.: Suzie, tell T. that the reason she, T., doesn't want to marry is
     because she thinks her mummy had trouble getting married
     and her aunt thinks it's wiser not to marry.

T.   (Suzie): See, dear? (Explains to T. in Spanish:) Your mommy
     got into trouble, you heard me? Your mama got into trouble
     when she got married. (T.:) Well, well, yah, see? (Suzie:) Well,
     tell me about it, I don't understand. (T.:) Well, you see, Suzie,
     when my mother got married she was a very young girl, she was
     about nineteen or twenty and she was very beautiful, and when
     she got married she got into trouble, see? (Suzie:) She got into
     trouble? (T.:) Yeh, she got into trouble. See, the first thing that
     happened was . . . was . . . see, the first thing that happened
     was . . . she. . . . (Suzie:) Yah, she what? (T.:) Well, she, uh,
     she, uh, well, uh, she just got into some trouble, see. (Suzie:)
     Oh. (T.:) She didn't, she just got married because she wanted
     to be a movie star, see, and I don't know how the trouble came
     but it just came. See, when she married my father he was a
     millionaire, like The Millionaire on the program on TV, and
     she thought that he would make her a movie star, see, like Rita
     Hayworth, but it didn't happen that way, because my mother
     didn't turn out to be like a movie star, like Rita Hayworth is
     one of her favorite movie stars, she always talks about Rita
     Hayworth. Rita Hayworth married this guy, she divorced this
     other one and now she's gonna get married again, she's the most
     beautifulest of Hollywood and who knows what? (Giggles:)
     Well, see, it became upside down, the world of Suzie Wong.
     (Suzie:) Gee, oh goodness, well, yah, things like that happen,
     oh yes. But with you I don't think it will happen, you're very
     lucky, you know, and you can get married any time you wish
     when you get older. Not when you're too young, you know,

right now you're a young kid, you know, but when you grow older, you'll be a woman, then you can find yourself a nice guy and marry him, you know like this song (sings): "I was born as others in August, I was born as Blueberry pie, lalalalalala, I'm in love with a wonderful guy." You know, I was in love with a wonderful guy in my picture, and I called him "Candy." (Sings:) "Candy, I call my sugar Candy, 'Cause he's as sweet as candy, and he's my candy dear. He treats me handy, my little sugar candy, 'cause he's as sweet as candy, and he's my candy dear."

E.: Suzie?

T. (Suzie): Yes?

E.: Suzie, I want to ask you something. But why would you want to tell T. to marry some day when she's scared of it?

T. (Suzie): To marry some day? Well, it isn't that she's scared, yes, she is scared of getting married, because she's afraid that her husband might then not really love her, that he might just have fooled her, see?

E.: Yah, but more than that, Suzie, haven't you heard, didn't T. ever tell you that she sometimes thinks that it's better to stay a little girl than to grow up and work hard to become an adult person?

T. (Suzie): Well, let's see, let's see, let's see. Well, I guess, I don't know, I don't know, I don't know, I don't know what's going on.

E.: Don't you think we should try to find out, Suzie?

T. (Suzie): Yes, I think so, why not?

E.: You think we could find out?

T. (Suzie): Yah, any time.

E.: Why don't you ask her? Go ask her.

T. (Suzie): Yah? What shall I ask her?

E.: Suzie, ask her why she thinks it's hard to grow up.

T. (Suzie): Well, why do you think it's hard to grow up anyway? (T.:) Well, because when you grow up . . . it isn't hard to grow up, that I think it's easy to grow up, you just want to grow up and that's all. You want to get married and you can get married, if you don't want to get married you don't have to get married, when you're old, no matter, look, there's a million beautiful girls in this world that don't get married. How beautiful they are, I believe there's more beautiful girls that are more beautiful than Elizabeth Taylor or Rita Hayworth, and they would never get married, they would always be living their own lives, living without marriage or nothing and they wouldn't even have boy friends. I'll bet all the boy friends in the world would look at them, but they wouldn't mind getting married and they would never get married. Well, why can't I be that one? (Suzie:) Well, that's true.

E.: But Suzie, tell T. that even if one doesn't marry one could still grow up to be an adult person rather than a child.

T. (Suzie): Well, that's right, you could grow up to be an adult person rather than a child, you heard, dear. (T.:) Yah, that's right.

E.: What does T. think about that?

T. (Suzie): Well, what do you think about that? (T.:) Well, I think about that . . . well, what do you . . . I think about that, well. . . . (Suzie:) Well, you see, I guess T. and I are friends, we became good pals for one? Right now, we're good pals, I guess, aren't we? (T.:) Yah, we're good pals.

E.: Who are good pals?

T. (Suzie): Well, me and T., we're good pals.

E.: Oh, Suzie, you and T. are good pals.

T. (Suzie): Yah, we're good friends. We became friends. Aren't we good friends? (T.:) Yah. (Suzie:) Yah, I guess we are, we're good pals, we're very good palsy-walsies.

E.: Well, Suzie, you're from the movies, that is, really from fantasy-land, and T. is from the childhood land, no wonder you're good friends.

T. (Suzie): Well, yah.

E.: How would the two of you get along with someone who is from the adult world?

T. (Suzie): Well, I'll give you an example. Like, have you ever heard of this program on TV of this guy that has this doll and he talks to this doll? He's a show guy on, on the show he comes on with this doll that he makes him talk to him.

E.: A puppet, yes, he works with a puppet.

T.: That's right, they're pals, no?

E.: Yes.

T.: That's the same, she and I are pals the same way, so what's wrong with that, it's just a little . . .

E. (interrupts): Nothing, it's excellent, excellent. But I was just wondering how the two of you would get along with someone who is. . . .

T. (Suzie): Well, I face reality, see, as she does, and she faces fantasy sort of a little, as I do, see? But we, we face reality more than fantasy, because we think it's best of all, that it's the better thing to do, see?

E.: Suzie? When will you go to school?

T. (Suzie): Well will I go to school? Well. . . .

E.:   You haven't finished high school yet.

T.   (Suzie): Well, well, uh, well, now I'm going to school, I mean I'm not going to school.

E.:   Does T. go to school?

T.   (Suzie): Well, do you go to high school? (T.:) No, I just go to school. I'm very back in my studies, that's why.

E.:   Are you back in your studies?

T.:   Well, why do you think I'm going to this school, to catch up, this school helps you catch up, so that then you can start going to high school, see?

E.:   You think you might catch up?

T.:   Sure I will. Naturally, Western Air Lines, the only way to fly.

E.:   Where does it say that? Where does it say Western Air Lines?

T.:   Well, have you ever heard of that owl?

E.:   What?

T.:   Well, have you ever heard of that bird that passes flying in an airplane on TV and say, "Naturally, Western Air Lines, the only way to fly."

The conflict and the modes of expression in this particular play interview are very much the same as in the hour when the puppet represented Liz the bunny. Again we find that the voices of interpretation, of reflection, and of adult demands toward growth are vested in the puppet. The struggle is again between three people, as it were, the therapist and Teresa, and the link between them, the puppet, who represents partly the introjected therapist and partly the transitional object, the extroject, as it were. Basically the conflict again involves an attempt to establish an object relationship, a struggle against the object, against the forces of growing up, and at the same time a kind of progression in terms of the playing out of normalcy.

The struggle again is a one-sided one; when the therapist starts to push toward action, tries to induce the patient to make some form of commitment, he again loses the struggle, and it becomes quite clear that it is still impossible for the patient to choose the actual realistic task. Although the therapist presented the choice as a question for the puppet to put to the patient, it is experienced as a frightening injunction.

However, there are also important differences between these two interviews. In the first puppet hour the theme is the struggle against orality, while the second puppet hour represents the conflicts between impulse and delay on a higher pseudo-phallic level. The bunny Liz, a compromise between the overeating animal and the beautiful tempting movie actress, now turns into Suzie Wong. The eating animal now is a tempting, man-eating lover of the screen. Suzie Wong introduces more openly the choice of the sexual partner, the temptation of adult sexuality. Liz, the bunny, contains more features of the hospitalized schizophrenic mother, once a beautiful aspirant for movie stardom, while Suzie Wong presents the features of the unmarried aunt who plays with adult sexual roles but cannot maintain them. Both female figures thus offer negative models for identification, although the image of the uncontrollable mother arouses more fear than that of the aunt, who in spite of her many difficulties has some sustaining strength (Ekstein, 1963b).

The interplay now is between Suzie Wong, who invites Teresa to look at boys, to think of marriage, to think of children, and Teresa who defends herself against temptation by pointing out that one could well grow up without making this choice which is so fraught with dangers. She has Suzie Wong explain to her or, rather, to the therapist the reasons in the history of the patient which might make her refusal to choose love and marriage understandable and rational.

When the therapist intervenes, we find that the pressure becomes too great. While he permits Teresa to take the stand she does, he wonders whether there isn't a way of growing up without the choices that Suzie Wong suggests and he refers to Teresa's schoolwork. This suddenly turns the play into a regressive move; the therapist's comment whether Teresa could catch up with her schoolwork is countered by the patient's telling remark that surely she would catch up: "Naturally, Western Air Lines, the only way to fly."

The nature of the puppet has changed somewhat in those last eight months. It must be realized that the puppet is but a slave of the illness, attains only temporarily some form of independence, fluctuates from toy to the projection of the introject, to the function of a transitional object, and a bridge to the real object of the therapist. One might also suggest that one sees the growth of an ego, a living link between the illness and the therapist, but an ego that is still weak, in the service of the id, and not differentiated from it.

During the following three months of treatment further changes, although of a subtle nature, make one feel that the playing with normalcy might move toward a point at which it might become genuine action, albeit frequently disturbed by more primitive maneuvers of powerful acting out as well as play acting.

The material raises the question whether one can expect to help such patients to move from play to action. Play is of course psychic work which can lead to the development of new functions in the ego organization and allow such patients to make a new and different commitment. On the other hand, one can only push people toward a choice when they have a capacity to choose. The material offers examples of a reintegrative process which leads toward the crossroad of choice. This example of psychotic puppet play can be considered to be a version of psychotic obsessionalism; its constructive purpose is to ward off destructive impulsivity on the part of the feared internal object which is experienced at times as the danger that lies in the external world and is confused at times with the angry reactions provoked in the environment (Ekstein, 1963b), both tending to push the child from the psychotic world of play into a world of age-appropriate action.

One may well say that the psychotherapist, as well as those who take care of such children, must bear with the nature of the puppet. The puppet not only is a transitional link but is in part the therapist himself. Can he give up the fantasy of power and allow himself to be for a while a helpless puppet who is manipulated by the forces of illness? Patients have their own ways of allowing the puppet to become alive. As they can allow the therapist to become a real person rather than a fragmented part of their delusional system, they develop a stronger ego and self organization in order to meet the challenge of objective reality.

When this challenge is met and recovery has been obtained, both patient and therapist may look back at the process that has taken place and may then feel identified with Collodi's statement at the end of *The Adventures of Pinocchio:* "After a long, long look, Pinocchio said to himself with great content: 'How ridiculous I was as the marionette! And how happy I am now that I have become a real boy!' "

BIBLIOGRAPHY

Cain, A. C. (1964), On "Playing Crazy" and Identity Problems in Some Borderline and Psychotic Children. Unpublished paper.

Colby, K. M. (1960), *An Introduction to Psychoanalytic Research*. New York: Basic Books.

Collodi, C. (1957), *The Adventures of Pinocchio*. New York: Grosset & Dunlap.

Ekstein, R. (1963a), The Opening Gambit in Psychotherapeutic Work with Severely Disturbed Adolescents. *Amer. J. Orthopsychiat.*, 33:862-871.

—— (1963b), The Parent Turning into the Sibling. *Amer. J. Orthopsychiat.*, 33:518-520.

—— & Friedman, S. W. (1957), The Function of Acting Out, Play Action and Play Acting in the Psychotherapeutic Process. *Amer. Psa. Assn.*, 5:581-629.

—— & —— (1959), On the Meaning of Play in Childhood Psychosis. In: *Dynamic Psychopathology in Childhood*, ed. L. Jessner & E. Pavenstedt. New York: Grune & Stratton, pp. 269-292.

—— & Meyer, M. M. (1961), Distancing Devices in Childhood Schizophrenia and Allied Conditions: Quantitative and Qualitative Aspects of "Distancing" in the Psychotherapeutic Process. *Psychol. Rep.*, 9:145-146.

Erikson, E. H. (1940), Studies in the Interpretation of Play: 1. Clinical Observation of Play Disruption in Young Children. *Genet. Psychol. Monogr.*, 22:557-671.

Freud, S. (1911), Formulations Regarding the Two Principles in Mental Functioning. *Collected Papers*, 4:13-21. London: Hogarth Press, 1948.

Klein, M. (1961), *Narrative of a Child Analysis: The Conduct of the Psychoanalysis of Children as seen in the Treatment of a Ten-year-old Boy*. New York: Basic Books.

Mahler, M. S. (1952), On Symbiosis and Schizophrenia: Autistic and Symbiotic Infantile Positions. *This Annual*, 7:286-305.

—— & Gosliner, B. J. (1955), On Symbiotic Child Psychosis: Genetic, Dynamic and Restitutive Aspects. *This Annual*, 10:195-214.

Rambert, M. L. (1949), *Children in Conflict*. New York: International Universities Press.

Schlesinger, H. (1964), A Contribution to a Theory of Promising: I: Primary and Secondary Promising. Unpublished paper.

Shakow, D. (1962), Psychoanalytic Education of Behavioral and Social Scientists for Research. In: *Science and Psychoanalysis*, ed. J. Masserman. New York: Grune & Stratton.

Waelder, R. (1932), The Psychoanalytic Theory of Play. *Psa. Quart.*, 2:208-224, 1933.

THE MOURNING REACTION
OF A TEN-AND-A-HALF-YEAR-OLD BOY

YVON GAUTHIER, M.D. (Montreal)

John was ten and a half when his father suddenly died of a heart attack. In the week that preceded the fatal seizure, the father had complained only of mild symptoms; he died shortly after arrival at the hospital where he was taken during the night. At that time the mother too was in the hospital for a minor operation. The children were sleeping and were not aware of anything unusual happening.

In this paper I shall discuss John's reactions to this completely unexpected event, as observed during analytic sessions over a period of about eight months. In attempting an analytic understanding of the boy's rich material, I hope to contribute to a more precise knowledge of loss reactions in childhood.

CASE PRESENTATION

The History

At the time of the event, John had been in analysis for eighteen months. Around the age of six, he had been treated by another analyst and had gradually stopped treatment as his main symptoms, enuresis and phobias, had disappeared. When he was eight and a half, enuresis had reappeared and the parents noticed the boy's difficulty in mixing with cousins and other children. An acute anxiety attack at a recreational center where the mother wanted to leave him

This paper was presented in briefer form to the Canadian Psychiatric Association Meeting, Vancouver, June 24-27, 1964, and in this version to the Conference on Depressive Illnesses, Montreal, February 5-7, 1965.

This child's analytic material was regularly discussed in a Child Analysis Study Group of the Canadian Psychoanalytic Society, under the direction of Dr. W. Clifford M. Scott, whose suggestions I wish particularly to acknowledge.

Director of Training, Child Psychiatry Department, L'Hopital Sainte-Justine pour les Enfants, Montréal, Canada.

with friends led his parents to seek help again, and analysis was resumed.

John's history revealed several traumatic factors. The relationship with his mother had been marked with much ambivalence. The oldest of four children (boy eight, girl four and a half, boy two), John seems to have been the one to bear the brunt of the mother's personal conflicts. She revealed that on several occasions she had severely punished him physically because she was enraged. Once, around the age of two, when he was crying, his mother is said to have beaten his head on the edge of the crib. When he was around three, she put his face into the BM he had just made on the living room floor. There were, during those early years, several separations (hospitalizations of the mother and trips) which were certainly traumatic, as we could see during the analysis: each new absence of the mother and each separation from the analyst stirred up intense anger and depression.

There is a history of the mother teasing the boy's penis, much to his dislike (according to the father). She was overprotective, always afraid he would be hurt in some way. The father also used to be very worried about John being hurt and did not even like him to be held by his own parents. There was evidence of a poor relationship between the parents. The mother openly expressed her scorn of her husband in the presence of the children. The father, having inherited a large fortune from his father, never seemed to have held a job consistently. It was only in the last two years of his life that he had found the type of work which seemed to channel his voyeuristic drives: he censored movies for a local TV station. Both parents were in analytic treatment when I first saw John.

John's analysis up to his father's death was most often centered around drawing maps of the section of town where he lived, of Australia, and gradually of an imaginary island in the Pacific, L'Ile Quatre Étages (he lived in a four-story home). This very unusual activity revealed, at one time or another, his feeling of loneliness when his mother left him and his attempt to make sure he could join her at any time; or his competition with father, who was considered to have no sense of direction and had to be directed by the boy when they drove together. This struggle with his father had been expressed in a significant dream, which told of John's feat in conquering Grand Coté, an enormous and dangerous hill (6,000 feet long and five times as high), in a bus driven by a friendly chauffeur. At the end, he was rewarded with decorations and a large sum of money, but it was hardly more than what his brother won for doing nothing.

After a vacation during which he went to camp for the first time, John resumed treatment, and was still involved in drawing maps of his imaginary island and of imaginary areas in Labrador. In the few weeks that preceded his father's death, there were frequent references to the idea of getting married. He used to say he would not get married "because it is too much trouble" and "one can be big without getting married." He seemed to be repeating the words of his father who had often said that he should not have married.

It is in this context of a struggle with his father, partly solved through identification with father's ideals, that this boy lost a warm figure to whom he had gradually become quite close.

The Initial Reaction

The boy was told about the death in my office by his uncle who had brought him to his regular session. At first, for a very short time, he cried. He said he had thought his father would live as long as his grandfather, who died in his seventies. He talked about a movie he had recently seen in which a Japanese emperor, dying in his youth, left a daughter who killed herself shortly afterward and a younger son who did not want to succeed his father lest the same fate befall him. He was worried about how they would live, how long the money which had been left to his father by the grandfather would last. He also wondered whether his mother would remarry. From this point, several themes gradually unfolded in the boy's sessions. I would like to summarize them before I discuss their meaning.

A few days after his father's funeral, John reacted angrily to a comment by the maid and was later found in his room, where he had taken the outside window off, threatening to kill himself by jumping out. In the following session he said, "Oh yes, I wanted to kill myself and go to see my daddy in Heaven." On another occasion I suggested that he had a feeling of not being very good and of having lost the struggle with his father who, in his own words, had become a powerful spirit; he answered: "Yes, but not for long—I am going to die too and I am going to be as good as he is."

The Search for Power

Hypnotism appeared frequently in his material. John believed he was a hypnotist and practiced his art with a friend whom he would place on top of the Statue of Liberty: but he feared that his power would be taken away, his friend killed, and he punished. The thought occurred to him that he might throw himself from my window and not hurt himself because he would pronounce a name, thus testing and showing his strength. He talked about India, "the land of hypnotism." His father was now a spirit and had all the characteristics of a spirit: he knew everything and was very powerful. "Spirits know everything but they don't have a body." One day he brought with him a statue of the Virgin with the globe under her feet, and he talked about spirits being very powerful, particularly the Holy Spirit because of His wings.

Knowledge of languages became a recurrent theme in John's sessions. His father had started to learn Italian before his death; John, who had not previously shown any interest in this language, started to learn it. For a long time, he could not leave the session without telling me a few sentences in Italian, which he had learned from the records left by his father. He recalled how angry he used to be at his father who would talk Italian to him or read newspapers in Italian. He often spoke English (the analysis was conducted in French) during sessions and considered it superior to know several languages. One day, he talked about a magic doll he had just seen on television, who could speak 116 sentences in seventeen languages. His father, now being a spirit, could speak more languages, all of them in fact, 6,000 maybe, including the African dialects. He wondered how many the analyst could speak, and again he said that he could speak three, French, English, and Italian, as well as "piglatin." German was added a few days later. John believed a universal language would be invented and used at the World's Fair in Montreal in 1967, and everybody, whatever their original language, would understand it without even learning it. It seems he used to pray in French to his father, but it was not enough, hence the need for a universal tongue: a way of being a spirit, to be strong like father, but not quite as strong as Jesus.

A far northern imaginary area somewhere in Labrador became prominent in John's fantasies. He spent many sessions drawing details of cities and villages in that area, ski slopes and skiing facilities that existed there. Chateau Bellevue, one of the northern villages, was the exact counterpart of his summer place and showed its value in being built on solid gold. It was remarkable in that everything there was bigger and wider. For several months, this area became a central theme around which other more specific themes became expressed.

The Continuation of Generations

A figure appeared in this northern area, M. de Sacholaka, a man of great stature, the owner of a vast area, who had come from Germany. John often talked about him, and finally said very openly that M. de Sacholaka stood for his grandfather who died a millionnaire. The money had been left to his father and now to them. He calculated how much money this was and compared it to the little money I made. He spoke of how his family went all the way back to a great French poet, and of the need to continue the generations, which will be done by the youngest brother since neither he nor the second brother wanted to get married.

A short while later, he brought with him five little cracked nuts, which he carefully painted in different colors and finally called his babies as he put them away in his drawer. He also called an airplane his "baby." My suggestion that he was worried about continuing the generations brought a sharp denial: he would not get married, women are no good, women only want to be better than you, they act as if they are superior. This clearly was an identification with feelings often expressed by his father—not about his mother, he said, but about other women. But he further wondered: "Who could it be that I would marry?" A few days later he told a joke he had made at a class party, in which kissing girls seemed an important element.

He began to talk about his plans to become a biologist when he grew up, and of building a very modern zoo for himself; he would be its architect and travel to far countries to find animals. In so doing, it was clear, he would become as big and powerful as his grandfather. Around the same time he became futuristic, talking about the houses of the year 2,000 which will replace the ones that now exist, houses which will be on pillars and could easily rise to 4,000 feet in the air. But it rapidly became clear that such fantasies were his way of warding off the very bad news that the summer house, which had belonged to his grandfather and to his father, would be sold.

The High Dangerous Mountain

In a story he described the struggle of a group of boys who wished to climb a high mountain and had to get rid of a giant Indian preventing access to the top. A younger boy had first tried and had been tied up by the Indian: rescued by the other boys, he helped in caging the man during his sleep and achieving his defeat. A nearby mountain was thought to be dangerous since a volcano lay under it. A new mountain appeared in Labrador, the highest of all, and it became clear that it was the symbol of Heaven. Heaven is the highest place, but there is no danger of falling from Heaven into Hell: "Hell is not within the earth as you think, like in China, the other side of the earth. It is on the same level as Heaven, and Purgatory is in the middle."

One of his cities, Chateau Bellevue, built on gold, was also seen to be a symbol of Heaven where God lived like in a palace. Heaven, like Chateau Bellevue, is enclosed by a high fence, so devils cannot get in. He spent much time drawing details of this Chateau Bellevue in a secret booklet, which he tore up one day because he did not like some minor details. Actually, as he was getting near to drawing the top of the mountain, there also emerged his fears of approaching the top, Heaven, of getting closer to his father, and of becoming his equal. Being the mayor of Chateau Bellevue, he would be like God if the symbol was pushed to its conclusion—"and of course he is not" as he readily realized.

Ambivalence Toward Father and Analyst

This material slowly revealed John's ambivalence toward his father. Talking about spirits and their power, he mumbled between his teeth, "But they are worthless." Once he talked about his father, saying he spent forty-six years on earth and would be in Heaven for forty years: "then he will go to Hell." Several months later he expressed with difficulty the doubts he had about his father's real situation, that he might not be in Heaven but in Purgatory or in Hell: "After all, he has committed so many sins." A few days later, I made an interpretation that he was afraid to let himself think that his father might not be in Heaven but in Hell; he said I was insulting his daddy and I was like a little man with horns and tail and in a very hot place. One day he brought with him a butterfly he had found in a drugstore near my office. He was worried that it might be stepped on and lack fresh air. He complained of having a pain in the heart and he talked of his own death. Returning to a map previously started of one of his cities, he left some space for an animal cemetery. Confronted with a suggestion that the butterfly was a symbol of himself, that he was actually afraid to die, either in an attempt to be as powerful as father in death or as a punishment for taking his place on earth, he spontaneously talked about his fear of going to Purgatory (for a few venial sins he had committed) and the precautions he took every day: by going to Mass every morning and reciting prayers which gave him indulgences. At the end of the session, he very carefully took the butterfly in his hands and called it Johnny, the name of his father.

John often expressed angry feelings toward the analyst in close relation to his feelings toward his father. For instance, about two months after his father's death, as the Christmas vacation approached, he expressed the desire to terminate treatment, apparently being afraid to get too close to the analyst. He called the analyst "moose, dumb, stupid, crazy," whereas his father was the powerful spirit. When confronted with the suggestion that such thoughts were an attempt not to feel that his father was not so good, he said, "I will tell my mother that you insult my father." He further accused the analyst of hearing an inside voice repeating "insult him" and of being jealous of his father's power. In the very next session, he accused the analyst of thinking that his father did not smell good.

At the same time as the vacation came nearer, John expressed his desire to get close to the analyst in several subtle ways. However, he was caught in an impossible struggle: in getting close to a person one becomes like him; to get close to the analyst meant he would become as stupid as he felt the analyst was. Upon his return from his vacation, John again missed no opportunity to belittle me, calling me stupid and *niaiseux* (dumb). The connection with father became clearer when he called the analyst "trash" and associated it with ashes and how his father's body turned to ashes, but not his spirit. Sometimes, however, the desire for closeness overcame his aggression. Once he said that he understood everything within himself as well as within me; the good qualities and the bad ones: he knew very well about the bad ones, about the good ones he specified that I was polite, a tiny bit friendly, and not jealous of his being better than I was. Another time, a drawing left by another boy stirred up anger against me and his desire to belittle me. Gradually, however, such material as playing with an airplane he called his baby, comparing my beard to his father's who did not shave on Sundays, led him to deny his wish to be close to me, "to be in the arms of dada," as he said.

It was only in the week that preceded the summer vacation, that is, six months after the death of father, that his mourning seemed to become less intense. There were suggestions of some fantasies involving growing up to be a teenager, and disgust at such ideas. The Pope's death, seven months after his father's death, brought out more doubts about the whole idea of religion and the power of dead people who have become spirits. Competitive games appeared in relation to me, and demonstrated his need to be better than me. At the same time, he seemed less involved in his faraway place, saying he had assistants doing his work for him. The approaching summer vacation stirred up his conflict about terminating the treatment or going on for a long time, years to come. He used the question of money to say he could not continue, again worried there would not be enough money left, then bringing out how much money had been left to him by his father. But in the last hour, he took home maps he had drawn in sessions, and emphasized again a volcanic area, saying, "I had died and father had died in it, and my father felt it was a very dangerous area," then further, "I would be on a planet and I would be resurrected."

DISCUSSION

The loss of his father drove John into painful, ambivalent feelings, with which he attempted to deal by using different mechanisms.

The feeling of loss underlay John's attempts to communicate again with his father. He tried in so many ways to get close to him; scarcely a day or two after the death, he suggested he wanted to throw himself out of his window. Actually he also tried to get closer to father by adopting his activities, his skills, the power he attributed to him; he attempted to identify with old attributes of his father or with the new powers with which he believed death to have endowed his father. He believed he had the special privilege of hypnotism, conceived as a power which could be used to put a friend on the Statue of Liberty. Languages assumed an important role soon after the father's death. He often spoke English in sessions, usually at times when the material was related to his father. Italian, which his father knew and spoke at home, became a new interest for the boy. He mentioned the thousands of languages that are spoken in the world, particularly in Africa; there was a short run of "piglatin," a language to which one must know the key to be able to communicate. Finally, he spoke of a "universal language" which will be spoken at the World's Fair (reminding us of the Day of Pentecost). All through these activities (and probably prayer is an important, more secret one, only alluded to) John wished to communicate with a special attribute of his father: the omnipotence of one who has become a spirit through dying. And he seemed to long for his own death, as the only means of becoming reunited with the long-sought-for power of his father.

John's desire for reunion with his father was also expressed in his attempts to get closer to the analyst as a father substitute, but he allowed himself very little satisfaction in this relationship. He suggested that the analyst was very intelligent, only to return quickly to a process of belittling him as a stupid fool, the opposite of his idealized father. He was afraid of liking me: to like somebody makes one become like the loved one, and this is childish. We may assume that he regarded his desire for close contact with his father as a dangerous submission to a now powerful figure and that he needed to belittle the analyst upon whom he had displaced his desires.

Actually John's relationship with his father had often been lived in ambivalent terms. A constant attempt to be better than father, to show father up with his knowledge of streets and geography, was a feature of the early part of the analysis. The "Grand Coté" dream revealed his efforts to overcome this impossibly high figure, his triumph marred by his brother's easy victory. At the same time, father was "a nice guy" who usually protected him against mother and spent time doing things with him. It should be no surprise that this ambivalence toward his father was stirred up by his sudden disappearance. Death, immediately construed in the religious teaching as a transformation into a powerful spirit, was felt to be the definite triumph of father and therefore stirred up his competitive strivings. The same activities which were different attempts at communication with the lost father were also aggressive efforts to become as strong and powerful as this ideal father. Hypnotism, the mastery of many languages, the flying spirit, the Chateau Bellevue built on and with gold, all symbolize in one way or another the struggle against the giant and the victorious overthrow and his thus reaching the dreamed-of power.

To be sure, at first, only suggestions of his father's worthlessness were made. Much later, John talked of his father's sins, that perhaps he was in Hell or on the verge of falling into Hell. There were symbolic allusions to his father's body turning to ashes, and denial of the bad smell of his father. Volcanoes, burning inside the earth, could be understood as the symbol of Hell waiting for father. Such allusions, however, were always very rapid, only touched upon: they were actually very dangerous to him. And all through his fantasies of power, the threatening danger was readily invoked. The hypnotist could place his friend on top of the Statue of Liberty, but he was immediately threatened with death if his power were suddenly to be taken away. Recurrent images of mountains were usually dangerous ones; they were often old, extinct volcanoes, still loaded with peril. The climbing expedition was a very dangerous one. Actually death was at every corner of his streets, somewhere in almost every theme he approached: death was regarded both as an ideal through which power would finally be granted and as the worst punishment for having wished to take over father's power in Heaven.

The anxiety stirred up by these hidden aggressive tendencies toward both the father and the self was met by this immediate idealization of the father's power and the gradual belittling of the analyst, the two facets of a splitting process. Helped in the idealization of his father by the religious teaching, he made sure that the aggressive urges did not overwhelm him. The belittling of the analyst pre-vented his getting too close to him (which could mean losing his father completely and accepting a substitute) as well as the upsurge of the aggressive drive against its true object, the father. However, such mechanisms, though useful, needed to be helped by reparative efforts, which were expressed in the good care given to the butterfly and his Lenten religious activities.

As John thus dealt with his ambivalent feelings, progressive trends gradually made their appearance. We can observe his drive toward the future in his struggle with ideas of having babies to con-tinue generations, his throwing airplanes from the window and call-ing them his "babies," his planning faraway cities and considering himself the mayor of them. He saw himself as a future planner, a zoologist and a biologist, perhaps as the builder architect of a large zoo. Possible sublimations were announced in such projects. The regressive trend toward communication with father and toward intro-jection of his power gradually led to a progressive utilization of the acquired skills in fantasied responsibilities and constructions. The return to the past not only was balanced by a strong turn to the future, it was used to prepare and insure its realization.

REVIEW OF THE LITERATURE

Few analytic observations have been recorded of a child's reac-tions to the loss of a parent.

Anna Freud and Dorothy Burlingham (1944) reported on the re-actions of young children who were observed in the setting of the Hampstead Nursery, after they had been separated from their parents during the war.

Bowlby, in a series of publications, has been particularly inter-ested in reactions of young children to the separation from their mothers. He finally assumed that the underlying processes are similar in child and adult mourning. In their discussion of Bowlby's 1960 paper, Anna Freud, Max Schur, and René Spitz suggest that Bowlby did not sufficiently take into consideration the age and the develop-mental stage of the child beset by the loss of a parent: as Anna Freud in particular stresses, the child's mourning will be approximately similar to the adult's only after he has reached the stage of object constancy.

Helene Deutsch (1937) believed that the mourning process must sooner or later, in one form or another, be completed; however, the total denial of painful affects is often used by the child who finds it difficult to bear the work of mourning and who thus lays the foundation for later pathological reactions. Rochlin (1953, 1959) placed the accent on the need the child feels for an object and on his efforts at identification with the lost object. He believes that the child uses mechanisms very similar to those used by the adult, but that the child shows no signs of a clinical depression.

Scharl (1961) compared the reactions of an eight-year-old girl and of her five-year-old sister to the sudden death of their father. She concluded that regression is more prominent in a younger child, whereas the older child, who has a more fully developed ego, stronger identifications, and more elaborate defenses, can better adapt to the loss. The significant difference in the reactions of these two children appeared to be determined mostly by the phase of psychic development during which the trauma occurred.

Shambaugh (1961), observing the reactions of a seven-year-old to the death of his mother, focused on the boy's attempts to deny the painful affects and on his resorting to regression rather than coping with the grief work.

Furman (1964) described the first seven months of the analysis of a six-year-old boy whose mother died shortly after the treatment had been started. The mourning itself unfolded in two phases, from the painful acceptance of the reality loss to the beginning decathexis of the inner-world representation. Contrary to Shambaugh's patient, denial was used little until the last month of the reported period of analytic work (about five months after the mother's death). Furman mainly outlined the technical problems raised by the event and did not see any reason to alter the basic analytic technique appropriate for a child of that age. He attempted to confine the analytic work to the interpretation of the defenses which the child used to ward off the painful loss. He discussed the indications of analytic work in a situation of loss. Furman clearly believes that treatment should not be considered only because of the imminent death of a parent, lest the analyst allow himself to replace the lost one; but he also sees no reason in a parent's death to alter the valid indications for a child analytic treatment.

Conclusion

The mourning reaction of this ten-and-a-half-year-old to the sudden loss of his father went through three main stages, closely interlocked in their complicated, most often very symbolic expression. At first, the child attempted to reunite with the lost one at almost any cost. However, such efforts at identification soon were seen to be an aggressive incorporation of the power of the ambivalently loved father: the splitting of the father image into the idealization of the good (spiritual) father and the depreciation of the bad analyst then appeared to be the main defense against such aggressive urges. When the splitting was interpreted, the child could abandon this omnipotent idealized object of identification and turn toward the tasks of the future.

At no point did this child become depressed. Using adult concepts, one might say he has used a massive denial of his painful feelings. My hypothesis is rather that the complicated processes used by this child to communicate and to identify with his father, as well as to work through his ambivalence toward him, constituted the mourning process and consequently prevented the appearance of a clinical depressive reaction. In this context, the analyst, representing the depreciated aspect of the father, played a very important role. The patient warded off the potential danger of turning aggression upon the partly introjected father: the analyst became the object upon whom the child could displace the aggressive feelings he might otherwise have expressed toward the introjected father.

The analytic situation provided us with a rare opportunity to observe a child's reaction to the loss of his father. It was much more important, I believe, to the child himself, in providing him with an object with whom he could partly identify, thus partly replacing the lost object, and upon whom he could turn his aggression, thus saving him the painful suffering of an attack against the powerful father in Heaven, as well as against the internalized father, that is, himself. Furthermore, I hope that the interpretation of the splitting process also enabled him to reunify the good and the bad object, thus saving him the often tragic and futile search for an ideal omnipotent image in the future.

BIBLIOGRAPHY

Bowlby, J. (1960), Grief and Mourning in Infancy and Early Childhood. *This Annual,* 15:9-94.

Deutsch, H. (1937), Absence of Grief. *Psa. Quart.,* 6:12-22.

Freud, A. & Burlingham, D. (1944), *Infants without Families.* New York: International Universities Press.

Furman, R. A. (1964), Death of a Six-Year-Old's Mother during His Analysis. *This Annual,* 19:377-397.

Rochlin, G. (1953), Loss and Restitution. *This Annual,* 8:288-309.

—— (1959), The Loss Complex. *J. Amer. Psa. Assn.,* 7:299-316.

Scharl, A. (1961), Regression and Restitution in Object Loss. *This Annual,* 16:471-480.

Shambaugh, B. (1961), A Study of Loss Reactions in a Seven-Year-Old. *This Annual,* 16:510-527.

SOME THOUGHTS ON THE TECHNICAL
HANDLING OF BORDERLINE CHILDREN

SARA KUT ROSENFELD and
MARJORIE P. SPRINCE (London)

This paper is a further report on the work undertaken by the group studying borderline cases,[1] but should not be taken as a final statement of our findings and views on the subject of technique. Working with borderline children appears to produce as many techniques as there are children and this figure can probably be multiplied by the number of therapists concerned.

If experience is pooled, however, certain common problems emerge. Although as a group we have learned to thrash out our problems and benefit from each other's experience, it has been easier to reach agreement on matters of theoretical formulation than on technique.

In this paper we have tried to show the divergences of opinion as well as the areas of agreement within the group. We have often

Material for this paper has been collected in the Hampstead Child-Therapy Clinic. The Clinic is maintained with the aid of grants by The Field Foundation, Inc., New York; The Anna Freud Foundation, New York; The Grant Foundation, Inc., New York; The Estate of Flora Haas, New York; The Walter E. Meyer Research Institute of Law, Inc., New Haven, Connecticut; The National Institute of Mental Health, Bethesda, Maryland; The Old Dominion Foundation, New York; The Psychoanalytic Research and Development Fund, Inc., New York; The Taconic Foundation, Inc., New York.

[1] The members of our group are: A. Bene, S. Baker, R. Edgcumbe, I. Elkan, A. Goldberger, H. Kawenoka, H. Kennedy, E. Shepheard Model, and the authors. S. Fahmy worked with us until recently. Over the years we have had many visitors who have made invaluable contributions. Of these we should particularly like to mention the recent visit of Gerd Jacobsen from Oslo, Norway. Miss Jacobsen worked with us over a long period and some of her thinking has been embodied in this paper.

This paper is the joint work of the authors based on the corporate thinking of the group. The group members have read the paper and have helped us to formulate ideas more clearly.

The children whose material is included as illustrations in this paper were treated by the following therapists: A. Bene, R. Edgcumbe, H. Kennedy, and M. P. Sprince.

worked on one case in great detail and again and again have returned to certain points, looking at them in different contexts. These meetings have been heated, stimulating, and exciting, and at the time we felt that we had achieved new insights into the functioning of the borderline child. When we collected the material for this paper, however, we wondered whether we had in fact learned so much that was new and we felt a bit like the mountain in labor who having shouted so loudly brought forth only a mouse. But this, we think, may be symptomatic of work with borderline children.

Characteristic Borderline Features

It has become increasingly evident that the therapist about to take on a borderline child has to be prepared for this in a special way, since his or her experience with neurotic children will be of limited help only. The techniques we are accustomed to employing can in fact hinder the establishment of a working rapport with the borderline schizophrenic child.

When we start to treat a neurotic child, our technique is guided by a diagnostic appraisal and by our experience with other similar cases. When we work with a borderline child, we will find no such safe frame of reference and often no diagnosis will be available. We must then slowly work out our own special technique for each case anew. This is necessary because the level of development in each area is different in each borderline child and the combinations of psychopathologies are infinite.

Accustomed to a relatively passive role which allows the material of the neurotic child to unfold and develop, we find ourselves confronted with a very different situation in the treatment of the borderline child: there we may be forced at once into a more active role, primarily because of the need to make contact wtih the child and sometimes because of the need to safeguard the child from impulsive behavior which may harm him, the therapist, or the environment. The technique must therefore vary in relation to a variety of factors, and these include what we already know about the borderline child's psychopathology in general, as described in the literature (see, e.g., our earlier paper [1963] and Ruth Thomas [1964]). Other factors such as specific characteristics of parental psychopathology and the impact of the material on the therapist must also be taken into account.

Our knowledge of the borderline child's psychopathology includes the following factors:

1. The precarious maintenance of object cathexis in most of these children and the ease with which it slides over into primary identification.

2. The disturbance in ego functioning, which has been found in all our cases and which may be due to inherent or traumatic factors. Although the origin of the defect cannot always be precisely pinpointed, there is evidence of its early existence. Moreover, there seems to be some connection with a disturbance in the infant's perceptive and integrative function, which manifests itself in a faulty capacity to select and inhibit stimuli. In spite of this, all our children show considerable high-level ego functioning, which is, however, characteristically unstable.

3. Anxiety is characterized in our cases by primitive feelings of disintegration and annihilation.

4. The bisexual conflict is always present, but it does not seem to be basic to the disturbance of the children we have studied; it is rather an aspect of the disturbance surrounding the question of identity. This means that uncertainty about sexual identity has a preoedipal connotation. It seems to us that the majority of our children have never attained a phase of phallic-oedipal dominance, that they remain basically on the preoedipal level, although some of the material looks as though it belonged to the phallic-oedipal phase. However, there appears to be a discrepancy in the development of the sexual and aggressive drives in the more severely disturbed children in our group.

The developmental process through which the infant passes from a period of closest union with the mother, to a stage in which a separate identity is gradually established has been referred to in our previous paper (1963).

For our purposes here it is necessary only to remind ourselves of the fact that the achievement of secondary identification presupposes the formation of an ego and the awareness of the self as a separate entity. The whole process of the building up of permanent object representations cannot take place unless there is a capacity to internalize. This process in turn depends largely upon the normal capacity to make an affective contact with the object and to maintain such cathexis.

Anna Freud, in a recent discussion on a borderline child,[2] added another dimension to this process when she drew attention to the fact that the growth and development of the normal child center around pleasurable experiences. This has an immediate bearing upon both instinctual and ego development. We have always accepted the mother's role as an auxiliary ego, but we have not sufficiently spelled out her function in offering herself as a mediator between instinct development and ego development. The normal child is able to make use of the object, thereby strengthening his capacity for object cathexis and further ego integration. Deprivation of such early pleasurable experiences interferes with these processes and must be taken into account in our handling of these children.

In the healthy child, the stages in the development of instinct and object relationships are reflected in the functioning of the ego. This is not so in our borderline children. Their ego development often appears to be at a higher level than one would expect from the stage of their object relationships, but the apparently high functioning in certain areas cannot easily be maintained. It follows from these observations that in therapy, stability in ego development may depend upon the child gradually becoming anchored in the appropriate phases in object relationship.

It is just in this area of object relationships and ego development that the borderline child's disturbance shows itself most clearly. It is not the function of this paper to examine causation or to decide whether ego disturbance threatens the capacity for object relations or is caused by their failure. We have to bear in mind, however, that what the child experiences as mothering will be reflected in his relationship with the therapist and will have repercussions upon the therapist's technique.

In our earlier paper (1963) we described how our findings confirmed Anna Freud's suggestion that our children are constantly on the border between object cathexis and identification. We described how their tendency to revert to identification with the object leads

[2] At the Hampstead Child-Therapy Clinic, February, 1965.

to the wish to merge and to defenses against this wish. In this connection we drew attention to the fact that most of our children are fixated predominantly at the oral phase of libido development and that their object relationships all show the characteristics of this phase—that is to say, a clamoring for satisfaction of their needs and a sporadic blurring of ego boundaries.

However, when our children are considered individually, it is clear that their capacity to cathect objects and to maintain cathexis varies from individual to individual. This may be due not only to the different points of fixation within the oral phase but also to the fact that many borderline children have touched or experienced later developmental stages, if only fleetingly, and then regressed. When regression, even from only a slightly higher level, has occurred, we may be taken in by what appear to be more sophisticated modes of object relationships, since we know that the borderline child simultaneously shows libidinal material from every stage he has ever reached. We may further be taken in by the fact that the borderline child appears to have an almost extrasensory sensitivity, which takes account of and responds to the smallest mood changes, mannerisms, dress, etc., and gives the impression of a much higher level of object relationship than has in fact been achieved. From our experience with most of our cases, this sensitivity actually indicates a very early state of object relationship in which the patient's self boundaries are temporarily interfered with, and merging with the object still plays a significant part.

We do not intend to repeat what has been widely described in the literature about the borderline child's ego development. We shall confine ourselves to mentioning only some of those aspects which have an immediate bearing on the handling of the borderline child. Some of our children are capable of high-level, even abstract thought, although their ego functions operate with relatively unneutralized energy, and they easily disintegrate under any kind of stress. Secondary thought processes easily regress to primary-process thinking with the accompaniment of concretizations, the tendency toward direct translation from fantasy into action or from drive impulse to action. We understand this tendency toward direct translation into action from the point of view of normal thought development; that is to say, action precedes and is gradually converted into thinking and speaking.

This arrest in thought development has to be considered together with the poor capacity to inhibit incoming stimuli and to select the relevant from the irrelevant. Another factor is that some of our children have no scale for judging relative importance. An example of this is Norma, aged ten and a half; she feels that if she can knock down a chair, she can equally well knock down a house. This has a bearing upon the poor impulse control noted in a number of cases. Although poor impulse control is in itself a specific problem for both the patient and us, it is quite clear that the wild behavior (sometimes mistaken for aggression) in fact expresses intense diffuse and panic-like anxiety which cannot be contained.

The borderline child, like the neurotic child, experiences anxiety as a danger signal, but the ego of the borderline child, unlike that of the neurotic, cannot find appropriate measures to reduce the level of anxiety. "Signal anxiety is therefore experienced as a threat which may lead to overwhelming feelings of disintegration" (Kut Rosenfeld and Sprince, 1963). The therapist's capacity to respond and indeed to bear the patient's anxiety is an essential part of therapy, but it is further complicated by the fact that in the initial period of treatment we do not know what situations or experiences may trigger an outburst of panic or how to alleviate such a panic. At this phase of treatment we do not even know whether the child's overwhelming anxiety is due to a re-experiencing of an infantile traumatic situation —whether it is set off by a fear of disintegration and a threatened loss of body boundaries—or whether it is caused by still other reasons to which we have no clue. We often do not even know the immediately precipitating cause, and sometimes an apparently irrelevant object has become attached to the anxiety, which is mobilized whenever the object appears, even long after the original link may have been lost. In Norma's case, the therapist was able to catch just such an associative link in the making.

It had long been observed that Norma was a child for whom certain words had a terrifying and incomprehensible meaning. She called these words "worry words" and would complain that they got in the way of her thoughts so that she could not remember or think of other things.

Once, while Norma was showing her therapist how to make a mechanical toy dog move, she became frightened by having to press the button because it was round. In this way she introduced "round" as a new worry word which she said reminded her of "roundabouts" (an old worry word). Very quickly this fear spread to all round objects, so that Norma refused to eat round biscuits and even had to avoid thinking of round things—an oval-shaped piece of cardboard was not round, she explained, so she was not afraid of it. At this point she wanted to plug her ears with cotton wool to keep the worry word out of her mind, thus indicating that under the impact of extreme anxiety she could not distinguish between external and internal stimuli.

The need to avoid round things caused Norma to initiate a game in which she and her therapist described things in a "round about" way to avoid mentioning their names.

The fear was so great, however, that Norma could not contain it in words and one day without warning she picked up a round ash tray and smashed it on the floor. The next day she lost her voice (not uncommon with Norma at times of anxiety). She was still troubled by the worry word and wanted to damage it by shouting it to get rid of it.

This acute anxiety which had become attached to all round objects related to an actual event when Norma had been driving from High Wick to her treatment at Hampstead.[3] On this occasion the driver had missed his direction and had driven round a roundabout twice. Via the worry word Norma communicated the terror of that moment when she had thought that they would go round and round and never stop and that she would never safely reach her destination —the Clinic. The panic associated with the actual event was so great that it had to be repressed or obliterated, but the memory of the terrible experience had been left, locked in the single word "roundabout." Although at the time of the incident the fear had been understood, discussion could not prevent it from spreading and attaching

3 Norma and Basil are treated as part of a combined project of the Hampstead Child-Therapy Clinic and the High Wick Psychiatric Unit (psychiatrist-in-charge Dr. George Stroh) for the investigation and treatment of borderline psychotic children. We should like especially to acknowledge the work of Ruth Thomas in coordinating and advising on this project.

itself to objects now having only an indirect link with the original trauma and worry word.

One of the difficulties involved in tracing such expressions of panic to their source is that attempts to get near to their origin seem to increase anxiety and confusion to an intolerable degree. This might mean that the original anxiety was so unbearable that the ego was temporarily put out of action. Attempts at reconstruction, especially at the height of anxiety, might then threaten similar disintegration. It is possible that at a later stage reconstruction, achieved primarily by the child herself, might therefore be less threatening and might bring with it real relief. On the other hand, even if one gets to the core of a traumatic event, in a borderline child there is no certainty that the trouble will be corrected.

The problem of dealing with outbursts of acute anxiety at the beginning of treatment often depends upon the therapist supplying the ego functions missing in the child. To follow the borderline child's material when one has not yet a true understanding of him is a formidable task and can only be likened to learning to speak an entirely new language. But knowing the borderline child's vulnerability to anxiety and the time it will take to understand him at least enables us to prepare ourselves and attempt to plan the therapeutic environment in such a way that a minimum of change and outside stimulation will be involved.

Our awareness of the borderline child's acute anxiety has many implications for technique. It helps us to tolerate the unreliability of his "object relatedness" and influences the development of a working alliance.

We do not here want to enter the controversy concerning the role of transference in child analysis except to point out that the swings from merging to identification and from identification to object cathexis influence the development of the treatment relationship. Our aim here is to highlight the difference in the treatment relationship of the neurotic child, whose ego is sufficiently developed to enable the therapist to understand conflicts from transferred features, and that of the borderline child, whose treatment relationship is governed by his fragmentary ego, his proneness to acute anxiety, and his low level of object relationship.

Often at the commencement of treatment it appears to some of us that we may represent little more than a piece of furniture to the child. At best he seems to regard us in terms of our ability or lack of ability to provide supplies. It is an immediate necessity, in appraising each new case, to decide upon the degree to which he will or will not actively satisfy such needs. Unlike neurotic children, with whom the work is carried out under conditions of relative frustration, borderline children cannot tolerate the severe demands made upon the neurotic by normal analytic techniques. They may regress still further if their needs are not given recognition in a phase-adequate form, that is to say, concretely. On the other hand, the treatment of borderline children, like that of any of our other children, does not progress under conditions of direct gratification. Sensitive to the child's minute increases in frustration tolerance, we have to find substitutes for the original demand, thus gradually furthering displacement. In this selection of substitutes for direct gratification, two important aims must be kept in mind; namely, that these substitutes will facilitate the emergence and reconstruction of underlying trauma and the furthering of ego development.

When Pedro first came into treatment, his overwhelming need for supplies was enacted in oral, anal, urethral, and phallic terms. Pedro would equate soap, money, and plasticine with feces; spools, watering cans, toothpaste tubes, and the bath shower were equated with the penis. Play with any such symbols would end by eating, sucking, or swallowing; he would eat and swallow plasticine, bits of plastic or tubing, and he would shower water into his mouth and throat—all accompanied by extreme excitement. His demands for food and drink were ceaseless and always equated with the need to fill himself up with strength-giving substances, as an engine is filled with petrol.

Since the material indicated an identification with and extreme jealousy of his baby brother, it was decided to offer him an empty plastic bottle and teat. This empty bottle he filled with water and used daily for many months. He eventually abandoned it by asking to throw the teat away since he no longer needed it.

The bottle provided gratification slightly removed from the original and offered opportunities for regression. Such concrete ways of working through oral conflicts so that they become meaningful may be necessary because of the difficulty these children have in cathecting words and ideas. It is suggested that the closeness of the bottle to the original object may indicate to the child that the therapist understands his specific needs and is attuned to him. In addition, it seems that since all libidinal stages overlap in these children, our therapeutic task may be to stimulate a temporary phase dominance so that the material of that phase can be worked through, thereby allowing the move forward (or back) to the next relevant material.

We have already referred to our difficulties in understanding the borderline children we are treating. Since all of them show a gross disturbance in object relationships together with ego regressions of varying severity, it is extremely difficult to establish contact with them. A particular difficulty is found in the children who step back into primary identification, since their real identity is concealed by the way they merge into whatever object or event has just impressed them. This could be seen most clearly with Derek whose identity changed rapidly within the session. Thus he was Mrs. Joe from Dickens's Great Expectations at one minute, a participant of a television play at another moment, and a drunken man from the pub where he lives at another moment—all in rapid succession. Most frequently, however, Derek feels, acts, moves, and talks as his mother does. The difficulty is to contact the affects. Defense interpretations concerning his need to hide his own identity are insufficient. We think that ideally the therapist should be able to follow these merging experiences with the child, if we are to be able to pick out with him those specific aspects which have triggered off his need to change his identity or to become a participant rather than an observer. This demands an emotional flexibility and understanding which we are not easily able to provide.

With Basil it was not a swing from object cathexis to primary identification but rather a blocking of affect. At the beginning of treatment Basil appeared to shut out the object to such an extent that "sameness" in the environment seemed to be more important than any one person.

These defensive measures were aimed at containing an undue amount of anxiety. The types of behavior described present very special technical problems because they are aimed at deceiving or misleading the therapist. This was equally true of those children who presented us with an overwhelming amount of fantasy material. If this was taken up, it would lead to further elaboration of fantasy, as has been stressed before. It therefore soon became clear that our technique had to be modified to facilitate repression and displacement, rather than to make unconscious material conscious. In other words, we had to help the children to build up defenses, whereas with neurotic children we do the very opposite. This need to direct proceedings is of considerable importance in technique since it places upon us the responsibility of actively guiding the material. To some extent, because of the nature of the borderline disturbance, our function as therapist must be different and has something of the quality of an auxiliary ego, at least in the initial phase.

METHODS OF DEALING WITH ACUTE ANXIETY
AT THE BEGINNING OF TREATMENT

Some of our childern cannot conceive of the possibility of a safe relationship—for them, a pleasurable relationship seems to imply an aggressive one. This means that the development of any new relationship brings the child into a dangerous situation in which he and the object may be at the mercy of aggressive drives. It is not always clear whether this difficulty is based upon real experiences of hostility in early childhood, or whether it is the outcome of later projections, which certainly are predominant by the time we meet the children.

It stands to reason that such a child will experience extreme anxiety in the building up of a tie to the therapist and may well express this anxiety by attacking either us, the environment, or himself. At first many of us tried to deal with this problem by interpretation in the usual way, but we found that the anxiety seemed to increase. This did not wholly surprise us since there are many examples in the literature of disturbed neurotic children who have been observed to stop talking and to act at the height of their fear. Berta Bornstein (1949) comments that at such moments of crisis, interpretations of anxiety could not have been accepted by the child. If this is so with a neurotic child, it might well be more so with a borderline child.

Many of our children seemed to seek active intervention from us to protect them from external dangers and the acting out of impulses. It is neither practical nor useful to give an interpretation to a child who is about to throw himself out of a window. This protection is more primitive than using ourselves as an auxiliary ego, and can best be compared with the function of the mother in the oral stage when she prevents her baby from swallowing dangerous objects or later from burning himself.

Every member of our group agreed that our children could really start to face their hostility only when they began to be anchored in a relationship to the therapist—that is to say, in a relationship in which the child could conceive of the possibility of libidinal attachment. However, this agreement did not extend to the methods which could be employed to bring about such an attachment.

Our discussions concerned the whole question of interpretation of aggressive conflict as against ego-supportive handling. One point of view was that such an attachment could not be brought about without the early interpretation of aggressive conflict. On the other hand, it was suggested that such interpretations at an early stage could be taken by the child as a siding of the therapist with the aggressive drives, acting permissively and leading to an increase in anxiety and therefore to an increase in aggressive behavior. This topic of early interpretation as against ego support has been a point of heated discussion. As we went along it became clearer that it was not one kind of approach versus another but rather the question of balance, timing, and the personality of the therapist. This latter point brings up the whole problem of the treatment relationship between therapist and patient, which is of specific importance in dealing with borderline children and will be referred to later.

During discussions on how to help the child to become anchored in treatment, an attempt was made to spell out some of the ways used to achieve this. They will be discussed under two headings: (1) the use of ego-supportive handling, and (2) the use and timing of interpretations.

Ego-supportive Handling

The acting out shown by our children has been found to be directly connected with the need for immediate discharge of tension due to an inadequate capacity to contain tension of any kind.

One of our aims is to help the child to become aware that tension can at least temporarily be contained, and to aid the development of an ego structure which will facilitate this. We all agreed on this, but once again found that there were different methods of approach. It did seem that our individual attitude was to some extent influenced by *the degree* of acting out in patients.

It has been pointed out that technical devices used with borderline children are similar to the educational methods used with very young children which aim at facilitating displacement.

Basil, aged nine and a half years when treatment started, the eldest of three children of a mixed marriage, was one of the High Wick children. One of the most striking features of his psychopathology was the undue amount of anxiety characterized by feelings of disintegration, depletion, and loss. He defended himself by blocking his affect completely, as mentioned earlier. When he began treatment, he made a list of toys which he asked his therapist to get for him; it included a machine which would give endless supplies of chocolate (to deal with his acute feeling of depletion). Since such a chocolate machine could not be provided, he was offered as an alternative a large and elaborate toy cash register, also on his list. Basil accepted this substitute which performed a useful function throughout the early period of his analysis. By providing an object slightly removed from the physically need-satisfying one he had demanded, the therapist was, he felt, discouraging straightforward instinctual gratification while facilitating displacement. The cash register retained, however, many of the characteristics of the chocolate machine. It offered opportunities for expressing and communicating problems surrounding supply and demand in the form of a pleasurable need-satisfying activity. At the same time it represented the turning of a passive infantile experience into an active one over which he felt he had control.

Pedro, aged six and a half, regressed to sexual and urethral acting out when anxiety was acute. This behavior was so gross that he would urinate and smear over the therapist's clothes and possessions. At its height, however, the urge to urinate itself reminded Pedro of his previous attempts to draw her into mutual activity in this way, and he would again feel impelled to urinate over her. Attempts to stop this either by interpretation or by physical force acted as a further stimulus. It was only when the therapist acknowledged his wish for a mutual activity by suggesting that she continue their joint game, whatever it may have been, while he urinated in the toilet, and report progress by calling out to him, that this particular piece of behavior decreased. It seems that she was establishing the mutual activity he desired at a higher level, that is, removed from his body and physical sensations.

We all made an attempt to arouse in the child the ambition to give up primitive gratification or direct discharge in order to understand his own troubles. Pedro enacted his feelings of helplessness and emptiness by identifying with a train engine which had to be kept full of petrol so that it would be the most powerful vehicle in existence and could protect itself from all danger. Not only had the engine never to run dry, but by drinking throughout the hour, Pedro proved that urinating did not weaken him and that he could replenish lost strength himself. He proved that his strength remained constant by jumping and climbing onto the window sills while whistling shrilly like an engine, pulling down the curtains, or threatening to jump through the windows. There seemed every likelihood that he might carry out this threat since he did not acknowledge danger and asserted that the most powerful trains could not be damaged. His therapist introduced the idea that a really powerful vehicle had brakes and that strength implied being able to use these brakes to stop and start at one's own command. Pedro's game now changed to one in which he would turn his brakes on and off thus providing welcome intervals during which the therapist could occasionally pop in an explanation or interpretation. The game was then elaborated by an introduction of a mechanic who sought to understand how the train worked and where it had gone wrong so that it could have more control and prevent breakdowns and damage. Similar devices, such as games in which Pedro would enter and leave the house by first predicting and then counting his own strides, enabled us to limit garden breakage at the time.

Those of us using these techniques do so in the belief that unless we can make affective contact with the child which will enable us to help him to control the excessive acting out, treatment cannot survive until the unconscious motives are understood and the correct interpretations can be given.

There are many possible disadvantages to this technique. We wonder whether ego-supportive methods might affect the development of transference and influence the use of interpretation as an effective tool in the treatment of our children. We have considered that ego-supportive techniques might block the emergence of affect, push ego development forward while libidinal development remains at its original unbound level, and thus enforce an artificial cover over a volcanic structure. It has further been suggested that a borderline child might need to relive early traumata through a type of treatment offering opportunities for regressively experiencing developmental processes anew. It may be that such therapy is compatible only with institutional treatment such as described by Bettelheim (1963) and Sechehaye (1951). This seems to be confirmed by reports about High Wick children prior to treatment. For example, mothering on an infantile level at High Wick brought about Norma's recovery of speech at the age of five.

We have considered how the reliving of an infantile experience could be brought about in treatment and how one could ensure that regression would be followed by a "good intake experience."

The Use and Timing of Interpretations

We have become increasingly aware of the importance of the whole question of communication between the borderline patient and the therapist. We do not know what these children understand of the verbal content of an interpretation; what reaches some of them may be only the affect or emotional aspect, perhaps the facial expression or tone of voice. Most of our children experience words in oral terms so that the mode of delivery must in some way be geared to their developmental level.

It has already been suggested that interpretation of aggression at the time of acute anxiety increases the anxiety and results in loss of control and violent behavior. We thought that this might be due to the fact that the therapist's words are experienced as concrete and magic, thus omnipotently turning the thought into the act. We have pointed out that at the time of an acute anxiety state the ego is weakened and in no condition to cooperate or fully comprehend interpretations. It seems, however, that the therapist's empathy comes across at such times through her attempts to understand, while at the same time acting as an auxiliary ego and creating some feeling of safety. It was also pointed out that our patients' anxiety had other contributory factors besides the projected aggression— reality events such as separation experiences, starvation, etc., have had to be taken into account. We have described elsewhere (1963) how the loss of objects or separation seems to produce experiences of body loss or disintegration in our children, a circumstance which also has important implications for technique.

The behavior and activities of some of the children had a stereo-typed character, such as has been described in the literature (Gold-farb, 1961). Basil particularly showed this behavior both at High Wick and at the Clinic. Stereotyped activities were observed when he first came to High Wick, but these decreased markedly during the two years there, prior to the beginning of treatment. At the be-ginning of treatment there was a recurrence of this behavior which could be noted both at the Clinic and at High Wick. It was thought that unlike a compulsive act, such activities were not associated with the *solution* of any internal conflict but more a manner of dealing with anxiety by providing a measure of "safety." They were aimed at defending against feelings of disintegration and they served the purpose of orientation to reality. Basil, for instance, spent long peri-ods at the Clinic and at home, opening and shutting a locker, or locking and unlocking doors. When interrupted he reacted as if he had been disturbed in a gratifying activity, but he did not react with any overt signs of anxiety. He asked whether it was good for him to continue with these activities everywhere or whether they were one of his worries. The therapist understood these activities as hav-ing associated links with many traumatic experiences, and much later in treatment it emerged just what some of these links were.

We spent quite some time in trying to understand this type of behavior which is not so very different from Norma's worry words, the origins of which are mostly untraceable. But in this one ex-ample of the roundabout which we have given, it is clear that a definite anxiety-arousing incident was instrumental in setting it off. We felt that Fenichel's (1945) term "emotional remainder" was a most appropriate term to describe just this type of behavior. We thought that the associative links contained in these actions might indeed have a content related to conflict, but the compromise solution of a conflict no longer seemed their main function as such compulsive behavior would be in a neurotic. Its main function was the mastery of anxiety, probably achieved by "sameness" (such as endless repetition) and by the fact that the action is completely under the child's control. Such behavior can take up all the child's attention cathexis, thereby avoiding anxiety-arousing contents and yet enabling him to keep some hold on reality. We all agreed that such behavior has to be treated as a form of communication, although there was a variety of opinion about the use we would make of it for therapeutic purposes. For instance, it was questioned why the locking and unlocking of doors was not interpreted in connection with Basil's probable fears of the treatment situation, particularly in view of the fact that this behavior which had subsided as he felt more safe at High Wick reappeared in an increased manner since he started treatment, and might thus be taken as an indication of increased anxiety related to the new and unfamiliar situation. His therapist explained that Basil's overtly positive attitude to his analysis as a treat and the apparent lack of *object relatedness* which he showed during the first year of treatment would have made such an interpretation of anxiety expressed in the transference meaningless to him.

Norma's disturbance in object relationships showed itself in a different way. She attacked the people to whom she became attached and demonstrated that she could not conceive of the possibility of any relationship not leading her into a dangerous situation similar to the real one with her mother, in which both were at the mercy of aggressive drives. She defended against making a new relationship partly because she dreaded the therapist's aggression and partly because of the terror of her own, which might destroy her therapist.

The situation was dealt with by the therapist presenting herself as a person totally different from the mother and at times assuring Norma that she would protect both Norma and herself from Norma's aggressive attacks. .Later in treatment when Norma imitated the Clinic dog, the defense aspect was left unspoken, but it was explained that Norma could safely remain a little girl by being the sort of girl who made things instead of breaking and destroying them. Another view was that the feeling that it is safer to be a dog when frightened could have been verbalized, although it was acknowledged that premature defense interpretations could be experienced by the child as exposing "nerve endings" which arouse excessive anxiety and provoke acting out.

Discussions of this sort led to an attempt to understand how the borderline child experiences interpretation of aggressive impulses. This appears to vary from child to child; thus when we verbalize these impulses, some children seem to take our words literally and think that they themselves are "bad." This could reinforce the already-existing bad self image. Other children, however, seem to react with increased acting out, taking the therapist's verbalization as permission. Another factor is that when a child's self-esteem is low, interpretations of aggression seem further to deflate the child, whereas when self-esteem is high, interpretations appear to act as a boost.

We have been discussing what happens when the anxiety is interpreted and thus channelized into the treatment situation at the beginning of therapy. While on the one hand the treatment situation with the borderline child, as with the neurotic child, may be said to represent a laboratory in which behavior responses can be scrutinized, the danger with the borderline child is that a mistimed interpretation may so increase anxiety that the child becomes either phobic or unmanageable. This is a problem that we certainly also meet in the treatment of neurotic children, but it may be that the primitive mode of thought development and object relationship in our borderline children makes it necessary for us to consider such dangers much more carefully.

The Impact of the Borderline Child upon the Therapist[4]

When we embark upon the treatment of a neurotic child, we do so with a certain basic conviction that we are relatively well equipped to understand emotional disturbances and that however disturbed the child may be at the outset, the nature of the disturbance will become clearer to us as the material unfolds. This is because our own, more or less integrated ego makes an alliance with an ego of similar quality. Thus our confidence in our understanding and

[4] The papers of H. F. Searles (1958, 1961, 1963) have helped us especially with the formulation of this section of the paper.

capacity to bring about an improvement is passed on to our patient and assists us over difficult periods of the analysis.

This self-assurance is lacking when we work with borderline children, a fact that must greatly influence our handling of them. We seek to make contact with our patient, but what the child makes of us or our tentativeness is difficult to speculate upon. The borderline child's sensitivity to mood and affect is likely to make him more aware of our uncertainty and bewilderment. When Pedro arrived after a particularly chaotic session and said with aggressive and menacing brightness, "And how are *you*, are you quite all right this morning?" he was expressing not only anxiety over guilt but also his fear that his therapist, like himself, might be overwhelmed by his chaotic behavior and anxiety and thus unable to help him. It is a fact that the terrifyingly chaotic world in which these children live has an overwhelming impact upon those of us who treat them. We know that in order to understand them we have in some measure to follow them into their world and accept its psychic reality. Very often, however, we find this world too frightening and we are tempted to impose order on it. Such measures are the more tempting since they may be followed by a period of apparently more integrated behavior, which may in fact reflect the child's primitive mechanisms of identification to which we referred earlier. In this way we seek to make the child more manageable and comprehensible, our own anxiety more tolerable, and the prognosis appear more hopeful. At times we take recourse to neurological and other examinations to counteract our helplessness.

The use of such defensive measures against the child's material will very soon communicate itself to the child, who will probably infer how anxious we are about being involved in his psychotic process. It is no good training ourselves not to appear shocked at the behavior or material since these children are too sensitive to be taken in. We have instead to work upon ourselves so that for brief periods we can genuinely meet the child's needs for symbiosis and follow his communications on a primary-process level. We have thought that this might be comparable to the mechanism in the mother of a young infant, who offers herself as a symbiotic object to her child, allowing herself moments in which her ego boundaries are blurred with those of her child. She, like the therapist, is always alert and ready to step back into a position in which she is able to protect and take over in case of need.

In the early stages of treatment especially, the therapist feels cut off from the patient because of the bizarre nature of the child's behavior and, in some children, because of the lack of relatedness. We must tolerate not only the borderline child's physical attacks but also his apparent denial of our existence. We could put up with being consciously ignored, but to be literally "unheard" can be experienced as a narcissistic hurt. This would be more tolerable if we knew what and whom we represented to the child. We have to remember, however, that the borderline child lives on the border between relatedness and lack of it—even those children who come to us apparently in contact suddenly switch into behavior which appears completely lacking in affect or object cathexis.

Once we find out whom or what we represent to the child, our task may become even more complicated. The borderline child often relates to us only on a part-object level and we then have to unravel the fragmented aspects which he has projected onto us from his infantile objects. Crazy behavior may sometimes represent both projections of aspects of his parents and externalizations of his own feelings of madness. In either case it is very hard for us to be treated as insane with such conviction, and we may find ourselves at times attempting to convince the child (and ourselves) of our sanity. Since a defect in neutralization is a feature in the psychopathology of our children, excessive ambivalence and aggression often accompany the struggle to become free of the symbiotic object. We may react to this with feelings of frustration and anger, or by attempts to hasten the process of individuation by setting ourselves up as a separate good object.

Another problem concerns the question of physical contact. Trained to work with neurotic children in a relatively nongratifying manner, we find it difficult to keep the balance between the child's need for physical proximity at some stages and for distance at others. Often our judgment may be interfered with by our own need to compensate for the lack of relatedness by physical nearness. Alternatively we might tend to avoid physical nearness on account of the child's age and sexual excitement, instead of responding to his primitive needs for maternal protection and care.

The process of differentiation, followed through in the treatment, often means that the child closely scrutinizes the therapist's physique and especially her face. Spitz (1955) has pointed to the role played by the mother's face in the process of differentiation. This may often mean that the borderline child in treatment needs to touch and feel us. Moreover, our mannerisms, tone of voice, inflections, sudden movements, and indeed emotional state are all of special significance to these children because at times they do not perceive the therapist as a whole person. By the same token it will be evident that our words are often experienced concretely and omnipotently, thus putting on us a special responsibility. In our work with neurotic children a wrongly timed or incorrect interpretation can usually be put right in the next session, but this is more difficult with borderline children because so often they react immediately to whatever is said. We must, therefore, think all the time about *the formulation* of our communications as well as the content because of this curious tendency to ignore our words on the one hand and to fasten to a detail that seems irrelevant to *us* on the other hand. The borderline child's difficulty in cathecting objects is well known, but we know less about their tendency to "stick onto a detail" which seems to be defensive and to absorb them so completely that everything else including ourselves is shut out.

SUMMARY

The body of this paper has been concerned with techniques used in the initial stages of treatment, which can extend over years and which aim at making the child more analyzable. We have not dealt with the later period of therapy when the borderline picture gradually changes and internalized conflict can become the center of treatment. We hope that at some future date other members of the group will describe just this process.

We have discussed the technique within the treatment situation, as it is in reality and not as we would like it to be. We would ask the reader to bear in mind that treatment in a clinic involves special problems such as consideration for other patients, for the building, and not least the question of transport.

We have described some of the problems peculiar to the treatment of borderline children and particularly how each child's level of ego and object relationship is at a different stage of development so that there are a variety of different psychopathologies.

We have spoken of the need to make meaningful contact with the borderline child and the difficulties of following him into his psychic world. We have described how we may be forced into a more active role than we are accustomed to and we have stressed that the treatment relationship with these children is governed by their fragmentary ego, their proneness to acute anxiety, and their low level of object relationship.

Different methods of dealing with acute anxiety at the beginning of treatment have been considered; we have discussed the use of ego-supportive techniques and the timing of interpretations. We have also tried to give a picture of the impact of the child's material on ourselves, emphasizing how each therapist reacts differently to the material and defends herself against it in a different way. We think that this must influence our handling of the cases and that it may explain why we have evolved no single technique.

It may be that work with borderline children involves some specific anxiety since we so often feel personally responsible for the slow therapeutic gains seen in our patients. Working with colleagues in a group has a special value for us since it not only offers opportunities for exchange of views but also provides us with the support and reassurance which enable us to look at the material objectively and to attempt formulations such as we have undertaken in this paper.

BIBLIOGRAPHY

Bettelheim, B. (1963), Unpublished paper on the case history of an autistic child, read at the Hampstead Child-Therapy Clinic.

Bornstein, B. (1949), The Analysis of a Phobic Child: Some Problems of Theory and Technique in Child Analysis. *This Annual*, 3/4:181-226.

Fenichel, O. (1945), *The Psychoanalytic Theory of Neurosis*. New York: Norton.

Goldfarb, W. (1961), *Childhood Schizophrenia*. Cambridge: Harvard University Press.

Kut Rosenfeld, S. & Sprince, M. P. (1963), An Attempt to Formulate the Meaning of the Concept "Borderline." *This Annual*, 18:603-635.

Searles, H. F. (1958), Positive Feelings in the Relationship between the Schizophrenic and His Mother. *Int. J. Psa.*, 39:569-586.

—— (1961), Anxiety Concerning Change, as Seen in the Psychotherapy of Schizophrenic Patients: With Particular Reference to the Sense of Personal Identity. *Int. J. Psa.*, 42:74-85.

—— (1963), The Place of Neutral Therapist-Responses in Psychotherapy with the Schizophrenic Patient. *Int. J. Psa.*, 44:42-56.

Sechehaye, M. A. (1951), *Symbolic Realization*. New York: International Universities Press.

Spitz, R. A. (1955), The Primal Cavity. *This Annual*, 10:215-240.

Thomas, R. (1964), Comments on Some Aspects of Self and Object Representation in a Group of Borderline Children: The Application of Anna Freud's Diagnostic Profile. In preparation.

NARCISSISTIC EGO IMPAIRMENT IN PATIENTS WITH EARLY PHYSICAL MALFORMATIONS

WILLIAM G. NIEDERLAND, M.D. (New York)

Since Freud's work, "On Narcissism" (1914) many analytic papers have been devoted to the study of narcissistic disorders. Few, however, have dealt specifically with narcissistic disturbances observable in one category of patients in whom such manifestations are encountered with a certain regularity and often, in fact, are found to be the predominant features of their psychopathology. This is all the more surprising in view of Freud's statement that prominently lists among the means of approach "by which we may obtain a better knowledge of narcissism . . . the study of organic disease" (p. 82).

From the group of patients loosely described as "narcissists," that is, individuals in whose pathology narcissistic phenomena play a major role, I have selected a special category for discussion, namely, patients in whom a particular type of body defect—irrespective of the clinical diagnosis and classification—can be recognized as a nodal psychological factor in their ego development as well as a pathogenic element in the formation and maintenance of narcissistic disturbances. In view of the prevalence of compensatory narcissistic self-inflation, fantasies of grandeur, etc., among such persons, their analytic study can be expected to yield information about the role such defects play in the genesis and perseverance of certain narcissistic disturbances.

In focusing attention on such cases, I took as my point of departure Freud's papers "On Narcissism" (1914) and "Some Character-Types Met with in Psycho-Analytic Work" (1916), Jacobson's (1959) elaboration of the latter, A Reich's (1960) contributions to the understanding of the regulatory processes involved in the maintenance of self-esteem, related studies by Bychowski (1943), Greenacre (1952, 1958), Murphy (1958, 1959), and others. I also wish to draw attention to the growing concern over birth defects—a concern which in recent years has dominated several international congresses on pediatrics, orthopedics, teratogenic effects of drugs, etc. While the tragedy of phocomelia that affected the fate of thousands of seriously deformed children has been the most alarming teratogenic malformation thus far produced, it is noteworthy that frequently the teratogenic anomalies observed have been less severe, many of them involving only fingers or toes.

Studying persons suffering from congenital malformations or physical defects acquired early in life, Freud (1916) commented on their refusal to accept the reality principle. "For reasons which will be readily understood," Freud tells us, "I cannot communicate very much about these and other case histories." He then supplemented his clinical observation with an illustration from *Richard III,* "a figure in whose character the claim to be an exception is closely bound up with and motivated by the circumstance of congenital disadvantage" (p. 313). From this first comment and from his example we may legitimately infer that Freud alluded to patients with gross physical pathology whose identity might have been revealed by a more detailed description of their case material. The "exceptions" described by Jacobson (1959) consisted of two groups of women characterized by conspicuous physical attributes: one group included patients with visible physical deformities, and the other included women of extraordinary beauty and charm. Similarly, Lussier's (1960) case report from the Hampstead Clinic refers to a severely malformed adolescent with readily visible body defects, while Blos's recent study (1960) on cryptorchism deals with an anatomically less obvious anomaly and concentrates exclusively on this disorder in children.

In contrast to these contributions, the present study is based on observations of adult patients who suffered from the consequences of minor physical anomalies or imperfections which were of secondary importance with regard to manifest anatomical involvement, inconspicuous in appearance, and scarcely or not at all noticeable without a medical examination. In this sense, the anomalies considered here should be understood as secret or hidden afflictions; indeed the patients tended to remain silent about their presence and to keep them concealed from themselves as well as from the outer world. It should be noted, however, that despite the relative inconspicuousness of these defects, several of them were associated with some degree of functional and other types of impairment in child-hood. This fact has to be kept in mind, especially in view of the frequently stated observation that "the psychological reverberations go far beyond the actual physical disability" (Kaplan, 1959). This observation is undoubtedly correct; but what strikes the clinician as disproportionate psychopathology in terms of later development may reveal itself as proportionate to the actual impairment in early life, to its phase-specific significance, and to its far-reaching elaboration in fantasy.

Included in the group studied are two patients with minor con-genital chest deformities, two with congenital umbilical hernias, one with a small bony exostosis below the clavicular region, one with inconspicuous residual cranial and thoracic deformities due to infan-tile rickets, one with barely visible imperfections of the left arm caused by a birth injury, and one with a congenital torticollis. Of these, only the last two patients had outwardly recognizable anom-alies. One of them, the patient with the torticollis, had undergone plastic surgery in adolescence and his deformity had been so well repaired that no trace of it was noticeable when he entered analysis in his early thirties. My study thus comprises eight cases, only four of which were or are in analysis; the other four were treated in pro-longed, analytically oriented psychotherapy. Five of the patients are men and three are women. In presenting my observations I shall focus on the findings pertinent to the prevalence of narcissistic phe-nomena in these patients and shall omit the discussion of other relevant material.

Though small in number, the present series and the data derived therefrom are not, I believe, without clinical and theoretical sig-nificance. Viewing the problem for a moment nonanalytically, it is perhaps worth mentioning that about 10 to 12 out of 100 newborn infants have congenital anomalies. Since the most frequent types of such defects are those involving the bones, joints, and other parts of the body surface—as in the cases under consideration—and since some kind of congenital defectiveness is thought to be present in about 30 per cent of the general population (if certain minor anom-alies of the skeleton, teeth, skin, etc., are included), the incidence and importance of clinical manifestations directly or indirectly connected with early physical malformations cannot be negligible. The relative paucity of psychoanalytic reports[1] on patients with such handicaps does not necessarily militate against the mounting evidence of their clinical importance in and outside analytic practice. If the current views concerning the incidence of teratogenic effects of drugs as well as the relation between increased radioactivity and a higher rate of congenital malformations are correct, it may be expected that the pertinence of these observations may soon become more obvious.

To return to the predominance of narcissistic phenomena in these cases, it is well to reiterate that Freud (1916) recommended "among the means of approach . . . by which we may obtain a knowledge of narcissism" the study of organic diseases and related conditions. The presence of an increased body narcissism and its significant implications for the psychopathology of the patients under scrutiny could, in fact, be demonstrated in all of them. The familiar, one may perhaps say, the classic features of a narcissistic or at least narcissistically tinged disorder—compensatory narcissistic self-inflation, fantasies of grandiosity and uniqueness, aggressive strivings for narcissistic supplies from the outside world, impairment of object relations and reality testing, excessive vulnerability—were apparent in the character structure of all eight patients, though in varying and analytically not equally accessible degrees. Moreover, at the time the patients came for treatment—that is, as adults—the psychological reverberations resulting from their essentially benign physical anomalies and the complex, usually less benign elaboration of the latter in fantasy strikingly outweighed the organic pathology.

In what follows I wish to discuss some of the principal features which characterized the narcissistic pathology of the patients.

THE NARCISSISTIC INJURY

Although each case is, of course, individual and presents its own specific pathology, it can be said that the presence of an unresolved narcissistic injury derived from basic physical experiences of an un-

[1] In the discussion of this paper Dr. van der Waals stated that he had never encountered similar cases (Fall Meeting of the American Psychoanalytic Association, 1960).

mastered and perhaps unmasterable kind resulted in certain characteristics common to all the cases studied. The nature and permanence
of the defectiveness lent to the latter a quality of nodal significance,
somewhat in the manner of an organizing and concretizing experience in Greenacre's sense (1952, 1958) for the entire ego and superego development. In contrast to a variety of psychic traumata in
childhood which often find a more or less spontaneous solution
(through mastery) in the course of further development, an early
body defect tends to remain an area of unresolved conflict through its
concreteness, permanency, cathectic significance, and its relationship
to conflictual anxiety (primitive body disintegration anxiety, castration fear). In my patients the physical defectiveness either had existed from birth or had occurred during the first year of life; therefore, the development of the body ego had been affected virtually
from the beginning. The result was a faulty, sometimes bizarre and
distorted body image with strangely disfigured body contours, incompleteness of body reality and, via projection, of external reality.
In this respect the site of the injury is pertinent. The man with the
thoracic deformities (pectus excavatum), a six-footer, saw himself as
a dwarfish hunchback, "bent in the middle," and spoke of his deformity as being a feminizing defect in the sense of providing him
with a gratuitous, nonmasculine extra cavity. One woman had a birth
injury which paralyzed her left arm; during her first year of life the
other arm became involved, though in a minor and not fully clarified way. This immobilization of the damaged arm had directly interfered with the formation and normal functioning of the "hand-
mouth-ego" integration (Hoffer, 1950). Moreover, in later life, she
showed poor reality testing as well as compensatory narcissistic self-
inflation: she saw herself as a world-famous artist (a man!) of immor-
tal greatness. At the same time, she repeatedly complained that she
could not "grasp" what was going on in the world; that, to her,
people were like shadowy figures "out of reach" or like "so many fish
floating by"; that at times she had no "contact" with people or
events. The patient's damaged arm had been in traction throughout
most of her first year of life during which time she had been forced
to lie flat on her back. Thus, a part of her own body as well as many
external objects had actually been "out of reach" for her, and during that period the significant figures of her immediate environment

had appeared to be "floating by" in shadowy fashion, as it were. Further aspects of this experience will be discussed below.

What I have called the nodal significance of an unresolved narcissistic injury due to some type of physical defect expresses itself clinically in various ways. Some of the features have already been mentioned: compensatory self-aggrandizement, heightened aggressiveness often accompanied by outbursts of aggression and hate in word and action, the castrative aspects of the defectiveness and its bisexual and sadomasochistic elaboration. I wish to call special attention to two more characteristics: the prevalence of revenge fantasies as well as florid birth-rebirth fantasies. They usually are part of the rich and secret fantasy life which in these patients is replete with narcissistic-exhibitionistic-aggressive themes, sadomasochistic fantasies (involving especially bodily mutilation, dismemberment, etc.), erotized megalomanic daydreams, conscious or semiconscious aspirations to greatness, immortality and eternal life. The "little man" patient whom I described some years ago (1956) saw himself as a massive conglomerate of the prominent statesmen and war leaders during the last World War. Another patient, the woman with the bony exostosis near the sternoclavicular area, dreamed that she was participating in the assembly of the eternal gods on Mount Olympus, a Greek god herself (a god, not a goddess!), looking down on the poor mortals from lofty heights.

The immortality aspects of such fantasies are of great interest, clinically and from another viewpoint as well. In several of these patients the fantasies of everlasting youth and eternal life were extraordinarily strong and, when associated with magic ideas of personal invulnerability and invincibility (in some cases, even immortality), as part of their narcissistic pathology, they appeared to assume the quality of semidelusional or even delusional beliefs—in these otherwise nonpsychotic patients. While this "eternal" feature, with its imperviousness to the passing of time and to other aspects of the reality situation, can present many therapeutic problems, especially with its implications of "interminable" analysis, the narcissistically held and often richly elaborated view of everlasting life can be readily recognized as a residue of the timeless grandiosity of infancy reinforced by later restitutive processes in which cathexes withdrawn from the object world were invested in the operations of the ego organization. It is worth noting, in this connection, that the narcissistic attributes of physical immortality and lasting value to the point of *aere perennius* appeared to be especially strong in the artistically gifted patients who ascribed such "eternal" qualities, if not to themselves, surely to their creative works. The fact that there were three painters, one writer, and one creative scientist among my eight patients with physical anomalies may be nothing more than a coincidence, of course. On the other hand, the presence of intense restitutive strivings which a hidden body defect experienced as a narcissistic injury of a virtually unchangeable type seems to produce; the interaction between such narcissistically imperative repair efforts, the usually strong bisexual elaboration of the bodily defectiveness, and the rich fantasy life in these people; the aggressive wish to express artistically what is concealed from the world (i.e., the physical defectiveness and the suffering it engenders)—all these strivings and psychological labors should not be ignored as potential sources of creativity in such individuals.

The unconscious reconstructive and restitutive aspects of the creative "labor" which goes into the artistic productions of some of these patients became apparent to me not only in their individual subject choice (e.g., the painting of many "naissance" and "renaissance" pictures in one case) but was also suggested by two observations. One refers to the timeless or "eternal" factor mentioned above, the other to the disproportionate disfigurement (in fantasy) of the damaged body contours. These two elements seem to find expression in the creative work as well as in the analytic productions of the patients. More specifically, the patients try to regress, in their restitutive efforts, to the time prior to the formation of the defect[2] or at least prior to their subjective discovery of their defect. This attempt may lead to marked pregenital preoccupation and pseudopsychotic symptomatology; but it *may also induce in the artistically gifted individual that regression in the service of the ego* which Kris (1952) emphasized as a requirement for creativity—here *brought about through regression in the service of ego restitution.* Since a narcissistic gain results from such restitution, though of course the physical defectiveness remains unchanged, the unconscious reconstructive

[2] A point made especially by Dr. Bettina Warburg during the discussion of this paper.

efforts tend to go on indefinitely and may in gifted persons lead *to continued creativity of an almost frantic or feverish type.* I believe I have observed this creative activity (which in the deepest sense is really a restitutive, re-creative one) in some of my patients and propose to deal with these complex processes in a separate study.

The second factor which refers to the damaged or unusual body contours also has ego-restitutive aspects. As will be described under the appropriate heading, there exists an uneven distribution of body cathexis as a result of the defectiveness. The peculiar stimuli provided by the congenital or early acquired injury may not only contribute to the psychology of the "exceptions," as Freud (1916) has shown; they may also play a role—as yet uncharted and unrecognized—in the creativity of some of these individuals. MacKinnon (1962), studying creative factors among architects, "found the unusualness of mental associations one of the best predictors of creativity." It remains to be seen whether the unusualness of associations reflects, albeit indirectly and in certain individuals, the unusualness or unevenness of cathectic stimuli emanating from the site of an unresolved and undisclosed narcissistic injury of very early origin. At any rate, the question of a possible connection between creativity and hidden physical anomalies invites further investigation. Similar views have been expressed by other authors, e.g., Freud (1916), quoting Adler's approach to the problem of the so-called "organic inferiorities," and Rickman (1940) in his paper on "Ugliness."

SECRECY AND MAGIC CONNOTATIONS OF A NONVISIBLE BODY DEFECT

Most of my patients showed what Blos (1960) has called "a mysterious exclusion" of the physical malformation from the rest of the clinical symptomatology. As in Blos's patient Joe, whose cryptorchism was "inadvertently" disclosed after three years of treatment, one of my women patients revealed a rhinoplasty only in her fourth year of psychotherapy.[3] Patients in analysis also kept their physical imperfections concealed for a long time, though derivatives and symbolic representations sometimes emerged quite early in the treatment. The first dream of a patient with a congenital funnel chest was about a car that had an indented front fender.

3 This patient is not included in the series of eight.

However that may be, the secrecy about the defect and the fact that, though a handicap, it is usually not a major physical one not only sets this type of defectiveness apart from the more visible type of malformation; these factors also add to their narcissistic and magic implications. The narcissistic significance of the secret is well known. The invisibility achieved through the use of a magic device (*Tarn-helm*), in the Nibelungen, makes invincible figures of Siegfried, the young hero, and of Alberic, the dwarf. Mahler's (1942) clinical material dealing with such fantasies included two patients with congenital deformities. According to Gross (1951), the secret ultimately refers to bodily organs and processes. Since the secrecy of a hidden body defect links it to other bodily secrets, especially to the rectum and to anal functioning with their familiar connotations of power, sadism, and magic, the concealment of the defect represents a narcissistic gain. Its narcissistic value is further enhanced by outwitting and outmaneuvering the environment. In the fantasy life of several patients a variant of the typical "Rumpelstiltskin" idea with its magic and grandiose connotations could be found ("Oh, how good that no one knows. . . !"), with the Rumpelstiltskin fantasy not just as "a pleasant pastime, but an intrinsic part of the personality" (A. Reich, 1960). Rumpelstiltskin could transform straw into gold; these patients, via the secret and its magic implications, strove to convert the defectiveness into a mark of distinction and a seat of power, thus magically undoing the narcissistic injury.[4] Sometimes magic oral incorporation fantasies are acted out in an attempt to restore intactness to the congenital body damage. One of my patients with a defective muscular area in the anterior abdominal wall licked and at times ate pages from sport magazines showing photographic reproductions of muscular men (a magical attempt at narcissistic replenishment). Or he would bathe for hours in a tub, retire, and awaken in the morning expecting the defect to be gone (rebirth fantasy). Such magic expectations greatly influenced the transference. The woman with the hidden bony exostosis, after having relinquished her secret,

---

[4] What can be found analytically in the fantasy life of such persons, can also be seen *in actu* in certain visibly deformed persons, e.g., in those hunchbacked cripples who, walking up and down before gambling houses in Italy, accost passers-by with the following words: "I am a hunchback, touch me, I shall bring you good luck." The magic property of the visible malformation, to be conveyed to the one who touches it, is obvious.

often turned to me imploring: "Make it go away!" words she remembered having addressed to her mother as a child when she discovered her malformation.

With regard to the anal and oral features, it may be recalled that Richard III, besides being "a lump of foul deformity," was also equipped by Shakespeare with teeth from the moment of his birth so that "he could gnaw a crust of bread when two hours old," a clear allusion to a hidden congenital defect in addition to his gross deformities.

BODY IMAGE, CATHECTIC CHANGES, AND DEFENSES

Body-image distortion is an inevitable outcome of early physical defectiveness. My observations appear to confirm Hoffer's statement (1950, 1952) that by the second year of life the infant has established an oral-tactile concept of his own body. It forms the basis of what later becomes the intact, relatively stable, and properly cathected body image of the healthy individual; among other determinants, it is characterized by a cohesive, fairly stabilized, predominantly libidinal cathexis of the body as a unitary whole. This mental representation of the body is always influenced by the interaction of physiological (dimensional-kinesthetic-postural) factors and psychological (sensorial-emotional-exquisitely personal) experiences. Though not simply identical with the actual body, it tends under normal conditions to approximate the actual body configuration. Perception of one's self, perception of others, reality testing, and other mental activities evolve against this background of an essentially bodily self image and its cathexis. For this reason the incompleteness or disruption of the body image is bound to have an impact on a number of important ego functions. The extent to which emotional experiences can interfere with the formation of an accurate body image is exemplified by Jacobson (1954) who points to the persistence "in women of the unconscious fantasy that their genital is a castrated organ, frequently with simultaneous denial and development of illusory penis fantasies" (p. 87).

Using this familiar body-image distortion as a kind of *tertium comparationis*, it should be noted that in cases of congenital (or early acquired) deformity there is usually a more marked, more distorted, and insidiously pervasive discrepancy between the realistic appearance and the concrete attributes of *the body in the flesh* and the fantasied appearance and attributes of *the body in the mind*. In other words, the faulty body image caused by very early physical defectiveness cannot be viewed in the same way as the persistence of the female castration complex with its specific body-image implications, however severe the latter may be. If, for example, one of my female patients consistently feels and sees her body from the neck down as a rubbery, gelatinous mass of "some cheap, hastily put-together fabric," this fantasy—while not necessarily delusional—expresses more than the usual refutation of her female genitals. The patient is the artist whose left arm, inconspicuously deformed as a result of a birth injury, is hypocathected; for her, it hardly exists and she never mentions it. The right arm (with which she paints) and her eyes are hypercathected. More precisely, it is of course the mental representations of these body parts which are directly affected. Yet the uneven balance of the body cathexis involves more and extends further; to her, the whole body image from the neck down is that of a rubbery, gelatinous mass. This type of body feeling appears to be closely related to Mittelmann's description (1960) of the body scheme in which the skeletomuscular system holds the position of an early, quasi-independent ego structure. My patient's image, moreover, included also the body surface, i.e., the representation of the cutaneous system. In this context it should be recalled that she had been in traction and immobilized for most of her first year of life.

Closer study reveals that patients with congenital or early acquired malformations are prone to suffer from a permanent disturbance of the self image, which in severe cases may assume semidelusional or almost delusional proportions, have archaically tinged psychological reverberations, and present distorted or even fragmented body-image features. In some of my cases the pathological body image observed resembled that of Keiser's patients: "The body image never coalesced into a unitary whole, but persisted as a number of discrete parts which functioned independently of each other." In two of my patients the withdrawal of cathexis from the object world and its concentration on the body led to a sort of "closed unit" or "closed circle" existence in feeling, thinking, and to some extent also in action, a condition called by the patients themselves their "cocoon state," "amoeba state" or "worm existence." I am inclined to view such formations as variants of the return-to-the-womb fantasy which automatically excludes any physical handicap and restores the earliest state of narcissistic perfection. This "closed unit" type of narcissistic retreat, which in these patients appeared to be connected with the regressive pull toward attaining the fantasied state prior to the defect in the restitutive effort previously discussed, thus served to undo the feeling of physical imperfection and incompleteness. Such strivings were especially intense in patients who had unusually strong castration fear and in whose pathology the threat of loss of body parts and physical intactness constituted a major element in their ego impairment. While noting these relations between disturbed ego development and early physical defectiveness, I wish to emphasize that I do not regard the latter as the sole pathogenic influence in their clinical picture. I believe, rather, that the defect, in addition to its significance as a concretizing and organizing experience of pathogenic import from early childhood, adds a "kernel of truth" quality and multidimensional aspects to the pathological fantasies which are likely to arise during the developmental phases.

The formation of a distorted, permanently incomplete and insecure body image appears particularly intense in male patients in whom inguinal or genital anomalies such as testicular malformations, penile deformities, congenital or early acquired varicocele, open inguinal rings, etc., exist. Overly strong bisexual identifications, florid fantasies of being a hermaphrodite, and compensatory narcissistic features—ideas of being unique, of possessing special powers, magic qualities, or the like—as well as intense exhibitionistic strivings are frequently encountered in such persons. In addition, strong anal preoccupations appear to prevail in them. Equally noteworthy are psychopathic impulses and behavior. On the whole, my observations tend to support those of A. Bell (1965) and Blos (1960).

Besides the notable increase in fantasy life, most of these patients used the defense mechanisms of denial, undoing, isolation, regression, reaction formation, displacement, and projection. Although the emotional responses to the handicaps, as was stated above, differed in every individual according to the many variables and vicissitudes involved, the defenses of denial and undoing (putting the defect "out of existence") were present in all patients and could be readily observed analytically. The deeper narcissistic defenses were much less accessible and attempts to deal with them required much analytic work and utmost prudence.

Another relevant factor seems to be connected with the distribution of body cathexis in a more specific way. While the faulty body image is characterized mainly by incompleteness, marked distortions, vague feelings of altered consistency and tonus to the point of partial emptiness or disembodiment—one patient's term "rubbery" describes some of this rather appropriately—the uneven distribution of the body cathexis sometimes finds expression in still another way. In a few of my patients I have observed phenomena which suggest that, within the improper balance of the total body cathexis, a compensatory "focal" hypercathexis exists in the body-self representation at the zone of confluence between the defective *bad* part and the adjoining *good* part or, by displacement, a zone of overcathexis which involves a corresponding body area distally (away from the defect). I have already mentioned the cathectic shift from the damaged arm to the undamaged one in the patient with the birth injury. In the woman with the bony exostosis the area surrounding the defect was hypercathected so that she felt she had a particularly attractive bust. In another patient, a very young man with a funnel chest, the altered cathexis of the total body-self was accompanied by a focal hypercathexis of the self image in the dorsal region opposite the defective area. His back region was posturally and affectively "phallicized," the patient holding himself stiffly erect like a Prussian officer (which he was not). This focal hypercathexis not only reinforces the overcathected phallic self image in the sense of the body-phallus equation, but also gives added impetus to the narcissistic-exhibitionistic-aggressive strivings which, through belligerent behavior, provocative action, boastfulness, arrogance, etc., make such individuals gradually obnoxious even to their devoted friends. According to Eidelberg (1948, 1959), the brash or crude actions lead to external narcissistic mortifications in an unconscious effort to undo the internal mortification. In fact, by his behavior the patient often does succeed in obtaining sufficient external punishment from the outer world, which may then serve as the external narcissistic mortification required to deny the internal one.

The phenomena suggesting the concept of "focal" hypercathexis require further investigation. Keiser (in a personal communication) commented on the fact that some afflicted persons are intensely preoccupied with their impaired body area. This preoccupation may well be the result of such focal hypercathexis of the surrounding zone rather than a masochistic fascination with the defect. Keiser suggests that the sensitivity around the body orifices or defects might be studied with these admittedly tentative findings in mind.

GENERAL REMARKS ON COMPENSATORY NARCISSISTIC FANTASIES

An analytic inquiry into the narcissistic pathology of individuals with certain inborn or early acquired malformations discloses a multitude and complexity of relations which, though not excluding some aspects of Adler's "masculine protest" approach to organic inferiorities, makes his formulation appear designatory rather than illuminatory. The fantasy life, in particular, which is such an intrinsic part of these personalities and is abetted by the secrecy, the self-image distortions, the compensatory megalomanic features, the magic connotations, and the attempted or factual denial of an important sector of body reality, tends to abound in florid, at times bizarre narcissistic formations. These fantasies influence the behavior of such individuals in various ways. In gifted persons an unresolved narcissistic injury derived from physical defectiveness may act as a permanent stimulus and restitutively become a source of notable creativity and artistry. Others, bristling with hidden conceit and lifelong rancor, may be revengeful and insufferable. All shades and nuances are likely to occur, of course, and to produce unusual pathological features.

Literature perhaps more than psychology has paid attention to the character structure and behavior of malformed persons. The line of literary endeavors depicting their actions and motivations and correlating these to their disturbed physique extends from Homer's Thersites in the *Iliad,* Shakespeare's *Richard III,* to some modern writers. A contemporary novelist, A. Dewlen (1961), writing about the selection of the jury in a murder trial, has the lawyer for the defense say: "He would avoid cripples, men of small stature and people with ugly faces. These, when exalted to life-and-death power, could become cruel jurors capable of doing to the defendant as had been done unto them." While oversimplification and generalization are obvious, the statement does not appear to be entirely devoid of some astute empirical observation.

One of my patients believed he had the most remarkable brain power in the world as well as a head several times its actual size. In three patients the continued presence of an unconscious, isolated, split-off self image of infantile origin and functioning in primitive fashion could be discerned. This self image in the form of a "little man" or dwarf fantasy preserved the primitive self representation of the person at the time when the recognition of the defectiveness resulted in the permanent narcissistic traumatization and in the subsequent compensatory setting up of a separate narcissistic ego structure within the total ego organization. The patients referred to this isolated, primitive segment as "little man," "the dwarf," "the imp" or the like within themselves. This split-off ego segment had remained essentially unmodified since its formation under the impact of the trauma in childhood and had not participated in the later development of the intact part of the ego. On the other hand, it had under certain conditions become the reservoir of the totality of the narcissistic-destructive-omnipotent fantasies. The analysis of the infantile features of invulnerability, grandiosity, timelessness, magic power, and other narcissistic attributes demonstrated the early split of the ego. Most of these findings have been reported in my earlier paper (1956) and in a paper by Kramer (1955) which preceded mine.

I should like to return once more to the altered cathexis of the self image and its focal concomitants mentioned above. With the sharpened and overly keen awareness, in a distorted way, of certain body parts, much of the cathectic distribution may center on and around the psychic representations of these parts. The cathectic distortions, through projection and further elaboration in fantasy, may then lend themselves to paranoid reactions and in severe cases to their further elaboration into bizarre and delusional or quasi-delusional formations. Less severe disturbances include sadomasochistic tendencies and behavior, difficulties in maintaining or regulating self-esteem (A. Reich, 1960), acting out, low frustration tolerance, belligerence and vengefulness, poor or volatile object relations.

The modifications of normal ego development usually set in at an early period of life. When a physical defect is found soon after birth or during the first months of infancy, there often ensues, from the time of the recognition of the defectiveness ("recognition shock") a marked disequilibrium in the relations between mother and child —a disequilibrium which hardly ever fully subsides. Some mothers go into a prolonged postpartum depression, which may later be followed by renewed depressions or anxiety states. Others become oversolicitous, seductive, or otherwise defective in their nursing functions. The children are thus further traumatized through the unsatisfactory mother-child interaction, overstimulation of the body, and various physiotherapeutic or orthopedic procedures (A. Freud, 1952). Indispensable as the latter may be, the psychological vicissitudes resulting from prolonged immobilization, the necessity of wearing corrective braces, etc., and the resultant inadequate discharge of aggressive and libidinal energy, and, finally, the factual or fantasied threats to bodily intactness—all accentuate the traumatic influences of physical defectiveness upon psychic development.

With their ego and superego pathology, infantile megalomania, faulty body image, bizarre and at times ominous-appearing symptomatology, persistent ego split and identity problems, some of these patients lend themselves to a diagnosis of psychotic illness. But a break with reality seems to be rare and the clinical picture, as I view it, appears to be that of a narcissistic, deep-seated, but not necessarily intractable character disorder. Prolonged analytic work with several of these patients, though not easy, has proved rewarding. Among the therapeutic tasks the correction of the faulty body image, for instance, that of being half-man, half-woman, is of considerable importance and curative value.

BIBLIOGRAPHY

Bell, A. I. (1965), The Significance of Scrotal Sac and Testicles for the Prepuberty Male. *Psa. Quart.*, 34:182-206.
Blos, P. (1960), Comments on the Psychological Consequences of Cryptorchism. *This Annual*, 15:395-429.
Bychowski, G. (1943), Disorders in the Body-Image in the Clinical Pictures of Psychoses. *J. Nerv. Ment. Dis.*, 97:310-335.
Dewlen, A. (1961), *Twilight of Honor*. New York: McGraw-Hill.
Eidelberg, L. (1948), *Studies in Psychoanalysis*. New York: International Universities Press, 1952.
—— (1959), Humiliation in Masochism. *J. Amer. Psa. Assn.*, 7:274-283.
Freud, A. (1952), The Role of Bodily Illness in the Mental Life of Children. *This Annual*, 7:69-82.

534 WILLIAM G. NIEDERLAND

Freud, S. (1914), On Narcissism: An Introduction. *Standard Edition*, 14:67-102. London: Hogarth Press, 1957.

—— (1916), Some Character-Types Met with in Psycho-Analytic Work. *Standard Edition*, 14:309-333. London: Hogarth Press, 1957.

Greenacre, P. (1952), Pregenital Patterning. *Int. J. Psa.*, 33:410-415.

—— (1958), Early Physical Determinants in the Development of the Sense of Identity. *J. Amer. Psa. Assn.*, 6:612-627.

Gross, A. (1951), The Secret. *Bull. Menninger Clin.*, 15:37-44.

Hoffer, W. (1950), Development of the Body Ego. *This Annual*, 5:18-23.

—— (1952), The Mutual Influences in the Development of Ego and Id: Earliest Stages. *This Annual*, 7:31-41.

Jacobson, E. (1954), The Self and the Object World. *This Annual*, 9:75-127.

—— (1959), The "Exceptions": An Elaboration of Freud's Character Study. *This Annual*, 14:135-154.

Kaplan, E. (1959), The Role of Birth Injury in a Patient's Character Development and His Neurosis. *Bull. Phila. Assn. Psa.*, 9:1-18.

Keiser, S. (1958), Disturbances in Abstract Thinking and Body-Image Formation. *J. Amer. Psa. Assn.*, 6:628-652.

Kramer, P. (1955), On Discovering One's Identity: A Case Report. *This Annual*, 10:47-74.

Kris, E. (1952), *Psychoanalytic Explorations in Art*. New York: International Universities Press.

Lussier, A. (1960), The Analysis of a Boy with a Congenital Deformity. *This Annual*, 15:430-453.

MacKinnon, D. (1962), The Nature and Nurture of Creative Talent. *Amer. Psychologist*, 17:484-495.

Mahler, M. S. (1942), Pseudo-imbecility: Magic Cap of Invisibility. *Psa. Quart.*, 11:149-164.

Mittelmann, B. (1960), Intrauterine and Early Infantile Motility. *This Annual*, 15:104-127.

Murphy, W. F. (1958), Character, Trauma, and Sensory Perception. *Int. J. Psa.*, 39:555-568.

—— (1959), Ego Integration, Trauma, and Insight. *Psa. Quart.*, 28:514-532.

Niederland, W. G. (1956), Clinical Observations on the "Little Man" Phenomenon. *This Annual*, 11:381-395.

Reich, A. (1960), Pathologic Forms of Self-Esteem Regulation. *This Annual*, 15:215-232.

Rickman, J. (1940), On the Nature of Ugliness and the Creative Impulse. In: *Selected Contributions to Psychoanalysis*. London: Hogarth Press, 1957, pp. 68-89.

INHIBITION OF EGO FUNCTIONS AND THE PSYCHOANALYTIC THEORY OF ACALCULIA

PIERRE VEREECKEN, Ph.D., M.D. (Antwerp)

While there is a great amount of information about disturbances of reading and writing, it is not easy to find psychoanalytic studies on arithmetic difficulties in the first grade. The examination of a large group of children with problems in arithmetic has shown that their difficulties with arithmetic are of a specific type, and that there are striking similarities in their psychodynamic backgrounds and the structure of their thinking. A typical case will be presented in detail to demonstrate the structure and the causes of this disturbance. I shall also describe a specific type of functional and intellectual inhibition and discuss several interesting features about the relations between the primary process and the functions of the ego.

CASE PRESENTATION

Background Information

Eddy was six and a half years old when he first came to see me. His parents told me that he had been in the first grade for five months and that he did nothing at school. There was no open rebellion, nor did he dislike going to school, but he paid no attention to what the teacher said and was "just dreaming." During the first days of school the teacher had noticed that Eddy was very anxious. At Christmas he scored only 30 points out of a total of 100. His reading and writing were satisfactory, but there was a severe inhibition in learning arithmetic. When his teacher or parents asked him to do addition or something else concerned with arithmetic, he gave no answer, he "blocked," it was "as if a curtain fell down between him and the adult."

Eddy was born in a foreign country to which his parents had moved one year before his birth. His mother did not adjust very well; she felt lonely and went through a mild depression. She could not bear to be alone, especially in the evening; when she left the house, she felt surrounded by the darkness of the night, which looked to her like "a big, dark hole." During the delivery, Eddy's mother was panicky; the obstetrician looked like a "butcher" to her. Immediately after Eddy was born, her depression disappeared. He was breast-fed for the first two weeks, after which the mother could not feed him enough. He ate very well. There were no difficulties during the first years of life. He was exceedingly quiet and lay motionless in his cradle and never complained or cried. One never heard him, so that one almost "forgot him." He showed astonishingly little motor activity; he did not move and did not sit. When the parents put him in the sitting position, he fell down immediately.

One morning when Eddy was eleven months old, his parents entered his room and were very amazed to see him standing up; they had never seen any preparation for it. He began to walk at the age of fourteen months, but did so with great circumspection.

He talked early and his language development was very rapid. Bowel training was very easy; at the age of fourteen months, his mother "had to try only a few times." Thereafter he did not like to have dirty hands and wanted to be quite clean all the time.

Eddy laughed as much as other children and could play with them. The parents never had educational difficulties with him, but they noticed that he withdrew from learning new skills and frequently said: "I can't do that." He was rather inactive and was not eager to have new experiences. When Eddy was five years old, his parents returned to Belgium. He went to nursery school for one year. He, as well as his brothers, experienced some difficulty in adapting to the new cultural surroundings. Eddy sometimes complained about being teased or attacked by other boys, but he liked going to school. His two brothers, identical twins who were one year older than he, excluded him somewhat from their play. There were also three younger siblings.

The Parents.—The father was a friendly, hard-working, and successful intellectual, who had very high ethical standards and an obsessional character structure. He tried very hard to be good to his children and spent as much time with them as he could. However, he was often irritable toward them. He was very dependent on his wife, and did not like to go anywhere without her. He very much wanted psychoanalysis for the boy because his sister had had a severe nervous breakdown, and because his own father had been overworked during his entire lifetime.

The mother was a courageous and warm woman, who enjoyed being active and domineering. Although she accepted the treatment after a few months, she maintained a strong inner resistance against the analysis of her son, since she was dimly aware that his disturbance was related to her. She denied the existence of any psychological problems and displayed the "normal" attitude to the psychiatrist who tried to complicate everything. In this she followed a trait which was very prominent in her own mother. Her father was a taciturn and withdrawn man, whom she had had to nurse for three months before he died of cancer. He never showed any gratitude and almost refused to talk to her. This was a severe blow to her and certainly caused deep inner resentment, which might have played a role in her rather castrative and sometimes humiliating attitude toward Eddy. She had no problems in handling him, but she was amazed that in the beginning phase of treatment he sometimes called her "bad mother."

The Examination.—Eddy was a good-looking boy, very inactive and inhibited, but not openly anxious. He was very obedient and passive. During the first two psychiatric interviews he did not play; he took the toys but put them back again. He had no personal initiative at all. In the psychometric examination, his initial behavior was equally obedient. However, when the first difficulties appeared, he blocked and began to dream. At first one might have thought that he had not heard the question, but it soon became evident that he was reacting with withdrawal and protest. One could not see any open rebellion in his behavior: the curtain, of which the teacher spoke, had fallen down. When the questions were easier, he answered again, but showed very little interest or desire to do well. He did not really engage himself. There was no effort to make a good impression. As soon as the problems became harder, Eddy blocked again and could not be induced to answer.

On the Terman-Stanford Test (Form L) he obtained an I.Q. of 94 (because the examiner had insisted very much). He succeeded on all subtests at the six-year level and solved subtest 5 at the seven-year level (Analogies). He missed the repetition of sentences at the level of four and five years (a factor of resistance was certainly present). Whenever he could answer more or less mechanically, he succeeded, but when any active mental elaboration or comprehension was required, he blocked. However, when the examiner insisted, he understood quite a few things, even at the seven-year level.

On the Rorschach Test he showed massive perseveration: he saw only a very big, bad, and wicked bird in the first eight plates. The bird bites (Plate I); the bird has red hands (claws) (Plate II); the birds catch and devour a chicken (Plate III); the bird has no head and no legs and a broken back (Plate VII). All but two answers were global W response, only a few of them having normal F quality. There were no H or M responses, but several C', even F + C' and one FM.

There was some retardation in constructive-praxic activities (examined with the tests described in my book, *Spatial Development,*

1961). The motor examination with the Oseretsky Test gave unreliable results because he was so inhibited. There were mostly psychomotor disturbances: a great lack of motor initiative and spontaneity
and some retardation in motor coordination which seemed to be due
to his inhibition and to the fact that he was not accustomed to use
his body.

The results in reading and writing were normal. The examination of arithmetic will be described in the second part of this paper.

Treatment

Eddy was seen three times a week, for two and a half years. I shall
briefly summarize the course of the analysis and emphasize only those
factors which may contribute to a better understanding of the inhibitions in learning and arithmetic.

The First Phase.—During the first weeks it was almost pitiful to
observe the inactivity and inhibition of this little boy. He did practically nothing. Whenever he tried to solve a puzzle or to build with
blocks, he went about it almost like a baby. He was very clumsy, did
not really look at what he was doing, and immediately abandoned
it. He often worked with his mouth wide open, and then looked like
an imbecile oligophrene. His first emotional communication came
after a few weeks. He took Leggo blocks and built a house that had
neither doors nor windows and was completely closed. He deliber-
ately tried to close every opening and then said: "This is a prison."
He built this house several times and sometimes put a small car in
it. This theme portrayed well his own position in the world: completely shut off from the surroundings, which he did not try to discover. Other elaborations of the same fantasy appeared repeatedly
during the analysis: there were many connections with his fantasies
about the night and darkness (which played a central role in his
mother's depression when she was pregnant with him).

The Second Phase.—One month and a half after the beginning
of the analysis the theme of "the wolf and the big black madam"
made its first appearance and held his central interest during more
than a year of the analysis. In the beginning it appeared only sporad-
ically and was accompanied by little affect. Gradually this theme
began to dominate all his activities, unleashing incredible amounts
of energy. It was elaborated exclusively in the puppet theater.
"John" was always confronted by a terrible wolf or a threatening

"big, black madam." His key or his treasure was stolen. Sometimes he was swallowed or devoured by the wolf; on other occasions it seemed that the devouring wolf stood for Eddy himself. His strong oral-aggressive fantasies contained defensive measures such as identification with the aggressor. This second phase was characterized by the extreme weakness of his ego. The poor soldier was at the mercy of terrible dangers, he had to pay attention all the time lest he be killed or devoured or his key be stolen. Gradually he began to fight back, but he could never win or contain the threatening forces. In this phase the theme of the prison, completely shut off from the world, reappeared repeatedly. He began to talk about strange fantasies which seemed to stem from deep layers of the unconscious and had only a minimum of ego elaboration. Night and blackness were dominant themes that evoked horror and intense emotions. The house had a chimney with a thick column of black smoke. There were many fantasies about the devil and nocturnal fears of devils and ghosts. The same state of undifferentiated and unstructured energy appeared in several drawings; e.g., he drew a big mountain with fire (a volcano) and everything around was "so black."

The Third Phase.—Gradually Eddy's ego gained some strength. "John" (the boy of the wolf fantasy) became more powerful and less helpless in the face of danger. The first indications of this could be seen when John received a gun from the police. He became a soldier who took his revenge and killed the wolf or put him in jail. Sometimes he was a butcher or a tiger who killed the big madam or the other participants in the play and ate them with groaning noises. For these deeds, however, John or the soldier were frequently thrown into jail themselves. After approximately seven months of treatment the material lost its archaic quality and became more related to the themes which we usually see in other children of this age. At that time the first behavioral changes in Eddy appeared. He gradually became more energetic, but also rather irritable and disobedient at home.

The theme of night led to a wealth of sexual and aggressive fantasies. The blackness no longer made him shudder, but became connected with erotic pleasures. For about two months he had many fantasies of rain during the night, of stars shining, of a church with a sparkling light on top of it. Gradually these fantasies became less cosmic and impersonal: thieves appeared who stole the treasure of the witch or killed her.

Eddy produced much oedipal and genital material. John and Mary played many games in bed and hid themselves when the mother came. (The parents noticed some masturbation and a tendency to exhibit his genital at that time.) At first the boy often stole the treasure of the father; he collaborated with the big madam in order to kill the enemies and then they ate together and danced. He began to show much sexual curiosity: the children went into their father's bed, the father did all sorts of things. Eddy asked me whether I had a wife and children. The children were afraid that a ghost might come into their beds during the night. Although there were a few indications of some anxiety that the father would punish the children, the main anxieties were still focused on the almighty mother.

After a year of therapy the theme of the "false" cowboy emerged for the first time: there was a false cowboy, who lied all the time. This fantasy can be considered a re-edition of the wolf theme on a more human level. It served as a defensive measure in an attempt to cope with the threatening figure: the cowboy told the wolf that he was not going to kill him, but he did. The horse said that it would not kick, but it did. Eddy frequently sided with the vicious figure, the thief or the false person, and showed in many other ways his refusal to accept the usual rules. His parents reported that he and his brothers played a game in which he liked to take the role of the false crook. Among many other factors, this fantasy was also related to difficulties in the formation of a good ego ideal. The identification with his good, ethical father occurred late in the treatment and remained relatively weak. To be good and kind, hard-working and conscientious like his father probably meant to him that he would be at the mercy of his domineering mother, exactly as his father was. The good person very often proved to be the weakling, who lost the battle. Only the brutal cowboy could resist the big, strong madam. Eddy consciously admired Till Eulenspiegel, the strong, amusing, and asocial figure who refused to conform and always fooled authority. At the same time there were many indications that this fantasy also served as an identification with the aggressor: he sometimes took the same attitudes as the big madam.

When the primitive anxieties began to be less prominent and when Eddy showed more aggression himself, an attitude of strong rebellion and opposition came to the fore. Some horses were in a meadow which was completely fenced in, but they broke through the fences or flew over them. They killed the other animals or even the farmer and his wife. A small horse kicked the police and refused to listen to any order. A car drove into the house and broke everything. Gradually the same attitude was taken by little children: John and Mary frequently hid themselves from the adults. They amused themselves and whenever an adult came to look for them, they hid themselves in another place. Eddy's parents told me that during this year he was rather rebellious at home; e.g., he slammed doors or broke things when he did not like something. In school he talked or played with other boys during class and ignored his teacher's warnings.

The Fourth Phase.—After I had helped Eddy to understand his struggle against the powerful madam, his fear of people and normal activities, his anxiety that the good boy would not be strong enough to resist his enemies, the nature of the material began to change, although there were still frequent relapses to the themes of the preceding phase. The father became much more important: he stole the money of the big foolish madam; he threatened to throw her out; he killed or mistreated her during the night.

Eddy produced many positive oedipal fantasies, expressed much rivalry and hostility against his father, and began to show signs of castration anxiety. The latter was elaborated in terms of a real incident: his father had a minor car accident, which had frightened Eddy very much. There followed many anxious scenes in which cars were damaged and people brought to the hospital. In some scenes he himself was attacked by the father, and occasionally he referred to other passive homosexual fantasies. However, he also had a positive relationship with his father. Eddy now wanted to be big. This desire was first expressed in oral terms: a few times he urged the workers to eat a great deal and become very fat; then they would be even stronger than their boss.

Eddy's ego had become much more efficient: he did better at school; his difficulties in arithmetic almost disappeared; he displayed much intellectual curiosity; he could accept help; and he showed pleasure in growing up. He began to discuss real events and his feelings about the home situation and he listened better to my interpretations (previously he had shut himself off, laughed timidly, and protested passively against talking). The wish to identify with his father, to be admired and helped by him, gradually came to the fore. The laborers worked for the architect and were pleased when the latter praised them. (At this time his father told me that Eddy began to ask a lot of questions "in order to become intelligent.")

However, disappointments were frequently followed by regressions: he again became a thief, the false cowboy who refused to work, or the strong figure who identified with the mother. A healthy masculine identification and the formation of a good, constructive ego ideal remained difficult, in part because of the reality situation at home. He could not genuinely admire his father, who was too dependent on the mother. The attitude of the mother still contained some humiliating aspects. The children of Eddy's fantasies often excluded themselves from the adults. His personality remained too introverted: the inner elaboration of events was very strong. The Rorschach Test at the end of the treatment showed the extraordinary richness and refinement of his impressions, but this hypercathexis of his inner life seemed to be related to some affective withdrawal from the external world.

However, the healthy forces had become stronger; he learned well and had made a good social adjustment; he no longer complained about being teased and enjoyed fighting. The push of the primary-process fantasies decreased, and many hours of the analysis were filled with typical latency activities and sublimated, conflict-free play. It seemed possible to terminate the treatment.

THE INHIBITION OF THE EGO FUNCTIONS

Disturbances of the Sensorimotor and Spatial Functions

During Eddy's analysis it became clear that there was a massive and generalized inhibition of ego functions. This inhibition was particularly clear in all manual, spatial, and constructive activities. During the first weeks of therapy it was almost pitiful to observe Eddy's inactivity. He sat silently on the floor. From time to time he tried to play with blocks or puzzles. He chose puzzles suitable for approximately four-year-olds. (These age levels are described in my book [1961].)

Eddy's work on the *Schowanek puzzles* is a good example. At the five-year level the child should be able to copy a simple design of a house, a bird, or a table with four to eight blocks. Most of these blocks are square, and two or three of them are triangular (to represent the obliqueness of the roof, the bill of the bird, etc.). Eddy managed to place a few of the square blocks, but he usually failed with the triangular blocks. He vaguely felt that something was wrong; the observer was aware of a painful, inner tension in Eddy, but Eddy did nothing to relieve it. He did not try to change the position of the triangular blocks, he did not rotate them. It was also evident that he did not really look at the model. He furtively glanced at it, but he did not explore it thoroughly.

The exact nature of Eddy's perceptual and sensorimotor inhibitions could also be clearly discerned in the "*Landscape Game.*" He was shown the photograph of a landscape, on which several houses, trees, cars, bridges, animals, an airplane, and the sun were placed in various positions. He was then given a similar landscape, and houses, cars, bridges, etc., and asked to place these objects on his landscape in the same positions as on the model. (As is shown in *Spatial Development*, this is a task for five-year-olds.) After he had found the sun, a few houses and trees, he needed the airplane and the bridge. The objects were fixed on two small cardboard pieces that were lying on top of each other. The airplane and the bridge were on the bottom piece of cardboard, which protruded and thus was partly visible. All he had to do was to remove the cardboard. Although Eddy wanted to find the airplane and the bridge, he was paralyzed. His hands did not move, he did not look in the box containing the game. His eyes did not explore the immediate surroundings; they moved only a few inches, but very slowly and against a great inner resistance. He looked at the upper piece of cardboard, but I could not tell whether he had discovered the piece underneath. He anxiously withdrew his eyes, but then came back to it, thus indicating that he knew about the second piece of cardboard. However, the expected actions did not follow. He had discovered the place, but this remained at the periphery of his mind (I shall return to this phenomenon when I describe the disturbances of awareness and "definite statement"). Only gradually did something become clarified in his mind: he then really knew that the objects could only be there. Yet, instead of simply removing the top piece of cardboard, he tried to look under it: he saw the airplane and the bridge protruding a little bit and very carefully tried to draw them in his direction. He could not allow himself enough freedom to remove the upper piece. On later occasions when he played this game, the same thing happened, but he finally could decide to remove the top piece of cardboard. The same phenomenon was observed when Eddy was playing with cards or toys. After he had placed one or two rows of cards, he found it difficult to place the third row. He only had to move the first row a few inches, but he dared not do so. He clumsily tried to place the next row in an impossible place and it was only after long hesitation that he removed the objects that were in his way. Only when he was making the fifth row, I heard him say: "These are in my way" and he then removed them quite easily.

These examples give us some idea about the meaning of Eddy's disturbance: there is a deep blocking of all mobility and movement. He cannot remove a piece of cardboard that is in his way. The visual exploratory activities are severely disturbed. He sticks to the same area of the model, he cannot freely move his eyes from one point to the other. He is paralyzed. When he has understood something, this insight is not followed by the expected motor activity. He cannot freely move in space with his eyes or with his body. However, the inhibition is not limited to the sphere of muscular movement. We shall see that the same disturbance appears in other mental activities as well (e.g., the verbal sphere and in the "Two-in-One Game").

The role of *motor phenomena* could also be observed during the process of recovery. As the treatment progressed, there was a striking parallel between the liberation of verbal or spatial functions and the emergence of motor fantasies or actual motor play. The greater freedom in motility did not remain confined to the motor sphere; it spread to all mental areas. It was fascinating to follow the various phases through which motor development passed (Mittelmann, 1954). In the beginning the liberation of motor activity could be seen almost exclusively on the level of the primary process. During the fantasy play around the theme of the wolf and the devouring mother, Eddy began to shout violently, made groaning noises, threw things, and knocked the enemies against each other. He enjoyed making large and violent movements. A little later the motor activity seemed to be on a level between the primary and the secondary process. For example, the horses jumped over the fences, they could not be restrained by anything. When the fence was too high, they broke through it or flew over it. The horses killed the farm personnel who tried to master them. These fantasies contained many ingredients of the primary process but also a strong ego component: the wish to become free, to break all the rules and barriers that kept him a prisoner. Still later the motor activities belonged more and more to the secondary process. This manifested itself in gross muscular activity: Eddy loved to knock with his hammer on the blocks (in construction games); his parents reported that he was no longer afraid to climb trees or to use the gym equipment on the playground. In the fourth phase of his treatment his fantasy play was full of motor themes: children climbed on roofs; they jumped from one roof to another; they walked on a rope fixed between two houses; acrobats in the circus performed reckless games on the trapeze. The liberation of motor activity could also be seen in the sphere of fine movements: he began to make all kinds of knots and to glue objects to each other. The visual exploratory movements also became entirely free (see the description of the Schowanek puzzle and the "Two-in-One Game").

Significant features of Eddy's mental inhibition could be seen in the *"Two-in-One Game."* This is a simplified edition of the game of Checkers that can easily be played by six-year-old children. The men of the first player should be directed toward the base line of the other player. Each child has only four men. Each man may advance one step at each turn, except when it meets the man of the other player. In that case (exactly as in Checkers) the man may jump over the man of the other player and eventually over two men. Eddy's rigidity in learning this game was striking in several respects:
1. He always moved his men in the same order, regardless of what I was doing. He first moved his first man until it had arrived at my base line; only then did he start to move his second man. This was a disadvantage that was obvious even to him: he saw that when he placed the first man exactly in front of mine, I could jump over his and win one turn. I saw him hesitate, but he still moved this man. The solution would have been very simple—to move his second man—but he did not do so. The scheme of action had been traced once and was always repeated. This is a clear sign of his mental rigidity.
2. His mental field was extremely narrow: for example, he concentrated only on his first man, disregarding his other men and my moves. In later phases when he had abandoned this trick of always moving the same man, his attention still remained fixed on one spot of the board. He moved the man nearest to it, disregarding better possibilities in other areas.

3. His attention lacked all mobility. This can clearly be seen in the preceding example: he concentrated on one spot of the board and, when his turn came, did not move his eyes in various directions over the entire field.

4. His awareness of structure was very limited and he had no insight into the whole. This follows from the two preceding points: when his mental field is so narrow and when his attention is given to only one aspect, he cannot play in accordance with the situation in the whole field. He isolated one part from the whole, could not simultaneously survey all the parts, and certainly was unaware of the relations existing between these parts (he did not say to himself: "I can do that, but this other move would be better").

5. Whenever he discovered a new possibility in the game, he was very slow to apply it. For example, he had seen that on certain occasions his man could jump over two of my men. However, previously he had learned to jump over only one of my men. There was a strong tendency to stick to that custom. After jumping over the first man, he stopped. Sometimes he was a little restless and looked at me. After some hesitation he would sometimes ask: "Should I now jump over this one too?" His comment clearly shows his awareness of this possibility, but he was blocked in using it.

6. There was an almost complete blocking of the mental activities of anticipation, invention, and planning. This phase in the development of intelligence has been described by Piaget (1941). From the age of five to seven years, the child's intelligence gradually becomes less static and more mobile. The child can weave a net of mental activities over the perceptual reality: he can make several assumptions and anticipate (in his mind) what will happen. Eddy never did this, he never made a plan, he never said to himself: "If I place my man here, I might be able to make a long jump next turn." He never stated: "The doctor comes along that side, he will be able to jump over two of my men, so I must try to stop that."

These six categories are all manifestations of the same basic disturbance: Eddy displayed a pronounced lack of mental mobility. It is striking that all these phenomena correspond closely to those described by Piaget (1941) for the level of intelligence characterized by operational correspondence (stage 3). Between the age of five and seven the child's intelligence undergoes a gradual change from a static form (closely bound to perception) to a mobile form (in which the child can transform the perceptual reality through a variety of inner mental operations). I shall again refer to Piaget's ideas when I discuss Eddy's disturbance of arithmetic. His case indicates that mental inhibitions need not affect all mental activities, but may be confined mainly to one level of intelligence—in this case, operational correspondence. Moreover, the emergence of specific stages of intelligence may be blocked by psychogenic factors.

The same lack of mental mobility appeared in other symptoms:

1. Eddy had a pronounced *aversion to the new*. He did not like to shift to new schemes of action. In the "Two-in-One Game" Eddy stuck to the same scheme of action and disregarded other methods, although he knew that they would be better. Whenever he was given new games or tasks, he wanted to apply old schemes regardless of whether they were appropriate or not. When I introduced a new rule, he understood it, but something still compelled him to maintain the old way. For this reason Eddy was so very slow in learning something new. He saw a coin and said: "It is one cent." He then asked me: "Is it one cent?" I told him that it was one franc. However, when he played with these coins he usually said: "One cent," although he asked from time to time whether it was one franc. This aversion to the new existed not only in learning situations but was evident in his general behavior. For example, during the first four months of the treatment his fantasy play was very repetitive: the puppet game was usually arranged in exactly the same manner; the "big, black madam" did the same thing every time; the stolen key was always hidden in the same place. (This factor played an important role in Eddy's arithmetic difficulties.)

2. Another characteristic symptom was *the reduction of his perceptual field* to a very small area and his *"piecemeal approach."* Eddy did not perceive the world as ordinary people do. When we enter a room or look at a group of soldiers in a field, we see the general configuration and do not perceive the tiny details of every object. Eddy noticed details of toys that other children and I had never seen. While playing with a Red Indian, he said: "This Red Indian is hiding behind a rock [indeed, in front of the Red Indian a dark piece of stone could be seen], he has a knife [a very small knife was painted on the back of his trousers]." He also noticed that one of the toy soldiers "was made for an airplane" [a tiny white bundle, representing a parachute, was painted behind his shoulders]. Why did Eddy perceive in this manner? He was very inhibited, he dared not move, his eyes did not freely scan his surroundings. Therefore,

he perceived not the totality of the external world but only a small area of it (as if he looked at the world through a tube). However, within this small area Eddy's perception was unusually precise.

This perceptual phenomenon had of course repercussions on his activities: e.g., in the "Two-in-One Game," he divided the field into separate parts. This can be compared to the "piecemeal approach," which Paterson and Zangwill (1944) described in the visual-agnostic disturbances of neurological cases. The same phenomenon is responsible for the lack of hierarchic structure of Eddy's perceptions. A normal person perceives the total situation and notices only the most important details. In contrast, the person who is unaware of the total situation lacks the necessary criterion to determine what is important.

Disturbances of the Verbal and Logical Functions

The same type of inhibition affected Eddy's verbal functions and thinking. He had never shown curiosity, he never asked questions. The first months of the treatment were characterized by a lack of verbal communication. He talked little, did not understand what I said, or shut himself off. Gradually he began to show some interest, to look at television or picture books, but real mental activity was essentially blocked. For example, he was looking at pictures of birds, of which one was drawn in two colors: on the first picture it was shown in a red "mating dress" and on the other the bird was in its "usual dress." Eddy asked what these terms meant. I told him that the bird wore the red "dress" when it is going "to mate." He accepted my explanation and continued to look at the book. Since I noticed some hesitation, I asked him: "Do you know what 'to mate' means?" He did not know. This happened again and again: whenever he did not understand a particular point or situation, he blocked, whereas another person would spontaneously inquire further.

Very often there was not only an inhibition of one or the other mental function, but a restriction of consciousness itself. When Eddy was on the verge of understanding something, when he had already taken the main steps, clear and precise knowledge or "awareness" nevertheless did not emerge. A beautiful example of this was described in the "Landscape Game." When Eddy had discovered that the airplane and the bridge were covered by another piece of cardboard, a kind of clouding of consciousness took place. He anxiously withdrew his eyes, then tried to come back to the cardboard, but he did not remove it. While he knew where the missing pieces were, this knowledge did not gain full awareness. Eddy was unable to proceed to a "definite statement." Nothing appeared clearly and unambiguously in the center of his mind. He kept the discovery at the periphery of his mental field. He knew it, and yet he did not seem to know it.

Eddy's verbal knowledge was adequate when he merely had to reproduce mechanically what he already knew. Whenever mental activity was required, he failed. All logical or connected thinking, all reasoning was blocked. For example, on the Terman-Stanford Test, seven-year-olds are expected to be able to answer in which way coal and wood, apple and pear, ship and automobile are similar. To find this similarity, the child must make all kinds of comparisons and permit the image of coal and wood to pass through his mind (coal is black, it is in our cellar, my mother uses it during winter for the stove . . . wood is white, it comes from the trees, it burns). The attention should wander freely from one point to the other. Many factors are of course required to solve such a problem, but it is clear that mental mobility is of paramount importance. When Eddy was asked this question, he was at a loss, seemed to be in a painful state of inner paralysis, and apparently did not think. He reacted in the same way as he had in spatial activities: he very anxiously clung to one aspect of the situation, without daring to let his mind move freely.

The recovery of these functions occurred somewhat later than that in the spatial and perceptual field. His parents reported that only after one and a half years of treatment had Eddy begun to ask a lot of questions. It was very interesting to see that during this phase various types of mobile and combinatory thinking made their appearance—though on the level of two- or three-year-old children. Eddy was especially interested in the "relations" existing between objects: e.g., shoes are made of leather and leather comes from the skin of cows. Later on he became interested in more complicated relations of causality and finality (e.g., he asked why there was a policeman at a particular street corner, why the streetcar had green and blue lights). He actively combined various bits of knowledge:

he connected something he had seen a week previously with current events. For example, he and his aunt, while driving to the session, were caught in a traffic jam. Eddy said: "There is a big truck that cannot pass through the tunnel" (this had happened the week before) and he even opened the window to see whether there was a big truck at the entrance of the tunnel.

Eddy also developed rich and mobile connections between his own functional systems, e.g., between the visual-motor and the auditory spheres. For example, while hammering small wooden nails into the holes of Matador blocks, he wondered whether he could not drive the nails somewhat deeper into the block. Suddenly I saw a flash of comprehension and he said: "No . . . that won't work . . . I hear it." Indeed, when he hammered on the nail, we heard a dull sound, indicating that the nail had arrived at the bottom of the hole and was hitting wood. This fact shows that the auditory stimulus could be connected with visual-motor activities. At an earlier phase the auditory stimulus would have remained isolated from the rest of his surroundings. It is also remarkable that at this time there was a sudden and immediate flash of insight: he no longer showed that painful, hesitating, and very slow approach until finally something began to dawn upon him.

Not only did he discover the relations between events, but he also began to realize that they could change. For example, he had seen the word "Ekla" (a Belgian beer) on the window of a pub and thought that "Ekla" was the name of that pub. However, he noticed the name "Ekla" on quite a few pubs. His father reported that this seemed to constitute quite a problem for Eddy, but he finally realized that "Ekla" could not be the name of the pub and then understood his father's explanation. This shows that he no longer adhered rigidly to his schemes, that he had become able to undo the preceding relations, and to shift to another combination. All this resembles the behavior of children between two and three years of age. They try to unravel the riddles of this world: they discover some regularities and then are amazed when some irregularity presents itself. Their faces then show the same mental effort that the now eight-year-old Eddy displayed.

The unfolding of Eddy's mental activity revealed itself also in another way: his perceptions or experiences were no longer made passively. When he perceived something, it spread to other mental activities and activated new mental connections.

The Causes of These Ego Inhibitions

Several findings obtained in the psychometric examination and the analytic treatment might help explain Eddy's deep inhibitions. I shall first discuss *dynamic* factors. Eddy suffered from intense castration anxiety, which in the beginning of the analysis had a strong oral coloring. His behavior and fantasies were characterized in the first months of treatment by a state of inactivity and later on by intense fears of being devoured, bitten or torn apart by the oral-aggressive mother, who would take his key away (phallic castration) and rob him of the treasure (anal castration). After these anxieties had become conscious, the blocking of ego functions began to subside very quickly. It seems that the oral-aggressive and orally colored castration anxieties constituted by far the most important block. This was confirmed by a reappearance of earlier symptoms at the end of the treatment. When Eddy had a strict female teacher, his lack of concentration and dreamy absence in school reappeared, and so did the oral-aggressive fantasies in the treatment.

Other factors were of course also involved. Early in the treatment there were veiled references to threatening and savage primal-scene fantasies (which might have been related to the fact that Eddy shared his parents' bedroom until he was one and a half years old). The blocking of curiosity and comprehension as well as the severe inhibition of looking and visual exploration were probably also related to this fact. All this must have been augmented by the specifics of his family situation: certain characteristics of his parents, the quick succession of the births of his brothers and sisters (with the inability to inquire about these events), his position as the younger brother of twin brothers who were only one year older. These boys excluded him from their games, which made Eddy feel weak and helpless. It was quite significant that the children of his fantasy games often appeared in pairs: John and Mary. They hid from their parents, they were rebellious, they engaged in more and more daring adventures. Eddy seemed to have the idea that to be strong one needed to be twins.

All this makes it understandable that Eddy tried to escape from the external world and did not use his ego functions. However, Eddy's difficulties were not just general inhibitions. They were much more specific and were characterized by the lack of motility, the mental immobility, and the difficulties with arithmetic. What were the causes of this motor inactivity and mental immobility? There were a number of psychodynamic factors which may have contributed to making all movements appear so dangerous: movement seemed to be tied to masturbation and sexual excitement (during the third phase of the analysis he played a great number of motor games, which were masturbatory equivalents). Movement also meant the desire for sexual exploration (when he tried to reach the bedroom of his parents, he had to do all kinds of reckless tricks on the roof, the chimney, and the windows). However, these meanings of movement became prominent only during the third and fourth phases of treatment, when the lack of motility and the mental immobility had greatly decreased. I believe that the main factors causing the motor inhibition can be found in the orally colored castration anxiety and to some extent also in the anal tendencies. In the first phase of treatment Eddy showed extreme inactivity and immobility, after which intense fears of the devouring mother appeared: the "big, black madam" might take his key. Schematically speaking, we might say that this reproduced the extreme inactivity of his first year of life, when he developed a very poor pattern of interaction with his mother, who was just coming out of a depression. Later he also showed strong tendencies toward rebellion and opposition within a framework of anal and obsessional characteristics. The aversion to the new, the immobility, and the difficulty in shifting to new behavioral schemes were also an expression of his stubbornness and obsessional rigidity. His introverted and very blocked behavior was related to his refusal to let things come out of him. For a long time he did not show any initiative, he did not communicate his feelings or thoughts: he held them back. His rigidity was due to his unwillingness to let his associations "flow" and take their natural course. As soon as he permitted his associations free reign in the richness of his fantasy games, his mental activity became much freer and the pattern of rigidity diminished. Some causes of these strong anal components can be discerned. Toilet training was instituted too early and "accepted" much too easily; it was soon followed by excessive cleanliness. There also were some indications of anal birth fantasies (around the birth of his younger brother), and identification with the almighty, anal mother (van der Leeuw, 1958).

It is important to note that Eddy not only feared to move, but he also used muscular as well as mental immobility as a *defense:* it became a general scheme of behavior which freed him from all dangers. This defense pattern was established in the very first months of life. Eddy's rigidity and aversion to the new can be considered to be primitive defenses, closely related to the obsessional defenses many children develop between the age of one and two: everything must remain in the same place and must be done in the same sequence. In Eddy's case it was very clear that he avoided the new because it meant entering an unknown, threatening situation.

In addition to the psychodynamic factors, certain *structural* considerations help to explain the nature of Eddy's difficulties. Although I shall briefly mention some structural deficiencies of Eddy's ego and ego ideal, I shall emphasize primarily the structural anomalies of his psychic energies and the disturbances of neutralization.

1. The anxieties and psychodynamic conflicts had such deep influence on Eddy's ego functions because his ego functions were not yet cathected with stable and sufficiently neutralized energies. When he worked so poorly on spatial tasks, when his eyes did not proceed to a series of exploratory movements, this was also caused by the fact that there was no neutralized energy available. He had never developed the capacity really to engage himself in spatial tasks. There had been no occasion to connect neutralized energies with these functions. This point is not only relevant to Eddy's case; it is an important principle for the understanding of learning inhibitions in general. Moreover, it explains in part why psychodynamic factors have such disastrous effects in cases of organic damage or general immaturity. The same psychodynamic factors play a much weaker role when the ego is well structured and when its functions are cathected with enough neutralized energy. For example, for another boy, intellectual performance represented a terribly aggressive destruction of the father. However, this did not impair his intellectual insight, because his ego functions could

work in the conflict-free sphere (it caused difficulty only in display-ing his intelligence).

Another aspect can be stated as follows: the influence of severe phallic-oedipal problems on ego function depends very much on the cathexis of these ego functions with neutralized energies before the child enters the phallic-oedipal phase. When the child has already experienced the free use of his functions in playful and enjoyable contact with his parents, the impact of the phallic-oedipal problems on intellectual performance is much less pronounced. Eddy, we can assume, left the preoedipal phase with a very poorly developed ego; its functions were not cathected with enough neutralized energies. Such an ego cannot fulfill the tasks of the phallic-oedipal phase: i.e., it cannot develop a positive identification with the father. Indeed, when a child cannot play, when he does not display the wish to solve small problems himself, when he is not proud of his first achievements at the age of two or three, how can he then become proud of his boyhood and try to compete with his father? Conse-quently there is a significant decrease in the amount of neutralized energies which would normally become available to the ego during the oedipal phase and also during its resolution and the formation of the ego ideal. Eddy's ego functions could not become strong and reliable tools for the affirmation of himself and for the stabilization of a healthy identification.

This formulation illustrates an interesting principle of genetic psychology: the multidirectional interrelations of growth factors (Kris, 1955). We used to attribute primary importance to instinctual development and to consider the growth or pathology of the ego as a consequence of instinctual conflicts. This example shows that the opposite is also true: when preoedipal ego development is not satis-factory, this will greatly disturb the further evolution not only of the ego but also that of the instinctual impulses on the phallic-oedipal level.

The ego functions were flooded with primary-process derivatives. The exercise of these functions had to be curtailed lest a dreadful primary-process fantasy be realized. For example, motor activity had to be inhibited because the motor act might mean killing the enemy. Even the mental images were blocked because they were too closely bound to the primary process: e.g., the child would think of the devouring mother. Visual exploration was forbidden because this activity might dangerously penetrate the object or lead to the discovery of awful primal-scene events. Both primary and secondary autonomy were impaired: each function was flooded by unneutralized energies and could not work in the conflict-free area of the ego (Hartmann, Kris, Loewenstein, 1946).

Why did Eddy's ego functions not become cathected with a sufficient amount of neutralized energy? This question has a direct bearing on important related problems of psychogenic learning inhibitions. When does an ego function remain sexualized, when does it not achieve sufficient autonomy, when does it remain too much in the realm of the primary process? As in all cases of unsatisfactory neutralization, the causes are manifold. I shall now attempt a hypothetical reconstruction of the disturbances of neutralization in Eddy's case.

a. First of all, there was a severe disturbance of the neutralization normally taking place during happy and playful contacts with the early objects. The ego functions did not become invested with libidinal energy. All forms of play during childhood were greatly inhibited. The functional inhibition had been unusually severe as early as the first year of life: Eddy never moved or cried or complained. When the parents tried to make him sit, he fell down immediately. Yet at eleven months he was able to stand, without any previous preparation. When he was a little older, he did not like to play; he did not seek admiration or attention from his parents; he did not ask questions. On the basis of these observations we may assume that even during the preoedipal phase there was a severe functional inhibition and that the conditions for neutralization were not satisfactory. His first sensorimotor experiences did not occur in playful contact with his mother. Therefore the motor basis for the development of his ego functions and the opportunities for neutralization were very weak. His ego functions were not satisfactorily object-related; he did not like to exercise them in contact with adults. In the first year of therapy his parents told me repeatedly that Eddy could answer a question when he was not looked at, but that he suddenly went to pieces when one looked at him. His mother would tell him: "Try again . . . I shall not look" and he then could recite his multiplication tables. The same attitude was evident in the psychometric examination: when he could not answer a test item and the examiner tried to help him in a friendly and encouraging manner, his responses did not improve and his performance fell apart. The same situation existed during the treatment: he did not like to be helped in his work, he did not desire to be praised. While some indications of this wish appeared during the third phase of treatment, it was still very weak even at the end of the analysis. He remained too introverted; the wish to affirm himself and to exercise his ego functions in the company of other people did not become sufficiently strong.

b. Another factor has already been described: when the ego functions are not cathected with enough neutralized energies during the preoedipal phase, the oedipal phase and its resolution are also disturbed. The child cannot develop a strong ego identification with his father and the ego ideal remains weak.

c. The process of neutralization was also threatened from the side of the impulses. The manner in which instinctual impulses cause disturbances of neutralization constitutes a problem per se (A. Freud, 1952; Kris, 1955). I want to stress the following points: the disturbances of neutralization originate not only on account of the instinctual vicissitudes themselves but primarily when the drives do not achieve a satisfactory cathexis of an external object or cannot be used in the process of identification. As has been shown, Eddy's object relations were shallow and his instinctual drives were not sufficiently directed toward external objects. During the treatment he developed a very extensive fantasy life, but he did not reach out for external objects; he remained too introverted. The aspect of identification is also very important: the normal child cathects external objects and identifies with them. The formation of these identifications is of paramount importance for the process of neutralization. In Eddy's case, the phallic-oedipal impulses were caught up in his fantasy life; they were not elaborated by strong ego identifications. Therefore, he lacked an essential impetus for further neutralization.

The fact that Eddy's phallic-oedipal impulses did not result in normal identifications has of course many other reasons: e.g., the mother image was too threatening and played too important a part in his psychic economy.

2. The structural anomalies of Eddy's psychic energies mentioned so far are concerned mainly with neutralization and do not seem to have a particular bearing on the specific symptoms of immobility and motor inhibition. However, here too the structural point of view may contribute to a better understanding. Let us again consider the state of Eddy's energies.

a. There were no stable cathexes of ego functions with neutralized energies. There was almost no feeling of self; the ego did not try to assert or realize itself; there was no solidly organized ego ideal, having at its disposal firmly bound energies. In normal latency children a great deal of their biopsychic energy is integrated in these well-organized functional systems. What happens with these energies when they are not bound in this way?

b. During the first two months of Eddy's therapy there was not only a great lack of ego activities, even the fantasies with primary-process content were extremely inhibited. During the following six months some fantasies began to emerge, but they were all on the same level: a little boy was confronted with a terrible, big madam or a wolf. What was the state of Eddy's energies during these first months of treatment? We can safely assume that there was a great amount of unneutralized energy, a great lack of structuralization and "binding" of the energies on both primary- and secondary-process levels. In the beginning nothing had really taken form in him. It was only gradually that one single theme (the big, black madam and the little boy) could establish itself in a stable way. Of course there was some structure and organization (e.g., Eddy did understand me, he could move and play), but underneath there must have been a "seething cauldron" of unstabilized energies. These might drift away in any direction, because they had never assumed stable positions. His energies must have existed in a formless, undifferentiated, and unbound state. A few drawings from the first months of treatment may illustrate this condition: e.g., he drew a big mountain with fire (a volcano) and around it he just smeared black color and said: "Everything is so black." Nor could his emotional state be characterized by a well-circumscribed feeling, although the tone with which he talked about the blackness indicated a vague feeling of horror. (This state of formless, amorphous, and unbound energies is related to the pure C and C' responses on the

Rorschach Test.) Any emerging energies thus had no pre-established pathway in which they might safely flow. Therefore I propose the following hypothesis: Eddy's immobility also served the function of structuralizing and stabilizing his inner world. (This phenomenon might have some bearing on the understanding of certain psychotic processes.)

THE DISTURBANCES OF ARITHMETIC

A description of Eddy's intellectual inhibition had to be given first because his problems with arithmetic can be understood only on the basis of these facts. The few analytic investigations of this subject usually emphasize the unconscious fantasies which are attached to all or a few numbers and interfere with their proper manipulation (Freud, 1923b; Jeffreys, 1936; Wegrocki, 1938; Pearson, 1952; Plank and Plank, 1954). Pearson and Plank described a number of specific conflicts and psychodynamic constellations responsible for difficulties with arithmetic. Hellman (1954) and Pearson, e.g., stress the importance of oral-aggressive factors. Pearson states that these children have great difficulties in taking in knowledge from adults. However, why these fantasies specifically involve arithmetic remains an unsolved problem. Frijling-Schreuder (1954) indicates that these children may have great anxieties about destruction or tearing apart. Therefore, arithmetical operations such as subtraction are inhibited because they represent the fulfillment of a dangerous act: the whole loses its integrity, something is taken away. We shall now describe Eddy's specific disturbance and attempt to demonstrate the point at which the psychogenic factor inserts itself (Bladergroen, 1954) to cause the arithmetic failures.

The psychometric examination revealed several problems with arithmetic. One of them was the difficulty in the global apperception of numbers. When Eddy saw 3, 4, 5, or 6 dots on a die, he could not say immediately how many he saw; instead he tried to count. Here, as in so many other situations, he became fearful, blocked easily, and withdrew. It seemed as if the act of verbalizing the result implied taking a great risk. He could count normally when he was allowed to start from 1. Oral counting (without seeing the objects) was very difficult, particularly when he was asked to start with a number other than 1. It soon became clear that he could do so, but only against great inner resistance. He wanted to start from 1, but somehow did not dare to. Counting backwards (from 10 to 1) was even more difficult, especially when he had to start from 6 or 9.

Eddy had great difficulties even in such simple tasks as adding or subtracting 1, whereas other children can do such sums immediately. He seemed to be in some kind of a cloud, which persisted for a long time before the right answer broke through. He had great trouble with all additions, surreptitiously tried to count on his fingers, and made many errors even with such simple sums as $3 + 2$, $3 + 1, 4 + 1$.

After five months of treatment Eddy was re-examined. While he was better at adding, he could not yet subtract. He even failed with $4 - 2, 5 - 1, 7 - 1, 4 - 1$. It was also evident that he had to stick very rigidly to the same type of sum. He could find $5 + 3 = 8$, but when the sum was written in another form (such as $5 + ? = 8$; $8 = ? + 3$) he gave up completely. His parents and the teacher noticed that the results were very irregular: sometimes he was unable to solve the simplest sums, whereas at other times he could do difficult sums (such as $18 + 5$). They found it very striking that he often worked better when he was not looked at. When the teacher asked him to do a sum, he blocked. He could not profit from help; all efforts in this direction only increased the breakdown of his functioning.

After about a year of treatment the situation began to change rapidly. His symptoms in arithmetic gradually disappeared and eventually it was no longer possible to detect any signs of rigidity and immobility, even with more difficult sums (1 to 100). However, his grades in arithmetic remained lower than his other grades. While some conscious aversion to arithmetic continued to exist, he no longer had difficulties with arithmetic thinking. He solved the problems appropriate for his age, and quickly knew when to add, multiply, or divide. When he was allowed to write his sums, he could do them easily. When he was not allowed to write, the results were less satisfactory. He easily solved sums such as $62 - 4, 58 + 5, 40 - 6$, but when he tried to do sums involving numbers such as $36 + 23$, $42 + 35$, a peculiar residual phenomenon could be demonstrated (see below).

Some areas of Eddy's understanding of arithmetic were not disturbed. He knew what a number is, the quantity it represents, its position in the row of the other numbers. The difficulty appeared when something had to be "done" with these numbers (Bladergroen, 1954). My basic hypothesis is that Eddy's problems in arithmetic are caused mainly by the great lack of mobility in his thinking. This rigidity and blocked mobility has already been described in several behavioral areas. For an understanding of how these characteristics hamper arithmetic operations, Piaget's ideas about the development of the number concept are especially important.

Piaget showed in great detail that a special type of intelligence is gradually established between the ages of five and seven. He speaks of the level of operational correspondence. Its main characteristic is mobility of psychic processes, in contrast to the more static form of earlier types of intelligence (intuitive intelligence). When the child is aware of a given structure, e.g., the drawing of a diamond or a house and a garden, he understands this pattern as a coordinated system of several characteristics (e.g., there are four lines in that diamond, they are oblique, two of them are parallel, etc.). On this level of operational correspondence, the child's insight is very mobile. In copying a diamond, the child no longer needs to start at the same point and continue in the same direction. He can start at any point, draw a line here, then a line there, etc. The child is no longer bound to any direction or sequence. At one time he may work in one direction, on another occasion he may work in the opposite direction. This is Piaget's principle of reversibility: when an operation has been performed in one direction, it can also be performed in the opposite direction. Moreover, on this level of intelligence insight no longer depends entirely on perception. The child can transform the perceptual model in his mind, he can add some details to his mental representations, and he can anticipate what the model would look like if one part were omitted. This also shows the mobility: structures can be quickly analyzed, resynthesized, and transformed by purely mental operations. Piaget (1941) beautifully described the dependence of the comprehension of numbers and arithmetic on this type of intelligence. I shall concentrate on Eddy's symptoms and show that in each case a lack of mobility is involved.

1. Oral counting (without seeing the objects to be counted) was very difficult, particularly when he was asked to start from 5, 8, 3, etc. This task requires sufficient mobility to abandon the old scheme of always counting from 1 to 10 and to shift immediately to another position. The same is true for his inability to count back-

wards, which requires that he move through the system of numbers in a completely new way. This would be an early form of Piaget's principle of reversibility. It necessitates a free exploring and "running through" the structural system of the numbers. Eddy was incapable of doing this. He showed only reluctance, wanted to stay on the customary and safe positions, and did not want to jump into the unknown.

2. Eddy had great difficulties in adding or subtracting 1, while other children can do such sums instantly. They only have to move one place in the row of numbers. They "possess" the row so thoroughly that they can immediately locate the position of a number and its immediate neighbors. Eddy, however, seemed to be in some kind of a cloud. There was an inner resistance to the immediate awareness of the place 5 in the row, and also to the free and quick shifting to the position one unit higher or lower in the row.

3. Eddy's difficulties increased with the more complicated mental operations, which require greater activity or mobility. We saw that the operation of addition was very disturbed. Although I cannot embark on a thorough analysis of the thought processes required for addition, a few relevant points will be mentioned. Addition requires a very mobile structural insight into numbers. The child must know that each number consists of equal units. Only this knowledge makes it at all possible to add two numbers to each other. One of the structural conditions that enables the child to know immediately that $3 + 2 = 5$ is the fact that the child considers 3 as three equal units, 2 as two equal units, and both numbers together as a group of five units. All these numbers are simultaneously experienced as global quantities and as consisting of units. This is characteristic of the level of operational correspondence: a structure is considered not as one single thing but at the same time under two different aspects. When the child tries to solve the sum $3 + 2$, he first considers 3 and 2 separately, and then unifies them in the number 5. The parts can be considered independently and also as comprising the whole. Another important factor in addition is the following: the various sums are not known independently from each other. The child knows that 5 can be the result of several sums: $3 + 2$, $4 + 1$, or $7 - 2$. This is a high form of mobility: 5 is not one static entity that exists unchanged once and for all. It can consist of all kinds of material. Shifting from one conception of 5 to another can take place very quickly. Eddy failed because he could not proceed to these quick shifts of structure. He could not risk imagining this fluid state in which things are easily decomposed, reunited, or changed.

The same type of structural insight is required for numbers between 10 and 100, but the level of complexity is still greater: the child must think of 32 as being made up of 3 tens and 2 units. Such sums as 32 + 19 require very intricate decompositions and reunifications.

4. Eddy had to stick rigidly to the same forms of sum. After he had learned to do additions rather easily (e.g., 5 + 3 = 8), he was completely disoriented when the sum was written in another form (e.g., 5 + ? = 8). The normal child can do this rather easily: once he understands the principle of reversibility, it does not matter very much in which direction he proceeds. Eddy felt secure only when he could rigidly work in the same way. When the form of the sum was changed, he withdrew into a state of anxious constriction and did not dare move.

5. After two years of treatment, the typical symptoms of his inhibition in arithmetic were no longer present even when he had to solve difficult sums such as 58 + 7 or 72 − 6. However, a peculiar behavior remained in doing sums such as 36 + 23, especially when he was not allowed to write the sum. He did not use the scheme 36 + 23 = 36 + 20 + 3 = 59. He did 36 + 23 = 36 + 10 + 10 + 3 = 59. He knew the right technique and applied it easily after a few minutes of exercise, but he showed some initial aversion to using it. This can be considered as a residual manifestation of the initial disturbance. He knew the exact technique, but he did not like to use it. If he had proceeded by way of 42 + 35 = 42 + 30 + 5 = 77, he would have been obliged to add 30 to 42. This is a big jump, freely and widely moving in the space of the numbers. He preferred to move more carefully: not 42 + 30, but 42 + 10 + 10 + 10. Here we see a discrete manifestation of his initial inhibition of movement, of his anxious sticking to rigid procedures, and of his old fear of free mobility in space.

All these findings clearly indicate that the lack of mobility plays an important role in Eddy's difficulties with arithmetic. The same type of behavior could be found in a number of children presenting difficulties in learning arithmetic. I shall briefly describe two of them:

Mary was seven and a half years old when she came to see me. Of normal intelligence, she was inhibited in arithmetic. During the psychometric examination she showed the same behavior that we had seen in Eddy: on certain occasions she "froze" and got into a silent but not openly rebellious state, from which it was impossible to move her. The first months of her analysis were also characterized by a state of extreme inactivity; she did not play at all, she did not talk. Like Eddy, she did not remove objects which were in her way.

When I asked her a question, she whispered a short answer. Her mother reported that Mary had had the following dream during this period: "I was very deep in the water. A great fish arrived and wanted to bite me and to tear me into little pieces. Then other fishes came and also tried to devour me."

Frank was a rather tense eight-year-old boy, who could not keep up with arithmetic in the second year of school. He was normally intelligent and he did well in other subjects. In the projective tests, we found a strong impact of orally colored anxieties and wishes. Working on arithmetic problems, he tended to persist in his errors, even when he had understood an explanation. After Frank had finally learned a new type of sum, a new "track of thinking," he tended to follow it and could not abandon it, even when easier sums (which he had known for a long time) were introduced. For example, he had learned to do sums such as $35 + ? = 38$. He then was given sums such as $15 + 19 = ?$, or $35 + 38 = ?$ Following the schema suitable to the preceding sums, he could not shift to a new way of thinking and wrote: $15 + 19 = 4$ and $35 + 38 = 3$. Frank showed the same rigidity and aversion to the new in his everyday life. He demanded that everything remain unchanged, that each cup or spoon always be put in the same place, that each person always have the same plate.

All these children were characterized by long-standing obsessional tendencies of a specific type. The main features were immobility, rigidity, and aversion to the new. Although most of them showed indications of a potentially better intelligence, the I.Q. on the Terman Test was usually a little lowered (between 90 and 100), probably for emotional reasons. The Oseretsky Test frequently disclosed the absence of true neuromotoric symptoms, but the prominence of psychomotoric difficulties such as slowness, lack of spontaneity, avoidance of free movement and risks (Bladergroen, 1954). The same lack of mobility can be found in some of their verbal functions: on the Terman Test they almost reach their age levels or even go beyond them, but they have difficulties when mobile and free combinatory thinking is required (e.g., Absurdities or Similarities, Sentence Construction).

These children stick to what they are familiar with. They are afraid of the new. They hesitate for a very long time before they can adopt a new method, even if they understand it quite well. For this reason they do not profit very much from explanations or other help. Of course, other factors are also involved: these children have difficulties in their object relations and unsatisfactorily developed ego functions. They cannot "take in" because of primitive oral fears. The psychogenic blocking with regard to arithmetic not only can be inferred from the analytic material; it can be observed directly in their performance of arithmetical tasks. Although I encountered a few children (especially older ones) who did not show this immobility, rigidity, and aversion to the new, I believe these characteristics are most frequently responsible for psychogenic difficulties with arithmetic.

General Remarks about Learning Inhibitions

Much psychoanalytic work has been devoted to learning disturbances. Pearson (1952) has surveyed the literature in this field. By far the most frequent type of interpretation is the following: any area of learning can be blocked by a specific unconscious fantasy; e.g., reading may be inhibited because it represents the child's attempt to see the dangerous events of his sexual fantasies. Eddy's case shows that the cause need not be a specific fantasy, although unconscious fantasies undoubtedly also played a role in his case; e.g., his aversion to arithmetic might be connected with anxieties of things being torn to pieces. However, this is not the main cause: it does not explain his blocking in other areas of functioning. The case presentation demonstrates that the main cause is the lack of motility and the blocking of all mobile processes. The oral-aggressive themes do not directly affect arithmetic (in the sense that arithmetic itself represents some dangerous and forbidden oral-aggressive activity). The oral-aggressive impulses and anxieties cause a deep paralysis and immobility of thinking; in this way they secondarily have such an effect on arithmetic, because arithmetic requires the highest degree of mobility. The psychogenic factors cause an impairment not so much of one specific area but of a general functional modality of the mind: mobility and the level of intelligence characterized by operational correspondence (Piaget).

SUMMARY

The examination of a large group of children with difficulties in arithmetic in the first grade revealed certain common features. The disturbances are not limited to arithmetic alone, but can be seen in all areas of behavior: there is a specific type of blocking, characterized by a lack of motor freedom and a paralysis of mental mobility. These inhibitions serve as a primitive defense against very strong orally colored castration anxieties. Anal factors also play a role. The inhibition of ego functions and arithmetic is especially severe because these functions have not been cathected with stable, neutralized energies. The immobility is also used in the attempt to bring about structuralization and stabilization of their inner world.

BIBLIOGRAPHY

Bladergroen, W. J. (1954), Children with Learning Difficulties. *Acta Psychother., Psychosom. & Orthopedagogica*, 2:42-51.

Freud, A. (1936), *The Ego and the Mechanisms of Defense*. New York: International Universities Press, 1946.

—— (1952), The Mutual Influences in the Development of Ego and Id: Introduction to the Discussion. *This Annual*, 7:42-50.

Freud, S. (1923a), The Ego and the Id. *Standard Edition*, 19:3-66. London: Hogarth Press, 1961.

—— (1923b), A Seventeenth-Century Demonological Neurosis. *Standard Edition*, 19:67-105. London: Hogarth Press, 1961.

—— (1926), Inhibitions, Symptoms and Anxiety. *Standard Edition*, 20:77-174. London: Hogarth Press, 1959.

Frijling-Schreuder, E. M. C. (1954), *Preventie van neurotische gezinsrelaties*. Assen: van Gorcum.

Hartmann, H., Kris, E., & Loewenstein, R. M. (1946), Comments on the Formation of Psychic Structure. *This Annual*, 2:11-38.

Hellman, I. (1954), Some Observations on Mothers of Children with Intellectual Inhibitions. *This Annual*, 9:259-273.

Jarvis, V. (1958), Clinical Observations on the Visual Problem in Reading Disability. *This Annual*, 13:451-470.

Jeffreys, H. (1936), The Unconscious Significance of Numbers. *Int. J. Psa.*, 17:217-223.

Kris, E. (1955), Neutralization and Sublimation: Observations on Young Children. *This Annual*, 10:30-46.

Maenchen, A. (1936), Denkhemmung und Aggression aus Kastrationsangst. *Z. psa. Päd.*, 10:276-299.

Mittelmann, B. (1954), Motility in Infants, Children, and Adults: Patterning and Psychodynamics. *This Annual*, 9:142-177.

Omwake, E. G. & Solnit, A. J. (1961), "It Isn't Fair": The Treatment of a Blind Child. *This Annual*, 16:352-404.

566 PIERRE VEREECKEN

Paterson, A. & Zangwill, O. L. (1944), Recovery of Spatial Orientation in Post-traumatic Confusional State. *Brain,* 67:54-68.

Pearson, G. H. J. (1952), A Survey of Learning Difficulties in Children. *This Annual,* 7:322-386.

Piaget, J. (1936), *The Origins of Intelligence in Children.* New York: International Universities Press, 1952.

—— (1941), *The Child's Conception of Number.* London: Routledge & Kegan Paul, 1961.

Plank, E. N. & Plank, R. (1954), Emotional Components in Arithmetical Learning as Seen through Autobiographies. *This Annual,* 9:274-293.

Rapaport, D., tr. & ed. (1951), *Organization and Pathology of Thought.* New York: Columbia University Press.

—— (1958), The Theory of Ego Autonomy: A Generalization. *Bull. Menninger Clin.,* 22:13-35.

Rubenstein, B. O., Levitt, M., & Falick, M. L. (1961), Déficiences dans l'Apprentissage et Distorsion du Moi. *Rev. Franç. Psychanal.,* 25:131-148.

Shentoub, S. A. (1963), Remarques sur la Conception du Moi et ses References au Concept de l'Image Corporelle. *Rev. Franç. Psychanal.,* 27:271-300.

van der Leeuw, P. J. (1958), The Preoedipal Phase of the Male. *This Annual,* 13:352-374.

Vereecken, P. (1961), *Spatial Development: Constructive-Practice Activities from Birth to the Age of Seven.* Groningen: J. B. Wolters.

Wegrocki, H. J. (1938), A Case of Number Phobia. *Int. J. Psa.,* 19:97-99.

CONTENTS OF VOLUMES I–XX

1945–1965

CONTENTS OF VOLUMES I–XX